D0941512

SANCTA SOPHIA

HOLY WISDOM

Or
**Directions for the Prayer of Contemplation
Extracted out of more than Forty Treatises**

**BY THE
VEN. FATHER F. AUGUSTINE BAKER
A MONK OF THE ENGLISH CONGREGATION OF
THE
HOLY ORDER OF S. BENEDICT**

METHODICALLY DIGESTED BY
R. F. SERENUS CRESSY
OF THE SAME ORDER AND CONGREGATION

AND EDITED FROM THE DOUAY EDITION OF 1657 BY THE
RIGHT REV. ABBOT SWEENEY, D.D.
OF THE SAME ORDER AND CONGREGATION

© 2007 Benediction Books

EDITOR'S PREFACE

PREFACE TO THE PRESENT EDITION

If it is a duty to apply to holy books the practice which the *Following of Christ* bids us observe towards holy persons, 'not to dispute concerning the merits of the saints, as to who is more holy than another, or greater in the kingdom of heaven,' it will not be right to give the preference to the work which we are now offering in a new form to the public, over the many, spiritual books which have helped on souls in the way of perfection. But it will not be right either to give to other books a preference over this. Certainly *Sancta Sophia* has been of great service in instructing beginners, in guiding proficients, and in securing those that have arrived at some degree of perfection, in the way along which Almighty God has called and led souls that have been highly privileged; and the Holy Spirit, *who breatheth where He will,* has through the words of the Venerable Father Baker whispered to these souls, and has drawn them on to a closer and closer union with Himself. Ever since the time that I first became acquainted with the writings of Father Augustine Baker, either in the epitome of them in which Father Serenus Cressy has so successfully presented them in his compilation, to which he gave the appropriate name which this book bears, *Sancta Sophia*, Holy Wisdom, or in their extended and full form, as they exist in various portions in some of our convents, I felt the desire to enter upon the task, which by God's blessing I have at last completed, of republishing with necessary annotations this golden treasury. Why should it be kept in the dark when, by being set up aloft, it could shed such light around?

Difficulties, which time has at last removed, have constantly been in my way. Duties of an imperative nature have ever attended me, and in the midst of them—though I have never lost sight of the task I had imposed upon myself—it has not been in my power to do more than a little at a time; and therefore the time has been long in proportion to the importance of the labour. In addition to reprinting the work, I felt that I ought to do two things,— to verify the quotations from the Fathers and spiritual writers, which are interspersed throughout the various treatises; and secondly to call attention to certain passages where explanation or even correction was demanded. The first of these tasks I have been compelled in great measure to abandon; the second, which is of greater importance, I have not neglected. But I must say a word upon both.

i

The task of verifying quotations from the authors referred to in the writings of Father Baker has been, as is the case with regard to all similar works, an exceedingly difficult and a hopeless labour. I have spent hours upon hours and with very little success. I remember many years ago reading in a note in some edition of the *Spiritual Exercises* of St. Ignatius, that the Scripture quotations of that holy Saint and great Master of the spiritual life are not always strictly correct; because it was evident the Saint quoted from memory, without referring on each occasion to the sacred text. Father Baker, in his reading of the Fathers and of spiritual writers, seems to have noted down at the time passages and words that struck him as bearing upon the subject on which he happened to be then engaged. And Father Cressy, in condensing the good Father's writings, cited the name, but without any reference to the special treatise; and thus in almost all instances no help is given towards a classical verification of the authority, upon which a truth or principle confirmed by the writer. To verify passages, therefore, to which no reference whatever is given, is a very laborious task. But in cases in which it is important that the special reference should be pointed out, I have done my best with whatever assistance I have been able to command; and I trust that no question has been left unnoticed in which the authority has been really of importance. To verify every quotation would imply an expenditure of time which I have not, and never can expect to have, at my disposal. This difficulty I have especially felt in the case of the writings of Thaulerus, whose works, as far as I know them, are in very closely-printed volumes, with limited and imperfect indexes. However, I feel that this is not a matter of practical value, as the good persons into whose hands this edition of *Sancta Sophia* will fall, and who will make the most use of it, will probably have no opportunity or desire of referring to the original, even if every chapter and verse were carefully recorded.

With regard to the second matter of explaining or even correcting certain passages, I hope I have not been negligent. The necessity of such explanations or corrections arises mainly from the circumstances of the period in which Father Baker wrote, and in which his writings were collected, condensed, and printed. Father Baker wrote his treatises and gave his instructions to the religious under his guidance, a short time before the Church was called on to pronounce on the doctrines of Quietism. The same difficulty, therefore, exists in regard to certain expressions of his, as exists with regard to the writings of the Ante-Nicene Fathers. Before the time in which the Church in the Council of Nicaea found it necessary to enter more fully into the definition of the terms of Substance, Nature, and Person, as predicated of the Mysteries of the Blessed Trinity and the Incarnation, expressions may have been sometimes used by perfectly orthodox theological writers, which were capable of a wrong interpretation. But when, under the guidance of the Holy Spirit, the Church defined with careful and logical precision what these sacred Mysteries implied in reference to the various terms used and required, with regard to unity of Substance and plurality of operations, a more exact terminology was strictly observed, in order that orthodoxy might be professed, and that through *the sound word that cannot be blamed, he who is on the contrary part might be afraid, having no evil to say* (Titus ii.8). If even St. Paul's own words, notwithstanding the inspiration under which he wrote, were *wrested to destruction,* no wonder that the words of faithful and wise theologians and martyrs were sometimes misinterpreted and wrenched into a defense of heresy. Father Baker, I have said, lived and wrote just before Quietism was condemned. For it was in the year 1687 that Pope Innocent XI. censured and pronounced sentence against the sixty-eight propositions of Molinos; and in 1699 Innocent XII. condemned the semi-Quietism of Madame Guyon and the illustrious Fénélon. Father Baker had already completed his labours, having gone to his reward in 1641, and Father Cressy in 1674.

Certainly some parts of *Sancta Sophia* would have been omitted or expressed otherwise, had these two holy Fathers lived to witness the controversy and its issue. Care has been taken to call attention to these points. I hesitated for a time whether I ought not altogether to omit such parts; but upon deliberation and after taking counsel, I thought it better not to interfere with the original, but to make the correction, or give a necessary explanation, in a note. An instance will be found in treat. iii. sect. iii. chap. vii. in reference to the prayer of silence of Don Antonio de Rojas, which has been condemned by the Church; though the censure was not affixed to it during Father Baker's lifetime. That Father Baker was no Quietist and had no sympathy with Quietism is especially evident from the prayer of Acts, which he so fully explains and so warmly recommends in the third section of the third treatise. And the collection of Acts at the end of the work is of itself an evidence how averse he was to the teaching of those, who, after Molinos, considered Contemplation to be a state of perfect inaction, in which the soul exercised none of its powers, and elicited no acts whatever, not even of hope, love, or desire; in other words that it was doing nothing at all, and therefore not praying nor adoring.

Although it may be safely said that there is no fear nowadays from Quietism in any general effect, for the active spirit of the time is so opposed to it, and even the prevalence and increase of vocations to active rather than contemplative orders in the Church render such a danger very unlikely, yet there may be a risk in individual cases of souls being misguided, unless they are on their guard, and receive caution from their directors against this possible evil. I trust that the danger signals which will be erected, where it seems necessary, will remove every objection which has been at any time felt, about allowing the free use in religious communities of this most useful and solid work on Mystical Theology.

A brief biography of the two good Fathers who have been respectively the author and compiler of the work will be appropriate. Some years ago, when I first undertook the task of preparing an edition of *Sancta Sophia,* I published a *Life of Father Baker,* and appended to it an essay on the Spiritual Life, mainly grounded on the venerable Father's teaching. As that work is accessible, though I believe it is not very easy to procure, I shall limit myself at present to but a few details.

David, known in religion by the name of Augustine, Baker was born in Abergavenny on the 9th of December 1575, of Protestant parents. He received his early education at Christ's Hospital in London, and at the age of fifteen went to the University of Oxford, and entered as a commoner at Broadgates' Hall, now known as Pembroke College. He remained at Oxford but two years, and then returned home to enter upon the study of the law under the instruction of an elder brother. This study he afterwards prosecuted with great attention in London, until upon his brother's death he once more returned to his native town. Here he worked under his father, who managed the estates of the Earl of Abergavenny. His religious education had not been attended to, and for a long time he seems to have led a thoughtless, though, from his own testimony, not a wicked life. But having been rescued by an extraordinary intervention of Providence from a most perilous position, in which his life was likely to be sacrificed, he entered into himself, and began to think seriously upon the affairs of his soul. He sought instruction at the hands of a Catholic priest, the Rev. Richard Floyd, was received into the Church, and abandoning the law he resolved to devote himself to the sacred ministry. He became acquainted with a Benedictine Father of the Cassinese Congregation, sought and obtained admission into the novitiate, and was clothed in the Abbey of St. Justina at Padua. He went through his year's probation; but being very much broken down in health he left Padua before taking his vows, and returned to England, where, having recovered his strength, he made his profession at the hands of some Italian Benedictine Fathers of the same Cassinese Congregation. He was then in the thirty-second year of his age.

For some years, before being promoted to the priesthood, he was employed by his superiors in various employments, in which his legal and historical knowledge was of great service. He devoted himself very earnestly also to prayer and the exercises of the spiritual life; and although he made such progress by his earnestness and perseverance—sometimes for six hours at a time in prayer—as to have been rewarded by ecstasies, yet in his case the course even of such love did not run over-smoothly, and from time to time he seemed to fall back again from his advancement. All this was the working of the Divine Spirit, both to ground him more perfectly in humility, and to give him an experience which he was to use afterwards in the guidance of others. After an interval of twelve years he went over to Rheims, where he was ordained priest in the year 1619, in his forty-fifth year; and in the following year he was appointed chaplain to the family of Mr. Philip Fursden, in Devonshire. Here, in a life of great retirement, he pursued with steady constancy the spiritual exercises, and by recommending to all inquirers into the Catholic faith the duty of prayer, in order to obtain light and strength, he succeeded in gaining many converts to the Church.

At this time the venerable Father's life was so thoroughly one of prayer, that he used sometimes to devote as many as eleven hours in the day to this holy practice. His health, however, was extremely delicate, and as he was threatened with consumption, he was ordered by his superiors to move to London, where it was hoped that occupation of a somewhat more active nature might be of advantage to him. He laboured, conjointly with Father Clement Reyner, in compiling the well known *Apostolatus Benedictinorum*, and began at that same period to write some of his spiritual treatises. He had to travel about to various parts of England and the Continent to consult documents, and at the same time that this change of occupation benefited his bodily health, it did not in the least interfere with his spiritual progress. He had now so perfectly grounded himself in the ascetical life, that no distractive employments could withdraw him from his habits of recollection. His life *was hidden with Christ in God,* and was what he himself so aptly calls such a life, 'a life of introversion.'

In Christmas of the year 3, Father Rudesind Barlow, President-General of the English Benedictine Congregation, founded a community of Benedictine nuns at Cambray, and in the following summer Father Baker was ordered to go and assist in training the young community in the ways of the spiritual life. Here he was in his true element; and the solid progress made by his disciples was a proof of his skill and success as a guide in these high paths. The two most noted amongst these holy souls were Dames Catherine Gascoigne and Gertrude More. The former of these was the most faithful and constant follower of Father Baker's instructions, and became herself so skilled in the practice of the duties of the Religious Life, that she was employed for some time by the Archbishop of Cambray in forming a convent in his diocese after the model of her own. She held the office of Abbess of Cambray from the fifth year of her profession, almost uninterruptedly till her death in 1676, two years after her jubilee in Religion. Her letter to Father Cressy prefixed to *Sancta Sophia,* and his answer prefixed to the third treatise, show what interest she, took and what part she bore in the drawing up of the instructions contained in this work. The other holy nun, Dame Gertrude More, a direct descendant of the martyred Lord Chancellor, was of a character more difficult to bring into that subjection to a spiritual guide, which seemed so natural to Dame Catherine Gascoigne. At first she refused the direction of Father Baker, and pursued a spiritual course of her own. But being one day vividly struck by a passage which he read to her from an ascetical work upon the exceptional guidance of souls in a state of aridity, she placed herself completely under his direction, and quickly advanced so far as to arrive at a very close union with God. Many of the Acts and Affections at the end of *Sancta Sophia* were found among her writings, gathered, it would appear, from Father Baker's suggestions. Her little work, called *An Idiot's Devotions* by herself, but by Father Baker more properly called *Confessiones Amantis,* expresses the spirit by which she was animated. She died young, it is said in the odour of sanctity, in the twenty-seventh year of her age in the year 1633.

During the nine years that the venerable Father remained at Cambray, he drew up many of his ascetical treatises at the earnest request of the community, who were anxious to perpetuate instructions which had been of such immense value to themselves. Many of them are lost, but several are preserved, and may be found in manuscript in the libraries of Downside, Ampleforth, Stanbrook, and St. Benedict's Priory at Colwich. They are best known, however, through the form in which Father Cressy drew them up in the work which is now presented once more to the public. Father Baker remained nine years at Cambray, and then was removed to the Monastery of St. Gregory at Douai, and became a conventual. There he continued his wonted exercises, and devoted himself also to his writings. After about five years' sojourn he was again sent on the mission into England, being then in the sixty-third year of his age, in the year of our Lord 1638. At that time a summons to the English Mission was a summons to go forth to martyrdom; and notwithstanding his love for conventual life, and his deep sense of the responsibility attending the career of a missioner, he at once set about preparing for his departure. He started—after a painful farewell—from his convent; and, on arriving in England, divided his labours between London and Bedfordshire. He was sought after by the pursuivants who were at that time particularly active in bringing Catholic priests to judgment and to execution; and was obliged, old and feeble as he was, to fly, according to our Divine Lord's advice, from place to place, in order to avoid the persecution. But nothing interfered with his devotedness to prayer.

The struggle between sickness and persecution, as to which was to conquer in his regard, went on for three years, and at last it was to end in 1641 in favour of sickness. The year 1641 was a fatal one for priests, but a rich one for martyrs. In that year Bishop Challoner enumerates eighteen priests who were condemned to death, and were either savagely executed or harassed to death in prison. Among them were two of Father Baker's *confrères*, Fathers Ambrose Barlow and Bartholomew Roe. He himself was on the point of being seized, when he was struck by a contagious fever, which scared away his pursuers. Though he did not actually die upon the scaffold, to which he was on the very point of being led, he may well be considered as a martyr. In concealment, and under the solicitous and affectionate care of a good Catholic matron—Mrs. Watson, mother of one of the nuns of Cambray—in constant prayer and acts of resignation, he resigned his soul unto the hands of his Creator on the 9th of August 1641, in the sixty-sixth year of his age and the thirty-seventh of his religious profession. *Defunctus adhuc loquitur*. Though dead, he continued to live, and has continued living ever since, in his spiritual writings; and it is to be hoped that his voice will be made to sound again, and be heard by a more numerous circle of hearers, through the means of the work which is now again going forth into the world.

It was in the year 1657, sixteen years after this holy Father's death, that his friend and disciple, Father Serenus Cressy, published the useful compilation of his writings, under the name of *Sancta Sophia*. This Father, called in baptism Hugh Paulin, and in religion Serenus, was born at Wakefield, in Yorkshire, in the year 1605, the eventful year of Fawkes's Gunpowder Plot, and the same year in which Father Baker was clothed in the Abbey of St. Justina in Padua. He went to the University of Oxford at the early age of fourteen, and in the year 6, at the age of twenty-one, became Fellow of Merton. He received orders in the Church of England, and was appointed chaplain to Lord Wentworth, afterwards Earl of Strafford of noted memory. A little later he was chaplain to Lord Falkland; then he became Canon of Windsor, and afterwards Dean of Leighlin, in Ireland. He travelled as tutor to a young English nobleman, and in the year 1646 became a convert, and was received into the Church in Rome, where he happened to be at the time. Next year, being in Paris, he published his *Exomologesis*, or Motives of his Conversion, which he dedicated to the Carthusian Fathers of Nieuport in Flanders, whom he at one time thought of joining. However, owing to their very secluded mode of life, he was directed to turn towards an Order in which his literary capacity might be of greater service, and he joined the Benedictine Community of St. Gregory's at Douai, where he took his vows in April 1649. He remained as a conventual for some eight years, having, however, spent about one year of that time in Paris, with an affiliation community from Cambray. This house in Paris, placed under the protection of our Lady of Good Hope, is now existing in its worthy successors at St. Benedict's Priory, Colwich, near Stafford. He was afterwards sent out on the mission into the South Province in England; and upon the marriage of Charles II. with the Infanta of Portugal in 1662, he became one of her chaplains, and resided for four years at Somerset House. Here, besides discharging zealously and edifyingly the duties of the sacred ministry, he devoted much time to writing several learned books on controversial subjects. During this time he was also engaged upon his great work, the *Church History of Britanny,* which he published at Rouen in 1668.

Father Cressy was greatly esteemed by his religious brethren, and held among them several offices of trust and responsibility, and was for many years a member of the General Chapter. His last missionary appointment was to the chaplaincy of Richard Caryl, Esq., of East Grinstead, in Sussex, where he died the death of the just on the 10th of August 1674, in the sixty-ninth year of his age. It was towards the end of the time of his residence as a conventual at Douai, that he drew up these instructions from the writings of Father Baker, which in a dedicatory letter to Father Laurence Reyner, President-General of the English Benedictine Congregation, he declares to have drawn up and published in obedience to his command. Not obedience only, however, he adds, but gratitude urged him on in his work of love; for to these instructions he, in that same letter, attributes the hastening of his conversion to the faith, and his call to join the Benedictine Order. May God in His infinite mercy grant that these same words of wisdom and piety may bring grace and inspire resolution into many a hesitating soul, and tend to *enlighten those that are sitting in darkness and in the shadow of death!* Any one who has had the opportunity of reading any of the Treatises of Father Baker in their original form, will be able to testify to the industry required for compiling them, as Father Cressy has done, and for the fidelity with which the more than forty different Treatises have here been preserved and interpreted.

It remains to make two or three observations in connexion with the teaching conveyed in the treasury of wisdom here laid open. Let me most earnestly recommend the reading of Father Cressy's *Preface to the Reader,* herein prefixed to the first Treatise. Possible objections are here anticipated and answered. Also I must invite very particular attention to the case of the holy Jesuit, Father Balthasar Alvarez, recorded in the 7th Chapter of Section 1, Treatise III., where we find a full and striking and most telling apology for the method of prayer, so strongly recommended by Father Baker. One great reason why so many break down in their attempts at arriving at perfection in the spiritual life is, because they are tied down too stiffly to the formal method of Discursive Prayer, and are not allowed free enough scope for the exercise of Acts and Affections. It is quite proper that upon the first entrance into the spiritual life, the soul should be well exercised in the use of the powers of the soul, and that the Understanding especially should be called into play. But to insist upon working the Understanding, even when the Will is ready at once to work, is not unlike insisting on the spelling of every word, or the parsing of every sentence, each time that we read a book or a newspaper. All our proficiency and skill would avail us nothing, if we were to be thus tied down; and the reading of books would indeed be anything but instructive and entertaining. Father Balthasar Alvarez, in the chapter just referred to, will be found to say: 'All internal discoursing with the understanding was to cease, whensoever God enabled souls to actuate purely by the will. And that to do otherwise would be as if one should be always preparing somewhat to eat, and yet afterwards refuse to taste that which is prepared. By this divine Prayer of the Will, the Holy Spirit of Wisdom with all the excellencies of it described in the Book of Wisdom (chap. viii.) is obtained, and with it perfect liberty.'

Undoubtedly, as we have said, on the first entrance into the spiritual life it is important to attend to the instructions given upon Discursive Prayer, or ordinary Meditation. But it is not to be understood that this method is to be rigidly adhered to throughout. When Almighty God calls the soul to the Prayer of Acts, and afterwards of Aspirations, the soul ought to be allowed liberty to obey and follow the call. It is quite true that we should not attempt to run, until we have become steady enough upon our feet to stand or walk. But it is equally true that if we content ourselves with only standing or walking, when there is occasion for greater speed and activity, we shall be outstripped by others, who have learnt that *where the Spirit of the Lord is, there is liberty:* who have heard the summons to work in the words: *Why stand you here all the day idle?* and have obeyed the command of the energetic St. Paul: *So run that you may receive.* For a great truth which Father Baker always keeps before us is, that we are not simply to satisfy ourselves that we devote a certain period each day to our mental prayer, but that we must aim at progress in Prayer, and that by becoming more practised and more perfect in that holy exercise, we may make corresponding progress in holiness of life, and ascending from virtue to virtue, may at last by closer union be allowed to *see the God of gods in Sion.*

In the same manner as Father Rothaan, S.J., in his most practical and excellent instruction on 'the Method of Meditation,' gives an example how to meditate on an eternal truth, and works out the meditation, in order that it may serve as a model on which to work out others, so will I submit an example, how the Prayer of Acts may be exercised, according to the instructions given in *Sancta Sophia.* We will take the truth suggested by Father Rothaan: *What doth it profit a man, if he gain the whole world, and lose his own soul!*

We must divide our Prayer into the ordinary divisions observed in meditation: 1. the Beginning; 2. the Body; 3. the Conclusion. In the BEGINNING we must, as usual, make our act of recollection of the Presence of God, pray for light, and by an act of sorrow remove sin, which obscures the soul, and then quiet the imagination, by picturing our Divine Lord standing before us, and addressing directly to us those words, which are His own.

Then passing on to the BODY of the Prayer, instead of arguing with myself, I address my words in the form of Acts to Almighty God, or to our Divine Lord; observing, usually, a method in the Acts, beginning with the lower ones grounded on Faith, and progressing towards the higher ones of Confidence and Love. Thus may I pray. *Faith.* O my God, I believe these words, and I accept in my soul the great truth they express. Thou hast made my soul eternal, and therefore I fully see its immense value. The world may try to convince and persuade me through its false principles to follow it, and forget Thee; but to whom shall I go but to Thee who hast the words of eternal life? &c. *Sorrow.* O my Divine Jesus, how sorry am I that I have not hitherto felt this truth and acted up to it! Every time I have sinned I have denied this truth by my own willful act and deed. Never let me sin again, &c. *Humility.* But who am I, that I should pretend to make such a promise? I am weak by nature, and have weakened myself still more by sin. I am Thy child: do Thou save me. Lord, save me, or I perish, and I shall never gain the end for which alone Thou hast made me, &c. *Supplication.* Give me grace, O my most powerful and generous God, that I may ever live up to what I now feel; and if this day any temptation come upon me, do Thou cry out in my ears, and make me hear Thy words: *What doth it profit*, &c. *Hope.* Now I feel that I have more courage, because Thou hast promised to assist me in my struggle. I rely on Thy power and Thy fidelity; and though I have a great work to do in striving to save my soul, Thou canst and wilt help me, and then we shall succeed, &c. *Confidence.* Nay, O my God, I have more than hope: *Certus sum.* I am sure that Thou canst conquer all my enemies, and that Thou, in saving my soul, wilt save what is already Thine. *Tuus sum ego, salvum me fac*, &c. *Love and Desire.* Since I belong to Thee, O God, I value Thee far beyond all the world, and all that the world can give me. I desire to be dissolved, and to be with Thee, Thou God of my heart and my portion for ever. Woe that my sojourning is prolonged! Draw me to Thee, and help me to run in the way of Thy commandments, &c. Thus, the soul speaks to God, and is continually actuated towards Him. The lower Acts of Faith, Sorrow, &c., will at first be more numerous, and will suggest themselves more readily than the higher ones of Confidence, Love, Resignation, and such like; but after a time these latter ones will prevail. At the end a devout, colloquy or address is made to God, and His blessing is humbly and fervently besought in behalf of all that the soul has been inspired to promise and resolve. A slow and patient perusal of the Exercises appended to this volume will facilitate the making of these Acts. And as the higher Acts become more easy and familiar, the soul will advance further in its union with God, and Prayer will become more affective. I may be allowed to refer the reader to what is said in the short Treatise upon the Spiritual Life, which I have appended to the *Life of Father Baker*, pp. 141, &c.

I feel that it is not necessary for me to say anything more by way of Preface. But, submitting everything to the judgment of the Holy See, I now commend the work which I have prepared, to the blessing of God; and beg that He, from whom comes down every good and perfect gift, will bestow, in behalf of those who make a good use of these holy instructions, a fresh harvest of the fruit which was gathered in such abundance when *Sancta Sophia* first made its appearance, and guided so many souls to Perfection.

J. NORBERT SWEENEY, O.S.B.

St. John's Priory, Bath,
Ash Wednesday, A.D. 1876.

APPROBATIONS

TO

OUR MOST REV. FATHER LAURENCE REYNER,

PRESIDENT GENERAL OF OUR HOLY CONGREGATION OF THE
ORDER OF   ST. BENEDICT,

AND TO ALL OUR VERY REV. FATHER SUPERIORS IN THE SAME.

VERY REV. FATHERS,

   Such being the distemper of this age, that only good books, and such
as are most proper to cure in the very root its disorders, do stand in need of
protection, you cannot in justice, as it seems to me, refuse yours to this, the
composing and publishing whereof at this time was an effect of your V. R.
Paternities' order and commands. Now those very commands, with so much
advice and zeal unanimously made, are a very strong proof that this book (for
as much as concerns the substantial doctrine therein contained) is such an
one, so perfectly good and medicinal, as that I need not doubt, and indeed
should be sorry, it should have any other fate than the hatred of all those who
love darkness more than light. As for whatsoever faults may have happened
through my want of skill in the compiling, I do not desire such patrons to
them. Yet truly there hath not been wanting all the diligence and care that I
was capable of, to provide that so excellent instructions should not be too
much disparaged by the second copying and new fashion and dress upon
them. The pains herein taken will appear to be not very ordinary to any one
that shall consider how difficult a matter it is out of such a world of Treatises
(written upon particular subjects for the special necessities and use of certain
devout persons, without any eye or design in the author of affording materi-
als for an entire body of spirituality) to frame such a body not at all defective,
and with parts not unproportionable. Now I must confess that though conscience alone and duty to your VV. RR. Paternities would have had sufficient
influence on me to prevent negligence, yet I had moreover one motive besides to heighten my diligence which was gratitude. For to the admiration
and love of these excellent instructions I owe not only the hastening of my
reconciliation to the Catholic Church (as on this very day, being the Vigil of
the Feast of St. Mary Magdalene, in the Office of the Holy Inquisition at
Rome), but also the happiness of being a member (though unworthy) of your
holy congregation. It may notwithstanding fall out, that with all my endeavours I may fail of giving satisfaction in the point of art; but that I have not
been wanting in the principal condition of faithfulness, besides the testimony
of my own conscience, I have that also of persons learned and pious, to

whom the writings of the venerable author have been perfectly known and familiar.

It will doubtless seem strange to others, but not to your Paternity (V. R. F. President) that so perfect instructions for contemplation should proceed from one that had spent almost his whole life in the laborious employment of the Apostolic Mission. But your V. R. Paternity by experience knows that those who sincerely give themselves to seek Almighty God by pure spiritual prayer, whatever their employments be, will, without any prejudice to them, never want opportunities to meet and converse with Him in solitude. Now from such conversations it is that there do proceed from the Father of Lights such illustrations as not only give a splendour to the persons themselves, but by reflection also serve to guide others.

The solitude that our Venerable Author enjoyed was, by his own election, among friends, penitents, and disciples. But God's Holy Spirit led your V. R. Paternity into a desert far more full of horror indeed, but withal far more instructive: a solitude of prisons and dungeons, among enemies to religion and humanity, where yet by the light and force not only of your learning, but also your devotion, &c., you could found churches of converts.

A more sufficient and proper patron, therefore, and judge, could not be found than your V. R. Paternity of instructions of this nature. So that from you it is that all others, your religious subjects, receiving them, will through God's grace daily with their increasing fervour, by their good practice and example, recommend them to others also.

VV. RR. Fathers,

Your VV. RR. Paternities' in all duty and service in our Lord,

Br. SERENUS CRESSY.

From my cell in the Convent of St. Gregory's in Doway, this 21st of July 1657.

Many grave authors have written of this subject, but in my opinion none more clearly (and with such brevity) than the R. Father Augustine Baker, of the holy Order of St. Benedict, sometime spiritual director to the English Benedictine Dames at Cambray. Who in his several treatises abridged in this book, entitled *Sancta Sophia*, probably out of his own ex-perience, hath methodically, solidly, clearly, and piously set forth such efficacious instructions for the attaining of true perfection, that all devout souls aspiring thereto, especially religious persons (whose daily practice of meditation and continual exercises tending to that end will, if well applied, much advance them), by their practice with great facility, may attain great perfection. Let them, therefore, read diligently the preface and first treatise, and practise exactly what is contained in the second; and I dare promise them by God's grace a happy progress in the third.

Wherefore I judge the work worthy to be published, as containing nothing opposite to the doctrine of the Church; but on the contrary, very profitable rules and rare instructions of piety and true devotion.

Given at Doway, in the Convent of the English Recollects, this 2nd of July 1657.

Br. ANGELUS FRANCIS, Lector Jubilate,
and Episcopal Censurer of Books.

I have read three treatises of that V. F. A. Baker, of an Internal Life, Mortification, and Prayer; and do approve and esteem of it as of a work that may much promote the perfection of a religious state and lead others to a competent reasonable participation of it, though living in the world. And, reader, if thou art seriously resolved to attempt this principal and main work of thy salvation, thou wilt find nothing to displease thee; but very many advices and instructions to advance thee in the way to perfection. But if spiritual conversation internally with Almighty God be either insipid or unsavoury to thy ill-affected palate, thou wilt easily find little straws, motes, or hairs to pick quarrel with, and cast away such food as this; and I wish thee to take heed, thou dost not cast more away.

Given this 21st of July, in our English College of Doway, A.D. 1657.

T. PRODGER, Prof. of Divinity.

To the foregoing approbations I esteemed it much for my advantage to adjoin the following testimony of my sincerity and faithfulness in delivering the doctrine of our V. Author. The excellent person from whom the letter came will, I hope, pardon this publishing, without a commission from herself, what she privately directed to me; since it is done for the better recommendation of the doctrine so worthily esteemed by her.

TO THE REV. F. SERENUS CRESSY.

REVEREND FATHER,

I must acknowledge the particular obligation that our convent hath to your R. P., for the great diligence you have used, and the very much labour you have bestowed in compiling the abridgment of our Venerable and dear

PREFACES

Father Baker's works, so exactly conformable to the sense and meaning of the Author; and as we well know the pains you have taken in perusing seriously all his books several times, and in collecting the substance of each, digesting and reducing them into a most convenient order and method; and that you refused not to undergo the labour to go through all this a second time, to give the most full satisfaction in rendering your abridgment more entirely conformable to his writings in the very expression as much as might be; so we may very well believe that it hath pleased God to assist very much your unwearied industry, since not any that hath read your book, and is versed in the Author's works, hath found any objections to make either of anything wanting or differing from him; but all acknowledge that you have most faithfully, clearly, and substantially delivered his doctrine. We cannot, therefore, but hope God will be the reward of your fidelity, care, and pains, in a work so acceptable to Him, as we shall not fail to pray; and none shall esteem themselves more obliged to testify their gratitude than,

R. Father,
Your unworthy sister and servant,
S. CATHARINE DE S. MARIA, Abbess Unworthy.
Cambray, July 7th, 1657.

AUTHOR'S PREFACE

The Sum of the Preface.

BELOVED CHRISTIAN READER,

Before thou proceedest to partake of what is promised thee in the frontispiece of this book, thou art entreated to permit thyself to be detained awhile in the entry. For perhaps a short delay here will make thy progress afterwards both more speedy and profitable.

2. This is to acquaint thee that the *immaculate doctrine* contained in this book, though it never met with any that opposed, or so much as questioned, the verities thereof, speculatively considered, yet there have not wanted some that have judged them not fit to be thus exposed to thy view, much doubting thou wouldst prove such an one as would make an ill use and perverse advantage from them.

3. Now the principal, yea only, point that gives some this jealousy is that which thou wilt find in the *Second Section* of the *First Treatise*, where is

treated touching divine illuminations, inspirations, impulses, and other secret operations of God's Holy Spirit in the hearts of internal lives. Concerning which the constant teaching of our Venerable Author (in brief) is this, viz. 'That the Divine Spirit, by virtue of the said operations, is to be acknowledged our only secure Guide and Master in these secret paths of divine love, discovered in some measure in the following treatises. And consequently that the most essential, universal duty to be aspired unto by every one that pretends a desire or intention to walk in the same paths is, to give up his soul and all his faculties to God's internal guidance and direction only, relinquishing and renouncing all other instructors and instructions, as far as they are not subordinately coöperating with this our Divine Master, for the receiving of whose celestial influences, the humble and devout scholar is obliged to prepare and dispose himself by prayer, abstraction of life, &c.; in solitude hearkening to His voice and call, and learning how to distinguish it clearly from the voice and solicitations of human reason or corrupt nature; till that by long familiarity and conversation with God, divine love alone will so clear his spiritual sight, that he will see at last no other light, nor receive motion from any other, but God only; and this in all actions, omissions, and sufferings, though in themselves of the smallest importance.'

4. This is our Venerable Author's doctrine, everywhere in all his treatises (whatever the subject be) inculcated, and even to the wearying of the readers, continually repeated and asserted. Indeed a doctrine it is so fundamental to all his other instructions concerning prayer and mortification, &c., that the least weakening of its authority renders all the rest unprofitable.

5. But little reason there is to fear that a doctrine, which is the very soul of Christianity, can be shaken by human opposition, or disparaged by jealousy. True it is, notwithstanding, that though this fundamental verity receives testimony abundantly both from Scripture and universal tradition, though it be constantly asserted in the schools, and sprinkled everywhere in almost all mystical writers, yet scarce hath any one since the ancient fathers' times (especially St. Augustine) so purposely, largely, and earnestly recommended it to practice. And, therefore, no great wonder it is, if such a way of delivering it hath seemed a novelty, even to those that speculatively and in theory acknowledge it to be the established doctrine of the Church; and whilst they willingly, and with applause, hear it asserted daily in the schools, yet meeting with it thus popularly spread, they are offended with it; I mean with the communicating it to the use and practice of the unlearned.

6. Now what it was that troubled them will appear from the only objection in the Author's lifetime made against it, which was indeed a mere jealousy, lest this doctrine so delivered should prejudice the authority of superiors. The which objection he answered to the full satisfaction of all that were interested in the matter. The sum of which answer follows in the ninth

chapter of the second section of the first treatise, and needs not to be here repeated.

7. But since his death, and especially after that, by a general unanimous agreement of all superiors among us, it had been ordained that the sum of the Author's spiritual doctrine should, for the good of souls aspiring to contemplation, be published; but the same objection hath been renewed, and others moreover added thereto. And all of them have risen from the like ground of jealousy, not so much acknowledged to be rational by the objectors themselves (who readily subscribe to the doctrine as Catholically true and holy) as feared from others; to wit, partly from ordinary not learned Catholics, who, it is suspected, will be suspicious of a doctrine that will seem new and, however, unproper to them; but principally from strangers and enemies to the Church, especially the frantic enthusiasts of this age, who, as is feared, will conceive their frenzies and disorders justified here.

8. These things considered, both zeal to truth, duty to superiors, and charity to thee, beloved reader, obliged me before all other things to beseech thee to abstain from reading the book, unless it can be demonstrated beforehand that it was fit to come into thy hands; that the suspected inconveniences and suspicions are evidently groundless; that it would be a greater frenzy in the enthusiasts of these days, or in any seduced or seducing spirits, to claim any right in this doctrine than that which already possesses them; and, in a word, that no objections, either against the doctrine or publishing of it, either have, or, as we suppose, can rationally be devised, to make us repent the printing, or thee the reading, of the following book.

9. Among the said objections this one is scarce worthy to find place, which yet by some hath been urged against the publishing to all Christians' view instructions about prayer and mystical practices proper to a few contemplative persons (for whom alone the Author intended them, without the least thought of having them communicated and exposed so generally): especially considering that this treatise discourses of sublime mystic matters, above the reach of vulgar capacities; and also, that whereas to such tender well-minded souls (as those were for whom the said treatises were meant) just liberty and condescendence were allowed in many cases, not to be permitted to others that either in the world, or else in a religious life, do walk in other ways; these, notwithstanding, will be apt to their own prejudice to make use of such liberty.

10. But surely, as it would be most unreasonable to forbid a physician to publish a book of remedies against some special diseases, for fear that some that are untouched of those diseases, or perhaps sick of the contrary, should hurt themselves with making use of medicines improper for them; or

Molina the Carthusian to publish his excellent instructions for priests, lest lay persons should assume the privileges belonging to that sublime calling; or Alvarez de Paz to print his volumes about the duties and exercises of religious persons, because they are improper for seculars; so neither upon such grounds ought these instructions be hindered from being public. Neither ought any to fear lest ordinary Christians will foolishly apply to themselves the relaxations about confessions, &c., necessarily allowed to well-minded scrupulous souls that pursue contemplative ways in an abstracted life and solitude. Or that souls that live distracted, solicitous, active lives, as long as they live so, will judge themselves interested in the ways and exercises of internal contemplative livers. Or, in a word, that those who are yet but beginners, or have made but small proficiency in internal ways of the spirit, will be so foolishly presumptuous as to aspire to exercises more sublime than belong to them; the which they cannot do without receiving infinite prejudice by their indiscreet ambition. Add hereto, that on several occasions there have been used and inculcated in this book the best preventions, cautions, and provisions that possibly could be devised, against all misunderstanding and misapplication of any doctrines contained in it. To conclude, it may seem a sufficient safeguard for me to have herein the example of the V. R. F. A. C., a person much esteemed for learning and piety, who hath not only published (in an additional treatise to *The Conflict of the Soul*) *Instructions for Contemplation,* but a great part of his Maxims (though brief) are very conformable to what is here expressed more largely.

11. The special feared inconveniences that may arise from the publishing of this doctrine touching divine inspiration, do regard partly some that live in the communion of the Church; but principally such as are strangers and enemies thereto. As for the former, it is suspected, that by urging so seriously the duty of attending to and following divine inspirations, some even of the more sober Catholics will be apt to be jealous, that the teachers and practisers of such a doctrine will seem thereby to exempt themselves in many things from the ordinary jurisdiction of prelates and magistrates, pretending to extraordinary illuminations and commissions, and to walking *in mirabilibus super se,* &c., by which a prejudice and contempt also may be cast upon the common orders and rules concerning faith and good manners established in the Church.

12. Now not to forestall what is copiously delivered in the second treatise (to wit, that due obedience to all kind of superiors is so far from being prejudiced by this doctrine, that it is only by this doctrine that it is perfectly established, and all possible suspicions, all imaginary cases to the contrary solved): hereto it is answered that, whereas it is said that by a pretending to divine illuminations, &c., a contempt may be cast upon the common doctrines and rules of faith and a good life, there is not the least

ground for such an apprehension. For never did any spiritual mystic writer pretend to receive any new or formerly unknown lights or revelations in matters of faith, beyond what have been known and universally received in the Church. The lights which such persons by God's gracious visits receive being only a clearer sight of ordinary mysteries; the which produces in them a firmer assent unto them, a greater love of them, an abhorring of all novelties of doctrines, and a most fervent zeal to the unity and peace of the Church, and to the reducing of all unbelievers, misbelievers, and schismatics, into its bosom and communion.

13. The like is to be said for the rules of practice, and a holy Christian conversation. They know no other but such as are common to all other Christians, which are revealed in the Gospel, and proposed by the pastors of God's Church in councils, and in the writings of the holy fathers. The only advantage that in this regard is pretended to, and acquired, by attending to divine inspirations, is a more perfect use and a more faithful application of the ordinary precepts of holiness, or of counsels of perfection, to those who profess the embracing of such counsels: an extending of them further, and to more particulars, than it is possible to be taught by books or attained by study.

14. All Christians know that to blaspheme, to lie, to defraud, to be rebellious, unchaste, revengeful, &c., are sins odious to God; and that the contrary virtues are to be practised. Yea, moreover, they know that we are obliged to love God with all our heart, with all our soul, and with all our strength; that we ought in all things to intend His love and honour, &c. Moreover, all know that besides the essentially necessary Christian duties, there are other counsels of perfection, which belong to those upon whom God hath bestowed an extraordinary vocation and grace, enabling them to cast from them all secular anxieties and other impediments to perfect charity, and to put themselves in a condition of solitude, obedience, &c.; the which affords them the best expedients and helps for the increasing of divine love and conformity to His will, even in the smallest matters. All this in gross is known to all Christians of any reasonable capacity and good education.

15. But yet the wisest, the most subtle and learned Christians will never be able, by any human endeavours of study or meditation, to put in practice even those essential precepts after a perfect manner; that is, with an intention not only right, but also pure and deiform. And much less will they by such weak helps, be enabled to discern in a thousand particular cases and circumstances what is most perfect, most acceptable to God, and conformable to His divine will. As for example: 1. How when two good or indifferent things are proposed, to make choice or preference of that which, in the pre-

sent disposition of the soul, will prove most advantageous to perfection. 2. How to spiritualise even the ordinary indifferent occurrences of our life, daily and hourly. 3. How to perceive what manner and degree of prayer is most proper and profitable to the soul in her present state. 4. Or what mortifications are in the present circumstances most advantageous. 5. Or how to discern the state, inclinations, and spiritual necessities of other souls committed to our charge. 6. Or lastly, to discover a thousand secret subtleties, close interests, and reservations of our corrupt nature, which mingle themselves, more or less, almost in all our best actions, &c. In these and a thousand like cases, not all the reading or study in the world will enable souls to carry themselves perfectly in the execution of those precepts or counsels, which in gross all know to be necessary, at least to the attaining to perfection. But a distinct actual supernatural light and grace is necessary; and this not to teach us new precepts or furnish us with new counsels, but circumstantially to apply those which are common and universally known. For want of which light it is that the true way to perfection is almost unknown, even to those who profess the seeking of perfection, and fill the world with books and instructions about it.

16. By what other means, then, is such light to be had? Surely by no other but by the exercise of divine love, which is most perfectly performed in internal prayer, in attention to and union with God in spirit. What an expert, persuading, and subtle master love is, beyond study or consideration, we see even in natural and secular businesses. One that is immersed in sensual love to any person, has no need of instructions or books to teach him the art of loving. We see how skilful on a sudden such an one becomes in the ways how to please the person beloved. He loses not, neither out of ignorance nor negligence, the least opportunity to ingratiate himself. He understands the mind and intention of the other by the least signs; the motion of a hand, the cast of an eye is sufficient to inform him, and set him on work to attempt anything, or procure anything that may content the party. The like subtlety and perspicacity we may see in those earthy souls which cleave with an earnest affection unto riches. What subtle ways do they find out to increase their wealth! Such trifling inconsiderable things they make use of for that purpose, as another would not take notice of, or could not see how to make profit by them. They have almost a prophetical spirit to foresee dangers where none are, and advantages probable or possible to happen many years after.

17. Now how comes it to pass that the eyes of love are so quick-sighted? Surely by this: that where love to any particular object is predominant, it subdues all other affections to all other objects, which would distract the thoughts, and seduce the will from contemplating and adhering to the thing so beloved.

18. Upon such grounds, therefore, as these it is, that St. Augustine calls Divine Love (*Luminosissimam Charitatem*) *most full of light, and most enlightening.* For a soul that truly loves God with a love worthy of Him, having the mind cleared from all strange images, and the will purified from all strange affections, is thereby enabled purely to contemplate God without any distraction at all. And being desirous in all things to please Him, knows how to make advantage of all occurrences. Light and darkness, consolations and desolations, pains and pleasures, all these contribute to the advancing of this love. Yea, there is nothing so indifferent, or, in its own nature, so inconsiderable, but that such a soul can perceive how use may be made of it to please God thereby.

19. Now since pure love is exercised immediately to God only in pure prayer, by which alone the spirit is united to Him, hence it is that prayer is the only efficacious instrument to obtain supernatural light, according to the saying of David: *Accedite ad Deum, et illuminamini: Approach unto God* (by prayer), *and* (ye shall) *be enlightened.* And hence also it is, that the same holy prophet so earnestly and frequently (above twenty times in one Psalm, 118) prays for such light to understand and discover the wonderful things of God's Law. And what were those wonderful things? Surely not to be informed that murder and adultery were sins; or generally that God was to be loved with the whole soul; for much more knowledge he had than this before he prayed. But being desirous to give himself wholly to God, and to perform His will alone in all things, he so often makes use of prayer for the obtaining an extraordinary light (to be had no other way but by prayer) that he might thereby be enabled to discover and find out the Divine Will in all manner of cases and doubtful circumstances.

20. Now only such inspirations and such illuminations as these do spiritual persons pretend to by the means of prayer and attending to God. And if they do exercise prayer with a due fervour and constancy, these they shall most certainly enjoy, and that in such a measure that whereas the greatest part of ordinary good Christians are so dim-sighted as to see the Divine Will only in circumstances where there is a necessary obligation (so that they spend the far greatest part of their lives in actions that do no way advance them in Divine Love, being wrought chiefly in virtue of the principle of self-love and interests of nature), those that are perfectly internal livers, being clouded by no vain images, and distracted by no inferior affections, do see the Divine Will clearly in the minutest affairs, which they accordingly make advantage of to improve themselves in the love of God. And, according to the degrees of love, so proportionably are the degrees of light. And thus, I

suppose, the pretended inconveniences suspected to flow from the publishing of this doctrine will appear to be only pretended and causelessly feared.

21. But the other objection at first sight seems more considerable, as implying a far greater and more certain inconvenience and danger that may ensue upon the publishing of this doctrine concerning divine inspirations, illuminations, and calls. For thus they argue. It is to be feared that the fanatic sectaries which now swarm in England more than ever, will be ready to take advantage from hence to justify all their frenzies and disorders; all which they impute with all confidence to divine inspirations, illuminations, and impulses. For can we forbid them to practise what we ourselves teach to be a Christian duty? And yet it is apparent what fearful and execrable effects the practice of this pretended duty doth produce among them. It was by inspiration, say they, that their progenitors did break out of the Church; and by inspiration they do still introduce endlessly new fancies and practices. It is by inspiration that they endanger the ruin of Christianity itself by infinite schisms and pestilent reformations. It is by inspiration that they employ the Gospel to destroy the Gospel; from thence preaching heresies in churches and chambers, sedition in states, rebellion against princes and prelates; so destroying all order, unity, and peace everywhere. These things considered, what can be more reasonable than that we should take heed how we furnish them thus with arms to maintain themselves, and to fight against God and His Church?

22. This is the objection which, though it have a fearful show, yet, being well examined, it will prove no less weakly grounded than the former. For the demonstrating, therefore, of the inconsequence of it, I will, by way of preparation, lay down these following undeniable principles, briefly mentioned before, viz.

23. First, that divine inspirations are so absolutely necessary in precepts for the avoiding of sin, and in counsels for the gaining of perfection, that without them no action of ours can be good or meritorious. Yea, the duties of obligation which we perform, or counsels of perfection freely obeyed by us, are only so far acceptable to God as they proceed from His inspirations and motions of His Holy Spirit. This is not only an undoubted verity, but one of the most fundamental verities of the Christian religion, which attributes all good in us to the Divine Grace. And what is grace but the divine inspiration of love spread abroad in our hearts by the Holy Ghost, as St. Augustine saith? To this verity give evident witness those expressions of the Church in her public devotions 'Da, Domine, famulis tuis, ut quæ a te jussa agnovimus, implere cœlesti inspiratione valeamus;' that is, 'Grant, O Lord, unto Thy servants, that those things which we acknowledge to have been commanded by Thee, we may, by Thy heavenly inspiration, accomplish.' And again: 'Auge populi tui vota placatus; quia in nullo fidelium nisi ex tua inspiratione

proveniunt quarumlibet incrementa virtutum;' that is, 'Increase in mercy, O Lord, the desires of Thy servants; for not the least progress in any virtues can be made by any of Thy faithful servants by any other means, but only by Thy (divine) inspirations.'

24. The second ground is consequent on the former, viz. that since such absolute necessity there is of divine inspirations, the necessity obliging us to correspond unto them is, and must needs be, equal. For, from no other root, but the neglect of this obligation, doth or can proceed all our mischief. The guilt of such neglect is so much the greater inasmuch as the gift of God's Holy Spirit imprinted in the hearts of His servants is of such an active nature that, were it not that the spirit of corrupt nature, cherished by us, doth deafen its call and weaken its efficacy, it would continually, being wakened by every occasion, incite us to love God only, and to raise up our souls to Him. Now by such neglect, we are said in Holy Scriptures to contristate the Holy Ghost; and by oft contristating Him we shall, in the end, come to quench Him. And the first indignation of God against such negligent despisers of His holy inspirations and calls is powerfully expressed in those words of his: *Quia vocavi et renuistis, &c.: Because I have called, and ye refused, I stretched forth My hand, and there was none that regarded, I also will laugh at your destruction, and I will mock when that which ye did fear shall happen unto you, &c. Then shall they call on Me, and I will not hear: they shall rise early, and they shall not find Me* (Prov. i. 24-28). Now though it be not indeed a mortal sin to resist the motion of the Divine Spirit inciting us to actions which are not of essential obligation, yet so doing we do contristate God's Spirit, and more indispose ourselves afterwards to observe and follow its directions. And mortal sins are seldom rushed into upon the sudden: they begin with lesser resistances, by which the mind is more obscured and less capable to obey it in greater matters. But as for perfect souls, they are in continual attendance and obedience thereto, being in continual prayer, or in good works and exercises begun and performed in virtue of prayer, and also accompanied by prayer.

25. The third preparatory ground follows, which is this: that since these so necessary internal inspirations must necessarily be hearkened to and corresponded with, and since there may be false suggestions, either of the devil or of our corrupt nature, which may counterfeit or subtly pretend to a divine original, therefore it is necessary that some possible, yea satisfactory, means should be afforded how to distinguish between true and false inspirations. For otherwise we shall have an impossible obligation to obey we know not whom, nor what. We shall be in as much danger to be actuated by the devil, and used as instruments of his illusions, as of the saving influxes of

God's Holy Spirit; and consequently shall not be able to distinguish the way between heaven and hell.

26. Neither will it suffice to say, that we do sufficiently perform God's will when we perform the commands of God expressed clearly in Scripture, likewise the precepts of the Church, and of all our lawful superiors. For neither will the doing of these things without an interior influx of grace avail us, since the devil can be content, yea will suggest the exercise of the greatest virtues to hearts which he knows will intend only the satisfaction of natural pride, or the interests of self-love, in them. And, besides, neither can any of these external rules extend to all our actions, so as to regulate them in order to contemplation and perfection.

27. The fourth and last ground to be premised is this: that since it is necessary to be enabled to distinguish the true inspirations of God from the false suggestions of our enemy, the only means imaginable that can be proper, natural, and efficacious to obtain such a supernatural light to discern God's will in all things is pure spiritual prayer exercised by a soul living an abstracted, internal, recollected life, spent in a continual attendance on God, &c.

28. This is a way suitable to reason, conformable to Scriptures and the doctrine of the holy fathers, and delivered both by ancient and modern mystic authors, as might copiously be demonstrated if there were any cause to think, that to pray perfectly, and by prayer to obtain divine grace, were suspicious exercises to any. In a word, this is a way, the which practised according to the instructions here delivered, all manner of good and no possible inconvenience can flow from it.

29. Here is no pretending to new or strange revelations. no walking *in mirabilibus super se:* no zealous seditious reformations, nor the least prejudice done or intended to peace, unity, humility, obedience, or any other divine virtue. Yea, on the contrary, all these heavenly graces are hereby not only fortified and increased, but by no other means can be perfectly obtained.

30. And indeed, since in a world of passages in Holy Scriptures we find ourselves obliged to a double duty, the one whereof perhaps in popular judgments seems to entrench upon the other, and yet neither of them is in due place and circumstances to be omitted, namely, obedience both to God's Holy Spirit inwardly directing, and also to superior outwardly commanding; by what other way can we reconcile such seemingly different and, as it may fall out, contrary precepts, but by joining this doctrine to that concerning outward obedience? Which is here done, and done without the least prejudice to either; yea manifestly to the advantage of both in their due circumstances. If, then, for any outward carnal respects, we shall conceal or discountenance this most necessary duty of following the inspirations of God, we shall efface the proper character of God's servants, who are said to be such as are *led by*

the Spirit of God, and that *by the unction are taught in all things.* Again, if, on pretence of following inspirations and internal lights which cannot be so absolutely certain, we shall transgress the most evident certain commands of lawful superiors, which are, therefore, God's also, there would quickly follow an end of all order, peace, and government. What other means, therefore, is left to comply with both these, but to obey God both ways; that is, commanding most certainly when His will is revealed by superiors; and also very securely when, in other internal things, or which tend to perfection, without the least wrong, yea to the great advantage of superiors, He doth communicate His light and directions to us? So as that saying of the Apostles with which they silenced the whole Jewish Sanhedrim, namely, that *God is rather to be obeyed than man,* commanding contrary to God, holds only when it can evidently be demonstrated (as the Apostles then did by miracles) that such a command did indeed come from God, or that the thing commanded by man is certainly unlawful.

31. These things considered, in all reason we ought to be so far from being deterred from publishing such instructions as these, because forsooth the frantic spirits of this age do falsely make pretended inspirations the cause and ground of all the miseries and mischiefs of late happening in our nation, &c., that for this very reason and motive every one ought to publish such wholesome doctrines, the which are the only possible means to undeceive them. For what other way does there remain to convince them of their errors and seductions, dangerous to all mankind, but most certainly pernicious to their own souls? Shall we tell them that there are no inspirations at all? We shall, in so doing, betray the Christian religion. Shall we say, though there be inspirations, yet they are never to be marked, never obeyed nor complied withal? Besides the ridiculous falseness of the assertion, which will expose us to their most just contempt and hatred, they will overwhelm us with unanswerable texts of Scripture and passages from the holy fathers. What other thing then can be done, but that (acknowledging both that there are inspirations, and that we are obliged to correspond unto them) we should inform those unhappy souls how to dispose themselves so as to be out of danger of diabolical illusions, and to be in a capacity of receiving inspirations truly divine? As likewise with what caution and prudence, but withal with what fidelity, they ought to comply with them. But especially we ought to demonstrate and inculcate this fundamental verity, that the general and most certain precepts of humility, obedience, unity, and peace must never receive any prejudice by any pretended inspirations or illuminations; since those which are truly from God do establish and increase all these virtues; yea, that the external order, authority, and subordination established by God in His Church (by which alone it becomes one body, and not a monstrous heap of

unlike, unproportionable members, fighting with and devouring one another) must be the rule by which to examine, and the judge to pronounce sentence for or against all manner of inspirations.

32. Therefore, instead of a human fruitless policy of hiding such divine fundamental practical truths as these, let us sincerely, faithfully, and plentifully teach them. And though it can never be prevented but that the devil will suggest to proud, ambitious, covetous, or sensual spirits to draw poison from the most perfect doctrines of Catholic Faith, yet then at least he and they will be the less able to seduce well-meaning souls to join with them; yea, by God's grace and benediction upon His truth faithfully taught, they will lose many such already seduced, when all their pretended lights being confronted before the Sun of divine verity and holiness, will either vanish quite away, or manifestly discover themselves to be the sulphurous gloomy lights of such wandering falling stars as are mentioned by St. Jude, to whom the tempest of darkness is reserved for ever.

33. Oh, therefore, that it were God's blessed will that they would be persuaded to examine themselves and their instincts by such characters, such signs so manifestly Christian, holy, perfect, and secure as are here contained in this treatise, and accordingly judge of their and our inspirations! 1. In the first place, here the only proper disposition towards the receiving of supernatural irradiations from God's Holy Spirit is an abstraction of life, a sequestration from all businesses that concern others, and an attendance to God alone in the depth of the spirit; whereas their lights never come more frequently than when either being alone they yield to discontented, unquiet passions and murmurings about the behaviour and actions of others; or, when in close meetings and conspiracies, they vent such passions by invectives against the governors of the Church or State. 2. The lights here desired and prayed for are such as do expel all images of creatures, and do calm all manner of passions, to the end that the soul, being in a vacuity, may be more capable of receiving and entertaining God in the pure fund of the spirit. Whereas their lights fill them with all tumultuous disquieting images and phantasms concerning the supposed miscarriages of all others but themselves: and not only heighten their passions, but urge them to most terrible desolating effects. 3. The prayer here acknowledged to be the most effectual instrument to procure divine light is a pure, recollected, intime prayer of the spirit. Whereas the prayer they glory in is only an acquired ability and sleight to talk earnestly to God before others, and oft thereby to communicate their passions and discontents to their brethren. 4. Here are no new speculative verities or revelations of mysteries pretended: no private newly-found-out interpretations of Scripture bragged of. Whereas amongst them every day produces a new fancy, which must gather new company. 5. Here the estab-

lished order of God's Church, and the unity essential thereto, is not prejudiced. Yea, the inspirations expected and obtained by pure internal prayer do more firmly and unalterably fix souls under this obedience, and to this order and unity; insomuch as whatsoever pretended lights do endanger the dissolving of unity, or do cross lawful authority, or shall be rejected by it, they are presently suspected and extinguished. Whereas those men's lights teach them nothing so much as to contemn and oppose all external authority, and to dissipate unity, dispersing the body of Christianity into innumerable sects and conventicles. 6. Our lights teach us to attend only to God and our own souls, and never to interest ourselves in any care or employment about others, till evidently God's inspirations force us, and external authority obliges us thereto. Whereas their lights render them incapable of solitude, and thrust them abroad to be reformers of others, being themselves impatient of all reformation and contradiction. 7. Our lights make us to fear and avoid all supereminence and judicature, all sensual pleasures, desires of wealth, honours, &c. Whereas their lights engage them violently and deeply in all these carnal and secular ways, and (for the attaining to these) in tumults, sedition, bloodshed, and war; in a word, in all manner of actions and designs most contrary to the spirit of Christianity. 8. And, lastly, our lights, if they should chance sometimes to be mistaken by us, no harm at all would accrue to others, and not any considerable prejudice to ourselves; because, as hath been said, the matters in which they direct us are in their nature indifferent, and are ordered only towards a more perfect loving of God, and withdrawing us from creatures. Whereas all the miseries, and almost all the disorders and enormous vices, of the nations are the effects of their misleading lights.

34. Thus stands the case between Catholic inspirations and the pretended inspirations of sectaries. Such is that spirit of charity and peace, and so divine are the effects of it directing the minds of good, humble, obedient, and devout Catholics; and such is the spirit of disorder, revenge, wrath, rebellion, &c., and so dismal are the effects of that spirit wherewith self-opinionated, presumptuous, frantic sectaries are agitated! What resemblance, what agreement can there be between these two? This evil spirit, though it sacrilegiously usurps the name, yet it does not so much as counterfeit the operations of the Good One. Or if with the name it do sometimes seem to counterfeit some outward resemblances, and to some persons show demure looks, &c., yet the equivocation and hypocrisy is so gross and palpable that they must put out their eyes that perceive it not.

35. Shall we, then, extinguish, and in some sort exorcise, the good Divine Spirit, for fear it should raise up the evil one with it? Or rather shall we not confidently assure ourselves that, upon the appearing of the Good

One, the evil one will either vanish, or the hideousness of it will affright all from hearkening to it? Shall we forbid the sun to rise, because in some unclean, rotten marshes some fogs will arise with it? We may as well annul the Sacraments, forbid prayer, extinguish the Scriptures, &c.; for from all these the devil has maliciously taken advantage to pervert and damn thousands of souls.

36. No doubt it is but that among those seduced and seducing people great numbers there are who, if they were charitably instructed in such ways of discerning spirits, they would be surprised and would start to see to what kinds of directors and guides they have unwaringly committed their souls. If such as these could be persuaded (and I beseech God they may), even whilst they are yet out of the Church, for a while to suspend the pursuance of their busy designs and reforming of others, and retiring themselves into solitude, would allow themselves the leisure to turn their eyes inward into their own spirits, and practise as well as they can the humble, self-renouncing, resigned way of spiritual prayer taught in this book, thereby to procure from God such lights as then may be trusted to, neither they nor we should ever repent that the publishing such doctrines as these gave them a happy occasion to do so.

37. And what greater satisfaction can Catholics have in their ways! And what greater advantage can they have over all those that are out of the Church than this proof made good by universal experience, viz. that whosoever sincerely and constantly gives himself to the practice of such perfect prayer as is here taught, if he be already a Catholic, he will most certainly ever remain so; and if he be not yet in the Church, he will be afraid of remaining his own pastor and guide? For never did any Catholic that exercised spiritual prayer cease to be a Catholic till he first ceased so to pray. And the spirit of such prayer, in any perfection, never rested upon any soul that was out of the Catholic Church.

38. And this, I suppose, may suffice not only to justify the truth and innocency of this our doctrine concerning divine inspirations, &c., but also the lawfulness, yea conveniency, yea even the necessity of publishing it to the world; and this for those very reasons wherewith others would deter us. For the objectors are afraid of the publication of it, lest frantic sectaries should think themselves justified in their pretences; and, on the contrary, I conceive the publication necessary, lest they should think themselves justified in their pretences, which, till they see how unlike to true divine lights and inspirations theirs are, they may have some show for. I do not intend, when I call it our doctrine, to appropriate it to any person or community; for it is the very same that hath in all ages been taught by all saints experienced in internal ways, as will be demonstrated by infinite testimonies ancient and modern, if God shall engage us to such a labour by the opposition of any one. True it is, that the pious and sublime Author of the treatises here abridged

hath (doubtless by the guidance and assistance of a supernatural light) spent more thoughts about this subject, and taken more pains in encouraging well-minded souls to fit themselves for the receiving of such light, in distinguishing it from false lights, and in showing the blessed effects of it, &c., than perhaps any other author formerly did. And that is all. For the doctrine in substance is as old as Christianity itself, and cannot seem strange or new but only to such to whom in these days antiquity seemeth the greatest novelty.

39. Having thus, by declaring the insufficiency of these objections against the publishing of the following instructions, opened the barriers to give this book a free scope to range abroad at liberty; and my only intention being (for God's glory) to benefit thy soul, dear reader; for as for the mean or sinister ends of gaining credit or esteem with others thereby, the ambition is so unworthy of my profession, and withal so poor and unreasonable, considering that I can appropriate nothing to myself but a little pains in transcribing and digesting another man's labours, that I cannot think myself liable to any suspicion with thee in that regard; therefore, to the end I may, according to the utmost of my ability, facilitate the receiving good to thy spirit hereby, though I have no more objections to answer, yet by conversing with certain pious and learned persons to whose perusal and judgment this book was presented. having found that some few passages in it were not so very clearly expressed, but that even an uninterested and dispassionate reader might, perhaps, stop a little at them, I thought it expedient to let thee, good reader, be acquainted what satisfaction I gave to them.

40. One point that seemed to require explanation is that (1st treat. 2nd sec. 2nd chap.) where is treated of what care a spiritual disciple ought to take in the choice of a fit director. For to leave a matter of such importance to the election of an inexperienced, and perhaps young and ignorant, soul, seemed to them neither convenient nor prudent. Besides that in religious communities such a permission would be an infringing of all due order and submission to superiors. But hereto was replied: 1. That religious persons were expressly excepted in the book; 2. and as for others, this very same advice was long since given by the Bishop of Geneva, Avila, &c. True it is, notwithstanding, that there may oft be found in the world many good devout souls that yet are not very capable of making a good choice. However, even such, as far as is allowed, ought to use their best endeavours, hoping that God will bless such their care for the advancement of their spirits. Notwithstanding such ought withal to take heed that from too nice a curiosity in choosing, there do not follow any disquiet in the families where they live, if several persons should be zealous each for a particular director; as St. Jerome chides a mother and a daughter that upon such an occasion separated from one an-

other. Therefore in such a case a good soul that will prefer peace before contenting her mind may, of all others, rely upon God, assuring herself that He will in a special manner assist and conduct her, supplying all other wants. And particularly such an extraordinary divine assistance may be most confidently expected by well-disposed souls in religious communities, where such freedom of choosing is not permitted. For, as Rusbrochius saith, God will rather send an Angel from heaven than that such humble, obedient, and sincere souls relying upon Him shall want due helps. Therefore, such as forbear a solicitous searching after a director, either for the preventing inconveniences, or out of an humble, sincere apprehension of the danger of erring in the choice, or a religious regard to the prejudice it might cause in a community to peace and good order, &c., such may well hope that God will not permit them to be losers thereby. Yea, moreover, such as in the fore-named cases think they have a true occasion, and that they may justly do it for the quieting of their consciences, resolving of their doubts, &c., had need be very wary that they proceed sincerely, and that they really seek their spiritual profit, and not natural contentment. For, as our Venerable Father Baker in a certain place adviseth, it is not sufficient to any souls, that it is permitted by the laws of the Church at certain times to require a special director (upon a consideration of the expedience and necessity that some souls in some circumstances may have), but they are to consider whether their case have these circumstances, and whether they do truly make use of the said permission for the right end.

41. A second point in the same chapter supposed to require explanation was that assertion, that a devout soul once set in a good and proper way of prayer, after she has made some progress in it, ought not to have recourse ordinarily to a director, but that she should practise the following of God's directions, &c. On the contrary, it was supposed that until a soul have made some considerable progress in the prayer of the will, she would not be subject to illusions, and, therefore, had thenceforward most need of advice from a prudent guide. But this difficulty is cleared towards the latter end of the third treatise, where it is taught that in the case and peril of illusion upon an opinion of some extraordinary illuminations, &c., it is necessary that souls, though never so much advanced, should distrust their own judgment, and never presume to add belief unto, and much less put in execution anything suggested by, any illuminations (true or pretended) without the advice and consent of superiors and directors. But, as for the ordinary practices of an internal life, as prayer and mortification, &c., it is very requisite that souls should be taught, as soon as may be, to quit an assiduous dependence on external guides, from whence would follow nothing but solicitudes, distractions, &c. There is a parallel advice, though in somewhat a different case in the 3rd treat. 4th sec., 3rd chap. §§ 36, 37, where, in a discourse concerning rapts and the like extraordinary favours, it is said of perfect souls that

they may judge of those matters by their own supernatural light, &c., and that they are not so absolutely obliged to resign their judgments and wills to others as utterly to neglect their own proper call received from God, &c. By which words it is not meant that any souls, though never so perfect, should be exempted from the obligation of submission to superiors, judging or ordaining, concerning such divine favours; but only that such perfect souls need not so often have recourse for advice about such matters, but may proceed by that divine light communicated to them; whereas the imperfect ought neither to yield belief nor execution further than they have advice and order for. Now who would find fault with St. Teresa, St. Catherine of Sienna, &c., if they should forbear consultations after every rapt of revelation, having formerly been sufficiently warranted by superiors, &c.?

42. In consequence to the story of V. R. F. Balthasar Alvarez's account given of his prayer to his general (mentioned in the 3rd treatise, 1st sect. 7th chap. at the end), where a relation is made of the general's orders, requiring all superiors to direct and assist the younger religious among them, so as that they might highly esteem and in their practice follow the manner of prayer most suitable to their institute, and prescribed in their exercises, I think myself obliged to acquaint thee, dear reader, that by two books published of late by two Rev. Fathers of the Society, and perused by me since the writing and printing of that passage, I find that the said orders of the general are not, at least of late, so rigidly interpreted as formerly they were.

43. The authors of the said books written in French are R. F. Ant. Civorá and R. F. Andr. Baiole, in which the whole doctrine of this book, especially concerning the excellency of affective prayer beyond discoursive, is most copiously and strongly asserted. Yea and moreover the instructions concerning the necessity of attending to and following divine inspirations, as likewise ways prescribed to distinguish them from false suggestions of the devil or corrupt nature, are so largely, clearly, and even in the very phrases of this book delivered by the former of the two in his book called *Les Secrets de la Science des Saints* (tr. iii. cap. ix. from p. 402 to p. 486), that, it not being credible that he had seen our V. F. A. Baker's writings, we may rationally infer that what he writes with such extraordinary exactness proceeded from a deep and experimental knowledge of these internal and secret paths of contemplation.

44. So that no doubt there are many devout persons in the society who, not being engaged in many external employments, and enjoying consequently both a solitude and liberty of spirit greater perhaps than will be afforded in many communities by profession purely contemplative, do permit

themselves to the divine conduct, and make wonderful progress in these divine ways.

45. True indeed it is that the other author (F. Andr. Baiole) seems to maintain that the spiritual exercises, according to the intention of St. Ignatius, will, by practice, become a prayer of contemplation and mystic union, an assertion in which I have not yet found any to join with him. But, however, he shows in his book (styled *La Vie Intárieure*) that he had a true notion of the prayer of mystic union. And that being so, he may freely enjoy the contentment of the former supposition.

46. Besides these, there may possibly be other passages that thou also, devout reader, if thou hadst had the perusal before the impression, wouldst perhaps have given us occasion to explain or interpret more at large. If it prove so, all we can do is to refer them to thine own candour and charity, promising upon a re-impression all satisfaction possible; and in the mean time requesting that our own good intention and the judgment of our superiors and approvers may be our safeguard. Only one suit we make unto thee (most reasonable and just), which is, that thou wouldst not proceed to the censure of any passage till thou hast read the whole book. The same points and matters do occasionally come in several places, and it would have been too great a tiring of thee to repeat in every place all the circumstances and phrases necessary for explanation or prevention of suspicions and objections. If it be for thine own good principally that thou art a reader, we shall stand in little need of preparing thee with apologies. And if it be for our hurt that thou art a reader, we thank God we are not guilty of the least ill design to make us fear, except only in thy behalf. All that we have to say is, God Almighty make thee (whosoever thou art) a practiser of the good that thou wilt certainly find in the following treatises; and then we shall have no cause to apprehend either for thee or ourselves.

47. Thus, truly, for aught appears to me, devout reader, thou mayest freely, and without the least apprehension of any danger, peruse and make thy best benefit of these following instructions; the which, moreover, as thou seest, have passed the censure and deserved the approbations of several pious and learned persons. Whatever opinion thou shalt, after reading, have of them, at least I will oblige thee to acknowledge that here (in the treatises that follow) is no manner of covert indirect meaning or design (according to the fashion nowadays) to broach any bold new-fangled inventions, and much less of maintaining unduly what shall be duly found fault with, since they are exposed to the common view by one that (as he hitherto hath so) here he doth (and by God's grace ever will) submit himself and his writings to the authority and judgment of the See Apostolic in the first place, and next to all other his superiors. This I profess, as is the duty of an humble, obedient son of the Church. And this, if I did not moreover expressly signify with reference to

the doctrines contained in the following treatises, I could not avoid some degree of guilt and imputation of not delivering candidly and faithfully our Venerable Author's sense, who in many places protesteth the like submission of all his writings to all lawful authority whatsoever.

Farewell, dear reader. Oremus invicem, ut salvemur. AMEN

Contents

THE FIRST TREATISE

OF A CONTEMPLATIVE LIFE IN GENERAL. THE NATURE AND END THEREOF, AND GENERAL DISPOSITION REQUIRED THERETO.

THE FIRST SECTION
OF A CONTEMPLATIVE LIFE.

CHAPTER I.

§§ 1-3. Continual union in spirit with God the end of man's creation, and practised by Adam in innocence.

§§ 4. 5. Man's fall and misery through sin.

§§ 6, 7. Which is transfused into us and all his posterity.

§§ 8, 9. The reparation of mankind by Christ.

§§ 10, 11. That all Christians are obliged to aspire to perfection in divine love by the ways of prayer, &c., as Adam did.

1. It was only infinite goodness that moved Almighty God to create the world of nothing, and particularly in this inferior visible world, to create man after His own image and similitude, consisting of a frail earthly body, which is the prison of an immortal, intellectual spirit, to the end that by his understanding, which is capable of an unlimited knowledge, and by his will, which cannot be replenished with any object of goodness less than infinite, he might so govern and order himself, and all other visible creatures, as thereby to arrive unto the end for which he was made, to wit, eternal beatitude both in soul and body in heaven, the which consists in a returning to the divine principle from whom he flowed, and an inconceivably happy union with Him, both in mind, contemplating eternally His infinite perfections, and

1

in will and affections eternally loving, admiring, and enjoying the said perfections.

2. Now to the end that man might not (except by his own free and willful choice of misery) fail from attaining to the only universal end of his creation, God was pleased to the natural vast capacity of man's understanding and will to add a supernatural light, illustrating his mind to believe and know Him, and divine charity in the will, which was as it were a weight to incline and draw the soul, without any defect or interruption to love God, and Him only. So that by a continual presence of this light, and an uninterrupted exercise of this love, the soul of man would in time have attained to such a measure of perfection of union with God in this world, as without dying to merit a translation from hence to heaven, there eternally to enjoy a far more incomprehensibly perfect and beatifying union with God.

3. Hence it appears that the means to happiness, and the end itself, are essentially the same thing, to wit, union of the spirit with God, and differ only in degrees. And the union which Adam during his state of innocence did and would always have practised was in a sort perpetual, never being interrupted (except perhaps in sleep). For, loving God only and purely for Himself, he had no strange affection to distract him, and the images of creatures, which either by his consideration of them, or operations about them, did adhere to his internal senses, did not at all divert his mind from God, because he contemplated them only in order to God; or rather he contemplated God alone in them, loving and serving Him only in all his reflections on them, or workings about them. So that creatures and all offices towards them served as steps to raise Adam to a more sublime and more intimate union with God; the which was both his duty and his present happiness, besides that it was a disposition to his future eternal beatitude.

4. But our first parents by a willful contempt and transgression of that one most easy command, which God for a trial of their obedience had imposed on them, not only broke the foresaid union, and deprived themselves of the hope of enjoying God eternally in the future life, but moreover were utterly divested of all supernatural graces, and extremely weakened and disordered in all their natural gifts. So that having lost that divine light, by which their understandings had been illustrated, and that divine love by which their wills and affections adhered continually to God, they were rendered incapable either of contemplating God (except only as a severe judge and avenger), or consequently of affording Him any degree of love. On the contrary, both their minds and affections were only employed on themselves, or on creatures, for their own natural, carnal interests or pleasure; and this with such a violent obstinacy and firmness, that it was impossible for them

2

by any force left in corrupt nature to raise their love towards God, being once so impetuously precipitated from Him towards themselves.

5. All these miserable depravations having been caused in all the powers and faculties of their souls by the forbidden fruit, the which utterly and irreparably disordered that most healthful, exact temper of their bodily constitutions; insomuch as the spirits and humours, &c., which before did nothing at all hinder their exercisings and operations towards God, but did much promote them, now did wholly dispose them to love and seek themselves only, with an utter aversion from God, and the accomplishing of His divine will; and all circumstant creatures, instead of being steps to raise them towards God, on the contrary more and more seduced their affections from Him, and raised all other inordinate passions displeasing to Him. Hereby in lieu of that peaceable and happy condition which they before enjoyed in this world by a continual union with God (the which was to be perfected eternally in the world to come), they became disquieted, distracted, and even torn asunder with a multitude of passions and designs, oft contrary to one another, but all of them much more opposite to God; so that by falling from unity to a miserable multiplicity, and from peace to an endless war, they were therein captived by the devil, readily yielding to all his suggestions, hateful to and hating God, and so contracted not only an unavoidable necessity of a corporal death, but also the guilt and right to an eternal separation from God after death in that lake of fire and brimstone burning for ever, and prepared for the devil and his angels.

6. Now the whole stock of human nature being thus totally and universally depraved in our first parents, it could not by any possible natural means be avoided, but that all their posterity should be equally infected and poisoned with all these disorders, all which were increased and daily heightened by ill education and actual transgressions. And consequently the same guilt both of temporal and eternal death was withal transfused upon them.

7. But Almighty God, the Father of mercies, pitying His own creatures thus ingulfed in utter misery by the fault of Adam, seduced by his and our common enemy, did in His most unspeakable mercy, freely and unasked, provide and ordain His own coeternal Son to be a Saviour unto mankind; who by His most bitter sufferings and death redeemed us from the guilt of eternal death; and by His glorious life and resurrection, having obtained a power of sending the Holy Ghost (communicated to us in His word and sacraments, &c.), He hath rectified all these disorders, shedding forth a new heavenly light to cure the blindness of our understandings, and divine charity in our hearts, the which abateth that inordinate self-love formerly reigning in us, and hereby He reinstates us (cooperating with His divine grace, and per-

severing therein) to a new right unto eternal happiness, (perhaps) more sublime than man in innocency was destined to.

8. Notwithstanding, it was not the good will and pleasure of God by this reparation to restore us to the same state of perfect holiness wherein Adam lived in paradise. And this we ought to ascribe to His infinite wisdom, and also to His unspeakable goodness towards us; for certainly, if we had been once more left, as Adam was, in the free power of our own wills, that is, in so casual an estate as Adam was, and assisted and fortified with no stronger an aid than the primitive grace, we should again have irreparably forfeited all our happiness, and plunged ourselves far more deeply in endless misery.

9. Therefore, Almighty God thought fit for our humiliation, and to keep us in continual vigilance and fear, as also thereby daily to refresh the memory of our primitive guilt, and our thankfulness for His inestimable goodness, to leave us in a necessity of incurring temporal death, which we are not now to look on as a punishment of sin, so much as a freedom from sin, and a gate and entrance to eternal glory. Moreover, though by His grace He hath abolished the guilt of original sin, yet He hath suffered still to remain in us many bitter effects of it, the which shall never in this life be so wholly extinguished by grace, or our holy endeavours, but that some degrees of ignorance and inclinations to that pernicious love of ourselves will remain in us; by which means we are preserved from our greatest enemy, pride, and also forced to a continual watchfulness and combat against ourselves, and our spiritual enemies; always distrusting ourselves and relying upon the medicinal omnipotent regenerating grace of Christ, far more helpful to us than the grace of innocence was, in that it not only more powerfully inclines our wills and conquers the actual resistance of them, by making them freely coöperate with it, whensoever they do coöperate (for it takes not away our liberty to resist), but likewise after it hath been weakened by venial sins, and extinguished by mortal, it is again and again renewed by the means of the sacraments and prayer, &c.

10. Our duty therefore in our present state, and the employment of our whole lives, must be constantly and fervently to coöperate with divine grace, thereby endeavouring not only to get victory over self-love, pride, sensuality, &c., by humility, divine love, and all other virtues; but also not to content ourselves with any limited degrees of piety and holiness, but daily to aspire, according to our abilities assisted with grace by the same ways to the same perfection for which we were first created, and which was practised by Adam in innocence; to wit, an utter extinguishing of self-love and all affection to creatures, except in order to God, and as they may be instrumental to beget and increase divine love in us; and a continual uninterrupted union in

spirit with God, by faith contemplating Him, and by love ever adhering to Him.

11. This, I say, is the duty and indispensable obligation of all Christians, of what condition soever, not only seriously to aspire to the divine love, but also to the perfection thereof suitably to their several states and vocations, for it is morally impossible for a soul to love God, as He ought to be loved (that is, as the only object of her love, and as the only universal end of her being and life, for the procuring of an inseparable union with whom and for no other reason the use and comfort of creatures was permitted and given to her), I say, it is morally impossible for such a soul so loving God deliberately and habitually to yield to the love of anything but God only, and in order to Him; or to stop in any inferior degree of love to Him. The frailty of nature and many unavoidable distractions and temptations may and generally do hinder most souls from attaining or even approaching to such perfection, to such uninterrupted attention and union with God, as was practised by Adam in innocency, and by a few perfect souls in all ages; but nothing but the want of true sincere love will hinder the aspiring thereto, according to the measure and strength of grace that each soul in her order enjoys. And both reason and experience witness this truth in all manner of loves, lawful or unlawful; for we see that wheresoever the love to riches, honour, empire, or pleasure is the tyrannising affection, so as to cause the person to place his supposed happiness in any of these, such persons neither will nor can, being so disposed, willfully surcease a continual progress in pursuing their designs endlessly; neither can they admit an habitual and deliberate adherence with affection to any other object, though (not ruinous, but) in an inferior degree prejudicial to what they principally affect.

Chapter II. Of Natural Propensions to Devotion

§ 1. Commonly those only are said to aspire to perfection that consecrate themselves to God.

§ 2. A natural devotion and propension to seek God, of which the degrees are infinitely various.

§§ 3, 4, 5. Yet all ranged under two states—Active and Contemplative.

§§ 6, 7. Generally most souls are of a mixed temper between both; hence comes the difficulty of the guiding of souls.

§ 8. At the first entrance into internal ways all souls seem to be of an Active temper.

1. Notwithstanding although all Christians are obliged to aspire to perfection, and to lead spiritual lives, sanctifying all their actions and employments by prayer, yet the effectual practice of this obligation is so very rare that in ordinary speech those only are said to aspire unto perfection who have been so highly favoured by God, as to have been called by Him from all solicitous engagement in worldly affairs, so as to make the only business and employment of their lives to be the serving, adoring, loving, meditating, and praying unto God, the attending to and following His divine inspirations, &c., in a state of competent abstraction and solitude; and this most ordinarily and perfectly in a religious profession, or if in the world, yet in a course of life divided and separated from the world.

2. There seems indeed to remain even naturally in all souls a certain propension to seek God (though not at all for Himself, but merely for the satisfaction of nature, and self-ends), which is a kind of natural devotion, and is to be found even in heretics, yea, Jews and heathens; and this more or less according to their several dispositions and corporal complexions, the variety of which is wonderful and almost incredible. Now when divine grace adjoins itself to such good propensions, it promotes and increases them, rectifying what is amiss in them, especially by purifying the intention and making them to seek God only for God himself, and no unworthy inferior ends of nature; but it doth not at all alter the complexion itself, but conducts souls in spiritual ways suitably to their several dispositions by an almost infinite variety of paths and fashions, yet all tending to the same general end, which is the union of our spirits with God by perfect love.

3. Notwithstanding all these varieties of dispositions and ways (of which we shall treat more fully when we come to speak of internal prayer) may commodiously enough be reduced in gross to two ranks, to wit, Active and Contemplative spirits: both which aspire to a perfection of union in spirit with God by perfect love; and for that purpose in gross practice make use of the same means necessary to that end, to wit, mortification and prayer. But yet the manner both of their union and prayer, and consequently of their mortification also is very different; and the root of such difference is the forementioned variety of propensions and natural dispositions to internal ways.

4. For, first, the propension which is in some souls to devotion is of such a nature that it inclines them much to busy their imagination and to frame in their minds motives to the divine love by internal discourse, so as that without such reasoning and use of images they can seldom with any efficacy raise or fix their affections on God. Such dispositions are not patient of much solitude or recollection more than shall be necessary to enable them to produce and maintain a right intention in outward doings and works of char-

6

ity, to the which they are powerfully inclined; and the mortifications most willingly practised by them are usually external, and oftentimes voluntarily assumed, the which make a great show and procure very great esteem from others. And proportionably hereto the divine love and union produced by such means is very vigorous, but less pure and spiritual, apt to express itself by much sensible devotion and tenderness. The state therefore and perfection of these souls is called the state and perfection of an Active life.

5. Again, others are naturally of a propension to seek God in the obscurity of faith, with a more profound introversion of spirit, and with less activity and motion in sensitive nature, and without the use of grosser images, yet with far greater simplicity, purity, and efficacy. And consequently such souls are not of themselves much inclined to external works (except when God calls them thereto by secret inspirations, or engages them therein by command of superiors), but they seek rather to purify themselves and inflame their hearts in the love of God by internal, quiet, and pure actuations in spirit, by a total abstraction from creatures, by solitude, both external and especially internal, so disposing themselves to receive the influxes and inspirations of God, whose guidance chiefly they endeavour to follow in all things. And the mortifications practised by them, though less remarkable, yet are far more efficacious, being profound and penetrating even to the most secret deordinations of the spirit. By a constant pursuance of such exercises, their spirits becoming naked and empty of all strange affections, images, and distractions, the Divine Spirit only lives and operates in them, affording them light to perceive and strength to subdue self-love in its most secret and, to all others, imperceptible insinuations; and by consequence they attain unto an union with God far more strict and immediate than the former, by a love much more masculine, pure, and divine. And the state and perfection of these happy souls is called the state and perfection of a Contemplative life.

6. Now, though all internal dispositions of souls (by which mankind is more diversified than by outward features) may conveniently enough be ranged under these two states, yet we are not to conceive that each soul is by its temper entirely and absolutely either contemplative or active; for, on the contrary, the most part are of a disposition mixed between both, and partaking somewhat, more or less, of each. But they receive the denomination from that whereto the propension is more strong.

7. And from hence comes that great difficulty that there is in the conducting and managing of souls in these internal ways; for each several disposition must be put in a way suitable to the spirit of the party, otherwise small progress can be expected. Now, that wherein the diversity of spirits is principally discerned is their prayer. If therefore an active spirit should be obliged to that internal solitude, to that quiet affective prayer of the heart

alone which is proper to contemplative souls; or if a contemplative spirit should be too long detained or fettered with the rules and busy methods of discursive meditation (which is a prayer chiefly of the head or imagination); or, lastly, if a spirit of a mixed disposition should be strictly confined to either of these sorts of prayer and not allowed to practise them interchangeably according as she finds profitable to her present temper of mind, &c., they would entangle themselves with insuperable difficulties, scrupulosities, and unsatisfaction, and be so far from any considerable advancement, that they would be in danger of giving over all thought of seeking God internally.

8. Notwithstanding, although the propensions of some souls to internal operations of the spirit, and consequently to contemplation, were never so strong, yet at their first entrance into a spiritual course they will, ordinarily speaking, seem to be of an active, extroverted temper, and consequently will not be capable of a long-continued rigorous solitude, nor of operations purely spiritual. They will therefore be forced to begin with exercises of the imagination and discursive prayer. And the reason is, because by their former secular, negligent, and extroverted life, their mind is so filled and painted all over with the images of creatures, and their hearts so disordered and divided with inordinate affections and passions, that the will alone, with its actuations, purposes, and resolutions, has not power to expel the said images and to assuage the said passions; so that there is a necessity by meditation and consideration, of introducing good images to expel the vain and bad ones, and of inventing motives to quiet passions by diverting them upon God. But this being once done by the exercises proper to an active life (which to such souls will not need to last long), they thenceforwards are to betake themselves, and always to continue in such internal exercises as are suitable to their natural propensions, to wit, the quiet, solitary, spiritual exercises of a *contemplative life.*

Chapter III. Of a State Contemplative and Active

§ 1. The contemplative state more perfect.

§ 2. And also more easy and secure.

§ 3. Of which yet the most simple and ignorant are capable.

§§ 4, 5, 6, 7, 8, 9, 10. The end of a contemplative life supereminently excellent above that of the active, and the union with God more Divine.

§ 11. Of passive unions therein, yet more supernatural.

1. Of these two states, the contemplative is by all acknowledged to be the more sublime and perfect, inasmuch as the operations and exercises of it are more spiritual, more abstracted from the body and its sensual faculties, and consequently more angelical and divine. It is represented to us by our Lord in the person of Mary, who is therefore said to have chosen the best part, which shall never be taken from her, being the beginning and imperfect practice of that which shall be our eternal employment and beatitude in heaven. As on the other side the active life is typified by the other sister Martha, who turmoiled herself with many exterior businesses and solicitudes, which though they were in themselves good and laudable, yet Mary's vacancy and inward attention to our Lord is much preferred.

2. And as the contemplative state is of the two the more perfect, so also is it far more easy, more simple, and more secure from all errors and illusions which may be occasioned by an indiscreet use of prayer. And the reason or ground of such security is evident, because a contemplative soul tending to God and working almost only with the heart and blind affections of the will pouring themselves upon God apprehended only in the obscure notion of faith, not inquiring what He is, but believing Him to be that incomprehensible Being which He is, and which can only be comprehended by Himself, rejecting and striving to forget all images and representations of Him, or anything else; yea, transcending all operations of the imagination, and all subtlety and curiosity of reasoning; and lastly, seeking an union with God only by the most pure and most intime affections of the spirit: what possibility of illusion or error can there be to such a soul? For if the devil should suggest an image (which is his only means and way to seduce a soul to error and a sinful curiosity of knowledge), she is taught and exercised to reject all manner of images, and to hold the internal senses almost wholly vacant during her spiritual actuations. Or, if by stirring up unclean or other unlawful affections in sensitive nature, he seek to assault her, what more secure remedy is there than with the whole bent and affections of the soul to adhere and be united to God, neglecting and scarce marking whatsoever disorders may unwillingly happen in inferior nature, above which she is exalted into a region of light and peace?

3. Now, for a further proof of the excellency and security of contemplative prayer beyond active, experience demonstrates that all the most sublime exercises of contemplation may as purely and perfectly be performed by persons the most ignorant and unlearned (so they be sufficiently instructed in the fundamental doctrines of Catholic faith) as by the learnedst doctors, inasmuch as not any abilities in the brain are requisite thereto, but only a strong courageous affection of the heart. Hence it is that we see that simple unlearned women are more frequently graced by Almighty God with the gift of high contemplation than men, and especially such men as are

much given to sublime speculations. A reason whereof may be (besides that God reveals Himself more willingly to humble and simple minds) because by means of that tenderness and compassionateness which abounds naturally in women, they are disposed to a greater fervour in charity, and their affections being once fixed on their only proper object, which is God, they do more vigorously and firmly adhere thereunto, and by consequence arrive both more easily and quickly to the perfection of contemplation, which consists (as shall hereafter be shown) in the fervour and constancy of the will united to God, and scarce at all in the operations of the understanding.

Now this present treatise being intended only for encouraging and instructing of persons that aspire to perfection in a contemplative life, and more especially for the discovering of the several degrees of prayer proper for that state, reason requires that, since in all doctrines which tend to practice the end is principally to be regarded as being that which, if it can be approved worthy the taking pains for, will give life and courage in the use of the means conducing thereto, we should treat more precisely of the proper end of a contemplative life, the which indeed is of so supreme an excellence and divine profection above anything that can be designed or sought after in any other doctrine or profession, that those who have eyes to see it and palates capable of a spiritual tasting of it, will think no difficulties, no tediousnesses, no bitternesses or labours too great a price to purchase it.

4. It was said before that the general end of man's creation, and which ought to be aspired unto by all Christians, and much more those whose more special profession is to tend to perfection, whether in an active or a contemplative state, is a perfect and constant union in spirit to God by love, which is uninterrupted perfect prayer. But the same end is differently sought and attained by active and by contemplative spirits; for in an active life the union is not so immediate, stable, sublime, and intime of the supreme portion of the spirit with God, as it is in a contemplative state. But as the exercises of the active livers are much in the imaginative and discursive faculties of the soul, so is likewise their union. The effects indeed of it are more perceptible, and therefore more apt to cause admiration in others; but withal, being much in sense, it is not so clear nor so peaceful, and by consequence not so stable nor immediate as is that of contemplatives. The charity of actives is strong and vigorous, and the outward effects of it dazzling the eyes of the beholders, and thereby causing great edification; they are withal frequently multiplied, for strong love is a passion that takes pleasure in labours. Whereas the deeds of contemplative souls (except when God by an extraordinary inspiration calls them to exterior employments) are but few, and in appearance but small, and little regarded or esteemed by others. Yet those mean actions of theirs in God's esteem may be preferred incomparably before the others, as being in a far more perfect degree supernatural and divine, as proceeding

10

from an immediate and most certain impulse of God's Holy Spirit, whose conduct, light, and virtue such souls do far more clearly perceive, and more faithfully and constantly follow, even in their daily and ordinary practices, than active livers do or can in their actions of highest importance. Lastly, the charity of contemplatives, though it be less stirring and busy, yet is far more profoundly rooted in the centre of the spirit, causing an union much more spiritual and divine.

5. St. Bernard, perfectly experienced in the internal ways of a contemplative life, writing to certain religious Fathers of the Carthusian Order, professing the same, excellently expresses this union in these words: *Aliorum est Deo servire; vestrum adhærere. Aliorum est Deo credere, scire, amare, revereri; vestrum est sapere, intelligere, cognoscere, frui;* that is, It is the duty of others (that live active lives either in the world or religion) to serve God; but it is yours to adhere inseparably unto Him. It belongs to others to believe, to know, to love, to adore God; but to you to taste, to understand, to be familiarly acquainted with, and to enjoy Him.

6. Constantly to this expression of St. Bernard, mystic writers do teach that the proper end of a contemplative life is the attaining unto an habitual and almost uninterrupted perfect union with God in the supreme point of the spirit; and such an union as gives the soul a fruitive possession of Him, and a real experimental perception of His divine presence in the depth and centre of the spirit, which is fully possessed and filled with Him alone; not only all deliberate affections to creatures being excluded, but in a manner all images of them also, at least so far as they may be distractive to the soul.

7. The effects of this blessed, perceptible presence of God in perfect souls are unspeakable and divine; for He is in them both as a principle of all their actions internal and external, being the life of their life and spirit of their spirits; and also as the end of them, directing both the actions and persons to Himself only. He is all in all things unto them: a light to direct securely all their steps, and to order all their workings, even those also which seem the most indifferent, the which by the guidance of God's Holy Spirit do cause a farther advancement of them to a yet more immediate union. He is a shield to protect them in all temptations and dangers, an internal force and vigour within them, to make them do and suffer all things whatsoever His pleasure is they should do or suffer. They not only believe and know, but even feel and taste Him to be the universal, infinite Good. By means of a continual conversation with Him they are reduced to a blessed state of a perfect denudation of spirit, to an absolute, internal solitude, a transcendancy and forgetfulness of all created things, and especially of themselves, to an heavenly-mindedness and fixed attention to God only, and this even in the midst of employments to others never so distractive; and finally, to a gustful

knowledge of all His infinite perfections, and a strict application of their spirits by love above knowledge, joined with a fruition and repose in Him with the whole extent of their wills; so that they become after an inexpressible manner partakers of the divine nature; yea, one spirit, one will, one love with Him, being in a sort deified, and enjoying as much of heaven here as mortality is capable of.

8. To this purpose saith the same St. Bernard: Amor Dei, vel amor Deus, Spiritus Sanctus amori hominis se infundens, afficit eum sibi, et amans semetipsum de homine Deus, secum unum efficit et spiritum ejus, et amorem ejus; that is, The love of God, or love which is God, to wit, the Holy Ghost pouring himself into the love of man (inclineth and) applieth man by love unto Himself; and thus God, loving Himself by man, maketh both his spirit and love one with Himself.

9. A most blessed state this is certainly, being the portion chosen by Mary, which our Lord Himself calls *optimam partem,* the very best of all divine graces which God can bestow in this life; and wherewith He enriched in a singular manner those His two most highly favoured and most tenderly loved friends, St. John the Evangelist, and St. Mary Magdalen; but in a yet more supereminent degree His own most heavenly Virgin-Mother.

10. Happy, therefore, are those souls upon which God bestows a desire and ambition so glorious as seriously and effectually to tend, aspire, and endeavour the compassing a design so heavenly: qualifying them not only with good natural propensions to those internal ways of love leading to this end, but also calling them to a state of life abstracted from the world, the vanities and solicitudes of it; and with all supernatural light to direct them in the secret paths of this love; and lastly, strong resolutions, and perseverance with courage to break through all discouragements, difficulties, persecutions, aridities, and whatsoever oppositions shall be made against them either from concupiscence within, or the world without, or the devil joining with both against a design of all others most hurtful to him and most destructive to his pretensions.

11. And for a yet further and greater encouragement unto them to embrace and prosecute so glorious a design, they may take notice that, besides this (hitherto described) happy union of a contemplative soul with God by perfect charity, in the which the soul herself actively concurs, not only as to the fruition, but also in the disposing herself immediately thereto, there are other unions entirely supernatural, not at all procured, or so much as intended by the soul herself, but graciously and freely conferred by God upon some souls, in the which He, after a wonderful and inconceivable manner, affords them interior illuminations and touches, yet far more efficacious and divine: in all which the soul is a mere patient, and only suffers God to work His di-

vine pleasure in her, being neither able to further nor hinder it; the which unions, though they last but even as it were a moment of time, yet do more illuminate and purify the soul than many years spent in active exercises of spiritual prayer or mortification could do.

Chapter IV. Of the Necessity of a Strong Resolution

§§ 1, 2, 3, 4. A strong resolution necessary in the beginning.

§§ 5, 6, 7, 8, 9. Considering first the length and tediousness of the way to perfection in mortification,

§§ 10, 11. And also many degrees of prayer to be passed,

§ 12. Therefore it is seldom attained, and not till a declining age,

§ 13. Except by God's extraordinary favour to a few.

§ 14. Yet old and young ought to enter into the way.

§ 15. A motive to resolution are the difficulties in the way

§§ 16 &c. And those both from without and within.

1. The end of a contemplative life, therefore, being so supereminently noble and divine that beatified souls do prosecute the same, and no other, in heaven, with this only difference, that the same beatifying object which is now obscurely seen by faith and imperfectly embraced by love shall hereafter be seen clearly and perfectly enjoyed, the primary and most general duty required in souls which by God's vocation do walk in the ways of the spirit, is to admire, love, and long after this union, and to fix an immovable resolution through God's grace and assistance to attempt and persevere in the prosecution of so glorious a design, in despite of all opposition, through light and darkness, through consolations and desolations, &c., as esteeming it to be cheaply purchased, though with the loss of all comforts that nature can find or expect in creatures.

2. The fixing of such a courageous resolution is of so main importance and necessity that if it should happen to fail or yield to any, though the fiercest temptations, that may occur and are to be expected, so as not to be reassumed, the whole design will be ruined; and therefore devout souls are oftentimes to renew such a resolution, and especially when any difficulty presents itself; and for that purpose they will oft be put in mind thereof in these following instructions.

3. It is not to be esteemed loftiness, presumption, or pride to tend to so sublime an end; but it is a good and laudable ambition, and most accept-

able to God; yea, the root of it is true, solid humility joined with the love of God; for it proceeds from a vile esteem and some degrees of a holy hatred of ourselves, from whom we desire to fly; and a just esteem, obedience, and love of God, to whom only we desire to adhere and be inseparably united.

4. Happy, therefore, is the soul that finds in herself an habitual thirst and longing after this union, if she will seek to assuage it by continual approaches to this Fountain of living waters, labouring thereto with daily external and internal workings. The very tendence to this union, in which our whole essential happiness consists, has in it some degrees of happiness, and is an imperfect union, disposing to a perfect one; for by such internal tendence and aspiring we get by little and little out of nature into God. And that without such an interior tendence and desire no exterior sufferances or observances will imprint any true virtue in the soul, or bring her nearer to God, we see in the example of Suso, who for the first five years of a religious profession found no satisfaction in soul at all, notwithstanding all his care and exactness in exterior regular observances and mortifications: he perceived plainly that still he wanted something, but what that was he could not tell, till God was pleased to discover it to him, and put him in the way to attain to his desire, which was in spirit to tend continually to this union, without which all his austerities and observances served little or nothing, as proceeding principally from self-love, self-judgment, and the satisfying of nature even by crossing it.

Let nothing, therefore, deter a well-minded soul from persevering with fervour in this firm resolution. No, not the sight of her daily defects, imperfections, or sins, or remorses for them; but rather let her increase in courage even from her falls, and from the experience of her own impotency let her be incited to run more earnestly and adhere more firmly unto God, by whom she will be enabled to do all things and conquer all resistances.

5. Now to the end that all sincerity may be used in the delivery of these instructions, and that all vain compliance and flattery may be avoided, the devout soul is to be informed that the way to perfection is, 1. both a very long, tedious way; and, 2. withal there are to be expected in it many grievous, painful, and bitter temptations and crosses to corrupt nature; as being a way that wholly and universally contradicts and destroys all the vain eases, contentments, interests, and designs of nature, teaching a soul to die unto self-love, self-judgment, and all propriety, and to raise herself out of nature, seeking to live in a region exalted above nature: to wit, the region of the spirit; into which being once come, she will find nothing but light and peace and joy in the Holy Ghost. The which difficulties considered, instead of being discouraged, she will, if she be truly touched with God's Spirit, rather increase her fervour and courage to pursue a design so noble and divine, for

which alone she was created; especially, 3. considering the infinite danger of a negligent, tepid, and spiritually slothful life, and likewise the security and benefit of being but truly in the way to perfection, though she should never attain to it in this life.

6. First, therefore, to demonstrate that the way to perfection must needs be long and tedious, even to souls well-disposed thereto both by nature and education (for to others it is a way unpassable without extreme difficulty), this will easily be acknowledged by any well-minded soul that by her own experience will consider how obstinate, inflexible, and of how gluey and tenacious a nature corrupt self-love is in her; how long a time must pass before she can subdue any one habitual ill inclination and affection in herself. What fallings and risings again there are in our passions and corrupt desires, insomuch as when they seem to be quite mortified and almost forgotten, they will again raise themselves and combat us with as great or perhaps greater violence than before. Now till the poisonous root of self-love be withered, so as that we do not knowingly and deliberately suffer it to spring forth and bear fruit (for utterly killed it never will be in this life); till we have lost at least all affection to all our corrupt desires, even the most venial, which are almost infinite, perfect charity will never reign in our souls, and consequently perfect union in spirit with God cannot be expected; for charity lives and grows according to the measure that self-love is abated, and no further.

7. Souls that first enter into the internal ways of the spirit, or that have made no great progress in them, are guided by a very dim light, being able to discover and discern only a few grosser defects and inordinations; but by persevering in the exercises of mortification and prayer, this light will be increased, and then they will proportionably every day more and more discover a thousand secret and formerly invisible impurities in their intentions, self-seekings, hypocrisies, and close designs of nature, pursuing her own corrupt designs in the very best actions, cherishing nature one way when she mortifies it another, and favouring pride even when she exercises humility. Now a clear light to discover all these almost infinite depravations not only in our sensitive nature, but also in the superior soul (which are far more secret, manifold, and dangerous), and a courage with success to combat and overcome them, must be the effect of a long-continued practice of prayer and mortification.

8. The want of a due knowledge or consideration hereof is the cause that some good souls, after they have made some progress in internal ways, becomes disheartened, and in danger to stop or quite leave them; for though at the first, being (as usually they are) prevented by God with a tender sensible devotion (which our Holy Father calls *fervorem novitium*), they do with much zeal and, as it seems to them., with good effect begin the exercises of

mortification and prayer; yet afterward, such sensible fervour and tenderness ceasing (as it seldom fails to do) by that new light which they have gotten, they discern a world of defects, formerly undiscovered, which they erroneously think were not in them before; whereupon, fearing that instead of making progress, they are in a worse state than when they began, they will be apt to suspect that they are in a wrong way. This proceeds from a preconceived mistake, that because in times of light and devotion the soul finds herself carried with much fervour to God, and perceives but small contradictions and rebellions in inferior nature, therefore she is very forward in the way to perfection. Whereas it is far otherwise; for nature is not so easily conquered as she imagines, neither is the way to perfection so easy and short. Many changes she must expect; many risings and fallings; sometimes light, and sometimes darkness; sometimes calmness of passions, and presently after, it may be, fiercer combats than before; and these successions of changes repeated, God knows how oft, before the end approacheth.

9. Yea, it will likely happen to such souls, that even the formerly well-known grosser defects in them will seem to increase, and to grow more hard to be quelled after they have been competently advanced in internal ways; and the reason is, because, having set themselves to combat corrupt nature in all her perverse, crooked, and impure desires, and being sequestered from the vanities of the world, they find themselves in continual wrestlings and agonies, and want those pleasing diversions, conversations, and recreations, with which, whilst they lived a secular, negligent life, they could interrupt or put off their melancholic thoughts and unquietness. But if they would take courage and, instead of seeking ease from nature (further than discretion allows), have recourse for remedy by prayer to God, they would find that such violent temptations are an assured sign that they are in a secure and happy way, and that when God sees it is best for them, they shall come off from such combats with victory and comfort.

10. Now, as from the consideration of the tediousness of a perfect universal mortification of the corrupt affections of nature, it does appear that hasty perfection is not ordinarily to be expected, and where there are appearances of extraordinary lights and supernatural visits in souls not thoroughly mortified, it is to be feared that there hath been some secret exorbitancy in the proceedings of such souls, some deeply rooted pride, &c., which hath exposed them to the devil's illusions, so that their state is very dangerous, the like will appear if we cast our eyes upon the nature and degrees of internal prayer, in the perfection of which the end of a contemplative life, which is perfect union in spirit with God, doth consist.

11. For a soul must, 1. ordinarily speaking, pass through the way of external and imaginary exercises of prayer, in the which she must tarry, God

knows how long; yea, without a discreet diligence and constancy in them, she may perhaps end her days therein. 2. Then when her affections do so abound, and are sufficiently ripe, so as that discourse is not needful or becomes of little efficacy, she is to betake herself to the exercise of the will, in the which a very long time must ordinarily be spent before she can chase away distracting grosser images, and before the heart be so replenished with the Divine Spirit that, without any election or deliberation, it will of itself almost continually break forth into aspirations and pure elevations of the superior will. 3. Being arrived to this happy state, only God knows for how long a time she is to continue therein, there being almost infinite degrees of aspirations, each one exceeding the former in purity, before she be ripe for the divine inaction. 4. And having gotten that, a very long time is like to be spent, very oft in most woeful obscurities and desolations, before she arrive, 5. to the state of perfection. Now all these degrees of prayer are to be attended with proportionable degrees of mortification; so that no wonder is it if so very few, even of those whose profession it is to aspire thereunto, do find or attain unto this end, partly out of ignorance and error, whilst they place perfection in an exact performance of outward observances and austerities, the which (though being well used they may be certainly very proper helps to perfection, and are accordingly to be duly esteemed, yet), if they be undertaken for any end of nature, and not for the purifying of the interior and disposing it for more perfect prayer, are of no value at all, but rather proceed from and nourish self-love, pride, &c., and partly out of want of courage and diligence to pursue constantly the way that they know leads thereto.

12. Upon these grounds mystic authors do teach that, though it be a very great advantage to a soul to tread in these internal ways from her youth, before she be darkened and made sick with vicious habits, the combating against which will cause great difficulty, pain, and tediousness to her, yet she will hardly arrive unto the aforesaid active union and experimental perception of God's presence in her till almost a declining age; by reason that though her natural ill inclinations may be mortified in a reasonable perfection before that time, yet till such age there will remain too much vigour in corporal nature, and an unstableness in the inward senses, which will hinder that quietness and composedness of mind necessary to such an union. Whereas some persons of a well-disposed temper and virtuous education have in a few years arrived thereunto, though they did not begin an internal course till their ripe age, but yet supplying that delay by an heroical resolution and vigorous pursuit of the practices proper thereunto; but as for those that have been viciously bred, there will be necessary a wonderful measure of grace and very extraordinary mortifications before such souls can be fitted thereunto.

13. Now what hath been said concerning the length of the way, and the multiplicity of conditions requisite to the attaining to the end of it, is to be

understood with relation to the ordinary course of God's providence. But God, who is the free Master and Disposer of His own graces, may bestow them upon whom and when He pleases, either miraculously increasing His grace in some souls, or conferring His supernatural favours before the time that they are ripe for them, as He did to St. Catharine of Siena (and some others), who, in their younger years, have been favoured with a passive union. Mystic authors, likewise, except from the ordinary course, the case where God upon the death of well-willed and well-disposed souls happening before perfection attained, supplieth after some extraordinary manner what was wanting, and effects that in a moment which would otherwise have required a long space of time; and this, say they, God frequently doth in regard of the serious and fervent wills that He seeth in such souls, which were resolved to prosecute the way of His love for all their lives, though they should have lasted never so long.

14. But be the way to perfection never so long, the design itself is so noble and the end so divine, that a soul cannot begin to aspire unto it too soon, nor take too much pains to procure it. Yea, the very desire and serious pursuance of so heavenly a design brings so great blessings to the soul, and puts her in so secure a way of salvation, though she should never perfectly attain unto it in this life, that there is none so old nor so overgrown with ill habits but ought to attempt, and with perseverance pursue it, being assured that at least after death he shall for his good desire and endeavours be rewarded with the crown due to contemplatives. For it is enough for a soul to be in the way, and to correspond to such enablements as she hath received; and then in what degree of spirit soever she dies, she dies according to the will and ordination of God, to whom she must be resigned, and consequently she will be very happy; whereas if, out of despair of attaining to perfection, she should rest and do as it were nothing, contenting herself with outward ceremonious observances, she will be accounted before God as having been wanting to perform that whereto her profession obliged her. Though the truth is, the soul being a pure spirit, consisting of mere activity, cannot cease doing and desiring something; so that if her desires and operations be not directed to the right end, they will go a wrong way; and if a soul do not continually strive to get out of nature, she will plunge herself deeper and deeper into it.

15. The second motive to induce a soul to arm herself with a great courage and strong resolution in her tendence to perfection is because, as the wise man says, *He that sets himself to serve our Lord* (especially in so high and divine an employment as contemplation) *must prepare his soul for temptations* greater and more unusual than formerly he had experience of; the which temptations will come from all coasts, both from without and within.

16. For an internal life, being not only a life hidden from the world, but likewise directly contrary to the ways of carnal reason, yea, even different from common notion of virtue and piety which ordinary Christians, yea, too many even in religion have also, who approve only of actions and ways which outwardly make a fair show, as solemn performance of divine offices, external formal regularities, mortifications, &c; hence it is that very sharp persecutions have almost always attended those whom God hath called to revive the true spirit of religion (too generally decayed, and in many religious communities utterly unknown), by teaching souls not to neglect, but on the contrary to be very careful in an exact performance and just esteem of such duties; but yet to place perfection in exercises of the spirit, and to esteem all other observances no further than as they serve to advance and increase perfection in spirit; since most certain it is, that if in and for themselves alone and without any interior direction for the purifying of the soul they be esteemed (and performed) as parts of real perfection, and not chiefly as helps of internal devotion and purity, they will rather become hindrances to contemplation, nourishing pride, contempt of others, &c., and be the ruin of true charity. Examples of such persecutions are obvious in stories, witness the sufferings of Thaulerus, Suso, St. Teresa, St. John of the Cross, &c.

17. Again, in the world, the lives of those that God hath called to the exercises of an internal life, being so different from and unlike to others, though ordinary, well-meaning Christians, by reason that they abstract themselves from secular businesses (except such as necessarily belong to their vocation), likewise from worldly conventions, correspondence, and vainly complying friendships; hence it is that the sight of them is unacceptable to their neighbors and acquaintance, as if they did silently condemn their liberties. For this reason, they are apt to raise and disperse evil reports of them, calling them illuminates, pretenders to extraordinary visits and lights, persons that walk in *mirabilibus super se*, &c.; or at least to deride them as silly, seduced, melancholy spirits, that follow unusual and dangerous ways.

18. All these, and many others the like persecutions, calumnies, and contempts, a well-disposed soul that purely seeks God must expect and be armed against. And knowing that they do not come by chance, but by the most wise, holy, and merciful providence of God for her good, to exercise her courage in the beginning, and to give her an opportunity to testify her true esteem and love to God and spiritual things, let her hence not be affrighted, but rather pursue internal ways more vigorously, as knowing that there cannot be a better proof of the excellency of them than that they are displeasing to carnal or at least ignorant men unexperienced in such divine ways. Let her not with passion judge or condone those that are contrary to her, for many of them may have a good intention and zeal therein, though a zeal not directed by knowledge. If, therefore, she will attend God, following

19

His divine inspirations, &c., she will see that God will give her light and courage, and much inward security in her way.

19. But her greatest and more frequent persecutions will be from her own corrupt nature and vicious habits rooted in the soul, the which will assault her many times with temptations and inward bitternesses and agonies, sharper and stranger than she did expect, or could perhaps imagine. And no wonder, for her design and continual endeavours both in mortification and prayer being to raise herself out of, and above nature, to contradict nature in all its vain pleasures and interests, she can expect no other, but that nature will continually struggle against the spirit; especially being enflamed by the devil, who will not fail to employ all his arts, all his malice and fury, to disturb a design so utterly destructive to his infernal kingdom established in the souls of carnal men. The well-minded soul, therefore, must make a general strong resolution to bear all with as much quietness as may be, to distrust herself entirely, to rely only upon God, and to seek unto Him by prayer, and all will assuredly be well. She will find that the yoke of Christ, which at the first was burdensome, will, being borne with constancy, become easy and delightful; yea, though she should never be able to subdue the resistance of evil inclinations in her, yet as long as there remains in her a sincere endeavor after it, no such ill inclinations will hinder her happiness.

Chapter V. Of the Danger of a Tepid Life

§§ 1, 2. A third motive to resolution is the danger of tepidity, of which the nature and root is discovered.

§§ 3, 4, 5. The miseries of a tepid religious person that is ignorant of internal ways.

§§ 6, 7. Or of one that knows them, but neglects to pursue them.

§§ 8, 9. How pestilent such are in a community.

§ 10. On the other side, an indiscreet passionate fervour may be as dangerous as negligence.

1. A third yet more pressing motive to a courageous resolution of prosecuting internal ways once begun, and a strong proof of the extreme necessity thereof, is the consideration of the extreme danger and miseries unexpressible of a negligent and tepid life, whether in religion or in the world; the which not only renders perfection impossible to be attained, but endangers the very root of essential sanctity and all pretension to eternal

happiness, as among other mystic writers, Harphius in his twelve mortifications earnestly demonstrates.

2. Tepidity is a bitter poisonous root fixed in the minds of negligent Christians, who though out of a servile fear they abstain from an habitual practice of acknowledged mortal actual sins, and therefore (groundlessly enough) think themselves secure from the danger of hell, yet they perform their external necessary obligations to God and their brethren sleepily and heartlessly, without any true affection, contenting themselves with the things however outwardly done; yea, perhaps knowing no perfection beyond this; but in the mean time remain full of self-love, inward pride, sensual desires, aversion from internal conversation with God, &c. And the ground and cause of this pernicious tepidity is want of affection and esteem of spiritual things, and a voluntary affection to venial sins (not as they are sins, but as the objects of them are easeful or delightful to nature), joined with a willfulness not to avoid the occasions of them, nor to do any more in God's service than what themselves judge to be necessary for the escaping of hell.

3. Such persons, if they live in religion, must needs pass very uncomfortable and discontented lives, having excluded themselves from the vain entertainments and pleasures of the world, and yet retaining a strong affection to them in their hearts, with an incapacity of enjoying them. They must undergo all obligations, austerities, and crosses incident to a religious state without comfort, but only in having dispatched them, with very little benefit to their souls, and with extreme wearisomeness and unwillingness. Now, what a resemblance to hell hath such a life, where there is an impossibility freely to enjoy what the soul principally desires, and where she is forced continually to do and suffer such things as are extremely contrary to her inclinations!

4. Whereas, if souls would courageously at once give themselves wholly to God, and with a discreet fervour combat against corrupt nature, pursuing their internal exercises, they would find that all things would coöperate, not only to their eternal good, but even to their present contentment and joy. They would find pleasure even in their greatest mortifications and crosses, by considering the love with which God sends them, and the great benefit that their spirit reaps by them. What contentment can be greater to any soul than to become a true inward friend of God, chained unto Him with a love, the like whereto never was between any mortal creatures? to know and even feel that she belongs to God, and that God is continually watchful over her, and careful of her salvation? None of which comforts tepid souls can hope to taste; but, on the contrary, are not only continually tortured with present discontents, but much more with a fear and horror, considering their doubtfulness about their future state.

5. If such tepid souls be ignorant of the internal ways of the spirit (which without some fault of their own they scarce can be), when they come to die, it is not conceivable what apprehensions and horrors they will feel; considering that a settled willful affection to venial sins brings a soul to an imminent danger of a frequent incurring actual mortal sins, the which, though they be not of the greater kind of enormous sins, yet they may be no less dangerous, because less corrigible, such as are those spiritual sins of pride, murmuring, factiousness, envy, ambition, &c.; besides which, how is it possible for them to give an account of sins of omission, of the want of perfecting their souls by prayer, &c., of the avoiding of which they never took any care, although their profession and vows obliged them thereto?

6. Again, if tepidity (though not in so high a degree) be found in souls that are acquainted speculatively with the internal ways of the spirit, and their obligation to pursue them in order to perfection, but either for want of courage dare not apply themselves seriously to them, or do it very faintly, coldly, or with frequent interruptions, and only are not resolved to relinquish and abjure such ways, such as though they have not a willful affection to venial sins, yet are for the most part willfully negligent in resisting them,—such souls ought to consider that their case in all respects approaches near to the miserable condition of the former, and they will have guilt enough to take away all comfort almost in a religious state, and to give them just apprehensions for the future life, of which they have no security.

7. For when such souls approach near unto death, they will then too late consider that for want of diligent prayer there may be, yea, assuredly are in them, a world of inordinations, impurities, and defects undiscovered by them, and therefore can neither be acknowledged nor bewailed; so that they cannot have any assurance of the state and inclinations of their souls; besides, they know themselves to have been guilty of a life spent in an uninterrupted ingratitude to God, who gave them light to see the ways to perfection which their profession obliged them to walk in, and yet willfully they neglected to make use of such light, or to make progress in those ways, &c. (and this is an aggravation of guilt beyond the former); they are conscious likewise of an unexcusable and long-continued unfaithfulness, never almost complying with the divine inspirations which daily urged them to put themselves resolutely into that only secure way of an internal life, nor ever vigorously resisting the sins and imperfections which they did discover in themselves, &c. Such sad thoughts as these pressing (as usually they do) one upon another near the approaches of death, what grievous apprehensions, what terrible uncertainties must they needs cause in tepid souls, then most sensible of dangers and fears! so that their lives will be full of anguish and continual remorse, and their deaths very uncomfortable.

8. Lastly, to all these miseries of a tepid life, this also may be added as an increase of the guilt, and consequently an aggravation of the dangerous state of souls infected with that poison, which is, that they do not only themselves most ungratefully withdraw their own affections from God and divine things, but by their ill example, by misspending the time in vain extroverted conversations, by discountenancing those that are fervourous in internal ways, &c., they infect their companions, and so treacherously defraud Almighty God of the affections of others also. So that a tepid religious person, though given to no enormous excesses, is oft more harmful in a community than an open, scandalous liver; because none that hath any care of himself but will beware of such an one as this latter is; whereas a tepid soul unperceivably instills into others the poisonous infection wherewith herself is tainted.

9. From the grounds and considerations here mentioned, it doth appear how necessary it is for a devout soul, both in the beginning and pursuance of a contemplative life, to excite and fortify her courageous resolution not to be daunted by discouragements either from within or without, but at what price soever, and with what labours and sufferings soever, with fervour to persevere in the exercises and duties belonging thereto, accounting tepidity and spiritual sloth as the very bane of her whole design, the which, if it be yielded unto, though but a little, it will gather more force, and at last grow irresistible.

10. But withal she is to be advised that such her courage and fervour must be exercised, not impetuously out of passion, or such impulses as a fit of sensible devotion will sometimes produce in her; but this fervour and resolution must chiefly be seated in the superior will, and regulated by spiritual discretion, according to her present forces, both natural and supernatural, and the measure of grace bestowed on her, and no further; for there may be as much harm by outrunning grace, as by neglecting to correspond unto it. Hence, it oft comes to pass, that many well-minded souls, being either pushed forward by an indiscreet passionate zeal, or advised by unexperienced directors to undertake unnecessarily and voluntarily either rigorous mortifications or excessive tasks of devotions, and wanting strength to continue them, have become able to do nothing at all; so that affecting too hastily to attain unto perfection sooner than God did enable them thereto, they so overburden themselves that they are forced to give over quite all tendence to it. Therefore we must be contented to proceed in such a pace as may be lasting, and that will suffice.

Chapter VI. The Parable of a Pilgrim

A confirmation of what hath been said, particularly of the necessity of a strong resolution and courage to persevere, shown by the parable of a pilgrim travelling to Jerusalem, out of *Scala Perfectionis.*

1. Now, for a further confirmation and more effectual recommendation of what hath hitherto been delivered touching the nature of a contemplative life in general, the supereminent nobleness of its end, the great difficulties to be expected in it, and the absolute necessity of a firm courage to persevere and continually to make progress in it, whatsoever it costs us (without which resolution it is in vain to set one step forward in these ways), I will here annex a passage extracted out of that excellent treatise called *Scala Perfectionis*, written by that eminent contemplative, Dr. Walter Hilton, a Carthusian monk, in which, under the parable of a devout pilgrim desirous to travel to Jerusalem (which he interprets the vision of peace or contemplation), he delivers instructions very proper and efficacious touching the behaviour requisite in a devout soul for such a journey; the true sense of which advices I will take liberty so to deliver briefly as, notwithstanding, not to omit any important matter there more largely, and according to the old fashion, expressed.

2. "There was a man," saith he, "that had a great desire to go to Jerusalem; and because he knew not the right way, he addressed himself for advice to one that he hoped was not unskillful in it, and asked him whether there was any way passable thither. The other answered, that the way thither was both long and full of very great difficulties; yea, that there were many ways that seemed and promised to lead thither, but the dangers of them were too great. Nevertheless, one way he knew which, if he would diligently pursue according to the directions and marks that he would give him,—though, said he, I cannot promise thee a security from many frights, beatings, and other ill-usage and temptations of all kinds; but if thou canst have courage and patience enough to suffer them without quarrelling, or resisting, or troubling thyself, and so pass on, having this only in thy mind, and sometimes on thy tongue, *I have nought, I am nought, I desire nought but to be at Jerusalem,*—my life for thine, thou wilt escape safe with thy life and in a competent time arrive thither.

3. "The pilgrim, overjoyed with these news, answered: So I may have my life safe, and may at last come to the place that I above all things only desire, I care not what miseries I suffer in the way. Therefore let me know only what course I am to take, and, God willing, I will not fail to observe carefully your directions. The guide replied: Since thou hast so good a

will, though I myself never was so happy as to be in Jerusalem, notwithstanding, be confident that by the instructions that I shall give thee, if thou wilt follow them, thou shalt come safe to thy journey's end.

4. "Now the advice that I am to give thee in brief is this: Before thou set the first step into the highway that leads thither, thou must be firmly grounded in the true Catholic faith; moreover, whatsoever sins thou findest in thy conscience, thou must seek to purge them away by hearty penance and absolution, according to the laws of the Church. This being done, begin thy journey in God's name, but be sure to go furnished with two necessary instruments, humility and charity, both which are contained in the forementioned speech, which must always be ready in thy mind: *I am nought, I have nought, I desire but only one thing, and that is our Lord Jesus, and to be with him in peace at Jerusalem.* The meaning and virtue of these words therefore thou must have continually, at least in thy thoughts, either expressly or virtually; humility says, *I am nought, I have nought;* love says, *I desire nought but Jesus.* These two companions thou must never part from; neither will they willingly be separated from one another, for they accord very lovingly together. And the deeper thou groundest thyself in humility, the higher thou raisest thyself in charity; for the more thou seest and feelest thyself to be nothing, with the more fervent love wilt thou desire Jesus, that by Him, who is all, thou mayest become something.

5. "Now this same humility is to be exercised, not so much in considering thine own self, thy sinfulness, and misery (though to do thus at the first be very good and profitable), but rather in a quiet loving sight of the infinite endless being and goodness of Jesus; the which beholding of Jesus must be either through grace in a savourous feeling knowledge of him, or at least in a full and firm faith in Him. And such a beholding, when thou shalt attain to it, will work in thy mind a far more pure, spiritual, solid, and perfect humility, than the former way of beholding thyself, the which produces a humility more gross, boisterous, and unquiet. By that thou wilt see and feel thyself, not only to be the most wretched filthy creature in the world, but also in the very substance of thy soul (setting aside the foulness of sin) to be a mere nothing, for truly, in and of thyself and in regard to Jesus (who really and in truth is all), thou art a mere nothing; and till thou hast the love of Jesus, yea, and feelest that thou hast His love, although thou hast done to thy seeming never so many good deeds both outward and inward, yet in truth thou hast nothing at all, for nothing will abide in thy soul and fill it but the love of Jesus. Therefore, cast all other things behind thee, and forget them, that thou mayest have that which is best of all; and thus doing, thou wilt become a true pilgrim that leaves behind him houses, and wife, and children, and friends, and goods, and makes himself poor and bare of all things, that he may go on his journey lightly and merrily without hindrance.

6. "Well, now thou art in thy way travelling towards Jerusalem; the which travelling consists in working inwardly, and (when need is) outwardly too, such works as are suitable to thy condition and state, and such as will help and increase in thee this gracious desire that thou hast to love Jesus only. Let thy works be what they will, thinking, or reading, or preaching, or labouring, &c.; if thou findest that they draw thy mind from worldly vanity, and confirm thy heart and will more to the love of Jesus, it is good and profitable for thee to use them. And if thou fndest that through custom such works do in time lose their savour and virtue to increase this love, and that it seems to thee that thou feelest more grace and spiritual profit in some other, take these other and leave those, for though the inclination and desire of thy heart to Jesus must ever be unchangeable, nevertheless thy spiritual works thou shalt use in thy manner of praying, reading, &c., to the end to feed and strengthen this desire, may well be changed, according as thou feelest thyself by grace disposed in the applying of thy heart. Bind not thyself, therefore, unchangeably to voluntary customs, for that will hinder the freedom of thy heart to love Jesus, if grace would visit thee specially.

7. "Before thou hast made many steps in the way, thou must expect a world of enemies of several kinds, that will beset thee round about, and all of them will endeavour busily to hinder thee from going forward; yea, and if they can by any means, they will, either by persuasions, flatteries, or violence, force thee to return home again to those vanities that thou hast forsaken. For there is nothing grieves them so much as to see a resolute desire in thy heart to love Jesus, and to travail to find Him. Therefore they will all conspire to put out of thy heart that good desire and love in which all virtues are comprised.

8. "Thy first enemies that will assault thee will be fleshly desires and vain fears of thy corrupt heart; and with these there will join unclean spirits, that with sights and temptations will seek to allure thy heart to them, and to withdraw it from Jesus. But whatsoever they say, believe them not; but betake thyself to thy old only secure remedy, answering ever thus, *I am nought, I have nought, and I desire nought, but only the love of Jesus,* and so hold forth on thy way desiring Jesus only.

9. "If they endeavour to put dreads and scruples into thy mind, and would make thee believe that thou hast not done penance enough, as thou oughtest for thy sins, but that some old sins remain in thy heart not yet confessed, or not sufficiently confessed and absolved, and that therefore thou must needs return home and do penance better before thou have the boldness to go to Jesus, do not believe a word of all that they say, for thou art sufficiently acquitted of thy sins, and there is no need at all that thou shouldst stay

26

to ransack thy conscience, for this will now but do thee harm, and either put thee quite out of thy, way or at least unprofitably delay thy travailing in it.

10. "If they shall tell thee that thou art not worthy to have the love of Jesus, or to see Jesus, and therefore that thou oughtest not to be so presumptuous to desire and seek after it, believe them not, but go on and say: It is not because I am worthy, but because I am unworthy, that I therefore desire to have the love of Jesus, for if once I had it, it would make me worthy. I will therefore never cease desiring it till I have obtained it. For, for it only was I created, therefore, say and do what you will, I will desire it continually, I will never cease to pray for it, and so doing I hope to obtain it.

11. "If thou meetest with any that seem friends unto thee, and that in kindness would stop thy progress by entertaining thee, and seeking to draw thee to sensual mirth by vain discourses and carnal solaces, whereby thou wilt be in danger to forget thy pilgrimage, give a deaf ear to them, answer them not; think only on this, *That thou wouldest fain be at Jerusalem.* And if they proffer thee gifts and preferments, heed them not, but think ever on Jerusalem.

12. "And if men despise thee, or lay any false calumnies to thy charge, giving thee ill names; if they go about to defraud thee or rob thee; yea, if they beat thee and use thee despitefully and cruelly, for thy life contend not with them, strive not against them, nor be angry with them, but content thyself with the harm received, and go on quietly as if nought were done, that thou take no further harm; think only on this, that to be at Jerusalem deserves to be purchased with all this ill-usage or more, and that there thou shalt be sufficiently repaired for all thy losses, and recompensed for all hard usages by the way.

13. "If thine enemies see that thou growest courageous and bold, and that thou wilt neither be seduced by flatteries nor disheartened with the pains and troubles of thy journey, but rather well contented with them, then they will begin to be afraid of thee; yet for all that, they will never cease pursuing thee—they will follow thee all along the way, watching all advantages against thee; and ever and anon they will set upon thee, seeking either with flatteries or frights to stop thee, and drive thee back if they can. But fear them not; hold on thy way, and have nothing in thy mind but Jerusalem and Jesus, whom thou wilt find there.

14. "If thy desire of Jesus still continues and grows more strong, so that it makes thee go on thy ways courageously, they will then tell thee that it may very well happen that thou wilt fall into corporal sickness, and perhaps such a sickness as will bring strange fancies into thy mind, and melancholic apprehensions; or perhaps thou wilt fall into great want, and no man will offer to help thee, by occasion of which misfortunes thou wilt be grievously

tempted by thy ghostly enemies, the which will then insult over thee, and tell thee that thy folly and proud presumption have brought thee to this miserable pass, that thou canst neither help thyself, nor will any man help thee, but rather hinder those that would. And all this they will do to the end to increase thy melancholic and unquiet apprehensions, or to provoke thee to anger or malice against thy Christian brethren, or to murmur against Jesus, who, perhaps for thy trial, seems to hide His face from thee. But still neglect all these suggestions as though thou heardest them not. Be angry with nobody but thyself. And as for all thy diseases, poverty, and whatsoever other sufferings (for who can reckon all that may befall thee?), take Jesus in thy mind, think on the lesson that thou art taught, and say, *I am nought, I have nought, I care for nought in this world, and I desire nought but the love of Jesus, that I may see him in peace at Jerusalem.*

15. "But if it shall happen sometimes, as likely it will, that through some of these temptations and thy own frailty, thou stumble and perhaps fall down, and get some harm thereby, or that thou for some time be turned a little out of the right way, as soon as possibly may be come again to thyself, get up again and return into the right way, using such remedies for thy hurt as the Church ordains; and do not trouble thyself over much or over long with thinking unquietly on thy past misfortune and pain—abide not in such thoughts, for that will do thee more harm, and give advantage to thine enemies. Therefore, make haste to go on in thy travail and working again, as if nothing had happened. Keep but *Jesus* in thy mind, and a desire to gain His *love,* and nothing shall be able to hurt thee.

16. "At last, when thine enemies perceive that thy will to Jesus is so strong that thou wilt not spare neither for poverty nor mischief, for sickness nor fancies, for doubts nor fears, for life nor death, no, nor for sins neither, but ever forth thou wilt go on with that one thing of seeking the love of Jesus, and with nothing else; and that thou despisest and scarce markest anything that they say to the contrary, but holdest on in thy praying and other spiritual works (yet always with discretion and submission), then they grow even enraged, and will spare no manner of most cruel usage. They will come closer to thee than ever before, and betake themselves to their last and most dangerous assault, and that is, to bring into the sight of thy mind all thy good deeds and virtues, showing thee that all men praise thee, and love thee, and bear thee great veneration for thy sanctity, &c. And all this they do to the end to raise vain joy and pride in thy heart. But if thou tenderest thy life, thou wilt hold all this flattery and falsehood to be a deadly poison to thy soul, mingled with honey; therefore, away with it; cast it from thee, saying, thou wilt have none of it, but thou wouldest be at Jerusalem.

17. "And to the end, to put thyself out of the danger and reach of all such temptations, suffer not thy thoughts willingly to run about the world, but draw them all inwards, fixing their upon one only thing, which is *Jesus:* set thyself to think only on Him, to know Him, to love Him; and after thou hast for a good time brought thyself to do thus, then whatsoever thou seest or feelest inwardly that is not He, will be unwelcome and painful to thee, because it will stand in thy way to the seeing and seeking of Him whom thou only desirest.

18. "But yet, if there be any work or outward business which thou art obliged to do, or that charity or present necessity requires of thee, either concerning thyself or thy Christian brother, fail not to do it; dispatch it as well and as soon as well thou canst, and let it not tarry long in thy thoughts, for it will but hinder thee in thy principal business. But if it be any other matter of no necessity, or that concerns thee not in particular, trouble not thyself nor distract thy thoughts about it, but rid it quickly out of thy heart, saying still thus, *I am nought, I can do nought, I have nought, and nought do I desire to have, but only Jesus and his love.*

19. "Thou wilt be forced, as all other pilgrims are, to take ofttimes, by the way, refreshments, meats and drink and sleep, yea, and sometimes innocent recreations; in all which things rise discretion, and take heed of foolish scrupulosity about them. Fear not that they will be much a hindrance to thee, for though they seem to stay thee for a while, they will further thee and give thee strength to walk on more courageously for a good long time after.

20. "To conclude, remember that thy principal aim, and indeed only business, is to knit thy thoughts to the desire of *Jesus*—to strengthen this desire daily by prayer and other spiritual workings, to the end it may never go out of thy heart. And whatsoever thou findest proper to increase that desire, be it praying or reading, speaking or being silent, travailing or reposing, make use of it for the time, as long as thy soul finds savour in it, and as long as it increases this desire of having or enjoying nothing but the love of Jesus, and the blessed sight of Jesus in true peace in Jerusalem; and be assured that this good desire thus cherished and continually increased will bring thee safe unto the end of thy pilgrimage."

21. This is the substance of the parable of the Spiritual Pilgrim travailing in the ways of contemplation; the which I have more largely set down because, by the contexture of it, not only we see confirmed what is already written before, but also we have a draught and scheme represented, according to which all the following instructions will be conformably answerable.

THE FIRST TREATISE
THE SECOND SECTION

IN WHICH IS DECLARED AND PROVED THAT GOD ONLY BY HIS
HOLY INSPIRATIONS IS THE GUIDE AND DIRECTOR IN AN
INTERNAL CONTEMPLATIVE LIFE.

Chapter I. Two Internal Guides in all Christians

§ 1. In internal contemplative ways a guide is necessary, and why?

*§§ 2, 3, 4. All good Christians have within their souls two internal guides. 1.
The spirit of corrupt nature, which is never wholly expelled. 2. The Spirit of
God. And these teach contrarily, and for contrary ends.*

*§§ 5, 6, 7, 8, 9. Divine inspirations, beyond the light of common grace, are to
be our light in internal ways.*

§§ 10, 11. In what special things such inspirations do direct internal livers.

*§§ 12, 13. They ordinarily teach rather cessation and not doing than much
doing.*

§§ 14, 15. Extraordinary inspirations, illuminations, &c., not pretended to.

1. Having hitherto treated of a contemplative life in general, the nature and end of it, together with the necessary disposition required in souls that, according to their vocation or profession, are desirous to pursue the exercises belonging thereto, the next thing that in relation to the said state deserves our consideration is the guide whose directions we may and ought to follow therein; for certainly a guide must needs be had, since it is evident that in our present state of corrupt nature, we have no light so much as to discover that there is any such way, and much less to direct and enable us to walk in paths so much above, yea, so directly contrary to the designs and interests of nature.

2. Now, since in every good, faithful, and true Christian (as truth and experience teach) there are two internal lights and teachers, to wit, 1. the

spirit of corrupt nature; 2. the Divine Spirit, both which, in all our deliberate actions, do offer themselves, and even strive for mastery, contending whether of them, with the exclusion of the other, shall lead us in the ways proper and pleasing to each, the which ways, as also the ends to which they conduct, are directly contrary to one another; for the spirit of corrupt nature only teaches us such things as are for the present pleasing or profitable to our carnal desires or sensual and secular designs, but pernicious to the soul or spirit; the which, following the light of nature, runs into endless errors and labyrinths, all which lead us from God and true happiness unto eternal misery. On the other side, the Spirit of God, discovering unto us the folly and danger of following so blind and pernicious a guide as nature is; teaches us that our happiness consists in forsaking such a wandering guide, and treading paths quite contrary; in renouncing present sensual pleasures and commodities so far as they are a hindrance (yea, not an advancement) to our knowing of God and spiritual things, the which only must be the object of all our desires and endeavours, and whereby only we shall arrive to eternal happiness and union with God.

3. Besides these two guides, we neither have nor can have any other within us, and with both these good Christians are continually attended. Whatsoever, therefore, is not the teaching of the Divine Spirit is the suggestion of the false teacher, who is His and our enemy, the which took possession of the souls of men upon Adam's transgression, whose fault was the not attending to the teaching of God's Holy Spirit (which then was the only internal teacher), but instead thereof, hearkening to the flattering temptations of his wife, seduced by the devil. And from Adam this false light is communicated to all his posterity, so as naturally we have no other. But the new heavenly teacher, the Holy Spirit, is freely given us by means of the divine word and sacraments; it being a new divine principle imprinted in our spirits, raising them to God, and continually soliciting us to walk in His ways.

4. Our misery is, that whereas by mortal sins the divine light is for the time wholly extinguished, so as to the producing of any considerable good effect upon the will, it is not so on the other side, that by grace the false teacher should be totally expelled or silenced, but it remains even in the most perfect, and God knows even the best are too much inclined often to hearken to it. Those that are less perfect, though in matters of necessary duty and obligation they follow the conduct of the Divine Spirit, yet in lesser matters they for the most part are moved with no other principle than that of corrupt nature, by which they incur defects, the which, though in themselves venial, yet do much obscure the divine light, and weaken its efficacy. Yea, even in

those things wherein such imperfect souls do for the substance of the action and its essentials follow the direction of God's Spirit, yet, by mixing of sensual interests and ends, suggested by the false teacher, they do diminish its lustre, beauty, and value. And so subtle is the spirit of nature, that it oft makes its false suggestions pass for divine inspirations, and seldom misses the insinuating its poison in some degree, either into the beginning or continuation of our best actions.

5. From these unquestionable grounds thus truly laid, it follows evidently that in all good actions, and especially in the internal ways of the spirit which conduct to contemplation and perfection, God alone is our only master and director; and creatures, when He is pleased to use them, are only His instruments. So that all other teachers whatsoever, whether the light of reason, or external directors, or rules prescribed in books, &c., are no further nor otherwise to be followed or hearkened to, than as they are subordinate and conformable to the internal directions and inspirations of God's Holy Spirit, or as God invites, instructs, and moves us to have recourse unto them, by them to be informed in His will, and by Him enabled to perform it; and that if they be made use of any other ways, they will certainly mislead us.

6. This is by all mystical writers acknowledged so fundamental a truth, that without acknowledging it and working according to it, it is in vain to enter into the exercises of an internal contemplative life. So that to say (as too commonly it is said by authors who pretend to be spiritual, but have no taste of these mystic matters), take all your instructions from without, from external teachers or books, is all one as to say, have nothing at all to do with the ways of contemplation, which can be taught by no other but God, or by those whom God especially instructs and appoints determinately for the disciple's present exigency. So that it is God only that internally teaches both the teacher and disciple, and His inspirations are the only lesson for both. All our light, therefore, is from divine illumination, and all our strength as to these things is from the divine operation of the Holy Ghost on our wills and affections.

7. Now, to the end that this so important a verity may more distinctly be declared and more firmly imprinted in the minds of all those that desire to be God's scholars in the internal ways of His divine love, they are to take notice that the inspirations which are here acknowledged to be the only safe rule of all our actions, though of the same nature, yet do extend further, and to more and other particular objects, than the divine light or grace, by which good Christians, living common lives in the world, are led, extends to; yea, than it does even in those that seek perfection by the exercises of an active life.

8. The light and virtue of common grace afford generally, to all good Christians that seriously endeavour to save their souls, such internal illuminations and motions as are sufficient to direct them for the resisting of any sinful temptation, or to perform any necessary act of virtue, in circumstances wherein they are obliged, though this direction be oft obeyed with many circumstantial defects, and their actions are so far and no further meritorious and pleasing to God than as they proceed from such internal grace or inspiration. But as for other actions, which in their own nature are not absolutely of necessary obligation, the which, notwithstanding, might be made instrumental to the advancing and perfecting of holiness in their souls (such as are the ordinary and usually esteemed indifferent actions of their lives), to a due improvement of such actions, they have neither the light nor the strength, or very seldom, by reason that they live distracted lives, not using such solitude and recollection as are necessary for the disposing of souls to the receiving such an extraordinary light and virtue. And as for those that tend to perfection by active exercises, even the more perfect, although they attain thereby a far greater measure of light and grace, by which they perform their necessary duties of holiness more perfectly and with a more pure intention, and likewise make far greater benefit for their advancement by actions and occurrences more indifferent; yet they also, for want of habitual introversion and recollectedness of mind, do pass over without benefit the greatest part of their ordinary actions.

9. But as for contemplative livers, those I mean that have made a sufficient progress towards perfection, besides the common grace, light, or inspirations necessary for a due performance of essential duties, the which they enjoy in a far more sublime manner and degree, so as to purify their actions from a world of secret impurities, and subtle mixture of the interests and ends of corrupt nature, invisible to all other souls—besides this light, I say (which is presupposed and prerequired), they walk in a continual supernatural light, and are guided by assiduous inspirations in regard of their most ordinary, and, in themselves, indifferent actions and occurrences, in all which they clearly see how they are to behave themselves, so as to do the will of God, and by them also to improve themselves in the divine love; the which extraordinary light is communicated unto them only by virtue of their almost continual recollectedness, introversion, and attention to God in their spirits.

10. More particularly by this internal divine light an internal liver is or may be directed: 1. In the manner and circumstances, when, where, and how any virtue may most profitably and perfectly be exercised; for as for the substantial act of such a virtue, and the necessary obliging circumstances in which it cannot, without mortal sin, be omitted, the light of common sanctifying grace will suffice to direct. 2. In the manner, frequency, length, change, and other circumstances of internal prayer. 3. In actions or omissions, which,

absolutely considered, may, seem in themselves indifferent, and at the present there may be, as to ordinary light, an uncertainty whether the doing or omission is the more perfect. This is discovered to the soul by these supernatural inspirations and light: such actions or omissions are, for example, reading, study of such or such matters, walking, conversing, staying in or quitting solitude in one's cell, taking a journey, undertaking or refusing an employment, accepting or refusing invitations, &c.; in all which things well-minded souls, by solitude and introversion disposing themselves, will not fail to have a supernatural light and impulse communicated to them, which will enable them to make choice of that side of the doubt, which, if they correspond thereto, will most advance them in spirit, and suit with the divine will; whereas, without such light, generally souls are directed by an obscure light and impulse of nature and carnal ends or interests, without the least benefit of their spirit, yea, to their greater distraction and dissipation.

11. Generally and ordinarily speaking, when there is proposed the doing or not doing of any external work, and that both of them are in themselves lawful, the divine inspiration in contemplative souls moves to the not doing; because the abstaining from much external working, and the increasing in internal solitude of spirit, is more suitable to their present state, and to that abstraction of life which they profess—except when the doing may prove a more beneficial mortification to self-love, or other inordinate affection of corrupt nature.

12. The special points and matters of omissions, which (among others) are usually the objects of such divine calls and inspirations, may be such as these, viz.: 1. To eschew unnecessary, though permitted, conversations and correspondences with others, either by speaking or writing. 2. To be very wary and sparing in the use of the tongue. 3. Not solicitously to avoid occasions of mortifications or afflictions 4. To avoid the encumbering ourselves with business not pertaining to us. 5. To fly honours, offices, care over others, and the like. 6. Not to crave this or that unnecessary thing or commodity, but to be content without them. 7. Not to question or expostulate why such a thing was said or done, but to hold patience, and to let things be as they are. 8. Not to complain of or accuse any. 9. In cases of supportable and not harmful oppressions, to abstain from appeals to higher superiors. 10. To avoid the voluntary causing or procuring a change in our present condition, employment, place, &c. 11. To quiet and compose all manner of passions rising in the heart, and all troubles in mind, and to preserve the soul in peace, tranquillity, and cheerfulness in God's service. 12. To avoid such things or doings as will distract our minds with dissipating images. 13. To forbear and break off all particular partial friendships and compliances. 14. To preserve convenient liberty of spirit, and to abstain from encumbering or ensnaring ourselves by

any voluntary assumed tasks, obligations, &c., though in matters in themselves good, but which may, becoming obligatory, prove hindrances to better things. 15. In a word, the divine inspirations, of which we here treat, do ever tend to a simplicity in thoughts, words, and deeds, and to all things which may advance the more perfect exercise of obedience, humility, resignation, purity of prayer, purity of intention, &c., so that whatsoever is contrary to any of these is to be rejected as a diabolical suggestion.

13. As for extraordinary supernatural inspirations, illuminations, apparitions, voices, conversations with spirits, messages from heaven, &c., a spiritual internal liver is forbidden to pretend to, or so much as desire them; yea, rather to pray against them, lest he should abuse them to vanity and pride; and, moreover, never to admit or esteem them for such, and much less to put in execution anything that seems to be such a way commanded, till they have been first examined, judged, and approved by superiors, &c. But of this particular we shall speak more hereafter.

14. The divine inspirations, lights, impulses, or calls, of which we here speak, are: 1. either such as are immediately communicated to the soul alone; 2. or also mediately with the concurrence of some other person or thing, to wit, by the mean of an external director; or also by the use and reading or hearing read spiritual or other pious books. We will, in the first place, treat of this latter way of understanding the divine will, because it is both more easy to be discerned, and also it is the way by which commonly imperfect souls are first instructed.

Chapter II. Of an External Director

§§ 1, 2. Why an external guide is necessary in the beginning.

§§ 3, 4, 5, 6. The conditions of such a guide; of which the principal is experience in the same ways beyond learning, &c.

§§ 7, 8. Active spirits cannot be fit guides for contemplative.

§§ 9, 10. Actual illumination oft necessary to external directors.

§§ 11, 12, 13. The office of a director may not be voluntarily assumed or sought.

§§ 14, 15. Lay persons may be spiritual guides to religious; yea, women.

§ 16. That is no prejudice to the spirit of an order.

§ 17. Conditions necessary in directors.

§§ 18, 19. Directors must teach their disciples to seek light from God.

§ 20. Sincerity and obedience necessary in the disciple.

§ 21. The gift of discerning spirits necessary in a director.

§ 22. His instructions must be general.

§§ 23, 24. Frequent consultations harmful.

§ 25. Two general remedies against difficulties: viz. 1. Riddance. 2. Patience.

§§ 26, 27. The director must not with unnecessary questions raise doubts.

§ 28. Great danger from unnecessary conversation of directors with women.

§ 29. More particular advices referred to other following places.

1. A soul that comes out of the world to a religious contemplative life, or that living yet in the world is abstracted from the world and aspires to a state of perfection, at the first ordinarily will stand in need of an external instructor and guide for most matters that concern her in that way. The reason is because that such souls, although being supposed to be in the state of grace, have sufficient internal light to direct them in the ordinary duties of a Christian life, for the avoiding of sin and performing the necessary acts of virtues requisite; yet, as to the proper practices of internal ways, and to the ordering of common actions to the advancing of themselves towards contemplation, they are indeed *penitus animales,* governed by sense and the obscure deceitful light of natural reason, scarce knowing what an internal inspiration (with regard to such matters) is, and however very much disabled are they to discern or correspond to such an inspiration. And for this reason their natural light and general knowledge that they have of their own insufficiency to be their own directors in a new unknown state, will tell them that they must have recourse to other guides skilled in those things of which themselves have no experience. Yet even this seeking and submitting themselves unto external directors is not to be esteemed merely an act of nature, or guided only by a natural light; but of such inspirations and supernatural light which attends the actions of all good Christians, by which they are taught and moved to distrust themselves, and not knowing as yet how to dispose themselves for the receiving supernatural lights from God (much less to merit them), grace directs them to use the mediation of others, and to hear and obey God, speaking and ordaining by them.

2. But the necessity of an external instructor is generally only at the beginning of a contemplative course. For after that souls, by the means of general directions given and a competent pursuit of internal exercises, have been once put and conveniently settled in a right way how to seek for more light from God alone, they must not afterwards, out of levity, curiosity, or a foolish proneness to discover their interior, nor without a just necessity, continue to seek instructions from without; nothing will excuse it but the want of internal light in some special doubtful cases, and then also, they having an

internal inspiration and motion to seek it from others; in which case it is indeed their divine internal Master that they obey, who speak unto them by the external director appointed unto them by God. The devout reader may further see what the fore-mentioned excellent author of *Scala Perfectionis* says to this purpose in the 2nd part and 91st chapter, as likewise the author of the book called the *Cloud of Unknowing,* chap. 49 and 54.

3. Now to the end to enable the soul to make a good choice (I mean such a soul as hath freedom to make her own choice), I will set down the qualities necessary to be found in a good director, by which title I do not mean simply a *Confessarius,* that is only to hear faults confessed, to give absolution, and there an end; for the ordinary qualities of learning and prudence are sufficient thereto. But by a spiritual director I intend one that, besides this, is to instruct the disciple in all the peculiar duties of an internal life; that is, to judge of her propension to contemplative ways, and that can at least teach her how she may fit herself with a degree of prayer proper for her; that knows all the degrees of internal prayer, and can determine how long she is to remain in such a degree, and when to change it for a higher; that can judge what employments, &c., are helpful or hindering to her progress in internal ways; but especially that can teach her how to dispose herself to hearken to and follow God's internal teaching, and to stand in no more need of consulting her external director, &c. Such are the proper offices of a guide, to enable him whereto there are generally by spiritual writers required three principal qualities: 1. a good natural judgment; 2. learning; 3. experience.

4. But because it is scarce to be hoped for in all places and for all souls to find a director absolutely perfect and qualified with all manner of fitting conditions, therefore the said writers do dispute what quality is the most necessary to make a director capable of a sufficient discharge of his office. Now forasmuch as concerns the first condition, to wit, a good natural judgment, though by all it be acknowledged to be insufficient alone, yet is it so absolutely necessary that without it no considerable experience can be attained; and learning, if it be joined with an extravagant capricious spirit, will prove rather pernicious than advantageous; therefore, the question remains between learning and experience, whether of the two is the most necessary?

5. But truly this scarce deserves to be a question. For though for the assoiling of ordinary doubts and cases of conscience, as about fasting, saying the divine office, confession, restitution, &c., learning be the principal condition to be looked after in one that is to be a guide for such purposes, notwithstanding, since the office of the spiritual director that now we seek after is to be exercised in such internal matters of the spirit as hath been said, to wit, contemplative prayer, attending to divine inspirations, &c., it is the

resolute judgment of Gerson, Avila, St. Teresa, B. John de Cruce, Seraphinus Firmanus, &c., that no trust is to be given to learning without experience, but much to experience though without learning. And to this purpose it is observable that for the most part the instruments that God hath been pleased, both in ancient and modern times, to employ in the instructing and guiding of souls to the perfection of contemplative prayer, have been persons of small learning but great experience, such as were St. Anthony, St. Benedict, St. Francis, St. Teresa, &c.

6. No learning, therefore, that may be got by study and reading, though of all the contemplative books that now are extant, will alone serve to enable any one to be a competent director for internal livers. But there is necessary experience and practice in the same prayer, and other internal exercises that are to be taught; for never so many years spent in discursive prayer will little avail to qualify any one to be a proper and profitable director for souls tending to contemplation, as all enclosed religious men and women are obliged.

7. Yea, it is much more safe for a well-meaning soul, the which, in solitude and abstraction, aspires to contemplation, to make use of that, though obscure, internal light which God has given her for the applying of such instructions as books which treat of effective prayer proper for her will afford her; or else to trust to the guidance of a virtuous humble-minded director, who, though he have but a very small proportion either of experience or learning, yet, out of humility, will not assume unto himself authority to judge of things above his reach, but will encourage the soul either to seek out one more intelligent, or to follow the directions of her own spirit illuminated by grace, than to confide in any directors, though never so learned, that would confine her all her lifetime to a form of discursive prayer, much busying the imagination, but not affording a scope free enough for the affections and holy desires, in which principally consists the good of prayer; and by consequence that will be apt to make her suspect all tracts and invitations wherewith God shall draw her to a more sublime, quiet, pure prayer in spirit, to the which, if she do not correspond, she will remain continually in multiplicity, distraction, and unquietness. The more learned that such improper directors are, the more incompetent are they for such an employment about souls whose profession is the aspiring to the prayer of contemplation; because, if either they be ignorant of such prayer, or unwilling to acknowledge any prayer more perfect than that which themselves practise and teach others, their learning will make them both more able and forward to keep souls under a certain captivity, chained with methods and forms, the which, though very profitable, even to these souls in the beginning, yet afterward become very painful

and even insupportable to them living in solitude and a quiet abstraction of life.

8. Truly it is not without some scruple and unwillingness that the present subject obliges me to deliver instructions, the which, perhaps, will to some appear displeasing and unwelcome. But the charitable reader is entreated to believe that here is not the least intention to reflect with censure upon any, or to inconciliate any directors to their disciples; our design being only to show what kind of prayer and practices we judge proper for internal livers; and this being so, we hope that, without offence to any, we may say that the most fit directors are such as are versed in the ways that they teach, as likewise that we may suggest to those that are of a contemplative profession that they would, in the exercise of prayer, abate, as much as may be, the busy work of the imagination, and enlarge that of affection. This is all we intend, both here and in whatsoever other passages of this book occasion is given to renew the like advices.

9. I may truly say that neither natural judgment, learning, nor experience all together are absolutely sufficient to qualify a person for the employment of guiding souls in all cases in the internal ways of the spirit, but very oft an actual supernatural illumination will moreover be requisite and necessary; though true it is that experienced persons have great advantages beyond what wit or learning can afford. And such, for matters beyond their experience, no doubt, will often remit souls to God and their own observation; the which is a quality and office not to be expected from persons that bring no better endowments with them to the managing of contemplative souls, but only subtlety of wit and learning, or experience in a quite different and much inferior exercise of prayer (such experience being, as I said, rather a disadvantage), for such will resolve all cases; and though the directions they give must needs be improper, yet they will be very absolute in requiring obedience. Whereas, a person experienced in the same internal ways, being humble withal (for else, saith Avila, he also will probably be faulty too), though he be not in all cases able to give a resolute judgment, yet, finding his own deficiency, he will make a doubt of the matter, and thereupon, out of humility, will not scorn but rather be desirous to consult and take advice from others more able to resolve.

10. Hereupon it is that St. Teresa (as it is recorded in her life) much complains of the hurt that such resolute and insufficient teachers did to her and will do to others. And Thaulerus (worthily styled the illuminate doctor) professeth of himself in a certain sermon that unless he were specially illuminated by God for the solution of a doubt proposed to him, he would remit the party to God himself, to be instructed in prayer what to do. And let not such a one doubt, saith he, but that God will be his faithful counsellor. More-

over, he finds great fault with those arrogant persons that reprehend souls for suffering themselves to be guided by the instincts and internal lights and motions proceeding from God's Spirit, and for their calling such by the titles of new spirits, or pretenders to extraordinary illuminations; whereas, saith he, those that take all their instructions from persons and books will with very small success pursue the ways of the spirit.

11. It is a miserable thing to see how this employment of directing souls (which above all other is most difficult, and exceedeth even the ability of an angel yet), out of an ambitious humour, is invaded by persons wholly unfitted for it, and that without any vocation from God voluntarily undertake it; so that no marvel it is if so little good come from such intruders. Not one of a thousand, saith Avila, is capable of so sublime a task. Nay, saith the holy Bishop of Geneva, not one of ten thousand. And most certain it is that those who so freely offer themselves to so divine an employment, do thereby show themselves to want the most necessary qualifications, to wit, humility and a true knowledge of its difficulty, and therefore their directions are most to be suspected.

12. Hereupon Thaulerus saith, that a soul intending perfection ought to seek out an experienced servant of God, though it cost her a journey of many German miles. But, saith he, if such a friend cannot be found, then will a simple Confessarius serve, though never so ignorant; for even by such men doth the Holy Ghost speak by reason of their office; so that they may securely be submitted to and obeyed, even in things which they do not well understand.

13. If a soul that is fearful and scrupulous be to choose a director, she ought to avoid one of the like temper, for passion which blinds the seeker will also blind the director, and so the blind will lead the blind.

14. It is not necessary that the persons consulted with about difficulties concerning internal prayer should be learned, or in holy orders (except doubts concerning matters of faith or cases of conscience intervene), for though lay persons and women be not allowed by the Church to preach publicly, yet are they not forbidden to give private instructions in matters of that nature to any that shall have recourse to them. And of the good success of such instructors we have divers examples, as in the layman that converted Thaulerus, a learned doctor and a religious man, and likewise in St. Catharine of Siena, St. Teresa, &c. And in a well-governed monastery of women, where a good course of internal prayer, approved by superiors and learned divines, is once well settled, it is very expedient that instructions concerning it should rather come from superiors within; because otherwise, by reason of the frequent change of directors, perhaps of contrary spirits, and many of

them little practised in such prayer, souls will be governed uncertainly, and be in danger to be put out of their way.

15. Though it seem evidently more reasonable and more proportionable to the spirits of persons professing a religious state to be conducted by others of the same profession (*cæteris paribus*) than by such as are strangers thereto, yet scarce any directors can be found more improper for such (supposing that they tend to contemplation) than are religious guides of active spirits, that know no further of prayer than meditation, and that show more zeal for an exact observance of ceremonies, or a multiplying of external voluntary austerities (the which of themselves, and unless they be guided by God's Spirit, have no special influence on the spirit, but only serve either for an outward show of rigour, or for keeping souls from misspending the time), than for the more essential internal duties of prayer, solitude of spirit, interior mortification, &c. Much more profitable to such souls would be a director, though not of any religious profession, that would impose on souls only such austerities as are essentially necessary to an internal life; such as are perfect abstraction, silence, solitude, convenient abstinence, &c. And for other matters not much necessary nor much effectual, leaving them in a due moderate liberty of spirit, especially such as will not impose on them any forms of mental prayer, however liked or practised by themselves, but for such matters rather leaving them to the conduct of God's Holy Spirit, and that will not torture them with painful, iterated customary confessions, &c.

16. And whereas it will be perhaps objected that probably such directors, being strangers as to the special distinctive spirit of such an order or community, may endanger in their disciples a loss of the said spirit, I must profess that I understand not what is meant by that so-much-talked-of spirit of an order; nor how several orders, though never so much distinguished by habits or certain external practices, if their profession be to tend to contemplation, can have any more than one spirit, which directs them to make their principal design to be the seeking of God in His internal ways of divine love, and to that only end besides conformable prayer to practise such observances and mortifications as will best promote this design. And surely this good spirit of religion and contemplation, a good director, of what profession soever, will very studiously endeavour to advance, yea, and moreover will no doubt oblige his disciples to be very regular and zealous in the observance of all good ordinances of the community, and principally of the rule according to their profession made; instructing them withal how they may use such things for the advancing of their spirit and the service of God, although in the mean time, perhaps, he be not cunning in all the particular observances that belong to them, and little or nothing at all to him.

17. All souls that live in contemplative orders are not naturally fitted for contemplative ways, nor the seeking of God in spirit. Those, therefore, that have not, and indeed are not capable of much light in their interior, and so are not so fit to be guided by divine inspirations, do the more need to have certain rules from without, at least for the exterior. And for such it is God's will and direction that they should more depend on external guides.

18. He that takes upon hire the office of a spiritual director, saith Thaulerus, ought for some reasonable space of time to converse with his disciples, especially at the beginning; for a few transitory conferences will not suffice to give him light concerning their propensions and dispositions, that he may fit them with a degree of prayer proper for them, both for the present and future. And his principal care must be to set them in such a way as that they may not need to have much recourse unto him afterward, the which is done by giving them general directions about their prayer, and especially how thereby to dispose themselves to receive light from God, Whose inspirations ought for the future to be their principal rule, especially for the interior. And for the practising in particular according to the general directions given, the disciples must use their own judgment, and for a help they may also make use of such instructions as they may find in books, so far as they shall be proper for their spirit. But in cases when neither their own judgment nor books will help them, if the difficulty be of greater moment, they may again have recourse unto their director.

19. And in this sort are writers that speak much of the necessity of an external director to be understood. For if such necessity were to last always, good souls should be obliged to spend their whole lives in conferring with directors, from whence would follow continual solicitudes, scrupulosities, and dangerous distractions, &c., most contrary to an internal spiritual life, which ought to be a state of much repose, cessation, introversion, and a continual attendance unto what God speaks within unto the soul; who, if souls will humbly and faithfully depend on Him, will clear and resolve difficulties, which external masters will never be able to penetrate into. But it is too general a humour in directors nowadays to make themselves seem necessary unto their disciples, whom they endeavour to keep in a continual dependence, to the great prejudice of their progress in spirit, besides many other inconveniences not needful to be mentioned particularly.

20. A soul that has recourse to an instructor provided by God for her, or that, using her best advice, she hath made choice of, must deal freely, plainly, and candidly with him, concealing nothing necessary to be known by him; and his directions she must follow in all things, assuring herself that if she do so in the simplicity of her heart, and as in obedience to God himself, God will enlighten him so that she shall not be misled.

21. The gift of discerning spirits is so necessary to a spiritual guide, that except thereby he be able to fit a soul with a sort and degree of prayer suitable to her natural disposition, not tying all souls to begin according to any general methods (for none such can be prescribed but will be prejudicial to some), and unless he teach how she may become illuminated without him, by God alone, by the means of prayer and abstraction of life (wherewith the mists of images and passions being dispelled, a light will spring forth in the soul far more clear and certain than any that can come from human instructions), not all the instructions of men and angels, joined with all mortifications imaginable, will be able to bring a soul to contemplation. For seldom or never doth God work contrary to our natural complexions; and till souls come to exercises in spirit and prayer, infused by God alone, they are far from contemplation.

22. Now at the first it is very hard for any director to know exactly the secret inclinations of imperfect souls; which are so infinitely various; and therefore, for the most part, their instructions about prayer and attendance to divine inspirations must be general, the which the disciples themselves must make a particular use of by observing their own abilities and inclinations, and by marking what more particular forms of prayer, &c., suit best with them and do them most good. And this if they be not able in a reasonable manner to do, or if they have not the courage to abide in a way in which they are put, it will be in vain for them to proceed in those secret internal ways.

23. If the way wherein a soul is put, and hath made a reasonable progress, be indeed proper for her, there will be little need of frequent recourse unto her director. Neither ought he to examine her about her internal exercises, of which he may judge well enough by her external comportment; for it is impossible for a soul to be in a wrong way interiorly, but of itself it will break out exteriorly, especially to the eyes of those who themselves are in a right way, as the spiritual director is supposed to be. And there is scarce any more certain sign that a soul is not interiorly in a good way, than is her being forward to trouble her director with a multiplicity of questions and doubts, and her readiness to discover her interior to others, whom she has heard or does believe to be skilful in spirituality.

24. The images and internal distractions raised by impertinent consultations about the interior are, of all other, most pernicious; for distractions from without are but superficial, whereas those being hatched and bred within the soul from some secret ill qualities, as fear, scrupulosity, curiosity, &c., they are more profound and destructive to true recollection.

25. The general remedies against almost all difficulties are these two: 1. riddance; 2. patience. The former consists in affording to the soul some ease and latitude, as far as a good conscience will permit, in such things as

are apt to perplex well-minded tender souls, as confession, saying of the office, obligation to the ordinances of the Church, and some kind of temptations; in all which things such souls are to be taught to neglect and transcend scrupulous nicety, and they are likewise to be prudently freed from the practice of customs not obligatory. And this remedy is proper against scrupulosity, disentangling the soul from many snares which otherwise would prove a great hindrance to her. The other remedy of patience and abiding is reasonable in case of aridities, desolations, and other such discouragements in an internal life; in which cases the devout soul is to be exhorted to behave herself as well as she can, and to be quietly resigned for what with all her industry she cannot help. Above all things, she is to be heartened to pursue courageously her appointed recollections in despite of all such oppositions raised by the devil or corrupt nature, and permitted by God for her good. The which if she do she will either disperse these temptations, or obtain a divine light to perceive that the way both most proper and most secure, by which God purposes to lead her to perfection, is the way of aridities and obscurities, as B. John de Cruce teaches in his treatise called *Mount Carmel*. And when she once perceives this, then they will not only be supportable, but even acceptable to her. However, if a soul did know, or could be persuaded how much better it were for her to suffer a little bitterness arising from such difficulties or perplexities, than to hasten for a remedy by seeking help from others, or by turning herself to unnecessary solaces in creatures, and also with what confidence she might expect satisfaction from her internal master, if she would seriously, by prayer, seek Him, she would save both herself and her director much trouble and inconvenience.

26. The instructor must use great wariness that he do not raise doubts and scruples in his scholars' minds by moving needless and indiscreet questions, or by impertinent discourses concerning spiritual matters, for thereby he may come to raise such doubts as himself shall not be able to resolve, and to put them so far out of their way as perhaps they will never be able to find it again. Therefore, in ordinary conversations, it is more fit that the subject of discourse should be some external and indifferent matters, wherein the parties are not much concerned, than such as regard the interior. Experience shows how much inconvenience doth come to souls by the conversations of such as are great pretenders to skill in spirituality, and therefore, out of vanity or a mistaken charity, are apt, when there is no need, to be offering instructions about spiritual matters.

27. Some souls do see their way before them far better than others, and therefore do move fewer questions. The instructor therefore is to behave himself towards them all according to the quality and need of each spirit, always remembering that his office is not to teach his own way, nor indeed any

determinate way of prayer, &c., but to instruct his disciples how they may themselves find out the way proper for them, by observing themselves what doeth good and what causeth harm to their spirits; in a word, that he is only God's usher, and must lead souls in God's way and not his own.

28. Of all other spiritual persons, it concerns women especially to be very sparing in consultations, and, when necessity requires, to be brief in delivering their difficulties, for otherwise many inconveniences will follow; as: 1. loss of time both to the disciple and instructor; 2. distractions far more hurtful than if they were busied about the most encumbering employments of the community; 3. danger of multiplying new perplexities, by fearing that they have not given a full and a right account of themselves, &c. Besides, one difficulty will be apt to beget a new one, so that instead of seeking peace by disburdening of the conscience, by their indiscretions they may come both to trouble the peace of their instructors and to plunge themselves in incurable perplexities and obscurities of mind; 4. great cause there is to fear that there may, upon such occasion of unnecessary consultations, ensue dangerous familiarities and friendships with such as may prove very unfit counsellors. Thereupon St. Francis Xavier saith, that seldom was there so much good to be expected from the frequent treaties between persons of different sexes as there was peril in them to both.

29. This may suffice concerning the qualities and office of an external director. As for more special duties belonging to him in more particular cases, as scrupulosities, mortifications, &c., it shall be treated when we come to speak of such particular subjects; as likewise of the obligation of superiors about the promoting the spiritual good of their subjects' souls (although they be not consulted with in the nature of spiritual guides), somewhat shall be said in the following discourse concerning the state of a religious profession.

Chapter III. Of reading Spiritual Books

§ 1. Of reading, which is next to prayer.

§ 2. Some books may be read for diversion.

§ 3. But spiritual books only for the soul's profit.

§§ 4, 5. Books proper for contemplatives, &c.

§ 6. Not to stop in obscure places.

§ 7. Not to practise directions, but such as are suitable to the spirit.

§§ 9, 10. Extraordinary practices of saints in mortifications not to be imitated without great caution.

FIRST TREATISE – SECOND SECTION

§ 11. Why mystic authors seem to write diversely.

§ 12. Some Authors indiscreetly require perfection at first.

§ 13. Reading must give way to prayer.

§ 14. How mortification is to be practised in reading.

§§ 15, 16. Divine inspirations to be observed in applying instructions; and particularly of those in this book.

§ 17. A soul following God may without books or instructors be led to perfect contemplation.

1. A second mean by which the Divine Spirit teacheth devout souls is the reading of pious books. And this exercise I esteem, for worth and spiritual profit, to be next unto prayer.

2. As for ordinary books, as ecclesiastical history, &c., it may be permitted to souls even in religion to read them for an innocent diversion and recreation, so that be not the principal end, but that the intention further be by such diversion to dispose a weary soul the better afterwards to pursue her internal exercises. And this permission now is the more reasonable, since that in religious communities of men bodily labour is almost out of date, and in place thereof reading and study hath succeeded, as now the principal daily employment of religious persons, who, living much less abstracted from the world, are almost forced to comply with the customs of the present times, in which learning is so valued and so abounding.

3. But as for spiritual books, the intention of an internal liver ought not to be such as is that of those who live extroverted lives, who read them out of a vain curiosity, or to be thereby enabled to discourse of such sublime matters, without any particular choice or consideration whether they be suitable to their spirit for practice or no. A contemplative soul in reading such books must not say, this is a good book or passage, but moreover, this is useful and proper for me, and by God's grace I will endeavour to put in execution, in due time and place, the good instructions contained in it, as far as they are good for me.

4. For such souls the books most proper are these following: *Scala Perfectionis,* written by F. Walter Hilton; the *Cloud of Unknowing,* written by an unknown author; the *Secret Paths of Divine Love;* as likewise the *Anatomy of the Soul,* written by R. F. Constantin Barbanson, a Capuchin; the book entitled *Of the Threefold Will of God,* written by R. F. Benet Fitch (alias Canfield), a Capuchin likewise; the works of St. Teresa, of B. John de Cruce; likewise Harphius, Thaulerus, Suso, Rusbrochius, Richard de St. Victor, Gerson, &c. And of the ancients, the *Lives of the Ancient Fathers living in the Desert,* and Cassian's *Conferences of certain Ancient Hermits* (rec-

ommended particularly unto us by our holy father), *St. Basil's Rules,* &c. Then for souls that tend to perfection in an active life, books most proper are, the works of Rodriguez, of *Perfection;* the Duke of Gandia, of *Good Works;* Mons. de Sales, Ludovicus de Puente, &c. And lastly, books of a mixed nature are Granada, Blosius, &c. Indeed, few spiritual books there are wherein there is not an intermingling of such instructions. Now I should advise souls in an active life not at all to meddle with instructions belonging to contemplation, but applying themselves to the precepts and exercises of an active life, to use them in order to the end thereof, the perfection of external Christian charity.

5. In all spiritual books, as likewise in all that treat of Christian morality, such instructions as concern the essential qualities and practice of virtues are to be esteemed proper to all souls, yet not so the motives, manner, and circumstances of exercising the said virtues.

6. In reading of spiritual books, if anything touching prayer, &c., occur (as ofttimes it will happen) that the spiritual disciple understands not, let him pass it over and neither unnecessarily trouble his own brains, nor make it a business to trouble others about the understanding of it. Perhaps in time, after more reading, and especially more experience in prayer, he will come to understand it.

7. And as for those things which he either does indeed, or thinks he understands them, let him not be hasty to apply them to himself by practice, out of his own natural judgment or liking, but let him observe his own spirit, way, and internal guidance by God, and accordingly make use of them; otherwise, instead of reaping benefit, such inconveniences may happen, that it would have been better he had never read, nor been able to read any books at all, but only to have followed his own internal light, as many good souls have done that never could read, and yet seeking God in simplicity of their hearts, and praying without any prescribed methods, practising likewise according to the invitation and impulse of the Divine Spirit, have attained to perfect contemplation.

8. Generally mystic authors write according to their own experience in their own souls, when they treat of the several degrees of prayer and the several manners of divine operations in souls in such degrees, as if the same instructions would serve indefinitely for all others. Whereas such is the inexplicable variety of internal dispositions, that the same course and order in all things will scarce serve any two souls. Therefore, if the indiscreet readers, without considering their own spirits and enablements, shall upon the authority of any book either tarry too long in an inferior degree of prayer, when God has fitted them and does call them to a higher, or in a foolish ambition

shall, being unprepared, presume to a degree of prayer too sublime and spiritual for them, there will be no end of difficulties, doubts, and consultations.

9. But of all errors the greatest and most dangerous is the indiscreet imitating the examples and practices of saints in particular extraordinary corporal mortifications, voluntarily (yet by God's special direction) assumed by them, as labours, fastings, watchings, disciplines, &c. For such a forwardness in others not called thereto, to be extraordinary likewise, it is much to be feared proceeds merely from pride and self-love, and will produce no better effects than the nourishing of the same inordinate affections. And if such have not the courage and patience (as it cannot be expected they should have) to persevere in such exercises, this will cause infirmity of body, dejection of mind, and weariness, if not an utter casting off a spiritual course.

10. The benefit that we ought and easily may reap from the reading of such extraordinary practices of others, is to admire God's ways in the conducting of his saints, and to take occasion from thence of humbling and despising of ourselves, seeing how short we come of them in the practice of their virtues; but no further to imitate them in such things than we may be assured that God directs us by a supernatural light, and enables us by an extraordinary grace, yea, and moreover, till we have obtained the leave and approbation of a prudent director. Till this be, let us supply with a good will what our forces will not reach unto. And above all things, we must take heed that we do not entangle ourselves by laying obligations or vows upon our souls about such matters, the which we shall have difficulty to discharge ourselves from when by trial we find the inconvenience.

11. Mystic writers, in expressing the spiritual way in which they have been led, do oft seem to differ extremely from one another; the which difference, notwithstanding, if rightly understood, is merely in the phrase and manner of expression. And the ground hereof is, because the pure immaterial operations of perfect souls in prayer, and especially the operations of God in souls in which they are patients only, are so sublime that intelligible words and phrases cannot perfectly express them, and therefore they are forced to invent new words the best they can, or to borrow similitudes from corporal things, &c., to make their conceptions more intelligible; and thus does each one according to the mariner that he finds or conceives in himself, or according to his skill in language. No wonder, therefore, if there seem to be diversity among them. Hereupon the author of *The Cloud* observes, that great harm may come by understanding things literally, grossly, and sensibly, which, howsoever they be expressed, were intended and ought to be understood spiritually.

12. Some good spiritual authors, intending to recommend certain duties necessary to be practised, forasmuch as concerns the substance of the

duties (as an entire self-abnegation, purity of intention, &c.), do urge the said duties in the greatest perfection universally upon all, and with such phrases of absolute necessity as if upon any defect in practising that virtue (so by them extended to the full, to the end to prevent all the most secret ways and shifts in which nature is apt to seek her own satisfaction) all the whole design of an internal life were ruined; they do by this overmuch exactness and care, instead of exciting the courage of their readers to the serious practice of so necessary a duty, quite dishearten them; yea, perhaps they make them suspect the state of their souls, who being conscious of their present infirmity and imperfections, lose all heart to adventure upon an attempt so unproportionable to their weak abilities. Whereas, if instructions had been tempered with regard to the capacity of each practiser, they would have gone on with courage and good success.

13. Voluntary reading must give place to prayer, whensoever the soul finds herself invited thereto.

14. The virtue of mortification may, and sometimes ought, to be practised in reading in this manner. When any book or subject is very gustful to a soul, she must be watchful over herself not to pour herself wholly upon it with an intemperate greediness, nor to let curiosity or delight too much possess her, but let her now and then stop the pursuit of reading, lifting up her mind by interruptions to God, and afterwards continue at least in a virtual attention to Him, so mortifying and qualifying the impetuosity of nature. And by no means let her give way to an unwillingness to quit reading for performing her appointed recollections or other exercises of obligation.

15. To conclude: whosoever in reading, &c., doth not chiefly observe his own spirit and divine call, and makes not the books, sayings, and examples of others to serve the said spirit and call, but, on the contrary, makes the divine inspirations subject to books, &c., it were better for him never to read such books, or receive human instructions, but that he should cleave only to God, who in case of necessity will most assuredly supply all other wants and defects.

16. And the same liberty that I have recommended to souls in the reading of other books, I advise them to use in these instructions also, that is, to apply to their own practice only such directions as their spiritual instructor and their own experience and reason, enlightened by grace, shall show them to be proper for them. Indeed, in all this book I know scarce any one advice which I can confidently say to be properly belonging to all souls that lead an internal life generally, except this, that they who aspire to perfection in contemplation must not content themselves nor rest finally in any inferior degree of prayer, but following the divine light and invitation (without obliging themselves to any forms or methods) they must from the lowest degree of

internal prayer (which is ordinarily meditation) proceed to a more sublime prayer of immediate affections and acts of the will, and from thence ascend to the infused prayer of aspirations.

17. Yea, I dare with all confidence pronounce, that if all spiritual books in the world were lost, and there were no external directors at all, yet if a soul (sufficiently instructed in the essential grounds of Catholic faith) that has a natural aptness, though otherwise never so simple and unlearned (being only thus far well instructed at first), will prosecute prayer and abstraction of life, and will resignedly undergo such necessary mortifications as God shall provide for her, observing God and His call exteriorly and interiorly, and so forsake herself, and propose Almighty God, His will, love, honour, for her final intention (which she will certainly do if she attend unto His inspirations), such a soul would walk clearly in perfect light, and with all possible security, and would not fail in due time to arrive at perfect contemplation. These are the two external means by which God teaches souls, discovering to them His will, to wit, instructors and books. And to these we might add another, to wit, laws and precepts of superiors (for God teaches also this way, and never commands contrarily). But of these we shall speak hereafter.

Chapter IV. Of Immediate Divine Inspirations

§ 1. Of the third and principal way by which God teaches internal livers, viz. immediate divine inspirations; the order of particular considerations following touching them.

§ 2. First, of the necessity of them, and the ground of such necessity.

§§ 3, 4, 5, 6. The said necessity proved by the testimony of St. Benedict in his Rule, &c.; as also by his example.

§ 7. A further demonstration of the said necessity.

1. The third fore-mentioned, and of all other the most principal means by which God instructs and directs internal livers in the secret paths of His divine love, and upon which do depend the two former, are interior illuminations and inspirations of God's Holy Spirit, who is to be acknowledged the only supreme Master; concerning which inspirations it hath already been shown in general what they are, how distinguished from the lights and motions of common grace, and what are the objects about which principally they are exercised, &c. I will now treat more particularly of them in this following order, viz.: 1. there shall be further shown the necessity of them; 2. that souls are obliged to dispose themselves for the receiving of them, and how this is to be done, to wit, by removing the impediments; 3. how God communicates

to the soul His light and grace for her instruction and direction; 4. that it is not hard to discern them, and very secure to rely upon them; 5. that by the use of them no prejudice at all comes to ecclesiastical or religious obedience.

2. Touching the first point, to wit, the necessity of them in an internal contemplative life, there is none that will deny or doubt, but that divine inspirations are necessary forasmuch as concerns the proper and essential actions of Christian virtues, which receive all their meritoriousness from the said inspirations. But some there are that will not allow the same necessity of expecting inspirations and calls for actions or omissions of themselves indifferent or of less moment. But surely, since it is generally agreed upon by divines following St. Augustine, St. Thomas, &c., that there are no actions done in particular circumstances which are simply to be esteemed indifferent, but since they must have some end, if the end be good they are to be esteemed good, and if evil they are evil (howsoever universally considered, they are in their own nature indifferent, because according to the intention and end wherewith they are done they may be good or evil): again, since there are no actions so inconsiderable but may, yea, ought to be performed out of the motive of divine love, and to the end to increase the said love in our souls, especially the ordinary actions and employments of a religious contemplative life; and lastly, since perfection in divine love cannot be attained by the simple exercise of charity in duties which are absolutely necessary, and without mortal sin cannot be omitted, the which duties do seldom occur, but it is moreover requisite for that end to multiply frequently and daily exercises of the said love in offices less necessary; yea, and to purify all our most ordinary actions from the stains of self-love which adhere unto them; hence, I say, appears the necessity of the influence of the Divine Spirit upon our actions which are not of such obligation, if we seriously tend to the perfection of divine love in our souls.

3. To this purpose it is worth the observing how seriously our holy Father St. Benedict enforces the necessity of hearkening to and obeying the inspirations of God's Holy Spirit, our only supreme Master, making this the foundation of all religious duties, in the prologue of his Rule, where he saith that we must (*nunquam discedere ab ejus magisterio*) never depart from the institution and direction of God; that we must have our eyes open (*ad Deificum lumen*) to the divine light. On which grounds he calls a monastery (*scholam Dominici servitii*) the school wherein God's service is taught, and (*officinam artis spiritualis*) the workhouse wherein the art of the Divine Spirit is taught and practised; namely, because all things, all observances, even those of the least moment in a religious life, do tend to withdraw us from all other teachers and all other skill, and to bring us to be (*Deo docibiles*) taught by God only. And therefore it is that our said holy patriarch lays this as the foundation of all religious practices, that they be done in virtue of

prayer; his words are, *Inprimis ut quidquid agendum inchoas bonum, a Deo perfici instantissima orations deposcas.* As if he should say, in the first and principal place, thou art to consider this to be the end why I invite thee to an abstracted religious life, that thou mayest thereby be brought to this happy and secure state, as to be enabled to obtain of God, by most earnest and assiduous prayer, to give a blessing and perfection to every action that in a religious state thou shalt apply thyself to. Now if according to our holy Father's principal intention prayer ought to prepare and accompany every action which we perform in religion, then surely it will follow that they ought all of them to be performed with relation to God, as upon His bidding and for His love and glory.

4. Moreover, more particularly concerning divine inspirations, our holy Father makes mention of several ones in special, as in the point of internal prayer, though in common he ordains that it should be short (in the 20th chapter of his Rule), yet so as that he leaves it to the liberty of any one to prolong it (*ex affectu inspirationis Divinæ gratiæ*) by an invitation and enablement from a divine inspiration and grace. And again, concerning abstinence, as also the measure of allowance for meat and drink, he professeth that he had a scruple how to proportion it, considering the variety of men's tempers and necessities. But, however, though he was willing to allow what might be sufficient for the strongest, yet he leaves every one in particular to the direction of grace, saying in the 40th chap. (*Unusquisque proprium habet donum ex Deo; alias sic, alius vero sic*), that is, every one hath a peculiar gift of God; one hath this, and another that (*Quibus autem donat Deus tolerantiam abstinentiæ, propriam se habituros mercedem sciant*), that is, those unto whom God hath given the strength to endure a sparing abstinence, let them be assured that so doing God will give them a peculiar reward. Besides these, several other passages might be produced out of our Holy Father's Rule to the same purpose.

5. Now in this last passage there is a document that well deserves to be considered. Every one, saith he, in St. Paul's words, hath his proper peculiar gift in the matter of refection. All good Christians have the gift to avoid therein a mortally sinful excess, but religious internal livers have moreover (or may have) a special gift to avoid even venial defects, and the perfect to advance themselves thereby towards perfection. Yet from thence we cannot conclude that God has obliged himself to discover unto every one, although seeking it by prayer, the exactly true state and complexion of his body. Whence it follows that if he, being mistaken in that which he is not bound to know, should demand more or less sustenance than is absolutely necessary, it is no sin, upon supposition that such desire did not proceed from a sensual

affection to meat nor a faulty neglect of health, but from the best light that reason could afford him to judge of his own necessity, and from an intention to benefit his soul by a moderate refreshing of nature. And it is God's will that we should follow reason in all external things in which God doth not usually otherwise illuminate his servants. Though natural reason, therefore, may fail and be mistaken, yet the person does not offend, but rather follows God by following the light of his reason, this being all the light in such cases afforded him. So for example, if a hermit, being infirm, and having none to consult with, should doubt whether it were unlawful for him to break a commanded fast, and having by prayer desired God's direction, should remain persuaded that it was, and thereby should prejudice his health by fasting, this would be no sin at all in him, yea, on the contrary it would be meritorious. For he would fail indeed in that for which he had no light, neither was light necessary to him, to wit, the exact knowledge of what had been requisite for corporal health; but he would merit in that for which he had light, to wit, the advancement of his soul. And ordinarily speaking, the inspirations that God affords to the more perfect in such cases are rather to abstain even from the more expedient commodities, yea, ofttimes to some prejudice of health, for the greater good of the soul; because, too anxious a solicitude for health is unbecoming an internal liver. Yea, a robustious health uninterrupted is not convenient for such a one. But leaving this digression:

6. Our holy Father teaches, as himself had been taught (for what other teacher had he from his infancy till the moment of his expiration but the Divine Spirit, by whose light and impulse alone he was directed into and in his solitude, and afterward enabled to direct all succeeding ages in a cœnobitical life?) to have recourse to the same teacher. The like may be said of all the ancient hermits and anchorites who could have no other instructor but God, and had no other employment during their rigorous solitude and silence, but to attend to their internal teacher, and put in execution His inspirations in all their actions both internal and external. To this purpose, saith a holy hermit in Cassian, that as it was by God's inspiration that we begin, when we enter into religion, so likewise (*magisterio et illuminatione Dei ad perfectionem pervenimus*) by the discipline, instruction, and illumination of God we attain to perfection. Another says that a soul can do no good at all unless she be (*quotidiana Domini illuminatione illustrata*) enlightened by a daily illumination from God. These are expressions that our holy Father himself uses, and it seems borrowed them from the same authors. And for this reason it is that in his Rule he contents himself with ordaining prescriptions for the exterior only, because he knew that the interior could only be directed by God. But withal, his ordinations are such as we may see his intention and only design was by them to dispose souls to be capable of observing and following the inspirations and inward instructions of God's Holy Spirit, without

which all exterior observances would never bring us to perfection; such were very rigorous solitude and abstraction from all intercourse either with the business or news of the world, almost continual silence but when we speak to God, &c. And withal, in several places of his Rule he signifies by the way that the reformation of the spirit ought to be the principal aim of a religious soul. So that in the conclusion of the Rule, having regard to the external observances expressly commanded therein (as a preparation to the perfection to be learnt out of the lives and conferences of the fathers), he professeth with great humility, but with great truth also, that his intention thereby was that those which observed it be enabled to declare in some sort (*honestatem morum, aut initium conversationis eos habere*) that they had attained to a laudable exterior carriage and the beginning of a holy religious conversation. But, saith he, whosoever shall tend to perfection, *Sunt doctrinæ Sanctorum Patrum;* as if he had said he must, according to the teaching of the holy Fathers, attend unto the divine Master by exercising, according to his instructions, that pure sublime prayer, &c., which they practised and discovered. And suitable hereto St. Francis likewise in his Rule advises his disciples thus: *Attendant fratres, quod super omnia desiderare debent habere spiritum Domini, et sanctam ejus operationem,* that is, the religious brethren must attentively mark that, above all other things, they ought to desire to have the Spirit of our Lord and his Holy operation in their souls.

7. To conclude: either it must be granted that perfection may be attained merely by avoiding mortal sins, and doing such actions of virtue as are absolutely necessary to all Christians (which to say were manifestly foolish and false), and likewise that actions more indifferent and not so universally obliging (such as are certain more profitable manners of prayer, external religious observances, refection, conversation with our brethren, &c.) cannot be rendered capable of a holy intention and of advancing us in the divine love (which is against experience); and moreover, that without internal grace actually operating (which is nothing else but divine illuminations and impulses) these ordinary inferior actions may be exalted to produce that effect which the greatest necessary virtues could not produce, which to say were impiety; or it must be granted that the teaching of God's Holy Spirit is the only principal necessary cause by whose virtue we are informed and enabled to improve and make use of these actions for the attaining of so sublime an end as perfection in contemplation is, and without which it is impossible to be attained. And indeed, so impossible to be brought under external rules, and so secret and undiscoverable are the internal dispositions of souls and their operations, that they cannot be clearly perceived nor consequently ordered, but by Him to whom alone (our *figmentum)* our hearts and all the secret inclinations and motions of them are naked and transparent.

Chapter V. Impediments to Divine Inspirations

§ 1. All internal livers obliged to attend to God's inspirations.

§ 2. Therefore the impediments to this duty are to be removed, which are two. First, distracting images, which are expelled by abstraction of life.

§ 3. The second impediment is unruly passions, which are calmed by mortification and peace of mind.

§§ 4, 5. The end why a religious state, especially of St. Benedict's institution, is undertaken, is the removal of these impediments.

§§ 6, 7, 8, 9. A third more special impediment: to wit, want of due liberty of spirit to follow God's directions, caused by voluntary burdens and customs assumed.

§§ 10, 13. Several such are exemplified.

1. The necessity of a divine internal teacher being established, there follows from thence an equal necessity for all those whose profession obliges them to walk in those ways towards the sublime end proposed, to attend unto and obey this only most necessary master. And because each one hath in his heart a false teacher that always urgeth us to hearken to his perverse teachings and to neglect the divine teacher, therefore, the way to become a diligent and obedient disciple to God's Holy Spirit will be: 1. to neglect, contradict, and, as much as lies in us, to silence the teachings and suggestions of corrupt nature; 2. and secondly, to be attentive to the voice of God's Spirit in our souls.

2. For the first: there are two general impediments that nature lays in our way to hinder us from attending to God. The first is distracting images; the second, unquiet passions. Now the remedy against the former is abstraction of life, a not engaging ourselves in business that belongs not unto us; the mortifying of the curiosity of knowing or hearing strange or new things not pertinent to our profession; the tempering of our tongues from vain, unprofitable conversations; the reducing our thoughts, as much as may be, from multiplicity to unity, by fixing them continually on the divine love which is that *unum necessarium, &c.*

3. Again, the only proper remedies against the other impediment, to wit, unquiet passions, are, first, mortification of all inordinate affection to creatures—of all vain encumbering friendships, all factious partialities, all thoughtful provision for the contenting of our sensual desires; but especially of that most dangerous, because most intimate and spiritual thirst of knowl-

edge unnecessary, and of all ambition to get victory or glory by disputing, writing, &c., as likewise of all anger, impatience, melancholy, fear, scrupulosity, &c.; and, secondly, a studious care to preserve our souls in all the peace, tranquillity, and cheerfulness possible, not suffering any passions to be raised in our minds during our imperfect state, no, not although they should be directed upon good and holy objects, because they will obscure and disorder our spirits. And, therefore, we must avoid all violence and impetuous hastiness in performing our best and most necessary duties, which are discharged most efficaciously and purely when they are done with the greatest stillness, calmness, clearness of mind and resignation. It is sufficient in this place only to touch passingly upon these impediments, because in the following treatise we shall have occasion to treat more largely and purposely of them.

4. Now to what end did we come into religion, but only to avoid all these impediments in the world, which withdraw us from attending to God and following His divine guidance? In this very point lies the difference between a secular and a religious state, that a secular person secularly minded, by reason of the noise, tumults, and unavoidable distractions, solicitudes, and temptations which are in the world, cannot without much ado find leisure to attend unto God and the gaining of His love even for a few minutes every day, or little oftener than the laws of the Church necessarily oblige him. And all the directions that he is capable of in God's service must come from without, for by reason that his soul is so filled with images vain or sinful, and so agitated with impetuous affections and designs, he cannot recollect himself to hear God speaking in him. Whereas, a religious person professes his only business to be attending to God's internal voice, for which purpose he renounceth all these impediments and distractions.

5. And surely, in a special manner, the disciples of St. Benedict, if they will cast a serious eye upon the frame of their Rule, will find that as it is very moderate, and prudently condescending in all matters of outward corporal austerities afflicting to nature, but not immediately helpful to the spirit, so, on the contrary, it is very rigorous in the exacting of silence, solitude, a renouncing of all proprietary solicitude for corporal necessities and all other mortifications which will hinder the dissipating of our spirits and thoughts, and indispose the soul to recollection and attention to God; but especially prayer, which he calls *Opus Dei* (to which all other works and observances are to give place), is most seriously and incessantly enjoined, by the practice whereof we do, above all other exercises, transcend grosser and sensible images in the understanding, and subdue unruly passions in the heart. So that it is evident that our holy Father's principal care in all the observances enjoined by him was to free his disciples from these two general and most powerful

hindrances to introversion, and a continual attention to and conversation with God: which may most properly be called the spirit of St. Benedict's Rule.

6. There is, moreover, one special impediment to the observing and obeying of divine inspirations which is not to be omitted, and the rather because it is less taken notice of in ordinary spiritual writers: this impediment consists in this, that many souls do indiscreetly prejudice, yea, oft take away quite, that indifference and liberty of spirit which is necessary to all that will seriously follow the divine guidance in all the ways that they then are led by it. For it were foolish to prescribe unto God the ways in which we would have Him to lead us: this were to oblige God to follow our ways and to do our wills, and not we to perform His. And this is done by those who obstinately adhere to preconceived opinions and fore-practised customs, whatsoever they be. For though such customs in themselves and to other souls may be never so good and profitable, yea, though formerly even to those persons themselves they have been never so proper and beneficial, yet this was only whilst they were in such a state and degree of spirituality; the which state altering (as in progress it needs must), then that which was formerly proper and conformable to the divine will and inspiration will become improper, inconvenient, and contrary to the present internal guidance of God.

7. This impediment must necessarily be removed, and devout souls must continually keep themselves in a free indifferency and suppleness of spirit, for otherwise they will become, in many cases and circumstances, indisposed to believe, and incapable to execute that which God's Holy Spirit shall dictate unto them; yea, they will oft contristate and endanger to extinguish the said Spirit in them by an obstinate doing of the contrary to what It moves them.

8. The reasonableness and necessity of this advice may be shown by this example: it may have been good and profitable for a soul when she entered into an internal life to appoint unto herself certain voluntary devotions and vocal prayers, &c., or afterwards to select certain peculiar subjects of meditation, as the four last things, the Mystery of the Passion, &c., or to prescribe unto herself certain times for some good external or internal practices, or to make frequent examinations of conscience, confessions, &c. All these things are good whilst the soul finds profit by them, and so long they are to be continued; but if God shall call her to a higher exercise, and to a more pure efficacious prayer, so that she begins to lose all gust in her former exercises, the which do not only abridge her of the time necessary for her more perfect recollections, but likewise dull the spirit and indispose it for such prayer and other more beneficial practices to which she is by a new, clearer, divine light directed or invited, and by divine grace enabled; in this case pertinaciously to adhere to former customs, because she finds them commended

in books, &c., or because she did formerly reap profit by them, this is to en-tangle, fetter, and captivate the spirit, to renounce the divine guidance, and to obstruct all ways of advancement in the paths of contemplation. The soul, therefore, in such or the like cases, must necessarily use some violence upon herself to recover a true and most needful indifference and liberty of spirit, that so she may freely follow God whithersoever He shall by His inspirations invite her, being assured that she shall never by Him be persuaded or tempted to do anything contrary or prejudicial to her duty, obedience to lawful author-ity, or any other necessary obligations.

9. This instruction reaches very far; yea, so far that even learned men, yea, some that pass for spiritual, if they be unexperienced in the true internal ways of God's Spirit leading to contemplation, would perhaps mis-like the freedom which in many cases must and hath been allowed by the best and most sublime mystic authors to souls of some peculiar dispositions and in certain circumstances. And as for unlearned persons, they would be in danger almost to be scandalised.

10. The special points, therefore, by which liberty of spirit in many souls is (or may be) much abridged to their great hindrance are such as these which follow, viz.: 1. A frequent scrupulous confession (and this merely to continue a custom) of certain venial sins causing a harmful anxiety to the person. 2. Customary solicitous examinations of conscience, and not content-ing one's self sometimes with virtual examinations. 3. A needless anxious reviewing of general confessions. 4. The forcing acts of sensible remorse, &c. 5. The overburdening one's self with a certain task of vocal prayers or other practices, to the prejudice of daily recollections. 6. Assuming and con-tinuing voluntary mortifications when the soul finds no benefit by them, but rather becomes disheartened and dejected. 7. Practising what is found in books, though improper for the spirit. 8. Imitating unwarily the good prac-tices of others, without a due consideration of one's own ability or weakness in regard of them. 9. Obliging one's self indifferently at all times, in all states and degrees of prayer, to a discursive exercise on the Passion, &c. 10. Doing things merely for edification. 11. Tying one's self to nice methods and orders of prayer, and to a determinate number of succeeding acts in recollections. 12. Exercising corporal labours and austerities without due consideration and necessity. 13. Adhering with propriety to any kind of internal exercise when the soul is enabled and invited to a higher. 14. The obliging one's self in all circumstances to a determinate posture in private recollections. 15. And (which is worst of all) an entangling of the soul by hasty and indiscreet promises or vows made during some fit of sensible devotion or in a passion of remorse, fear, &c. Hereto other points may be added of a like nature, con-taining practices, though in themselves good, and to some persons very

beneficial, yet, considering the state of abstraction proper (yea necessary) to a contemplative liver, which may prove very prejudicial by engaging such a one in duties and offices to be performed alone or in association with others, by which images and solicitudes may be multiplied, &c. By these, and other such practices as these, which are supposed not to be of obligation, many souls in desire tending to perfection may so overburden and entangle themselves that they either cannot observe the operations of the Divine Spirit in them, or have not the liberty to follow whither It would draw them; and thereby remain in their imperfect state without hope of making any progress, unless they will renounce their own preconceived judgment and preassumed self-imposed obligations.

11. Hitherto it may suffice to have spoken of the impediments by which souls are hindered from attending to and obeying their internal divine teacher, who only knows what is best for every one in all circumstances, and will not fail to direct for the very best every soul that with humility and resignation hath recourse to Him.

12. Now such is the nature of the reasonable soul (which is all activity, and will be continually thinking on and loving somewhat) that if these impediments, caused by impertinent images of creatures, inordinate affections to them, and by a voluntary shackling the soul with assumed opinions and customs, were once removed, she would see clearly what she ought to follow and love, which is God only; for creatures being removed and forgotten, nothing remains but God: no other light for our understanding, nor other object for our wills and affections, but He only.

13. And the general, of all others most efficacious, means to remove all these impediments is, by abstraction and prayer in spirit, to aspire unto an habitual state of recollection and introversion; for such prayer, besides the virtue of impetration, by which God will be moved according to His so frequent and express promises to be a light to the meek and humble, it hath also a direct virtue to procure this illumination, inasmuch as therein our souls see Him and nothing else, so that they have no other guide to follow but Him; and especially inasmuch as by prayer in spirit divine charity is most firmly rooted in our hearts, which makes them insensible to all other things that would divert our attention or affection. And we see by experience that love (of what object soever) doth more clear the mind, and confers in a moment, as it were, more skill to find out the means by which the object beloved may be obtained, than never so much study or meditation.

Chapter VI. How God Communicates Internal Light

§§ 1, 2. The gift of the Holy Spirit is the principle of all good actions in us.

§§ 3, 4, 5, 6. It doth not work of itself, unless excited by actual grace and our endeavours.

§ 7. By the using and employment of this gift, there is raised in us a supernatural light of discretion, as prudence is increased by the practice of virtue.

§ 8. How the exercise of love causes illumination.

§§ 9, 10. Supernatural light is, 1. actual; 2. permanent.

§ 11, The effects of supernatural discretion.

§§ 12, 13, 14, 15. Contemplative and active livers, both guided by a supernatural light, but differently.

§ 16. How imperfect souls may do their ordinary daily actions in light.

1. The third point before proposed for our consideration in this matter of internal inspiration, is the manner how God communicates His light and grace to our understanding and wills for our instruction and directions, in the mystic ways of contemplation.

2. Now for a clearer explication of this point we are to consider that that fundamental grace, which in Scripture is called *donum Spiritus Sancti* (the gift of the Holy Ghost), and which is conferred on all in baptism, and being afterward by actual sins smothered or extinguished, is renewed by penance, prayer, &c., and cherished or increased by the worthy use of the holy Eucharist and other virtuous practices of a Christian life: this grace, I say (whatever it be physically in its own nature, if it were examined scholastically, which is not my intent), is a certain divine principle or faculty, partaking somewhat of the nature of a permanent habit, infused into the spirit of man, by which he is enabled, whensoever the free will concurreth actually, both for knowing, believing, and practising to do the will of God in all things. For the virtue thereof extends itself through all the faculties of the soul, curing the distempers, wants, and deordinations that sin had caused in them.

3. This new divine faculty therefore (which seems to be expressed by the prophet David, when he saith, *signatum est super nos lumen vultus tui, Domine,* that is, the light of thy countenance, O Lord, is like a seal stamped on our souls) doth not, neither is it sufficient of itself alone actually to produce any saving effects: as we see that a musician or a poet, though never so skilful, do not therefore ever actually sing or write verses until some certain occasions or circumstances do actually determine them thereto, as gain or

requests of others, or praise, or a mind to please themselves, &c. For the actual employment and exercise of such grace there is, moreover, necessary an actual aid from God, who by a special divine providence doth often administer occasions, hints, and enablements, exciting the will to waken this grace in the soul, which otherwise would lie vacant and unuseful.

4. And proofs of this daily experience shows us, both in ourselves and others, how a sermon or any other word reasonably spoken, or any object occurring with due circumstances, doth incite us to lift up our souls to God by prayer, to perform some acts of charity, to mortify some inordinate affection, &c., yea, sometimes from a desperate sinful state, to convert our souls to God. And this doing we (as St. Paul exhorts Timothy, ἀναζωπυρεῖν) raise and blow into a flame the grace which before lay in our hearts like coals of fire smothered in the ashes. And if this be frequently done, that Grace which at the first imparting was but weak, and needed strong endeavours to excite it, becomes the more active and more easy to be excited; so that upon any the least occasion offered it is ready to bestir itself and disperse its odours and virtue, till at last it gets so perfect a dominion in perfect souls that it quite subdues the contrary principle of corrupt nature; and is scarce ever idle, but the least hint being given, it turns the soul presently to God, and keeps it almost continually fixed on Him: insomuch as those things which formerly had no effect at all upon them, now presently and even violently inflame them.

5. Yea, in some supereminently perfect souls this gift of God's Holy Spirit comes to be so vigorous that it subdues even reason itself, and leads it captive after itself, pushing the soul to heroical actions without any precedent act of reason or the least deliberation, though in the act the soul, by consenting, merits. Thus we read of the ancient martyrs, how they by an impetuous impulse of the divine spirit, rushed before the persecuting judges to confess the name of Christ. Yea, and St. Apollonia cast herself into the fire: the love of Christ burning in their hearts and constraining them, as St. Paul says. From the like efficacy of the Divine Spirit proceeded that spiritual gift of prayer by which the holy primitive Christians in their public meetings conceived and poured forth prayers without any concurrence thereto of their own invention, God's spirit itself (in St. Paul's expression) praying in them. And in this sense principally it is that, I suppose, the schools do understand the gifts of the spirit, although most certain it is that all holy actions, internal or external, are effects of the same Spirit, though in a less degree.

6. This fundamental grace, therefore, is that talent or stock that has God's image on it, and not Cæsar's, which God bestows upon every one in baptism, &c., to trade withal, which till the will coöperates with the actual aid of God is, as it were, wrapped in a napkin and hid under ground, but, being well managed, multiplies into many talents. This is that very small but

divine seed of which the Evangelist speaks, which, being cast in our hearts, by labour and cultivation produces many and precious fruits: this is that *(Fermentum) leaven,* which, being enclosed in the three faculties of our souls, as in three measures of meal, doth disperse its virtue throughout the whole mass.

7. Now, to the end I may approach more close to the present matter, we may further consider, that as by the exercise of moral philosophical virtues there is generated and daily increased by perseverance in the same exercise, that most noble universal virtue of moral prudence which no study or speculative learning, how great soever, could have produced, the which prudence, as the philosopher says, is the skill most properly conversant about particular acts (not general notions or definitions of things), and enlightens the soul to judge and determine in what circumstances and with what concurring qualities an action of virtue ought and may with the best advantage and perfection be exercised: so that by the help of this virtue of prudence, when it is arrived to an excelling degree, a virtuous person will never omit a due occason to practise a virtue, nor will he ever do it unseasonably and indiscreetly (for then it would not be virtue); and when he exercises it he will not be deficient in anything requisite to give a lustre thereto. The very same in a due proportion is seen in the exercise of divine virtue or charity; for by a constant practice thereof, not only charity itself is exalted, multiplied, and increased, but there is likewise kindled in the soul by the Spirit of God a light of spiritual prudence far more clear and more certain to conduct us in the divine ways than moral prudence is in the ways of moral honesty; which divine light has this great advantage above prudence, that whereas moral wisdom can only teach the exercise of virtue in those occasions (which do not every day happen) in which such virtues ought to be exercised, neglecting to give any rules to lesser indifferent actions, this divine light, which teaches us to love nothing at all but God, accounts no actions at all in particular indifferent, but teaches us to direct all to the service and love of God, and can discern how one may concur thereto more than another, and accordingly choose the best.

8. Now the reason why, by the exercise of charity alone (and not by any study or speculative considerations), this divine light can be kindled, is because the blindness and darkness which is naturally in our understandings comes principally from the perverse deordination which self-love causes in our wills; by means of which we will not suffer the understanding to see what it does see; for even when by the light of faith we are in general instructed in the offices and rules of virtue and piety, yet, in many particulars, self-love adhering to that side which we ought to refuse, will either forbid and hinder the understanding from considering what is evil or defectuous in it, or if there be any the least ground of doubt, it will cast such fair glosses on

it, and so seduce the understanding to find out motives and pretences for the preferring thereof that, in fine, the light itself which is in the understanding will mislead us. But when by perfect divine charity all these distortions of the will are rectified, and that all the subtle insinuations, false pretexts, close interests, and designs of self-love are discovered and banished, then the mind beholds all things with a clear light, and, proposing God as the end of all actions whatsoever, it sees where God is to be found in them, and may best be served and obeyed by them; then the will is so far from clouding or casting mists before the eyes of the understanding, that if there were any before, it alone dispels them; for it is only the now-sanctified fervent will that draws the soul in all its faculties from all other inferior seducing objects, and carries them in its own stream and swift course towards God: it will not suffer the soul to choose anything but what is good, yea, the best of all, because God would have that to be chosen alone. According, therefore, to the measure of charity, so is our measure of divine light. If charity be but warm and imperfect, our light in particulars is obscure, and can show us only such things as are necessarily to be practised under the penalty of being separated from God, the object of charity; but if charity be inflamed, how great is the light which that heavenly fire casts! not a step we set forward but we see the way perfectly before us, and can avoid all the uneven, rough, miry, or crooked steps in it, and so run apace without stumbling, delaying, or declining, so approaching daily nearer and nearer to the end of our heavenly race.

9. Moreover, this divine light is either an habitual, permanent light, or actual and transitory. The permanent light is the virtue of spiritual discretion, without which the actions that to the world give the greatest lustre are of little or no profit. Such as are great voluntary austerities, performing of solemn offices, almsgiving, &c., all which, unless they come from the principle of true charity, and are designed for the increasing and deeper rooting thereof in the spirit, are so far from being of any worth that they do rather prejudice and diminish that virtue. Both these conditions are requisite to make an action perfect and acceptable to God; it must both proceed from Him and also be directed to Him: He must not only be the end, but the principle also. It is not therefore sufficient for a soul (especially if she seriously tend to perfection in contemplation) that the action which she does now is in itself good and directed to a good end, unless her divine light inform her that in the present circumstances it is God's will that she should perform that determinate action rather than another, perhaps in itself and in other circumstances, better than it: for, as Thaulerus says, God will reward no actions but His own, that is, such as He gave order and commission for.

10. This being a most certain truth, what a world of actions, in themselves of no ill aspect, are there done by imperfect, extroverted souls, which, having no other fountain, principle, or light from which they are at first de-

rived but the light of human reason, they will find at God's hands no accep-tance at all; such souls lose all benefit by all their doings but those which are of absolute necessity, and by many of those likewise. Nay, how many are there which, being driven to some actions by a violent unlawful passion for or against some person, yet, because before the action is ended they can cozen themselves with proposing some good end, do therefore think them-selves excused? Whereas such a proposing of a good end to an action beginning only from corrupt nature rather aggravates the fault by adding hy-pocrisy to it; the which themselves might easily discover if they would at the same time consider that such objects and persons had been changed. How small a proportion of this spiritual light have such souls!

11. This permanent light of supernatural discretion informs the soul generally in all things efficacious to her advancement towards contemplation. It teaches her in religious observances culpably to neglect none, and to per-form them with a pure intention for her spiritual good: in mortifications, to support the necessary ones willingly and profitably, and assume only such voluntary ones as God directs her to, therein considering the infirmity of the body as well as the fervour of the will, lest by overburdening nature unneces-sarily, she be rendered unable to bear even those which are of obligation: in prayer it teaches the soul what degree is proper for her, and how long she is to continue in it without change till God invite her to a higher, and then read-ily to accept of His invitation. Likewise, what proportion of time is requisite to be spent in prayer, so as to make a discreet and sufficient progress therein. It teaches her to suspect sensible devotion, and not to glut herself with the honey of it, nor to follow it too fast to designs of seeming perfection and ex-traordinary tasks, which, when such devotion ends, would be burdensome and harmful: in a word, it teaches the soul that due moderation in all things which makes them laudable and meritorious.

12. Now whereas I have called this a permanent and habitual light, it is to be observed that, as it is habitual only, it does not direct; because, unless it be in action, it is as it were veiled over until God, by some occasion admin-istered, do move the soul to reflect and consult Him, and hereupon the light is unveiled and shines forth, giving direction in the present action and neces-sity. So that it is God, or the gift of his Holy Spirit (very predominant in such souls) that is their actual director.

13. There is none that hath a good will and seeks God in sincerity of heart but is capable of such a guidance by the light communicated to souls by the Holy Spirit; so that the duty of attending to and obeying it has place not only in a contemplative, but also in the exercises of a devout active life; for doubtless such likewise have a supernatural light answerable to their state, by

which they are enabled to perform their actions with much purity of intention.

14. Notwithstanding, in respect of the degrees of purity of intention, the doings of contemplative souls do much excel those of active livers, by reason of the deeper entry that they make into their interior in their more profound, pure, and imageless recollections, by which they discover the depth of their most secret intentions, and accordingly purify them from whatsoever is amiss in them. Besides, they, according to their state, dealing in fewer exterior, distractive employments, do both keep themselves in a better disposition to attend to the voice of their internal teacher, and also contract fewer blemishes; and those that they do contract, they do more easily discern and rectify; lastly, being exercised for the most part in internal operations, their continual task is to cleanse the very fountain, which is the spirit itself, the seat of divine light and grace.

15. In a contemplative life, likewise, according to the degrees of proficiency, so is the attendance unto, and the performance of, the divine inspirations; for to perfect souls the divine voice and light is in a manner a continual guide, and they have a continual correspondence with it, even in their most ordinary smallest actions. Whereas the imperfect receive it seldom (forasmuch as concerns the purifying and supernaturalising their ordinary actions), except in their recollections, yea, perhaps only when they are in the height of their exercise. And the like may be said of devout souls in an active life. And they do at other times put in execution the directions received in prayer by virtue of the light remaining in their minds. But as for other actions, for which they have received no light at all in prayer, those they perform with the help of their natural reason, or at best by the general habitual light of grace only, by virtue of which they avoid grosser sinful defects; but yet their actions are stained with great impurity of intention, and a mixture of natural and sensual interests. The reason is, because imagination and passion being yet very predominant in them, do push them hastily to perform their actions without sufficient reflection and consulting their internal teacher; and if they do endeavour to adjoin a good intention, it comes late after the action is either begun or resolved upon for other motives; so that the divine love is but an accessory and attendant, not the prime mover or principle of the action.

16. The best means, therefore, that imperfect souls have to cleanse their ordinary actions from the impurity of natural interests, is in a general manner to forethink daily of their employments of obligation, and to foreordain the future employments of the day (I mean such as are left to their own voluntary choice and judgment, and that are likely to take up any considerable part of their time and thoughts, as certain determinate studies, &c.), and

thereupon, at their morning recollections begging the assistance of the Divine Spirit, let them make good purposes to perform them out of the motive of divine love and for God's glory; and let them take heed not to change the order resolved indiscreetly; yet withal, on the other side, let them avoid the entangling themselves with any such resolutions, so as that the transgressing of them should cause disturbance or remorse in them. Thus doing, and sometimes during the day quietly reflecting upon the promise made in the morning recollection, the divine light will grow more and more familiar to them, extinguishing by degrees the false light by which they were formerly for the most part misled.

Chapter VII. How to Obtain Light in Doubtful Cases

§§ 1, 2, 3, 4, 5, 6, 7. How a soul is to behave herself to obtain light in doubtful cases of moment.

§ 8. She must not pretend to extraordinary matters.

§ 9. God signifies His will two ways: first by clearing the understanding.

§§ 10, 11. Why and how prayer disposes thereto.

§§ 12, 13. The second way is by a blind reasonless moving of the will.

§§ 14, 15. The same confirmed out of St. Thomas and Aristotle.

§ 16. A confidenoce that these operations are of God.

§ 17. In what faculties the said operations are wrought.

§§ 18, 19. What a soul, not perceiving either of these operations in her, is to do.

§§ 20, 21, 22. Constancy in a resolution once made requisite; but yet in some cases it may be altered.

§§ 23, 24. Purposes not to be made in the very time of prayer, except of resignation.

§ 25. A soul must not be troubled if the issue be not as she expects.

§ 26. Evident certainty not to be expected.

§ 27. In known cases the declaration of God's will is not to be expected.

1. But now, because, as I said, those that are imperfect have but a dim light, insufficient to direct them in many occurrent actions, and those that have attained to an habitual supernatural light of discretion do find that there are many cases to which their light doth not extend, yea, in the most perfect it will fail them in some, therefore, in such a case of uncertainty,

wherein a well-minded soul has a considerable doubt about some matter of moment, either in the course of her prayer or in any other thing that concerns an internal life, and that she cannot find an experienced person to whom she can confidently propose her difficulty, or perhaps has not an interior invitation to seek for resolution from any one,—I will endeavour, by the best light that God has given me, to instruct such a soul how she is to behave herself in such circumstances that she may obtain from God an actual illumination or direction; and then I will declare in what manner such light is ordinarily conferred upon internal livers.

2. The matter of the doubt is supposed to be of some weight; for as for ordinary inconsiderable difficulties, she may, in the name of God, despatch them the best she can with her natural judgment, doing with a good intention that which it shall dictate to be the best, troubling herself no further about them; because it would be more prejudice to a soul to lose time and disquiet herself with a curious and solicitous examination of every small difficulty, than if by determining quickly she should chance to choose that which in itself were the less perfect (it being supposed that sin lies on neither side of the doubt).

3. Again, some cases there are of such a nature that they are to be resolved only by an external director or superior, so that a soul ought not, and will in vain expect a resolution from God, who sends her to His substitutes. Such are the cases which concern external observances, as fasting, saying the divine office, interpreting the Rule, laws, or constitutions, &c. The office of the internal Master is chiefly about internal matters, or the not doing of external which are not of obligation.

4. In such doubtful cases of moment, especially if they concern something to be done, or omitted, or suffered in the future, a devout soul is to avoid all sudden and unadvised resolutions; and this especially when she is in any kind of passion, whether it be fear, anger, grief, or else of tenderness, compassion, and kindness, &c.; and chiefly when herself has an interest of nature, or when persons are concerned to whom she bears a sensible affection, or from whom she has an aversion. In such cases it is good to defer the resolution as long as well may be, to the end that she may have the more space to consider of it with her natural reason, and to free herself from passion, and so with resignation to consult God in her recollections, thereby to obtain light from Him to discern His holy will. And another reason and motive to defer the matter may be, because it may happen that, before a determinate resolution be needful, some new circumstance may spring and intervene that will perhaps alter the state of the difficulty.

5. In case the soul in her nature be inclined more to the one side of the doubt than the other, she must enforce herself, especially in prayer, to an

indifference and resignation in the matter; rather forethinking (and accordingly preparing herself) that God will declare His will for the contrary to that to which her nature is more inclined.

6. In seeking to know the divine will by prayer, let not the person make the subject and business of his recollection to be the framing a direct prayer about the matter; neither let him in his prayer entertain any discoursing, debating thoughts in his imagination or understanding about it, as if he had an intention to account that to be God's will which by such discourse seemed most probable. 1. Because, by such proceedings, our prayers, which should be pure and internal in spirit, will be turned into a distracting meditation upon all external affair, and so the mind comes to be filled with sensible images, and passions perhaps will be raised. 2. Because by so doing we incur the danger of being seduced, by mistaking our own imagination or perhaps natural inclination for the divine light and motion, whereas such divine light is most effectually and securely, yea, and seldom otherwise, obtained than when the imagination is quiet and the soul in a profound recollection in spirit. 3. Because such discoursing in time of prayer is anything else but prayer, being little more than human consideration and examination of the matter, the which, if at all, ought to be despatched before prayer.

7. Let not the soul, therefore, that is desirous by prayer to obtain light from God in a doubtful matter, for that end alter anything in the order and manner of her accustomed recollections, but let her pursue them as she was wont before; only it may be permitted her secretly and briefly to wish that God would teach her His will about the said difficulty.

8. But let her be sure to take great care she do not give way to any hope or desire that God should reconcile His will unto her by any extraordinary way, as by the ministry of angels, strange revelations, voices, &c.; for as nothing but pride can ordinarily nourish such foolish hopes or desires, so it is to be feared that if such desires should be granted, it would be to her prejudice, and would increase that pride from whence they flowed.

9. Now there are two ordinary ways by which God intimates His will to his servants that, with humble and resigned prayers, address themselves unto Him. The first is by clearing of the understanding, thereto adding a supernatural light, by which natural reason comes to see something that it saw not before, or at least did not esteem before so considerable; for by this new light of supernatural discretion such obscurities as did before hinder reason from discerning truth are removed. The which obscurities are generally caused by sensible images which have prepossessed themselves of the fancy, or by interests of nature which have engaged the affections; by both which reason is precipitated to hasten a judgment and election before she have considered maturely and without partiality all circumstances fit to be considered

in an action; so that reason wanting this supernatural light kindled by charity determines itself to choose that part to which passion inclines.

10. Now since there are no means so efficacious to free the soul from both these impediments as pure spiritual prayer, in which the soul transcends all gross sensual images, and withal contradicts and renounces all motions and interests of nature, we may securely rely upon the light and dictamen which is suggested by our understanding so cleared, purified, and freed from all noise and distraction from the sensible faculties and appetite; and this being the best and safest light that man can have, we may and must acknowledge it to be supernatural, because it illuminates us in supernatural things, discovering the proportion between the present action and our supernatural end, and extinguishing the light of carnal reason, by which the things which are of God are either not seen at all, or esteemed foolishness. It is therefore to be accepted as the very light of God's Holy Spirit, a light that cannot be obtained by study, nor instilled into another by the most spiritual person in the world. Yea, moreover, it is a light that exceeds the efficacy of the ordinary light of faith which is permanently in us, by which we are only illuminated to perceive in a general manner supernatural objects, and the means leading to them; whereas, by this lamp newly kindled in our understandings by prayer and charity, we clearly discern in each particular actions and circumstances in what manner and how far they have relation and efficacy to dispose us to a perfect union by love with God.

11. If a soul before her recollections hath advised and considered of the difficulty, and that afterward upon her prayer she do find herself inclined to do what before she, consulting with her own reason or with any other counsellor, had judged to be the best, I should esteem it now to be a divine inspiration: not for the former debating's sake, but for the subsequent confirmation of it in virtue of recollection.

12. The second way by which God doth immediately signify His will to the intellective soul in virtue of prayer is by imprinting a blind, reasonless motion into the superior will, giving it a weight and propension to one side of the doubt rather than to the other, without representing actually and at the present to the understanding any special motive or reason sufficient to determine the will. This also, coming, in virtue of spiritual prayer, may confidently be esteemed the work of God, since no creature can immediately move the superior will.

13. Pertinently hereto we read that the holy Abbot Nisteron (who was a familiar friend of St. Anthony), being asked by one what kind of work he would advise him to exercise for the good and advancement of his soul? answered, God only knows what is good for thee to do, and therefore look

70

what thou findest that thy soul, according to God, would have thee to do, that do thou.

14. Certainly, if ever God will show that He stands to His promise of granting the petitions of His children in all things which they ask according to His will, this promise is in no case so infallibly made good as when a sincere humble-minded soul, being urged merely out of spiritual necessity, doth with all resignation beg at His hands the light of his Holy Spirit for resolution of the difficulties that concern her purely in order to His service and honour, and for the perfecting her in His divine love. When can a soul be said to ask according to God's will, but when, withdrawing herself from all interests of nature and fixing her eyes and heart upon God only, she makes her requests known unto Him?

15. The doctrine here delivered, and particularly touching this reasonless and indeliberate moving of the will to good, is excellently and fully confirmed by St. Thomas (part 1, q. 1 a. 6), where to the third objection made against his position, that the doctrine of scholastic divinity is [*Sapientia*] wisdom, which objection was thus conceived: this doctrine is attained by study; but wisdom is had by infusion (and thereupon it is reckoned among the seven gifts of the Holy Ghost—Isa. xi.): therefore this doctrine is not wisdom. Hereto he answers thus: "Since judging pertains to a wise man, according to a twofold manner of judging, wisdom is understood in a twofold sense. For one may judge: 1. Either by way of inclination: as he that hath the habit of virtue doth rightly judge of those things which are to be done according to virtue, inasmuch as he is inclined unto such things. Whereupon it is said in the tenth Book of Aristotle's Ethics, that a virtuous man is the measure and rule of human actions. 2. By way of knowledge: as any one that is skilled in moral science can judge of the acts of virtue, although himself be void of virtue. The former way of judging of divine things pertains to wisdom, which is affirmed to be a gift of the Holy Ghost, according to that saying of St. Paul (1 Cor. ii. 15): "The spiritual man judgeth all things;" as likewise St. Denys saith in his 2nd chap. De Div. Nom.: 'Hierothus is instructed, not only learning, but also suffering divine things. But the latter way of judging pertains to this doctrine, inasmuch as it is gotten by study, although indeed the principles thereof come from divine revelation.' Thus far are the words of St. Thomas.

16. Yea, even Aristotle himself, though a heathen, could observe (lib. ii. Magn. Moral. c. 7) that to that good which is honest (and virtuous) there is first required a certain reasonless impulse, and thereby the reason is enabled to discern and determine. But more pertinently and expressly in the following chapter he saith thus: Good fortune is without any precedent act of reason; for by nature he is indeed fortunate that, without the exercise of reason, is

impelled to good or virtuous things and attains them. Now this is to be ascribed to nature; for such (an inclination) is naturally imprinted in our souls, by which we are impelled to such things as will render us happy without any exercise of reason: insomuch as if one should ask any person so disposed, Why doth it please thee to do so? he would answer, Truly I know not, but so it pleases me to do. The like happens to those that are divinely inspired and agitated, for such are impelled to the doing of some things without the exercise of reason. Lastly, the same philosopher, observing that sometimes there are suddenly injected into some souls certain good thoughts and desires, from which many following good actions do proceed; and hereupon inquiring from what principle such good thoughts may be judged to proceed, he resolves that the soul herself is not the cause of them, because they precede all exercise of reason; therefore the cause of them must be somewhat better than the soul, and that is only God.

17. The forementioned illustration is supposed to be not in the imagination, but purely in the understanding; as likewise the motion and inclination to be in the spiritual will, and not in the sensitive appetite, for otherwise they would not deserve so much to be relied on, because the workings of the imagination are so inconstant and irregular, and the sensible motions of the inferior appetite (being in corporal nature, producing a warmth about the heart and a stirring of spirits and humours) are so disorderly, that they are very justly suspicious and scarce to be trusted to. Therefore, although in a fervent exercise of much sensible devotion the sensual nature do after her manner carry herself well towards God, yet the superior soul, being not in a state of due tranquillity and stillness, is less capable of divine illustrations and influxes; and therefore the soul's inclinations, resolutions, and designs at such times are less to be regarded.

18. Now if it should happen that, after such trials by prayer made for the knowing of the divine will, the soul should yet perceive no sufficient light, nor any considerable inclination, propension, or preponderation towards one side more than another, in this case, according to Thaulerus's judgment, she may freely and confidently, as it were by lots, make choice indifferently of whether she thinks fit; and a choice so made, whenever it happens, she may and ought to believe to be according to God's will, since, having done her part to know His will, after all this is the result of her recollections, in which she has to her utmost power carried herself with resignation and indifference.

19. Notwithstanding, in making a choice in such circumstances, she may do well to use, or at least to advise upon these cautions: 1. Generally speaking, when two things seem in all respects to be equal, it were better, at least safer, to choose that side on which lies the greater mortification to na-

ture. 2. She may do well to make choice of not doing rather than doing, especially if the doing be likely to engage the soul in any distractions or solicitudes; for the election of not doing is more suitable to the perfection of a contemplative state and the spirit of our order and rule, that tends to God by abstraction, silence, solitude, &c. 3. Let her choose that side which she thinks would be more agreeable and better approved by virtuous and devout friends. 4. Let her follow the example of any one of whom she has a good opinion, in case the matter concerns others, as if the question be about giving a suffrage in the election of superiors, &c, 5. If the business concern herself and her own soul's good only, she is not always obliged to choose that which in itself is most perfect, but therein she is to consider her own present state and degree, and whether the choice will be likely to produce good or ill effects and inconveniences for the future as well as the present. For example, it is certainly in itself the most desirable perfection that a soul can aspire to, and to which she is also obliged to tend, to keep herself always in the divine presence, and in a constant state of recollectedness, or to renounce all manner of satisfactions to nature, &c. But if an imperfect soul should therefore attempt the exercise of internal prayer without interruption, or to practise so universal a mortification, she would overthrow corporal nature utterly, and in a short time, by indiscreet overdoing, come to an inability to do anything at all. To her, therefore, in such a state, that is to be esteemed most perfect which in itself is less perfect, to wit, a fervent but moderate exercise both of prayer and mortification, by which she will be enabled by little and little to get ground upon nature, and at last to do that which will be both in itself most perfect, and to her also.

20. A soul having, after the manner aforesaid, made a resolution and election, it is the advice of Michael Constantiensis, a devout prior of the Carthusians, that she should persevere in it, yea, though afterwards something by some others should be suggested to her contrary to such a resolution; although also that which is so suggested should seem to be more profitable and of greater perfection. Just after the same manner that a soul, having once advisedly submitted herself to the direction of a spiritual guide, is not to hearken to nor accept from any other any reason contrary to his directions, nor any discouragements from obeying him. And surely, saith he, a much greater obligation hath a soul to follow the interior counsel of God sought by a resigned, persevering prayer, to which our Lord has given an express promise, saying, Whatsoever ye shall ask in my name, believe that ye shall receive it, and it shall happen unto you. And such was the practice of B. Angela de Foligno, &c.

21. To this purpose it is very observable, in the life of the same B. Angela, that God commanded her to set down in writing this passage (which

is the only one for which she received such a command), to wit, that He would take away His light and grace from those who, being brought immediately to their internal master, would be so ungrateful as to forsake Him, and betake themselves to an external one; yea, and that moreover such should have a curse from Him, namely, if they did persist in receding from the divine conduct, constantly preferring human directions before God's.

22. Yet this advice of being constant to a resolution so made is to give place. 1. In case a superior should command anything contrary thereto; for a superior must be obeyed, even against such an interior counsel; because a soul is not only counselled, but also commanded to obey her superiors. So that whensoever a superior does deliberately disapprove a counsel so received, a devout soul is to believe that now it is God's will that His former counsel should cease from being any further obliging. 2. In case that any other different circumstances shall occur, which may perhaps alter the state of the difficulty; notwithstanding such a change is not to be made upon this last ground, without new recurring to God for light. Yea, though the reasons for a change be never so clear, yet it is best it should be made in virtue of prayer, to the end it may be done with greater purity of intention.

23. Now in all cases of such like nature, the purpose and resolution is seldom to be made in the very time of our recollections; both because (as hath been said) the thinking on such matters is not the proper subject of prayer, but is very distractive; and likewise because the internal illustrations and motions of God's Spirit are better perceived after prayer, when the soul, having been recollected, doth reflect on them.

24. But it is otherwise in matters of resignation, or when we pray for patience and tranquillity of mind in crosses and difficulties. For in such cases we are to make our good purposes in our prayers themselves, and oft are to renew them afterwards; because such purposes do of themselves presently appear to be clear and obligatory, and besides, they are proper matter for prayer.

25. After that a soul hath made a resolution in the cases, and after the manner aforesaid, and likewise hath put the same in practice, let the issue be what it will, whether profitable or harmful to nature, yet must she never esteem the election to have been amiss; nor must she hearken to any suggestions of nature, the which, finding in such practices something contrary to her inclinations, will be apt by subtle insinuations to move the soul to repent and to undo what she hath done. Such an erroneous judgment, procured by corrupt nature, is to be despised and deposed; for well may we happen to err in the manner of executing such counsel given us by God, and thereby, or by some other means, inconveniences or harms may sometimes befall us; but the election in itself, made in the manner aforesaid, was good,

and it would be an act of immortification to blame it, or to be sorry for it. God for our good doth often turn our best deeds to our greatest mortification, and thereby we reap a double benefit.

26. In such doubtful cases as have here been spoken of, a soul must not expect an apparent evident certitude, as spiritual writers say; for God, to keep the soul in humility, does not use to give an absolute assurance of the matter itself simply considered, but only a certainty of being directed and drawn more to one side of the difficulty than to the other; the which side, in the judgment of the said authors, is to be chosen and followed as the divine will. So that any advantage or preponderation, though never so little, towards one side more than another, maketh certitude enough of God's will as for standing to it. If there be no perceptible difference or leaning either way, the soul is either to take advice from some other, or to supply it with her natural impartial reason, or even, as it were, by lots to choose which she thinks good. And what she doth after this manner, she may equivalently be said to do as by the direction and impulse of the Divine Spirit; because it is God's will and appointment that, when Himself does not direct us immediately by His Spirit, we should make use of other inferior external ways the best we can for our direction: in all things always intending His glory and increase in His love only.

27. It would be a vain, presumptuous, and dangerous tempting of God to go and pray to the end to know His will in things commanded by known laws and by lawful superiors, for they are appointed by Him as the most assured interpreters of His will; and to expect any more is to pretend to extraordinary illuminations and calls, which are neither to be desired nor trusted to, because there will be great danger of illusion by the devil's counterfeiting a good angel; and he that is so presumptuous in his practice, deserves that God permit such illusions.

Chapter VIII. What is the Certainty of Divine Inspiration?

§§ 1, 2, 3. Sufficient assurance may be had that inspirations are from God.

§§ 4, 5, 6, 7. A soul, therefore, may securely commit herself to God's guidance; and why?

§ 8. No danger if a soul should sometimes be mistaken, taking that for an inspiration which is not so.

1. Now all these instructions and exhortations to attend unto and depend on the divine inspirations would be vain; yea, all the promises of God, that He would give His Holy Spirit to those that pray for it as they ought, would be as vain, if there were no means to be assured of such inspirations

that they are from God—by an assurance, I mean, of hope: for a certainty of faith (without extraordinary revelation) cannot be had of such matters which necesssarily suppose the like assurance of being in the state of grace. Hence it is that Thaulerus, Blosius, Michael Constantiensis, &c., do teach us how we may discern, and with confidence judge resolutely what is a divine inspiration; saying, That the devout soul which proceeds with recollection and resignation in all doubtful matters of importance, may and ought to take that to be the divine will, to which she is interiorly moved in or after her recollection (when as passions do not prevail in her), so long as the matter is not otherwise contrary to external obedience, or other law of God or man.

. For it is certain, yea, and faith obliges us to believe, that in all the good actions we do, or good thoughts we entertain, we so do and think in virtue only of a precedent and concomitant illumination of our understanding and inclining of our will, both which are immediately caused by God. Reason, likewise, and experience tell us, that whilst vain or sinful distracting images or inordinate passions cloud the mind, God's illuminations are either unperceived or neglected by us, and His motions ineffectual. If ever, therefore, the soul be in a fit disposition to receive those blessed effects of God's Holy Spirit, and if ever God will make good His so serious and frequent promises, it is then when by a profound recollection, an humble soul withdraws all her affections from herself and all other creatures, yea, and endeavours to expel all the images of them, transcending all created things, and raising herself according to her power to a strict union with Him, and withal pours forth her desire to be informed in His will, only intending thereby His glory and the increase of His divine love.

3. Now though imperfect souls, not being able as yet to drive away distracting images and to still all unruly passions, are forced to content themselves with their natural light in many matters of less importance, so that a great part of their ordinary actions do not at all contribute to their advancement in spirit, yet perfect souls walk almost continually in a supernatural light, perceiving and resisting the subtle insinuations of self-love, and not suffering themselves hastily to be pushed forwards to actions, before they have consulted their internal guide, and much less contrary to His directions.

4. Most securely, therefore, may we, yea, with all confidence ought we to yield ourselves to be disposed of by God, and to follow Him in any ways that He will lead us, both for the exterior and interior, through light and darkness, through bitter and sweet. And what doubt can there be of erring, having such a guide, which always leads the soul through the paths of mortification and renunciation of self-will? although sometimes some special ways may to our or others' natural judgments seem strange and perhaps impertinent.

76

5. The grounds of which duty and the security attending it are these: 1. Because we, through the ignorance of our interior complexion and temper of soul, as likewise of our present wants (incomprehensible to human knowledge got by sense), can neither know the special ways either of prayer or mortification proper to us; nor can we be assured that others do sufficiently know them; whereas, of God's omniscience and equally infinite goodness, none can doubt. 2. Because, the end whereto we aspire being supernatural, consequently the ways leading thereunto, and the light directing in those ways, must likewise be supernatural. 3. Because if we knew the most proper and most direct ways leading to contemplation and divine union, yet they being most contrary to our natural inclinations, without a divine impulse we should not choose the fittest, that is, those which are the most opposite to our nature.

6. Yet we are to consider that there are degrees of security, according to the several manners by which God communicates unto us His inspirations. For, 1. Though in sensible devotion the good thoughts and affections given us are in themselves and according to their substance the effects of God's Spirit, and ought with all security to be complied withal (yet with discretion, so as that out of gluttonous pleasure conceived by them we do not yield unto them so far as thereby to weaken our heads or prejudice our healths), notwithstanding the resolutions of undertaking any practices for the future, grounded on such sensible devotion, are to be mistrusted, as having in them more of nature and self-love, and wanting sincerity or resignation. Besides that the senses being principal workers, the reason is rather obscured than illuminated thereby; yea, and by God's permission, the devil may have some influence in such devotion and subsequent resolutions. 2. Of the like uncertain nature may the seeming inspirations or lights be, which are gotten by the working of the imagination and discourse upon the matter, either in prayer or out of it; the person thereupon concluding this or that side to be more likely to be God's will. 3. But if without such working of the imagination, or if after it, the soul in recollected prayer made with resignation and submission of her natural judgment, and renouncing all interests of nature, comes, as it were, unexpectedly to have one part of the question presented to her mind as truth and as God's will, God then giving a clarity to the reason to see that which it saw not before, or otherwise than it saw it; or if the soul do find a blind and reasonless motion in the will to one side of the matter: in such cases the soul may most securely and confidently judge it to be a divine inspiration and motion, being wrought without any trouble in the exercise of the imagination, senses, or passions.

7. Let not a soul, therefore, be discouraged from committing herself to God's internal direction, though it should happen that those who pass for

the most spiritual persons, and that are most forward to usurp the conducting of souls to perfection (whilst themselves know no further than the exercises of the imagination), should declaim against it, and out of an apprehension that it would be a disparagement to them if God should be acknowledged the principal guide, they should accuse the doctrine here delivered as fantastical, unsafe, and pretending to enthusiasms. No wonder is it if such, being strangers to the contemplative ways of the spirit, should be ignorant of these secret paths by which God leads souls to perfection; in the which none can tread, or at least make any considerable progress, till, quitting a servile dependence on external teachers, they rely only upon the divine guidance. And for this purpose devout souls are seriously and oft to be exhorted to keep themselves in a disposition of as much abstraction both external and internal as may be, to the end they may be enabled to hear and discern the divine voice; to the directions of which if they will in practice faithfully correspond, God will be wanting to them in nothing.

8. And for a further security that there can scarce happen any considerable danger to a soul proceeding this way for knowing the divine will, though she should sometimes mistake in the thing itself, both she and also the opposers of this doctrine are to consider that (as hath formerly been said) the only matters that are here supposed to be proposed for a resolution are, and must be, of the nature of those things which of themselves and in the general are indifferent, but yet which, being well chosen, may and will advance the soul; for in no other things but such can there be any doubt. And surely if we be capable of knowing God's will in such things (as who can question it?), certainly the proceeding thus with indifference and resignation, and without suddenness of resolution or motion of natural passions, or self-love, is the most secure and most assured way to come to that knowledge.

Chapter IX. Divine Calls do not Prejudice Authority

§ 1. Objections prevented.

§§ 2, 3. Difference between the terms 'Inspirations' (being only internal) and 'Calls,' which are also external.

§§ 4, 5. How inspirations direct us about external calls and obligations.

§ 6. External calls are to overrule internal.

§§ 7, 8. Authority of superiors ought to overrule inspirations, even in things not of obligation.

*§ 9. Inconsiderate commands of superiors in such things to be obeyed,
though superiors will be severely accountable to God.*

*§ 10. Decay of true spirituality arises from the ignorance or neglect of this
doctrine touching attending to divine inspirations.*

1. Lastly, to prevent all misunderstanding of this most holy and most necessary doctrine touching our obligation to attend unto (and to practise accordingly) the divine inspirations directing us to acts of perfection, as likewise to prevent all misapplication thereof by souls that ought and are willing to follow it, I will here take away the pretended grounds upon which some who, either out of ignorance, passion, or interest, have declared themselves to be enemies thereto, do declaim against it, supposing that they have a great advantage against it, whilst they pretend that by the teaching and practising of it great prejudice will come to the due authority of superiors, from which their subjects, following these instructions, will endeavour to exempt themselves, upon a pretext of divine inspirations to the contrary.

2. For the clearing, therefore, and dissolving of this supposed difficulty and inconvenience, we are to consider that, though in this discourse we have promiscuously used the terms of inspirations, lights, impulses, divine calls, &c., yet the former are only such operations of God as are internal; whereas the term of divine calls imports both an external ordination of God, and also His internal operation in our souls suitable to the external call. And both these are properly termed calls, because by both of them God doth signify His will to souls; for by the external ordination and commission given by God to all in lawful authority under Him, God by them doth reveal His will unto us, which we obey whilst we submit unto and execute the commands and wills of His substitutes. And by His internal operation He directs us to perform such obedience, in a spiritual manner, for the good and advancement of our souls in His *divine love.*

3. All laws, therefore, all constitutions, precepts, and commands of superiors, and all external or internal duties of obligation by virtue of our state of life as Christians, or moreover as religious or ecclesiastical persons, &c., are, indeed, and so to be esteemed by us, true divine calls, necessarily to be attended to, known, and performed by us.

4. And as for internal inspirations which have regard unto those external calls, the end for which they are given us is not only simply to direct and incline us to perform all our Christian, regular, or other duties with readiness and cheerfulness but to do them with perfection and purity of intention, in and for God only, as if He had immediately and visibly imposed them upon us. And forasmuch as concerns the not doing (to which I said that in a contemplative life the divine inspirations do invite us), that is meant only in matters either indifferent, or at least to the which we have no obligation by

virtue of any external law. Yea, on the contrary, we may say that our holy rule (the end whereof is to dispose and lead us to a perfect union with God by contemplation) doth in general oblige us to such abstraction and not doing, wheresoever it doth not require the doing of anything of us.

5. Therefore, whatsoever internal suggestions, motions, or impulses we may find that shall be contrary or prejudicial to such external calls to obedience and regularity, we are to be so far from hearkening to them or esteeming them for divine, that we ought to despise and reject them, judging them to be no better than diabolical illusions. Yea, this is to hold, although the said external laws, commands, or observances be such as we in our private judgment cannot think to be very proper or convenient for us in particular.

6. Now the reason why no internal suggestion ought to take place of external obligations is evident and convincing; because such external calls to obedience being of themselves both manifest and certainly unquestionable tokens and expressions of the divine will, they ought not to give place to any supposed internal significations of the same will whatsoever, which are not nor can be so manifest, but rather to prescribe rules unto them and overrule them. We know the former to be God's will, and to proceed from Him, and therefore we cannot rationally believe that those things that are opposite thereto can be acceptable to Him. Besides, God's will revealed to a subject by the mouth of his superior, or by established laws, has a kind of public authority, being derived by a public person and mean, and therefore must needs take place and be preferred before an inspiration or signification of the divine will to a private person alone.

7. Yea, moreover, so indispensably careful and even scrupulous ought we to be that exterior order and due subordination appointed by God should not upon any pretence be prejudiced, that we are to regard the authority of superiors even in doing or omitting those things which are not within the compass of any special laws or commands, but are left to our own liberty and judgment. So that we ought not to put in execution anything to which we are by an internal inspiration invited or directed, without the approbation and leave (either express or interpretative) of our superior; and if the matter be of considerable moment, his express permission is requisite.

8. Yea, I will add further, that if a religious subject shall have an inspiration which he confidently believes to be divine, by which he is invited to the doing of anything, yet if his superior shall declare such an inspiration not to be divine, and forbid the executing of what it directs, the subject ought not only to obey his superior by forbearing to do according to such an inspiration, but he is also obliged to submit his judgment and to believe his superior. And this he may sincerely and securely do; because though it were so that in

truth the inspiration came from God, and did direct to the doing of a thing more perfect or to a more perfect omission, yet all this is to be understood only conditionally, that is, upon supposition that a lawful superior did not judge and command otherwise. For in such a case it would be an act of greater perfection in the subject to obey him forbidding the doing or forbearing of anything, though in itself (and such prohibition not considered) more perfect. Yea, and a divine light and a new inspiration will inform and direct the subject to obey and believe the superior declaring against the former inspiration. For though nothing that a superior in such circumstances can say will make the former inspiration not to have come from God, yet his declaring against it will show it not to be of force now, since that all such inspirations do and ought to suppose the consent, or at least the nonopposition, of the superior, before they be put in practice; and therefore they are to give place to an inspiration of obeying, which is absolute. True it is that in such a case it may happen that the superior may commit a great fault, and must expect to be accountable to God for it; but howsoever, the subject, in obeying such an undue command, shall not only be innocent, but also merit thereby; because in both cases he doth well —first, in being prepared to obey the former inspiration, which was conditional, and afterwards in contradicting that, to obey a second inspiration of submitting to his superior, which was absolute.

9. As it concerns, therefore, particular souls to depend principally upon their internal director, so likewise are superiors and spiritual guides no less obliged to penetrate into the dispositions of their subjects and disciples, and to discover by what special ways the Spirit of God conducts them, and suitably thereto to conform themselves and to comply with the intention of the Divine Spirit. And this duty our holy patriarch, in the 64th chapter of his Rule, requires from all abbots or superiors, forbidding them to use rigour in the correction of their subjects, or so rudely to scour the vessels as thereby to endanger the breaking of them. He would not have them likewise to be restlessly suspicious and jealous over their subjects, but in their impositions to use great discretion (which he calls the mother of virtues), considering each one's ability, and saying with Jacob, 'If I force my flocks to travel beyond their strength, they will all of them die at once,' &c. If the superior, therefore, in a humour of commanding, on his own head, should impose commands on his subjects without any regard to the divine will and guidance, such commands will probably prove unprosperous as to the subject, and certainly very dangerous to the superior. Yet so it may be, that the subject may reap spiritual profit by them; for then it may please God to give him an interior enablement to turn such undue commands to his own good and advancement, by increasing in him the habit of resignation and humility. It will, indeed, be very hard for imperfect souls to reap benefit by such inconsiderate superiors;

but as for perfect ones, they have both light and spiritual strength to convert all the most unreasonable commands of superiors to the benefit and advancement of their own souls.

10. In case a superior should forbid a subject to pray at this or that time, or should command him to spend no longer than such a small space of time in internal prayer as would not suffice for his advancement in the internal ways of the spirit, the Rule of Perfection requires the subject to obey his superior; yet he may with all humility remonstrate to him his spiritual necessities, acquainting him with the great benefit that his soul finds in a constant performance of his recollections, and in attending to divine inspirations, and what prejudice it might be to him to be forbidden or abridged of them. But if the superior do persist, he must be obeyed, and God will some other way supply the loss the subject finds in such particular obediences. Now though a superior can no more forbid in general the use of internal prayer and of observing divine inspirations than he can forbid the loving or obeying of God, yet whether prayer shall be exercised at such certain appointed times, or for such a determinate space of tune, that is within the limits of a superior's authority; and how he employs that authority, it will concern him to consider. For if he guides souls according to his own will and not God's (and surely God's internal inspirations are His will), besides the guilt that he shall contract by the abusing of his authority, he must expect that all the harm or prejudice that his subjects' souls, through his miscarriage, shall incur, will be heaped and multiplied upon his soul.

11. But concerning the duties and obligations of superiors towards souls whose profession is to tread these internal ways of contemplation, more shall be said hereafter in its proper place; where it shall be demonstrated, that these instructions are so far from prejudicing their authority, that true cordial obedience will never, nor can be, perfectly performed to them but by such souls as are most zealous and constant in the essential duties of prayer and attending to the inspirations of God's Holy Spirit.

12. To conclude this whole discourse concerning divine inspirations: As these advices are not curiously to be applied to the practice of fearful scrupulous souls, whose unquiet thoughts make them in a manner incapable of either light or impulses of God's spirit in matters about which their scrupulosity is exercised, so in those cases they are to follow instructions peculiarly proper to them. But forasmuch as concerns all other well-disposed souls that lead contemplative lives, this doctrine ought to be seriously recommended to them, and they are to be taught how to practise it. For by this and no other way can they assuredly understand or perform the divine will, in which alone consists spiritual perfection. By these inspirations alone the interior is regulated, without which all exterior good carriage is little available to

perfection. No external director can order the interior operations of the soul, either in prayer or mortification; none but God alone, who knows and searches the hearts of men. And His principal way of directing is by His inspirations, which, by the acknowledgment of all good Christians, are necessary, to every action to make it good or meritorious. These inspirations, therefore, we must follow; therefore they may be known, for we cannot be obliged to follow an invisible and undiscernible light, we know not what. And if they may be known, surely the rules here prescribed for that purpose (to wit, abstraction of life, and pure, resigned prayer) are the most secure and most efficacious means to come to that knowledge, and to procure grace to work accordingly.

13. And it may very reasonably be believed that the principal ground and reason why true spirituality is in these days so rare, and why matters go so amiss among souls that pretend to aspire to contemplation, is because this most necessary duty of observing and following divine inspirations is either unknown or wilfully misunderstood, and suspected (if not derided) by some who, in popular opinion, are held and desire to pass for chief masters in spirituality. And no wonder is it that such should be disaffected to this doctrine, of the perfect practice whereof themselves are incapable, by reason of their distractive employments and imperfect degree of prayer; and consequently, neither can they, nor perhaps if they could would they, teach it to others, since thereby many souls would quickly be discharged from any necessity of continuing in a dependence on their managing and directions.

14. If any there be that, notwithstanding all that hath been here written touching divine inspirations and the necessity of attending to them, shall yet be unsatisfied, or at least suspect that the publishing of such doctrine may not be convenient—such a one, for further satisfaction, may consult the Appendix adjoined at the end of the treatises.

[The Appendix here promised was not given. But, as will be seen at the end, Father Cressy partly supplies the omission in an Advertisement and a Postscript to the Reader.—J. N. S.]

THE FIRST TREATISE
THIRD SECTION

TOUCHING THE SCHOOL OF CONTEMPLATION, VIZ. SOLITUDE
AND A RELIGIOUS PROFESSION.

Chapter I. All Conditions Capable of Contemplation

§§ 1, 2. That the proper school of contemplation is solitude.

§ 3. Which may be enjoyed in the world.

§§ 4, 5, 6. Contemplation is by God denied to no states. Yea, in some regards women are rather better disposed thereto than men. And why?

§§ 7, 8, 9, 10, 11, 12, 13. The condition of ecclesiastics in the world is of great perfection. What dispositions are required to the undertaking and executing of that sublime charge.

1. Having hitherto treated of the nature and end of an internal contemplative life in general, as likewise of the general quality and disposition requisite to all those who by a divine vocation do undertake that sublime course of life; and, in consequence thereto, having demonstrated that the only sufficient master and guide in such a life is God and His divine inspirations, by whom alone both disciples and also masters and guides must be directed, it remains, in the third place, that I should show what and where the school is, wherein ordinarily this Divine Master instructs His disciples in this so heavenly divine doctrine and science.

2. Now, by the unanimous acknowledgment of all mystic writers, the only proper school of contemplation is solitude; that is, a condition of life both externally freed from the distracting incumbrances, tempting flatteries, and disquieting solicitudes of the world; and likewise, wherein the mind internally is in a good measure, at least in serious desire, freed also from inordinate affection to all worldly and carnal objects, that so the soul may be at leisure to attend unto God, who deserves all our thoughts and affections,

and to practise such duties of mortification and prayer as dispose her for an immediate perfect union with Him.

3. Now though this so necessary solitude be found both more perfectly and more permanently in a well-ordered religious state, which affords likewise many other advantages (scarce to be found elsewhere), for the better practising the exercises disposing to contemplation, yet is it not so confined to that state but that, in the world also, and in a secular course of life, God hath oft raised and guided many souls in these perfect ways, affording them even there as much solitude and as much internal freedom of spirit as He saw was necessary to bring them to a high degree of perfection.

4. And indeed it is an illustrious proof of the abundant, most communicative, overflowing riches of the divine goodness to all His servants whatsoever that in truth of heart seek Him, that this state of contemplation (being the supremest and most divine that an intellectual soul is capable of either in this life or in heaven also) should neither be enclosed only in caverns, rocks, or deserts, nor fixed to solitary religious communities, nor appropriated to the subtlety of wit, profoundness of judgment, gifts of learning or study, &c.; but that the poorest, simplest soul living in the world, and following the common life of good Christians there, if she will faithfully correspond to the internal light and tracts afforded her by God's Spirit, may as securely, yea, and sometimes more speedily, arrive to the top of the mountain of vision than the most learned doctors, the most profoundly wise men, yea, the most abstracted confined hermits.

5. Yea, both history and fresher experience do assure us that in these latter times God hath as freely (and perhaps more commonly) communicated the divine lights and graces proper to a contemplative life to simple women, endowed with lesser and more contemptible gifts of judgment, but yet enriched with stronger wills and more fervent affections to Him than the ablest men. And the reason hereof we may judge to be, partly because God thereby should, as is most due, reap all the glory of His most free graces, which if they did usually attend our natural endowments would be challenged as due to our own abilities and endeavours; and partly also, because as substantial holiness, so the perfection of it, which is contemplation, consists far more principally in the operation of the will than of the understanding (as shall be demonstrated in due place). And since women do far more abound, and are far more constant and fixed in affections and other operations of the will than men (though inferior in those of the understanding), no marvel if God doth oft find them fitter subjects for His graces than men.

6. And for this reason it is (besides that women are less encumbered with solicitous businesses abroad, their secular employments being chiefly domestical within their own walls) that they do far more frequently repair to

the churches, more assiduously perform their devotions both there and at home, and reap the blessings of the sacraments more plentifully (upon which grounds the Church calls them the devout sex); insomuch as a very spiritual and experienced author did not doubt to pronounce that (according to his best judgment, which was grounded on more than only outward appearances) for one man near ten women went to heaven. Notwithstanding true it is that the contemplations of men are more noble, sublime, and more exalted in spirit; that is, less partaking of sensible effects, as raptures, ecstasies, or imaginative representations, as likewise melting tendernesses of affection, than those of women.

7. Now though the true and immediate motive of the writing of these spiritual instructions was the directing of certain devout religious souls in the way of contemplation, to the aspiring whereto their profession did oblige them—and for this reason most of the said instructions are intended to be most proper for such—yet being a debtor to all well-minded souls whatsoever that desire to tread in the said internal ways, I will here briefly show how they also may make use of my writings for the same end, from thence selecting such special directions as may also as well belong to them, and passing over those that are more peculiarly proper to souls in a religious state.

8. In the world, therefore, there are two sorts of persons that do, or may, aspire unto contemplation or perfection in prayer, to wit: 1. Ecclesiastics; 2. Lay persons.

9. First, as for ecclesiastics (I mean especially priests, to which all other inferior orders do tend), they not only may, but ought seriously to aspire thereunto, yea, perhaps more than simple religious; for their most sublime, and by all ancient saints deemed so formidable an office (by which they are empowered and obliged, with immaculate sacrifices and fervent prayers, to be daily intercessors with God for the whole Church), presupposeth them to have already attained to a good recollectedness in prayer. And if, moreover, they have a charge of souls, they will need a far greater stability therein, that their various employments may be performed purely for and in God, and not break their union with Him. Moreover, by their profession their obligations come near to the vows of religious persons, for: 1. They owe an obedience to superiors, though not in every ordinary action. 2. They profess the same chastity. 3. They ought to have little more propriety in their goods, for whatsoever is beyond their moderate necessity and obligation of hospitable charity, they can little more dispose of without wrong to the poor, &c, than religious. 4. Though their employments require from them more conversation with others than the state of religious does, yet they are as well obliged to disengage their affections from all love or solicitude about riches, &c., as

the others are, and in like manner to free themselves from all distractive employments not belonging necessarily to their calling.

10. And upon these grounds it was, that in the ancient and best times of the Church, scarce any durst presume to undertake so high and perfect a calling as the charge of souls is, till after many years first spent in a kind of religious abstraction of life, solitude, silence, great mortification, and assiduous prayer, &c. Witness St. Basil, St. Gregory Nazianzen, St. Gregory Nyssen, St. Chrysostom, St. Augustine, St. John Damascene, &c. And yet after they had done all this, it is a wonder with what unwillingness and fear they suffered themselves to be forced to accept of such a charge; what excuses, prayers, flights into the deserts to avoid it! And when they were compelled by God or men thereto, they were far from thinking themselves disobliged from a continuation of their contemplative exercises of abstraction, mortification, and prayer, &c. But, on the contrary, they stole time even from their necessary refections and sleep to employ in their recollections, as knowing that nothing they could do would be acceptable to God further than it proceeded in virtue of grace obtained by prayer.

11. But the best proof and example of the obligations of an ecclesiastical person is our blessed Saviour Himself, who, though by virtue of the hypostatical union He was replenished with all manner of graces without measure, and therefore had no need at all, as for Himself, to pray for more, yet to show an example most necessary to us, He took not on Him the employment of converting others till He had spent the former thirty years of His life in solitude, silence, and all the most holy internal exercises at home, where He lived unobserved and unknown unto the world. And during all the time of His most laborious execution of His prophetical office, besides much prayer exercised openly before others, the gospel expressly says that His custom was at night to retire Himself with His disciples to prayer; yea, and whensoever any great work was to be done, as before the mission of the disciples and apostles, that He spent whole nights alone in prayer. Add hereunto that He utterly refused to meddle in secular affairs or controversies, He frequented the deserts, &c.

12. So that an ecclesiastical person, both for his own sake and out of a tender love for his flock, ought to think himself more obliged than before to the practice of all internal contemplative exercises, and above all others, of pure spiritual prayer, which alone will sanctify and make successful both to himself and others all other actions belonging to his profession. And hence it is that St. Florentius, an ancient holy bishop, first of Utrecht and afterwards of Münster, when he was reprehended by some for spending so much time in prayer, as if thereby he was hindered from a more perfect discharge of his episcopal function, returned them an answer very becoming a perfect illumi-

nated bishop, saying, *Quid? Vobis insanire videor, si cum multas oves habeam, multum orem?* that is, 'What, do you account me mad, because, having so many sheep under my charge, I bestow so much time in prayer?' implying that it was only by prayer that he could hope for enablement to perform his episcopal duty, and for a blessing after the performance of it.

13. Such is the duty and such the obligations of ecclesiastical persons. But if there be any conscious to themselves of neglect in this matter, and desirous to repair past omissions by future diligence, they may, if they think good, make use of these simple instructions, which generally in the substance are proper enough for them, if they will only separate certain circumstances and respects in them which are peculiar to religious.

Chapter II. These Instructions Profitable to Seculars

§§ 1, 2. How a secular person may make use of these instructions, some of which do equally belong to such an one as well as to religious.

§ 3. What benefit such an one may also reap from instructions here peculiarly belonging to religious.

§§ 4, 5, 6, 7, 8, 9. Such a soul needs not to apprehend want, if, consecrating herself to God, she shall relinquish worldly solicitudes.

1. In the next place, as concerning a secular person not in holy orders, that lives a common life in the world, of what sex or condition soever (for with God there is no difference or acceptation of persons), to whom the Divine Spirit shall have given an effectual call to seek God in these internal ways of contemplation, yet so as that they do not find themselves obliged to forsake a secular profession and to embrace a religious life (of which state, the person perhaps being married or otherwise hindered, is not capable, or, however, finds no inclination thereto), such a soul may make benefit also of these instructions, though purposely written for religious, inasmuch as many of them do generally belong to all persons tending to perfection; and those that seem more peculiar to religious, yet with some qualifications and applications (such as ordinary discretion will teach), these instructions also may afford unto them some good help and useful benefit. And for that purpose they may do well to take into their consideration, and apply unto their own advantage in practice, these following advises:

2. A devout soul, therefore, being inspired by God to such a course, and living in the world, ought to conceive herself obliged as truly and as properly (though not altogether equally) as any of a religious profession to the practice of these substantial and essential duties and instructions follow-

ing, viz.: 1. A strong resolution, notwithstanding any contradictions and difficulties, to pursue, by the divine assistance, the ways tending to contemplation. 2. An equal care to observe, and faithfully to execute, all divine inspirations, and to dispose herself likewise (as is here taught) for the better receiving and discerning of them. 3. The practice both of external and internal mortifications (I mean those which through the divine providence are sent her, or do belong to her present state and condition of life. And as for voluntary mortifications, she is likewise to behave herself according to the following directions). 4. The exercise of internal prayer, according to the several degrees of it. In these general duties there is little or no difference between the obligation of religious from that of secular persons.

3. But whereas, in the next place, there are in this book many instructions that seem peculiar to souls of a religious profession; such I mean as are grounded upon and referred unto a life abstracted from the world, confined unto solitude, and there limited with a strict enclosure of special laws, constitutions, observances, &c.; even in these also, a secular devout person tending to contemplation, may think himself in some proportion and degree concerned and interested; and from them he may reap much benefit, applying to his own use so much of the spirit of religion as discretion will show to be fruitful to him. Now, for a better application of this advice, I will exemplify certain peculiar duties of a religious life, and therein show in what sort a secular person may do well, yea, and in some proportion is obliged, to imitate them.

4. First, therefore, such a soul, though she be not obliged really and personally to withdraw herself from worldly conversation, and to retire herself into a solitude as strict as that of religion, yet so much solitude and silence she must needs allow herself daily, as may be necessary for a due practice of internal prayer. Neither must she engage herself in any businesses of solicitude and distraction that do not necessarily belong to her vocation; and even those also must she perform with as much internal quietness and recollectedness as may be, carefully avoiding all anxiety of mind, care of multiplying riches, &c. And as for vain conversations, complimental visits, feastings, &c., she must not think to permit unto herself such a free scope as others do and as formerly herself did. But she must set a greater value upon her precious time, as much whereof as she can borrow from the necessary employments of her calling ought to be spent upon the advancing of her spirit in the way of contemplation. And she indeed will find the great inconveniences that do attend vain conversations, as dissipation of thoughts, engagements in new unnecessary affairs, sensual friendships, &c., all which she ought carefully to prevent and avoid.

5. Secondly, such a soul is by virtue of her new divine vocation obliged studiously to imitate especially the internal solitude belonging to a religious person, abstracting her spirit as much as may be both from all affection to outward things, as riches, pleasures, &c., and likewise from the images of creatures and worldly objects. For which purpose she is to perform all the duties of her external vocation in order to God, and in subordination to her principal design, which is the perfectionating of her spirit in the divine love. She is therefore not to account herself as absolute mistress of the riches that God had given her, but only as His steward to manage them so as may be most to His glory. So that in the midst of them, she ought to exercise true poverty of spirit, renouncing all propriety joined with affection to them, so as not to be disquieted if God should take them from her, and making no more use of them for her own sensual contentment or for show in the world than shall in true discretion be necessary. This internal solitude, introversion, and nakedness of spirit she must increase, as much as may be, both in her affection to it and practice of it, so that it may become habitual to her. Because without it she will never be in a fit disposition to attend unto the divine inspirations, or to exercise the internal duties of prayer, &c., belonging to a state tending to contemplation.

6. Thirdly, in conformity to religious obedience, she is to behave herself to all those in the world whom God hath set over her with a most profound submission of spirit, obeying them, or rather God in them, with all purity of intention. And moreover, she is, at the first especially, to put herself under the government of a spiritual director, if such an one be to be had, who is to teach her how she may discern the exercises of prayer and mortification proper for her. And in the choice of such an one she is to use the utmost of her prudence, recommending withal an affair of such importance in her prayers to God, that He would provide her one of sufficient abilities and virtue, and especially one that is experienced in those internal ways much exalted above the ordinary exercises of prayer commonly taught and practised. And when God has found out such an one for her, she is with all sincerity and humility to obey him, yet without prejudice to the duty which she principally owes to her divine internal Master, as hath been taught in the foregoing section, the doctrine and practice whereof doth as well belong to her as to any religious person.

7. Fourthly, although such a soul be not by any vow or otherwise obliged to any rule, or restrained by any constitutions or regular observances, notwithstanding she is to reduce the whole course of her actions and behaviour to a certain order, regularity, and uniformity, observing in her retirements, reading, praying, as also her refection, sleep, &c., an orderly practice both for times and manner, according as prudence and her spiritual guide shall ordain. This order and uniformity observed discreetly (yet with-

out any nice scrupulosity), is very requisite in an internal course; for otherwise, a soul being left at large will be unstable and uncertain in her most necessary duties.

8. It will not be necessary to exemplify in any more particulars; for the same reflections and the like applications may a soul make from any other instructions and duties peculiarly designed for religious persons. Besides, if she pursue diligently and constantly her internal prayer, God will not be wanting to afford her sufficient internal light, and likewise strong impulses and spiritual force to follow such light; to which if she faithfully correspond, she will find that since God has not given her a vocation to religion, yet He has not deprived her of the means of enjoying in the world in a sufficient manner the principal advantages of a religious state (except the solemn vows themselves), yea, in this case she may, not altogether unprofitably, think that it was for her own particular good that God did not give her an opportunity to enter into religion.

9. And whereas it was required of such souls that they should quit all solicitudes about temporal riches, let them not fear any great inconveniences by complying with this duty. For as the author of the *Cloud of Unknowing* observes, and confidently professeth, those whom God effectually calls from secular solicitudes to an internal abstracted life, may more than any others be confidently secure of His divine providence and special care over them and all that belong unto them, forasmuch as concerns a sufficient and contentful subsistence in this life. For though He should have called them into a wilderness, where no means of procuring corporal sustenance did appear, or if in the midst of a city He should call any one to lead an abstracted solitary life there, they are obliged to follow such a call, and may most securely do it, referring all care of their subsistence wholly to His divine providence, who infallibly, some way or other, either by ordinary or extraordinary means, will not be wanting to provide convenient maintenance for them, which, if it should happen to be with some scarcity, He will abundantly recompense that with feasting their spirits with far more desirable internal and celestial delicacies. And examples of God's wonderful care over such peculiar servants of His are plentifully afforded us in ecclesiastical history, both ancient and modern. So that to the end of the world that will appear to be a most approved truth, which the Psalmist so long since delivered. *Divites equerunt, et esurierunt: inquirentes autem Dominum non minuentur omni bono,* that is: the rich in the world have been brought to want and hunger; but such as truly seek our Lord shall not be unprovided of any kind of good things.

Chapter III. The Great Advantages of a Religious State

§ 1. Of a religious state.

*§§ 2, 3, 4, 5. How we are to understand and interpret, the great commenda-
tions and privileges given to a religious state by St. Bernard, &c.*

*§§ 6, 7. A religious state is secure and happy, but yet to those only that are
careful to reform and purify their interior.*

1. Hereafter the instructions following are most especially to be directed to souls living in a religious profession (I intend especially such an
one as is, according to the rule of St. Benedict, St. Bruno, &c.,) the most
proper school of contemplation. A state of life certainly the most happy,
quiet, and secure (if rightly undertaken and accordingly pursued), of any in
God's Church. Concerning which my purpose is in this place to treat, not in
its whole latitude (for a great volume would scarce suffice for such a discourse), but only with relation to the end designed in it, to wit,
contemplation, intending seriously to press the obligation that religious persons have to aspire thereto, and the great advantages afforded therein for that
purpose.

2. But as St. Augustine worthily finds fault with those that do too indiscreetly and excessively commend to secular persons living in the world,
either a monastical or a clerical profession; yea, and to heretics or infidels,
even the Church itself; taking notice only of the perfections of those who in
each of these are the most perfect, and forgetting or purposely omitting to
forewarn men that they are not to be scandalised if they meet with some also
who have no part in those commendations and felicities; by which it comes
to pass that, finding what they did not expect, they fall back, not only to a
disesteem, but also to a hatred of that which was so excessively and unwarily
commended to them: upon the same grounds I think myself obliged to forewarn my readers that they do not too inconsiderately read and attend to all
that they find written in commendations of a religious state, lest being too
much taken with what they read, imagining the outward habit and interior
virtues inseparable companions, and thereupon, having undertaken such a
profession, and there missing in some what they in all expected, they be in
danger either of living discontented lives, or perhaps even of finding themselves in a worse estate for their souls (because improper for them and
unproportionable to their forces), than if they had continued in the world.

3. Moreover, devout souls when they read modern spiritual authors
treating of a religious state, dilating much upon the great blessings attending
it, and with choice passages out of the ancient holy Fathers, pleasing histories, and elegant characters describing: 1. the nobleness and excellency of
that life, wherein honours, pleasure, empire, and whatsoever the world can
tempt mankind withal, are trampled under foot; 2. the great security that it

affords unto souls, which thereby are exempted from the devil's snares, living continually in the presence, favour, and familiarity with God; 3. the inexpressible sweetness and consolations enjoyed by His conversation, &c.;—in reading such passages, I say, just and reasonable it is that well-meaning souls should thereby be encouraged to aspire to such eminent blessings truly attributed to the same state, if God by His divine providence shall give them a free way thereto. But yet they are withal to know that such privileges do not belong to the exterior profession of the said state; for the more noble and excellent it is when the obligations thereof are duly corresponded with, the more do they abase themselves that live negligently and unworthily in it. And though it be a great step to a happy security to be secluded from the world's temptations, yet unless in religion we fly from ourselves also, we will find but danger enough. And lastly, true it is that the consolations that attend an assiduous conversation with God in prayer are most desirable and admirable; but they are withal purely spiritual, and not to be expected till souls have lost the taste of sensual pleasures and ease.

4. Hereupon it is observable how prudently, and withal how ingenuously, our holy patriarch St. Benedict deals with souls newly coming to a religious conversion. He commands that his Rule be several times read to them, that so they may be sufficiently informed what God and superiors expect from them through the whole following course of their lives. In the which Rule, though the prologue does with winning promises invite the readers to a participation of the inestimable blessings of a religious life, yet (in the 58th chapter, where is set down the discipline and order to be observed in the admission and profession of new-comers) he ordains that such shall not without great difficulty be admitted; yea, that they shall be treated rudely, with contempt and opprobrious usage; all manner of unpleasant, harsh, and rough things must be inculcated to them, &c. And all this is done to the end to try whether they bring with them that courageous resolution and patience, by which alone the incomparable blessings of a religious state are to be purchased.

5. In the same sense, and with the same conditions, we are to understand the nine privileges that St. Bernard affirms are to be found in a religious state. For surely it was far from his meaning to apply the said privileges to any but industrious souls, whose principal care is to purify themselves interiorly, and not at all to tepid persons that neglect to correspond to their profession. For who but the industrious and vigilant: 1. do live more purely than men do in the world; 2. or fall more seldom; 3. or rise more speedily; 4. or walk more warily; 5. or rest more securely; 6. or are visited by God more frequently; 7. or die more confidently; 8. or pass their purgatory more speedily; 9. or are rewarded in heaven more abundantly? On the contrary, it is justly to be feared, yea, too certain it is, that habitually tepid and

negligent souls in religion are in a far worse state, more immortified, more cold in devotion, more estranged from God every day than others, considering that, in the midst of the greatest advantages and helps to fervour and purity, they will continue their negligence; and therefore they must expect, for their obstinate ingratitude and for their offending against so great light, that they shall be more severely punished by Almighty God than others the like that live in the world.

6. How ridiculous, therefore, would it be for any to boast and say, God be thanked, I have been so many years a professed religious person, in an Order that hath produced so many thousand saints; that hath had so many popes; that received so many emperors, kings, queens, and princes; that hath so flourished with riches, learning, piety, &c. As if those good successes to some were sufficient security to all, so that they should need no more than only to be of such an Order.

7. For the undeceiving, therefore, of such as are strangers to a religious profession, and for the admonishing and encouraging of those that have already embraced it to comply with the obligations of it, that so they may enjoy all the incomparable privileges and perfections then indeed belonging to it—I will employ the following discourse, principally demonstrating that the principal thing to be intended in a religious profession is the incessant purifying of the interior, which is an attempt the most glorious, but withal the most difficult and most destructive to sensual ease and contentment of all other. This ought to be the motive of those that enter into it, and the principal, yea, almost the sole, employment of those that live in it. Whereto I will add a few instructions more especially belonging to superiors, officers, private religious, and novices respectively.

Chapter IV. A State of Introversion is the End of Religion

§§ 1, 2, 3, 4, 5. Motives inducing to religion to be examined. False security of tepid religious persons. Of false and true motives.

§ 6. An habitual state of introversion and recollectedness is the principal end of a religious life; wherein such recollectedness consists.

§§ 7, 8. Perfection in prayer is the perfection of a religious state.

§§ 9, 10, 11. The wonderful sublimity of prayer to which the ancient hermits attained.

§ 12. Advantages thereto enjoyed by them beyond these times.

§§ 13, 14, 15, 16. That St. Benedict chiefly intended by his rule to bring his disciples to purity of prayer.

§§ 17, 18, 19. False glosses and interpretations of St. Benedict's rule in these days.

§§ 20, 21. St. Bernard's excellent declaration of the design of St. Benedict's rule.

§§ 22, 23. That the only sure way of introducing reforms into contemplative orders is by the teaching of true contemplative prayer, and not multiplying of external forms and austerities.

1. It concerns a soul very much to examine well the motives inducing her to enter into a religious state; for if they be not according to God, it is to be feared she will not find all the profit and satisfaction that she promises to herself. For: 1. If such a profession be undertaken merely out of worldly respects, as to gain a state of subsistence more secure (and perhaps more plentiful); 2. or to avoid suits, debates, or worldly dangers, &c. (unless such incommodities have given only occasion to a soul to reflect on the vanities and miseries of the world, and from thence to consider and love spiritual and celestial good things, which are permanent and without bitterness); 3. or if such a state be undertaken out of a general good desire of saving one's soul according to the fashion of ordinary good Christians, and no more, but without a special determinate resolution to labour after perfection in the divine love, either because such souls know nothing of it, or, if they do, have not the courage and will to attempt it, but resolve to content themselves with being freed from worldly temptations and dangers, and with a moderate care to practise the external observances of religion, yet without sufficient purity of intention or a consideration of the proper end of a religious contemplative life, &c. I cannot tell whether persons living and dying in religion, without further designs of purifying their souls, shall find so great cause to rejoice for the choice they have made; since their beginning and continuing is indeed no better than a stable course of most dangerous tepidity.

2. However, as for souls that for external respects have embraced a religious life, let them not therefore in a desperate humour conclude that no good can come to them by it so unworthily undertaken; but rather hope that by a special providence of God they were, even against their own intentions and wills, brought into a course of life to which, if, however, afterward they will duly correspond, it will prove an infinite blessing unto them. For such ofttimes have proved great saints, after that God gave them light to see their perverse intentions and grace to rectify them, by which means they, beginning in the flesh, have ended in the spirit.

3. And as for the third sort of tepid persons, it much concerns them, at least after their solemn profession, to search well into their souls, and there

rectify what they find amiss, taking great heed how they rely upon external observances, obediences or austerities, the which, though they be necessarily to be performed, yet cannot, without great danger and harm, be rested in, but must needs be directed to a further and nobler end, to wit, the advancement of the spirit.

4. Neither let them conclude the security of their condition and good disposition of soul from a certain composedness and quietness of nature, the which, unless it be caused by internal mortification and prayer, is but mere self-love. And much less let them rely upon the esteem and good opinion that others may have of them, nor likewise on their own abilities to discourse of spiritual matters and give directions to others; since no natural light nor acquired learning or study can be sufficient to enable any one to tread in contemplative ways without the serious practice of recollected prayer. A sufficient proof whereof we see in Thaulerus, who was able to make an excellent sermon of perfection, but not to direct himself in the way to it, till God sent him a poor ignorant layman for his instructor.

5. What is it, therefore, that a soul truly called by God to enter into religion looks for? Surely not corporal labours; not the use of the sacraments; nor hearing of sermons, &c. For all these she might have enjoyed perhaps more plentifully in the world. It is, therefore, only the union of the spirit with God by recollected, constant prayer; to the attaining which divine end all things practised in religion do dispose, and to which alone so great impediments are found in the world.

6. The best general proof, therefore, of a good call to religion is a love to prayer, either vocal or mental. For if at first it be only to vocal prayer, by reason that the soul is ignorant of the efficacy and excellency of internal contemplative prayer, or perhaps has received some prejudices against it; yet if she observe solitude carefully, and with attention and fervour practise vocal prayer, she will in time, either by a divine light perceive the necessity of joining mental prayer to her vocal, or be enabled to practise her vocal prayer mentally, which is a sublime perfection.

It is a state, therefore, of recollectedness and introversion that every one entering into religion is to aspire unto, which consists in an habitual disposition of soul, whereby she transcends all creatures and their images, which thereby come to have little or no dominion over her, so that she remains apt for immediate coöperation with God, receiving His inspirations, and by a return, and, as it were, a reflux, tending to Him and operating to His glory. It is called recollectedness, because the soul in such a state gathers her thoughts, naturally dispersed and fixed with multiplicity on creatures, and unites them upon God. And it is called introversion, both because the spirit and those things which concern it, being the only object that a devout soul considers and values, she turns all her solicitudes inwards to observe defects, wants, or inordinations there, to the end she may remedy, supply, and correct them; and likewise, because the proper seat, the throne and kingdom where God by His Holy Spirit dwells and reigns, is the purest summit of man's spirit. There it is that the soul most perfectly enjoys and contemplates God, though everywhere, as in regard of Himself, equally present, yet in regard of the communication of His perfections present there, after a far more noble manner than in any part of the world besides, inasmuch as He communicates to the spirit of man as much of His infinite perfections as any creature is capable of, being not only simple Being, as He is to inanimate bodies; or Life, as to living creatures; or Perception, as to sensitive; or Knowledge, as to other ordinary rational souls: but with and besides all these, He is a divine light, purity, and happiness, by communicating the supernatural graces of His Holy Spirit to the spirits of His servants. Hence it is that our Saviour says (*Regnum Dei intra vos est*), 'The kingdom of God is within you;' and therefore it is that religious, solitary, and abstracted souls do endeavour to turn all their thoughts inward, raising them to (*apicem spiritus*) the pure top of the spirit (far above all sensible phantasms or imaginative discoursings, or grosser affections), where God is most perfectly seen and most comfortably enjoyed.

7. Now the actual practice of this introversion consists principally, if not only, in the exercise of pure internal spiritual prayer, the perfection of which, therefore, ought to be the chief aim to which a religious contemplative soul is obliged to aspire. So that surely it is a great mistake to think that the spirit of St. Benedict's Order and Rule consists in a public, orderly, protracted, solemn singing of the Divine Office, which may be full as well—yea, and for the external is with more advantage— performed by secular ecclesiastics in cathedral churches; a motive to the introducing of which pompous solemnity might be, that it is full of edification to others to see and hear a conspiring of many singers and voices (and it is to be supposed of hearts too) to the praising of God. But it is not for edification of others that a monastical state was instituted or ought to be undertaken. Religious souls truly monastical fly the sight of the world, entering into deserts and solitudes to spend their lives alone in penance and recollection, and to purify their own souls, not to give example or instruction to others. Such solitudes are or ought to be sought by them, thereby to dispose themselves for another far more profitable internal solitude, in which, creatures being banished, the only conversation is between God and the soul herself in the depth of the spirit, as if besides them two no other thing were existent.

8. To gain this happy state a devout soul enters into religion, where all imaginable advantages are to be found for this end—at least anciently they were so, and still ought to be. But yet, though all religious persons ought

to aspire to the perfection of this state, it is really gained by very few in these times; for some, through ignorance or misinstruction by teachers that know no deeper nor a more perfect introversion than into the internal senses or imagination: and others, through negligence or else by reason of a voluntary pouring forth their affections and thoughts upon vanities, useless studies, or other sensual entertainments, are never able perfectly to enter into their spirits and to find God there.

9. But it is wonderful to read of that depth of recollectedness and most profound introversion to which some ancient solitary religious persons by long exercise of spiritual prayer have come; insomuch as they have been so absorbed and even drowned in a deep contemplation of God, that they have not seen what their eyes looked on, nor felt what otherwise would grievously hurt them. Yea, to so habitual a state of attending only to God in their spirit did some of them attain, that they could not, though they had a mind thereto, ofttimes fix their thoughts upon any other object but God, their internal senses (according as themselves have described it) having been, in an inexpressible manner, drawn into their spirit, and therein so swallowed up as to lose in a sort all other use,—a most happy state, in which the devil cannot so much as fix a seducing temptation or image in their minds to distract them from God; but on the contrary, if he should attempt it, that would be an occasion to plunge them deeper and more intimately into God.

10. And this was the effect of pure, spiritual, contemplative prayer; which was not only practised by the holy ancient hermits, &c., in the most sublime perfection, but the exercise thereof was their chief, most proper, and almost continual employment, insomuch as the perfection thereof was by them accounted the perfection of their state. A larger proof whereof shall be reserved till we come to speak of prayer. For the present, therefore, I will content myself with a testimony or two related by Cassian, out of the mouths of the two most sublime contemplatives. Thus, therefore, speaks one of them (in the ninth conference, chap. 7), *Finis monachi et totius perfectionis culmen in orationis consummatione consistit,* that is: The end of a monastical profession and the supreme degree of all perfection consists in the perfection of prayer. And (in the tenth conference, chap. 7) another saith: *Hic finis totius perfectionis est, ut eo usque extenuata mens ab omni situ carnali ad spiritualia quotidie sublimetur, donec omnis ejus conversatio, omnisque volutatio cordis, una et jugis efficiatur oratio,* that is: This is the end of all perfection, that the mind becomes so purified from all carnal defilement, that it may be raised up daily to spiritual things, till its whole employment and every motion of the heart may become one uninterrupted prayer.

11. Now what a kind of prayer this was that they aspired to, how sublime in spirit (though ofttimes joined with their vocal prayers), may ap-

pear from that description given of it by a holy hermit in these words (in the tenth conference, chap. 20): *Ita ad illam orationis purissimam pervenit qualitatem, quæ non solum nullam deitatis effigiem in sua supplicatione miscebit, sed nec ullam quidem in se memoriam dicti cujusdam, vel facti speciem seu formam characteris admittet,* that is: Thus by much practice the soul will arrive to that most sublime purity of prayer, wherein no image at all of the Divinity is mingled, and which will not admit the least memory, nor a character or representation of anything either spoken or done. The strange subtlety and spirituality of which prayer considered, there is applied unto it that saying of St. Anthony (in the ninth conference, chap. 31): *Non est perfecta oratio, in qua se monachus, vel hoc ipsum quod orat, intelligit,* that is: That prayer is not a perfect one, unless the religious person that exercises it, be not able to give an account of his own thoughts that passed in it (or does not perceive that he prays).

12. What great advantages the ancient hermits and other religious persons enjoyed for the more certain and more speedy attaining to this internal purity of prayer and wonderful cleanness of spirit (the end of their profession), how much more able their bodily complexions were to support that most rigorous solitude, those long-continued attentions of mind, &c.; and how much more efficacious hereto were their manual labours beyond our employments in study; and lastly, how by such like means they, with the only exercise of vocal prayer, attained to perfect contemplation, shall be shown more fully when we come to the last treatise concerning internal prayer.

13. In this place I will content myself with showing that, by the Rule of our holy Father St. Benedict, all his disciples are obliged to propose to themselves no other end of their religious profession, but only such purity both of soul and the operations of it in spiritual prayer; so that how exact soever they be in outward observances, unless they be referred unto, and efficacious also for the producing of, this internal purity in some reasonable measure, they shall not be esteemed by God to have complied with their vocation and profession.

14. To this purpose we may observe that it is from those ancient holy hermits and religious that our holy Father borrowed the greatest part of his Rule and ordinances, which, in the conclusion, he professes to be meant only by him as a disposition whereby we may be enabled to imitate them in their most perfect internal practices. It is from them that he borrows the phrase of (*oratio pura*) pure prayer (in the 20th chap.). The exercise whereof, besides the reciting of the office, he appointed daily, as appears both by the same chapter of the Rule and also by the story related by St. Gregory, of one of his monks whom the devil in the shape of a blackamore, tempted out of the community in the time of such recollections. By which may be perceived the

great fruit and efficacy of such prayer; for the devil could be contented he should be present at the office, because during that exercise he could more easily distract his mind; but knowing the force of internal prayer, how recollective it is, and what light it affords to discover the inward defects of the soul, and to obtain grace to correct them, his principal aim was to withdraw him from so profitable an exercise. And, therefore, to countermine the devil's malice, our holy Father thought it worth a journey expressly to cure the infirmity and prevent the danger of one of his seduced monks.

15. For this end it is that our holy Father, in the 58th chap., ordains superiors in the examination of the spirits and dispositions of new-comers, that they should most especially have an eye to this most necessary condition (*Si deum vere quærit*): If he be such an one as truly seeks God. And more particularly (*Si solicitus est ad opus Dei*): If he have a solicitous care duly to perform the work of God, which he interprets to be prayer; and this so principal a work that he ordains that (*Nihil operi Dei præponatur*) Nothing must be preferred before it.

16. For the advancing of this prayer, that it may become such as is suitable to a contemplative state, all other exterior observances are appointed. 1. By the twelve degrees of humility, by frequent prostrations, acknowledging of secret imperfections, &c., pride, self-love, and all other our corrupt affections, hindering our union in spirit with God, are subdued and expelled, and (as our holy Father says at the end of the last degree) that perfect charity which most immediately unites the soul to God is produced in the soul. 2. By perfect obedience, self-judgment and self-will are abated. 3. By fastings, watchings, and other austerities, sensuality is mortified. 4. By religious poverty, all distracting cares about temporal things are expelled. 5. And for the gaining of an habitual state of recollectedness and introversion, so great silence and solitude were so rigorously enjoined and practised, all objects of sensual affections removed, all conversation with the world, all relating or hearkening to news severely prohibited. All this surely for no other end but that souls might be brought to a fit disposition to imitate those solitary and devout saints (proposed by our holy Father for our examples), in their continual conversation with God, attending to His divine inspirations, and uninterrupted union of spirit with Him by pure spiritual contemplation.

17. Therefore, though our holy lawgiver doth not in his Rule give his disciples any special instructions for ordering their interior spiritual prayer (touching such matters referring them to the inspiration of the divine Spirit, as himself saith; as likewise to the advices of the ancient fathers and hermits professing contemplation), yet it is evident that His principal design was to dispose His disciples by His ordinances to aspire and attain to such internal

perfection, without which the external observances would be of no value, but rather (being finally rested in without further application to the spirit) empty hypocritical formalities. And more particularly as touching the Conferences of the Fathers (written by Cassian, and expressly recommended to us by our holy Father), we reasonably may and ought to judge that his intention was, we should in a special manner make use of the instructions and examples there delivered by prudent, holy, and experienced contemplatives, as a rule and pattern to which we should conform ourselves, principally in our internal exercises, as being much more useful and proper for as than any instructions about such matters to be found in the writings of others, far more learned holy fathers of the Church, who generally direct their speeches to such as lead common lives in the world.

18. This obligation being so manifest and unquestionable, how can those new interpreters of our holy Rule be excused, that extend the profession of a religious person no further than to the performance of exterior obediences and observances literally expressed in the Rule, or signified by the express commands of superiors? Surely they forget that it is to God only that we make our vows, and not to man, but only as His substitute, and as appointed by Him to take care of the purifying of our souls. For the destroying, therefore, of so unreasonable an interpretation (yet too likely to be embraced by the tepid spirits of this age), it will suffice only to look upon the form of a religious profession instituted by our holy father In the 58th chapter, in these words, *Suscipiendus autem, in oratorio, &c.*, that is, Let him that is to be received to a religious profession promise in the presence of the whole community assembled in the church, before God and His saints: 1. a constant stability in that state; 2. a conversion of his manners; and 3. obedience. Now of the three things so solemnly and with such affrighting circumstances vowed, conversion of manners can signify no other thing but internal purity of the soul; obedience, indeed, seems to regard the outward observances of the rules, yet surely with an eye to the principal end of all external duties of all Christians, and much more of those that aspire to the perfection of divine love. And as for stability, it regards both these, adding to them a perseverance and a continual progress in both to the end.

19. These things considered, if God so earnestly protested to the Jews, saying, *My soul hates your new moons, your solemn feasts and sacrifices* (which yet were observances ordained by Himself); and this, because those that practised them with all exactness rested in the outward actions, and neglected inward purity of the heart, typified by them; much more will God despise and hate an exact performance of regular observances commanded by man, when the practisers of them do not refer them to the only true end regarded by the Instituter, which was by them to dispose and fit souls to internal solitude, aptness to receive divine light and grace; and, lastly, to the

practice of pure contemplative prayer, without which a religious state would be no better than a mere outward occupation or trade; and if only so considered, it is perhaps less perfect than one exercised in the world, by which much good commodity may be derived to others also.

20. Again, when such condescending interpreters do further say that all our obligation by virtue of a religious profession is to be understood only (*secundum regulam*) according to the Rule, we must know that this phrase (*secundum regulam*) is to be annexed to the vow of obedience only, importing that a religious superior hath not a vast unlimited authority, but confined to the Rule; whereas, there are no limits prescribed to conversion of manners, to Christian holiness and perfection, in which we are obliged daily to make a further progress. To the which duty, as by becoming religious we have a greater obligation, so likewise have we a greater necessity. For though by entering into religion we do avoid many occasions and temptations to outward enormous sins, yet we can never be freed from our thoughts, which will pursue us wherever we are, and more impetuously and dangerously in solitude than in company, being indeed the greatest pleasure of man, whether they be good or bad. For in solitude the soul hath her whole free scope without interruption to pursue her thoughts. So that a religious person that can think himself not obliged, and that actually doth not restrain and order his thoughts, by diverting and fixing them on heavenly and divine objects, such an one, if, for want of opportunity, he guard himself from outward scandalous crimes, yet he will more and more deeply plunge himself in corrupt nature, contracting a greater obscurity and incapacity of divine grace daily; and such inward deordinations will become more dangerous and incurable than if he had lived in the world, where there are so frequent diversions. Now a poor and most ineffectual remedy against these will he find in an exact conformity to any external observances whatsoever, yea, perhaps they will serve to increase such ill habits of soul, by breeding pride and security in it.

21. A much better and more profitable interpreter of our holy Rule, therefore, is devout St. Bernard, in many passages in his works, and particularly in those words of his in an epistle to William, an abbot of the same order: *Attendite in regulam Dei,* &c., that is, Be attentive to the rule of God. The kingdom of God is within you; that is, it consists not outwardly in the fashion of our clothes or manner of our corporal diet, but in the virtues of our inner man. But you will say: What? dost thou so enforce upon us spiritual duties as that thou condemnest a care of the external observances enjoined by the Rule of St. Benedict? No, by no means. But my meaning is, that the former spiritual duties must necessarily and indispensably be done, and yet these latter must not be omitted. But otherwise, when it shall happen that one of these two must be omitted, in such case these are much rather to be omitted than those former. For by how much the spirit is more excellent and

noble than the body, by so much are spiritual exercises more profitable than corporal.

22. Neither will it avail the fore-mentioned interpreters to say that their meaning is not to prejudice the obligation of religious persons to internal duties, but only to show that such obligation is grounded on the divine law imposed on them as Christians, and not on an external law made by man and voluntarily undergone. For in opposition to this excuse, besides what hath been said concerning the making of our vows to God, and the express obligation therein to an internal conversion of manners, we are to know that, by virtue of our religious vows, we are obliged to a far greater perfection of internal purity than we were formerly as Christians, answerable to the greater helps and advantages thereto afforded in religion; and particularly we have an obligation to aspire to the perfection of internal contemplative prayer, the practice whereof is (at least) of extreme difficulty in an ordinary, distracted, solicitous secular state.

23. And from what hath been said may be collected this most true and profitable observation, to wit, that whosoever would attempt the restoring of the true spirit of religion (which is contemplation), miserably decayed in these days, will labour in vain if he think to compass his holy design by multiplying of ceremonies, enlarging of offices, increasing of external austerities, rigorous regulating of diet and abstinences, &c. All which things will have little or no effect, unless the minds of religious persons be truly instructed in the doctrine of contemplative prayer, and obligation to attend and follow the internal guidance of God's Spirit, which is rather hindered than advanced by the excessive multiplication of outward observances. And for this reason St. Benedict (who surely had a most perfect light and an equal zeal, at least, to advance the spirit of contemplation) was very moderate in these things, and, on the contrary, very severe in requiring the observation of silence, solitude, and abstraction of life, which do most directly and efficaciously beget an habitual introversion and recollectedness of spirit. The ineffectualness, therefore, of these new ways of reformation we see daily proofs of, by the short continuance of them. For minds that are not enlightened, nor enabled by the spirit of contemplative prayer suitable to their state to make a due use of such great austerities for the increasing of the said spirit, become in a short time, after that the first zeal (much caused by the novelty and reputation gained in the world) is cooled, to grow weary, not finding that inward satisfaction and profit which they expected, and so they return to their former tepidity and relaxation.

Chapter V. How Far Ignorance will Excuse Religious Persons

§§ 1, 2, 3. A religious person is not perfect by his profession.

§§ 4, 5, 6, 7. Whether, and how far, ignorance of the true end of religion will excuse.

§§ 8, 9. The danger of those that knowing, will not pursue internal ways of recollection, which are the true end of a religious state; and much more of those that discountenance it.

§§ 10, 11, 12. Vain pretences of those that discountenance internal prayer, &c.

§ 13. A Description of an external and an internal monk out of Hesychius.

1. Our obligation, therefore, to tend to perfect internal purity and simplicity being so great and so indispensable, what account, think we, will some religious persons be able to give to Almighty God for their miserable deficiency in this so essential a condition?

2. Religion is by all acknowledged for a state of perfection, not that by the mere taking a religious profession or habit a person is thereby more perfect than he was before, but because by renouncing those distractive impediments which are in the world he puts himself into a condition in which he not only may far more easily aspire to the perfection of divine love, but moreover, by assuming such a state, he obliges himself to employ all those advantages which he finds in religion, as means to approach nearer to this perfection daily, more than if he had continued in the world he either could or was obliged. Which if he do not, he will be so far from enjoying any privilege in God's sight by the perfection of his state, as that he will be accountable to God so much the more for his ingratitude and negligence in making use of such advantages and talents given him.

3. St. Paulinus excellently illustrates this truth by this similitude. He compares the world to a dry, scorched, and barren wilderness, and celestial happiness to a most delicious paradise, divided from this desert by a deep and tempestuous river, which must necessarily be passed by swimming. The securest way to pass over this river is by quitting one's clothes; but few there are that have the courage to expose themselves to the injuries of the weather for a while, and therefore adventure over clothes and all; and of them, God knows, a world miscarry by the way. Some few others (such are religious persons), seeing this danger, take a good resolution to divest themselves of their clothes, and to make themselves lighter and nimbler by casting away all impediments, how dear soever to flesh and blood. But yet, this being done, it remains that they should labour, naked as they are, with swimming, to pass

the river. But this they neglect to do, or take so little pains or strive so negligently against the waves and stream, that all they do comes to nothing, they are in as much danger and as far from paradise as they were before. And whereas they glorify themselves because they are naked; that will rather aggravate their folly and make their negligence far more culpable, in that, having so great an advantage, they would not take a little pains to do that for which they cast off their clothes.

4. Now the impediments either much delaying or quite hindering many souls that live in religion, and are naturally apt enough for the exercises of a contemplative life, from complying with this most necessary obligation, are partly in the understanding and partly in the will. Concerning this latter, which is self-love, a settled affection to creatures, negligence, &c., much hath already been said and more will hereafter be added. But concerning the other impediment seated in the understanding, which is ignorance of the true way leading to that perfection which is the proper end of a religious contemplative life, I will here take into consideration whether and how far such ignorance may excuse a religious person that does not aspire to that perfection to which his state obliges him.

5. For the clearing of this doubt we may observe that there may in this case be a twofold ignorance. 1. An ignorance in gross that there is any such obligation. 2. On supposition that a soul is informed that she hath such an obligation, an ignorance of the means and ways proper and necessary for the acquiring of this perfection, which in the present case are Mortification and (principally) internal Prayer.

6. First, therefore, for the former sort of ignorance, it is so gross and even wilful that there can scarce be imagined any excuse or qualification for it. For what other thought can a soul have, quitting the world and all the pleasures and commodities therein, to embrace poverty, obedience, solitude, &c., but thereby to consecrate herself entirely to God, shown by the solemn circumstances of her admission and profession, the questions proposed to her, and her answers, her habit, tonsure, representation of a death and burial, solemn benedictions of her habit, and prayers of the community, &c. All that are witnesses and spectators of such an action do no otherwise understand it; and indeed, except it were so, what difference is there between a secular and religious state?

7. But in the next place, touching the second sort of ignorance, to wit, of the ways most proper and efficacious to bring a religious soul to perfection. It is to be feared that such an ignorance will be but a small excuse, and that but to very few. For since both faith and experience teach us with what great defects, what inordinate affections, &c. we enter into religion, with an intention there to abate and mortify them; and since even natural rea-

son and daily experience likewise show us that perfection of the soul cannot consist in external observances, which do not penetrate into the interior; yea, without prayer and purity of intention (to be had only by prayer), they do rather nourish self-love and self-esteem; since, thirdly, the same experience convinces us that such vocal prayers as we use and join to our other observances do not produce in us a sufficient purification of soul; no, nor that any other painful methods of meditation (unknown to the ancient contemplatives) do afford us sufficient light and grace for such a purpose, because they pierce not deep enough into the spirit; what reasonable soul but will hence conclude that there must needs be some other efficacious means for the acquiring of the end which we propose to ourselves? And since God will infallibly give light and grace to all those that have recourse unto Him in spirit and truth, it must necessarily follow that the only culpable ground of such ignorance must needs be a neglect of such prayer, and the root of such neglect a sensual tepid disposition of the will, hating to raise itself to God. And let any one judge whether an ignorance so grounded can excuse us; especially considering that our holy Father requires the practice of such prayer in all our smallest undertakings, and teaches us that his Rule is only a preparation to perfection; he refers us further to the examples of the ancient hermits, whose manner of prayer if we would imitate, we should make some approaches at least to that perfection—to the almost inconceivable sublimity and purity whereof they attained.

8. Now if ignorance will not be a sufficient excuse to any religious person for either not endeavouring after interior purity of soul by prayer in spirit, or endeavouring after a wrong improper manner and way, how much less excusable, nay, how deeply culpable, before God will those be who are sufficiently instructed in the only true internal ways leading to contemplation, and withal are furnished with all helps, leisure, and advantages for that purpose, and yet out of a settled slothfulness and fixed love to sensual objects have not the courage or will to walk in them, yea, perhaps having once comfortably walked in them, do most ungratefully and perfidiously forsake and turn out of them? Reaping no other benefit by their knowledge, but perhaps an ability to talk of them to the help of others, it may be, but to the increasing of their own pride and self-love; so that their knowledge of their obligation and end of their profession helps to lead them further from it.

9. But, above all, most miserable will their condition be who, living in contemplative orders and not having either sufficient knowledge or grace to practise themselves the exercises of true internal prayer and abstraction of life, shall deter others therefrom, and discountenance or perhaps persecute those whom God hath inspired to renew the only proper exercises of contemplation, the decay of which has been the decay of the true spirit of monastical religion.

10. True it is that to justify such undue proceedings and to gain an esteem to their own inferior exercises, partiality has suggested to them certain seeming reasons and pretences against the practice of contemplative prayer, as if it were dangerous, and did expose the exercisers of it to illusions, or as if it were prejudicial to regular observances and obedience; or that perhaps it may diminish the credit which some religious orders have gained in the world by their long solemn offices laboriously celebrated. But (as I shall in due place in the last treatise demonstrate) all these accusations made against contemplative prayer are most unjust and groundless. On the contrary, those that practise such prayers as they ought are most careful of conformity to religious duties, and especially the Divine Office appointed by the Church; and this is out of conscience and with great purity of intention.

11. Indeed, true internal livers are not very solicitous for gaining credit and esteem with the world, and much less would they make that an end of their religious observances. On the contrary, their cordial desire is to live unknown and excluded from the world, approving their souls to God only. Neither are they forward to usurp offices abroad not belonging to them, as of preaching, hearing confessions of seculars, &c., by which the most necessary solitude and recollectedness, which by their profession ought to be prized above all things, are interrupted and oft utterly destroyed. And the more confidently do they express a zeal for these essential things, as being assured that God will not be wanting to supply them sufficiently with all things necessary to their corporal sustenance, as long as they prefer the care of purifying their souls and complying with the obligations of their profession before such inferior things. St. Anthony was so careful of preserving this spirit of solitude and disengagement from all treating with the world, that he forbids his monks to enter into churches frequented by multitudes, and much less would he suffer them to invite and call seculars into their own churches. And St. Stephen, of Grammont, upon experience of what extreme prejudice the spirit of religion had received by neglecting a solitary abstracted life, forbids his disciples in his Rule to have public churches or to admit into their oratories the presence of seculars, or so much as to let them take holy water home with them, or to quit their desert to preach to others. He commands them to avoid confraternities, &c.; and to prevent complaints and fears, lest by so rigorous a sequestration from the world they should be in danger of penury, be most assuredly protests unto them that it is impossible that God should neglect to provide for them that for His sake quit all pretensions to the world.

12. But the true cause of bitterness shown by some against internal prayer (restored by several most illuminated and glorious saints in these latter times) may be feared to proceed partly from some kind of pride and an unwillingness to acknowledge any religious exercises to be more perfect than those practised so long by themselves, or to see that power which they had

gained in the managing of the consciences of religious persons, &c., to be in danger of ceasing.

13. To conclude this point. Those that place perfection of a religious profession in anything but in the purity and simplicity of spirit, such may call themselves monks and contemplatives, being yet able to show no signs of such a profession but the habit, and a certain outward, formal, solemn, and severe comportment, under which may be hidden a secret most profound self-love and pride. And they may do well to meditate seriously on that memorable saying of Hesychius, a holy illuminated monk: He that hath renounced the world, saith he, that is, marriage, possessions, and the like, such an one indeed hath made the exterior man a monk, but not as yet the interior; but he that hath renounced his own thoughts and affections, such an one hath made truly the interior man a monk also; and verily any one that hath never so small desire thereunto may easily make the outward man a monk, but it is a task of no small labour to make the interior man so too. Now a sign of an interior monk, saith he, is the having attained to the dignity of pure spiritual prayer.

Chapter VI. The Contemplation of the Primitive Monks

§ 1. That internal prayer was the practice of ancient hermits; what kind of prayer that was.

§§ 2, 3, 4, 5, 6. How it came to pass that vocal prayer became to them internal, and brought many souls anciently to perfection. And why it will not now do so ordinarily.

§§ 7, 8, 9, 10. The great help that the ancients found by external labours to bring them to recollection.

§§ 11, 12, 13. How manual labour came to give place to studies; the which are defended.

§§ 14, 15. The late practice of internal prayer recompenses other defects.

1. That internal spiritual prayer was seriously and almost continually practised by the ancients is apparent both out of the Lives and Conferences of the Ancient Fathers. But indeed there are but few proofs extant that appointed times were set for the exercising it conventually, except in the forementioned story of the monk tempted by the devil to retire himself from his brethren when they were in such prayer. I suppose, therefore, that superiors and directors of souls tending to contemplation were in these latter days obliged to enjoin daily recollections, by reason that the daily, private, and

continual employments of religious persons are not so helpful and advantageous to the procuring of that most necessary simplicity and purity of soul as anciently they were; and, therefore, they were forced to make some supply for this defect by such conventual recollections, the which they instituted to be performed in public, because they perceived or feared that religious souls, if they were left to themselves, would out of tepidity neglect a duty so necessary and so efficacious.

2. Now to the end that, by comparing the manner of living observed anciently by religious persons with the modern in these days, it may appear what great advantages they enjoyed towards the attaining of perfection of prayer beyond us, we may consider: 1. their set devotions, what they were; and, 2. their daily employments during the remainder of the day.

3. As concerning the first, their appointed devotions, either in public or private, was only reciting the psalter, to which they sometimes enjoined a little reading of other parts of scripture. For as for the fore-mentioned conventual mental exercise of prayer, it was very short, being only such short aspirations as God's Spirit did suggest unto them in particular, as it were the flower of their public vocal prayers. Yea, and in private, when they did purposely apply themselves to prayer, they seldom varied from the manner of their public devotions; for then they also used the psalter.

4. Now how it came to pass that vocal prayers alone were in ancient times available to bring souls to perfect contemplation, which in these days it neither does nor, ordinarily speaking, can do, I shall declare more fully when I come hereafter to treat of prayer; and in this place I will content myself to point only at the reasons and grounds of difference, viz. 1. one reason was their incomparably more abstraction of life, more rigorous solitude, and almost perpetual silence, of the practice of which in these days, it is believed, we are not capable; 2. a second was their fasts, abstinences, and other austerities beyond the strength of our infirm corporal complexions; 3. a third was their external employments out of the set times of prayer, the which did far better dispose souls to recollection, to attendance on the divine inspirations, &c., than those ordinarily practised in these days.

5. No wonder, then, if vocal prayer, exercised by such pure, resigned, humble, mortified, and undistracted souls, had the efficacy to produce in them an habitual state of recollected introversion, which doubtless in many of them was more profound, not only whilst they were busied in their vocal exercises, but also during their external business, than it is ordinarily with us in the height of our best recollections.

6. But a more large handling of this matter I refer to the last treatise, where we speak purposely of prayer. And for this present I will only take into consideration the third fore-named advantage of corporal labours, which to

the ancients proved a help to contemplation far more efficacious than the general employments of religious in these days.

7. For the demonstrating whereof it is to be observed that anciently souls embracing a religious life were moved thereto merely out of the spirit of penance, without any regard at all to make use of their solitude for the getting of learning or for the disposing themselves to holy orders. Being likewise poor, unprovided of annual rents or foundations (the which they were so far from seeking or desiring that, in our holy Father's expression, chap. 48, they did then only account themselves to be *vere monachi, si de labore manuum suarum viverent*—true monks, whilst they lived by the labour of their hands), they were both by necessity and choice obliged to corporal labour.

8. But their principal care above all other things being to attend unto God, and to aspire unto perfect union in spirit with Him, they ordinarily made choice of such labours as were not distractive, and such as might be performed in solitude and silence, so that during the said labours they kept their minds continually fixed on God. Such labours were the making of baskets, or some other works of the like nature, that required no solicitude and very small exactness and attention. And as ecclesiastical histories inform us, such was the charity of bishops and other good persons their neighbours, that to ease them of all care about the disposing or selling of their work, as likewise to hinder them from having recourse to markets for the sale thereof, order was taken that such works should be taken out of their hands, and a competent price allowed them for them.

9. By this means it came to pass that their external labours, being exercised in order to the advancement of their spirits, proved a wonderful help thereto, disposing them to prayer and almost continual conversation with God. And indeed it was God Himself who, by the ministry of an angel, taught St. Anthony this art and most secure method of aspiring to contemplation, when, being unable to keep his mind continually bent in actual prayer, he grew weary of solitude, and in a near disposition to quit it; at which time an angel appearing to him busily employed in making baskets of the rinds of palms, signified to him that it was God's will that he should after the same manner intermit his devotions, so spending the time that he could not employ in prayer.

10. Such were the external daily employments of the ancient contemplatives, and so great virtue did they find in them for the advancement of their spirit. By which means so many of them attained to so sublime a degree of contemplation; yea, and generally most of them arrived to very great simplicity of spirit and almost continual recollectedness.

11. But when afterwards by the most plentifully flowing charity of devout Christians there was not only taken from religious all necessity of sustaining themselves by corporal labours, but they were moreover richly furnished, and enabled to supply the wants of many others, we may well judge that it would become a hard matter to persuade a continuance of much manual labour, purely and only for the greater good of the spirit, when otherwise it was both needless and afflicting to the body. Hence it came to pass that since necessarily some employment besides prayer must be found out for the entertaining of those solitary livers, learning as the most noble of all other, was made choice of, yet so that for many ages corporal labours were not wholly excluded.

12. Yet this was not the sole, nor I suppose the principal, grounds of so great and almost universal a change as afterward followed in the manners and fashion of a cœnobitical life. But we may reasonably impute the said exchange of labours for studies in a principal manner to the good providence of God over His Church, that stood in such extreme need of another sort of labourers in God's vineyard; and consequently to the charity of religious men themselves, who, during that most horrible ignorance and depravation reigning over all the world almost besides, thought themselves obliged to repay the wonderful charity of good Christians, by extending a greater charity, in communicating to them spiritual and heavenly things for their temporal. Hence came a necessity of engaging themselves in the cure of souls and government of the Church, the which indeed, for several ages, was in a sort wholly sustained by them; yea, moreover, by their zeal, labours, and wisdom the light of divine truth was spread abroad among heathens also, and many provinces and kingdoms adjoined to the Church. These things considered, no wonder is there if the introducing of reading and studies in the place of manual labours was unavoidably necessary.

13. But perhaps some there may be not so well affected or pleased with the present reputation or commodities enjoyed by religious persons that, assenting to what hath been here said, will notwithstanding infer that, since learning is now become so much dilated in the world by the zeal and charity of ancient monastical religious, there is no longer any the like necessity of their interesting themselves in ecclesiastical affairs, and therefore that they ought to return to their old corporal employments and labours.

14. Hereto it may be replied that even still there is much need of them, considering the far greater frequentation of sacraments in these days above the ancient times. But moreover, if in these times, wherein learning and knowledge is so exposed to all sorts of men, religious persons should quit studies, returning to their ancient employment of manual labours (from which, as hath been said, God Himself did doubtless withdraw them), besides

that their ignorance would render them the universal objects of contempt through the whole Church, it would likewise expose them, as for their states, as a prey to all that either envied or coveted the scarce subsistence left them; and as to their souls, they would be obnoxious to be turned hither and thither by the variety of directors that would undertake to guide them; and by these means all men would be deterred from adjoining themselves unto them for continuing a succession.

15. Now though, as hath been said, such a change hath been after this manner made in the external employments of religious persons, yet still the same essential indispensable obligation of aspiring to contemplation remains; for the attaining to which, although studies joined with prayer seem in some regards to be less advantageous than anciently such labours as the Egyptian monks, &c. undertook were, yet it hath pleased God in goodness to His servants in a good measure to recompense that disadvantage by raising up several holy persons to teach more accurately than formerly the knowledge and practice of pure internal contemplative prayer. For since it cannot be denied that to persons far more distracted by studies than anciently they were by labours, (which did not hinder a moderate quiet attention to God) vocal prayer, though never so much prolonged, has not ordinarily speaking sufficient force to recollect the mind habitually, or to suppress and cure the many inordinate affections of corrupt nature: hence it is that the use of appointed daily recollections hath seemed to be of absolute necessity, without which the spirit of contemplation would be quite lost. So that to such prayer we may most principally impute the great lights and helps for contemplation afforded by some later saints in religious orders, and in the world also, to the great benefit of God's Church; that sole exercise in a good measure making amends for all other defects in which we seem to come short of the ancients.

Chapter VII. The Special Duties of Religious Persons

§ 1. Of special duties of religious persons.

§ 2. A religious person ought to desire to be always under obedience.

§§ 3. 4. Qualities necessary in a religious superior.

§§ 5, 6, 7, 8, 9. That active spirits are very improper to govern such as are contemplative. The grounds of the difference.

§ 10. A fearful example in Bernardinus Ochinus, showing how dangerous the neglect of internal prayer is in a religious superior.

1. Having thus largely set down the proper and only end of a religious profession, to wit, purity and simplicity of soul, to be obtained by recollected contemplative prayer alone, I will further add some more special duties belonging to religious persons, according to their several relations and qualities, as superiors or other subordinate officers, subjects, &c. For as for the proper virtues of a religious state, as obedience, poverty, humility, &c., the handling of them is referred to the following treatise.

2. Now with what mind a devout soul ought to embrace a religious profession is signified to us in that notable passage in our holy father's Rule, where he saith, *In coenobio degens desiderat sibi abbatem præesse,* that is, Whosoever lives in a religious community is desirous that an abbot should be set over him. From whence we ought that infer that the intention of a religious person ought ever to be to live in subjection to the will of another, and in such a mind to continue all his life. And, therefore, those that readily accept, and much more those that ambitiously seek, government and prelature may reasonably be judged to be led by a spirit directly opposite to the spirit of religion. And surely he that shall seriously consider of what difficulty and of what extreme danger the office of a superior is, what terrible threatenings our holy Father so often denounces from God against a negligent, partial, and unfaithful discharge of such an office, will think it far fitter to be the object of his fear and aversion than of his desire. Therefore that superior that does not find himself more willing to give up his place than to retain it, ought to suspect that he is scarce in a good state.

3. Now to the end that both subjects may be informed what qualities they are to regard in the electing of superiors, and also superiors be put in mind what is expected from them in the discharge of such an office duly imposed on them, I will, from St. Bernard, set down three necessary conditions or endowments by which superiors are to direct their subjects, the which are: 1. *verbum*; 2. *exemplum*; and 3. *oratio*; that is, exhortation, good example, and prayer; adding, moreover, *Major autem horum est oratio. Nam etsi vocis virtus sit et operis; et operi tamen et voci gratiam efficaciamque promeretur oratio;* that is, Of those three necessary qualities the greatest and most necessary is prayer; for although there be much virtue in exhortation and example, yet prayer is that which procures efficacy and success to both the other.

4. From which testimony and authority, yea, even from the light of natural reason, we may firmly conclude that the spirit of prayer is so absolutely necessary to a religious superior, that without it he cannot exercise his charge profitably either to himself or to his subjects; and consequently that to a superior in an order whose spirit is contemplation, it is necessary that he have attained to a good established habit of contemplative prayer. For (as hath been said in the foregoing discourse concerning spiritual guides) how

can such a superior, without knowledge gained by experience, inculcate the so necessary duties of recollection and prayer? Nay, rather will he not be more likely to discountenance those exercises in which he is not skilled, and from which perhaps he has an aversion?

5. Therefore that too ordinarily maintained position of some, that active spirits are more fit for superiorities and external employments than contemplative, which are to be left to the solitude and sequestration to which their spirits incline them, is indeed most unreasonable and groundless.

6. On the contrary, no doubt there is but that the decay of religion hath principally proceeded from this preposterous disorder, viz. that in most religious communities active spirits have got the advantage to possess themselves of prelatures and spiritual pastorships over the contemplative, though the state of religion was instituted only for contemplation. And this has happened even since contemplative prayer has been restored by persons extraordinarily raised by God, as Rusbrochius, Thaulerus, St. Teresa, &c., so that religious communities have been ordered even in the point of spirituality by spirits of a quite different and contrary temper to that for which they were intended.

7. Indeed, it is not to be wondered at that active spirits should so prevail, considering that those who are truly of a contemplative disposition and design, knowing well the difficulty and danger of superiority, how full of extroversion, distraction, and solicitude it is, and what occasions and temptations there are in it to raise, nourish, and satisfy sensual affections, pride, &c., to the peril of extinguishing the spirit of prayer (except in souls far advanced in prayer and mortification), such, I say, are therefore justly afraid of, and do use all lawful means to avoid, the care and government of others. Whereas active spirits that live in religion, not being capable of such prayer as will raise them much out of nature, have not the like apprehensions of such employments; but, on the contrary, being led by natural desires of preëminence and love of liberty, and believing that those who are true internal livers will not submit themselves to all the ways and policies used for the increasing the temporal good of their communities, do not fear to offer themselves, yea, and ambitiously to seek dominion over others, falsely in the mean time persuading themselves that their only motive is charity and a desire to promote the glory of God and the advancement, both temporal and spiritual, of their convents or congregations. But what the effect is experience shows.

8. True it is that it cannot be avoided but that many unfit spirits will oft be admitted into religious orders, very different from the dispositions requisite (though it belongs to superiors to provide as well as may be against such an abuse): but such being admitted, of active dispositions, the best were

to employ them in active exercises and external matters, as in the offices of procuration, dispense, building, and the like; but as for prelacies, the charge of instructing novices, or other offices pertaining to the directing of souls, it is to the destruction of the spirit of contemplation to employ active dispositions in such. For how can they, without light or experience, direct souls in ways unknown to themselves, yea, which through ignorance or mistake they perhaps disapprove?

9. Besides, upon exact consideration it will be found that, in the point of government, contemplative spirits that have made a good progress in internal prayer have great advantages above the active. For such being careful themselves to use all due abstraction will less molest themselves and others with impertinent businesses; not prying too narrowly into all passages, as if they sought occasion of showing their authority and ability in making unnecessary reprehensions, to the disquieting of communities; but for peace sake they will sometimes even *silere a bonis*, passing over many things which do seem a little amiss, wherein they show great prudence and also cause much profit to subjects. 2. Such being diligent about their own recollections, do, out of a love for patience, silence, and peace, forbear the doing or imposing of a multitude of unnecessary tasks upon others. 3. By means of prayer they obtain light to order all things to the benefit of their subjects' souls; and in case they have erred or been defective in anything, they discover and amend it in their next recollection. 4. In the manner and fashion of their whole comportment a certain divine grace shines forth, which is of great efficacy to win their subjects' hearts to obedience and divine love. 5. Yea, if by corporal infirmity they be disabled to attend to many external observances, yet a view of the patience, quietness, and resignation shown by them is more edifying to souls under their care than all the most exact external regularities and severities of active spirits. 6. Yea, even in regard of temporal benefit to communities, contemplative spirits are more advantageous than active. Because they, not putting any confidence in their own industry, prudence, and activity, but only in the divine providence (which is never wanting to those that for temporal regards will not do anything unseemly or misbecoming their abstracted state), do enjoy the effects and blessings of God far more plentifully, whilst they prefer His love and service before any human distracting solicitudes for outward things. Memorable examples of great blessings attending such a confidence in God we find abundantly in the life of our holy Father and of the ancient monks, and more lately in the life of Suso, St. John of the Cross, &c. Now the want of such confidence in active spirits proceeds merely from defect in divine love, and that from the want of internal prayer. And hence proceed hurtful and unseemly compliances with the world, a regard rather to wealth than good wills to serve God in the souls that enter into religion, &c.

10. A fearful example of the mischief following the neglect of internal prayer in a superior, we find in Bernardine Ochinus, a superior in a most strict order, who was a famous zealous preacher, and, as might be judged by outward appearance, of more than ordinary sanctity; yet withal, to comply with those outward employments, a great neglecter of internal conventual recollections. And when he was sometimes charitably admonished of such his tepidity, his ordinary answer was: Do you not know that he who is always in a good action is always in prayer? Which saying of his had been true, if such good actions had been performed in virtue of prayer, and by grace obtained thereby, for then they had been virtually prayers; whereas actions, though in themselves never so good, if they want that purity of intention which is only to be had by pure prayer, are in God's esteem of little or no value,—the principal motives of them being no other than such as corrupt nature is likely to suggest. Ochinus, therefore, continuing in the same neglect, was by one of his brethren prophetically warned that he must expect some terrible issue thereof, in these words: *Cave ne te ordo evomat,* that is, Take heed that our order be not hereafter constrained to vomit thee out of it. The which unhappily fell out; for notwithstanding all his other specious qualities and endowments, he, first forsaking God, was afterwards forsaken by Him, and became a wretched Antitrinitarian apostate. And it is very probable that the greatest part of the apostates of these times (such I mean as have formerly lived in religious orders) do owe their apostasy and perdition to no other cause so much as to such neglect and apostasy first from prayer; the which holy exercise if they had continued, they would never have been weary of their habit first and afterward of their faith.

Chapter VIII. The Duties of Superiors

§ 1. Superiors ought carefully to examine the dispositions of those that they admit to religion.

§§ 2, 3. Great danger to communities from loose spirit.

§§ 4, 5. Other ill qualities to be avoided.

§§ 6, 7, 8, 9. Of a good nature; what it is, and how to be prized.

§§ 10, 11. Inconveniences by admitting active spirits into contemplative religions.

§§ 12, 13, 14, 15. Sufficient time for recollection is to be allowed to all religious.

§ 16. Superiors will be accountable for disorders in their flock.

1. Now one of the principal points of a superior's care for the welfare of his community consists in providing or admitting into it only such spirits and dispositions as are likely to promote the good of it, by living according to the spirit of it. And in this all such officers and counsellors are concerned, to whom the laws have referred the examination and trial of such as offer themselves to a regular life, and are afterward, upon their approbation, to be professed; and a greater consideration of this point is more necessary in these days than anciently it was; for it is not now as in our holy Father's time, when incorrigible persons might be expelled the congregation.

2. It is not, I suppose, needful to advise such as are in those offices to take care how they admit loose spirits into religion among them, who will not so much as intend God or His service—all whose actions have no other motive but either fear of penance or hope of gaining reputation, preferments, &c.; whose bodies are prisoners in religion, but their minds and desires wandering in the world; who must enjoy all privileges and corporal helps equally with the best, yea, and generally use them most wastefully, without consideration of others; who, finding no taste or contentment in spiritual matters, are even forced to seek satisfaction in sensual pleasures, and for the passing of time, to frame designs, to raise and maintain factions, and this especially against those that they see do most intend God, on whom they will cast from off themselves all the burdens of a regular life; who will think themselves excused from all duties for the least corporal incommodity; who will desire and endeavour to make others like themselves, that their party and power may be greater; lastly, who reap so little good to their own souls, and are likely to do so much prejudice to others, that probably it had been much better for them to have continued in the world, the state of religion only serving to increase their guilt and misery.

3. Such loose spirits are worse in a community where the knowledge of true spirituality is common than in other places, because there they are wilfully nought, and do resist amendment. If by the severity of laws and constitutions they may come to be kept in some tolerable order, yet this reaches only to the exterior, and lasts no longer than the superior's eyes are upon them. And indeed the superiors themselves will in all probability feel the greatest smart from such undue admissions, being likely to find daily great bitterness from their obstinacy. Such loose spirits are the cause of such a burdensome multiplicity of laws, all which, notwithstanding, are little available for their amendment, and yet do abridge the due liberty of spirit necessary to devout well-minded souls, nourishing scrupulosity, &c., in them.

4. Let the best care that is possible be used, notwithstanding some unfit persons will, through easiness, partial affection, or other respects in the examiners, slip in. If, therefore, those who are apparently bad be received, what a community will there be provided? Many that seem good will prove bad, but seldom or never will those that appear bad become good. God indeed can change the worst; but yet an uncertain hope in extraordinary grace is not to be relied upon, especially where public good is concerned.

5. Generally there is great fervour in souls at their first entrance into religion. Therefore, if any show unruliness, obstinacy, and indevotion during their noviceship, small good is to be expected from them.

6. A little devoutness will not serve to countervail ill inclinations to lying, dissembling, factiousness, a humour of calumniating, &c.; for a great and scarce-to-be-hoped-for measure of grace will be requisite to subdue such pernicious qualities. On the contrary, a good nature, even where there is not so much devotion, yet will bear up a soul, and make her a tolerable member of a community. It is likewise a great disposition for grace, which it may well be hoped will one day follow, and that such an one will become devout. Especially this may be hoped for in those that have naturally a good sound judgment, which is much to be considered.

7. Now by a good nature I mean not such an one as is generally in the world styled so, to wit, a facility and easiness to grant a request or to comply with others. On the contrary, forasmuch as regards a cœnobitical life, I account such to be an ill nature, being easily seduced and perverted. By a good nature, therefore, in this place, I mean such an one as is endued with modesty, gentleness, quietness, humility, patience, love of truth, and other such morally good qualities, which are good dispositions for Christian perfection. Now a person of an ill nature, that will make a good show out of hope to steal a profession, ought the rather for his dissimulation to be rejected.

8. And indeed subtle natures are much to be taken heed of. Some novices will behave themselves so cunningly as at the end of their probation none can be able to produce any special accusation against them, and yet they may in their conscience believe them to be unfit. In this case every one is to follow his own judgment; and especial heed is to be taken of the judgment of the master or mistress of the novices, who are most to be credited, as having the opportunity and means to espy and penetrate more deeply into their interior dispositions.

9. This goodness or virtuousness of natures is an essential point, and far more to be regarded than those accidental ones, as strength of bodily complexion, acuteness of wit, gracefulness of behaviour, skill in singing, no-

hility, portion, &c. And particularly for this last, how far religious souls ought to be from regarding riches or gain in matters of this nature, or for such carnal ends to admit those that are unfit, or whom God hath not sent, the General Decree of the Church in the first Œcumenical Council of Lateran (can. 64) will show; besides, the practice of antiquity, as we may read in an epistle of St. Augustine. Surely the only way of founding convents securely, even in regard of temporalities, is by making choice only of those to whom God hath given fitting dispositions, whereby we may engage His omnipotence in their preservation.

10. Those, therefore, upon whose suffrages the admission and profession of new-comers do depend, are to consider that they are intrusted by the whole congregation with a matter of such consequence as not only the present but future welfare or ruin of convents is interested in their proceedings: all which trust they shall betray if any undue consideration of friendship, kindred, gain, &c., or a zeal of multiplying convents (which is but carnal), shall corrupt their judgments.

11. Surely, therefore, in all reason none should be admitted into communities professing the aspiring to contemplation, but only such as are disposed thereto, and that are willing, yea, desirous, to spend their whole lives in solitude, prayer, and regular observances, without any designs or thoughts of ever being employed abroad (yet always with an entire submission to the ordinances of superiors).

12. And Indeed (as was said before concerning superiors, that active spirits being to direct the contemplative do endanger the extinguishing of the spirit of contemplation; so likewise) if such be without choice admitted, the same mischief will follow. Yea, I am persuaded that many active spirits, though of a good seemly outward carriage, are no less harmful to a community than a lesser number of loose spirits. And the reason is because by their good exterior show they will seem worthy of superiority, to which also their activity will incline them. And those are they indeed, saith Thaulerus, that are persecutors of contemplation; for having a good opinion of themselves and their own ways (which loose spirits have not), they think themselves even obliged to depress those other good souls that do not judge those external exercises and fashions suitable to their profession. And for this reason they will by faction seek to increase their number; yea, and to strengthen their own party, they will not spare to join, with loose spirits, for their own interests yielding to their disorders. Neither when they have compassed their ends by the ruin of the spirit of contemplation will unquietness cease; for in a community wholly consisting of active spirits factions and partialities for several ends and designs will never be wanting.

13. Now the same care that superiors ought to have about the choice and admission of virtuous and fit souls into communities, must be continued in the managing and directing of them being admitted. Great care, therefore, is to be taken that the misbehaviour of novices do not proceed from want of knowledge and instruction in matters of the spirit; that so it may appear that, if they do not well, it is for want of good will, and not of light. Now it is not to be expected that novices should be perfect; it will suffice that they seriously tend to it by a constant pursuance of internal prayer and abstraction of life.

14. Above all things, therefore, superiors ought to allow to their subjects a competent time daily for their recollections, which is the food of the soul, and to deny which would be a greater tyranny than to refuse corporal food to slaves after their travail. He deserves not the name of a religious man, saith Cajetan, no, nor of a Christian, saith Thaulerus, that doth not every day spend some reasonable space in his interior. St. Bernard would not excuse even Pope Eugenius himself, in the midst of those continually most distractive weighty affairs of the popedom, from this duty; the want whereof is more harmful to the soul than that of corporal food is to the body. For he that fasts one day, besides the present pain he finds, will the next have a better and more eager appetite; but a soul that through neglect is deprived of her daily food of prayer will the next day have a less stomach and disposition to it, and so in time will come willingly and even with pleasure to starve in spirit; and to such neglect and loathing of prayer she will come, if superiors do hinder, or indeed not encourage her to a constant exercise of it.

15. Now this care of superiors must extend itself as well to lay brethren or sisters as those of the choir. For they also have the same obligation to aspire to contemplation; and if the appointed vocal prayers of the Divine Office without the joining of daily recollections will not avail to procure in these the spirit of recollectedness, much less will those short prayers or offices to which the others are obliged.

16. To conclude this point: It concerns most deeply superiors to take care that their subjects live according to their profession and obligation; for if it should be by their fault that they fail, it will be no excuse to the subjects, but a great part of the burden and punishment will light upon superiors. And it were far better they had never come under their direction, but stayed in the world, where, not having the like obligation to the perfection of Christian virtues, their guilt would have been the less. Hence St. Augustine saith that as he never saw better souls than those in religion, so likewise he never saw worse. And the reason is because it argues a most maliciously ill habit of soul when, in the midst of so great light and such helps to piety, spiritual sloth and

tepidity reign. And where tepidity is in religion, although carnal open sins may be avoided, yet the more dangerous sins of the spirit, pride, factiousness, envy, &c., do find occasions of being raised and nourished, perhaps more than in the world. Add hereunto that irreverences and profaning of the sacraments are not so common in the world, where the obligations and commodity of participating are not so frequent. And lastly, which is most considerable, those who in religion are sluggish and indevout do grow continually worse and worse, being more and more hardened by the daily heartless exercise of prayer and tepid communions; for where the sacraments do not produce the good effects for which God gave them, they do occasionally increase hardness of heart and impenitency. Hence, saith Thaulerus, it were better to take into one's body a million of devils, than once to take the Body of our Lord, being in an unfit disposition. And so it is a very extraordinary and almost miraculous thing, if God give the grace of a new conversion to souls that in religion are become habitually tepid and stained with known impurity, for they, being insensible of their soul's good in the midst of all advantages possible to be had, cannot by any change to a better state be amended; and, therefore (it is to be feared), such do generally die in the state wherein they lived. Whereas, in the world, an ill liver may far more probably meet with helps of conversion by change of state, place, &c., or by sickness: whereupon St. Bernard professed that he would not doubt to give a present absolution to the most enormous sinner living in the world, if he would promise to enter into a religious life; but what hopes can be of him that after he has left the world so habitually neglects God? What change, what new occasions, can be afforded to him for his conversion?

Chapter IX. The Duties of Novices

§ 1. Advices to novices.

§§ 2, 3, 4, 5. Of the 'Fervor Novitius.' Why God gives it at the beginning of our conversion; and what use is to be made of it.

§§ 6, 7. How they are to behave themselves after their noviceship.

§ 8. Superiors ought not to employ young religious in distractive employments.

§ 9. How they are to be ordered about their studies.

1. There will be occasion in the following treatises to speak of several special duties of religious persons, as how they are to behave themselves in exterior offices, in sickness, refections, &c. I will therefore content myself

to adjoin here a few directions and cautions, addressed particularly to beginners or novices in religion.

2. Daily experience confirms that which spiritual writers observe, that God in great goodness to souls does usually upon their first conversion bestow upon them a great fervour in divine and religious duties, which, therefore, our holy Father calls *fervorem novitium*. Yea, even naturally the inbred liking that our infirm nature has to all novelty and change causes a more than ordinary pleasure, diligence, and earnestness in any new begun employment.

3. To this purpose there is, in the annals of the Franciscans, related a passage touching a devout brother called Michael Magothi, by which we may learn the ground and intention of Almighty God in bestowing such a fervour. The story is this: There was one of the religious brethren in his convent that observed of himself that, ordinarily when he was in any external employment of study, labour, &c., God did present his soul with His blessing of sweetness and an affection of tender sensible devotion; the which, whensoever he set himself purposely to prayer, forsook him; whereupon he addressed himself to this good brother Michael to demand his counsel; who answered him thus: When you are walking at leisure in the market-place thinking of nothing, there meets you a man with a vessel of wine to sell. He invites you to buy it, much commending the excellency of it; and the better to persuade you, he offers you gratis a small glass of it, to the end that, being delighted with the colour and fragrancy of it, you may be more tempted to buy the whole vessel, which, you must expect, will cost you very dear. Even so our Lord Jesus, whilst your thoughts are wandering upon other matters, either in reading, or hearing a sermon, or working, by a secret inspiration invites you powerfully (instilling a few drops of His sweetness into your heart) to taste how delicious He is. But this is but transitory, being offered, not to satiate or inebriate you, but only to allure you to His service. And therefore, if you expect any more, you must consider it is to be sold, and a dear price paid for it. For spiritual sweetness can be obtained in no other way but by corporal affliction, nor rest but by labour.

4. Good souls, therefore, are often to be exhorted to make good use of this fervour, and to improve it diligently (yet with discretion), thereby to produce in their hearts an unshaken resolution to proceed in the ways of the divine love, notwithstanding any contradiction or pain that may happen. They must not expect that this fervour will be lasting; for, being seated in the inferior grosser part of the soul, it is not of long continuance, since it may easily be altered, even by any change made in the bodily humours, or by external occurrents. So that if it be not well managed, and good use made of it

to fix holy and resolute desires in the spirit (which are more lasting, as not depending on the body or outward things), it is justly to be feared that God will not bestow the like afterward.

5. A noviceship is a golden time for the learning and practising matters of the spirit. In that short space, therefore, a religious person is to raise a stock for his whole future life; so that if a noviceship be negligently and improvidently spent, he will scarce ever have the like opportunity to promote his spiritual good; for after his profession he will, besides liberty, have many more distractions, more freedom of conversation, and more intercourse with the news and affairs abroad. Besides, he will not utterly be out of danger of some offices and employments, for the discharge of which some, perhaps, will suppose him already fit and prepared in spirit.

6. At the going out of the noviceship, the person is to be very careful with whom he converses, so as to become an inward acquaintance, lest, being so tender as he is yet, he happen quickly to be corrupted with the society of negligent tepid companions. For want of this care too often it happens that all the good gotten in a noviceship is clean lost in a short time, since usually things are no other way preserved but by the same means that they were first gotten. Therefore, since it was by prayer and abstraction of life that a novice procured all the little proportion of divine love that he is possessed of, he must expect that it will no other way be preserved. For this reason it is very requisite that the superior should appoint such an one his companion.

7. A soul must consider that it is not a little diligence, nor yet the space of a year or two, that will, ordinarily speaking, suffice to get a habit and stability in mortification and prayer. And, therefore, a young beginner ought to imprint deeply in his heart this most important truth and advice, that his duty is never to abate or slacken, but rather continually to increase in firmness of mind and resolution, to proceed courageously during the whole course of his following life in the internal exercises of spirit. For he is to consider that his noviceship being once ended, he must never expect such advantages thereto afterward, such stillness, such want of interruptions and temptations, such clear light, and such calmness of passions, as he enjoyed before. Therefore, lest by a change of his state from a rigorous solitude and silence to ordinary conversings, and perhaps employments or studies, he should come to endanger a decay in spirit, and so be miserably reduced to his first natural state or worse (for, indeed, worse it will be if such a decay happen), let him be very vigilant and industrious to avoid all things that may hinder him from prosecuting internal prayer, and let him be careful to continue, according to the utmost of his ability, to use all abstraction possible, as if he were still in his noviceship.

8. Indeed, superiors ought to be very careful not to put their young religious into distractive employments or studies, either sooner, or more than can well stand with their spirit, or before they be reasonably well grounded in prayer. For how is it possible for an imperfect beginner, having such hindrances, to make progress in spirit? Whereas, if a good foundation of spiritual prayer were once laid, such a soul, by being applied to his studies or external offices, will suffer no decay; yea, moreover, he will probably profit in studies above the proportion of his natural abilities, by reason that passions which must distract and darken even the natural understanding will be much abated by prayer; and, moreover, he will undertake his studies as a duty and matter of conscience, which will increase his attention and diligence. Yet perhaps, by reason of his abstinence and exercises in spirit, his bodily strength will not be vigorous enough to enable him to support very much study; and if it should prove so, the loss is not great, since the divine love will sufficiently recompense all other wants. So it fared with our holy Father, who, as St. Gregory says, was *sapienter indoctus;* his wisdom consisted in despising all learning which was not helpful or not necessary to his advancement in the divine love, which alone is the true wisdom and learning.

9. Truly, so great harm comes to young religious after a noviceship well spent by being put immediately to schools, and for that purpose dispensed with in a great measure about their monastical duties of prayer, abstraction, silence, &c., that it were very good and fit when persons of tender age come to demand the habit to put them off; and in the first place to inform them well about prayer, and to endeavour to persuade them that before they undertake a religious state they should despatch their course of philosophy and divinity, and during such a course to use as much abstraction and recollection as well they can, for which they will then find more time than if they had been religious, because they shall not be interrupted by the choir and other regular observances. So that if studies be then a hindrance to prayer, how much more would they be so in case they had been religious? Having done all this, then in God's name let them demand the habit. By this means good souls would not be interrupted in their religious course, nor put in danger never again to recover the spirit of prayer. And if, following such directions, they should come to die before the time of taking the habit, they may assure themselves that in God's account they shall be esteemed as religious souls, wholly consecrated unto Him.

Chapter X. Of the Apostolical Mission into England

§§ 1, 2. Of the obligation of the English Benedictines to the Mission. The sublime perfection of that employment.

§§ 3, 4. The care of it belongs only to religious superiors, and not at all to particular religious.

§§ 5, 6, 7, 8, 9, 10, 11. Great danger of seeking that employment, and false pretences to obtain it, &c.

§ 12. How the said charge is to be performed.

1. It will not be amiss to adjoin to this section concerning a religious state certain considerations and advices touching a subject which, though it pertain not to religious persons in general, yet is annexed to our profession in the English congregation of St. Benedict's Order, and that is the Apostolical Mission into England, which all the professed do by a particular vow oblige themselves to undertake whensoever they shall be commanded by superiors.

2. An employment this is of high importance, and most sublime perfection, if duly undertaken and administered. But the care thereof only belongs to superiors; and indeed it is worthy both of their prudence and zeal,—by a right managing whereof they may procure great glory to God, and good to souls miserably misled by infinite and most pernicious errors.

3. But as for particular religious, they are merely to be passive in the business—they are to submit themselves to the undergoing of all the pains, incommodities, and dangers of it, whensoever it shall be imposed on them. But this being only an accessory obligation and capacity, they are not to suppose that when God gives them a vocation to a religious life, this doth make any alteration at all in their essential design, most secure and profitable to their own souls, which is the leading a solitary, devout, and abstracted life, and therein aspiring to contemplation. This only must they aim at, and to this must they order all their thoughts and actions, as if they were all their lives long to be imprisoned in their cloisters. Therefore, neither entering nor afterwards, must they entertain any thoughts or designs about anything that is out of the limits of their convents, in which, forasmuch as concerns themselves, their desire and intention must be to live and die. Particularly they ought to banish out of their minds all meditations and inclinations to go in mission into England. Yea, if they will indeed comply with their essential profession, they must resolve, as much as lies in them, and without offence to God or disobedience to their superiors, to prevent such an employment (of which they cannot without pride think themselves worthy, or able to encounter all the temptations and dangers accompanying it), simply and sincerely confining all their thoughts and affections to that life of solitude, abstraction, and

prayer which they have vowed, and in which their souls will find truest comfort and security.

4. Consequently, neither must they (with an intention to approve unto their superiors their fitness for that charge, thereby, as it were, inviting them to make use of them for it) apply themselves after such a manner to the studies proper for such an employment, as in any measure thereby to hinder or interrupt the reading of such books as are most beneficial to their souls, and much less to hinder their daily serious recollections. In case their superiors (who are only concerned in that business) shall require of them to apply themselves diligently to such studies as may fit them for the mission, they are obliged therein to submit themselves to obedience. Yet even in that case, if they find that much time cannot be spent in them without hurt to their spirit and a neglect or prejudice to their appointed recollections, they ought to acquaint their superiors with their ease, who no doubt will prefer the good and advancement of their souls by solitude, purity of spirit, and internal prayer, before any other considerations whatsover. Yea, they will judge prayer to be a better disposition, and to procure a greater enablement, even for such a calling than study, and will take heed how they send any abroad that for their studies neglect their prayer. For what blessing from God can such hope upon any endeavours of theirs? Is it not more likely that themselves will be perverted, than others by them converted?

5. It cannot easily be imagined how mischievous to many souls the neglect of such advices may be. Some will perhaps have a mind to take the habit for that end and intent principally of going afterward into England. What miserable distractions would such a resolution cause during all the time of their abode in their convent! for all their thoughts, almost all their affections, hopes, and designs will be carried abroad into another country; so that the place of their profession will be esteemed a place of exile to them. And so far will they be from procuring a divine light and grace to enable them for so terrible an employment by the means of prayer, that prayer and solitude will be distasteful to them. Regular observances will be a burden, and anything that may delay their intention, which they say is of converting souls; but, alas! perhaps with the loss, or at least imminent danger, of their own.

6. Nay, some that at the beginning have simply and with a good intention taken the habit, yielding afterward to the spirit of tepidity (which turns their happy solitude into a prison), will look upon the mission as a means to free themselves from their profession, and therefore will not fear to use all means, by friends and solicitations of their superiors, that they may be suffered to quit it and go in mission. God only knows into what dangers and temptations they wilfully thrust themselves, being utterly unprovided of light or grace to resist them. And what other issue can be expected but that God

should give them up to such temptations, unto which (out of a sensual affection to the world, pride, and a weariness of prayer) they have exposed themselves, without any call from Him, yea, contrary to His will?

7. Now it is not only particular religious, but much more superiors, that ought to think themselves concerned most deeply in these matters; for in case such unwary rash souls shall come thus to destroy themselves, they cannot but know that those souls shall be required at their hands. They ought, therefore, to root out of the hearts of their subjects all such pernicious designs, by showing that they esteem them least worthy that are most forward to offer themselves. And great care and wariness ought they to use how they send or permit any to go abroad, before they be sufficiently furnished, not so much with learning as with the spirit of mortification and prayer, and with zeal proceeding from an established charity, that so they may not, by undertaking and executing active employments, prejudice and perhaps ruin their contemplative state.

8. Our examples ought to be our first holy converters of England, who did not undertake such a charge till they were grown old in the exercises of solitude and contemplation; and not then till an absolute command was imposed on them by the Supreme Pastor. And in the execution of their charge, they never suffered their labours and solicitudes to dispense with them for the continuing of their accustomed austerities and the exercise of prayer, but borrowed from their employments as much time as could possibly be allowed, to spend in abstraction, solitude, and contemplation. Yea, though they conversed only with pagans and barbarous souls, yet so zealous were they of their monastical life and profession that they would not so much as quit the habit; and when they were consecrated and exalted to the episcopal function, yet still they retained both the exercises and fashions of monastical contemplative persons, as St. Bede declareth.

9. Moreover, in latter times, experience hath witnessed that some humble and devout, though not so learned, missioners have prospered better in converting souls than the most acute and cunning controvertists, and have by their humility, modesty, and edifying conversation, but especially by the practice and teaching of internal prayer, gained to Catholic unity those souls that many other, most skilful in disputes, and withal enabled with experience, have for long time in vain attempted.

10. Notwithstanding all this, I do not deny but that to a religious soul an impulse and interior invitation may come from God to go into the mission. This is possible; but most certain it is that such an invitation will very rarely, if ever, come but to souls established in a spiritual life. And in this case it will be sufficient for the person to propose the matter humbly and modestly to his superiors; yet withal with an entire resignation, and almost a desire to

be refused. If it be God's will actually to make use of such a religious person in an employment of that nature, He will no doubt facilitate the business, and in His own time incline the will of the superior, without the subject's solicitation, to permit him to go.

11. But whatever pretences are made by others for going into England, whether it be converting of souls, and particularly of some special friends or kindred, or of recovery of bodily health, gaining of temporal commodity to the community, &c., the true motives indeed ordinarily proceed from tepidity; which tepidity ought to be corrected by prayer and perseverance in religious duties, and not further increased and perhaps changed into open libertinage and profaneness by such an exemption from all regularity and order, by which a poor, unprovided, sensual soul will become deeply engaged in the world, exposed to innumerable temptations without spiritual armour, and, as it were, cast headlong into a pit of darkness, and of a forgetfulness of all things that concern a holy religious life.

12. As for their obligations in the discharge of that so terrible employment (when they are once engaged in it), it will suffice to put them in mind that the said charge doth not dispense with the essential obligations that lie upon them as religious. If in their convents they ought to be humble, abstinent, devout, &c., much more ought they, being still religious, but now exposed to innumerable temptations, to increase a vigilance over themselves, to avoid all unnecessary vain conversations, all solicitudes about external things, &c., and to practise all possible abstraction of life, solitude, both external and internal; but especially not to neglect the principal duty of all, which is pure spiritual prayer, which alone can procure security to their own souls and blessings upon others. For surely, if prayer be necessary in a convent, much more is it necessary to such persons living in the world.

THE SECOND TREATISE
OF THE FIRST INSTRUMENT OF PERFECTION VIZ. MORTIFICATION.

THE FIRST SECTION.
OF MORTIFICATION IN GENERAL; AND OF NECESSARY AND VOLUNTARY MORTIFICATIONS.

Chapter I. All Duties Contained in Mortification and Prayer

§§ 1, 2, 3, 4, 5. All the duties of a contemplative life reduced to two heads, viz. 1. Mortification; 2. Prayer. And the grounds of that division.

§ 6. The necessity of each of these.

§ 7. How they do advance each the other.

§§ 8, 9, 10. Of the two, Prayer is the more noble.

1. Having so largely treated of the nature and end of a contemplative life in general, as likewise of the only Divine Master from whom it is to be learned, and the school of solitude in which He gives His directions, order requires that we now treat of the special instructions touching the means or instruments conducing to the obtaining of the supernatural end aspired to by us. Concerning which our discourse will not need to be so diffused, considering the large scope that we have allowed to ourselves in the first general treatise, in which mention also was made of much of that which is to follow.

2. Several mystical authors, each one abounding in his own sense, and raising a frame of spirituality as suited best to his own imagination and design, have made several partitions of the duties of a spiritual life, and it is not a matter much considerable which of them should be preferred. But to the end the best ease and help may be afforded to the devout reader's memory, the division of them shall be the shortest that may be, yet sufficiently and

clearly enough comprehending all necessary duties, namely, under these two heads of—1. Mortification; 2. Prayer.

3. Now to the end that the grounds of the fitness of this division may be better understood, we are to remember that the glorious end of a contemplative life, to wit, union in spirit with God by love, is entirely supernatural and divine, so that it is impossible for man by any natural ability and strength, although he were free from sins, to attain unto it; and much more is this impossible to him in his present state, since he is naturally most averse from it, being wholly possessed and filled with nothing but self-love, propriety, and pride, absolutely inconsistent with such an union. Therefore, the foundation of all our spiritual duties must be a true knowledge—1. of ourselves, our own nothing, our unprofitableness, vileness, and misery, which is to be the object of our aversion and hatred; and 2. of the all-sufficiency, universal being, infinite perfections, and incomprehensible beauty and goodness of God, who is to be the only object of our contemplation and love; and, consequently, upon this knowledge all our endeavours towards this end (being directed by a Divine light and assisted by Divine grace) must be employed, first, in removing those impediments; and next, consequently, in approaching directly to God, an immediate union with whom is aspired to, as the only end of our creation and perfection of our intellective nature. We must renounce and fly from ourselves, that we may draw near unto God; we must destroy self-love in our souls, that so the Divine love may be raised and increased in them. Now, it is by Mortification that self-love and all other our natural deordinations, which hinder a divine union, are removed; and it is by Prayer that we directly tend to a divine union. By the former we exercise all duties and practise all virtues which regard ourselves (for virtues are so far only to be esteemed worthy of that name, inasmuch, and as far as they are mortificatory to our inordinate passions and affections, as humility of pride, patience of anger, temperance of sensual desires, &c.), and prayer (in the notion in which it is here understood) includes all our duties directly pertaining to God, as comprehending all manner of internal actuations and operations of the soul towards God, by the understanding, contemplating, and admiring Him; by the will and affections adoring, obeying, loving, and adhering to Him; and, in a word, the whole soul resigning and submitting itself, and the body also, with all things belonging to each of them, to be disposed according to His divine will, both for time and eternity.

4. This division deserves the rather to be approved, because Hesychius, an ancient illuminated monk, in his treatise *De Puritate Cordis,* hath conformably reduced all spiritual duties to: 1. temperance; 2. and prayer. By temperance understanding the very same that is here meant by mortification; for, as he expresses his meaning, this temperance is a general abstaining from all things that would any way disorder the affections, or obscure the light of

the soul. He calls it likewise *Custodiam Cordis,* a guard or watch set over the heart, forcing it to repel all vain and unprofitable thoughts, which, if they be too freely admitted, do hinder from observing the snares and suggestions of the devil or of our corrupt nature, and do withal disturb the tranquillity of the soul.

5. In those two duties, therefore, of mortification and prayer, all good is comprehended; for by the exercise of mortification those two general most deadly enemies of our souls, self-love and pride, are combated and subdued, to wit, by the means of those two fundamental Christian virtues of divine charity and humility. And prayer, exercised in virtue of these two, will, both by way of impetration obtain, and also with a direct efficiency ingraft, a new divine principle and nature in us, which is the Divine Spirit; which will become a new life unto us, and the very soul of our souls, by degrees raising us higher and higher out of our corrupt nature, till at last we be made one with God, by an union as perfect, constant, and immediate as in this frail life an intellective soul is capable of.

6. And both these duties of mortification and prayer are so absolutely necessary that they must neither of them ever cease, but continually increase in perfection and virtue to the end of our lives. For though self-love and pride may by mortification be subdued, yet as long as we are imprisoned in mortal bodies of flesh and blood, they will never be totally rooted out of us, but that even the most perfect souls will find in themselves matter enough for further mortification. And again, our union with God by prayer can never either be so constant but that it will be interrupted, so as that the soul will fall from her height back some degrees into nature again; nor is there any degree of it so perfect, pure, and spiritual, but that it may, and by exercise will, become yet more and more pure without all limits.

7. The diligent exercise of each of these doth much advance the practice of the other. For as mortification is a good disposition to prayer, yea, so necessary that a sensual immortified soul cannot raise herself up so much as to look to God with any cordial desire to please Him, or to love and be resigned to Him, much less to be perfectly united to Him; so, likewise, by prayer the soul obtains light to discover whatsoever inordinate affections in her are to be mortified, and also strength of spiritual grace actually and effectually to subdue them.

8. Hence it may easily appear that of these two prayer is much the more valuable and noble exercise. 1. Because in prayer of contemplation consists the essential happiness both of this life and that which is to come; so that mortification regards prayer as the means disposing to an end; for, therefore, a devout soul is obliged to mortify her inordinate affections, to the end she may thereby be disposed to a union with God. 2. Because mortifications

are never duly and profitably undergone but only in virtue of prayer. Whereas, possible it may be, that prayer alone may be considerably advanced without any other notable mortifications, in case that God hath provided none for the soul. 3. Because prayer is withal in itself the most excellent and effectual mortification; for in and by it the most secret risings of inordinate passions are contradicted, yea, the mind and superior will are wholly abstracted and elevated above nature, so that for the time all passions are quieted, and all creatures, especially ourselves, transcended, forgotten, and in a sort annihilated.

9. Notwithstanding, in case that God, as He seldom fails, do provide for us occasions of mortification out of prayer, if we be negligent in making good use of them to the promoting of ourselves in spirit, we shall decrease both in grace and prayer; as, on the contrary, by a good use of them we shall both certainly and speedily be advanced in the ways of the Spirit. So that neither of them alone is to be relied on. Mortification without prayer will be but superficial, or, it is to be feared, hypocritical; and prayer, with a neglect of mortification, will be heartless, distracted, and of small virtue.

10. The subject, therefore, of this and the following treatise being a recommendation of these two most necessary and most excellent instruments of contemplation, reason requires that of the two mortification should, in the first place, be treated of, inasmuch as it is not only the less perfect, but because, also, the proper use of it is to dispose and make even and plain the way to the other, by levelling the mountains of pride, raising the valleys of sloth, and smoothing the roughness and inequalities of our passions, but especially by removing out of the way that general impediment, which is propriety of our natural carnal wills.

CHAPTER II. Mortification of an Affection to Venial Sins

§ 1. The mortifications here treated of in particular are not of such sinful deordinations of passions as are acknowledged to be sins, either mortal or venial.

§§ 2, 3, 4, 5, 6, 7, 8. But of such deordinations as are commonly called imperfections, and which may occasion sins.

§ 9. That sin consists in the enjoying of creatures instead of using them.

§§ 10, 11, 12. All venial sins cannot be avoided, but affection to them must.

§§ 13, 14, 15, 16, 17. Wherein such affection consists; and how it is inconsistent with perfection.

SECOND TREATISE – FIRST SECTION

1. Now intending to treat of Mortification, first in general, and afterwards of the special kinds of it, at least such as are more peculiar to internal livers, my design is not to discourse in particular of such deordinations as are generally acknowledged to be in themselves sinful, either mortally or, in a grosser manner, venially; that is, such as that the actions or omissions to which they adhere can in no circumstances be lawful or permitted; although the end or pretended intention of them were never so good. Such as are officious lies, smaller revenges, or calumniations. For it is supposed that the souls for whose benefit these instructions were intended are not in a state to stand in need of advices concerning such matters, but are supposed to be entered into a way of perfection; being desirous—yea, through God's grace resolved—to abandon all things, and to cast away all adhesions and affections whatsoever that are inordinate, not only such as will endanger to kill the soul, but also such as would make it sickly and infirm, or stain the lustre and brightness of it.

2. The objects, therefore, of mortification which I shall chiefly handle, are such defects as though indeed in themselves they be sinful, yet are not acknowledged by all to be so, but are called only imperfections; being such sins as, considering the frailty of our nature, can hardly be avoided, and never totally rooted out; being conversant about objects which we may lawfully and most necessarily use, but the fault is, that we do with some deordination either adhere to or are averted from such objects. In a word, such sins they are that, except when they are more gross, it would be an endless and unprofitable labour to make them matters of confession, although the correcting and abating of them ought to be the object of our daily care.

3. I will endeavour to explain my meaning more fully in this matter, because it is the ground of the whole following discourse. We must know, then, that the duty of a Christian (much more of a soul that aspires to perfection) is to love nothing at all but God, or in order to Him; that is, as a mean and instrument to beget and increase His divine love in our souls. All adhesion to creatures by affection, whether such affection be great or small, is accordingly sinful, more or less; so that, if being deprived of anything or persons whatsoever, or being pained by anything, we find a trouble and sorrow in our minds for the loss or suffering of the thing itself, such trouble, in what degree soever, argues that our affection was sinful, not only because the affection was excessive, but because it was an affection, the object whereof was not God.

4. But yet withal this affection, which I say is unlawful, is not simply such an one as resides and is confined to sensitive nature, for that is impossible to be rooted out; neither is there any fault at all in it, considered as such.

For to Adam in the state of innocency, yea, even to our Lord Himself, many objects were pleasing and delightful to sense: His sight and taste took contentment in pleasurable objects, and there was in nature an aversion from pain, and an earnest desire to prolong natural life; and in all this there was not the least imperfection. The affections to creatures, therefore, which we affirm to be sinful, are such as are seated in the superior soul or rational will, by which the mind and will consider and adhere unto creatures, and knowingly and willingly pursue the attaining and enjoying of them, as if they were the good, not of sense only (for so they are), but of the person, which indeed they are not; for the only good of an intellectual nature is God, who alone is exalted above it; whereas all other creatures are but equal or inferior to it. To the superior will, therefore, all things but God must be indifferent as in and for themselves, and only to be loved as they are serviceable to the spirit. So that if things which are unpleasant, yea, destructive to inferior nature, do yet advance the spirit in her tendence to God, or if by the will and providence of God they are presented to her to suffer, she must with all indifference and resignation accept of them, though sensitive nature do never so much struggle and contradict.

5. A most perfect example hereof is given by our Saviour, which we are obliged, to the utmost of our capacity and enablement, to imitate. Though sensitive nature in Him took contentment in life, and in the actions and functions thereof, and above all things did abhor a dissolution by death, especially such a death accompanied with such inexpressible torments and shame; and though, for our instruction, He voluntarily gave way to inferior nature to express such her innocent inclination and aversion, yet, when the will of His Father opposed itself; and presented Him a cup in the highest degree mortal to nature and all the inclinations thereof, He most willingly, quietly, and cheerfully accepted it, then subduing all reluctances in nature; which reluctances in Him were to the thing itself considered in itself, and not at all to the dictates of the superior soul, the which had so absolute a dominion over sensitive nature that it never opposed itself, or expressed the least unwillingness to conform itself to the dictates of reason, though with its own destruction.

6. Whereas, therefore, there are continually presented to our outward and inward senses infinite objects pleasing and displeasing to them, and that the functions of life, which we are bound to preserve, cannot be exercised without admitting the use of many things delightful to sensitive nature— meats, drinks, recreative conversations, and relaxations of mind, &c.—we are to consider and resolve that none of these things, pleasing to the appetite, are given to be possessed of any affection at all, or fruition, but the mere simple use of them is allowed us for the good of the soul, and the contentment that the appetite naturally takes in them is no further, nor with other

intention to be admitted, than inasmuch as thereby the spirit, or rational will, is, or may be, enabled more cheerfully to pursue its supreme good. And with this end and intention, to admit sometimes with caution and discretion, of moderate comforts and contentments to inferior nature, is not in itself at all unlawful; on the contrary, it is fitting, requisite, and necessary.

7. But withal, considering the most miserable and inexpressible corruption of our nature, the violent adhesion of our appetites to sensually pleasing objects, the uncertain and weak dominion that the superior faculties of the soul have over sensitive nature, it is our duty and obligation, not only to be watchful over the sensitive appetite, that it do not with too much greediness pursue the contentments proper and necessary to it, but also, as much as may be, to abridge the number of them, making as few necessary as may be, and not suffering it to accept all the lawful contentments offered to it, yea, oft to re-strain and contradict the inclinations of it. In a word, to use all the industry we can, not to suffer it to run on blindly before, or without the conduct of reason, to things pleasing to it; and when we perceive it does so, to call it back, however, not to suffer reason to favour it and join with it in its desires, but to reserve all our rational inclinations and affections to God only.

8. For the case with us is far different from that it was with Adam during his state of innocency. For then it was no inconvenience, but rather perhaps a help to him, freely to make use of the pleasures afforded him in paradise. Because, though sensual pleasures were to him, considering the exquisiteness of his temper, far more pleasurable than they can be to us, yet his appetite did not so much as desire or wish the least excess; and his spirit was so replenished with divine love that, by admitting of such innocent satis-factions to nature, it rather increased than diminished or interrupted its fervour in tending to God and expressing its gratitude, love, and obedience to Him; whereas, we find all the contrary effects, and therefore must take a quite contrary course.

9. This is the ground of mortification, so proper and necessary in a spiritual life; and these are the venial sins or imperfections that we are con-tinually to combat against. In this point of distinction, between the using of creatures for the good of the spirit, and the enjoying of creatures for the pleasure of sense, without regard to the soul's good and advancement, lies the difference between the children of God and the children of Belial. Yea, in the degrees of such using or enjoying, between perfect good Christians and imperfect; yea, moreover between those that are perfect in an active, and those in a contemplative state. For wicked men give way deliberately to an habitual enjoying of creatures, without regard to their souls or God, yea, con-trary to His command. And imperfect good Christians have no care to root out of their souls an habitual love to creatures, except it be such a love as

endangers the soul by expelling charity. And lastly, those that are perfect in an active life, for want of a constant state of recollection do not enjoy a sufficient light to discover how in many things of less importance they give way to sense, preventing reason, and enjoying outward contentments without that purity of intention which contemplatives, being far less distracted, do much more frequently and perfectly exercise.

10. Now, having mentioned this diversity of venial sins and imperfections, before I come to speak further of the mortification here intended, I will add some few considerations touching venial sins, with relation to a contemplative state.

11. If it were required to perfection in a contemplative life that a soul should be entirely free from venial defects, it would be impossible to attain unto it, considering the incurable frailty of our nature, the frequency of temptations, and the incapacity which is in a soul to be in a continual actual guard over herself. True it is that, by perseverance in spiritual prayer, accompanied with mortification, such defects become for number more rare, and for quality less considerable; but though prayer and mortification should continue never so long, a soul will find occasion and a necessity to be in continual resistances against her perverse inclinations, and in such combats will sometimes come off with loss.

12. Venial sins, therefore, are not inconsistent with perfection, although they should be committed never so oft out of frailty, subreption, or ignorance. But if they be committed deliberately, advisedly, customarily, and with affection, they render the soul in an incapacity of attaining to perfection in prayer, &c. This is a point of great moment and consideration, and therefore, that we may distinguish aright between sinning out of frailty, surprise, or infirmity, and the sinning out of affection to the objects of venial sins, we must know:

13. First, that those are said to fall into venial sins out of frailty, which commit them only when an occasion or temptation unwillingly presents itself, and then are surprised with a sudden passion, or deprived of sufficient vigilance and reflection, but upon an observation of their fault they presently return to themselves, and find a remorse and self-condemnation for it, and an aversion (at least in their superior will) from such things as hinder their approach unto God; or if this be not done presently, however, in their next recollection such offences, if they be of any moment, will be brought into their minds, and will procure a sorrow, and consequently a pardon for them. But when they are out of such occasions or temptations, they do not give way to a pleasure conceived in the objects of them, and much less do they voluntarily seek or intend such occasions.

14. Those, in the second place, are said to sin venially out of affection, who both before and after such faults do deliberately neglect them, yea, and are so far from avoiding the occasions of them that they do oft procure them; and this out of affection, not to the fault, but to the things which they see do often occasion the fault. Such are those that love curiosity in apparel, delicacy of meats, hearing of vain discourses, and that contrive meetings of jollity, from whence they never escape without incurring many defects. Now such souls may perhaps have remorse for the sins so committed, and mention them with sorrow in confession; but yet such remorse and confession is not from the whole heart, not being sufficient to make them avoid the occasions, when this may be done without much inconvenience or trouble. Yea, they do not sufficiently consider that the very love unto those vanities which occasion greater defects, if it be a deliberate love, is in itself a sin, though no other defects were occasioned by it. Such can make no progress in spiritual prayer; yea, on the contrary, as long as such known voluntary affections, either to the sins or occasions, are not mortified, they do every day decline, and grow more and more indisposed to prayer; which thereby is so distracted, and so full of disquieting remorse, that it is almost impossible to persevere constantly in an exercise so very painful.

15. A hundred imperfections, therefore, though of some more than ordinary moment, are not so contrary to perfection whilst they are incurred by surprise or infirmity, as is an affection retained to the least imperfection, though it be but an unprofitable thought. A well-minded and courageous soul, therefore, at her first entrance into the internal ways of the spirit, must and does in an instant, cut off this deliberate affection to all venial sins and their occasions, with discretion seeking to avoid them; although it may happen, without any great prejudice to her progress, that she may find herself very oft surprised and overcome by many and great faults.

16. Neither ought any soul vainly to flatter herself with a hope of reserving this affection without prejudicing her pretensions to perfection, because one or two examples (almost miraculous) are found of some souls that, notwithstanding such affections, have been visited by God with supernatural favour and exalted to a very sublime prayer, as a late eminent saint writes of her own self. For besides that there was perhaps some excusable ignorance in her of the unlawfulness of such affections, we may say that God was pleased to confer on her such extraordinary favours, not so much for her own sake, but rather for the good of others, inasmuch as she was destined by Him to be the mistress and teacher of true contemplative prayer, then almost unknown to the world.

17. But most certain it is that, according to the ordinary established course of Divine Providence, perfection in prayer is accompanied with a pro-

portionate perfection in mortification. And therefore such souls as, during a voluntary habitual affection to venial sins (as to the objects and occasions of them), do seem to have great lights and profound recollections in prayer, (if the said lights and recollections do not urge and incite them to quit such harmful affection), such ought to suspect that all goes not right with them, but may justly fear that the devil hath some influence into such devotions, so utterly destitute of true mortification.

Chapter III. Absolute Necessity of Mortification

§ 1. Naturally we love ourselves only.

§ 2. Even the best and most composed tempers are deeply guilty of self-love.

§ 3. The benefit of such good dispositions.

§ 4. Self-love and propriety must universally be avoided.

§§ 5, 6. A state of afflictions and crosses alone is secure.

§ 7. What use is to be made of prosperity.

§ 8, 9. The great benefits of mortification.

§ 10. A great courage is necessary to the due practice of mortification.

§§ 11, 12, 13, 14. The advice of some writers to raise passions, to the end afterwards to repress them, is dangerous.

1. Naturally we love and seek nothing but ourselves in all things, whatsoever we love and seek. We are our own last end, referring all things, even supernatural—yea, God Himself—to our own interest and commodity. We seek things pleasing only to our senses, outward or inward, as if the felicity of our souls and persons consisted in sensual pleasures, opinion of honour, profit, or curiosity of knowledge, &c. Therefore there can be no merit in nature, or actions proceeding from nature.

2. Yea, they who naturally have much interior composedness and stillness of passions, and seem not much to be troubled with rebellion in sensuality, and that moreover have in them a kind of natural devotion, yet even these, whatsoever they appear outwardly in show, are full of self-love, which is the principle of all their actions. If they love quietness, it is because nature takes a contentment in it; and their self-love is more abstruse and more deeply seated in the root of the spirit itself; and therefore ofttimes is hard to be cured because not so easily discovered. Neither indeed is there any hope of remedy, till by prayer they get a light to discover the said secret self-love, and grace by mortification to subdue it.

3. It is true such good natural dispositions may be beneficial to souls in two respects especially: 1. in that by means thereof they fall into fewer sins than more passionate impetuous natures do, and consequently do not put so many impediments to grace. But yet it is to be feared, unless they practise prayer and mortification, they will increase in spiritual pride; for certain it is that nature not restrained will, one way or other, grow more and more inordinate. 2. A second benefit is, that such dispositions are better fitted for internal prayer, yea, to the perfectest kind of it, which is prayer of aspirations; so that they may with less labour get out of nature, elevating themselves to God.

4. An absolute necessity, therefore, there is for all souls to mortify nature, and especially to rectify this general depravedness of propriety, by which we are to ourselves our last end, the which is done by the infusion of divine charity, by which ourselves are directed to God as our last end; and a necessary disposition thereto is the mortification of self-love. And thus far all Christians are obliged to mortify themselves, namely to cure the mortally sinful disorders of their souls. A necessity likewise there is (upon supposition of aspiring to perfection) to mortify all deliberate affections to any the least venial defects and deordinations of our souls. This duty of mortification requires of us that, deliberately and customarily, we neither admit into our minds internally vain thoughts, nor outwardly speak or exercise acts of vain love, vain hope, vain fear, or vain sorrow; and all is vain that is not referred to God, or is not done for Him.

5. Mortification tends to subject the body to the spirit, and the spirit to God. And this it does by crossing the inclinations of sense, which are quite contrary to those of the Divine Spirit, which ought to be our chief and only principle; for by such crossing and afflicting of the body, self-love and self-will (the poison of our spirits) are abated, and in time in a sort destroyed; and instead of them, there enter into the soul the Divine love and Divine will, and take possession thereof; and therein consist our perfection and happiness.

6. For this reason the soul is in a far more secure state when crosses and afflictions do exceed worldly contentment and sensual ease; for wonderful seldom it happens that a soul makes any progress in a spiritual course by means of outward prosperity. Some perfect souls may perhaps keep the station in which they are, notwithstanding an easeful, contented, and abounding condition in the world; but it is almost miraculous if they thereby advance themselves in spirit,—so naturally and almost necessarily doth ease of nature nourish self-love, pride, security, a spiritual sloth, and a distaste of spiritual things.

7. Indeed, the only possible way for a soul to make prosperity an occasion of improvement in her, is by a voluntary crossing and diminishing of it; that is, by taking advantage even from thence to mortify nature: as, for

example, in case of riches and honours, by carrying ourselves both exteriorly and interiorly to God and man with more humility and modesty, as if we were not at all in such plenty and eminency; also by suppressing vain joy and complacency in such things, by acknowledging that we are not lords and proprietaries, but only stewards and dispensers of such things, from whom a severe account shall be required for the talents intrusted to us for others' sakes, not our own. So that it is most true that all the security, solidity, and fulness of our souls' good consists in a right use of those things which are contrary and afflicting to our nature.

8. In general, mortification includes the exercise of all virtues; for in every act of virtue we mortify some inordinate passion and inclination of nature or other; so that to attain to perfect mortification is to be possessed of all virtues.

9. The benefit and blessings that come to our souls by exercising of mortification are many and most precious; as, 1. There is thereby avoided that sin which otherwise would have been committed. 2. It causes a degree of purity to the soul. 3. It procures greater grace and spiritual strength. 4. One act of mortification enableth to another; as, on the contrary, by yielding any time to our corrupt nature, we are enfeebled and less able to resist another time. 5. It diminisheth our suffering in purgatory, because so much of suffering is past, and a little pain for the present will countervail and prevent sharp and long pains for the future. 6. It procures internal light by dispelling and calming the unruliness of passions. 7. It produces great peace to the soul, the which is disturbed only by unquiet passions. 8. It helpeth the soul much in her advancement in spiritual prayer and contemplation—the end of all our religious and spiritual exercises. 9. It is of great edification to our brethren and neighbours. 10. It increaseth all these ways our future happiness and glory.

10. The duty of mortification being so absolutely necessary and so infinitely beneficial, and moreover so largely extended as that it reaches to all manner of natural inclinations, insomuch as nothing does an imperfect soul any good, further than it is cross and mortifying to some inordination in her natural inclinations, it follows from hence that a soul that intends to walk in these ways of contemplation had need have a great courage, since her design must be to combat her own self in all manner of things to which she naturally bears an affection. For the maintaining of this courage, therefore, it will behove her both to use much prayer, and oft to think seriously on the blessings accompanying and following the due practice of it; remembering withal that custom will make that tolerable and even pleasant which at first seemed insupportable.

11. More particularly, forasmuch as concerns those that are beginners in an internal course, they are to consider that in such a state their souls are so full of impurities and defects, that scarce in any actions of theirs at all they do intend God purely, no not even in those that they perform with most advice and preparation, and with the greatest calmness of spirit; much less in actions, though substantially good, in which their passions are engaged. Therefore it is best for them during such state of imperfection in all times and occasions, as much as lies in them, wholly to suppress all passions, not suffering them to rise and swell in them, though with an intention by them the better and more fervently to perform their duties and obligation. The reason is because such imperfect souls, being not as yet masters of their passions, cannot prevent them from causing a disorder even in the superior rational faculties also; so that though reason can raise them at pleasure, yet it cannot so calm them again, nor hinder them from pursuing those objects out of motives of corrupt nature, against which they were employed at first upon superior and spiritual motives.

12. I do the more earnestly recommend the practice according to this advice, because I find that some good spiritual authors do counsel a quite contrary proceeding, as a remedy and means to subdue passions. For they would have souls willingly and purposely to raise them in sensitive nature, and when they are come to a certain height, then by the strength of reason and motives of religion to quiet and pacify them again. As for example in case of an injury received, they advise that we should call to mind all the circumstances and aggravations that are apt to kindle indignation and resentment; and as soon as the passion is inflamed, then to suppress it by considerations of the example of our Lord, and His precept of charity to enemies, of the dangerous effects of revenge, and the blessed rewards of patience, &c. The like they say concerning a sensual desire to any object, they would have it represented with all its allurements and charms, so as to move a strong inclination in sensitive nature, and this being done, presently to suppress such inclinations by strong resolutions and by contrary practices. Only they forbid this practice in the passion of sensual impurity, which must not be revived upon any pretence whatsoever.

13. To perfect souls this advice may be proper, who have an established dominion over their passions; but as to the imperfect, if they should conform themselves to it, two great inconveniences could scarce be prevented, viz.: 1. that they would be in danger either to be unwilling or unable to restore peace unto their minds once much disquieted; 2. by an advised and earnest representation of such objects as do raise passions in their minds, they do thereby fix more firmly in the memory the images of them, and by that means do dispose the said images to return at other times against their wills, when perhaps the reasons and motives to repress them will either not

be ready, or the soul in no disposition to make use of them; or if she should be willing it is to be doubted that then such motives will not prove efficacious. Therefore imperfect souls may do best to deal with all passions as they ought with those of impurity, namely, to get the mastery over them by flying from them, and, if they can, forgetting them.

14. Yet this advice of preventing all passions and disturbances in sensitive nature may sometimes cease, when just reason and the necessary care of the good of others shall require that some things be done with eagerness, as it may happen in the case of superiors correcting their subjects, &c.; for then it may be convenient to give some discreet way to passion, without which their reproofs would perhaps have but little effect. Yet even then also care is to be had that they do not thereby prejudice their own internal quiet of mind, and much less endanger to diminish true charity.

Chapter IV. General Rules of Mortification

§ 1. Certain general rules for mortification sufficient for some.

§§ 2, 3. By practice, according to these rules, is exercised: 1. a continual presence of God; 2. a continual thinking on our own nothing.

§§ 4, 5, 6, 7. Mortification is only perfectly exercised in virtue of internal prayer. And why?

§ 8. The difference between the mortification of contemplatives and of active livers.

§ 9. External practices or exercises of virtues not sufficient to cause mortification.

§ 10. How imperfect souls are to practise mortification.

§ 11. God's care in dispensing matters of mortification proportionable to each one's strength.

§ 12. The effect of each act of mortification.

§§ 13, 14. It may happen to an internal liver (in religion) some mortifications may be more difficult than if he had lived a common life in the world.

1. To discreet well-minded souls these three following general directions may be sufficient to instruct them in the duties of mortification, viz.: 1. to do or forbear whatsoever any law, divine or human, shall require of them to do or forbear. And where order has been taken by no such laws, there to follow the supernatural light and motions that God, by the means of prayer, shall afford them; doing or forbearing such things as they find will promote

or hinder them in their spiritual course, without captivating themselves to any particular examples, customs, or instructions. 2. To suffer with the best patience and resignation they can all the crosses and contradictions to self-will which by God's providence shall be sent to or upon them; whether such crosses regard external things, as injuries, disgraces, sickness, loss of friends, or of goods, &c., or internal, as aridities, obscurities, inward distresses, involuntary rising of passions, temptations, &c. All these things must be quietly suffered, whether they proceed immediately from God or from creatures. 3. If anything pleasing to nature be to be done, as in refections, recreations, &c., or anything displeasing to be omitted, to do or omit such things, not because they are agreeable to nature, but because they are conformable to God's will. By a constant and careful observing of these directions, a devout soul may be brought to a good established state of mortification, and yet withal be left in a convenient liberty and ease of mind to go on cheerfully in internal ways.

2. Moreover, if in practice according to these points a well-minded soul will be careful to have at least a virtual intention to the love and glory of God (that is, such an intention as follows in virtue of a precedent actual intention made in prayer, &c.), in so doing she shall perform, after the best and securest way, the exercise of the continual presence of God (so much commended by spiritual authors), and particularly by our holy Father, in the first degree of humility. By the which exercise surely it cannot be intended that a soul should be obliged to have continually an actual remembrance of God; for this, being the same with actual internal prayer, would so much endamage the heads of imperfect souls especially, that they would quickly be disabled from making any progress in spirit.

3. The same practice likewise doth, after the securest manner, supply that other exercise (oft recommended) of a continual thinking of our own nothing; for by conformity to the aforesaid directions, propriety and self-will (by the which alone we would fain seem to be something more than we are or ought to be) are not only in thought, imagination, or desire of mind, but really and effectually abandoned, and the inordinate affections of the soul mortified and annihilated. And it is only for this end that the said exercise is so much magnified. In a word, by such practices, joined with an intention to the glory of God and His divine love, a soul will be very well disposed to the most perfect prayer of contemplation.

4. Such a world there is of conditions and circumstances required to the perfection of every action, both touching the substance, manner, motive, principle, and end thereof, and corrupt nature is so subtle to insinuate her own interests, seeking them in everything we do, and persuading us that we renounce propriety even when we most earnestly intend it, that without an

extraordinary light from God (to be obtained only by spiritual prayer) we cannot discover the inclinations of our own hearts; and the reason why this light can be had only by prayer is, because then alone every the least defect and most secret suggestion hinders our view and contemplation of God and our tendence to Him, and by consequence is easily discernible as being set between our eyes and the sun. Whereas, in our ordinary vocal prayers and external good actions, only greater temptations are able perceptibly to distract us.

5. Those, therefore, that do not pursue internal prayer can only so far mortify their passions that they break not forth into outward expressions or actions. But the evil root remains still alive, causing inward disorders very displeasing to God.

6. As for crosses and adversities which a soul undergoes out of the strength of reason, and not in virtue of divine grace and prayer, the chief effect of them is only to vex and trouble nature, or at most they serve to mortify the superabundant activity and vigour of the internal senses and natural affections, by which means the persons may become more judicious, prudent, and temperate; but they pierce not to the spirit itself, to cause any purity therein, or really to diminish self-love. Moreover, the like crosses, undergone by virtue of such a common grace as ordinary good extroverted Christians do enjoy, though they may be helpful to prevent the mortally poisonous effects of self-love which is in us, yet are far from expelling that secret self-love which lurks in the inmost centre of our souls; so that they may remain grievously full of stains and infirmities, and the divine love feeble and easy to be extinguished, notwithstanding the effects of such crosses.

7. Whereas difficulties undergone by virtue of grace obtained by internal prayer, do, as it were, scour and purify the spirit itself from the rust of inordinate affections, and so do spiritualise all the faculties of the soul, causing it to become a pure spirit, exalted and separated from sensible objects and all adhesion to them, from which all vicious impurity proceeds. This is that division of the soul and spirit mentioned by St. Paul, by which the pure spirit works as a spirit, not obscured nor infected with sensual ends and interests.

8. The way of mortification, therefore, practised by internal contemplative livers is different from that of active, though living in a religious state, and well advanced in active exercises; for these endeavour to mortify their inordinate affections by combating them purposely and directly, to wit, by meditating discursively on the motives afforded by Christian doctrine to oppose them, as a consideration of their deformity, danger, &c.; and also by exercising an act of virtue contrary thereto, so repressing the inordinate passion. Whereas contemplative souls do indirectly, yet far more efficaciously, mortify their passions by transcending them, that is, by elevating and uniting

their spirit to God, with the help of pure intellectual actuations; by this means forgetting and drowning both their sensual desires, yea, all created things, and chiefly themselves in God; so that in a temptation they do not turn themselves towards the object, to the end to resist and contradict it, but by a vigorous act of resignation and love they convert their spirits unto God, scorning even to cast a regard or glance upon creatures that would allure their affections from God, and which cannot be considered, except in God, without leaving some tincture and imperfection in the soul.

9. It is not, therefore, the external practice of virtues, nor much less customary frequent confessions, communions, obediences, austerities, &c., but pure spiritual prayer, and the sublime degrees of it (to wit, aspirations, pure elevations of the will, and other such divine operations), that must be the principal instrument to bring a soul to a state of perfect freedom from exterior and interior immortification; for by such operations only she is enabled to transcend inferior nature, and to live in the quiet, secure, and illuminated region of the spirit.

10. But in the mean time, till a devout soul do attain to such perfection of prayer, she must be content to work according to her present light and enablement, so endeavouring to correct her defects by less perfect exercises, and such as partake of the active way; and she must, with patience and quietness of spirit, bear with her own imperfections as she would with others', expecting God's good time, and endeavouring to hasten the approach of that time by assiduous prayer, by means of which alone she may come to expel those defects which do now so much exercise and trouble her, and also to discover and correct many others which as yet her eyes are too infirm and dim to see.

11. Indeed, the provident care that God generally hath over His children, both perfect and imperfect, is wonderful, being carefully suited to their present state; for He does not usually send to imperfect souls any mortifications but such as are ordinary and proportionable to their infirmity, namely, such as do gall and afflict their sensitive nature, but do not pierce into the quick and centre of the spirit, that remains free to support the other. But as for souls arrived to the state of perfection, or near it, God doth usually provide for them strange inexpressible mortifications, most subtle temptations, privations, and desolations, the which, being worthily undergone, do wonderfully purify the spirit. The former mortifications St. Paul expresses thus: *'There hath no temptation taken you but such as is according to ordinary human nature,'* &c.; but the latter thus: *'Our wrestling is not against flesh and blood* (the usual temptations of God's imperfect children), *but against principalities and powers, against the governors of the darkness of this world, against spiritual wickedness in high places* (or things).'

12. Every act of mortification performed by virtue of internal prayer doth increase in us the grace of God, and dispose us to a more perfect future prayer; as, on the contrary, every act of immortification doth increase in us self-love, and doth make us more indisposed for future internal prayer. Again, prayer enables us for future mortifications, teaching us how to undertake and support them. So that these duties must never be separated. These contain all that an internal liver is obliged to.

13. I will conclude this discourse concerning mortification in gross with one observation, which may serve for a caution to a well-minded soul that lives an internal life to prevent an inconvenience which otherwise might perhaps surprise her. It is this: that it may happen that religious or spiritual persons will find a greater difficulty in mortifying and renouncing some sensual contentments after they have entered into a spiritual course than they formerly found whilst they led an extroverted secular life in the world. Now this happening to them may perhaps suggest either scrupulous or at least disquieting thoughts, as if the change that they have made were not for the better, or as if something (they well know not what) were amiss with them; but if they will well consider of the matter, they will find that this is no strange thing, nor deserving that they should much trouble themselves about it.

14. For the reasons hereof are: 1. Because if such an one had not pursued an internal life, he would have perhaps enabled himself to quit one pleasure by diverting himself from thence to some other, which would have recompensed and satisfied for that loss, taking away the present difficulty; whereas, in a spiritual life, a soul having in resolution abandoned all sensual pleasures, as such, that can be abandoned, she cannot recompense the bitterness found in mortifying one by a deliberate yielding to another, the pleasure felt in enjoying whereof might make her less sensible of the loss of the other. 2. Again, an imperfect soul will judge it necessary for the sustaining of corporal infirmity, and to prevent an uncheerful discontented habit of mind, to allow unto herself some contentments recreative to sense; and therefore, when such are denied her, she will be apt to be impatient, or if she endeavour to contradict and resist such impatience of nature, she will do it more feebly and faintly. 3. Because it is impossible that a soul can live and not take pleasure in something or other that affords contentment either to the sense or the spirit. Now a spiritual person being yet in an imperfect state has but little present sensible pleasure in the exercises proper to his way, except God now and then visit him with sensible devotion, for the chief pleasure that spirituality affords is in hope only, and that without any regard to the body—it regards the spirit alone. Now hope is not so attractive as present sensual contentment is. 4. Besides all this, such a soul, not having yet chased out of the superior faculties all affection to sensual pleasure, and finding for the present

little or nothing but pain in all her exercises, both of mortification and prayer, no marvel if, when pleasure sometimes comes in her way, that she finds difficulty in rejecting it. Indeed, the greatest pain comes not from the particular objects of mortification, but rather from tediousness and irksomeness in being continually in a condition of suffering which she judges must last till her life's end. This is very painful to an imperfect soul; but yet, by a constant practice of mortification and prayer, she will find daily an abatement of this tediousness, and, in the end, the renouncing of all contentments of sense and nature for themselves will become easy and pleasurable to her. 5. Lastly, such a soul is to consider that it is a proof of God's goodness to her to suffer her to feel so much difficulty now, not experienced before, to the end to humble her, and to teach her not at all to rely upon herself, nor to promise herself the least good from her own forces.

Chapter V. Of Mortifications, Voluntary and Necessary

§§ 1, 2, 3, 4, 5. Mortifications divided into: 1. Necessary, and 2. Voluntary. And what each of these is.

§§ 6, 7, 8, 9. Extraordinary or supernumerary mortifications are not to be assumed without great advice. They are seldom allowed in the rule of St. Benedict.

§§ 10, 11. The advice of some, that we should always in everything be crossing our natural inclinations, dangerous.

§§ 12, 13. The inconveniences of extraordinary mortifications unadvisedly assumed.

§§ 14, 15. What extraordinary ones are least dangerous.

§ 16. Signs by which to discern when such are proper and beneficial.

§ 17. Generally speaking there is little need that extraordinary mortifications should be assumed.

1. Having spoken in general of mortification, come we now to the division and kinds of it; and the most general division of mortification is into those which are: 1. necessary; 2. voluntary. This is a division of which we shall have great use through this whole treatise, and therefore it deserves to be explained more distinctly and accurately.

2. First, therefore, within the notion of necessary mortifications are comprehended: 1. not only such crosses and afflictions to nature as we cannot, though we would, avoid, whether they be external or internal, as sickness, want, disgraces, loss of friends, temptations, desolations, &c. (the

which, indeed, are the most proper and beneficial mortifications of all other, as being sent or suffered to come upon us by the most wise and good providence of God for our good); 2. but those also that we do or suffer by virtue of our assumed state of life, either by occasion of any law or human constitution, or by obedience and subjection to our superiors, conversation with our equals, inferiors, &c.; 3. those also that we undertake by the direction of our confessarius or spiritual guide (to whom, notwithstanding, our obedience is but voluntary, being to last only as long as we think good); 4. those works that true discretion requires of us, and which to leave undone, or to do contrary, would be against prudence; 5. likewise, whatsoever it befalls us to suffer from any creature whatsoever, not excepting the devil himself, yea, though it were by our own fault that such things happened to us, or were brought upon us; 6. lastly, those things that we accept willingly of, by virtue of an interior divine impulse, with the approbation of our spiritual father.

3. Secondly, on the other side, voluntary mortifications are such as on our own heads, and without the advice and judgment of those that are acquainted with our interior, we voluntarily assume or impose on ourselves, either because we have seen or read of others that have done the like, and thereupon, without further due consideration of our own state or abilities, we will hope they will advance us as much in the way of perfection: such are the voluntary corporal fasts beyond what the Church or regular observance do require, wearing of haircloth, chains, &c., obstinate silence during the times that the orders of the community do appoint conversations, &c. To these may be added an assuming of the task of saying so many vocal prayers, rosaries, &c.

4. This distinction being premised, the devout reader is to take notice that whatsoever hitherto hath or shall be spoken of the use, end, and benefits of mortification is to be understood and applied only to mortifications of necessity, and not to such as are voluntary; and, moreover, that all these instructions and directions are intended only for such souls (whether religious or others) as are entered (or desirous to enter) into an internal course, tending to contemplation.

5. As touching, therefore, the former sort of necessary mortifications, according to the whole latitude before expressed, a devout soul is to be exhorted (as being her duty and obligation) with all courage and fervour to accept and cheerfully undergo them, considering that, besides the forementioned inestimable benefits attending them, they are of great security, free from all peril of error, indiscretion, or pride.

6. But as for voluntary mortifications (those I mean which are properly such) we have nothing to do with them, yea, moreover, I should never persuade a spiritual disciple to assume any considerable mortifications be-

sides such as attend his present state of life, till he can assure himself that he has a good call to them; that is, till after that having spent a considerable time in internal prayer, he have received light to judge of their fitness for him, and grace or spiritual strength to undertake and pursue them cheerfully, and withal has the approbation of his superior or spiritual director. Yea, though he had a body as strong as Samson, and withal a very good inclination to internal ways, I should hardly be the first proposer, mover, and inciter of him to extraordinary mortifications, unless some special occasion required them for a remedy against any special temptations then assaulting him; in which case they are not indeed to be esteemed extraordinary and voluntary (although supernumerary), but, considering the present state, ordinary and necessary. Yea, and if such an one should ask my counsel about the use of such mortifications, and upon examination I should find it to be doubtful whether it was upon a Divine inspiration that he was moved to desire them, I should take the surer course, that is, to dissuade him from the undertaking of them.

7. It is true we find in reading the lives of saints that most of them have practised them, and many even from their infancy. But this shows that spirits fit for extraordinary mortifications are rarely to be found, being only such as God Himself leads after an extraordinary manner, to make them examples of the power of His grace, to the edification of many, using them for His instruments in great works. As for us, we are not to suppose that God esteems us fit, or intends us for such extraordinary matters. Therefore it may suffice us to undergo such mortifications as God Himself has provided for us, believing Him to know what is best for us and most proportionable.

8. In all our holy Rule there is no provision or order made for such extraordinary or supernumerary mortifications, but only (in the 49th chapter) about diet and in the time of Lent, &c. And then it is forbidden to undertake such without the approbation of the superior, the neglect of which approbation is imputed to rashness. For our holy Father, as he knew the inestimable benefit of mortifications which come from God, and therefore he is exact in requiring conformity to the austerities commanded in the Rule; so, on the other side, was he not ignorant of the great inconveniences that probably attend the undertaking such extraordinary ones by imperfect souls, which are commonly induced thereto merely out of a fancy, humour, or sudden passion; for such are seldom attended with any blessing from God, who neither is obliged nor ordinarily will bestow His grace and spiritual strength for the undergoing of any mortifications but such as are sent by Him, or evidently ordained by His inspiration; and experience witnesses this, because we seldom see souls to persevere in those which they assume by their own free election, and while they perform them it is with little or no purity of intention; hereupon it is that our holy Father expressly declares that the Divine

inspiration and grace is to be acknowledged the root of all religious voluntary austerities, by those words of his (chapter 40), *Quibus donat Deus toleran-tiam abstinentiæ;* that is, To whom God hath given the courage or strength to suffer extraordinary abstinence, adding withal, that such voluntary absti-nences must be offered to God (*cum gaudio Sancti Spiritus*) with joy of the Holy Ghost.

9. Great caution, therefore, is to be used in the reading and making use of instructions and examples found, especially concerning this point, in spiritual books; because otherwise a soul will be in danger to plunge herself into great inconveniences and difficulties; for whilst she does imitate such extraordinary practices, it is to be feared, being yet imperfect, she will enter-tain a proud conceit of herself, and not receiving grace to persevere, she will be apt to draw from thence matter of scrupulosity and dejection, so far as perhaps to become disheartened from further tendence in the ways of the spirit. Yea, such a soul will be liable to contract thereby an obscurity in her understanding (especially if she be unlearned), by which she will become disabled to distinguish necessary mortifications from voluntary.

10. It is a very hard, and to many souls would prove a dangerous, ad-vice, which some spiritual authors give, viz. that a spiritual disciple should in everything that is of itself indifferent (in case that several objects be offered to choice) take that which is most contrary to his natural inclination; as if many several dishes were set before us, to eat only that which we least like, &c., and thus to live in a continual contradiction and crossing of nature.

11. Surely no souls but such as are in a good measure perfect are ca-pable of making good use of such advices, for only such can with facility, discretion, and profit, practise them; as for the less perfect, if they practise them with any willingness, it is to be feared that the true ground is because thereby they do covertly comply with nature some other way, nourishing self-esteem, contempt of others not so courageous, nor affording so great edification, &c.

12. It were folly and inexcusable pride for souls not diligently and faithfully pursuing internal prayer, and not yet perfectly practising patience and resignation in crosses and necessary mortifications sent by God, or at-tending their present condition of life, to attempt the undertaking of those which belong not to them, but are merely devised by themselves; for, want-ing a Divine light, how can they perceive or judge them to be proper for them? And if they be unable to encounter difficulties which are ordinary and necessary, why should they think themselves prepared for extraordinary ones? So that there is nothing which makes these to be supportable, but only that they proceed from self-judgment and self-will, and by consequence are more pleasing than distasteful to nature.

13. The inconveniences attending the indiscreet passionate use of such mortifications are much greater in an internal life tending to contemplation than in an active, because liberty of spirit is much more necessary in the former than in this latter, which liberty is extremely prejudiced by such unnecessary obligations and fetters laid by a soul upon herself.

14. And for this reason the supernumerary mortifications which may prove more useful, and which are least prejudicial to this liberty, are those that least work upon the mind; as corporal labours, not of obligation, are more beneficial than the overmultiplying of voluntary vocal prayers, the practice whereof will probably prejudice the true exercise, not only of internal recollections, but also of such vocal prayers as are of obligation. And of all others, the most beneficial are those that regard *not-doing*, as more silence, more solitude, &c., than a person by regular ordinances is obliged to. Such mortifications as these, if the person use discretion and abstain from imposing on himself an obliging necessity, may sometimes be profitably undertaken by more imperfect souls.

15. I do not, therefore, wholly exclude even imperfect souls from the use of extraordinary mortifications, for such may be God's will that they may undertake them; and upon that supposition most certain it is that they will much hasten their advancement to perfection; as he that runs, if he be able to hold on, will sooner come to his journey's end than he that contents himself with an ordinary travelling pace. But if indiscreetly he will force himself to run beyond his breath and strength, that advantage which he got for a little while will not countervail the loss he sustains afterward.

16. Now the signs and marks by which a soul may inform herself whether the extraordinary mortifications assumed by her do proceed from a safe and good principle, that is, from a Divine motive, and not an impulse of nature and passion, may be these. She may esteem them to come from God: 1. if she bear herself well in the ordinary mortifications of necessity, supporting cheerfully and courageously both the usual austerities of her religious state and also all accidental crosses; 2. in case it be with the advice and approbation of her spiritual director, that is skilful in discerning spirits; 3. if the soul in the continuance of it find a cheerfulness and resoluteness—for if there follow any discontentedness or melancholy, that is a very ill sign; 4. if the occasion of undertaking it was a quiet, constant, internal invitation, and not some sudden humour of passion, remorse, or some fit of sensible devotion, or an ambition to imitate others, &c., especially if the matter of the mortification have any peril in it to corporal health, &c., for then the impulse to undertake it had need be very certain and strong; 5. if by perseverance in it the virtue of humility be increased; 6. lastly, if it dispose the soul to better recollection and to a greater constancy and fervour in prayer.

17. But to conclude this point: there are very few that need complain of want of mortifications, or that are put to a necessity of seeking them. All observances whatsoever, even the least that are practised in religion, or in the submission to a spiritual director, and much more all contradictions, humiliations, and penances, are profitable mortifications. Yea, even the acts of authority practised by superiors, if they be done (not out of nature, or a love of commanding, but) in obedience to the Rule, and with a foresight that God will expect an account concerning them, are such also. And if all these be too little, a faithful pursuance of internal prayer, together with abstraction of life, will sufficiently abate nature, and will, no doubt (generally speaking), be effectual to bring souls to perfection, if they live out their due time; and if not, yet death, finding them in the right way, will bring them to their desired end. And, lastly, such is the care and tenderness of God towards souls that truly and cordially consecrate themselves to Him, that if these mortifications be not sufficient, He will by a special providence procure others, and such as shall be most proper. Yea, a very sublime mystic author confidently protesteth, that rather than such a soul shall receive prejudice by the want of them, God will by a miracle immediately provide them, or by a supernatural light and forcible impulse direct and move her to find them.

Chapter VI. Of Abstraction of Life, and Solitude

§ 1. Of certain sorts of mortification which are more general.
§§ 2, 3, 4. The first is abstraction of life. Wherein it consists, &c.
§§ 5, 6, 7, 8, 9, 10, 11, 12, 13. The second is solitude. Several kinds of solitude. The benefits of it, and the means to procure it. The strictness of St. Benedict's Rule in requiring it. Perfect solitude is only for such as are perfect.

1. After this general distinction of mortifications, before we come to the special kinds regarding the several passions or affections of the soul to be mortified (for indeed the only subject of mortification are our affections, and not any other faculties but only in order to our affections), I will briefly set down more universal and unlimited mortifications, that is, such as regard not any one single passion, but many; yea, either the whole person, or some member that is the instrument of many passions, as the tongue. Such indefinite mortifications are these: 1. abstraction of life; 2. solitude; 3. silence; 4. peace, or tranquillity of mind.

2. First, therefore, for abstraction; the duty thereof consists in this, that we abstain: 1. from intermeddling with things not pertaining to us; and 2.

for such things as belong to us to do, that we do them with a reservedness of our affections, not pouring them out upon them (being due only to God Himself). Yet this does not hinder us from doing our duty with a sufficient attention and care. 3. That we not only relinquish all unnecessary conversations and correspondences, complimental visits, &c., but likewise all engagement of affections in particular friendships. This last is necessary in religious communities, because from such friendships proceed partialities, factions, murmurings, and most dangerous distractions and multiplicity; for the avoiding whereof it is very requisite that the allowed conversations should be performed in common, for from the singling out of persons by two or three in a meeting, will flow personal engagements, designs, divided from the rest of the community, discourses tending to the prejudice of others, &c.

3. The true ground of the necessity of abstraction is this, because the Divine union in spirit (which is the end of an internal liver) cannot be attained without an exclusion of all other inferior strange images and affections; therefore, by the means of abstraction, the soul is obliged to bring herself to as much unity, vacancy, and simplicity as may be. For this end a religious soul leaves the world, and if she practise not abstraction in religion, she does as good as return to that which by profession she has renounced. To this purpose is that sentence of the Wise man: *Sapientia in tempore vacuitatis, et qui minoratur actu, sapientiam percipiet;* that is, 'Wisdom is found in a state of vacancy, and he that diminishes external employments shall attain unto her' (Ecclus. xxxviii. 25).

4. I shall in the next treatise speak more on this subject, especially giving advices how an internal liver may without prejudice to his recollections behave himself in distractive employments and offices imposed on him, and therefore I will say no more here.

5. The next general mortification is solitude, which differs from abstraction only in this, that solitude regards the exterior, as abstraction does the interior; abstraction being an internal solitude of the spirit, and solitude an external abstraction of the person. Abstraction may by fervent souls be practised in the midst of the noise and trouble of the world, preserving themselves from all engagement of their affections in businesses or to persons, and ever remaining free to attend unto God. And on the contrary, some souls, even in the most retired external solitude, do wholly plunge their minds and affections in thoughts and solicitudes about persons and businesses abroad, by continual endless writing and answering letters, giving advices, inquiring after news, &c.; by which means they do more embroil their minds, and are less capable of spiritual conversation with God than many that live in the world, by reason that their retired state keeping them in ignorance and uncer-

tainty about the success of their advices and correspondences, they are in a continual solicitude about anything but their own souls.

6. So that if with external solitude there be not joined internal abstraction and prayer, it is rather a hindrance than an instrument of advancing spiritual perfection. Because such a soul is moreover always at leisure to attend to the object of her solicitudes, and so roots more fixedly all internal deordinations of faction, anger, pride, self-love, &c. Hence we see that factions grow sometimes to a great violence in many retired communities, because of the vacancy there to attend to them, the objects of their passions likewise being, in a manner, continually present before their eyes.

7. There is another, which may be called a philosophical solitude, made use of by religious persons, not with a design the more freely to seek God, but to attend to their studies and the enriching their minds with much knowledge. Indeed, study and reading used with discretion, and if the matters about which study is employed be not such as are apt to puff up the mind with pride, or a forwardness to dispute and maintain topical opinions, &c., may be no inconvenient diversion for a contemplative spirit, especially since that manual labours have been disused; but otherwise an inward affection to curiosity of knowledge is perhaps (*cæteris paribus*) more prejudicial to contemplation, and produces effects more hurtful to the soul, because more deeply rooted in the spirit itself than some sensual affections.

8. The solitude, therefore, here recommended, and which is proper to a religious life, consists in a serious affection to our cell, at all times when conventual duties do not require the contrary; and there admitting no conversation but God's, or no employment but for God. Keep thy cell, saith an ancient holy Father, and thy cell will teach thee all things. A soul that by using at first a little violence shall bring herself to a love of this solitude, and that shall therefore love it because there she may more freely and intimately converse with God, it is incredible what progress she will make in internal ways; whereas, from a neglect of such solitude, nothing proceeds but tepidity, sensual designs, &c.

9. Now to the end that solitude may in the beginning become less tedious and afterwards delightful, religious persons not only may, but ought to, preserve a convenient and discreet liberty of spirit about their employments and entertainments of their minds in private, prudently using a variety in them, changing any one, when it becomes over-burdensome, into another more grateful; sometimes reading, sometimes writing, other times working, often praying; yea, if they shall find it convenient, sometimes remaining for a short space in a kind of cessation from all, both external and internal working, yet ever being at least in a virtual attention and tendence to God, referring all to Him and His glory. For so they can truly say with the Psalmist

(*Fortitudinem meam ad te custodiam*), 'I will reserve my principal strength to be employed for Thee, O my God;' all other employments (not of obligation) are both for the manner and measure to be ordered as shall be most commodious for the spirit, that it may come with cheerfulness and an appetite to the appointed recollections. Suitable hereto is the counsel given by an ancient holy hermit to one of his brethren, demanding to what he should apply himself in times out of prayer; he answered, 'Whatsoever thy mind according to God shall bid thee do, that do thou.' And indeed, after a reasonable time well spent in solitude, by the help of internal prayer, a soul will receive a Divine light, by which she will clearly see what shall be most convenient and proper for her at all times to do.

10. Notwithstanding, this caution is to be used, that if in any employment a soul does find herself carried to it with too much eagerness and affection, she is to qualify such eagerness by forbearing and a while interrupting her present exercise, with a resignation of her will to be quite debarred from it, if such be God's will for her good, and actually referring it to God.

11. It is very remarkable the great and studious care that our holy Father in his Rule takes to recommend solitude, and to show the necessity of it, as likewise to imprint deeply in the minds of his disciples not only a great aversion but even a fear and horror of the world. All things must be provided and executed within doors (*ut non sit necessitas evagandi*), that no necessity may force the religious to be gadding abroad. And in case there should be an unavoidable necessity thereto, prayers are appointed to be made for those that are to go abroad, and the like when they return home; whither, when they come, they are strictly forbidden to tell any news of their journey. All this, as if by only stepping out of their inclosure they were exposed to immediate peril, and that it were not possible to have been in the world without contracting such stains, as that for the washing them away, public prayers of the community were needful. Such was the care expressed by our holy patriarch, who by his own experience had learned the wonderful benefit and extreme necessity of solitude for the attaining to contemplation, according to that of the prophet, by whose mouth God says (Osee ii. 14), *Ducam eam in solitudinem, et loquar ad cor illius;* that is, 'I will lead the devout soul into a solitary place, and there I will speak words of kindness and intimacy to her spirit.' And to the same purpose another prophet saith (Lament. iii. 28), *Sedebit solitarius et tacebit quia levavit se super se:* 'The solitary person will sit still and hold his peace, because he hath raised up his spirit above himself' (and all creatures).

12. Indeed, whatsoever spiritual employment a soul hath, and whensoever she desires to have any conversation with God, solitude is the state

most proper for it, whether it be to bewail her sins, to exercise penance, to meditate on the Holy Scriptures, to prepare herself for any employment, but especially to exercise spiritual prayer freely. Thither most of the ancient saints, yea, many holy bishops, oft retired themselves; because they knew that in solitude God's dwelling was especially fixed; and after a free, immediate, and inexpressible communion with Him there, they returned more enabled and enlightened to discharge the solicitous duties of their callings.

13. But absolute solitude (such as was that of ancient hermits) was never permitted to souls till after a sufficient time spent in the exercise of a cœnobitical life (except to a very few miraculously called thereto out of the world, as St. Anthony, St. Hilarion, our holy Father St. Benedict, &c.); because a wonderful firmness of mind, confidence in God, purity of soul, &c., are requisite to him that without the comfort and assistance of any shall oppose himself single to the devil's assaults, which in such a solitude are more furious; and likewise an unusual measure of spiritual light is needful to such a soul, to enable her to be her own director and disposer in all things.

Chapter VII. Of Silence

§§ 1, 2, 3, 4, 5, 6, 7, 8, 9, 10, 11. The third kind of general mortification is silence; the which is strictly enjoined in St. Benedict's Rule. But in these days cannot so rigorously be observed; and why? The conditions of it.

§§ 12, 13, 14, 15. Of recreations now permitted.

§§ 16, 17, 18. Conditions to be observed in conferences.

§§ 19, 20. Of melancholic dispositions; and how they are to be treated.

1. The third general kind of mortification is silence, which is one of the most profitable mortifications in a spiritual life, preventing a world of inconceivably pernicious damages which the spirit of devotion and recollection receives by the superfluity and intemperance of the tongue: the ordinary subject of unnecessary conversations being murmurings, detraction, at least vain and distractive disputes, professions of friendships, news, &c. *Upon the guard of the tongue* (saith the Wise man) *depends life and death; and whosoever accounts himself religious and refrains not his tongue, that man's religion is vain,* saith St. James; of such infinite importance is the well-ordering of so small a member—and this even in the world, much more therefore in religion.

2. Hereupon our holy Father deals with his disciples as God did with a certain devout and holy monk, to whom He left no power at all to use his tongue but only for prayer in the community, being absolutely dumb on all other occasions and times. For in our holy Rule there seems no permission allowed to particular religious for any voluntary or recreative discourses at any times; no, not to superiors themselves. And for spiritual discourses by way of teaching, those were only allowed to the abbots, or to certain seniors and officers by the abbot's express appointment or leave. And when there happened a necessity that an answer should be given by any of the private religious, they were to deliver it as briefly as was possible—if yea or nay would serve the turn, they must add no more. And it seems answering only was permitted—not asking of questions, except when necessary business required.

3. But in these latter days superiors have conceived themselves obliged to remit much of this rigorous silence, not only permitting, but even appointing set times for recreative conversations and entertainments; therein complying with the indispositions and general infirmity either of our complexions or minds.

4. Now whether it were true real necessity or no that hath caused such dispensations, I will not inquire. But this is certain, that no ancienter than St. Bernard's days, the rigorous silence of the Rule was most exactly observed; yea, even in these our days, and that in communities of women, there is little wanting of the like rigour. And if religious persons had truly good wills to seek God, they would find many things not very difficult, which in their present dispositions seem impossible, both in the point of silence and also of dict, &c.

5. However, this is certain, that much and willing speaking is the effect of tepidity, self-love, and pride. For commonly it flows from an opinion that we can speak well, and consequently out of a desire of gaining estimation from others, by showing our wits and abilities. But such intentions and designs as these the disciple of true humility and spirituality will abhor.

6. It is very requisite for an internal liver, therefore, at least to observe that moderate and qualified silence required in his community, not transgressing either in the appointed places, or at the determinate times in which speaking is forbidden.

7. A young religious person must not without necessity be the first mover or proposer of a discourse, nor ordinarily speak till he be asked, unless it be to propose a question or doubt in a matter of concernment. Yea, this advice may likewise concern the more ancient, unless we do conceive that they are disobliged from humility and necessary abstraction. Indeed, more

perfect souls can, when an occasion of necessary discourse is administered, speak more with incurring fewer and less defects than the imperfect.

8. When prudence and charity require of us to speak, we must be very careful not to make the imperfections of others any part of the matter of our discourse, and especially not the imperfections of those from whom in our natures we seem to have an aversion. And principally we must take heed of speaking or doing anything to breed a dislike between any. Therefore, all secret informings and accusations are most carefully to be avoided, as the ruin of Christian charity in communities.

9. And this concerns superiors as well as others, who ought to be very far from favouring this perniciously officious and uncharitable humour of accusing or informing in any of their religious. Much less ought they to esteem that their authority can extend to the prejudice of brotherly charity, so far as to excuse, or however to oblige, any one to be an accuser or informer against his brethren. A pretence of doing good to their subjects' souls will be alleged by such superiors as are of a curious, inquisitive disposition, and are continually searching into the behaviour of their religious; but little good reformation will ever be wrought by such a humour of jealous curiosity. On the contrary, the effects of it are the breeding of discontents generally in all, and the greatest mischief to the souls of private uncharitable informers.

10. It is more secure for one that is apt to offend in his tongue to be in company with many than of one or two whom he affects. Therefore, particular intimacy and private correspondences between religious is much to be avoided, both for the peace of communities and the good of each private religious person.

11. No words are to be spoken nor action done merely upon the motive of edifying others. And indeed, where recreative conversations are allowed, the most commodious subjects of discourse are purely indifferent things, and such as are neither apt to move passions nor to leave distracting images in the hearers' minds.

12. Upon this occasion I conceive it necessary to add some advices touching religious recreations; the which are not to be concluded fit to be prohibited because we said that the duty of mortification extends itself universally to the whole soul, and that it is to be continued to the end of one's life. On the contrary, not only reason, but the examples of the most perfect among the ancient saints, famous for contemplation, show that it is profitable, yea, at due times necessary. To this purpose seems the story of St. John the Evangelist, the first doctor and example of contemplation, whose custom was to recreate himself with a tame dove; for which, being censured by a hunter that passed by as for an action that was beneath his gravity, and not

beseeming one that professed a continual conversation with God, he defended himself to the conviction of the reprover by showing that as a bow, if it be always bent, would lose its force, so the mind likewise would become utterly incapable of Divine thoughts if no relaxation were allowed to it, considering the infirmity of the body, that cannot always supply fit spirits to actions, especially to such as are so contrary to its inclinations.

13. True it is that in our holy Rule there are extant no orders about conventual recreations, which argues that none were practised in those days. Yea, our holy Father takes a particular care how every hour of the day should be employed in common. Notwithstanding after refection he enjoined the religious to retire each one into his cell, permitting them a convenient time to refresh themselves alone, either with sleep, as the custom was in that warm climate, or otherwise as they found themselves disposed, if they had no inclination to sleep, for no certain employment is then appointed.

14. But because in these latter days our complexions are not supposed able to support so great solitude and attention to the spirit as hath been said, therefore hath superiors allowed and ordained daily certain times for recreative conferences, almost obliging each particular religious person to be present at them and besides, at certain seasons monthly, or as the custom is, they have afforded an addition to the diet.

15. Neither doth this prejudice the duty of continual mortification, which is not to be interpreted in extreme rigour, because then nature, even in the ablest complexions, would be destroyed. And besides, recreations are appointed that mortification may be better and more fervently exercised afterward. Add hereunto that, even in recreation itself, mortification may and ought in some reasonable degree to be discreetly exercised, so as that the mind is not to pour itself forth upon that which is pleasant to nature, but to keep a moderate watchfulness over itself, and to refer the contentment found therein to the good of the spirit.

16. To speak a little, therefore, particularly touching such conferences: decency is in gross to be observed, but it will be difficult to prescribe any set order or manner for the talk, as not to speak unasked, not to exceed such a limitation of words, &c. (to omit many particular cautions which at other times are to be observed). Here some more freedom must be allowed, so it go not too far.

17. Among women there can scarce be any recreation if the tongue be too much stinted. Neither is it to be expected that their talk should be of spiritual matters, both because such talk is far from being recreative, as likewise because none but expert persons ought to discourse of such subjects. Indeed, to make such the subject of ordinary discourse even between the most able experienced persons, either men or women, is not convenient at all,

except some special occasion makes it expedient. For it usually proceeds from pride, or a willingness to interest one's self in the guiding of the consciences of others, and may produce inconvenient effects in both.

18. The matter and conditions of recreative discourse, therefore, may be: 1. That the matter do not particularly refer to the interior of any of the parties; but if it regard a religious state, that it be about less considerable external matters, as ceremonies, customs, &c.; 2. that it may be something that may be apt to cause cheerfulness, though not laughter (which our holy Father would have banished from his communities). Now discourses about such matters are not to be reputed idle words; 3. it were better to talk of the occurrences of former times than of the present, because our holy Father forbids the inquiring or telling of news in the world, for fear lest the hearers, being interested, may become distracted with solicitudes; 4. it must not therefore be of anything that probably will leave in the minds any hurtful images; 5. the hearer is not to suffer the subject of the discourses to enter so deep into his mind as that it should raise any passions there; 6. it must by no means be of anything by which any one present or absent may be prejudiced or contristated, nor indeed afterwards distracted, &c.

19. As touching those that are naturally of melancholic dispositions, they ought to be exceedingly watchful over themselves that they give not way to so pestilent a humour. Nature will incline them to avoid all recreations and diversions, and being very subtle, it will suggest pretences to justify a froward loneliness, and a humour not able to support innocent conversation, as if this were done out of a love to a religious solitude and recollection. But in all likelihood such a perverse solitude is employed in troublesome disquieting imaginations and reveries, far more distracting than any conversations. Therefore they, or rather their superiors, ought to take a special care that such a dangerous humour be not nourished by discontented retirements, at the times when others are conversing together, and that at all other times they should be busied in such kind of employments as should not be apt to nourish solicitude. Such dispositions, if prudently managed, may prove proper for contemplation, because their thoughts being not easily dissipated, they are disposed for recollection. Whereas, on the contrary, the same dispositions, being neglected and suffered to follow the bent of their natures, they will be in danger to fall into terrible extravagances.

20. St. Teresa in her Foundations hath a particular discourse containing excellent advices how melancholic spirits are to be managed, saying that they ought not to be dispensed from mortifications or employments from which they are averse, notwithstanding this frowardness of their humour. Yet withal, that the superior in his carriage towards them ought to make it appear

that all that he imposes so on them proceeds from pure charity, and not any crossness or aversion, &c.

Chapter VIII. Of Tranquillity of Mind

§§ 1, 2, 3. Of the fourth kind of general mortifications, viz. tranquillity of mind.

§§ 4, 5. It may be in the superior soul during the time that there is disquiet in the sensitive.

§§ 6, 7, 8. How peace and tranquillity of soul may be procured.

§§ 9, 10, 11. Of a state of perfect peace; which is the end of a contemplative life.

1. The fourth general mortification is a constant peacefulness and tranquillity of mind, maintaining itself against all disquieting passions of grief, fear, despair, &c.; of which I shall in this place speak briefly, and only in a general manner, being shortly in the following section to treat largely of the chief enemy thereof, which is fear and scrupulosity, where I shall take notice of the special motives or instruments of procuring such peace of mind, and of restoring it when it is lost.

2. Without a reasonable proportion of such tranquillity obtained, a soul will be quite disabled from internal prayer. Therefore she is to use all care to preserve it, and when it is disturbed or lost she must endeavour as soon, and after the best manner she can, to regain it, till she be able to say, 'None shall take my peace from me;' and to use the words of the Psalmist (*Anima mea in manibus meis semper*), 'My soul is always in my hands and disposition, and not captivated by the corrupt passions of nature.'

3. The subject of this peace is the soul according to all its faculties, both knowing and affecting, and both in the superior and spiritual, as also in the inferior and sensitive portion; for not only the affections of the will and passions of sensuality, but also the reason and imagination, may be disturbed; and, therefore, a composedness and calmness is to be procured through all. But yet the ways and means hereto necessary are not the same; neither does it follow that when the inferior faculties are in disorder that the same disorder should be communicated to the superior also. It does not always lie in our power wholly to suppress the instability and obstinacy of the imagination, nor the unruliness of sensuality, which ofttimes do resist our superior reason. But we are always enabled by the ordinary grace of God to keep in repose our superior soul, that is, to hinder it from attending to the suggestions of imagination (which we may reject), or to deny consent or approbation to the motions of sensuality; and this at least it must be our great care to do.

4. Neither ought a well-minded soul to be discouraged or dejected at the contradiction that she finds in sensuality; but resisting it the best she can, she must be resigned and patient with herself, as she would be at the refractory humours of another, till that, by God's blessing, a longer exercise of prayer and mortification do produce a greater subjection of sensual nature to reason and grace. In the mean time she may comfort herself with this assurance, that all merit and demerit lies in the superior will, and not at all in sensuality considered in itself, and as divided from the will.

5. During the conflict between reason and sense, or appetite, there may be a real tranquillity in the superior region of the soul, although the person be not able to discern that there is any such quietness; yea, on the contrary, to fearful natures it will seem that whensoever the sensitive part is disturbed, the spiritual portion doth also partake of its disorders; and this uncertainty, mistake, and fear that a fault has been committed is the ground of much scrupulosity, and by means thereof, of great unquietness indeed, even in the superior soul, to persons that are not well instructed in the nature and subordination of the faculties and operations of the soul.

6. However, a well-minded soul may conclude that there is a calmness in the reason and in the will a refusal to consent to the suggestions of sensuality, even in the midst of the greatest disorders thereof, whilst the combat does not cease, and as long as the outward members, directed by reason and moved by the superior will, do behave themselves otherwise than the unruly appetite would move them. For example, when a person being moved to anger, though he find an unquiet representation in the imagination and a violent heat and motions about the heart, as likewise an aversion in sensitive nature against the person that hath given the provocation, yet, if notwithstanding he refrains himself from breaking forth into words of impatience to which his passion would urge him, and withal contradicts designs of revenge suggested by passion, such an one practising internal prayer and mortification is to esteem himself not to have consented to the motions of corrupt nature, although besides the inward motion of the appetite he could not hinder marks of his passion from appearing in his eyes and the colour of his countenance.

7. When we seek to retain such quietness in the midst of unquietness, we do it by exercising an act of mortification proper to the occasion. Every act whereof doth in some degree abate impetuous nature, disposing us for better and more quiet recollections, which will procure us a clearer light and more efficacious grace to resist sensuality afterwards. As, on the contrary, each act of immortification doth increase in us self-love (the cause and root of all unquietness), and causes a greater obscurity in the soul, indisposing it likewise to prayer.

8. To the end to procure an habitual peacefulness of mind, we must be careful not to do any of our actions (I mean even our actions of duty) with impetuousness and an inward hastiness, but with a composed calmness; for all acts of impetuosity and violence are so far but effects of self-love, and proceed not from the Divine Spirit, which is altogether stillness, serenity, and tranquillity. And let us not suspect that such a calm performance of our duty argues a tepidity and want of fervour. On the contrary, such actions so done are of more virtue and efficacious solidity; for the fervour that is indeed to be desired is not a hasty motion and heat in the inferior nature, but a firm and strong resolution in the will, courageously (yet without violence that is outwardly sensible) breaking through all difficulties and contradictions.

9. All the duties of mortification (and consequently the exercise of all virtues) may be reduced to *custodia cordis,* which is a wary guard of our heart, and it consists in not pouring forth our affections inordinately upon creatures, nor admitting into our souls any inordinate love: it is a chariness over our interior, to keep it in as much quietness as we can. In cases of suffering, it is patience; in occasions of fear and disquiet, it is the practice of resignation. It is in effect abstraction; for it requireth that we restrain ourselves from meddling with what doth not appertain unto us, and in what doth belong to us to do, it requireth a reservedness of our loves and affections for God, to whom they are only due; also, that in speaking, hearing, and seeing, &c., we be wary they carry no inordinate affections into our soul It is in effect solitude; for, though we be in company, yet having such a guard and care over our passions and affections, we are as it were alone. It is a passing over all creatures with a farther tendence to God. It is the practice of love, obedience, humility, and resignation to God; for these virtues we exercise virtually when we reserve ourselves and our affections for God. It is a principal mean to overcome all temptations of what kind soever, for it permits not the temptation to make any entry into the soul, which is kept as the dwelling-place of God and His love. It requireth that we look not after superfluities of meat, drink, clothing, &c., and that we desire not superfluous knowledge of what belongs not to us, nor is necessary for us. It forbids all childish immortified complaints or expostulations, or anything wherein we merely satisfy the inclinations of our corrupt nature. It forbiddeth us to do anything impetuously or with inward anxiety. It is termed an interior silence or an interior peace or concord; and for the better knowledge and practice of it, regard the teaching of the little treatise of the *Quiet of the Soul,* written by Bonilla, of the Order of St. Francis.

10. True peace of mind, when it is in perfection, is the supreme state in an internal life, being a stability in one and the self-same tenor—an immutability, indifference, and insensibility as to ourselves and to all creatures and events, by which the soul transcends all, living in God only, and not being

concerned in any other thing besides. And the root of it is the perfection of Divine charity and the destruction of self-love; for as long as self-love is active in us it carries us to multiplicity, urging us to seek contentment in anything pleasing to nature and all her appetites, which being crossed or not fully satisfied are restless and unquiet. Whereas, Divine love alone reigning unites and concentrates all our thoughts and affections in one only object, which is God, carrying all other affections in that one stream; so that there being no diversity of designs there must necessarily follow perfect unity and peace. This is a state to which the soul aspires in a contemplative life; the gaining of which will deserve and abundantly recompense all the sufferings and tediousness that nature is likely to find in the way.

11. Yet even this state in the most perfect is not absolutely and entirely exempted from all trouble in inferior nature. But such trouble is small and scarce considerable; for notwithstanding it, the superior soul partakes nothing of it, but reigns in that upper region of light and peace, and from thence looks down upon sensuality, either as a thing divided from itself, in whose imperfections and disorders she is nothing concerned, being as it were safe locked up from them in a strong tower, or else she suppresses all such motions in their first breaking out, in virtue of that dominion which, by long practice, she hath gained over them. In such a state of perfect peace (yet without the least contradiction of sensual nature) Adam lived during his innocency. And how far any other mere man hath, or may attain thereto in this life, is not for me to determine.

THE SECOND TREATISE
THE SECOND SECTION

TOUCHING CERTAIN SPECIAL MORTIFICATIONS OF THE
PASSIONS, ETC.

Chapter I. Of Special Mortifications

*§ 1. Mortification properly is not of the senses or cognoscitive faculties, but
of the affections.*

*§§ 2, 3. The special mortifications treated of are: 1. of the principal cardinal
passions; 2. of the affections of the superior will.*

§ 4. The first passion is love.

    1. Intending now consequently to treat of the special kinds of morti-
fications, those especially which are most proper for a religious
contemplative life, I take this as a ground that, though mortifications do regard the whole soul with all the faculties of it (and consequently the whole
person) universally depraved, yet, precisely and exactly speaking, it is only
the affective part of the soul that is immediately mortified, and only in consequence thereto the knowing faculties or organs. For though ignorance be a
defect in the soul, yet we do not say that knowledge or faith is properly a
mortification, though it be a cure of that defect. But an inordinate love to
knowledge unnecessarily, which is curiosity, deserves and is a deordination
proper and fit to be mortified. The like we may say of the outward senses; for
it is not seeing or tasting, &c., that are to be mortified, but the inordinate affections to those objects which delight the eyes or taste, &c. Therefore, my
intention is to distinguish the several sorts of mortification according to the
several passions or affections of the soul, both as to the sensitive and rational
portion of it, and to refer thereto the respective mortifications of the several

senses (without speaking distinctly and separately of them, which would force me to repeat over again the same advices, when I came to treat of the mortification of affections).

2. This, therefore, shall be the order according to which I will treat of the mortification of affections, viz.: In the first place, I will begin with the sensitive portion of the soul, in which there are four principal passions, comprehending all the rest, which are to be mortified, viz.: 1. Love, to which desire and joy have relation, being only a progress of love. Now the object of love being either persons or things, and those either material or spiritual, there are many virtues required to the mortifying (that is, the rectifying) of it, as against the love of riches, poverty; against impure delectations, chastity; against the pleasures of taste, temperance; against excessive (although not unclean) love to persons, friends, &c., the love of God and spiritual things, &c. But my purpose here is only to treat of that universal virtue which is the cure of all inordinate loves, to wit, the love of God, and in Him, and for His sake only, of our brethren; and of purity of intention (which in substance are the same); and because the temptations about taste are such as adhere to the most spiritual persons, daily and unavoidably assaulting them, I will add some instructions about our behaviour in refection; 2. the next passion is Anger. (Some instead hereof do put in Hope; but howsoever, for our present purpose, the passion of anger deserves more to be considered by us, for hope may be referred to desire or love.) Now the remedy or mortification proper against anger is the virtue of patience; 3. the third passion in sensitive nature is Fear; 4. and the fourth is Sorrow. And because it is not needful (as to our present purpose) to divide these two, since among internal livers it is fear that is the most tormenting passion, and that which causes excess of sorrow; therefore the same remedies will serve to cure both; for which purpose I will discourse largely concerning scrupulosity, the causes and remedies of it, &c.

3. In the next place, as to the superior portion of the rational soul (besides the same affections of love, anger, fear, and sorrow, which in the inferior soul are called passions, and having the same objects, &c. are to be comprised in them), there are more particularly two distempers in the will, to wit, pride or self-esteem, the remedy whereof is humility; and next, obstinacy and a violent retaining of liberty, to which the proper remedy opposed is obedience. As for a love of superfluous knowledge or curiosity, enough hath been said touching the mortifying of it, where we treated of the regulating of the studies of religious persons.

4. In this order, therefore, I will now treat of the passions or affections to be mortified, and the manner how to do it by the virtues opposed, beginning with the sensitive passions and so proceeding to the special inordi-

nate affections in the will. First, therefore, of inordinate love either to persons or things, and the remedy of it, which is Divine charity.

Chapter II. Of the Mortification of Love

§ 1. Love is the root of all other passions.

§ 2. The wonderful depravity of our natural love.

§ 3. The only universal remedy is charity or Divine love.

§§ 4, 5, 6, 7. Of the distinction of love into: 1. a love of desire or concupiscence; 2. a love of friendship. The which are never separated.

1. The principle of all our actions, both external and internal, and that which both begets and sets on work all other passions, is only love—that is, an internal complacence and inclination to an object from the goodness or beauty that is believed to be in it; which object, if it be absent, the first effect of love is a desire or tendence to it. But if it be present, then the effect of love is joy, rest, and fruition of it. Not only grief and anger, &c. but even hatred itself is set on work by love; for therefore a person is angry, discontented, or displeased, because something comes in the way, hindering him from what he loves; therefore he labours and works all that he does work. So that, according as love is regulated and placed upon a worthy or unworthy object, so is the whole person disposed, according to that saying of St. Augustine: *Non faciunt bonos vel malos mores, nisi boni vel mali amores;* that is, 'It is only a good or ill love that makes our actions and conditions to be good or ill.'

2. Hence will appear how inexpressibly depraved both our nature and all our actions, outward and inward, must be, since whereas we were created only to love and enjoy God, yet we love and seek nothing but ourselves. Our sensitive affections are carried to nothing but what is pleasing to sensuality; and our spiritual affections to nothing but propriety, liberty, and independence, self-esteem, self-judgment, and self-will, and to those things only that do nourish such depraved affections. By this means we are quite diverted from our last end and felicity: every thought that naturally we think, every word we speak, every action we do, carries us further from God, our only last end and perfection; and, consequently, nothing can we reap from them but increase in misery.

3. Now the only possible remedy for this horrible and universal deordination in us, proceeding from the only root of self-love, is to have a new contrary Divine principle imprinted in our hearts, by which we should be averted from the falsely seeming happiness that self-love promises us in creatures, and converted to our first and only end, which is God; and this can be no other but Divine love or charity shed abroad in our hearts by the Holy

Ghost. This charity is an universal cure of all our disorders, producing the like effects in us with respect to our true end that self-love did to a false end. It raises and employs, when need is, all other passions: anger against our own negligence, ingratitude, &c.; hatred against the devil and sin, that hinder our conversion to God, &c. And it is the root of all our good actions, for giving us an inclination, desire, and tendence to union with God; from thence it is that we regulate and direct all our actions to Him. Hereupon St. Paul ascribes to charity the acts of all other virtues: 'Charity,' saith he, '*is patient, it is kind, long-suffering, it doth nothing unseemly, it rejoiceth in the truth,*' &c.

4. Now to the end we may have a distinct and clear notion of the nature of true charity, which is one and the noblest species of love, we may take notice that in general love regards: 1. either a thing that we desire to be possessed of, or to procure for ourselves, or some other that we love, as pleasure, profit, honour, knowledge, &c.; 2. or else a person, either ourselves or any other, to whom we bear an affection, and to whom we wish any good thing. The former of these two loves is called a love of desire, the latter a love of friendship. The difference between these two is this: that when we love anything distinct from ourselves, or the person of our friend, our love does not rest in the thing, but in the person; for it is not the thing is loved, but only for the person's sake, in whom love is finally terminated, and to whom that thing is loved and sought. So that when we seek pleasure and riches, &c. to ourselves, the love that we bear unto them is indeed self-love, because it is only for our own sakes that we love them, to give satisfaction to our natural desires. Yea, when we love a person only for sensual pleasure's sake and not for virtue, it is ourselves only that we love in such a person, whom we then love not properly as a person but as a thing pleasurable to us. But by a love of friendship we do, at least we profess to, love the person for the person's sake, and to seek therein, not our own good, but only the person's for whose greater good we are willing to neglect our own; yea, sometimes for the person's contentment, safety, &c. to sacrifice our own contentment or may be our life also. Thus far friendship hath been described in ancient and latter times; and charity is by all acknowledged to be a love of friendship to God, and for His sake only to men or ourselves.

5. Indeed, if we narrowly examine the matter we shall find that there neither is nor can be any other true friendship but charity, or the love which we bear to God or for God; and that all other pretended friendships, either among heathens or Christians, are mere sensual self-love. For though in some friendships (as they are called) some have professed so absolute a purity and freedom from self-interest as, for their friends' sake, to neglect not only all temporal respects of riches, honour, pleasure, &c. but also willingly exposed their lives; yet indeed the true motive of all was a sensual love unto themselves; for therefore, for their friends' sake, they made choice of death, rather

than to live deprived of them, because the want of so great a sensual contentment was far more bitter and insupportable to them than the pain of suffering death, which would quickly be finished, whereas the languor and torture of the other would never have ceased till death.

6. But charity is only and in the most strict sense a friendship, because therein all our love is terminated in God only: we love nothing but Him or for Him; yea, we direct the love, not only of all other creatures, but also of ourselves only to Him.

7. Now in what sense it is usually said that our love to God must be a free unconcerned love, renouncing all interest or expectation of reward as a motive thereto, and how this purely free love may, notwithstanding, consist with, yea, be grounded upon, a hope of retribution in heaven, consisting in the vision and fruition of God, see appendix at the end of the last treatise.

Chapter III. The Nature and Acts of Divine Charity

§§ 1, 2. The proper seat of charity is the superior will, not the sensitive affections, though oft in beginners it operates much there.

§§ 3, 4. Several acts or fruits of charity

§§ 5, 6. The securest practice of Divine love is by self-abnegation.

§ 7. Propriety makes and fills hell; and resignation, heaven.

1. The most precious virtue of charity resides not in sensuality; neither is it a painful longing of the soul which causes motions in the heart; yea, though it become such a love as mystics call a languishing love, yet it is not such as sensual loves are used to be, a troublesome unquiet passion. But it is seated in the superior soul, being a quiet but most resolute determination of the superior will to seek God and a perfect union with Him; the which resolution she will not give over for any distractions or occurring difficulties whatsoever. Yea, then, it is oft most excellent and perfect, when the heart or inferior nature receives the least contentment by it; yea, on the contrary, feels the greatest disgusts and desolations. And such a resolution is grounded on a high esteem we have by faith of the infinite perfections of God, and the innumerable obligations laid by Him on us. This makes an inflamed soul to despise all things whatsoever for God, and to tend to Him with a resolution of enjoying Him, though with the loss of pleasure, riches, honour; yea, and the life itself.

2. Yet so generous a love as this is not gotten suddenly. At the first it is very imperfect, and much allayed by self-interest, and seeking contentment

to nature even in the actions done for God; so that were it not that ordinarily during such a state of imperfection God cherishes the soul with sensible comforts and gusts which she feels in the exercise of her love to Him, she would scarce have courage enough to proceed.

3. The acts, effects, and fruits proper to pure charity or Divine friendship are: 1. to be united in affection to God as our chief and only good, with whom in some sort we are one; 2. out of love to Him to take joy in His perfections, congratulating with Him therefore, and exulting that He is adored and glorified by angels and saints; 3. to will and consent to the immutability of those perfections; 4. to desire and, occasions being given, to endeavour that all creatures may love and adore Him—that infidels and sinners may be converted to Him, that so He may reign by love in all; 5. to be sorry for all offences, both our own and others', committed against Him; 6. in pure love to Him to determine faithfully and unchangeably to serve Him; 7. to take joy in all things that please Him; 8. with indifference to accept of all things from His hands, as well things displeasing to our natures as pleasing; 9. to be sorry for all things that are contrary to His holy will; 10. to love all things that belong to Him merely for that reason; 11. for His sake to love all men, yea, even our enemies and persecutors; nay, moreover, to endeavour to express some effects of love more to them than others, as being special instruments of procuring greater good to us than our friends are; 12. to do all the honour we can to Him, and all the service we can to others for His sake; 13. in nothing to seek temporal commodity, but only to please Him; 14. to imitate Him in all His perfections that are imitable, and particularly for His sake to love others with the like freedom of love wherewith He hath loved us, not seeking any commodity to ourself thereby; 15. to endeavour to serve Him the best we can, and yet withal to rejoice that He is served more perfectly by others; 16. to serve and love Him only in the service and love that we show to superiors, equals, or inferiors; 17. to resolve never to accept of any contentment but in Him, nor other happiness but only Him, and therefore not to rest with affection in any of His gifts, but only in Himself; 18. never to set bounds to the measure of our love, but still to endeavour to love Him more and better; 19. to desire to suffer for Him here, being for the present contented with hope only of enjoying for the future; 20. to hate ourselves, our corrupt natures, our insensibleness of His goodness, &c. with a most perfect hatred, never being weary in persecuting and mortifying ourselves; 21. to love Him equally in His commands as in His rewards; 22. to congratulate and take contentment in any act of temporal severity exercised by Him on us; 23. never to cease praying that God would show us the defectiveness of our love, and that He would daily give us grace more and more to increase it both in the degrees of fervour and purity; 24. to transcend in loving Him all thoughts of ourselves and of our own happiness, &c. These are marks, signs, and fruits

of pure charity; but, alas! where shall we find a soul that can show them all? However, we are to aspire to as many of these perfections as may be, and to be resigned in our imperfections, since such is God's permission.

4. Among all the expressions of our love to God, those which are generally the most profitable for us are: 1. to depend with an entire confidence on Him, both as to our temporal subsistence and spiritual progress, not relying on our own cares or endeavours, but casting our care on Him, living a life of faith. 2. To have hearts not only obedient to His commands, but inwardly affected to them, so that though they be never so contrary to our corrupt natures, yet to account the obeying Him to be both our necessary and most delicious meat and drink. 3. To practise a perfect resignation to His will in all occurrences that befall us to suffer. These are secure testimonies of our love, because they do exclude the interests of nature; whereas ofttimes affective love is mingled with natural gusts and complacency.

5. Now though this most secure practice of love by abnegation and annihilation of all propriety and self-will be at the beginning full of difficulty, because all the comfort of nature lies in self-will, yet by custom it will be less uneasy, and in the end delightful. For most certain it is that Christ's yoke, by constant bearing, becomes easy.

6. The smallest act of love and service to God, performed with a perfect self-abnegation, is more acceptable and precious in His eyes, than the working of a thousand miracles or the conversion of nations, if in these there are mixed interests of nature.

7. In a word, the difference between heaven and hell is, that hell is full of nothing but self-love and propriety; whereas there is not the least degree of either in heaven, nor anything but the fulfilling of God's will and seeking of His glory. This is the beatitude of all saints and angels, and no other way do they nor can they love themselves but by loving God only.

Chapter IV. Of Purity of Intention

§§ 1, 2, 3, 4. Of charity, as it is the same with Purity of intention. How God is the only end of all our actions. Of a pure and right intention.

§§ 5, 6, 7, 8, 9. Instructions how to get purity of intention; especially by the means of prayer.

§ 10. The dangerous state of those who do not practise prayer.

§§ 11, 12. Of the exercise of offering our daily actions and sufferings, and how far such an exercise may conduce to purity of intention.

§ 13. Rules prescribed by a late contemplative author not much approved.
§§ 14, 15. Other advices.
§§ 16, 17, 18, 19, 20, 21, 22, 23. Difference of purity of intention in contemplative and active livers, &c.

1. We will now consider charity under another notion, as it is the director of all our actions; and so it is called Purity of intention, by which we do refer all that we do or suffer to the love and glory of God, which is of all other the most necessary condition. For God rewards no deeds but such as are done purely for His sake. So that whatsoever other end we propose which is not subordinate to this makes the action so far unacceptable to Him.

2. I say subordinate, for doubtless there are and must needs be, besides this, other immediate ends and intentions of many of our actions, as the temporal or spiritual good of ourselves or others; but we are not to rest in those inferior ends, but to refer both the actions and them also finally unto God. So our Saviour commanded St. Peter to give tribute-money, lest the Jews should be offended.

3. Whereas, therefore, some spiritual authors do advise us to exclude the thought of all other ends but only God's glory from all our doings; yea, so far as that they would not scarce permit one in praying to mention himself (saying, O that I could love thee, O my God, &c.), we are to suppose their meaning to be that, considering how forward and subtle nature is to intrude itself and its interests in our best actions, even to the exclusion of God (though we pretend otherwise); therefore, being so imperfect as we are, our best course were to study, as much as may be with discretion, to forget ourselves quite, and all other creatures. But surely if we were perfect, we might, without wrong to God, yea, with the increase of our love to Him, cast an eye on all intermediate ends.

4. Harphius makes a difference between a right intention and a pure intention. The former he appropriates to good active livers, who, according to the substance of their actions, and the general purpose of their hearts, do indeed in all things desire to seek God's glory; but yet, for want of the practice of pure spiritual prayer, they mix many undiscovered designs of nature in their good actions, the which do so far abase the value of them. But the intention of perfect contemplative livers he calls a simple or pure intention, because it proceeds from a purified interior.

5. Now for the obtaining of such a pure and simple intention, I will endeavour, according to my small experience and the best light that God has given me, to yield the best information and help I can in the following instructions, the which do properly belong to souls in a contemplative course. And they are to be regarded, and use in particular made of them, only so far

as devout souls shall find them to be proper and profitable for them in particular, and as they are suitable to their Divine calls respectively, which are much more to be regarded than all human instructions.

6. First, therefore, let a well-minded soul that leads an internal life, by reading, conferring, considering, and praying, get to understand the best she can, what the true and perfect love of God is, and wherein it consists.

7. Secondly, this being done, let her (by the grace of God assisting her) seriously purpose with herself (yet so that she do not fetter herself by any vows or obligations), by all the best means she can, to labour for the attaining to the said love of God, and also purely for God's sake and to His glory, and no natural interests of her own, to intend the doing and suffering of all things that she shall afterwards do or suffer.

8. Thirdly, since this love is only to be obtained by the means of prayer and mortification, let her resolve to abide in the prosecution of these, according to the directions here given, to her life's end; not voluntarily resting in any degree of love already attained, but still proceeding further without all limits. And this good resolution let her accordingly with courage put in execution daily, often renewing it when she finds herself to become slack or negligent.

9. Lastly, in the execution of these duties and of all other her employments, she must always have at least a virtual intention of directing them all to God, making Him the final end of all, and oftentimes likewise she must frame an actual intention of the same. Now when God is indeed, and in the true disposition of the soul, the end of her actions, He communicates a supernaturality and a kind of divinity unto them, and unless He be truly the end, they have no merit at all.

10. Now it being certain that only by the practice of internal prayer this purity of intention can be obtained, in what danger are those souls that do wholly neglect it? Neither will a few interrupted occasional offerings of our actions to God be sufficient to procure a stable habit of such purity, without constant set exercises of prayer and mortification. All the virtue that such oblations have is a little to diminish the impurity of those particular actions, but they do not at all (or very inconsiderably) increase or strengthen the habit of Divine love in the soul. The virtue therefore of such acts is to be measured according to the state that the soul is in.

11. If an internal liver do practise such occasional offerings of daily actions, I should advise him: 1. not to multiply such acts too thick one upon the other, so as to endanger to hurt the head, or distract the imagination, or hinder the necessary liberty of spirit; 2. let them not be a hindrance to other more perfect and profitable elevations of the spirit to God, or aspirations, if the soul find herself invited thereto, or if they be relishing to her.

12. It is unquestionable that the offering of our sufferings to God will be far more profitable to the soul than the offering of mere works that have in them little or nothing contrary to our natural inclinations. Yet even that also, without constant prayer, will be of little force.

13. I dare with confidence profess, that the observing of the aforesaid simple directions will be far more available to the procuring purity of intention in most souls, than such a curious examination of our daily works as is prescribed by a late worthy contemplative of our nation, who requires in every work six qualities punctually to be observed, viz.: that it be done—1. actually; 2. only; 3. willingly; 4. assuredly; 5. clearly; 6. speedily for the love and glory of God. And he exacts of a soul carefully to search whether any of these conditions have been wanting, and consequently to be more circumspect in the future,—which surely would be an employment extremely distractive and full of solicitude. Though it may be he himself found much good by such a practice, and was able to do it with simplicity.

14. It is far more easy for an imperfect soul to exercise purity of intention in actions that are of obligation, and done either in order to any law, or any command of superiors, than in those that are left to her own choice; and therefore it would be good for such an one either to have her daily and ordinary employments prescribed to her by her spiritual director, or to ordain them to herself upon good consideration beforehand, yet so as not to prejudice due liberty of spirit.

15. In every recollection the soul doth either directly and expressly, or at least virtually, renew her first fundamental purpose of tending in all her actions, external and internal, to the perfect love of God; and then also she discovereth and correcteth such defects and transgressions of this purpose as have passed out of the times of prayer. Our recollections, therefore, are the fountain and root whence all our future works have their virtue and merit, and in them purity of intention is most perfectly exercised.

16. The doings or sufferings of a contemplative liver, though ofttimes with much repugnance in inferior nature, yet do partake more of purity of intention and merit than the voluntary actions of active livers, or of one that does not constantly pursue internal prayer; albeit the actions of these do seem to be done with greater alacrity and facility, and to the doer seem to proceed purely out of charity, and withal cause great admiration in the eyes of the beholders. The reason is because the actions of the former are done purely out of a Divine inspiration, and also in great simplicity and unity, their regard to God being not hindered by the images accompanying such actions; whereas, active livers immediately contemplate multiplicity—yea, in prayer itself they are not without multiplicity, though they do direct that multiplicity more directly to one than in actions out of prayer.

17. Now since purity of intention consists in regarding God with simplicity, that is, without mixture of images or affections to creatures, it concerns internal livers to use as great care and discretion as may be not to intrude themselves unnecessarily into distractive employments.

18. Even the most perfect souls are apt to have less purity of intention in things grateful to nature than in such things as are mortifying; therefore, in the former they may do well to frame an actual upright intention.

19. The repugnancy that contemplative livers do find ofttimes in the discharge of external employments, proceeds not so much out of any unwillingness to obey, as out of an averseness from leaving their internal solitude and abstraction; yet such repugnancy in inferior nature is easily subdued, at least so far that it shall not be a hindrance to obedience and duty.

20. True purity of intention is best discerned in the beginning of an action; for ordinarily we set upon external works out of a sudden impulse and liking of nature, and afterwards we cozen ourselves with a forced good intention fastened upon them, so thinking that in them we do purely seek the glory of God, and faintly renouncing our interests of nature. It is indeed better to do thus than to continue such actions upon the same motives upon which they were begun. But no actions are perfectly meritorious and pure, but such as have for their first principle a Divine light and impulse, and are continued in virtue of the same.

21. Therefore a certain ancient holy hermit was accustomed before he set upon any work to make a pause for some time, like one whose thoughts were busied about some other matter, and, being asked why he did so, he answered: 'All our actions are in themselves nothing worth; but, like a rough unshapen piece of timber, they have no gracefulness in them, unless we adorn and gild them over with a pure intention, directing them to the love and glory of God; or as one that is to shoot at a mark doth first carefully fix his eye upon it, otherwise he will shoot at random,—so do I fix my eye upon God, who is to be our only mark; and for this reason, before I begin any work, I do seriously offer it to God, begging His assistance.'

22. Active livers had need, in almost all their actions of moment, to frame an actual intention; but not so the contemplative, who are always habitually united to God; for such iterations of actual intention would cause too much distraction to them.

23. To conclude: how difficult and uneasy soever to nature the attaining to purity of intention be, because thereby the very soul of corrupt nature (which is propriety) is rooted out; yet, since it is absolutely necessary

in an internal life, therefore considering God's promise that He never will be wanting to our endeavours, souls of good wills will find it neither impossible nor of so great difficulty as at first it appeared, if they will attempt it with a strong resolution. To quicken and fortify which resolution I will end this discourse with that piercing saying of Harphius: 'O how great and hidden deceits of corrupt nature will appear,' saith he, 'and be discovered' (and consequently be severely punished) 'after this life, for that souls have not here been purified and made deiform in their intentions! God Almighty give us the grace to discover now and reform this perilous and secret self-seeking of nature, to the glory of His Holy Name! Amen.'

Chapter V. The Order and Degrees of Charity to Others

§§ 1, 2. Of the loving of God in ourselves and other creatures; and how the love to ourselves is to be ordered.

§ 3. Even that love which is duty in heathens, &c., is defectuous.

§ 4. We cannot love others truly and meritoriously till we first love God.

§§ 5, 6, 7. All affections not proceeding from charity are to be mortified.

§ 8. All intellectual creatures are the objects of our charity, except the damned souls and devils.

§ 9. Of the order of charity.

§§ 10, 11, 12, 13, 14. Those are most to be loved (even above ourselves) whom God loves most. Yet certain duties proceeding from love, as honour, sustenance, alms, &c., are first to be extended to parents, friends, &c., and especially to ourselves.

§§ 15, 16, 17. Further proofs of this.

§ 18. Whether beauty, &c., may be a motive of love.

§§ 19, 20, 21, 22. Of love extended to enemies. Who are esteemed enemies.

§ 23. Great grace required to practise this duty aright.

§§ 24, 25. Degrees of love to (supposed) enemies, and the fruits thereof.

§ 26. Of a special kind of love called Philadelphia, or love of the fraternity of believing, holy, Christian Catholics.

1. Before we end the subject of Divine love, something is to be said of love to ourselves and our neighbours, in and for God. For as for the love which out of God we bear to ourselves or any others, it is not worth the treating of, as being altogether defectuous and grounded in nature, and the more vehement it is the more defectuous is it.

2. The right ordering, therefore, of our love to ourselves and our brethren consists in this: 1. That the motive of our love must be the Divine will and command. 2. The ground thereof must be the relation in which we stand to God, as capable of the communication of Divine graces and beatitude. 3. The end must be to bring ourselves and others (either by our endeavours, exhortations, &c., or by our prayers) to God, that He may be loved and glorified by us, in the doing of which consist our perfection and happiness. 4. Lastly, the subject of this love must be the superior will especially: as for tenderness of nature, distracting solicitudes, and unquiet images in the mind touching those we love, the best and safest course would be to mortify and diminish them as much as may be, as proceeding from a natural sensual affection, the which, as far as it does not flow from the superior soul, and is not subordinate and directed to the love of God, is defectuous.

3. Hence appears, first, that affections in persons that are strangers from the true faith, are full of defectuousness in all the particular respects before mentioned. For though, for example, the love which children owe to their parents, and the affections mutually due between husbands and wives, &c., be for the substance according to the law of nature and right reason, and consequently so far conformable to the Divine will, so that the want or refusal of such love, and the neglect of the duties and offices required by such relations is a great sin; yet there can be no merit either in such love or the effects of it, by reason that it is neither from the motive of Divine charity nor directed to the glorifying of God by perfect love, from which all merit proceedeth.

4. Secondly, it follows from hence that we can neither meritoriously love ourselves nor our brethren, till first we are firmly rooted in the love of God, because charity to ourselves or others is indeed only love to God by reflection, or the loving of God in things belonging to Him, and which He either loves or may love.

5. Therefore an internal liver ought to mortify all sensual affection to creatures,—I mean all particular friendships and intimacies which are not grounded upon the necessary foundation of the Divine love; and as for such affections as are necessarily due by virtue of some respects and relations that God has put between ourselves and any others, such an one ought, as much as may be, to root them out of the sensual portion of the soul, because there they will cause great distractions and hindrances of our most necessary love to God.

6. A serious care to practise according to this advice is very necessary, especially in religious communities, both for our own good and others'. For besides that sensual friendships grounded on external or sensual respects are most unbeseeming persons that have consecrated themselves only to God,

and infinitely prejudicial to abstraction and recollectedness of mind, and much more if they be between persons of different sexes, such particular intimacies cannot choose but cause partialities, factions, particular designs, &c., to the great disturbance and harm of the community.

7. The least defectuous amongst the grounds of a particular friendship may be the resentment and gratitude for benefits, especially spiritual ones, that have been received. But yet even in this case also we ought to prevent the settling of amity in the sensual part of the soul, and content ourselves with requiting such obligations by our prayers, or by a return of proportionable benefits.

8. Now charity is to be extended to all intellectual creatures, that is, to all angels, and all men whether alive or dead, except only the reprobate angels and damned souls, which are not objects of our charity, inasmuch as they are not capable of enjoying God, which is the ground of charity. And the effects of our charity to the glorified saints and angels must be a congratulation with them for their happiness, and for the love which they bear to God, and which God will eternally bear reciprocally to them. To all Christians dying in the faith of our Lord, and not yet purified, we must testify our charity by praying for them, and doing all other Christian offices of sacrifices, alms, &c., for the assuaging and shortening of their sufferings in purgatory. For all Christians alive, yea, all men, we must pray for graces suitable to their necessities; for conversion to unbelievers or misbelievers, and also all those that are of ill lives; for increase of grace to those that are in a good state, with whom likewise we must rejoice for the mercies of God showed to them, and beg eternal happiness to all. Neither must we rest in mere desiring such blessings to all men (our neighbours), but also upon occasions offered do all we can to procure or effect the things we pray for, by exhortations, reproofs, &c. And if to others, much more must we express all these effects of charity to ourselves. And as for temporal good things (as they are called), we are to desire (and procure), both for ourselves and others, so much of them as God knows shall be best for the advancement of our souls in His love.

9. Notwithstanding, though the same charity ought to be extended to all, yet not in the same order nor degree, but to some more than others, and to some also certain effects of it which are not due to others. Now how to determine this order and degrees, though the disputes of many about it are very intricate, yet if we stand firm to the ground before laid, viz. that only God is to be loved by us in and for Himself, and ourselves with all other creatures only for and in God, it will not be difficult to clear this point sufficiently.

10. It is evident that some effects and expressions of love are due to parents, brethren, &c., which belong not to strangers; and some to superiors which are not proper for inferiors or equals, and much more to husbands and

wives, which are not due to any other,—yet love, generally taken, is due to all. Now our love to creatures being, as I said, only the love of God as reflected or reverberated upon those that belong to Him, this variety of effects of love is according to the various impressions of the Divine perfections in several of His creatures; for besides His graces and beatitude, which are common alike to all (at least of which all are capable), and consequently the objects of our love, God, in the first place (as being His own being, and nearest to Himself), has in a small degree imprinted being in us, the conservation and perfectionating of which being ought to be the first object of our desires and endeavours. Again, God as a creator and cause of being is imperfectly exemplified in our parents; and for that reason our parents, next to ourselves, may challenge our affections, and besides our affections, reverence and gratitude, in providing for their subsistence, as they formerly did for ours (except when public good interposes). Again, God as an universal supreme governor has imprinted the character of His power in superiors, for which, besides love, we owe them obedience and respect, &c.; in the paying of which duties we are not to rest with our minds and affections in any of these, but to pass through them to God, in whom resides that perfection in an infinite plenitude for which we express the said respective offices to several of His creatures, so that it is the universal Creator that we honour in our parents, and the supreme King of kings that we obey in magistrates, &c.

11. But, moreover, we are to consider that though no duty that we perform has any merit but as it proceeds from charity, and is commanded and ordered by it, yet love as love, and the proper effect of love as such, may be separated from these duties, the which are to be paid although we did not inwardly love the persons to whom we pay them. Yea, even in regard of God Himself we may distinguish these things.

12. Although God had no farther relation to us than that we have our being from Him—nay, though we knew not so much—yet if we knew how infinite His power, wisdom, dominion, &c., were, we could not choose but admire His wisdom, tremble at His power, &c.; but these would not produce love in us towards Him, the object of which must be good—that is, such perfections as are amiable and render a subject beautiful or agreeable; and withal there must be a possibility, at least in the imagination, that the person loving may in some sort participate of such perfections. Now in God there being acknowledged all the possible perfections that can compose an inconceivable pulchritude, and, moreover, He having signified His readiness to communicate unto us, by an affective identification or union, all those perfections, if we will approach unto Him by love, so requiting the love which He first bears to us—this is it that makes God properly the object of our love. To which purpose St. John saith that God loved us first, not because we deserved it, but to the end to make us deserve His love, and because we were

179

His creatures, capable of enjoying His perfections and happiness; and we love Him because He loved us first, proposing Himself and His happiness to be enjoyed by love. But because we are not to look upon God as a friend standing upon even terms, but infinitely supereminent and exalted above us, therefore with love we pay most submissive obedience, adoration, humiliation of ourselves, admiration, &c., with regard to His other perfections and relations, which duties are only meritorious because proceeding from love; and they proceed from love because these other perfections are the perfections of a friend, and such as, in all our needs, shall be exercised and employed for our good.

13. Proportionally in creatures those are most to be loved in whom the qualities producing love do most reside, or in regard of which especially we love God and God us—that is, goodness, purity, justice, charity, and the like; or, which is all one, we are by a pure affection of charity (simply considered as charity) to love those most that God loves most, and in whose souls God by His graces, deserving love, doth most perfectly dwell, and which most partake of His happiness. The supreme object, therefore, of our charity among creatures is the most blessed humanity of our Lord, and next thereto His heavenly Virgin Mother, and after them the heavenly Angels and blessed Saints, and on earth the most perfect of God's children.

14. Now though this assertion doth seem to contradict the common opinion that charity is to begin after God with ourselves, and that after ourselves it is to be next extended to those that have the nearest relations of nature, &c., to us, yet indeed it does not; for although the affection of charity simply considered in itself is only to regard God, and for His sake those that have near relation to Him, and are most like Him in the graces properly deserving love, yet several effects of charity, and of other virtues or qualities in us flowing from charity, are in the first place, after God, to be exhibited to ourselves, and afterward to those that God hath placed near to us respectively, according to the degrees of nearness.

15. For charity being an affection rather of the will than the sensitive faculties, seems to be a certain esteem and value set upon persons, and consequently an adhesion of the will and tendence to an internal union of spirit with them. Now questionless this esteem though due to all (inasmuch as all either do or may participate of God's graces and happiness), yet in the highest degree of it it is most due to those that most deserve it, or that are most like unto God. So that to value ourselves or any mortal friends or kindred before the glorified saints would be irrational and unseemly; charity would then be disorderly, contrary to what the Holy Ghost saith (*Ordinavit in me charitatem*), 'He hath fitly and duly ordered charity in me.' True it is that, by reason of self-love and self-interest (which is never wholly rooted out of us

in this life), as likewise of the great dominion that sensitive nature oft takes in our actions, we can hardly prevent or hinder love from showing a greater regard to ourselves and our nearest friends; yet as far as it is an affection of the will, so it may be, yea, in perfect souls it is stronger towards those that are nearest to God.

16. But as for some special offices and duties which in us do or ought to flow from charity, they are to be exhibited according as God hath placed persons in several relations to us. Now it being evident that God hath made us nearest to ourselves, and hath intrusted to every particular person the care of his own soul before all others, therefore every one is obliged to bestow his chief solicitude and endeavours upon the adorning of his own soul, and the directing of it to happiness. As for other men, certain general duties of this nature are upon occasions only to be exhibited towards all. Hence we are generally commanded to exhort, edify, reprove, &c., one another. But these duties are to be the employment and particular charge only of those that God hath called to the care of souls, yet so as that no souls are so strictly intrusted to any one as his own, so that upon no pretence can it be lawful for any one to neglect the care of his own soul. And in the extending of these offices of spiritual (or corporal) charity, reason requires that (other circumstances being equal) we should prefer those that have nearest relation to us, except when strangers do stand in far greater necessity, for they are then to be accounted as nearest to us, and, as it were, committed to our charge.

17. Therefore external works of charity and other offices, though they ought all to be paid out of charity (*honour to whom honour is due, fear to whom fear,* &c.), yet they are not to follow the order of charity, but of proximity; so that in equal necessity we are to prefer our parents, kindred, near neighbours, special friends, in regard of giving alms, &c., before those that may challenge the preference in the affection of pure charity, as being more holy and more beloved of God. It may, notwithstanding, happen that in some cases there may be a doubt how the order of charity is to be observed. But a soul that follows internal prayer will not want a light to direct her. To give particular rules would be tedious and impertinent to the present design; this, therefore, may suffice concerning the order of charity in general.

18. It may be demanded, whether external corporal endowments, as youth, beauty, gracefulness, &c., may be permitted to enter as a motive into the love that we bear to others? I answer that such corporal perfections, being gifts of God, may lawfully, as such, be motives of love, namely, to those that are so perfect as that they can use them as steps to ascend by them to a higher and purer love of God in and for them, who is beauty itself. But as for imperfect and sensual persons, it would be unlawful and a tempting of God to give a free and deliberate scope to their love of others (specially of different

181

sexes), for the regard of beauty, since we know it will powerfully withdraw their affections from God and fix them on creatures after the foulest manner. Therefore the necessary care of ourselves requires that we should not so much as look steadily and fixedly on the temptation of beauty, much less favour the attraction of it.

19. Before we conclude this so necessary a point concerning charity, somewhat is to be said touching the most Christian duty of love to our enemies. True it is that the love of Christ will not permit us to exercise enmity towards any person in the least degree, since charity is to be universally extended to all; but enemies I call those that are in their nature averse from us, or incensed by some provocation, or that are indeed enemies to our holy profession, or that would draw us to sin, &c.

20. As for these latter sort of enemies, they are indeed truly such, and their actions we must abhor, and also with discretion avoid their company; but we must not hate their persons, nor be wanting in any office of charity towards them when occasion is offered.

21. But touching the former sort, of those that (as it is to be hoped), without an utter breach of charity, do in external matters do ill offices to us, or are contrary to our designs, such we ought to esteem as indeed our friends; and, perhaps, if we regard the profit of our souls, we could less spare them than those we call our most officious friends, who do but flatter or nourish self-love in us. It is only as to the feeling of nature that we esteem such to be enemies, but really we are to behave ourselves towards them as God's instruments for our great good; yea, and as far as prudence will permit, we are to judge and believe that they love us, and intend our good in things that they do cross to our nature.

22. Now till we come to a perfect simplicity of thought (which will not be till we approach to a state of perfection), we must be careful neither by words nor deeds to procure them the least harm in any kind; no, not so much as in thought to wish it them. On the contrary, we must love them still, and principally for this, because God loves them and desires their salvation, which (it is to be hoped) He will effectually procure.

23. But to do an office so necessary, yet withal so contrary to the inclinations of corrupt nature, a great measure of grace is requisite, the which is not to be had without answerable efficacious internal prayer seriously pursued; the which, joined with good carriage towards them forth of the times of prayer, will in time abstract the soul from inferior passions and that inordinate self-love which is the root of hatred to such enemies; and Divine love increasing, it will proportionally subdue all other affections to itself, and even compel us to love our enemies for God, according to the most perfect example of our Saviour. And he that thinks to get this necessary love to ene-

mies (or indeed any other Christian virtue) in any considerable perfection without spiritual prayer will find that he will lose his labour.

24. The degrees of our love to (supposed) enemies are such as follows: 1. The first and lowest degree is not to revenge ourselves on them, nor to render evil for evil, by word or deed, in their presence or absence, privily or publicly, &c. (Indeed we ought to behave ourselves with much wariness towards those that in nature we find an averseness from, so as that if we cannot as yet conquer the resentments of nature, we were best to eschew meddling in matters that concern them.) 2. Not to be angry or offended for any ill offices that they may seem to have done us. 3. To forgive them whensoever they crave pardon. 4. To forgive them before they acknowledge their fault or seek to make amends. 5. Not to be contristated at their prosperity, nor deny any offices of charity to them, but to pray for them, to speak well of them, and to do kindnesses to them, to congratulate for any good successes of theirs, and be cordially sorry for their misfortunes, &c. 6. To seek occasions of doing them some special good, yea, and for the procuring of such good, to undergo some discommodity, loss, or prejudice. 7. To take part in their prosperities or adversities as if they were our own. 8. After the example of our Lord, to hazard, and even lay down our lives for their souls' good. 9. To conquer all resentment, even in inferior nature, and in simplicity of soul to judge all their ill offices to be effects of their charity, and not averseness. (Yet I doubt whether even in the most perfect the love to enemies can come to be transfused into inferior nature from the superior soul, as our love immediately to God sometimes may be.) 10. To do all this purely for the love of God. These things we ought to do the best we can, and God will accept of our good-will, though our actions be not so perfect as we would wish they were.

25. By such Christian and charitable behaviour towards our enemies, such a Divine virtue will proceed from our actions, that we shall come to gain them perhaps to be our best friends, yea (which is far more considerable), we shall probably gain them to God, if before they were estranged from Him.

26. To conclude this whole discourse, we are to know that there is a peculiar species of charity, which St. Peter makes the next step to perfection, which he calls *Philadelphiam,* or love of the fraternity, being a certain spiritual affection to all God's children, the which subdues all other inferior regards of nature, and makes our union with them to be purely in God, transcending all other kinds of obligations. And the offices of this virtue are such as cannot be extended to any but such as we know to be truly the servants of God, such as are an inward communion in holy duties of prayer, &c., and a communication of certain charitable offices, which out of an ardent love to

God we desire to express to Him, by a choice that we make of His special friends, as it were in them endeavouring to oblige Him after a more than ordinary manner.

Chapter VI. Of Temperance in Refection

§ 1. Of the mortification of sensual love to meats, &c., by temperance in refection.

§§ 2, 3. This is a lasting continual temptation even to the most perfect, and therefore to be especially regarded.

§ 4. Defects in refection which are to be avoided.

§ 5. Of disaffection to sensual pleasures to be aspired to.

§ 6. Feasting to be avoided.

§ 7, 8, 9. Inconveniences inseparably attending refection. Yet are we not therefore to abridge ourselves of a necessary measure of sustenance.

§§ 10, 11. Advices touching care to be had in refection.

§ 12. The body to be esteemed an enemy.

§ 13. In what case, and how, we may seek more delicate meats, &c.

§ 14. Certain benefits to the soul by refection.

§ 15. The subtlety of temptations in refection.

§ 16. Perfect souls have an aversion from necessary pleasures and refections.

§§ 17, 18. A sublime kind of mortification exercised by certain holy persons.

§ 19. Of attention to reading at refections.

§ 20. Of Physic.

§§ 21, 22, 23, 24, 25. Advices touching sleep.

    1. The love of God is a sufficient and most efficacious universal remedy against all other inordinate affections; and therefore I should have contented myself with that one general mortification of the passion of sensual love, were it not that the matter of corporal refection and pleasure felt in meats and drinks has something in it very considerable in a spiritual life, and therefore requires particular advices about it: 1. Because it is a temptation which unavoidably accompanies us through our whole life, forasmuch as the occasion of it, to wit, food, is absolutely necessary. 2. There is scarce any temptation more subtle, for it doth so cloak itself under the title of necessity that even the most perfect souls which have abandoned all other occasions,

yet being imprisoned in bodies that need daily refection, are continually exposed to this, and oft surprised and in some measure overcome by it, not being able to distinguish excess from necessity. Hence St. Augustine in his Confessions (lib. 10, c. 13) most elegantly yet passionately complains of it, describing the subtleness and importunateness of this temptation, which passage being commonly known and obvious it is not necessary to set down in this place.

2. The natural appetite desires food merely for the sustaining of nature. The sensual merely for pleasure, not considering benefit either to soul or body, nor regarding the seasonableness of the time nor any other due circumstance; but the rational appetite or will directed by grace, though it cannot hinder sensuality from taking pleasure in food, &c., yet desires and receives it out of a necessary care of supporting the body for the good of the soul according to the will and pleasure of God, and this in such order, measure, &c., as reason judgeth fit, and not as sensuality would have it. So that if the rational part give way to the inordinate desires of sensuality so far there is a fault committed, the which is not to be imputed to sensuality, but to the superior soul, whose office it is to restrain and bridle sense.

3. This temptation, as it is the last that is perfectly overcome, so it is the first that is to be combated against. For there is no virtue had (saith Cassian) till a soul come to have some degree of mastery over herself in the point of gluttony. And the main mischief of the temptation is prevented, when we are come to cast off the habitual affection to eating and drinking, especially to feasting, the which brings many inconveniences to an internal liver, as: 1. loss of time; 2. peril of intemperance and other misbehaviour; 3. hurtful distractions; 4. indisposition to prayer; 5. intemperance likewise in another use of the tongue, to wit, talking, &c.

4. Imperfect souls, therefore, must make it their care in refections to avoid these special defects, to wit, eating or drinking: 1. too much; 2. with too great earnestness; 3. too hastily, preventing the due times; 4. delicately; 5. with precedent studiousness to provide pleasing meats, &c. In respect of the two first qualities or defects, such souls may happen to offend who yet in a good measure have attained to a spiritual disesteem and neglect of those things that please sensuality; for they on occasions may be tempted to eat with some excess and ardour. But rarely do such offend in the following qualities.

5. Now the marks by which a soul may discern whether she have in her a disaffection to sensual pleasures are: 1. if her chief delight and esteem be in exercises of the spirit, and that she diligently pursues them; 2. if she seeks not after nor willingly admits extraordinary feastings; 3. if being alone she does not entertain herself with the thought of such things, nor talks of

them with gust; 4. if when she is forced to take refections she takes them as of necessity and duty; 5. if she could be content, so that God's will were such, to be deprived of all things that might please taste, &c.

6. In case that necessary civility shall oblige a spiritual person to be present at a feast, he may do well to be watchful over himself at the beginning. And this he may the more easily do because then others being more eager to their meat will less mark him. And to entertain the time, which is ordinarily long, let him choose such meats as are the lightest and of the easiest digestion; for so doing he may both seem to avoid singularity in abstaining more than others, and yet in effect eat far less. In a word, let him go thither with a mind and affection to abstinence, and retain such affection.

7. This one unavoidable misery there is in eating and drinking, how temperately soever, that a soul, for such a time and for some space afterwards, is forced to descend from that height of spirit that she had attained to by virtue of her precedent recollection. So that if before she had a sight and experimental perception that God was all, and herself nothing, she will afterwards have no other sight of this but her ordinary sight of faith, by reason that her spirits are more active, and her internal senses filled with images and vapours.

8. Yet a soul is not to abridge herself of a necessary quantity in refection, for her prayers' sake, or other internal exercises, for that would for a long time after do more harm to the spirit by too much enfeebling the body. Neither is she to judge that she has offended by excess, because she finds a heaviness, and perhaps some indigestion, for some space after refection; for this may proceed from that debility of complexion which ordinarily attends a spiritual life, since, as St. Hildegarde saith, the love of God doth not usually dwell in robust bodies.

9. It is not our petty failings through frailty or ignorance, and much less our supposed failings (judged so by our scrupulosity), that can cause God to be averted from us, or that will hinder our union with Him. For, for such defects we shall be atoned with God in our next recollections, or, it may be, sooner. But those are indeed prejudicial defects which proceed from a settled affection to sensual objects.

10. To correct the vice of eagerness in eating, Abbot Isacius advised his monks that when they stretched forth their hands for the receiving of their meat or drink, they should do it with a certain mental unwillingness.

11. Let every one content himself with what God by superiors provides for him, accounting that, how mean or coarse soever, to be the very best for him, and not that which cannot be procured without solicitude and impatience. Neither ought any to justify or excuse his impatience, out of an opinion of obligation that every one has to take care of the body for the ser-

vice of the spirit; for the spirit is far more endamaged by such impatience and solicitude than anything they can desire for the body can do it good.

12. We have small reason to love the body, for it is that which one way or other is the cause of almost all the sins which the soul commits. To cherish, therefore, and satisfy its inordinate desires, is to make provision for sin, as if our natural corruption did not sufficiently incline us thereto.

13. The infirmity of our body may sometimes require not only healthy but also well-tasting meats, not for the satisfying of our sensuality, but the upholding of our strength, as St. Augustine saith. In which case meats of good relish, even as such, may be sought for, yea, ought to be so, and this for the recreating and comforting of nature; and such corporal consolation may also have a good effect upon the spirit. But where no such necessity is, to seek for such meats is against the rules of religious temperance. And even during such necessity, to seek them either with solicitude or so as may be prejudicial to the community is contrary to religious poverty and resignation.

14. As many defects and hindrances to spiritual progress do flow by occasions of refection, so, on the contrary, to well-minded souls it may be the occasion of some advantages for their progress in spirit. For: 1. It obliges a soul to watch and pray that she be not overcome by the temptation. 2. It may give occasion for the exercise of patience in case of the want of things contentful to nature, as likewise of temperance in the use of them. 3. The experience of our frequent excesses beyond true necessity may afford great matter for the exercise of humility. 4. By the means of refection there are given to souls certain pausings and diversions from spiritual workings, necessary to enable them (making good use thereof) to work afterwards more vigorously and intensely.

15. *Vix perfectus discernit*, &c., saith St. Gregory. A perfect soul doth scarce discern the secret temptations and subtle subreption of sensuality, urging souls to take more than necessity or obedience requires; and the only light necessary for such discerning comes from internal prayer. And, moreover, till the soul by prayer be raised above sensuality, she cannot have strength enough to resist all the inordinate desires thereof which she doth discern. And when souls are arrived to perfect prayer of contemplation they oppose such desires rather by neglecting and forgetting the body than by direct combats against the appetites of it. And only from the decay and ignorance of such prayer hath it proceeded, that spiritual directors have been forced to multiply such and so many nice observances about diet and other duties of our Rule; all which, notwithstanding, without prayer have but small effect to produce solid virtues in the soul.

16. A soul perfectly spiritualised, if she might have her wish, would willingly be freed, not only from all pleasures taken in refections (consider-

ing the daily temptations to excess), but even from the necessity of them, being forced to cry out with David (*De necessitatibus meis erue me, Domine*), 'O Lord, free me from these my corporal necessities;' for were it not for them she might always, like an angel, be in continual contemplation, and enjoy a never-failing internal light, the which is obscured by the fumes raised even by the most temperate refections, by which also passions are in some degree quickened. Such souls may indeed properly be said to have a disaffection to refection. And the best way besides and out of prayer to beget such disaffection, and to prevent the harms that may come from any corporal necessities, will be, not only to practise the mortifying of sensual contentment in going to the refectory, but, upon serious consideration of the temptations there to be found, to go with a kind of unwillingness and fear.

17. A most noble kind of mortification in refection is that mentioned by Harphius of a certain holy brother of the order of St. Francis, called Rogerius, who, by means of elevating the powers of his soul, and suspending them in God during refection, lost all perception of taste in eating; and when he found himself unable so to elevate his soul, he would for so long forbear to eat of anything that might afford any gust. But this practice belongs only to the perfect; it may prove prejudicial and dangerous to the ordinary sort of less perfect souls, or any that have not an especial and certain inspiration to imitate it.

18. The like may be said of the manner of mortification practised by some of the ancient hermits, who used to mix a few dops of oil (esteemed by them a great delicacy) with their vinegar, to the end thereby to provoke the appetite to desire more, the which they denied to it. Or of another who, having received a bunch of grapes, ravenously devoured them, partly to make the gustful pleasure so much the shorter, and partly (as he said) to cozen the devil, to whom he desired to appear a glutton.

19. A soul that practises internal prayer may content herself with a moderate attention to what is read during refection. And the like may be said of that part of the office which in some communities is said immediately after dinner. Because too earnest an attention and recollectedness at such such times would prejudice the head and stomach. A soul, therefore, may esteem this to be as a time of desolation, as indeed there is some resemblance.

20. Concerning the use of physic, and cautions to be used about it, some instructions shall be given in the last treatise, where we come to speak how a soul is to behave herself in regard of her prayer during sickness.

21. Lastly, the matter of sleep is not unworthy the care of a spiritual person. For certain it is that a full repast doth not so much plunge a soul in sensuality, nor so indispose her for spiritual exercises, as a long and profound

sleep; from whence even a perfect soul will not be able to raise herself into exercises of the spirit without much difficulty and long striving.

22. And on these grounds, doubtless, it was that the midnight office was appointed, to the end to interrupt sleep; yea, anciently the three nocturns were therefore divided, namely, to prevent the immersing of souls in sensual nature.

23. For imperfect souls, it may be very prejudicial for them to be deprived of a convenient measure of sleep, yet it is very fitting it should be interrupted. It is likewise good for them to go to bed with an affection and desire to be early up, for such an affection will cause their sleep to be mixed with a little solicitude, which will dispose them both to wake sooner and to rise with less unwillingness.

24. In case that one being in bed cannot sleep, it is very dangerous to continue in a state of mere negligence and idleness, because then not only vain but very hurtful and pernicious thoughts will be apt to pass into the mind. For a prevention or remedy against which, I should by no means advise one to betake himself to any seriously-recollected thoughts or exercises of devotion, for that would quite hinder sleep for the future and spoil the next day's recollections. (The like I say of the time immediately going before bedtime.) But in case they be simply vain thoughts that then wander unsettled in his mind, let him not willingly pursue them, but rather neglect them. Whereas, if they be sinful imaginations, let him, as well as he can, divert quietly his mind from them, and now and then without much force lift up his mind unto God, or use some familiar prayers, or say the beads without much forced attention; yet more attention is required against sinful than vain thoughts.

25. As for perfect souls, their prayer in such a case will less hinder sleep, by reason it is both so pure and so facile that it is become almost as natural as breathing, and performed without any agitation of the spirits, or revolving of images in the internal senses.

Chapter VII. Of Patience

§ 1. Of the mortification of anger by patience.

§§ 2, 3, 4, 5. Here is treated of smaller impatiences chiefly, scarce observable but by recollected livers.

§ 6. Patience to be exercised at all times, even in joy and prosperity.

§§ 7, 8, 9. We ought to aspire to an indifference.

§ 10. Patience towards God afflicting us is easier than towards man.

§§ 11, 12, 13, 14, 15, 16, 17, 18. Seven degrees of patience.

§ 19. Examples of seemingly extravagant kinds of patience.

§ 20. Prayer the only efficacious instrument to get patience.

§ 21. All actions except prayer are in some degree defectuous.

1. The next passion to be mortified is anger, the which whosoever willingly suffers to arise and increase, or that deliberately yields to trouble of mind for any matter that concerns the body, health, fortunes, life, &c.—yea, or pretended soul's good—such an one really makes more esteem of them than of the solid good of his soul; for, as far as anger gets a mastery over him, so far he loses that dominion that his soul ought to have over all other things, and puts reason out of its throne. Hereupon our Saviour saith: *In patientia vestra possidebitis animas vestras;* that is, 'By patience ye shall keep the possession of your souls,' as implying that by impatience we lose that possession; and what greater loss can we have? Hence it is also that almost in all languages he that is in any great impatience is said to be out of himself.

2. Now the advices which I shall give for the repressing of impatience do not regard those great excesses of fury too common in the world—though it is to be hoped unknown in an internal state—but only those lesser inordinate passions of impatience and irresignation, or those smaller impetuosities of nature which may sometimes befall devout souls, by which the necessary peace of mind is disturbed, the habit of propriety increased, and the merit even of our best works of obligation diminished.

3. As we said that love (which is the root of all other passions and affections) is due only to and for God, so consequently all passions contrary to love, all aversions, impatiences, &c., are to be directed only against that which is directly contrary to God: the which no persons are, nor no actions or sufferings, which are not sinful. Therefore all such passions, against any persons whatsoever, or any accidents befalling us from any, are inordinate and sinful to the proportion and measure of the said passions.

4. Even the most solitary liver will not have reason to complain of want of occasions to exercise patience, for, besides the crosses happening by God's providence from without (against which all impatience is interpretatively impatience against God Himself), a soul aspiring to perfection must observe even the smallest motions passing in the heart, the which will be apt to rise even against the vilest creatures, as vermin, flies, &c.—yea, inanimate things, as pens, ink, &c. There are also certain propensions in the will without any perceptible motion about the heart, so secret and subtle that they can hardly be expressed, the which perfect souls, by the light proceeding from prayer, do discern and contradict. None are wholly free from these inordina-

tions; even the most quiet natures will find unequal inclinations which they ought to mortify.

5. Such is the difference, saith Cassian, between a perfect internal liver and one that is imperfect, as there is between a clear-sighted man and one that is purblind. A purblind man in a room sees only the grosser things, as chairs, tables, &c., but takes no notice of an infinite number of smaller matters, with their colours, distances, order, &c., all which are plainly distinguished by a clear-sighted man, who will observe many defects and inequalities invisible to others. So it is in regard of our inward defects. An imperfect soul only takes notice of grosser imperfections, and strives to amend them only, and that being done, conceives herself arrived to great perfection, when, alas, there yet remains a world of imperfections, only visible to eyes enlightened with supernatural grace (to be obtained only by pure internal prayer), the which will discover how strongly rooted and deeply fixed all passions are in the soul, and how souls deceive themselves who in prosperity do so wholly abandon themselves to joy, as if nothing could happen that could diminish it; and contrarily in sorrow; as we find examples in Suso, and the monk cured from a great inward affliction by St. Bernard, as likewise in David, who saith of himself: *Ego dixi in excessu meo,* &c.; that is, 'Being in an excess of mind through Divine consolation, I said, I shall never be moved.' But he found presently how he was mistaken, for it follows (*Avertisti faciem tuam,* &c.), 'Thou only didst turn thy face from me, and presently I became troubled.'

6. Therefore spiritual persons at all times must exercise patience, even in times of joy, by expecting a change thereof; which perhaps is to be desired, because the way to perfection is by a continual succession of mountings and descendings, to all which they must be indifferent, or rather they must think their more secure abode to be in valleys than on mountains.

7. All commotion of anger or aversion is according to the degree of self-love remaining, the which is never to be accounted subdued till we be in a perfect indifference to all creatures, actions, or sufferings, as considered in themselves. I say, as considered in themselves, for if such actions, sufferings, &c., be of obligation, we are not to be in such indifference, but are to be more affected to the obligation, for that is but to affect God, from whom all our obligations do proceed. Yet if a work of obligation be agreeable to our nature, we must take heed of tying our affections to it under that notion, the which we express by doing such works with more than usual diligence, haste, and impetuosity. In such case, therefore, imperfect souls ought to perform such a work as pausingly and mortifiedly as the work will well permit; and if it require haste, let them endeavour to do it with internal resignation and indifference, at least in the superior will. On the contrary, if it be a work from

which their nature is averted, then the more cheerfully and speedily they perform it, the more perfectly do they behave themselves, so that such speed do not proceed from a desire of gaining favour, or to have it despatched quickly out of the way.

8. The profession of aspiring to perfection in a contemplative life requires, not only patience and indifference in such crosses as we cannot avoid, but also that we be not solicitous in seeking to avoid them, although lawful means were offered; on the contrary, to entertain and make much of them, in case the soul finds inward strength sufficient to entertain them.

9. A spiritual person living in perfect abstraction may rather have need and hath more leisure to exercise himself sometimes in supposed imagined difficulties devised by himself than one that lives a distracted life. Such an one, therefore, may judge of his impatience either by remembering some injury passed or feigning one present, and thereupon observing whether, or how far, anger is stirred in him.

10. Matters about which patience is exercised if they come from men, as hurts, injuries, persecutions, &c., are generally more bitter than those that come from God, though in themselves greater, as sickness, losses, &c.; because other men are but equal to us—we know not their secret intentions, but are apt to suspect the worst—therefore we take such things worse at their hands than we would at God's, who, besides that He is omnipotent and has the supreme dominion over us, we know that His goodness is infinite, so that we can assure ourselves that all His dealings towards us are meant for our good, though sometimes we do not see how they can contribute to it. And as for matters of affliction that through imprudence or any other defect we bring upon ourselves, we are less moved to impatience by them (though often to a secret shame), because that, besides that we are too apt to excuse and favour ourselves, we are secure that we mean well to ourselves.

11. We may conceive these following degrees to be in patience, all which must be ascended before we can attain to the perfection of this virtue.

12. The first degree is to have a serious desire of patience, and however in the superior will to endeavour to hold patience upon any provocation; and if this cannot be had at first, yet to procure it as soon as may be, at least before the sun pass, or in the next recollection; and, however, to restrain the tongue and outward members from expressing impatience, though perhaps as yet anger cannot be prevented from showing itself in sour looks. A person therefore that ordinarily cannot abstain from deliberate angry speeches, or, which is worse, from passionate actions (in which the deliberation is greater), has not as yet attained the lowest degree of patience.

13. The second is, to use all endeavours to guard the heart, not suffering the contradiction or cross to enter into it, or move passions in it, but to

esteem the provocations as not worth the considering, or rather as a matter from which we may reap much good.

14. The third is, to use the mildest words and friendliest looks we can to the person provoking us, and not only to desire but endeavour also to procure his good, and to lay obligations upon him.

15. The fourth is, to imitate the prophet David, who said *(Improperium expectavit cor meum et miseriam)*, 'My soul expected scornful upbraiding and affliction.' This degree does not oblige us to seek voluntary mortifications, but only not to be solicitous to avoid them. And God oft inspires into His servants a desire that occasions of exercising their patience may be afforded them, yea, and sometimes to seek them, as St. Syncletica begged of St. Athanasius to assign unto her a cross ill-natured person to be attended on by her, the which being granted her, she came to attain this virtue in great perfection, suffering all her froward insupportable humours with facility and joy.

16. The fifth degree is showed in bearing with resignation and peace internal crosses, aridities, &c., which are far more grievous than external ones, especially that great desolation sent by God for the purifying of perfect souls, of which we shall speak in the following treatise.

17. Sixthly, a great addition is made to the grievousness of these internal crosses, and consequently to patience in bearing them, when they are accompanied with external afflictions also. This was our Lord's case on the cross, when to the intolerable torments of His body was added internal desolation.

18. The seventh and supreme degree of patience is to suffer all these things, not only with quietness, but joy. This is a degree more than human, being a supernatural gift of God, by which, not only the superior will without any repugnance doth receive and embrace things most contrary to nature, but the sensuality makes no opposition neither, though they should come suddenly and without preparation. Now I know not whether ever any mere creature (except our Blessed Lady) hath ever arrived to so high a degree of perfection in this life as to become wholly impassible.

19. St. John Climacus mentions two examples of two holy persons that seem somewhat extravagant. The first is of one that having received an injury, and being not at all moved with it, yet desiring to conceal his patience, made great complaints to his brethren, expressing a counterfeit great commotion of passion. The other was of a very humble soul that abhorred ambition, yet pretended an impatient desire and pursuit after offices and great irresignation when they were refused. But (saith our author) we must take heed lest, by imitating such practices, we come much rather to deceive our own souls than the devil or others.

20. All other means whatsoever used for the procuring of patience without pure internal prayer, will produce little better than a philosophical mortification mixed with secret undiscovered interests of nature. But by prayer joined with exercise of patience out of it the very soul will be rectified, and in time come to such an established peacefulness that nothing will be able to disturb it; no, scarce the persons themselves, if they had a mind to it. This amendment will be imperceptible, as progress in such prayer is; but after some convenient space of time there will be a certain general sense and feeling of it, and this ere we be aware. And the way that perfect souls take for the perfecting of themselves in this virtue, is not so much by a direct purposed exercise and combat against special defects or passions, as by a universal transcending of all created things, by means of an elevation of spirit and drowning it in God.

21. Hereupon a holy hermit in Cassian seems to account all our actions whatsoever, except only the actual exercise of contemplation, to be defectuous. His reason I suppose to be, because only during the time that a soul is in actual contemplation she is in God, perfectly united in spirit to Him, and consequently entirely separated from corrupt nature and sin. Whereas out of contemplation she is, at least in some measure, depressed in nature, and painted with the images of creatures which cannot but leave some small stains in the soul.

Chapter VIII. Of Scrupulosity

§§ 1, 2. *Of mortification of fear and scrupulosity, which is the most disquieting passion.*

§§ 3, 4. *What scrupulosity is.*

§§ 5, 6. *Advices here given only belong to such as truly desire to lead internal lives. And why?*

§ 7. *Scrupulosity, though a pernicious passion, yet is only incident to the tenderest consciences.*

§§ 8, 9. *Souls at the beginning of a spiritual course are usually very tender and scrupulous. And why? Therefore it is necessary (and easy) to prevent scrupulosity in the beginning.*

§ 10. *The order according to which the following advices are disposed.*

1. The next passion to be mortified is fear; to which we will add grief, not as if they were not quite different passions, but because ordinarily

the grief which is in well-minded souls that lead internal lives, proceeds from fear and scrupulosity, and not from such causes as procure griefs in secular minds, as loss of goods, friends, &c., or the feeling of pains, &c.

2. Now fear seems to be, of all other passions, the most disquieting; for though grief regarding the same object really adds this excess to fear, that it supposes the evil to be present, which to fear is only future; and a present ill, as such, is more afflicting than an evil only expected. Yet fear respecting the evil in the imagination, and as yet unknown, apprehends it according as the imagination will represent it, which ordinarily is far greater than in reality it is, yea, as in a sort infinite. And, moreover, such an apprehension sets the understanding on work, either to contrive means to avoid it, or if that be difficult, to invent new motives of unquietness and anxiety, which is far greater in evils in which we are uncertain how great they may be, and how soon they may befall us.

3. The special kind of fear, the mortification of which we are now to treat of, is such an one as is incident more particularly to tender devout souls (especially women) that pursue the exercises of a contemplative life, the which is usually called scrupulosity, which is a mixed kind of passion, the most contrary to that peace of mind necessary in a spiritual course of any other, as being envenomed with whatsoever causes anxiety and inward torments almost in all other passions. It regards sin and hell the most abhorred and most terrible objects of all others; and it is composed of all the bitternesses that are found in fear, despair, ineffectual desires, uncertainty of judgment, jealousy, &c.; and penetrating to the very mind and spirit, obscuring and troubling the understanding (our only director), and torturing the will, by plucking it violently contrary ways almost at the same time, it causes the most pestilent disorders that a well-meaning soul is capable of, insomuch as if it be obstinately cherished, it sometimes ends in direct frenzy, or, which is worse, a desperate forsaking of all duties of virtue and piety. And where it is in a less degree, yet it causes images so distracting, so deeply penetrating, and so closely sticking to the mind, and by consequence is so destructive to prayer with recollectedness, that it deserves all care and prudence to be used for the preventing or expelling it.

4. For which purpose I will here, according to the best light that God has given me, afford such tender souls as are upon this rack of scrupulosity the best advices I can; and such as if they will have the courage to practise accordingly, I do not doubt, but through God's help, they will be preserved from the dangerous consequences of such a passion. I shall insist with more than an ordinary copiousness upon this subject, because this so dangerous a passion is but too ordinary among souls of the best dispositions.

5. But in the first place I must make this protestation, that these following instructions (in which a great yet necessary condescendency is allowed in many cases) do belong unto, and application of them only to be made by such tender fearful souls as desire and intend sincerely to follow internal prayer and other duties of a spiritual life, with as much courage and diligence as their frailty will permit. Such do indeed too often stand in need, and are worthy of all assistance and indulgence that reason and a good conscience can possibly allow, as being persons that will probably turn all to the glory of God and good of their souls, and not to the ease or contentment of sensual nature (which they account their greatest enemy), and much less to unlawful liberty.

6. I do protest, therefore, against all extroverted livers, or any of different tempers and exercises that shall presume to apply or assume unto themselves any indulgences, &c., here not belonging to them; for they will but mislead themselves, and reap harm by so doing. It seldom falls out that such persons have a fear of a sin committed, or of the mortal heinousness of it, but that it is very likely that it is such an one, and has been committed; and therefore, for no difficulty of nature, nor for the avoiding of trouble of mind, ought they to expect any dispensations from due examinations of their conscience, express confessions, &c. Whereas a thousand to one the forementioned tender souls do take those for mortal sins which are mere temptations, yea, perhaps pure mistakes; and therefore to oblige them to such strict examinations or confessions would only nourish their most distracting anguishes of mind and furnish them with new matters of scrupulosity.

7. Now to encourage such tender well-minded souls to make use of these or any other the like advices proper for them, I desire them to take notice that that very disposition, to wit, a tender fearfulness of offending God, which renders them obnoxious to this so pernicious a passion, is such an one as, if they can avoid this inconvenience, will be the most advantageous of all others to enable them to make a speedy progress in internal ways, and to attain to purity of heart, the immediate disposition to contemplation above all other. So that this is the only snare that the devil has to hinder them, namely, by taking advantage from such tenderness to fill their minds full of multiplicity and unquiet apprehensions; with the which snare if they suffer themselves to be entangled, they will find that scrupulosity will be far from being effectual to cure any of their imperfections; yea, it will make contemplative prayer impossible to be attained, and God grant that those be the worst and most dangerous effects of it!

8. Such tenderness of conscience that is natural to many, frequently happens to be much increased immediately after the entering into an internal course of life; and therefore, then, especial care ought to be used for the pre-

venting of the fearful apprehensions which are the usual consequences of it. And the ground of such increase of tenderness at that time is not so much a conscience of former sins, as too severe a judgment of their present imperfections, which seem to be multiplied, by reason of the continual opposition that corrupt nature gives to their present exercises, as likewise because by the practice of such exercises they have a new light to discover a world of defects formerly invisible to them, Hence they become fearful of their present condition, and knowing as yet no other remedy but confession, they torment themselves with anxious preparations thereto; and their fears yet not ceasing by having received absolution, and besides, the same opposition of sensuality against internal prayer continuing, they begin to suspect their former confessions, which therefore they renew; so that all their thoughts almost are taken up with these suspicions of themselves, unsatisfactions in their confessions, &c. And by giving way to such anxious customary confessions, to which also perhaps they are encouraged by their indiscreet guides, they endanger themselves to contract an incurable disease of most pernicious scrupulosity and servile fear, from which terrible anguishes, dejectedness, and heartlessness in all spiritual duties do follow, with danger of rendering the state of religion, or at least of an internal life begun, a condition less fruitful, yea, more dangerous than a common extroverted life in the world would have been.

9. Devout souls, therefore, are earnestly wished to make timely provision against these inconveniences, and courageously to resist scrupulosity in the beginning, according to the advices here following; and above all things to use their best endeavours and prudence (as far as it belongs to them), as likewise their prayers to God, that they fall not into the hands of directors that will feed this humour (to them in such a state most pernicious) of frequent iterated confessions, either particular or general. If such care be had in the beginning, there is no disease more easily curable; whereas by progress it gathers such strength, disordering the imagination, disquieting the passions, and corrupting even the judgment also, that it is scarce possible to find a remedy.

10. Now to the end that the following advices may be more clear and distinct we will sort them according to tha several grounds from which usually scrupulosity doth proceed; the which are: 1. either internal temptations by suspected sinful thoughts and imaginations; 2. or certain defects, or supposed defects, incurred about external obligations, as saying the office, fasting, &c. In both which cases there is a strong suspicion of sin incurred, and an uncertainty of what heinousness that sin is, from whence follow unquiet examinations, scrupulous confessions often repeated, &c. First, therefore, we will treat of fear and scrupulosity arising from inward temptations by ill imaginations or thoughts, and afterward of the other.

Chapter IX. Of Scruples arising from Inward Sources

§ 1. Of scrupulosity arising from certain inward temptations.

§§ 2, 3. Temptations are not in themselves ill, but rather a mark of God's love. Yet they are not to be sought.

§ 4. Internal temptations very purifying.

§§ 5, 6, 7, 8. Of inward temptations resting only in the mind; and advices against them.

§ 9. Likewise touching those that cause also effects and motions in corporal nature.

§§ 10, 11, 12, 13, 14, 15, 16. Prayer is by no means to be omitted for temptations, as being the best and securest remedy, inasmuch as all temptations are most efficaciously and perfectly resisted by conversion of the soul with love to God.

1. The special kinds of inward temptations which do ordinarily afford matter of fear and scrupulosity to well-minded tender souls are, first, either such ill imaginations or thoughts as rest in the mind alone, without any other outward effect, such are thoughts: 1. of infidelity; 2. of blasphemy; 3. of despair, &c.; or, secondly, such as withal have, or may cause an alteration in the body, such are thoughts of impurity, anger, &c.

2. Now concerning temptations in general, the devout soul is to consider that it is no sin to have them; yea, being sent us by God, they are meant for our good, and to give us occasion to merit by them. And those which God sends us are the most proper for us; for if they were in our own choice we should choose least and last of all those that are most fit to humble us, and to withdraw our affections from ourselves and creatures; so that the more displeasing to us and afflicting that any temptations are the more profitable are they. Let none, therefore, be dismayed at the approach of temptations, but since self-love cannot be cured but by application of things contrary thereto, let us accept of them as a special gift of God, assuring ourselves that it would be perilous to be long without them. And if we cannot clearly see how our present temptation can turn to our profit we ought to content ourselves that God sees it; and otherwise He who is infinite wisdom and goodness would never have permitted them to befall us; therefore let faith supply knowledge or curiosity.

3. Nevertheless, we must not voluntarily seek temptations, for (*Qui amat periculum peribit in eo*), 'He that loves danger shall perish therein,'

saith the wise man. God will not deny spiritual strength to resist and make good use of temptations that by His providence befall us; yea, although it was by some precedent fault and negligence of ours that they befell us; but He has made no promise to secure us in a danger into which we voluntarily run.

4. More particularly internal temptations are more beneficial and purifying, and they do more profoundly humble us than do outward pains or persecutions: 1. because they discover unto us (not the malice of others but) our own sinful natures, prone of themselves to all abominations; 2. and by them we come to be delivered, not from other creatures, but from ourselves, in which separation our chiefest and last conquered difficulty consists; 3. they send us for remedy to none but God; for what effect can any assistance, medicines, or other helps of creatures have against our own thoughts.

5. And as for the special forenamed temptations a well-minded soul ought to consider that the simple passing of such thoughts or imaginations in the mind is no sin at all, though they should rest there never so long without advertence, but only the giving a deliberate consent unto them. Neither is it in the power of a soul either to prevent or banish them at pleasure, because the imagination is not so subject to reason as that it can be commanded to entertain no images but such as reason will allow, but it is distempered according to the disposition of the humours and spirits in the body; and sometimes the devil also is permitted to inject or raise images to the disquieting of tender souls, but he can force none to consent to the suggestions proceeding from them.

6. There is less danger of consenting unto temptations merely spiritual, such as are thoughts of blasphemy, despair, &c., and consequently less likelihood of scrupulosity from a suspicion of such consent. Though sometimes they may be so violent and so obstinately adhering that the fancy will become extremely disordered, and the soul will think herself to be in a kind of hell where there is nothing but blaspheming and hating of God.

7. Her best remedy is quietly to turn her thoughts some other way, and rather neglect than force herself to combat them with contrary thoughts, for by neglecting them the impression that they make in the imagination will be diminished. She may do well also, by words or outward gestures, to signify her renouncing and detestation of them, as in a temptation of blasphemy let her pronounce words and express postures of adoration of God, praise, love, &c.; let her be also the more diligent in frequenting the choir, continuing more carefully in postures of humility before Him. And doing thus, let her banish all suspicions of having consented as being morally impossible.

8. Certain it is that however troublesome and horrid soever such temptations may seem to be, yet they, being quietly resisted, or rather ne-

glected, do wonderfully purify the soul, establishing Divine love most firmly and deeply in the spirit. Moreover, by occasion of them the superior soul is enabled to transcend all the disorders and tumults in inferior nature, adhering to God during the greatest contradictions of sensuality.

9. As for the other sort of inferior temptations, which are more gross, causing oft disorderly motions and effects in corporal nature, it will be more difficult to persuade timorous souls that they have not consented, both by reason that such imaginations are more pertinacious and sticking to the corporal humours and spirits, and also because inferior nature is powerfully inclined to a liking of them, insomuch as that real effects and alterations may be wrought in the body before that reason be fully awake to resist them; yea, and after the resistance made by reason, yet such images continuing in the fancy and such motions in the body, the mind will be stupefied, and the resistance of reason will ofttimes be so feeble as that in the opinion of the person it will pass for no resistance at all; yea, rather the soul will be persuaded that she has deliberately consented, considering the continuance of them, after that she was fully awake, and had reflected on them.

10. Notwithstanding, unless in such souls the reason do not only reflect upon the sinfulness of such impure thoughts, if consented to, but likewise unless in the very same instant that she makes such a reflection the will be deliberately moved to the approving of them, they may be assured that there has passed no culpable consent to them. Again, if the general disposition of such souls be such as that seldom or never either speeches or deliberate actions do proceed from them comformable to such impure imaginations, they may confidently judge that there is no danger of having incurred a mortal sin.

11. Above all things the devout soul is to be careful that she be not disheartened by occasion of such temptations from pursuing constantly her appointed recollections the best she can, notwithstanding that then, above all other times, such thoughts will throng into her mind, so that she will think it almost unlawful to appear before God, being full of such impure images. But she is to consider that now is the proper time to show her fidelity to God. No thanks to her if she adhere to God when nature makes no opposition, but rather finds a gust in it. But if amidst these tempests of corrupt nature she will firmly adhere to God when such adhesion becomes so extremely painful to her, this is thanksworthy; then she will show herself a valiant soldier of our Lord, and worthy of that testimony that He gives of her, who has judged her fit and capable of encountering such furious enemies.

12. A great blessing and happiness it is that in all internal confusions, obscurities, &c., we can always make an election of God with the superior

will, which being effectually done, whatsoever disorders are in the imagination or in inferior nature, they do rather increase than prejudice our merit.

13. Indeed this is that great, most efficacious, and universal remedy against all temptations, to wit, an actual conversion of the soul to God in prayer; for thereby the soul being united to God, either she will lose the image and memory of the temptation for the present, or, however, she doth with far more efficacy oppose and work contrary to such temptations, than if she had fixed her eyes with a direct renouncing and detestation of them; for in an actual union with God is included a virtual detestation of all things contrary to Him, both for present and future, and also thereby the soul adheres to her only good, with whom they are absolutely inconsistent.

14. This remedy, therefore, which contains in it all the virtue of all other particular remedies, is often and seriously to be recommended to internal contemplative livers (for, indeed, none but such as live abstracted lives can, without great force and difficulty, be in a disposition at pleasure to introvert and recollect themselves). However, let every soul that is capable thereof use it. It is the plainest, easiest, securest, and most infallible cure of all others.

15. Those that are thoroughly practised in prayer cannot only be united in will to God, but perceive themselves to be so united, whilst in the mean time both the representation of these temptations remain in the imagination and understanding, and much trouble likewise in inferior nature, all which, notwithstanding, are not any hindrance or prejudice to such union; yea, by occasion of these things a more perfect and intense union may be caused.

16. The light obtained by prayer for the discovering of the causes, grounds, and remedies of such temptations, and the grace to resist them, is wonderful and incredible to those that do not practise prayer; by neglect of which many live in the midst of temptations, and yet do not know them to be such, or knowing them, yet have no strength nor will to resist them. But most certain it is, that a soul which duly prosecutes internal prayer, according to her present abilities, can scarce possibly be overcome with a temptation as habitually to yield to it, or, however, to die in it. Indeed, there is no security that a soul ordinarily is capable of in this life but by the means of prayer.

Chapter X. Of Scruples concerning External Duties

§ 1. Of scrupulosities about external duties, as the Office, fasting, &c.

*§ 2. Tender souls ought to seek full information touching such obligations,
which is not out of politic ends to be denied them.*

§§ 3, 4, 5, 6. Several cases of indulgence about the Office.

*§§ 7, 8, 9, 10. Some learned doctors do free particular religious persons (not
in holy orders) from a necessary obligation of saying the Office in private.*

§ 11. An advice touching the same.

1. In the next place, the special external duties about which tender
souls are apt to admit scrupulosities are many; yea, some are so inordinately
timorous that they can give way to unsatisfaction in almost everything that
they do or say. But the principal and most common, especially in religion,
are these: 1. the obligation of religious persons to poverty, obedience, regular
fasting, saying of the Office in public or private, &c.; 2. the duty of examination of the conscience in order to confession, and confession itself, with
communicating afterward.

2. The general proper remedy against scrupulosity arising upon occasion of any of these matters is a true information of the extent of the said
obligations. And surely spiritual directors are obliged to allow as much latitude to well-minded timorous souls in all these things as reason will possibly
admit, considering that such are apt to make a good use of the greatest condescendency. Therefore it would be a fault inexcusable before God, if
confessors, out of a vain policy and to the end to keep tender souls in a continual dependence and captivity under them, should conceal from them any
relaxations allowed by doctors or just reason. And timorous souls, when they
have received information from persons capable of knowing, and unlikely to
deceive them, ought to believe and rest upon them, and to account all risings
of fear or suspicion to the contrary to be unlawful.

3. More particularly forasmuch as concerns the Divine Office, since
all that understand Latin may acquaint themselves with all the dispensations
and largest allowances afforded by doctors, I conceive it most requisite that
such ignorant tender souls (especially women) as may come to see or read
these instructions, should not be left in an ignorance or uncertainty here-
about; for why should any additional burdens of a religious life lie more
heavy on those that are least able to bear them, and such as will be far from
being less careful in obliging observances, less submissive to authority, and
less assiduous in the service of God?

4. Therefore, forasmuch as concerns the public conventual reciting of
the Office, they may take notice that the obligation thereto does not at all lie
upon particular religious under sin, except when they have been *pro tempore*
expressly commanded by superiors to frequent the choir at such or such a
determinate time; at other times they may be penanced for negligence, and

202

ought to submit willingly thereto. But the obligation under sin to see that duty discharged lies only upon superiors.

5. Again, when they are in the choir, in case that when others are re-peating the Office they are employed about anything that concerns the church, as lighting of candles, fetching or turning of books, music, &c., they are not obliged to repeat such parts of the Office as have passed during such their employments. Neither is it necessary, in case of any considerable fee-bleness, that they should strain their voices to the tone of the convent, unless by reason of the paucity of the religious the Office through their silence can-not be solemnly discharged. Moreover, if any reasonable occasion concerning the Office require their going out of the choir, they are not bound to repeat afterwards what shall have been said in the mean time, but at their return they may content themselves to join with the community, &c.

6. But as touching the saying of the Office in private, it is the general vote of learned men: 1. that a very ordinary indisposition will suffice to dis-pense; 2. that the mistake of one office for another is not considerable, since it is only a day's office is enjoined, and not such a determinate office; 3. that if a few verses now and then were omitted, that being but a very small part of the whole, is not valuable; 4. that none are obliged to repetition for want of attention, or for not exact pronunciation, &c.; 5. that scrupulous souls being in an uncertainty whether they have said such a particular hour, or other con-siderable part of the Office, are not obliged to say it, 6. as for the times of saying each part, the liberty allowed is fully large enough. Other indulgences there are generally permitted, of which they may do well to inform them-selves. These will suffice to show that the burden is not so great as many good tender souls do apprehend.

7. But the root of all these and all other scrupulous difficulties in this matter is taken away by the positive assertion of certain learned doctors, not censured or condemned by any, viz. that no religious persons, except they be in holy orders, are bound to the reciting of the Divine Office in private under mortal sin (and if it were any sin at all to omit it, it would be a mortal sin, being evidently *in materia gravi*).

8. The principal authors of this assertion are Lessius—a very learned Jesuit—and Marchantius—a most prudent, learned, and conscientious Pro-vincial of the holy Order of St. Francis, who, being taught by long experience in treating with tender souls, professes that he thought himself obliged in conscience, in duty to God, and charity to timorous souls, to publish this as-sertion. And the reasons given for it seem to be very pressing and concluding, because the simple not reciting of the Office being not in itself evil—for then all seculars not reciting it should sin (mortally)—there can be named no title under which it can be made obligatory.

9. For, 1. all those that would maintain the contrary opinion do profess that there is no law for it; for although our holy Rule advises that in case any considerable number of religious by means of any employment should be hindered from the choir, they should in the place of such their employment recite the Office in common, yet it gives no order at all to single religious persons in that case; 2. the foundation and sustentation of religious communities is not as that of cures or canonries, to which there is correspondent by a debt of justice and virtual contracts the reciting of the canonical Office, so that restitution is due in case of omission. But to foundations of monasteries and pious oblations are correspondent only the performances and observances of religious vows, fasts, austerities, conventual prayer, aspiring to contemplation, &c., with respect to which only oblations were made to convents, not under a title of justice, but charity.

10. There remains, therefore, no other pretence for an obligation of particular religious not *in sacris* to a private reciting of the Office, but only custom that has the virtue of a law. Now Cajetan doubts whether *de facto* there be any custom of it at all; for certain it is that it is not universally received, neither is it by privilege that some do not receive it. However, if there be a custom, yet that it has not the force of a law may appear: 1. because if it had been introduced by authority of superiors it would have been established by constitutions, which yet hath never been done, neither hath any inquisition been made at visits of the breach of such a custom as a fault; 2. because those doctors that most urge the obligation thereto, yet never pretend the omitting to be a mortal sin: and surely if it be not a mortal sin it is none at all; 3. because several learned men have publicly, without censure, protested against any obligation flowing from such a custom, which would never have been permitted if prelates and superiors had an intention that their subjects should esteem such a custom obligatory; 4. because there are certain orders, as the Franciscans, the nuns of the Annunciata, &c., which by their Rule and an express vow are obliged to the reciting of the Office in particular, in case of absence from the choir, which would he ridiculous if the general custom was presumed to be sufficiently obliging; 5. the same is proved by a parity; for whereas a custom had been generally introduced among the Cistercians by the ancients of the Order of reciting the Office of our Blessed Lady and of the Dead, yet in General Chapter, A.D. 1618, it was declared that this custom, though introduced by the ancients and superiors, yet had not the force of a law.

11. All this notwithstanding, according to the opinion of the said authors we may conceive this to be a custom very laudably practised by devout souls, and has been indeed received under title of piety and a convenient holy

exercise, which if it should be causelessly neglected, contemned, or trans-gressed, a person so transgressing, if he did it out of indevotion and want of fervour in matters of piety, might justly be condemned, or at least esteemed a person indevout and negligent; the which fault yet may be remedied some other more commodious way than by laying a snare upon tender souls, or misinforming them.

Chapter XI. Of Scruples concerning Confession

1. Whatsoever the matters or occasions are that cause scrupulosity in tender souls, the bitterness thereof is felt especially in confessing of them, or preparing themselves to such confession. For then it is that all former unsatis-factions recur to their memory, and new examinations are made, and not only all the supposed faults, but also the former examinations and confessions are again examined and confessed; for to such souls, partly out of ignorance in

the nature, degrees, and circumstances of sins, and partly having their minds darkened by fear, all sins appear to them to be mortal, or for ought they know they may be mortal, and that suspicion, or even possibility, is sufficient to pierce them through with grief and fear.

2: The misery of such self-afflicting souls is much increased and rendered almost irremediable by indiscreet counsellors, unwary writers of spiritual matters, and such as are inexperienced in internal ways, who in the practice of Penance and Confession use the same rules and measure towards all souls indifferently, giving advices in general terms, which yet are proper only for the common sort of souls living in the world; who commend the repetition of general confessions, prescribing nice rules for examination; who enjoin all their penitents in a case of uncertainty and doubt, whether a sin be mortal or no, to choose that which appears to their prepossessed judgments the safer side, and therefore to be sure not to omit it in Confession; who recommend daily and almost hourly examinations of conscience; who extol the virtue and efficacy of sacraments without sufficient regard to the dispositions, and therefore indifferently encourage souls to frequent confessions, yea, even when they can find no present matter; in such a case advising them to repeat the mentioning of any one or more sins formerly confessed, merely to continue a custom of confessing, and to gain a new access of grace by virtue of the keys, &c. Now such advices and instructions as these may possibly be good for some negligent souls living extroverted lives (if that a proportionable care were also taken that penitents should bring due dispositions to the sacraments, without which the effects wrought by them will be far from their expectations); but that which is a cure for ordinary souls may, and frequently doth, prove poison to such tender scrupulous persons as we now treat of.

3. Therefore, surely a confessor or director that has any taste of internal ways, and any spiritual prudence and clarity, when he is to treat with souls that he sees have truly a fear of God and a sensible horror of offending Him, even in a proportion beyond what charity and due confidence do require, and that were it not that they are dejected by too great an apprehension of their guilt, would make great progress in the Divine love; perceiving likewise (after some experience and insight into their lives, exercises, and manners of their confessions) that such souls accuse and judge themselves and their actions, not by any light of reason or knowledge in the true nature and degrees of sins, but only by their own passion of fear, which corrupts their judgment, &c.; such confessors, I say, in these and the like circumstances, will not surely think it fit to deal with these as with the ordinary sort of tepid or negligent souls in the world that have need to be terrified, to have their consciences narrowly searched into, to be frequently brought before the spiritual tribunal. The like prudence is to be exercised also to such tender

souls leading internal lives, who, though they are not actually scrupulous, either have been formerly or easily may be cast into it by rough or indiscreet usage.

4. Therefore, surely these timorous and tender souls are to be told: first, that the end of their coming into religion, or of consecrating themselves to God in a life of contemplation, was not to enjoy the sacraments, which they might have had free use of in the world, but in the quietness of silence and solitude to seek God, and daily to tend to Him by internal exercises of love, resignation, &c., as also by a calming of all manner of passions; and that all external duties are only so far to be made use of as they contribute to the increase of this love, quietness of mind, and confidence in God. 2. That the Sacrament of Penance and Confession is a holy ordinance indeed, instituted by our Lord, not for the torment but ease of consciences, and to the end to bring souls to have a confidence in Him, and not a horror of approaching to Him. 3. That the administration of this sacrament is left to our Lord's priests, who alone are to be judges what sins are to be confessed, and in what manner. 4. That since it is evident that confession is their chiefest torment, causing effects in them so contrary to what our Lord intended, that therefore they should either abstain wholly from so frequent a custom of confessing, or to make their confessions only in the form that should be prescribed them. 5. That such examinations of sins will abundantly serve their turn, as they would think fit to be used in any ordinary matter of importance, and as may be made in a very short space. 6. That oft it is far more profitable for them to exercise rather virtual acts of contrition and sorrow for sin, by converting themselves directly to God with acts of love, than by reflecting with passion upon their sins. 7. That those common maxims, viz. that it is the sign of a good conscience there to fear a fault where none is, and that nothing is to be done against conscience; likewise, that in doubtful cases the securest side is to be chosen, &c.: these maxims, I say, though in gross true, yet if they should be strictly applied to scrupulous persons, would utterly ruin the peace of their minds; for they are altogether incapable of judging what is against conscience, or what may be said to be doubtful, accounting everything that they fear (without being able to give any tolerable reason of their fear) to be against conscience, and to be doubtful. It is therefore the spiritual director or experienced confessor only that is to be judge of these things, who has no interest at all in the business but the good of his penitent's soul, who can judge without passion, who is appointed by God to be judge, and whose unfaithful dealing the penitent hath no reason to suspect.

5. There is no possible way to be rid from scruples (besides the having immediate recourse to God by humble resigned prayer) but an entire indispensable obedience to prudent confessors, proceeding according to these or the like grounds and instructions, according to which if such tender souls

take the courage to practise, notwithstanding any fears in sensitive nature, they will find their fears to decrease. Whereas, if they neglect or obstinately refuse to put them in practice, their fears will not only grow far more dangerous, but they will become inexcusable before Almighty God, and contract the heinous sin of disobedience, ingratitude, and wilful obstinacy and resistance against the light which God has given them.

6. But withal they must know that they will never have sufficient strength and grace to obey against passion except they seriously practise internal prayer, which alone will make their obedience to become by custom far more easy, and also freed from that horror which at the first they will feel in sensitive nature.

7. Neither ought they to suspect that their confessors, set over them by God for their good, do not understand their case aright. True it is they do not feel the pains they suffer, no more than corporal physicians do their patients', but yet they know the causes of it better than they do themselves, proceeding by a supernatural light not clouded by passion. And why should they pretend to know the causes, being ignorant of them? What interest is likely to corrupt their judgment? Would they for no reward or gain incur the displeasure of God?

8. Notwithstanding, so subtle such souls are to their own prejudice, that though they should yield that their confessor knew their past state, yet they see some new circumstance which was either forgotten, or they doubt so, which may perhaps alter the whole case. As likewise every new sin or defect has something in it, to their seeming, different from the former, by which they make a shift to escape from obedience, yet they must know that not all these shifts will excuse them before God.

9. Yea, they ought to consider that though indeed it were true that the confessor should happen to be mistaken, notwithstanding, the penitents practising *bonâ fide* according to his orders in a point of this nature about his confession (which is not a moral precept), should commit no sin, nor incur the least danger by it; yea, being an act of obedience for God's sake and in opposition to natural passion it should be an occasion of merit to them; so that though the sins suspected by them were indeed mortal, yet, he judging otherwise, they would not be obliged to confess them.

10. But it is wonderful to see in souls very distrustful of themselves in all other matters, such an obstinate self-judgment in this, that they will neither be persuaded that they are scrupulous, though their wits be almost perished by scrupulosity; for if this were once admitted, plain reason would convince them that they ought not to be their own judges. As likewise in souls otherwise very innocent, humble, and most pliable to obedience, the

pertinacious disobedience in this point of abstaining from confessing or renewing confessions of things forbidden them to be confessed is very strange; so that against the command of their present confessor and the advice of all the most learned doctors they will persist in their reluctance; and if their confessor will not admit them, they will forbear no means to find out others, though wholly unacquainted with their state, to hear their scrupulosities. And what other ground can there be of such disorder but only self-love deeply rooted in corrupt nature, and ofttimes the suggestion of the devil, to which such souls by reason of their disordered imaginations and passions are miserably exposed? They had rather confess their virtues for faults (as their having resisted their fears in compliance with obedience), than their really greatest fault, which is self-judgment and disobedience.

11. A scrupulous fearful soul having been commanded to forbear examination and confession of such particulars as do cause unquietness in her, when she comes to put this in practice a double fear will present itself to her, the one of disobeying her confessor and the other of going against her natural judgment, which is contrary to her confessor's. But she ought to consider that the former fear has nothing of nature in it, yea, that it contradicts nature in its most sensible part, and therefore is far more worthy to take place. As for the fear of going against her own judgment, it proceeds wholly and only from nature, self-love, and a desire to be rid of her present pain that the memory of her faults causes in her, or the suggestions of the devil urging her to disobedience. Therefore, if she cannot expel this fear out of sensitive nature, she must accept it as a pain, but withal contradict it as a temptation.

12. She ought to assure herself that more harm comes to her, and incomparably greater impediments in her exercise of prayer, &c., by indiscreet confessions, or examinations made merely to satisfy scrupulosity, than by all the defects that she would confess, which, being generally incurred out of frailty, do far less estrange her from God than such confessions do, by which she is habituated in self-will, self-judgment, and servile fear; all which are the more perilous, inasmuch as they have a pretence of duty to God and to the orders of His Church, as also of humility, and a desire to receive benefit by the sacrament, &c.

13. Common reason will dictate that it is most unfit that, any one should be judge of his own state just at a time when a temptation or violent fear is actually predominant, the which do put the soul in a strange confusion and darkness. What a folly, therefore, and presumption would it be for a woman, ignorant, passionate, and fearful, to challenge the office of a judge in this case, and to think to regulate the judge that sits in God's seat!

14. Let, therefore, fearful souls that are forbidden the usual ways of curious examinations of conscience and nice confessions, whensoever any

scruple or suspicion concerning a mortal sin comes into their minds that would urge them to run for ease to confession, or that would affright them from communicating,—let them, I say, content themselves with asking their own consciences in one glance of their minds: Do I certainly know the matter of this fear to have been a mortal sin, and that it was really committed, and never confessed in any sort, defectively or exactly? And if their consciences do not answer that they are most certain of this, they may not only securely judge that they are not guilty, but they are obliged under sin to abstain from confession, in case they have been so commanded, and to proceed to communicating. For it is morally impossible that such tender souls should commit a mortal sin, but without any examination it will appear evidently to be mortal.

15. This way of self-examination I (being warranted by learned authors) do seriously recommend to those souls that find that a punctual examination doth destroy the quiet of their minds, so that if after one short self-questioning they do not resolutely and positively determine that they have deliberately consented to a temptation, and committed a sin unquestionably mortal, let them resolve never after to trouble their thoughts with it; but if they should press them for a reëxamination, let them neglect them and consider them as pure temptations.

16. Such souls are not to esteem that a fear or suspicion that anything is a sin or mortal can be sufficient to make the case to be doubtful; for a doubt is when two opinions are represented to the mind, and the contrary reasons for each are so even and equal, that the judgment cannot determine itself to assent to either. Now a firm assent may be where there is a violent fear of the contrary at the same time. And a scrupulous person cannot ofttimes give any other reason or account of her fear, but that, for ought she knows, the matter is according to her fear.

17. Amongst other subjects of scruple, one is a doubt in such souls whether they have true contrition for their faults or no. Whereas, if there be anything that hinders their sorrow from being true contrition, it is the excess of servile fear mixed with it, which they wilfully nourish with their scrupulosities; but, however, considering they are supposed to practise internal prayer in such manner as they are able, there is hardly any doubt to be made but that they have the true love of God, which makes sorrow for sin to be true contrition. The which may be performed either directly, by framing an efficacious act of sorrow and detestation of their sins, as offensive to God, and for His love; or only virtually (yet efficaciously), by producing an act of pure love to God, for thereby they do really avert themselves from whatever doth offend Him, or is contrary to such love (as sin is).

18. And from hence may appear the great security that a soul has which pursues internal prayer, because every act of love or resignation performed purely for God doth restore a soul to the state of Grace, in case that by any precedent sins she hath fallen from that state. And if she hath not, it doth advance and establish her the more in Grace.

19. There is not, therefore, a more assured general remedy against scrupulosity and all such inordinate fears than constancy in prayer. This alone will produce a courage to despise such fears, whensoever they would hinder a soul from performing obedience to the orders of her spiritual director.

20. The security and necessity of which obedience, as likewise the culpableness and danger of proceeding according to the suggestions of fear, a devout soul may evidently collect from hence, viz. by observing that she never disobeys in virtue of light obtained by prayer, the which always dictates obedience and renouncing her own judgment, and contradicting her fears to her; and on the contrary, that she is tempted to transgress the orders of her confessor only at the time when fear is so violent upon her, and makes so deep an impression of her supposed faults in her mind, that she cannot then pray with resignation, and believes that then to obey her confessor would be to go against her own knowledge. Her security, therefore, must come from prayer, to which her humble obedience will dispose her; and on the contrary, scrupulous fears will render her utterly unfit. Therefore, souls which wilfully nourish their fears and scruples by frequent unpermitted confessions have very much to answer for before Almighty God for their wilful plunging themselves into a state which makes a perfect union with God impossible, thereby defeating the whole design of a religious internal life, as also for forsaking the ways of obedience, which almost in all possible cases are most full of security.

21. It is far from my purpose to deter souls from frequent confessions, even of venial sins, when they find such confessions profitable to them and helps to their amendment; but otherwise, if by the means of such confessions they endanger themselves to run into mortal sins of the highest nature, as desperation or a wilful renouncing of all ways of piety, through the horror arising from their ignorance and incapacity to distinguish between mortal and venial sins,—then surely it were better for them to make use of other ways appointed by God for the expiating and purging of venial sins (such as are saying our Lord's Prayer, acts of humiliation and contrition, giving of alms, devout taking of holy water, &c.). And if they are desirous in some good measure to observe the ordinary times of confession, they may content themselves with expressing some such faults as they can with assurance and

without disquietness declare, and all other faults may be involved in some general phrase or expression.

22. If it be objected that by practising according to these instructions such souls will find nothing new to confess, and so will be deprived of the blessing and comfort of absolution, hereto I answer that it were happy if souls could find nothing expedient to be confessed. And surely the most effectual means to bring them to such happiness is according to these advices to free them from their dejecting scrupulosities, for as long as they remain, little effect of blessings can proceed from the best exercises or use of sacraments. We know that in ancient times innumerable saints attained to perfection with little or no use of confession (considering their remoteness from places where priests inhabited), by serious practice of prayer, abstraction of life, mortification, &c.; which means will doubtless have the same effect now, and without them confessions and communions, though daily practised, will have but small effect thereto. Now there is not in the world a mortification more effectual, more purifying, and more proper for such souls, than to obey God in their confessor, contrary to their own violent fears, scrupulosity, and seeming judgment.

23. The proper season of the trial of obedience and submission of scrupulous souls is the time of communicating, because they know that there is necessary thereto not only the condition of being free from mortal sin, but likewise that a greater preparation is requisite; for in all states they may pray, say their Office, exercise mortification, &c., without a precedent confession (though it is with great dejection, heartlessness, and most grievous distractions that such souls apply themselves to internal prayer, &c.); but above all, communicating during their suspicions is most grievous and full of horror to them.

24. In this case, therefore, a well-minded soul coming to communicate according to order prescribed by her confessor, and finding a fear to seize upon her, let her take courage, lifting up her heart to God in this or the like manner: 'My God, it is not by mine own choice, but in obedience to Thee speaking to me by my confessor, that I presume to approach to Thy altar. In Thy name, therefore, and hoping for Thy blessing, I will communicate, notwithstanding the horror and frights which I feel in my soul. These I accept as a pain, and I do resign myself to the continuance of them, as long as it shall be Thy pleasure for my humiliation. I hope and am assured that Thou wilt not condemn me for obedience, and for resisting the violent impulsions of my corrupt passions. It is only for the comfort of my soul that I desire to receive the precious Body of my Lord. If I did not think it to be Thy will that I should communicate now, I would abstain, though this were Christmas or Easter-day, and whatsoever confusion or shame I were to suffer

for abstaining.' Having said or thought to this effect, let her freely communicate, and be assured she shall not incur the least danger, but, on the contrary, merit in a high degree. And in the same manner she may lift up her heart to God, whensoever in confession she abstains from mentioning such faults as do cause unquietness to her.

25. Such souls may also do well to practise very often in private spiritual communicating, preparing themselves thereto by the forementioned brief and quiet examinations. Frequent practising after this manner will beget a confidence to it really upon occasions.

26. Those souls to whom these instructions have been, or shall be, esteemed proper in the judgment of their spiritual directors must not be discouraged from following them by anything that shall be said by others, or by anything that they shall find in books; for there is nothing written here which may not be confirmed by the testimony and authority of learned and unquestioned doctors. They must therefore abstain from making consultations with others, or demanding their judgments or opinions, for otherwise there will be no end of troubles and distractions. Neither willingly or purposely ought they to read books made for the common sort of souls, and that give different advices, for that would be to put themselves wilfully into a temptation. But let them content themselves with these or the like instructions, reading them oft, and seriously resolving in and with prayer to practise accordingly, and they may, through God's blessing, expect a good success.

27. Now they must not from hence expect advices to fit all cases, which are almost infinite. But according to their particular necessities they must apply these general instructions: observing the divine inspirations (especially in the time of prayer), their own experience, and sometimes likewise serving themselves of their natural judgment. For of this let them assure themselves, that if they will not resolve to obey till satisfaction be given them to all their scrupulous objections and fears, their case is desperate. If nothing will serve them but a riddance from the pain of the temptation, an angel from heaven will never be able to quiet and satisfy them. They must either obey, though with their eyes shut, or they will live and die in the same self-love and servile fear, which is a very dangerous state to die in.

28. Yet those who must of necessity at the first be helped with relying upon the warrant of their confessors and directors must not finally rest there, but make use of such peace as by their means they can obtain, to dispose them to have recourse to our Lord, to learn confidence in Him, which will arise from frequent conversing with Him by prayer.

29. To conclude this matter of scrupulosity: a general good way to cure it is by opposing it in its root and cause, which is either spiritual or corporal. The spiritual cause of scrupulosity is tepidity; for though it seems to be

a humour full of solicitude, haste, and eagerness, yet the true ground ofttimes of it is an unwillingness and lothness to give God more than we must needs. Now the measure and rule of what is absolutely necessary being uncertain, from the ignorance thereof grows a general fear (just enough, the heart being so corrupted by self-love) of falling short of what is necessary almost in everything, either for want of right intention, or some other important circumstance, which fear being servile is perplexing, confounding, and darkening. The proper remedy, therefore, is (as hath been said) an humble recourse to God by prayer to correct in us what is amiss, and to supply what is defective; as also a submission and resignation of ourselves sincerely and entirely to do to our uttermost what He requires; and when all this is done, not to judge of our soul's estate, its hope or danger, so much by a view of our own perfections, or a conceit of the diminishing of our imperfections, but only by our relying and affectionate dependence on God. For the greatest and most perfect servants of God, the more they grow in perfection, the more light have they to discern innumerable imperfections in themselves, which causes great humility, but yet does not abate their independence and confidence on God, grounded in His only goodness. Whereas, imperfect tepid souls hoping to gain security by diminishing their imperfections (which arises from pride), when they see their defects rather to increase, they become dejected, fearful, and scrupulous.

30. And such scrupulosity arising from tepidity doth much increase it, through a kind of despair of expelling our own imperfections by our own abilities, and neglect of the true means of dispelling them, which is serious prayer to God. If such souls, therefore, would take this for a ground, that it is impossible in this life that they should ever see themselves otherwise than full of innumerable defects, of which they are not able so much as to give any account; and yet, notwithstanding, they ought even, for that very impossibility's sake, to have recourse unto God and to rely upon His pardon, as also His help and concurrence to remove our defects, as far as His good pleasure shall be: again, if they would not expect a certainty or security touching their state, but be content to stand to God's good pleasure and mercy, by which not only perfection but salvation is to be obtained, they would shortly be freed from their painful wearisome fears and scrupulosities.

31. Again, ofttimes this humour of a timorous scrupulosity is very much to be attributed to the present indisposition in the body (especially in women), when by reason of some special infirmities, through the ascending of ill vapours to the head, there are raised melancholic and afflicting images in the fancy, which, without the help of the corporal physician, can hardly by counsel be expelled.

Chapter XII. Of Scruples concerning Vocation

§§ 1, 2. Of a scruple concerning a soul's vocation to a religious life.

§§ 3, 4, 5, 6, 7. Of several grounds and motives by which souls may be induced to undertake a religious state.

§§ 8, 9. What motives are perfect and what unfitting; and how a soul once engaged has then a necessary divine vocation to continue, &c.

1. Before I quit this passion of fear, it will neither be impertinent nor unprofitable, I hope, to speak somewhat of a temptation taken notice of by Thaulerus, the which affords great matter of fear to some tender souls, and regards their vocation to a religious life. The case stands thus:

2. Some tender souls in religion, that have good minds and wills to persevere in seeking God, but being unsatisfied with themselves because they see so many imperfections not yet amended, yea, some that they had not observed before they entered into that state, impute all their unsuccessfulness in curing their defects to God's judgment upon them, for having upon light or vain grounds of their own choice undertaken such a state of life for outward, and perhaps unworthy, ends, as to avoid worldly troubles, wants, persecutions, &c., and not out of a pure intention to seek God, nor from any inspiration from Him.

3. But to show the groundlessness of such scrupulous apprehensions, such suspicious souls may do well to consider, first, that in these wicked times, in which there is such a decay of charity in the world and of fervour in religion, such heroical enterprises and such admirable calls to a religious state are not every day to be expected as we read of in former times, when kings and princes, sometimes even in the prime vigour of their age, out of a loathing of transitory things and a longing after God, renounced all the abundance of wealth, pleasure, and glory that the world could afford, inasmuch as they were impediments to their holy designs of embracing solitude, poverty, and all other penitential austerities in religion. So that it is much to be doubted, that if the greatest part of those that now enter into religion had met with the like temptations and offers in the world as those despised, most of our cells would be empty, and our convents become true deserts. Yet all this does not argue that because the calls to religion usual in these days are not so extraordinary as formerly, therefore they are insufficient, or not at all divine. For though our intentions now are not so heroical and deiform (because our

charity is not so inflamed), yet for the substance of them they may be upright.

4. Secondly, they ought to consider that God is often pleased, in love to certain souls that perhaps would be in danger to make shipwreck of that imperfect charity which is in them if they continued in the world, to permit by an especial providence certain external casualties to befall them, by which they may be in some sort compelled to retire into the secure solitude of a religious state. For which purpose also He removes many impediments to such a course, depriving them of their dearest friends, riches, &c., crossing also their designs, which if they had succeeded would have chained them to the world. Hence it is that some for want of a comfortable subsistence; others to avoid suits and other troubles, or even for want of bodily strength, and being disabled to taste the pleasures of the world; others out of a tediousness and satiety of sensual contentments; lastly, some out of a deep remorse for some special crimes, or other respects no better than these, are induced to embrace a religious state. None of which respects notwithstanding, without some degree of charity, would probably have been sufficient to have produced this change, as neither would charity alone, had it not been actuated and quickened by such considerations. Now these vocations, though mixed with much impurity, yet are far from being unlawful.

5. In the third place, it may possibly happen that some may have come into religion, induced merely and only by outward, yea perhaps unlawful, respects. They had much rather have stayed in the world, the pleasures of which, if they could have enjoyed them, they preferred far before God. But God debars them from such pleasures, sending them great crosses, which they can no otherwise avoid but by the refuge of a religious state. In which also, it may be their first design is to seek themselves only, and not God; yea, we read of one that adjoined himself to a religious community merely for this wicked end, to get an opportunity to commit sacrilege by stealing a chalice. But being there, God touched his heart to repent and acknowledge his criminal hypocrisy, after which he led a very religious holy life.

6. Again, fourthly, some do come into religion, it may be, with a good harmless meaning, but, meeting with tepid or perhaps irreligious companions, they grow weary of their condition, the difficulties of which they have not yet spiritual strength to support and improve to their soul's advancement; so that if they were again freely to dispose of themselves, they would choose to return into the world, were it not that they are chained by a vow and ecclesiastical laws. Now although these came into religion uncalled by God, yet now the impossibility of changing their present condition is an effectual call from Him to keep them constant and faithful to Him.

7. Lastly, some come into religion as it were unawares unto themselves, and without any election of their own parts, which is the case of many persons of noble families (especially virgins), that are even forced to such a state by the tyranny of their parents, or inveigled into it by the subtle avaricious insinuations and persuasions of others engaged in the same state, &c. By which means they engage themselves in a state of life unknown to themselves, relying wholly on the wills and judgment of others; and being once a little engaged, the opinion of honour, and to avoid the imputation of inconstancy, forces them to persevere.

8. Now among all these varieties of cases and vocations to religion, shall we say that only those perfect souls mentioned in the beginning have a true call to religion? If so, how much the smaller number of religious could be judged to have had a lawful call! What reason, therefore, have any souls that now desire to seek God in religion, however they come thither, to disquiet themselves? Is it because they were not perfect in charity before they entered into religion? (For a perfectly pure intention cannot proceed but from a perfect habitual charity.) Is it therefore strange to them that nature, as long as it is alive in them, should mix its own interests even in the most holy actions? Or rather is this possible to be wholly avoided, unless we were perfect in an instant? If there were any undue or unlawful external motives that induced them in the beginning to betake themselves to such a state, since it now pleases God to show unto them that such a state is so secure and so happy a condition for their souls, surely they ought rather to employ their tongues and thoughts to bless Him, who dealt with them mercifully and graciously beyond their deserts, rather than to trouble and disquiet themselves. Are they afflicted because God made them happy against their wills? Or that, by His special and most merciful providence, He discouraged them from abiding in the temptations and snares of the world? Or that He took advantage from their imperfections to bring them into the way of perfection? Or that He changed their neglect into a desire of seeking Him, though with many defects?

9. They ought, therefore, to consider that, in the present state they now are, nothing can so much harm them as such unreasonable and unquiet apprehensions. If they were now in a capacity to begin to make a free choice, they would, with an undoubted good and right intention, renounce the world, having oftentimes freely confirmed their first profession. And surely this ought to satisfy them; for God looks upon all His servants according as their present condition is, so that if they now seek Him in truth, whatsoever the motives were that brought them to their present state, they shall be no prejudice to them: if they were impure, they are forgiven, and shall never be considered; if good, they shall be considered for their good only. If they still have imperfections, it is no wonder: who does not complain, and justly, of

imperfections? When they are more perfect they will have lesser defects, but they will see many more and be more humbled, though less disquieted for them. However, certain it is that scrupulosity and fear is their far greatest and most harmful imperfection; for this alone will make perfection in the divine union impossible to be obtained as long as the soul acts according to its inclination. And the way to cure it is not to dispute or contest with the cause of it, but to neglect, transcend, and work quite contrary to it; and doing so, though the pain continue in sensitive nature, yet such will prove a very purifying mortification.

Chapter XIII. Of Humility

1. Having thus largely treated of the mortification of the principal passions in sensitive nature, we are consequently to speak of the mortifications of the will or appetites of the superior soul, the general inordination

whereof is pride, the root of all other vices, and which of all other is the last cured, as being fixed in the inmost centre of the spirit. Now pride doth generally express itself one of these three ways: 1. in curiosity of knowledge, or seeking to enrich the understanding with sciences not profitable, and sought only out of an ambition of excelling. This is mortified by a nameless virtue which St. Paul describes by this circumlocution, when he exhorts us that we would (*sapere ad sobrietatem*) *be soberly wise;* concerning which duty we have treated sufficiently when we spoke of the regulating of our reading and studies; 2. in a love and desire of self-esteem, which is mortified by that most divine fundamental virtue of Humility; 3. in a love of liberty or independency, and a desire of prelature or authority over others, which is mortified by the religious virtue of Obedience. It remains, therefore, that we conclude this treatise of mortification with instructions touching these two eminent virtues of Humility and Obedience.

2. Humility may be defined to be a virtue by which we, acknowledging the infinite greatness and majesty of God, His incomprehensible perfections, and the absolute power that He hath over us and all creatures (which are as nothing before Him), do wholly subject ourselves, both souls and bodies, with all their powers and faculties, and all things that pertain to either, to His holy will in all things, and for His sake to all creatures, according to His will.

3. Properly speaking, humility is only exercised towards God, and not to creatures; because all creatures are in themselves nothing as well as we, and so deserve as well to be despised. And on these grounds the heathens were incapable of this virtue, because they did not, nor could, intend God, who was unknown unto them; yea, it was not without ground that they disgraced and condemned this virtue (by which men compared themselves with others, preferring all before themselves) as a hindrance to other perfections; because the undervaluing one's self compared with others was, in their opinion, a means to deject men's spirits and hinder any heroical attempts of raising one's self above others; and also because if the person comparing had indeed an advantage in perfections, it would be both unreasonable and unjust not to prefer himself. But what an inconsequent way of arguing this is, I shall hereafter show.

4. In this virtue of Humility, God, towards whom it was exercised, may be considered: 1. as absolutely and abstractly in Himself; 2. as compared with creatures; 3. as in His creatures, and in several degrees participated by them.

5. In this latter regard, we for God show Humility towards men, preferring others before ourselves, contenting ourselves with the meanest things

in diet, clothes, books, &c., yea with the meanest parts and endowments of nature, flying all honour, authority, or esteem, &c.

6. If humility were thus practised by religious persons, &c., all other duties also would be cheerfully and readily practised; for if we did indeed esteem ourselves to deserve no honour, kind usage, &c., but the contrary, how could we be impatient for injuries received, unresigned in afflictions, infected with propriety, &c.? with what sweetness and peace would we live towards all! with what tenderness and charity would we embrace all, &c.!

7. Now the principal act of this Humility is that which is recommended by our holy Father in these words: 'The eleventh degree of Humility,' saith he, 'is when a soul shall not only pronounce with her tongue, but likewise in the most inward affection of the heart believe herself to be inferior to and more vile than all others, humbling herself and saying with the prophet, *I am a worm and no man, the shame of men, and an abject among the common people; I was exalted by Thee, but I am humbled and confounded.* And again, *It was good for me that Thou didst humble me, that I may learn Thy commandments.*'

8. Such true Humility is so rare to be found, that there are few that make profession of this act even in the tongue, insomuch that a man should be esteemed a hypocrite that should only pretend thereto; whereas, in truth the very essence of Humility, as regarding men, consists principally in the exercising this act; for we are not to conceive that any one is become truly humble by any one or more of the degrees of it, till he have attained (at least in preparation of mind) to the highest degree, with which our holy Father begins. Certain therefore it is, that true Humility requires this acknowledgment from us, that we believe ourselves to be inferior and more vile than all others.

9. Now though to ordinary human reason it may seem an offence against prudence and truth for one (for example) that knows himself to be skilled in arts, prudent, noble, &c., to prefer before himself those that are ignorant, silly, ignoble, &c.; or for a soul that by the Grace of God perceives herself to be free from mortal sins, and to live unblamably, yea, with edification, and perhaps is favoured by Almighty God with supernatural graces, sublime prayer, &c., to esteem herself inferior to persons that she sees abandoned to all vice and impiety; for doing so she would seem to lie against her own conscience and God, and to be extremely ungrateful to Him,—notwithstanding Humility is not at all opposed to truth, for if it were so, it could not be a virtue. Yea, it is pure divine truth itself that forces such a confession from the perfectest soul; insomuch as that he that does not know, yea, and endeavours not experimentally to feel himself to be, the most vile and

wretched of all creatures, does in vain challenge the title of being humble or true.

10. And this will appear by discovering the grounds upon which, and the means by which, true Christian Humility is built and to be attained, the which are these:

11. In the first place, we are to know that God created all things for Himself, that is, in order and subordination to Himself, so that the perfection of their natures respectively consists in the preserving of this subordination, or in taking a true measure of themselves considered in themselves, and also as compared with God; and so doing we shall in very truth, without flattery or vanity, acknowledge that we ourselves and all creatures with us are in and of ourselves simply and in propriety of speech very nothing: we have nothing, we deserve nothing, we can do nothing, yea, moreover, that by all things that proceed from ourselves, as from ourselves, we tend to nothing, and can reap nothing but what is due to defectuousness; and on the contrary, that God alone of Himself is, and has being, and that illimited, replenished with all the perfections that being can possibly have.

12. This is the main, universal, unalterable ground of Humility, by virtue of which all intellectual creatures in all states and degrees are obliged to refer to God alone, not only themselves and all manner of things (because without Him they have no being at all, and only by Him they continue to enjoy that being), but also all endowments that are in them, all operations that flow from them, as far as they are not defectuous, and the success likewise of all their actions; so that to acknowledge any good to come from any but God only, or to ascribe excellency or praise to any other but God, is a high injustice, a breach of that essential order in and for which creatures were made and are preserved.

13. By virtue of this indispensable subordination, or comparing of God with His creatures, the most perfect, most holy, and most sublime of all God's creatures do most profoundly humble themselves in His presence. The glorified saints do prostrate themselves before Him, casting their crowns at His feet; the Seraphim cover their faces, and our blessed Lord as Man, having a most perfect knowledge, perception, and feeling of the nothingness of creatures, and the absolute totality of God, did more than all saints and angels most profoundly humble Himself before the Divine Majesty of His Father, remaining continually plunged in the abyss of His own nothing. Moreover, in virtue hereof, He submitted Himself to all creatures, yea, forasmuch as concerned suffering, even to the devil himself. As a creature, He saw nothing in Himself but the nothing of a creature, and in all other creatures He saw nothing but God, to whom He humbled Himself in all, accepting as from Him whatsoever persecutions proceeded from others. True indeed it is, that with-

out offending truth He could not believe any other creature to be more holy and perfect than Himself, and so could not in that regard humble Himself to them; but he considered all His own perfections as not His own, but God's, and therefore assumed nothing to Himself for them; yea, He did not at all consider them, but only to humble Himself and renounce all pretensions to them; and the least perfection that was in others He considered as belonging to God, and so humbled Himself to God in them.

14. But in the second place, although this consideration of the not-being of creatures out of God, and the all-being of God, be indeed the true and most proper ground of perfect Humility, yet because a great supernatural light and grace is required to make a soul sensible of this (for by discourse we may come to know it in an imperfect manner, and to believe it; but to taste, perceive, and feel it, this we can never do till we be entered far into God by our prayer), therefore we are in the beginning to make use also of another more sensible, and to the weakest eyes perceivable, ground of humiliation, which is the consciousness of our many imperfections and sins, joining therewith that imperfect discursive knowledge of our own nothing and God's totality, endeavouring by these two to humble and abase ourselves, so by little and little diminishing that natural pride which is in every one of us, by which we are apt not only to think better of ourselves than of any other, to excuse our own faults, and to accuse even the best actions of others, &c., but also to raise up ourselves against and above God Himself, considering ourselves as if we were both the principle and end of all good, challenging to ourselves the praise of all either real or imaginary good in us, and referring all things to our own contentment.

15. By a serious and frequent consideration of these things, way will be made for the introducing of true solid Humility into our souls; but yet these alone will not suffice, except thereto we join: 1. abstraction of life, by which we will come to overlook and forget the imperfections of others, and only look upon our own, thence flying employments, charges, and dealing with others; or when necessity requires a treating with others, doing it with all modesty, charity, and a cordial respectfulness, being confounded at our own praises, &c.; 2. a care to practise according to what Humility obliges us, with quietness of mind accepting humiliations, contempts, &c., from others, endeavouring to welcome them, and even to take joy in them, &c.; 3. but especially internal prayer, by which we not only get a more perfect light to discover a world of formerly unseen imperfections, but also we approach nearer to God, and get a more perfect sight of Him, in whom all creatures, ourselves and all, do vanish and are annihilated.

16. Now when by these means Humility begins to get a little strength in us, it is wonderful to see how inventive and ingenious it is in finding ways

to increase in perfection. Then this degree of preferring all others whatsoever before ourselves will appear not only possible, but easily to be practised, as being most conformable to reason and duty.

17. For then a devout soul knowing how valuable and necessary a virtue Humility is, by which alone that most deadly poison of our souls, pride, is destroyed: 1. she will become scarce able to see anything in herself but what is truly her own, that is, her defectuousness and nothing, nor anything in others but what is God's; and thus doing she cannot choose but humble herself under all others, preferring all others before herself, and this without fiction, with all sincerity and simplicity; 2. she will never compare herself with others, but to the intent to abase herself; 3. if there be in her any natural endowments wanting to others, she will consider them as not her own, but God's, committed to her trust to the end to trade with them for God's glory only, of which trust a severe account shall be required; and being conscious of her negligence and ingratitude, she will be so far from glorifying herself for such endowments, that she will rather esteem them happy that want them; 4. if she have any supernatural graces which others want, yea, or if others are guilty of many open sins, she will consider that she may, according to her demerits, be deprived of them, and others enriched with them, who in all likelihood will make better use of them; for she knows by many woful experiments the perverseness of her own heart, but is utterly ignorant of others, and therefore cannot, without breach of charity, suspect that they will be so ungrateful; 5. she will not take notice of lesser imperfections in others, yea, not knowing their secret intentions, she will judge that those things which seem to be imperfections may perhaps be meritorious actions; 6. in a word, considering that God has made her a judge of herself, only to the end to condemn herself, and of others only to excuse them, and knowing that there can be no peril in judging (if it be possible) too hardly of one's self, but much in judging the worst of another in the smallest thing, though others be never so wicked, yet at least she will judge this, that if God had afforded them the light and helps that she enjoyed, they would have been angels in purity compared with her, and however that at least they are not guilty of such ingratitude as she is.

18. By such considerations as these, a devout soul will fix in her understanding a belief of her own vileness and baseness. For to make Humility a virtue it is the will that must even compel the understanding to say, 'I will believe myself to be inferior to all, according as I find just cause by these considerations,' and the same will will upon occasion force practices suitable to such a belief. It will make the soul afraid to seek things pleasing to her, yea, content with all hard usage, as knowing she deserves far worse, and ought to expect to be trodden under foot by all creatures; so that in love to justice and equality she will even desire and rejoice in all affronts, persecu-

tions, and contempts; or if certain circumstances, as infirmity of body, &c., shall require, and that she be necessitated to choose or desire, any consolations, she will accept them in the spirit of humility and mortification; that is, purely in obedience to the Divine Will, and not at all for the satisfaction of nature, being far from thinking herself worthy of anything but want, pain, and contempt.

19. Now a superior is not to be judged to offend against this degree of Humility when he discovers, objects, reprehends, or punishes the faults of his subjects; for in so doing he sustains the person of God, to whom alone it belongs to exercise the office of a judge, yet withal the superior ought not therefore to esteem himself better than the person reprehended; for though perhaps in that one respect he cannot much condemn himself, yet for many other faults which he sees in himself and cannot see in others, he may and ought to remain humbled, yea, to be more confounded whensoever the duty of his place requires of him to be a reprehender of others, whilst himself doth far more deserve reprehension.

20. When by serious practice of humiliation joined with prayer a soul is come to a high degree of purity in spiritual exercises, then is attained that more admirable kind of Humility which regards God; in which the soul contemplating His totality and illimited universality of being, and thence reflecting on her own nothing (of which now she has a more perfect sight), she most profoundly humbles and annihilates herself before Him.

21. And when prayer is come to perfection, then will the soul also mount to the supreme degree of Humility, which regards God considered absolutely in Himself, and without any express or distinct comparison with creatures; for hereby a soul fixing her sight upon God as all in all, and contemplating Him in the darkness of incomprehensibility, does not by any distinct act or reflection consider the vacuity and nothingness of creatures, but really transcends and forgets them, so that to her they are in very deed as nothing, because they are not the object which with her spirit she only sees, and with her affections only embraces.

22. This most heroical Humility can only be exercised in the act of contemplation, for then only it is that a soul feels her own nothing, without intending to reflect upon it. At all other times she in some degree feels the false supposed being of herself and creatures, because it is only in actual pure prayer that the images of them are expelled, and with the images the affections to them also.

23. Notwithstanding, a great measure and proportion of the virtue of such prayer remains, and is operative also afterwards out of prayer; for if the soul do see creatures, she never sees them as in themselves, but only in relation to God, and so in them humbles herself to God and loves God in them;

and if she reflect upon herself, and turn her eyes inward into her spirit, desiring to find God there, there will not be any considerable imperfection, obscurity, or stain that will darken her view of God, but she will discover it and most perfectly hate it.

24. As for sins or imperfections in others, though never so heinous, they are no hindrance to her seeing of God, because either she transcends and marks them not, or is by their means urged to a nearer and more fervent love of Him for His patience—to a greater zeal for His honour impaired by the sins of men, and to a greater compassion towards sinners.

25. But the least imperfection in herself being really a hindrance to her immediate union with God and perfect sight of Him is, in so great a light as she then enjoys, perfectly seen and perfectly abhorred by her; yea, such faults as to her natural understanding formerly appeared no bigger than motes, do in virtue of this supernatural light seem as mountains; and defects which she before never dreamed or imagined to be in herself, she now sees not only to be, but to abound and bear great sway in her. To this purpose saith St. Gregory (1. 22, Moral. c. i.): *Sancti viri quo altuis apud Deum proficiunt, eè subtilius indignos se deprehendunt, quia dum proximi luci fiunt, quidquid in illis latebat inveniunt:* that is, Holy men the higher that they raise themselves approaching to God, the more clearly do they perceive their own unworthiness, because, being encompassed with a purer light, they discover in themselves those defects which before they could not see.

26. Hence it appears that there is a great difference between the knowledge of our own nothing, and the feeling or perception of it. The former may be got by a little meditation, or by reading school divinity, which teaches and demonstrates how that of ourselves we are nothing, but mere dependences on the only true being of God. Whereas the feeling of our own nothing will never be attained by study or meditation alone, but by the raising and purifying of our souls by prayer. The devil hath the knowledge of the nothingness of creatures in a far greater perfection than any man, and yet he hath nothing at all of the feeling. Now it is only the feeling of our not-being that is true perfect Humility, as, on the contrary, the feeling of our being is pride.

27. Now this feeling of our not-being has two degrees: 1. The first is in regard of the corporal or sensitive faculties, to wit, when the soul is so raised above the body and all desires concerning it that it hath lost all care and solicitude about it, having mortified in a great measure all inferior passions. This is a high degree of Humility, but yet not perfect, as may appear plainly by this, that after a soul hath attained hereto by a passive union, there ordinarily follows the great privation or desolation, in which she finds herself

to be yet full of herself and her own being, combated with many risings and repugnances. 2. The second degree follows after that the said privation ceases, in which the soul exercises herself after a far more sublime manner, and begins then to have a more perfect feeling of her not-being, consisting in an abstraction from the soul herself and all her faculties and operations, all which are so lost and annihilated in God, that in her exercises of most pure prayer she cannot perceive distinctly any working either in the understanding or will, not being able to understand or give an account of what she does when she prays.

28. The author of *Secrets Sentiers* saith that souls which are arrived to this state of perfect union are yet ordinarily permitted by God to descend oft from their high abstractions into their inferior nature, even as they were during their state of entrance into a spiritual course. So that (according to his doctrine) during such a descent they must needs be full of the feeling of their own being. But then, saith he, they from this descent do by little and little through their internal exercises ascend higher than they were ever before, and such ascents and descents interchangeably continue all their lives. Thus saith Barbanzon, perhaps out of experience of what passed in his own soul. But whether from thence he had sufficient warrant to apply these observations so generally, I leave to the determination of the perfect, who only can judge of such matters.

29. But alas, these contemplations, and consequently the said blessed fruits of them, are very rare, and not at all in our own power to come at pleasure, inasmuch as a soul does not arrive to the perfection of prayer till after a passive union or contemplation, whereto well may we dispose ourselves according to our power; but it is in the free will and pleasure of God to confer it on whom, when, and in what manner it pleaseth Him.

30. But, however, let not beginners nor proficients in spirituality be discouraged, for that as yet they cannot find in themselves (or at least very imperfectly) a perception of their not-being, not having as yet a supernatural intellectual species evidently and even palpably representing to their minds God's totality and their own nothing, the which species it is not the nature of active exercises to produce. It is a great blessing of God to them that He has given them the courage to aspire thereunto. And persevering in the ways leading thither, they will certainly arrive to the partaking of the substance of this sublime Humility, in virtue of which alone all other virtues will be perfectly exercised by them; inasmuch as by it they will come to know both God and themselves aright, and be in an immediate disposition (as our holy Father says) to that perfect charity which expels all fear, for which reason he only treats particularly and largely of this virtue, and of Obedience, which is a branch of it.

31. We ought therefore never to cease praying that God would reveal unto us our own nothing and His all-being: for prayer is the only effectual means to attain unto it. As for exterior acts and expressions of Humility, if they flow from prayer, they may be profitable and acceptable to God; however, for the peril of pride, which will insinuate and mingle itself even in Humility also, we should not be too forward to exercise voluntary outward affections of Humility out of a pretence of giving edification to others. And when we do such as are commanded in the Rule, and conformable to our state, we ought in them, as well as we can, to purify our intention.

Chapter XIV. Of Obedience

§§ 1, 2. Of the mortification of our natural inclination to liberty or independency, by the virtue of Obedience.

§§ 3, 4. Obedience likewise regards God, either mediately or immediately. And that it is easier to obey God than man.

§§ 5, 6, 7, 8. The obligation laid by our holy Rule on subjects to discover their internal defects to superiors is now much out of use. And how this is come to pass.

§ 9. Obedience earnestly pressed by St. Benedict.

§ 10. It ought to proceed from the soul.

§§ 11, 12. Of the doctrine of casuists limiting or dispensing with regular Obedience; and what use is to be made of it.

§§ 13, 14. Special advices thereabouts to scrupulous souls.

§ 15. Truly perfect obedience has no limits.

§§ 16, 17, 18. Several defects in obedience.

§§ 19, 20, 21, 22, 23. How a soul is to behave herself in obediences, in things prejudicial, and in such as are pleasing to nature.

§ 24. An example of perfect simplicity in obedience.

§ 25. Of obedience to brethren required in our Rule.

§ 26. Prayer a necessary means to beget obedience.

1. The second depravation of the will which is to be mortified is a natural love of liberty and independence, as also an ambition to dispose and rule others; and the proper virtue whereby this is mortified is (religious) Obedience, which is a branch of Humility, as the aforesaid depravation is of pride.

2. Obedience, therefore, as well as Humility, doth principally regard God, even when it is performed to man. And indeed unless our obedience to creatures do flow from our obedience due to God, it will never advance or perfectionate the soul, but rather nourish all depraved affections in it, as having its root in self-love, servile fear, yea oft in pride itself; whereas, if it be grounded on our duty to God, the soul thereby will become so humble, supple, and pliable, that it will not refuse to subject itself to the meanest creatures, it will cheerfully suffer all crosses, contradictions, and pressures, both external and internal.

3. Obedience is performed either: 1. immediately to God alone; 2. or immediately to man, but for God's sake. We will in this place only treat of this latter; for as for the other, it comprehends all the duties of piety and devotion, whether external or internal, and therefore needs not be spoken of particularly.

4. To submit one's self to man for God's sake, or out of love to God, is much harder than to do it immediately to God (and consequently it is in that regard more meritorious, and will most efficaciously and speedily bring a soul to perfection). The reasons of the greater difficulty in our obedience to men are: 1. Because we acknowledge our superior to be God's substitute, yet we are not always convinced that his particular commands proceed from him as such, but rather from passion, natural interests, aversion, &c., so that we cannot see his commands to be so reasonable (as God's are acknowledged to be), nor that obedience to them will produce so much good to the soul. 2. Because we know our superior cannot see nor judge the heart, but may err and be mistaken, so that it is not easy to submit the mind to one that has no right over it, nor power to see his commands perfectly executed.

5. For this reason it is that our holy Father, knowing the wonderful virtue and efficacy of obedience proceeding from the heart, requires in his holy Rule that subjects should in a sort communicate to their superiors that proper attribute of God, who calls Himself a seer and searcher of the heart; with humility and simplicity discovering unto them all their considerable imperfections in thoughts; and this he does not only out of an eye to the benefit that may come by the sacrament of penance, for this was to be done though the superior were no priest (as anciently oft they were not), but the ends of this obligation were: 1. For the more perfect humiliation of the subject, and a mortification of that natural aversion that we have from the discovering and submitting to the censures of others our secret defects. 2. To the end that the superior might be enabled to govern his subjects for their spiritual advancement.

6. We may reasonably impute to the disuse of this obligation the great decay of religious discipline and perfection in the world; because now,

generally speaking, superiors know no more of their subjects but what they chance to observe in their outward behaviour, for as for internal matters (which are the principal), they all pass between each religious person and a private chosen confessarius.

7. But withal the disuse of the said obligation we are to impute: 1. Partly to the tepidity of subjects and their want of care to be governed by a way absolutely the best for themselves, however very heavy to corrupt nature. 2. But principally to the incapacity and insufficiency of superiors, in regard of which such a change of the said custom was esteemed even necessary.

8. Surely this most excellent practice had never been brought into disuse, or would again be restored, if superiors (according as our holy Rule requires, and as in the primitive times they were) had continued, or generally now were: 1. Themselves practised in a spiritual course of prayer and contemplation, and would consider that their duty is to direct their subjects' souls in the same way. 2. If they had the spirit of discretion and light to discern the several dispositions and capacities of their subjects' souls in order to their principal end. 3. If in whatsoever impositions they lay on them beyond the observances of the Rule, they would regard whether thereby their subjects (considering their several tempers) are likely to be advanced or hindered in their spiritual course, and not esteem that it is a sufficient justification for them that the things in themselves are not ill, and their end therein is to mortify their subjects' wills and passions; for such mortifications there may be as will endanger to extinguish the light that is in their subjects' souls, by drawing them to multiplicity, &c., so that no other impositions or mortifications are excusable but such as right reason enlightened by grace would judge necessary, and such as God Himself would ordain for them. 4. Especially if they would abstain from laying such encumbrances on their subjects as are lasting, and regard not only the exterior but interior also, distracting the memory, confounding the understanding, and breeding perplexity in their minds, or, in a word, that are prejudicial to internal prayer (for indeed impositions are to be accounted only so far to be encumbrances). 5. Lastly, if they did require obedience from their subjects, not to show their own authority, but only to benefit their subjects' souls thereby (without which intention their office becomes merely secular, &c.). If, I say, superiors had remained thus qualified, there would never have been any sufficient occasion to dispense with such an order prescribed by our holy Father, touching the subjects' revealing to the superior their most secret imperfections, even in thoughts.

9. But however, matters standing as they now do, and obedience being divided, as it were, between a regular and a spiritual director, the subject is to perform to each the obedience which is due; yet with this difference,

that he is to consider that the obligation of obedience to a spiritual director, voluntarily chosen by the subject and changeable at pleasure, is far less strict than to a superior, who has God's authority communicated to him, confirmed by the Church, ratified by a solemn vow, by virtue of which we have given up our wills wholly to the wills of our superiors. Insomuch as that our holy Father (in the 5th chap. of the Rule) requires a performance of this duty on no meaner motives than the hope of heaven, the fear of hell, and, which is the most perfect of all other, the love of God; for, with he, obedience without delay is proper to them who esteem nothing dearer to themselves than Christ.

10. Now since the only principal end why a religious person has engaged himself in a life of obedience is the good and advancement of his soul, and not any temporal convenience, as in secular governments, therefore, notwithstanding the common saying that our souls are exempted from human jurisdiction, and notwithstanding that in these days, as hath been said, superiors are not always the directors of their subjects' consciences,—yet unless their commands be obeyed in purity of heart, as for God's sake, and with submission not only of the outward but inward man also, that is, both the will and judgment, such obedience is not at all meritorious nor conformable to the general design of a religious life and to their vows of profession. For if all Christians, as St. Paul teacheth, be obliged to obey secular superiors, and servants their masters, not for fear of wrath or punishment, but for conscience' sake, and in order to God, who hath invested them with authority, intending principally the good of their souls in all manner of exterior obligations, surely this doth much more strictly hold in religious obedience, which was ordained and hath been undertaken only for the benefit of the soul.

11. Therefore, whereas later doctors and casuists have found out exemptions in many cases abridging the authority of superiors, and disobliging subjects from obedience, a religious subject that seriously aspires to perfection according to his profession will be very wary how he makes use of the advantages and dispensations afforded him, considering that although by such disobedience he may perhaps escape the punishment of external laws, yet he will not esteem himself quit from his obligation to obey, unless the things unduly commanded be such as are inconsistent with his duty to God, and manifestly prejudicial to his soul.

12. Moreover, a truly humble internal liver will very rarely, and not without extreme necessity, make use of that just liberty of appealing from an immediate superior allowed by the laws of the Church; and this he will never do for the ease of nature, or the satisfying of any passion, but purely for the good of the soul. Indeed, I do scarce know any case in which an appeal may be fit to be used by such souls, except perhaps when they find that their immediate superior, either out of ignorance or a disaffection to spiritual prayer,

shall abridge their subjects of time and means necessary for the exercise of it, either by overburdening them with distractive and solicitous employments, or as it were purposely; and this frequently and customarily imposing on them obediences at the times appointed and proper for prayer. Yet surely the case must needs be extraordinary if a soul cannot, by using her dexterity and prudence, recover each day two half-hours for recollection.

13. Notwithstanding, some good use may be made of the opinion of doctors, touching the limits and bounds prescribed to the authority of superiors, and the degrees of obligation to such authority, for the necessary ease of devout, tender, and scrupulous souls. Not that such are to be encouraged to dispense with themselves in the duties required thereby, but lest they, out of tenderness in suspecting oft a mortal sin to have been committed by disobedience where perhaps there was scarce any fault at all, should be disquieted, perplexed, and hindered from reaping any benefit by prayer or any other duties. And indeed little danger is there that souls so disposed should from any larger interpretations make advantage to the ease of nature or the satisfaction of an inordinate passion.

14. Such souls, therefore, may know: 1. That the authority of superiors is not illimited, but confined to certain conditions, as that it must be *juxta regulam,* neither besides nor above the Rule, and that their command must be *ad edifacationem,* and not *ad destructionem, &c.* 2. That disobedience to their commands which are according to the Rule is not a mortal offence, unless the matters commanded be in themselves of more than ordinary importance, and that a command be expressly given, and with signification that their intention is that it should so oblige, and that the subject has not ground to judge that if the superior were present he would not have urged such an obedience so strictly. 3. That in matters of lesser moment a disobedience mortally sinful is not committed, unless it be done with manifest contempt, that is, as St. Bernard (lib. de Precept. et Dispens.) interprets it, 'When the subject will neither obey nor submit to correction for disobedience.' So that all faults that are committed by one that really has a mean or contemptuous opinion of his superior, and which without such a precedent unfit opinion would not have been committed, are not to be called in this sense sins out of contempt, unless the subject renounce correction—a fault that such tender souls are incapable of committing, &c.

15. Perfect obedience, saith the same St. Bernard, knows no ends or limits: it extends itself to all lawful things pertaining either to body or soul, and to all actions, both external and internal (as far as these last are voluntarily submitted to him), insomuch as that our holy Father, to cut off all pretences of disobedience, does not except even things impossible; so that if such things as not only in the faint-hearted opinion of the subject are es-

teemed such, but really are impossible, should be seriously and considerately imposed by a discreet superior (for trial), the subject is obliged to do his endeavour toward the effecting of them, so they be lawful and not destructive to the subject's life. Yea, we find examples of saints that upon commands of superiors have cast themselves into rivers, or leaped down precipices, or taken coals of fire into their hands, &c. But we are to suppose that, in these cases, there was a special divine instinct both in the superior commanding and the subjects obeying, as the events showed, the said subjects having never miscarried, but been miraculously delivered from any harm by what they so did in obedience; and therefore the like examples cannot be drawn into a rule.

16. The several defects in point of obedience (the avoiding of which defects constitutes several degrees of true religious obedience) are reckoned by Turrecremata to be these which follow, viz.: 1. To do some, but not all things enjoined. 2. If all, yet imperfectly and incompletely. 3. Or not in the manner requisite. 4. Or not upon the first simple bidding, but expecting a second command, or perhaps one in form and in virtue of obedience. 5. Or to do it with reluctance and unwillingness. 6. Or after discussing the reasonableness and lawfulness of the command. 7. To go slowly and lazily about it. 8. To do it rashly and without fit preparation. 9. For want of a resolute purpose beforehand to obey absolutely and universally, to be in a readiness to contradict when commands come upon the sudden, rather than to hasten to obey. 10. Then to obey indeed, yet not without repining, or at least a show of it in the countenance. 11. Or, however, with sadness and dejectedness. 12. To obey in greater matters, but not so readily in small. 13. To obey in the substance of the thing commanded, but not according to the intention of the superior or law. 14. The command being unpleasing, to suspect or judge ill of the superior's intention. 15. To make pretended excuses of insufficiency. 16. To be of so troublesome and froward an humour as to discourage the superior from imposing any commands. 17. Out of an opinion of one's own judgment or sufficiency, to slight the superior's way of government. 18. To seek to draw the superior to one's own way and opinions, and so in effect to become as superior. 19. When one does the thing commanded, to do it with a willing fraudulent insufficiency. 20. Not to do it with all cheerfulness and readiness. 21. Lastly, not to obey with a perfect intention for God's glory and love.

17. Now lest a beginner should be discouraged, seeing so many conditions requisite to perfect obedience, and so many defects to be avoided, he must consider that God does not expect at the first from him an obedience in all points perfect. It is well that he do the command without sin, that is, not making the principal motive to be outward sensual respects, and without behaving himself with a deliberate defectuousness, murmuring, &c. By practice in obeying according to one's power, a soul will by little and little wear out

the defects, as it is in the learning of any art or trade. An obedience, though imperfect, so it be not sinful, meriteth somewhat; and besides, it disposeth the person to amend it the next time, by taking notice of the defect and being willing to be admonished.

18. It is no marvel, neither is it a fault, that the body being wearied and exhausted with many obediences, there should thereupon be found in inferior nature a reluctance. But the mind or will should never be weary or backward, but remain ever invincible, forcing inferior nature to comply to the utmost of her power, but yet according to discretion.

19. In case a superior command a subject things not only heavy and grievous to nature, but even such as are apparently contrary to health and corporal strength, as a rigorous conformity to regular abstinence, fastings, watchings, &c., the subject must neither refuse the command nor show any unwillingness to obey; but having, after good consideration and experience, found himself unable and infirm, he may lawfully declare unto the superior such his infirmity, so he do it (as the Rule expresses it, *patienter et opportune*) with patience, and taking an opportune time for it, not suddenly, querulously, and in a passion. But in case the superior do persist, the subject must obey, submitting both body, will, and judgment, and so committing the issue to God; and then the success, whatever it be, cannot but be good.

20. If the thing commanded be grateful to nature, honourable, pleasing, &c., it is not good nor secure to be over-forward in obeying; it were better, so it might be done without offence, to seek to avoid it, wishing that others might rather be employed, or, however, to undertake it as obedience only, and, as it were, against our wills. But if the matter be harsh to nature, we are to do it with all possible readiness and cheerfulness, being desirous that others should be exempted from it.

21. It is not very hard internally to resolve universally to forsake one's own will, submitting it to another. But really and actually to perform this at all times, whensoever obediences are imposed, and that frequently; and when the things are of difficulty and contradiction to nature (and it may be), imposed by a superior against whom the subject hath some disaffection in nature, or of whom he hath a mean opinion, and when the subject himself is in an ill-humour of obeying, or when the obediences, though performed never so cheerfully and exactly, yet are usually ill-accepted, censured, &c.,— this requires a great courage and perfect self-denial, and much more to persevere in such obedience to the end of one's life with meekness and patient subjection.

22. And a yet greater degree of perfection is it (to which notwithstanding internal livers ought to aspire) for a religious person that is hardly and injuriously treated by his superior to be content and desirous that he

should continue to use him so or worse, so it might be without offence to God, and so that no harm might come to the superior's soul thereby.

23. There are no commands, though never so impertinent or distracting, that can prejudice perfect souls that are come to an established state of recollection, and habitually enjoy the Divine presence. But great harm and danger may come thereby to the imperfect, the which, notwithstanding, by patience, quietness, and meekness in obeying, may come to make their profit even from them also, so that, though they lose one way by a hindrance to their recollection, they may repair that loss by rooting these virtues more firmly in their souls. However, the superior must expect to have a severe account required of him for indiscreet and harmful impositions laid upon his subjects.

24. A memorable example of obedience, joined with a mortification very sensible to humble souls (to wit, a mortification caused by an obligation to accept undue and unproportionable honour), we read of in the story of the great St. Basil, who, having obtained at his own request from a neighbour bishop a priest to attend him, recommended as an humble and obedient person, St. Basil, for a trial of these virtues, required of him to prepare some water for the washing of his feet. The good priest with a modest cheerfulness obeyed, and having quickly brought the water, St. Basil, sitting down, commanded him to wash his feet, who readily and diligently performed that command. That being done, the saint commands the priest to sit down, that so he in exchange might also wash his feet. The humble and virtuously simple man, without any excuses or contestations, quietly and calmly, as it became one perfect in obedience, suffers his feet to be washed by him, who was then the most eminent and most reverend prelate in the Eastern Church. Upon this proof, St. Basil was satisfied that he had found an attendant fit for the employments to which he destined him, and, with many thanks to the neighbour bishop, took the priest with him for his inseparable companion.

25. There is mentioned in our holy Rule another sort of obedience, of great efficacy to bring souls to perfection, to wit, an obedience not out of obligation and duty to superiors, but only from respect to brethren (specially ancients) in religion, and this out of charity, and in conformity to St. Paul's advice (which is very general) that we should in honour prefer every one before ourselves. This kind of obedience, as receiving proper commands from such, is now out of practice. And whether this disuse has proceeded from want of simplicity and humility in the younger sort, or from imperfection and want of discretion and gravity in the more ancient, or perhaps from jealousy and love of being absolute in superiors, it is hard to say; but surely it is a great loss. There were likewise obligations imposed upon all juniors, after any the least offence taken by the ancients, to make present satisfaction by

prostrations, the which were to continue till that pardon and a benediction were given. Indeed, in those times, in which so much abstraction of life and so seldom mutual conversations were used, offences were so rare that it would be no hard matter for such simple humble souls as most religious persons then were to comply with these obligations. So that the only way to restore them is to restore that most profitable abstraction, solitude, and silence again.

26. It is vain for any one to seek the attaining to the perfection of obedience (which, besides the outward work, requires a submission of the spirit itself to God alone, in the superior, and a renouncing of one's own judgment upon the dictates of the most ignorant or indiscreet superior) but by the serious and constant practice of internal prayer, which alone purifies the soul and makes all other things but God invisible to her. So that, without such prayer, all other exterior practices of an officious humiliation will be of little or no virtue or efficacy thereto.

Chapter XV. Of Virtues in General

§ 1. We do not here treat of all kinds of mortification or virtues; but principally such as are most proper and most necessary to be known and practised in order to an internal life.

§§ 2, 3, 4, 5, 6, 7, 8, 9, 10, 11. Several advices and observations touching virtues in general.

1. Hitherto we have treated of the first instrument and mean of perfection, to wit, Mortification; at least, so far as we conceived proper to the design of this book, that is, in order to internal prayer of contemplation. And therefore it is that we have not enlarged the discourse to comprehend universally all moral virtues (the which are mortifications to all our distempered affections), but only such as are more peculiar to religious or internal livers. For the rest the reader is referred to other books of Christian morality, which abundantly treat of that subject, the doctrine of which may be applied to the present purpose, if reflection be made on the advices which have already been given concerning the special virtues hitherto treated of. To the which I will, for conclusion of this treatise, add a few more touching virtues in general.

2. The first advice is this, that before a soul can attain to perfect contemplation it is necessary that she be adorned with all sorts of Christian virtues, not one excepted, according to the saying of the Psalmist: *Ibunt de virtute in virtutem: videbitur Deus Deorum in Sion*—that is, They shall go from one virtue to another, and then (and not till then) the God of gods shall

be contemplated in Sion. So that if a soul make a stop at any virtue, or willingly favour herself in any inordinate affection, it will not be possible for her to ascend to the top of the mountain where God is seen.

3. The second regards the manner of attaining to virtues; for we are not so to understand these words of the Psalmist as if a soul's progress to perfection was by a successive gaining of one virtue after another; for example, first possessing herself of the virtue of temperance, and, having got that, then proceeding to patience, humility, chastity, &c. But they are all in the root gotten together, and we make no progress in one virtue, but withal we make a proportionable progress in all the rest. And the reason is, because charity is the root of all Christian virtues, they being only such duties as charity (which alone directs us to God, our last end) would and doth dictate to be practised on several and different occasions.

4. True it is that, either by our natural tempers or by having more frequent trials and occasions of exercising some virtues, certain passions opposite to them may be, according to the material disposition in corporal nature, more subdued and regulated than others; yet, in regard of the disposition of the spiritual soul (that is, the judgment of the mind and resolution of the will), the soul (according to the merit of the object) is equally (by an equality of proportion) inclined to all good, and equally averted from all ill. Because divine love is equally inconsistent with all mortal sins, and doth combat and subdue self-love in all its branches. Our progress, therefore, expressed in the phrase *de virtute in virtutem,* is to be understood to be from a lower and more imperfect degree of charity, and all its virtues, to a higher, till we come to the mount of perfection.

5. The third advice is, that this progress and increase in virtues is neither equal at all times—for the soul, by resisting stronger temptations and in virtue of more efficacious prayer, doth make greater strides and paces— neither is it always observable either by the traveller himself or others. Yea, it is neither necessary nor perhaps convenient that we should much heed the rules that are given by some for examination of our proficiency. Such inquiry seems not very suitable to humility, and probably will not produce any good effect in us; it may suffice us that we go on, and that God knows perfectly our growth in piety and love, and will most assuredly reward us proportionally, though we should be never so ignorant to what degree of perfection we are arrived.

6. Fourthly, all increase of sanctifying grace, by whatsoever instruments it be produced, as by regular austerities, temperance, exercises of mortification, &c., is performed according to the good internal dispositions and actuations of soul accompanying the use of them. Yea, the same may

also, in a certain proportion, be affirmed even of the sacraments themselves *(in adultis),* the which, although, by their own intrinsical virtue, and (as the Council of Trent, sess. vii. can. 8, expresses it) *ex opere operato,* they do confer a peculiar grace and aid, and this, *quantum est a parte Dei,* at all times and on all persons that duly receive them (see sess. vii. can. 6 and 7), yet, withal, the quantity and measure of the said grace is in the same council (sess. vi. cap. 7) said to be *(Secundum propriam cujusque dispositionem et coöperationem)* according to the peculiar disposition and coöperation of each person respectively; that is, those that come with more (or less) perfect, intense, continued, and multiplied internal acts of faith, hope, charity, devotion, &c., do accordingly receive a more (or less) plentiful measure of sacramental grace. Now what are all these dispositions and preparations but the exercising of internal prayer? Whence appears how wonderful an influence internal prayer, both by way of merit or impetration, and likewise by a direct efficiency, hath in the producing and increase of divine virtues in the soul.

7 . Fifthly, if a soul out of the times of prayer shall in occasions (for example) of contradictions, persecutions, &c., neglect to exercise patience, she must necessarily exercise impatience, and, by consequence, will make little or no progress by her prayer; yet, if then she shall use any reasonable care, diligence, or watchfulness over herself, though not for the getting of much, yet not to lose much out of prayer, God will, by means of her prayer seriously prosecuted, infuse such a measure of grace as will cause a progress, notwithstanding frequent failings through frailty or inadvertence, &c., but it will be late ere the effects of such infusion will appear.

8. Sixthly, increase in virtue doth purely depend on the free grace and good pleasure of God conferring the said grace in prayer, &c., in a measure as Himself pleaseth, and also by His holy Providence, administering occasions severally of exercising several virtues, the which occasions ordinarily are not at all in our own power or disposal.

9. Seventhly, according to our progress in virtues so is our progress in prayer; and till

the soul be in a very high degree purified from self-love she is incapable of that perfect degree of prayer which is called contemplation. According to that saying of our Saviour (Matt. v.), *Beati mundo corde, quoniam ipsi Deum videbunt;* that is, 'Blessed are the pure in heart, for they shall see God.' And the reason is evident, because until the internal eye of the soul be cleansed from the mists of passion and inordinate affections, it neither will nor can fix itself upon so pure and divine an object. True it is, that in every the most imperfect degree of prayer (by which the soul is proportionally purified) God is, in some qualified sense, contemplated. But we do not apply the term Contemplation except only to the most sublime degree of prayer; the which yet is never so perfectly absolute in this life but that it may, without limitation, increase; because the soul is never so perfectly freed from the bitter fruits of original sin (ignorance and concupiscence), but there will ever remain matter and exercise for further mortification or purification.

10. Eighthly, virtues are in no other state of life so perfectly established in the depth and centre of the spirit as in a contemplative state, because all the exercises thereof do principally and directly regard the exaltation, spiritualising, and purification of the spirit by a continual application, adhesion, and union of it to God, the Fountain of light and purity.

11. Lastly, by the means of contemplative prayer in an internal life, virtues are most easily obtained, most securely possessed, and most perfectly practised. In an active life a person that aspires to perfection therein stands in need of many things to enable him for the practice of the duties disposing thereto; for the exercise of external works of charity there are needful riches or friends, &c.; and for spiritual almsgiving there is required learning, study, disputation, &c.; and if by the help of these there be acquired an established habit of solid charity, it is not very securely possessed in the midst of so many distractions, solicitudes, and temptations. But a contemplative life (as St. Thomas, 22 q. 182 a. i. c., observes, even from Aristotle himself) stands in need of very few things, being to itself sufficient. Such a person alone, without needing either assistance or favour from abroad, can both purchase and exercise all virtues; yea, and liberally dispense all kinds of charity to others also. For by prayer alone, exercised in solitude, he can employ and engage God's omnipotence, wisdom, and all the treasures of His riches for the supplying all the necessities, external and internal, of His Church. The light that is gotten by prayer will be more than equivalent to long and laborious study (not sanctified with prayer) for the enabling him to discharge efficaciously a pastoral charge over souls when they shall be committed to him, though no doubt prayer will also incite to sufficient study. And in the mean time, though he were deprived of all conversations and books—yea, fettered and buried in the obscurity of a dungeon—prayer alone would be a sufficient entertainment to him. There he would find God and His Holy Spirit as present and as bountiful to him as ever; yea, the greater solitude there is, at the more freedom is the soul to run speedily and lightly in the course of virtues, for nothing doth indeed fetter her but self-love and propriety. And lastly, virtues once gotten are evidently most securely possessed in solitude, from whence all distraction and almost all temptations are excluded.

THE END OF THE SECOND TREATISE OF MORTIFICATION.

THE THIRD TREATISE
OF PRAYER

TO THE VENERABLE AND R. LADY D. CATHERINE GASCOIGNE

THE LADY ABBESS OF THE RELIGIOUS DAMES ON THE HOLY ORDER OF ST. BENEDICT, IN CAMBRAY;

AND TO ALL THE RR. DAMES, ETC., OF THE SAME CONVENT.

MADAME,

If I had not any pressing obligation (as I have many) to take all occasions to acknowledge both my worthy esteem and resentment also for your many favours, yet without injustice I could not but return unto Your Ladyship, &c., these instructions about the prayer of Contemplation, which from your full store I first received. I could wish it had been in my power to commend them to the liking and practice of others, as the admirable piety of the Venerable Author (whose memory will always be in benediction with you) did to yours. But being able to boast no other virtue in this matter, but only diligence and fidelity (asserted by Your Ladyship's own testimony), I should doubt that the unworthiness of the compiler would to their disparagement prevail against the excellency of the Author, and his argument, were it not that I am confident that a view (apparent to all that know that Convent) of the many most blessed effects that they have produced there, will have the force to recommend them to strangers, and to defend them against contradictors. Your great charity (RR. DD.) makes you think yourselves not unbeholding to me for dispersing thus abroad to all that will accept them these your richest jewels, your most delicious provisions, your most secure armour, that is, all that makes your solitude and scarcity, &c., deserve to be the envy of princes' courts, the habitation of angels, and temples of God Himself. For prayer is all this, and more good than yourselves can express; and yet you can express more than any others but such as yourselves can understand. Since, therefore, you have been pleased to say I have obliged you by this publication, let my recompense, I beseech you, be to be sometimes thought of in your prayers, that I may become seriously mine own disciple, and learn by this book to pray as you do; and that this work may invite the readers, whoever they be only to make a trial (though at first but even out of curiosity) whether we have boasted too largely of the treasures here exposed. This, if through the Divine assistance they shall do, it may be hoped that many unawares to themselves will become converts not only to piety, but even to Catholic Truth and Unity. And surely none will suspect that any danger can come from pure spiritual prayer.

Madame and RR. DD.,

Your servant in our Lord most humbly devoted,

Br. SERENUS CRESSY

Doway, this 23rd of July, 1657.

THE THIRD TREATISE
THE FIRST SECTION

OF PRAYER IN GENERAL, AND THE GENERAL DIVISION OF IT.

Chapter I. The Excellency of Prayer in General

§§ 1, 2, 3, 4. Of Prayer in general. What it is.

§§ 5, 6, 7, 8. It is the most excellent and most necessary of all duties.

§§ 9, 10. The division of prayer into mental and vocal, improper.

1. The whole employment of an internal contemplative life having been by me comprehended under two duties, to wit, Mortification and Prayer, concerning (the former) mortification we have discoursed largely in the precedent treatise. We are now henceforward to treat of the other most noble and divine instrument of perfection, which is Prayer; by which and in which alone we attain to the reward of all our endeavours, the end of our creation and redemption—to wit, union with God, in which alone consists our happiness and perfection.

2. By prayer, in this place, I do not understand petition or supplication, which, according to the doctrine of the schools, is exercised principally by the understanding, being a signification of what the person desires to receive from God. But prayer here especially meant is rather an offering and giving to God whatsoever He may justly require from us—that is, all duty, love, obedience, &c.; and it is principally, yea, almost only exercised by the affective part of the soul.

3. Now prayer, in this general notion, may be defined to be an elevation of the mind to God, or more largely and expressly thus: prayer is an affectuous actuation of an intellective soul towards God, expressing, or at

241

least implying, an entire dependence on Him as the Author and Fountain of all good, a will and readiness to give Him His due, which is no less than all love, obedience, adoration, glory, and worship, by humbling and annihilating of herself and all creatures in His presence; and lastly, a desire and intention to aspire to an union of spirit with Him.

4. This is the nature and these the necessary qualities which are all, at least virtually, involved in all prayer, whether it be made interiorly in the soul only, or withal expressed by words or outward signs.

5. Hence it appears that prayer is the most perfect and most divine action that a rational soul is capable of; yea, it is the only principal action for the exercising of which the soul was created, since in prayer alone the soul is united to God. And, by consequence, it is of all other actions and duties the most indispensably necessary.

6. For a further demonstration of which necessity we may consider: 1. That only in prayer we are joined to God, our last end, from whom when we are separated we are in ourselves, wherein our chief misery consists. 2. That by prayer grace and all good is obtained, conserved, and recovered; for God being the Fountain of all good, no good can be had but by recourse to Him, which is only by prayer. 3. That by prayer alone all exterior good things are sanctified, so as to become blessings to us. 4. That prayer does exercise all virtues, in so much as whatsoever good action is performed, it is no further meritorious than as it proceeds from an internal motion of the soul, elevating and directing it to God (which internal motion is prayer); so that whatsoever is not prayer, or is not done in virtue of prayer, is little better than an action of mere nature. 5. That there is no action with which sin is incompatible but prayer. We may, lying in our sins, give alms, fast, recite the Divine Office, communicate, obey our superiors, &c.; but it is impossible to exercise true prayer of the spirit and deliberately continue under the guilt of sin, because by prayer, a soul being converted and united to God, cannot at the same time be averted and separated from Him. 6. That by prayer alone, approaching to God, we are placed above all miseries; whereas, without prayer, the least calamity would oppress us. Therefore prayer is the proper remedy against all kinds of afflictions, guilt, remorses, &c.

7. And hence it is that all the devil's quarrels and assaults are chiefly, if not only, against prayer; the which if he can extinguish, he has all that he aims at—separating us from the fruition and adhesion to God, and therewith from all good. And hence likewise it is that the duty of prayer is enjoined after such a manner as no other duty is, for we are commanded to exercise it without intermission. *Oportet semper orare et non deficere,—We must needs pray continually and never give over.*

8. In the precedent description of prayer in general, I said that it was an affectuous actuation of an intellectual soul, by which words is signified: 1. That it is not prayer which is performed by the lips only, without an inward attention and affection of the soul—that is, that prayer which is not mental is not indeed properly prayer; 2. That whatsoever employment the mind or understanding exercises in prayer, by discoursing, inventing motives, &c., these are only preparations to prayer, and not prayer itself, which is only and immediately exercised by the will or affections adhering to God, which shall be showed hereafter.

9. Hence it follows that the ordinary division of prayer into vocal and mental is improper, because the parts of the division are coincident; for vocal prayer, as distinguished from (and much more as opposed to) mental, is indeed no prayer at all; and whatever it is, what esteem God makes of it, He shows by His prophet, saying: 'This people honours Me with their lips, but their heart is far from Me. In vain do they honour Me,' &c.

10. Yet both a good sense and a good use may be made of that division, being explicated after this manner, viz.: that though all true prayer may be mental, yet, 1. Some prayers are merely mental without any sound of words; yea, there may be such pure blind elevations of the will to God, that there are not so much as any express internal words or any explicable thoughts of the soul itself. 2. Other prayers may be withal vocally expressed in outward words, the soul attending to the sense of the words pronounced, or, at least, intending to do so, and this is properly vocal prayer.

Chapter II. Of Vocal Prayer

§ 1. Of Vocal prayer.

§§ 2, 3, 4, 5, 6, 7, 8, 9. By vocal prayer the ancients attained to perfect contemplation. And why this cannot so well be done in these times.

§§ 10. How voluntary vocal prayers may he made instrumental to contemplation.

§§ 11. That vocal prayer of obligation is upon no pretence to be neglected.

§§ 12, 13, 14, 15, 16. Of attention required to vocal prayer, and of the, degrees of it.

1. The design of this Treatise being to deliver instructions concerning internal contemplative prayer, therefore little shall be said of Vocal prayer, and that little also shall be of it considered, as it may among others be, an instrument or mean to bring a soul to contemplation.

2. It cannot be denied but that in ancient times many holy souls did attain to perfect contemplation by the mere use of vocal prayer; the which likewise would have the same effect upon us if we would or could imitate them both in such wonderful solitude or abstraction, rigorous abstinences, and incredible assiduity in praying. But for a supply of such wants, and inability to support such undistracted long attention to God, we are driven to help ourselves by daily set exercises of internal prayer to procure an habitual constant state of recollectedness, by such exercises repairing and making amends for the distractions that we live in all the rest of the day.

3. Notwithstanding God's hand is not shortened, but that if He please He may now also call souls to contemplation by the way of vocal prayer, so as that they are their general and ordinary exercise; which, if He do, it will be necessary that such souls should, in their course, observe these following conditions:

4. The first is, that they must use a greater measure of abstraction and mortification than is necessary for those that exercise mental prayer. The reason is, because internal prayer, being far more profound and inward, affords a far greater light and grace to discover and cure the inordinate affections; it brings the soul likewise to a greater simplicity and facility to recollect itself, &c., and therefore vocal prayer, to make amends, had need be accompanied with greater abstraction, &c.

5. The second condition is, that those who use vocal prayer must oblige themselves to spend a greater time at their daily exercises than is necessary for the others, to the end thereby to supply for the less efficacy that is in vocal prayer.

6. The third is, that in case they do find themselves at any time invited by God internally to a pure internal prayer (which is likely to be of the nature of aspirations), they then must yield to such an invitation, and for the time interrupt or cease their voluntary vocal exercises for as long time as they find themselves enabled to exercise internally. These conditions are to be observed of all those who, either in religion or in the world, desire to lead spiritual lives, and cannot without extreme difficulty be brought to begin a spiritual course with any kind of mere menial prayer.

7. And, indeed, if any such souls there be to whom vocal prayer (joined with the exercise of virtues) is sufficient to promote them to contemplation, certain it is that there is no way more secure than it, none less subject to indiscretion or illusions, and none less perilous to the head or health. And in time (but it will be long first) their vocal prayers will prove aspirative, spiritual, and contemplative, by their light and virtue illustrating and piercing to the very depth of the spirit.

8. But in these days this case is very extraordinary, and indeed unknown; and therefore contemplative religious persons ought not, upon any pretence, to dispense with themselves for the exercise of mental prayer, whatever pretensions or temptations they may have thereto. They may, perhaps, find their vocal prayers to be more clear and undistracted, and, on the contrary, their recollections to be painful and disturbed; but yet, in time and by constancy in pursuing internal exercises, they will find the contrary, and perceive that the ground of the difference was either some present corporal indisposition, or perhaps a temptation of the devil, to move them to a neglect of exercising in spirit. Since certain it is, that little less than a miracle will cause vocal prayers, to imperfect souls, to become contemplative, or sufficient to produce profound recollection; the which effects even those that have long practised internal exercises do not find in the reciting of the Office. Such seeming extraordinary contemplations, therefore, as seem to come to souls, none knows from whence, without any great merit or due disposition on their part, are not much to be esteemed, but rather to be suspected; and, however, they deserve not that therefore the solid exercises of internal prayer should be neglected.

9. To the like purpose we read that St. Ignatius found extraordinary illustrations in soul being at his study of human learning; whereas at his ordinary mental prayers he could find no such effects, but, on the contrary, much difficulty and obscurity; but this in time he discovered to be the working of the devil.

10. The use of voluntary vocal prayer in order to contemplation may, in the beginning of a spiritual course, be proper: 1. For such simple and unlearned persons (especially women) as are not at all fit for discoursive prayer; 2. yea, even for the more learned, if it be used as a means to raise and better their attention to God; yet so that it must always give place to internal prayer when they find themselves disposed for it.

11. But as for that vocal prayer, either in public or private, which is by the laws of the Church of obligation, no manner of pretences of finding more profit by internal exercises ought to be esteemed a sufficient ground for any to neglect or disparage it; for though some souls of the best dispositions might perhaps more advance themselves towards perfection by internal exercises alone, yet, since generally, even in religion, souls are so tepid and negligent that if they were left to their own voluntary devotions they would scarce ever exercise either vocal or mental prayer; therefore, inasmuch as a manifest distinction cannot be made between the particular dispositions of persons, it was requisite and necessary that all should be obliged to a public external performance of divine service, praising God with the tongues also (which were for that end given us), that so an order and decorum might be

observed in God's Church, to the end it might imitate the employment of angels and glorified saints in a solemn united joining of hearts and tongues to glorify God. This was necessary also for the edification and invitation of those who are not obliged to the office, who perhaps would never think of God, were they not encouraged thereto by seeing good souls spend the greatest part of their time in such solemn and almost hourly praying to and praising God.

12. Now, whereas to all manner of prayer, as hath been said, there is necessarily required an attention of the mind, without which it is not prayer, we must know that there are several kinds and degrees of attention, all of them good, but yet one more perfect and profitable than another; for, 1. there is an attention or express reflection on the words and sense of the sentence pronounced by the tongue or revolved in the mind. Now this attention being, in vocal prayer, necessarily to vary and change according as sentences in the Psalms, &c., do succeed one another, cannot so powerfully and efficaciously fix the mind or affections on God, because they are presently to be recalled to new considerations or succeeding affections. This is the lowest and most imperfect degree of attention, of which all souls are in some measure capable, and the more imperfect they are the less difficulty there is in yielding it; for souls that have good and established affections to God can hardly quit a good affection by which they are united to God, and which they find gustful and profitable for them, to exchange it for a new one succeeding in the Office; and if they should, it would be to their prejudice.

13. The second degree is that of souls indifferently well practised in internal prayer, who, coming to the reciting of the Office, and either bringing with them or by occasion of such reciting raising in themselves an efficacious affection to God, do desire without variation to continue it with as profound a recollectedness as they may, not at all heeding whether it be suitable to the sense of the present passage which they pronounce. This is an attention to God, though not to the words; and is far more beneficial than the former. And therefore to oblige any souls to quit such an attention for the former would be both prejudicial and unreasonable. For since all vocal prayers, in Scripture or otherwise, were ordained only to this end, to supply and furnish the soul that needs with good matter of affection, by which it may be united to God, a soul that hath already attained to that end, which is union as long as it lasts, ought not to be separated therefrom, and be obliged to seek a new means till the virtue of the former be spent.

14. A third and most sublime degree of attention to the divine Office is that whereby vocal prayers do become mental; that is, whereby souls most profoundly and with a perfect simplicity united to God can yet, without any prejudice to such union, attend also to the sense and spirit of each passage

that they pronounce, yea, thereby find their affection, adhesion, and union increased and more simplified. This attention comes not till a soul be arrived to perfect contemplation, by means of which the spirit is so habitually united to God, and besides, the imagination so subdued to the spirit that it cannot rest upon anything that will distract it.

15. Happy are those souls (of which God knows the number is very small) that have attained to this third degree, the which must be ascended to by a careful practice of the two former in their order, especially of a second degree! And therefore in reciting of the Office even the more imperfect souls may do well, whensoever they find themselves in a good measure recollected, to continue so long as they well can, preserving as much stability in their imagination as may be.

16. And the best means to beget and increase such a recollected way of saying the Divine Office is the practice of internal prayer, either in meditation or immediate acts of the will, the only aim and end whereof is the procuring an immovable attention and adhesion of the spirit to God. And this, as to our present purpose, may suffice concerning vocal prayer.

Chapter III. The Excellency of Internal Affective Prayer

§ 1. Of internal prayer in general, and principally of internal affective prayer.

§§ 2, 3, 4, 5. The excellency and necessity of affective prayer, and that it was practised by the ancients; and not discoursive prayer or meditation.

§ 6. The great necessity of it in these days.

§§ 7, 8. The testimony of Cardinal Bellarmine to show that vocal prayer, &c., sufficeth not.

§§ 9, 10, 11, 12, 13, 14, 15. Five admirable virtues of internal affective prayer.

§§ 16, 17. An exhortation to constancy and courage in pursuing the exercise of it.

1. Internal or Mental prayer (which is simply and merely such, and) which we made the second member in the division of Prayer in general (if indeed it be a distinct kind), and of which only we shall treat hereafter, is either, 1. imperfect and acquired; 2. or perfect, and that which is called properly infused prayer. The former is only a preparation and inferior disposition, by which the soul is fitted and made capable of the infusion of the other, to wit, the Prayer of Contemplation, which is the end of all our spiritual and

religious exercises. I shall therefore, in order, treat of them both and of their several special degrees, beginning with the lowest, and thence ascending orderly till we come to the highest, which will bring a soul to the state of perfection.

2. But before I come to deliver the special instructions pertinent to the exercise of the several degrees of internal prayer, it will be very requisite, by way of preparation and encouragement, to set down the necessity and excellency of internal prayer in general; I mean especially of that which is Affective. For as for discoursive prayer or Meditation, the world is but even burdened with books, which with more than sufficient niceness prescribe rules and methods for the practice of it, and with too partial an affection magnify it, the authors of such books neglecting in the mean time, or perhaps scarce knowing what true internal affective prayer is, which, notwithstanding, is the only efficacious instrument that immediately brings souls to contemplation and perfect union in spirit with God.

3. Some there are that, because they do not find in the writings of the ancient Fathers and mystical Doctors such exact instructions touching the practice of internal prayer as are now common and abounding in the Church, do therefore undervalue and despise it as a mere human invention, not at all necessary, but rather, on the contrary, subject to great inconveniences, exposing souls to illusions, errors, &c. And therefore they, in opposition to it, do only recommend and exact vocal prayer, and a solemn protracted performance of it.

4. Notwithstanding, to any one that shall heedfully read the writings, not only of the ancient solitaries, but likewise of St. Augustine, St. Basil, St. Gregory Nazianzen and others, it will evidently appear that they both knew and practised most profound and recollected devotions internally, yea, and exhorted souls to a continual attendance to God and His divine presenoe in the spirit; sufficient proofs whereof shall occasionally hereafter be inserted.

5. True, indeed, it is that they have not delivered any exact methods for the practice of such prayer, which in those times were not at all necessary, or at least not at all needful to be communicated to the world. For to souls that lived (as anciently they did) entirely sequestered from all worldly business or conversation, in continual laborious and penitential exercises, having no images of creatures to distract their minds, and much less any inordinate affections to creatures to depress them from mounting to spiritual union with God, it was more than sufficient for such to know that their duty and the end of their solitude was to live in a continual conversation with God, suffering themselves to be conducted and managed by His Holy Spirit. To such, all other more nice or particular instructions would have proved but distractive and entangling; and therefore we see that our holy Father, though

he ordained daily conventual short recollections for the exercise of (that which he calls) pure prayer, yet he neither interprets what be means by such prayer (for all his disciples understood that sufficiently), and much less does he deliver any instructions how to exercise it.

6. But in these days, in which religious persons and others that aspire to spiritual contemplation do either want the means to enjoy, or have not the courage and strength to support, such solitude and austerities, lest the spirit of contemplation should fail in the world, God raised up first in Germany masters of contemplative prayer, as Suso, Harphius, Eschius, Thaulerus, &c., in former times, and more lately in Spain, St. Teresa, St. John of the Cross, &c., who, no question, by the direction of God's Spirit (as the grace of miracles conferred on them may witness), have judged it necessary to supply the want of the foresaid advantages, by adding a certain obligation to the daily practice of internal recollected prayer, prescribing orders and times for the performance of it. They have likewise more exactly discovered the degrees and progress of prayer, and, in a word, most earnestly do they exhort souls to a diligent pursuance of it, professing that without it, it is impossible to comply with the essential design of a spiritual or religious life.

7. I will content myself in this place to express the grounds and sum of the exhortations of those and other illuminated persons (the glorious instruments of God for the reviving of decayed spirituality in the world) by producing a passage of Cardinal Bellarmine's, which may be applied to this purpose, taken out of one of his sermons (in fer. 2. Rogat.), which is this, *Ego illud mihi videor verissime posse affirmare, &c.*—that is, 'This I believe I may most truly and confidently affirm' (saith he) 'that without a diligent pursuit of internal prayer none will ever become truly spiritual, nor attain to any degree of perfection. We see many which oftentimes in the year do approach to the Sacrament of Penance, and, as far as human frailty and infirmity will permit, do with sufficient diligence endeavour to purge away all the stains and uncleanness of sin; and yet they make no progress, but are still the very same that they were, and having been at confession, if a week after they come to the same tribunal again, they bring neither fewer nor lesser faults than such as were formerly confessed. Yea, without offending against truth, I may add somewhat more strange than all this, to wit, that we see sometimes religious persons and not a few priests which by their vocation and habits profess sanctity, and, moreover, do assiduously read divine Scriptures and books of piety; they do often (if not daily) celebrate the most holy Sacrifice; they nave neither wives nor children, but are free from all cares and solicitudes which may distract them from a continual attendance to divine things; and yet, after all this, they are so void of all devotion and the Spirit of God, so cold of Divine love, and so earnest in the love of secular vanities, so replenished with impatience, envy, and all inordinate desires, that they seem

not one jot to differ from secular persons wholly engaged in the world. Now the only cause of these disorders is that they do not seriously enter into their own hearts by exercises of introversion, but only esteem and regard the exterior,' &c. Thus far are the words and too just complaint of the learned and pious Cardinal.

8. This, with very great reason, may be further extended, even to those religious who by their profession ought to aspire to contemplation, and being mistaken in the true way thereto, erroneously believing that by an exact performance of outward observances and the solemn saying of the Office, adjoining the exercises of such internal discursive prayer, do yet find but little fruit as to any interior reformation or simplification of their souls, by reason that they rest in such active exercises (which in a short time, to solitary livers, lose all their virtue), and do not from them proceed to the truly enlightening exercises of internal affective prayer (which is a prayer of the heart or will, by good affections quietly and calmly produced, and not with the understanding), a prayer made without those distracting methods or that busying of the imagination and wearying of the soul by laborious, discourses, which are only inferior and imperfect preparations to true prayer.

9. Now to a consideration of the necessity of internal affective prayer we will add certain virtues, benefits, and preëminences thereof, compared with all other sorts of prayer, either vocal or discoursively mental, the which virtues are indeed admirable and inestimable, deserving to be purchased with all the cares and endeavours of our whole lives.

10. The first excellency of internal affective prayer above all other is, that only by such prayer our union in spirit with God (in which our eternal happiness consists) is perfectly obtained. For therein the will with all the powers and affections of the soul are applied and fixed to the loving, adoring, and glorifying this only beatifying Object, whereas in vocal prayer there is a continual variety and succession of images of creatures suggested, the which do distract the souls of the imperfect from such an application. And meditation, in which discourse is employed, is, so far, little more than a philosophical contemplation of God, delaying this fixing of the heart and affections on God, which are only acceptable to Him.

11. The second virtue is this, that by this prayer of the will, the soul entering far more profoundly into God, the fountain of lights, partakes of the beams of His divine light far more plentifully, by which she both discovers God's perfections more clearly and also sees the way wherein she is to walk more perfectly than by any other prayer; and the reason is because, when the soul endeavours to apply all her affections entirely on God, then only it is that, being profoundly introverted, a world of impurities of intention and inordinate affections lurking in her do discover themselves, and the obscure

mists of them are dispelled, the soul then finding by a real perception and feeling how prejudicial they are to her present union in will with God; whereas, when the understanding alone, or principally, is busied, in the consideration of God or of the soul herself, the imagination (which is very active and subtle) will not represent to the soul either God or herself so liquidly and sincerely; but being blinded and seduced by natural self-love, will invent a hundred excuses and pretexts to deceive the soul, and to make her believe that many things are intended and done purely for God, which proceeded principally, if not totally, from the root of concupiscence and self-love.

12. A third admirable perfection of internal affective prayer is this, that not only divine light, but also grace and spiritual strength to put in practice all things to which supernatural light directs, is obtained principally by this internal prayer of the heart, and this by a double causality and virtue, to wit: 1. By way of impetration, grounded on the rich and precious promises made by God to prayer above all other good actions. 2. By a direct and proper efficiency; for since all the virtue and merit of our external actions does depend upon and flow from the internal disposition and operations of the soul exercising charity and purity of intention in them, and conquering the resistance of nature, and since all internal exercises of all virtues whatsoever are truly and in propriety of speech direct prayer of the spirit, hence it follows that as all habits are gotten by frequency and constancy of exercise, therefore, by the persevering in the exercise of internal prayer, the soul is enabled with facility to practise perfectly all virtues.

13. To this may be added that such prayer is universal mortification, and a mortification the most profound, intime, and perfect that a soul can possibly perform, entirely destructive to sensual satisfaction. For therein the will forces inferior nature and all the powers of the soul to avert themselves from all other objects pleasing to them, and to concur to her internal actuations towards God; and this oftentimes in the midst of distractions by vain images, during a torpid dulness of the heart, yea, a violent contradiction of sensuality, when there is, according to any sensible perception, a total disgust in the soul to such an exercise, yea, when the spirit itself is in obscurity, and cannot by any reflexed act reap any consolation from such an exercise. Such an *exilium cordis,* such a desertion and internal desolation is a mortification to the purpose; yet, as of extreme bitterness, so of unexpressible efficacy to the purifying and universal perfecting of the soul and spirit. Therefore St. Chrysostome (Tract. de Oratione) had good reason to say: It is impossible; again I say it is utterly impossible that a soul which with a due care and assiduity prays unto God should ever sin.

14. A fourth excellence of internal affective prayer is that it is the only action that cannot possibly want purity of intention. Souls may, from an

impulse of nature and its satisfaction, exactly observe fasts, perform obediences, keep the choir, approach to sacraments, yea, exercise themselves in
curious speculations during meditations, or in the exercise of sensible devotion they may comply with self-love, &c. (and, indeed, they have no farther
any purity of intention in any of these duties than as they do proceed from
internal affective prayer, that is, the will fixed by charity on God). Whereas if
any oblique intention should endeavour to insinuate itself into internal prayer
or the will it would presently be observed, and unless it were contradicted
and expelled there could be no progress in such prayer. So that it is not possible to find an exercise either more secure or more profitable, since it is by
the virtue of it alone that all other exercises have any concurrence towards
the perfecting of the soul.

15. Lastly, affective prayer of the will is that alone which makes all
other sorts of prayer to deserve the name of prayer; for were that excluded,
meditation is but an useless speculation and curiosity of the understanding,
and vocal prayer but an empty sound of words; for God only desires our
hearts or affections, without which our tongues or brains are of no esteem at
all. Yea, there is not so much as any profitable attention in any prayer further
than the heart concurs. For if the attention be only of the mind, that will not
constitute prayer, for then study or disputation about divine things might be
called prayer. Hence, saith an ancient holy hermit, *Nunquam verè orat quis-
quis etiam flexis genibus evagatione cordis etiam qualicumque distrahitur;*
that is, that man does never truly pray who, though he be upon his knees, is
distracted with any wandering or in attention of his heart. And likewise the
learned Soto, to the same purpose, conclusively affirms, *Orationi mentali
deesse non potest attentio, cum ipsa attentio,* &c.; that is, attention cannot
possibly be wanting to mental prayer (of the heart) since the attention itself is
the very prayer. And therefore it is a contradiction to say that one prays mentally and is not attentive, as is of itself manifest; for as soon as ever the mind
begins to wander it ceases to pray. Therefore vocal prayer is only that prayer
which may want attention, namely, when the thoughts diverting themselves
to other objects, the tongue, without the concurrence of the mind, gives an
uncertain sound. And we may add that the attention of the mind, which cannot be separated from discoursive prayer, is little valuable except it be
accompanied with, or performed in order to the causing an attention (as we
may call it) of the heart or affections.

16. These inestimable benefits (to which more may be added, as shall
be shown), which flow from internal prayer of the will, being considered, a
well-minded soul will think no pains too much that may avail to purchase so
invaluable a jewel. And religious superiors will esteem that nothing does so
essentially belong to their duty as to instruct and further their subjects in the
practice of it: according to the counsel of St. Bernard, *Docendus est incipiens*

spiritualiter orare, et a corporibus vel corporum imaginibus cum Deum cogi-tat quantum potest recedere; that is, whosoever begins a religious course of life must be taught spiritual prayer, and in elevating his mind to God to transcend all bodies and bodily images. And with just reason did the holy Grecian Abbot Nilus (a disciple of St. John Chrysostome) say, *Beata mens quæ dum orat,* &c. Happy is the soul that when she prays empties herself entirely of all images and forms; happy is the soul that prays fervently and without distraction: such a soul increases continually in the desire and love of God; happy is the soul that, when she prays, does altogether quit the use and exercise of all her senses; happy is the soul that during the time of prayer loses the possession and interest in all manner of things (but God)!

17. And, indeed, a soul must expect to pass through a world of difficulties before she attain to such a purity in prayer, for as the same author saith, *Universum bellum quod inter nos et dæmones conflatur, non est de alia re quam de oratione;* that is, all the war and controversy that is between us and the Devil is about no other thing but prayer, as being most necessary to us, and most destructive to all his designs. And hereupon a certain holy Father, being asked what duty in a religious life was the most difficult, answered, to pray well. The reason is because prayer can never be perfectly exercised till the soul be cleansed from all manner of impurities, yea, not only from the affections, but all images also of creatures.

Chapter IV. Of Prayer without Ceasing

§§ 13, 14, 15, 16. Whether the habit of continual prayer may be attained by prolonged vocal offices.

§§ 17, 18. That the sure means to attain to it is a constant practice of daily recollections.

§§ 19, 20. Who they are that shall he accounted by our Lord to have satisfied the obligation of this precept.

1. Having showed the necessity and excellency of Affective Prayer, I will now treat of certain qualities and conditions requisite thereto, of which I will at the present insist only on three, to wit: 1. The first, regarding the extension of it; 2. the second, the intension or fervour of it; 3. the third, the cause or principle from which it must proceed, to wit, the Divine Spirit.

2. As touching the first point, to wit, the extension of prayer, it is our Lord's command that we should never omit this duty of prayer (*oportet semper orare et non deficere*), we ought always to pray, and not to cease (or faint in it). And St. Paul exhorts indifferently all Christians (*sine interinissione orate*), pray without intermission. Now in this precept of our Lord there is an obligation so express, so universal, and so confirmed, and repeated both affirmatively and negatively, that all exception and derogation seems to be excluded, and that it binds both *semper et ad semper*. In all the Gospel we can scarce find a precept so fast-binding and so unquestionable.

3. This being evident, how can any one without grief and indignation read the strange dispensations and escapes invented and allowed by some late writers to defeat this so necessary a duty? Because, perhaps, no man can positively say that, *hic et nunc,* actual prayer is necessary and obliging under mortal sin, therefore they conclude that, except two or three moments of our life, it is not at all necessary to pray; that is, in the first moment that a child comes to the use of reason, and in the last moment when a soul is ready to expire; for then, indeed, some of them (not all) acknowledge that without mortal sin a soul cannot deliberately and wilfully neglect to lift up itself to God. As for the Divine Office, those to whom the reciting of it is of obligation, such (say they) are only bound under mortal sin to the external pronunciation of the words; as for the mentality of it, that is only a matter of counsel of perfection.

4. In the ancient times there was a certain sect of heretics that wandered as far wide the contrary way; who, upon a mistaken interpretation of this precept of our Saviour, neglected, yea, condemned all other things besides prayer, despising the sacraments, omitting the necessary duties of their vocation, refusing to do any external acts of charity, &c.; and from this frenzy they were called Euchitæ, that is, persons that did nothing but pray.

5. But the truth lies between these two extremes; for most manifest it is that we are obliged to aspire unto uninterrupted prayer, and yet most certain also it is that besides simple prayer there are many other duties required of us. The sense, therefore, and importance of our Lord's precept of praying continually without failing may be cleared by two passages of St. Paul. The first is this (1 Tim. iv.), *Cibos creavit Deus ad percipiendum,* &c.; that is, God hath created meats to be received with giving of thanks by His faithful servants, and those which have known the truth. For every creature of God is good, and nothing to be rejected which is received with giving of thanks; for it is sanctified by the word of God and by prayer. The second is (1 Cor. x.), *Sive ergo manducatis sive,* &c.; that is, therefore, whether you eat or drink, or what other thing soever you do, do all to the glory of God. From which text it appears, 1. That all creatures are in their use unsanctified unto us, that is, profane, unless they be used with prayer. 2. That we are obliged not only in the use of creatures by eating and drinking, &c., but also in all our other actions whatsoever, to join prayer and a consecrating of them to God's glory, so that if we comply with these our obligations and duties, we must continually either be in actual prayer or busied in something done in virtue of prayer.

6. Now, as we said in the first Treatise, that although all are not obliged necessarily to attain unto the perfection proportionable to each one's state, yet all are necessarily bound to aspire thereunto; because no man can love God with a sincere love, and such an one as may be accounted worthy of Him who is our only God and beatitude, that shall fix any limits to his love, or that shall not aspire continually to a further and higher degree of his love; so here, likewise, we are to conceive that this precept of praying continually so indefinitely expressed, so earnestly pressed, so universally applied, both by our Lord and His apostle to all Christians, doth infer an indefinite and universal obligation, so as that although none but the perfect do really fulfil it, yet all, even the most imperfect, cannot without danger dispense with or neglect the endeavouring and aspiring to the fulfilling of it. Every one must exercise as much prayer as shall be necessary to sanctify his vocation, and make the works and duties of his life acceptable to God and helpful to the procuring of his eternal felicity.

7. And the ground of this obligation is both very firm and manifest, which is this, that even reason dictates that all the things we do we ought to do them in order to our last end, which is God; that is, with a sanctified intention (for whatsoever is not done with a right intention in order to God is of no worth at all, being only a work of corrupt nature). Now, since there are only two things which do sanctify all things and actions, to wit, the word of God and prayer: the word of God generally, that is the certain and revealed will of God, that the thing is in itself lawful to be used or done, and prayer in particular, proceeding from faith or assurance that the thing is lawful, and

thereupon acknowledging it to be God's gift, desiring His blessing on it, and referring it to His glory, &c.: hence it evidently follows that since without prayer all things are unsanctified or profane, not at all conducing to our last end, but rather prejudicial to it, therefore all are bound to endeavour to sanctify all their actions and works by prayer.

8. Hence we may infer that the degrees of grace and sanctity in any man are to be measured according to the virtue that prayer has upon his actions, for the more and more frequently that his ordinary actions are performed in virtue of prayer, the more perfect and holy such an one is, and the more approaching to his chief end; and he whose actions do not, for the most part, flow from the virtue of prayer is not yet right disposed towards his last end.

9. Now, though perhaps scarce any man can say that, *hic et nunc*, actual prayer is necessarily obliging under mortal sin, yet withal, most certain it is that that man has reason to doubt that he is in a mortally sinful state that does not use so much prayer as thereby to sanctify and render meritorious the generality of his more serious actions, or (which is all one) he is in a state mortally sinful that for the most part lives wilfully and habitually in a neglect of grace, which can no way be obtained without prayer. Therefore it is observable that the disciples of our Lord never asked any instructions but how to pray, for that skill being once had, all other good things are consequently had; and when all other actions are performed by grace obtained by prayer, and for the end proposed in prayer, then a person may be said to lie in continual prayer, and much more if they be accompanied with an actual elevation of the spirit to God.

10. This is the perfection of prayer to which our holy Rule obliges us to aspire, namely, besides the set exercises either of vocal or internal prayer, to preserve our souls in an uninterrupted attention to God and tendance in spirit to Him, so as that whatsoever actions we do, they should be accompanied (*instantissima oratione*) with a most fervent and perseverant prayer. And that this perfection of continual prayer in a supreme degree has been really attained to by the ancient contemplatives, and accounted by them an essential duty of their vocation, is evident out of what we read in several places in Cassian: *Hic finis totius perfectionis est*, &c. (saith a holy hermit there.) This is the end of all perfection, to have the soul become so extenuated and purified from all carnal desires, as that it may continually be in an actual ascent to spiritual things, until all its conversation and employment and every motion of the heart become one continual prayer. We mentioned, likewise, before a hermit, whose spirit was so continually fixed on God that he could not, though he endeavoured, to depress it for so small a time as till he might fetch from the other end of his cell some small thing that his

neighbour desired of him. The like continual attention to God Gregory Lopez acknowledgeth to have been in himself by long practice of recollection, so that though he would, he could not but think on Him, the which attention and union no work, conversation, or study could interrupt. Another hermit, likewise in Cassian (in 19 conf.), called John, saith of himself, how he forgot whether he had taken his daily sustenance, so continual was his prayer, by which their senses became so stupefied that they saw not what was before their eyes. To this purpose it is reported in the Lives of the Fathers that when a certain religious man, in a journey, met with a little troop of religious women, and seeing them, purposely turned out of the way to avoid them, the abbess said to him, 'If thou hadst been a perfect monk, indeed, though thou hadst seen us, thou wouldst not have known that we were women.'

11. Now it is impossible for a soul to continue without interruption in vocal prayer, there being so many necessary occasions hourly occurring to employ the tongue other ways, besides that, it would utterly exhaust the spirits. And as for meditation, the exercise thereof is so painful that it would destroy the head to force the imagination continually to invent and discourse internally on divine or spiritual objects.

12. Therefore by no other manner of prayer but the internal exercise of the will in holy desires, &c., can this precept of our Lord be perfectly accomplished. For the soul is naturally in a continual exercise of some one desire or other, the which are not at all painful to her, being her natural employment, so that if by practice we can so rectify our desires as to place them upon their only true and proper object, which is God, it will necessarily follow that the soul should be in continual prayer. *Si semper desideras, semper oras,* saith St. Augustine; if thou dost continually desire (God) thou dost continually pray. Such desires, by custom, will become easy and as it were natural to the soul, and consequently, without any force used on the imagination or understanding, they may be continued without interruption, for they will flow as freely as breath from the lungs; and where such desires do abound, flowing from a holy inward temper of soul, there no employment will be undertaken that shall cross or prejudice such desires; on the contrary, they will give a tincture to all actions, directing them to the object of those desires, and thereby adding to the fervency of them.

13. Now a question may be made, whether in contemplative orders, where likewise there is used much abstraction, solitude, and other austerities, souls may attain to this uninterrupted prayer by the way of meditation, or else of long-continued vocal prayers alone, without appointed recollections of internal affective prayer constantly exercised?

14. Hereto it may be answered, first, that as for meditation, it is an exercise so disproportionable to the nature of such a state (except as a prepa-

ration for awhile in the beginning), that it is not possible to be the constant and continued exercise of such persons; for, as shall be shown, the imagination and understanding, by much exercise thereof in an undistracted life, will become so barren, and it will produce so small or no effects in good affections in the will, that it will be disgustful and insupportable, so that all use of meditation must be for a long space passed and relinquished before the soul will be brought to this good state of having a continual flux of holy desires.

15. But in the second place, touching long-continued vocal prayers and offices, without any set exercises of internal recollection, no doubt it is but by them such religious persons may be brought to this habit of continual prayer; so that, 1. They hold their minds to as much attention as reasonably they can. 2. So that out of choir they keep their minds from distractive affections or solicitudes either about studies or any other employments, voluntary or imposed. 3. So they be watchful over themselves not to give scope to thoughts which may be harmful to them. (Thus the ancient hermits arrived to this perfection.) 4. A fourth condition may be that such persons content themselves with the public office, &c., not overburden themselves with a surcharge of voluntary vocal prayers; for Turrecremata saith well (on the Decr. d. 92.), that the voice and other external doings are in prayer to be used only so far as by them to raise internal devotion, so that if by the excess of them it should be hindered or the mind distracted, they ought to be abstained from. And St. Augustine (no doubt from experience as well as judgment) saith, *Quantum proficis ad videndam sapientiam, tantò minus est vox necessaria;* that is, the greater progress thou makest in contemplative wisdom, so much less necessary will vocal praying be. Such persons, therefore, if in their solitude they do not appoint to themselves any set recollections, yet ought they to keep their minds in a state of as much recollectedness as may be, by interrupted good desires, at least begetting in their minds an affection to prayer and an appetite to the succeeding office.

16. Notwithstanding, certain it is that vocal prayers though never so much prolonged and in never so great solitude, yet will never produce this effect where the true spirit of contemplative prayer is not known, and such ignorance hath been even in orders of the greatest abstraction and austerity; thus we see that Germanus and Cassianus, though practised many years in a strict cenobitical life, yet were astonished when they heard the holy hermits discourse of pure spiritual prayer, free from images, &c.

17. It remains, therefore, that, ordinarily speaking, the only efficacious and immediate disposition to the habit of uninterrupted prayer is a constant exercise of internal prayer of the will, by which the soul being daily forced to a serious attendance and tendance to God in spirit, by little and little

becomes more and better affected to a frequent conversation with Him, and in time loses all relish or taste of pleasures in creatures.

18. This, I say, will be the effect of such constant and fervent exercise of recollections; for as for those which are commonly called ejaculatory prayers, that is, good affections now and then, by fits, and with frequent interruptions exercised, though they are very good and profitable, and withal very fit to be used in the midst of reading especially, or any other external employments, yet they alone will, though joined to the ordinary use of the Divine Office, be insufficient to produce such a habit of soul. And the reason is because being so short and with such interruption exercised, the virtue of them is presently spent, and will have little or no effect upon subsequent actions; but as for the ejaculatory prayers mentioned and worthily commended by the holy hermits in Cassian, the nature of them is quite different from those forementioned, for they are indeed not different from infused aspirations, being the effects flowing from the habit of continual prayer already acquired, and not imperfect preparations thereto.

19. To conclude, none can account themselves to have satisfied (in that perfection that they ought) the obligation imposed upon them by this necessary precept of our Lord (*Oportet semper orare et non deficere*); but, 1. Such as do actually exercise as much prayer as may consist with their abilities, and as is necessary to produce contemplation (if such be their state of life), and, moreover, such actual prayer as is suitable thereto, yet not indiscreetly straining themselves beyond their power to perform it perfectly at first, lest it happen unto them, according to the saying of the prophet (Jerem. xxviii.), *Quia plus fecit quam potuit, ideireo periit;* that is, because he did more than he was able, therefore he perished. 2. Such as when discretion or other necessary employments do withdraw them from actual prayer, yet do preserve in their minds a love and desire of it, and a firm resolution courageously to break through all discouragements and hindrances to it. 3. Such as do endeavour to do all their actions in virtue of prayer, that is, with the same holy and pure intention, as God gave them in their precedent prayers. 4. Such as do abstain from all voluntary employments as do indispose their minds for prayer, keeping their souls in such a disposition as to be able presently to correspond to an interior divine invitation to prayer, if God shall send it, and to be in a capacity of receiving and perceiving such invitations. Now this is done by keeping a continual guard over our passions that they break not forth so as to indispose us even for present recollection, and much less for the appointed recollection which is to follow. 5. Such as do practise mortification in a measure suitable to their state, thereby rooting out those inordinate affections which cause distraction in prayer and are hindrances to a state of recollectedness. For as that fundamental precept of loving God obliges a soul

at least never to do anything contrary thereto, so does that of prayer oblige that we should always be in a disposition and readiness to it.

20. Therefore let souls consider in what an insecure and dangerous state they remain that content themselves with a few heartless distracted vocal prayers, since not any temptation can be resisted without an actual exercise of prayer, and that the best prayer that the soul can make. Besides, it is not with prayer as with other arts or habits; a student by cessation from study doth not presently lose nor so much as diminish the knowledge that he had before, but a soul that is not in actual prayer, or at least in an immediate disposition and an habitual desire of prayer, sinks presently into nature and loses much of that strength that she had formerly. There are not always occasions to exercise particular virtues, as temperance, patience, chastity, &c.; because temptations do not always assault us; but we may always pray, and always we have need so to do, for a soul, except she be in prayer, or that the virtue of prayer be alive in her, is in a state of distraction and disunion from God, and, consequently, exposed to all manner of enemies, being withal deprived of the only means to resist them, so that the dangers and miseries of an unrecollected life are inexplicable.

Chapter V. Of Sensible Devotion

THIRD TREATISE – FIRST SECTION

§§ 21, 22. Vocal prayer and meditation not so much subject thereto.

§§ 23, 24. More good comes from prayer of aridity courageously pursued than from prayer of sensible devotion.

§ 25. The superior soul and its good disposition does not depend on the temper of sensitive nature.

§§ 26, 27. Means to beget courage in the prayer of aridity.

§ 28. How a soul is to behave herself in the most violent distresses in prayer.

§ 29. The prayer exercised by imperfect souls during aridities is not properly in spirit.

1. As, 1. Prayer, for the quantity or extension of it, is to be incessant, at least the virtue of it is to be an ingredient in all other works, whether they be study, labour, conversation, &c. (the which may be without any prejudice at all to the work, yea, to the great improvement and super-naturalising of it so far that where prayer is wanting the most specious works are of no value at all), so in the next place; 2. As to the quality or intention of it, it ought to be (*instantissima,* saith our holy Father in Prolog.) with all possible fervour and earnestness; for prayer being the most immediate and most perfect act of charity to God, ought, like charity itself, to proceed (*ex toto corde, ex tota anima; et ex totis viribus*) from the whole heart, the whole soul, and the whole strength. Therefore as he offends against the precept of charity that employs either his spirit, sensitive soul, or corporal strength on anything but God, or which has respect to God, His love or glory; so, if in our prayer we do willingly suffer our thoughts to wander upon anything but God, or if we harbour any desire in sensitive nature that would hinder the free tendence of our spirit to God in prayer, or if we employ our corporal strength about any other matter but such as may and ought to be intended for God in our prayer, we do so far neglect to correspond to this duty of fervour and instance which ought to be in prayer.

2. Notwithstanding this is not so to be understood, as if we were obliged either to employ our corporal forces or members, or to force our sensible affections to concur in our prayers to God, or as if God did require that this fervour should always be in sensitive nature, for that is not always in our power; yea, on the contrary, the sensual part moves often against our wills, being insensible, averse, and impatient of accompanying our spiritual actuations, which commonly do mortify and contradict the desires of nature. 2. And, moreover, when sensible fervour and devotion doth insinuate itself in our recollections (especially in imperfect souls) it does rather endanger to depress the operations of the spirit than advance them, and does, perhaps, more nourish self-love than contribute to the increase of divine love.

3. It is sufficient, therefore, if this fervour be in our superior will alone, though sensitive nature seem to partake nothing of it. So that our prayers may then be said to be instant and fervourous when the will, out of a worthy and high esteem of this most necessary and most excellent duty, resolutely and with perseverance pursues them, notwithstanding any contradiction in nature or discouragements from without, for that must needs be a great fervour of spirit that contradicts the contrary malignant fervour of nature, and undervalues all sensible ease and contentment compared with the spiritual good that is caused by prayer.

4. This is that good quality which our Saviour, in the parable of him who at midnight went to his neighbour to borrow three loaves of bread for the entertainment of a friend that was then arrived, calls by a homely name, to wit, *improbitatem,* or, as it is in the original, impudence; which quality, notwithstanding, he requires in our prayers to God, and promises an infallible success thereto. Now that improbity or impudence implies an importunate earnestness, a resolution to take no denial nor to stand upon nice civilities, but rather than to return empty, to force out a grant even by wearying out the person to whom we address ourselves; so that it includes both a great fervour and an incessant perseverance in such fervour, which is in a high degree in those who spend their whole lives as it were in one continual prayer, yea, in one only petition, which is, to be united in will and affection to God only.

5. These, therefore, being two qualities requisite in prayer, 1. Earnestness or fervour, and 2. Perseverance (both which are likewise included in the term [*instantissima*] given to prayer by our holy Father), imperfect souls will be apt to suspect ofttimes that their prayers are inefficacious, as being deprived of these conditions. 1. The former, when they do not perceive a tenderness and melting devotion in sensitive nature. 2. And the latter they will fear is wanting whensoever they find themselves (though unwillingly) distracted. Therefore to the end to prevent mistakes, and that a right judgment may be made of these two, to wit, sensible devotion and distractions, I will treat of them both, showing what good or ill effects may proceed from the former, and what remedies may be applied to hinder any inconveniences from the latter.

6. There is a twofold sensible devotion. 1. The first is that which we now speak of, which is found in good but imperfect souls, and it begins in sensitive nature, causing great tenderness there, and from thence it mounts up to the spirit, producing good and melting affections to God and especially (in discoursive prayer) to the humanity and sufferings of our Lord. 2. Another sensible devotion there is of perfect souls, the which begins in the spirit, and abounding there, overflows, and by communication descends into inferior

sensitive nature, causing like effects to the former. Now there is little need to give cautions or instructions concerning the use of this; because perfect souls walking in a clear light, and being established in a generous love of the superior will towards God, are not in danger to be transported with the pleasing effects which it is apt to produce in inferior nature, nor to fall into spiritual gluttony, by which their affections may be withdrawn from God and fixed on such mean gifts of His as these are. That, therefore, which I shall here speak concerning sensible devotion is to be applied unto that which is found in souls less perfect, for for such only all these instructions were meant.

7. Such souls then are to be informed that though sensible devotion be indeed at the first a good gift of God, intended by Him for their encouragement and advancement in His pure love, as it is therefore not to be neglected, so neither is it over highly to be prized. For as very good effects may flow from it, being well and discreetly used, so, on the contrary, without such discretion it may prove very pernicious, endangering to plunge them more deeply in self-love and corrupt nature (in which it is much immersed), and so it would produce an effect directly contrary to that for which prayer was ordained. A soul, therefore, is to separate that which is good and profitable in such devotion from that which is imperfect and dangerous, renouncing and mortifying this latter, and with discretion giving way and making her profit of the other.

8. The special signs and effects of such sensible devotion are ofttimes very conspicuous in the alteration caused by it in corporal nature, drawing tears from the eyes, producing heat and redness in the face, springing motions in the heart (like to the leaping of a fish in the waters, saith Harphius), and in some it causes so perceivable an opening and shutting in the heart, saith he, that it may be heard. And from such unusual motions and agitations about the heart, a windy vapour will now and then mount up to the head, causing a pricking pain there, which, if the head be not strong, may continue a good space; yea, if good care be not taken to interrupt such impetuosities of the spirits, the blood will first boil, and afterwards will grow thick and congealed, incapable of motion. And this once happening, the inward sweetnesses formerly felt will be turned into sadness, dejection, and stupidity; thence will follow complaints that the soul is forsaken of God, yea, she will be in danger desperately to renounce all further seeking of God; and the more that she shall endeavour to recover her former sensible affections, the farther will she be from it, and impatience for this will render her still more disposed, more darkened in the understanding, and more stupefied in her affections.

9. Now all these inconveniences proceed from self-love and a too gluttonous delectation in sensible sweetnesses, which, if they be accompa-

nied with any extraordinary visits, there will follow (it is to be feared) yet far more dangerous effects in unprepared souls, the which will probably take occasion from thence to nourish pride in themselves and a contempt of others.

10. To abate the too high esteem that unwary souls may have of this sensible fervour and devotion, it may be observed that it is not always a sign of a good disposition or holiness in the soul, for we read of several impious persons that have enjoyed it; so history makes mention of a certain wicked tyrant called William Prince of Juliers, how at his devotions, in the midnight of our Lord's Nativity, he twice or thrice felt so great an internal sweetness in divine visitations, that he professed afterward that he would be content to purchase with the loss of half his dominions such another consolation. Yet after his death it was revealed to a certain holy person that he was in hell, condemned to torments equal to those that that wicked persecuting Emperor Maxentius suffered.

11. The root of such sensible sweetnesses is oftentimes a mere natural temper of body; yea, by God's permission, the devil also will be forward enough to raise and increase it in unmortified self-willed souls, knowing that they will make ill use of it, either to the augmenting of their pride, or to a presumptuous undertaking of mortifications above their strength, by which in a short time their spirits will be so exhausted and their forces enfeebled, that they will become unable any more to correspond with divine grace, even in duties necessarily belonging to their profession; and when this happens, then all sweetness of devotion ceases, and in place thereof succeed anguishes, scrupulosities, pusillanimity, and perhaps even desperation. Therefore well-minded souls are to take special care of preventing these effects of sensible devotion which, without great vigilance, they are in danger to incur. And thereupon Harphius advises earnestly such to moderate with discretion the violent impulses of their internal desires to God; for (saith he) if they shall always to the utmost extent of their ability pursue them, they will find themselves in a short time quite exhausted and disabled to perform even easier and more necessary obligations.

12. The true use and benefit, therefore, that imperfect souls ought to make of sensible devotion (when God sends it) is this, that without resting much on it, or forcing themselves to continue it, they should make it an instrument to fortify and establish the solid true love and esteem of God in the superior soul, and to confirm an unshaken resolution in themselves never to desist from seeking Him by the internal ways of the spirit, even in times of desertion and aridity.

13. And if they will make this use of it, then from what cause soever it proceeds—yea, though the devil himself helping or changing the body

should have caused it—no harm can come unto them thereby; for a soul is most secure while she neglects and disesteems the effects of sensible devotion as far as they are pleasing to sensitive nature, and transcending it, shall endeavour to exercise herself towards God quietly yet resolutely in the superior will; and by the like practice may a soul obtain the like security in all extraordinary doubtful cases of visions, ecstasies, &c.

14. More particularly forasmuch as concerns tears (which are usual effects of sensible devotion), a soul must be wary that she give not free scope unto them, whatever the object or cause be, whether it be compassion to our Lord's sufferings or contrition for her own sins, &c. In all cases it is best to suppress them rather than to give them a free liberty to flow, for otherwise, besides the harm that may outwardly happen to the body by impairing the health or weakening the head, they will keep her still below in sensitive nature and immortification, with little or no advancement towards the true love of God. On the contrary, they do hinder the elevation of the spirit by obscuring the mind, that it cannot discover her secret defects, nor what would best keep her in her way. Let her therefore exercise these acts in the superior soul and will, from whence all merit comes, and by which they are performed with quietness and stillness, yet withal more efficaciously than in sensitive nature.

15. The case is otherwise in perfect souls, when God by an extraordinary grace bestows on them the gift of tears (as to St. Arsenius, who is said to have flowed almost continually with them), for in this case they do begin from the spirit, whose operations inferior nature doth not at all hinder, but rather promote in them. And such tears flow (*tanquam pluvia in vellus*) like a shower of rain into a fleece of wool, without the least disturbance and bitterness in inferior nature; which is a grace very rarely, if at all, granted to imperfect souls, and therefore those upon whom it is bestowed may, and no doubt will, without any danger comply with it, since it can flow from no other cause but God only, and the effect of it will not be to depress the spirit, but rather to draw sensitive nature upward into the spirit, causing it likewise to concur in the exercise of divine love; so as that the soul may say with David, *Cor meum et caro mea exultaverunt in Deum vivum*, sensitive nature not only joining with the spirit in serving and loving of God, but likewise finding its contentment therein, without the least prejudice to the spirit; and the way to attain to this solid and secure sensible fervour is by a discreet undervaluing and repressing of that which is originally and merely sensible.

16. Now it will not be impertinent on this occasion to take notice of another sort of temper in prayer of quite a contrary nature, in which the inferior soul seems to have no part at all in the actuations of the spirit towards God—yea, is not only inactive but very repugnant unto them, finding a great

deal of uneasiness and pain in them, so that the whole prayer seems to be made by the spirit, the heart or sensitive appetite in the mean time finding much bitterness in it, and the imagination in a sort refusing to suggest necessary images thereto, any further than as the superior soul, by virtue of the dominion it hath over it, doth even by mere force constrain it.

17. There are scarce any souls that give themselves to internal prayer but some time or other do find themselves in great indisposition thereto, having great obscurities in the mind and great insensibility in the affections. So that if imperfect souls be not well instructed and prepared, they will be in danger, in case that such contradictions in inferior nature continue long, to be dejected, yea, and perhaps deterred from pursuing prayer, for they will be apt to think that their recollections are to no purpose at all, since, forasmuch as seems to them, whatsoever they think or actuate towards God is mere loss of time and of no worth at all, and therefore that it would be more profitable for them to employ their time some other way.

18. Yea, some souls there are conducted by Almighty God by no other way, but only by such prayer of aridity, finding no sensible contentment in any recollections, but, on the contrary, continual pain and contradiction, and yet, by a privy grace and courage imprinted deeply in the spirit, cease not for all that, but resolutely break through all difficulties and continue, the best they can, their internal exercises to the great advancement of their spirit.

19. It will indeed be very hard and morally impossible for any souls but such as have naturally a good propension to introversion to continue constant to their recollections when aridities, obscurities, and desolations continue a long time. For it is this propension alone, assisted by divine grace, that holds them to their recollections, and that enables them to bear themselves up in all their difficulties and temptations.

20. The causes of this aridity and indisposition to prayer, ordinarily speaking (for sometimes God, for the trial of His servants, may, and oft doth, send or permit such temptations to fall on them), are principally a certain particular natural complexion of some, and especially of those who by their corporal temper are most fitted for the exercise of sensible affections; for of all others such are most obnoxious to these aridities and obscurities, because the Humours and spirits of the body, together with the change of weather, &c., have a far greater influence upon these sensible affections than upon the mere operations either of the understanding or will, which do not so much depend upon the body. And therefore, whensoever the said corporal disposition comes by any accident to be altered, such affectionate souls are apt to fall into these internal distresses, and being in such an afflicting disconsolate

condition, they are not able to help themselves by any discourse to which ordinarily they are indisposed. From this ground it is that devout women, who naturally do more abound with sensible affections than men, are more subject to be afflicted and persecuted with these aridities.

21. Such discouragements do least appear in Vocal prayer, which befits all kinds of spirits and all sorts of tempers, whether they discourse internally or not, and whether they can produce internal acts of the will upon conceived images or not; for all these at all times, and howsoever they are corporally disposed, may make their profit, more or less, of vocal prayers.

22. The prayer of Meditation likewise, in those for whom it is proper, is not usually much assaulted with such aridities, except it be sometimes towards the end of such prayer, when souls would endeavour to draw good affections from a precedent motive considered by the understanding; for then the heart may sometimes prove barren or averse from such affections. But, however, they that practise meditation may find some remedy by surceasing the producing of affections, and may either betake themselves to exercise mere acts of the will, which are not so affective, or retire themselves to their internal discourse.

23. The pain and anguish that good souls suffer from these aridities is very grievous, being a kind of continual martyrdom; and therefore the merit of constancy in prayer, notwithstanding such discouragements in nature, is the greater, and souls to whom God shall give such constancy will find their exercises both much more secure (however disgustful they be), yea, and much more profitable than if they had flowed with sensible affections. For all manner of good is gotten by prayer of aridity courageously prosecuted; all virtues are exercised in it: it is both prayer and most efficacious mortification too.

24. And indeed the only general effectual remedy against any inconveniences that may be caused by such aridities is this generosity of resolution not to seek contentment in nature by internal exercises, nor to quit them for any dulness, coldness, or aversion whatsoever. Let but souls do the best they can or know, and they will find that their spiritual progress in the true, solid, and only meritorious love of God will not at all be hindered, but rather advanced by such froward indispositions of corrupt nature.

25. And such courage and effectual resolution may well enough consist with these discouragements; for the spirit, whose operations do not much depend on the corporal disposition, may in the midst of all sensible aridities and obscurities perform its functions with great efficacy. The intellectual faculty is at all times capable of illumination, and the will of receiving grace and strength from God, and the light and grace which we receive at such times are far more pure and divine than when corporal affections do abound,

for then they are communicated purely to the spirit; and consequently the operations performed in virtue of such light and grace are more noble and meritorious, because it is apparent that nature neither does nor can mingle her own interests in them, so that they may confidently he adjudged to be supernatural and divine. The essential profit of a soul consists in the light and love of the spirit; such light and love therefore, which are got with so much difficulty and in such a struggling of nature, is far more pure, generous, and withal more solidly rooted in the soul, than that which is got by the exercise of sensible affections; because all the while there is a continual combat against self-love, and all the most secret, subtle, and deeply-hidden snares of it; so that all virtues becoming thus rooted in the depth of the spirit, and having been produced by the means and in the midst of the sharpest temptations there is less fear that they will be extinguished by other following trials.

26. Now at the first, to the end to attain unto this most necessary courageousness of mind, such souls may do well to help themselves during their aridities with the best motives and most efficacious affections that they can furnish themselves withal, either out of their own invention or by collection out of books, as likewise frequently to urge and even force themselves to the love of God by such ejaculatory prayers and desires as these: O my God, when shall I love Thee as Thou deservest? When shall I love as I am loved by Thee? O, that I were freed from myself, that I may only love Thee! *Excita potentiam Tuam et veni; veni, Domine, et noli tardare. Exurgat Deus et dissipentur inimici, ejus*, &c.

27. Such affections as these let a devout soul exercise in her recollections likewise the best she can (in case she cannot see how other ways to do better), although without any gust or sensible contentment, and God will not fail to accept and plentifully reward her good will, and thereby promote her in such manner as He best knows. She may be sure that since He has given her the generous courage to serve Him without present wages, He will at least in the next life multiply rewards upon her infinitely above her expectation, and she ought to account it a proof of His especial love and esteem of her that He has selected her to be a martyr of love, and a soldier to whose courage He commits the most difficult and hazardous employments.

28. In case that internal distresses in prayer be so violent, that the soul, to her seeming, can only keep herself in an outward posture of prayer; all that she thinks or does appearing to her so utterly void of all spirit of devotion, love, and reverence to God that she may rather suspect it to be injurious to Him; let her be patient and abstain from disquieting her mind with murmuring complaints, and by all means let her be sure not to betake herself to consolation in creatures or recreative diversions in times appointed for recollection, and then all will be very well. God will require no more of

her than she is well able to do, and He knows that it is not in her power always to subdue nature, yet she may and must always withdraw her consent from its sinful suggestions, and doing so, there will be no danger; therefore for what she cannot do let her be humbled and resigned, and such humble resignation will prove a very efficacious prayer.

29. Now it is not to be supposed that internal prayer exercised by imperfect souls during aridities, through the advantage of a natural propension, is a truly pure and spiritual prayer; because as yet their exercise is indeed in sense, yet it is in the nobler and supreme part of sensuality tending much toward the spirit, whereby they in that case do enjoy an internal light more clear and pure than whilst they exercise with flowing affections, insomuch as their operations are then abstracted from grosser sensuality, and the more strong that their propension to introversion is, the more easily and quickly do they raise themselves to that clear superior region of light; and the reason is because such a propension and aptitude to internal ways draws the persons endowed with it more and more deeply towards the spirit, in the perfect operations whereof consists the consummation of an internal life.

Chapter VI. Of Distractions

1. The second discouraging temptation opposite to the second quality requisite in prayer (to wit, perseverance), by which well-minded souls are oft much afflicted in their recollections, and also exposed to grievous scrupulosities, is Distraction in prayer, caused by images which oft, against their wills, press into their imaginations. These draw the mind from contemplating God,

and, consequently, the affections from embracing Him by love at such times when the soul desires and intends to contemplate and love Him.

2. I do not, therefore, here under the term of distractions comprehend all manner of interruptions from a direct actual tendence to God (for such, sometimes, considering the infirmity of our nature, may be necessary to the end that by a discreet relaxation, the head being refreshed, we may be enabled afterwards to produce more efficacious affections; and, therefore, those authors are too indiscreetly rigorous who oblige souls not yet perfect to a continual recollected attention to the divine presence, not considering the corporal infirmity and incapacity of their disciples' spirits, especially in these days). The distractions, therefore, here intended to be treated of are such as are involuntary, and which happen at times when souls do apply themselves either to vocal or mental prayer.

3. Now it is an effect of original sin (much increased also by actual) that souls are generally, some more some less, subject to this deordination, because by sin that due subordination of the sensitive faculties (the imagination, memory, and appetite) to the superior soul is impaired, so that the reason has not that absolute dominion over them that it had in innocence; but they often wander towards objects not prescribed by reason, yea, and sometimes seduce and even compel reason itself to comply with their disorders. Add hereunto, that the body being gross and lumpish cannot long endure that the soul, its companion, should remain in its proper exercise by which it becomes as it were a stranger to the body, contradicting its motions and desires; and, therefore, till the soul, by practice of spiritual operations, be enabled at pleasure to command the inferior faculties or to abstract itself from the images suggested by them; the said faculties do strive to depress the spirit and to call it down to attend to the necessities and desires of sensitive nature; yea, even in the most perfect the soul will not be able to continue long in the height of its elevation.

4. As for these distractions which, generally speaking, are hurtful and to be avoided (among which, notwithstanding, I need not reckon in this place such as are simply sinful, being about unlawful objects), the most harmful to our spiritual progress are those which are about objects to which we cleave with affection, because by such distracting thoughts not only the mind is diverted from God, but the heart also inordinately carried to creatures.

5. For, as for thoughts merely about vain objects, to which we have little or no affection, and which proceed wholly from the instability of the imagination, imperfect souls ought not to be discouraged with them, although they should be never so importunate during their recollections, since the most abstracted liver must be content now and then to suffer them.

6. And the most powerful remedy to prevent them is, with as much prudence and dexterity as one can, to cut off the occasions of entertaining such images as do most frequently and pertinaciously recur to the mind in prayer. And more particularly for those images to whose objects the soul cleaves by inordinate affection; the practice of abstraction and voluntary disengagement from unnecessary business is requisite, and a restraining of our affections from wandering abroad and fixing themselves upon any external objects; for certain it is, that if by the exercise of mortification and prayer we could restrain our affections from creatures and fix them on God only, we should scarce ever have cause to complain of distractions, for we see that we can easily and constantly fix our thoughts on such objects as we love; so that perseverance in prayer and mortification being the most assured instruments to increase divine love and diminish inordinate love to ourselves and creatures, consequently they are the most sure remedies against distractions.

7. But if after all due care had they do still persist, the most effectual expedients to hinder any considerable inconveniences from such distractions are: 1. Sometimes to use a discreet and reasonable industry in contradicting and expelling them, yet forbearing an over-violent anxious resistance of them, out of an opinion that by such violence they may be extinguished, whereas, on the contrary, such an eagerness of contending with them by the inflaming of the spirits makes those images more active and full of motion, and rather multiplies than diminishes them; and, however, it imprints them deeper in the imagination. Let a well-minded soul rather endeavour, according to the expression of the author of the Cloud, to look over their shoulders, as if she looked after some other object that stood beyond them and above them, which is God. 2. Let her (as hath been said) fix in her mind and superior will a strong resolution, notwithstanding the said distractions, yea, in the midst and press of them, not to relinquish prayer, but to persevere in it to the best of her power and skill. 3. Let the well-minded soul execute this resolution with all possible quietness, stillness, and patience, not troubling herself with any fears or scrupulosity, as if they came from her own fault, whereas ordinarily they are increased, at least, by the distemper of the body, or the natural instability of the imagination. 4. Sometimes it may be requisite for her (not being able, to her own satisfaction, to pursue her appointed exercise) to change it into acts of patience and quiet resignation, to suffer without murmuring such an affliction and visitation from God's hands; and so doing, she will, perhaps, more advance herself in pure spiritual prayer than if she had no such distractions at all; for besides that such prayer being made with an actual contradiction to the inclinations of nature, has in it the virtue of a most purifying mortification. Also, a perseverance in this practice will bring her to that pure prayer of the will without any perceivable help or concurrence of the understanding, in which the will is firmly united to God, whilst

the understanding is in no such union, yea, when both it and the imagination are never so extravagant and wandering.

8. And surely a matter of great comfort it is to a soul (and ought so to be esteemed) that in her will (which is her principal faculty, and, indeed, all in all) she may be united to God in the midst of all distractions, temptations, and desolations, &c., and that being so united, she will be so far from receiving any harm by them that she will, by their means, increase in grace, so that though she do not receive any extraordinary illuminations nor any satisfaction to her natural will by such distracted prayers, yet doth she get that for which such illuminations and gusts are given, to wit, a privy but effectual grace to adhere unto God and to resign herself to Him in all His providences and permissions concerning her; and grace gotten by such an afflicting way of abnegation is far more secure and merits more at God's hands, than if it had come by lightsome and pleasing consolations; since this is a way by which corrupt nature is transcended, self-love contradicted and subdued, even when it assaults the soul most subtlely and dangerously, to wit, by pretending that all solicitudes and anxious discouragements, caused by distractions, do flow from divine love and from a care of the soul's progress in spirituality. Lastly, this is a way by which charity and all divine virtues are deeply rooted in the spirit, being produced and established there by the same means that the devil uses to hinder the production of them in negligent and tepid souls, or to destroy them when they have been in some measure produced.

9. As for more particular advices, expedients, and sleights to be made use of in special cases and circumstances, none can teach but God only, who by means of experience and perseverance in prayer will undoubtedly give unto a soul light and grace sufficient.

10. To conclude, therefore, this point, this difference may be observed between distractions in perfect souls from the same in the imperfect, viz. that in perfect souls distractions proceed only from some unwilling distemper in the cognoscitive faculties, but in the imperfect they are rather from some degree of inordinate affection to the objects of the distractions; and, therefore, a well-advanced soul hath little difficulty in putting them away as soon as she reflects upon them, for without contending with them she can presently unite herself with her superior will to God, even whilst her knowing powers are busy about impertinent objects; whereas imperfect souls in the inferior degrees of prayer, having as yet an express and perceptible use of the understanding and imagination, cannot but receive some prejudice by distractions, inasmuch as those faculties cannot at the same time be employed upon different objects that have no subordination or relation to one another.

11. There remains a third condition or quality which I said was necessary to true internal affective prayer, to wit, the divine inspiration, from which if it do not proceed, it is of little efficacy or merit. Now though in the general division of internal prayer I seemed to appropriate the title of infused prayer to the prayer of perfect contemplation, the meaning thereof was, that such prayer is merely infused, the soul by any deliberate preparation or election not disposing herself thereto; whereas in the inferior degrees there is necessary both a precedent and concomitant industry in the soul to make choice of matter for prayer, and to force herself to produce affections corresponding to the said matter, by reason that as yet God's Holy Spirit is not so abounding and operative in the soul as to impel her to pray, or rather breathing forth prayers in and by her. But in all cases that is most true which St. Bernard saith, *Tepida est oratio, quam non prevenit inspiratio;* that is, that prayer is a tepid prayer which is not prevented by divine inspiration; and St. Augustine, *Bene orare Deum, gratia spiritalis est;* that is, it is a special grace of God's Holy Spirit to be able to pray aright.

12. Now the ground of the necessity of a divine inspiration hereto is expressed in that saying of St. Paul (*Quid oremus sicut oportet nescimus,* &c.), We know not how to pray as we ought, and therefore the Spirit of God helps our infirmity, yea, saith he, *the Spirit itself makes requests in us and for us,* and this oft *with groans which cannot be expressed,* and which the soul itself cannot conceive. It is this inspiration only which gives a supernaturality to our prayers, and makes them fit to be heard and granted by God.

13. But of this subject much hath already been said, and more will follow when we treat of the several degrees of prayer (especially the perfect prayer of aspirations), where we shall show how these inspirations are attempered according to the natural good propensions of souls; so that those which are naturally inclined to introversion are usually moved by God to seek Him by pure spiritual operations, without images or motives, yet this by degrees, according to the state of the soul; where also I will show how necessary liberty of spirit and a freedom from nice methods and rules of prayer are to dispose the soul for these divine inspirations, and therefore I will forbear any further enlarging of myself on this point in this place.

14. Now a due consideration of these excellencies and most heavenly effects of internal affective prayer ought to give us a suitable esteem and valve of it above any other employments whatsoever. An experience hereof it was that made an ancient hermit, called Jacob (in Theodoret. de Vit. PP.), resolutely to persist in refusing to interrupt his appointed prayer, or to delay the time of it for any other business or civilities in visits whatsoever. He commanded all to depart when the hour was come, saying, 'I came not to this solitude to benefit other men's souls, but to purify mine own by prayer.'

Chapter VII. The Doctrine of Fr. Baltazar Alvarez, S.J. Defended

§ 1. Internal affective prayer (of contemplation) hath always been enter-
tained at first with jealousy and rigour.

§§ 2, 3, 4. An illustrious example in the person of the late R. Father Baltazar
Alvarez, of the Society of Jesus.

§§ 5, 6, 7, 8, 9, 10, 11, 12, 13, 14, 15. An account required and given by him
to his general, touching his prayer of contemplation. The order and manner
of God's guidance of him thereto and therein: and the excellency of that
prayer declared.

§§ 16, 17, 18, 19, 20, 21, 22, 23, 24, 25, 26, 27, 28, 29. The substance of a
discourse written by him in answer to seven objections made against internal
prayer of contemplation.

§ 30. The success of this tempest.

1. It is so far from being a just prejudice against this most excellent of God's gifts (internal prayer of the will), that it is rather a proof of the more than ordinary eminency of it, that it has always found some, even among the learned, and ofttimes among such as have been the most strict and severe about religious observances, that have and do oppose it. God forbid that this should always be imputed either to malice, envy, &c., but rather to want of experience in the mysterious ways by which the Spirit of God ofttimes conducts His special servants. It is well known what calumnies and persecutions Suso, St. Teresa, St. John of the Cross, &c. found when God enlightened them and moved them to communicate to the world this heavenly light, all which they accepted as a certain proof that it came from God, that it was beneficial to souls, and therefore odious to the Devil; for so have all such things been ever at the first entertained.

2. But among all the late masters of pure spiritual contemplative prayer, there is none deserves more our esteem, nor is more proper to be produced in this place, than the late R. F. Baltazar Alvarez, of the Society of Jesus, well known unto and most highly esteemed by St. Teresa (who was much assisted and comforted by him during her troubles and difficulties). The special benefit that may be reaped from his story is, that by occasion of his trial and examination about his prayer all the suspicions and allegations against it are well cleared, and the whole substance of this treatise worthily confirmed and asserted.

3. This venerable person, after he had with great diligence spent about fifteen years in meditation and the spiritual exercises (peculiar to his order), and yet received but little profit to his spirit by them, being, on the contrary, tormented with extreme doubtfulness and unsatisfaction, was at last guided powerfully, by God's Holy Spirit, to quit meditation and to betake himself to a serious practice of prayer immediately in the will, by corresponding to which divine motion he presently received abundance of light, and a perfect remedy against all his anguishes and perplexities.

4. But his internal troubles ceasing, outward difficulties began; for others of his brethren and companions perceiving that he walked in ways unknown to them, earnestly required an examination of this new spirit, insomuch as that out of Spain these complaints came to the ears of their then General, the most R. F. Everardus Mercurian, resident at Rome; by order from whom his study was sealed up and afterwards searched by learned fathers thereto appointed, and all his papers examined, which, affording no matter of just accusation at all, but, on the contrary, of great edification, a second command comes from the General to him to give a full account of the order and manner of his prayer.

5. This command obliged him to make a free and ingenuous apology for himself, the which, because it is most pertinent and conformable to the spirit of these instructions, and besides is not common in many men's hands, I will here set down the substance of as it is related with most commendable candour and ingenuity by F. Ludovicus de Puente, of the same society, his scholar, who wrote his life.

6. Now, in his said Apology, he freely and humbly declares 'That near sixteen years he had laboured like one that tills the ground without reaping any fruit, that his heart was much strained with grief, observing that he wanted the talents for which he saw others esteemed, and particularly that he was much troubled that he had not space enough allowed him for prayer. But this temptation he overcame, resolving to employ no more time in prayer than holy obedience permitted, and rejecting that foolish ambition of excelling therein, or of pretending to divine favour, which others better deserving enjoyed. Notwithstanding, he still found his defects to multiply, and rather to disquiet than humble him; yea, they made him in an incapacity to comply with the internal counsels and invitations of God; moreover, that by reason of this unquietness the defects of others also under his government did much increase his distemper, so that he judged it a point of right government to make his subjects perform all things (like himself) with a melancholy dejectedness of mind.

7. 'That at the end of fourteen years he found himself in a practice of prayer, by which he placed himself in God's presence as a beggar, saying

little, but only expecting an alms; but by reason that he could not keep his mind fixed on God, but did overmuch reflect upon himself, his troubles, dejection, and utter despair of approaching to perfection increased, since God had showed him no marks of His favour, which it seems he expected, but (as he confesses) very foolishly, since his coming to God with such an expectation was a greater fault than his former deserting Him; yea, hereby he was brought to that extreme confusion, that for mere shame he durst not for a good space in prayer say anything to God at all, but only that He would punish, forgive, and assist him.

8. 'But when sixteen years were passed he found his heart on the sudden unexpectedly quite changed and dilated, all his disquietness vanished, and his soul, freed from all created things, being filled with an astonishing joy, like that of those which say, "Lord, when we see Thee, we have seen all good, and are entirely satiated." Here he found himself in a congregation of persons destined to beatitude, the way whereto seemed plain and easy; now he received a spiritual discretion to sever between the precious and the vile; new notions and intelligence of verities were given him, which fed his soul with joy and peace; yet such illuminations, at the first, were somewhat rare, but at the time of the writing of this Apology they were become much more frequent.

9. 'Instead of that anxiety that he had formerly, because his ambitious desire of being eminent was not satisfied, now he was content to live under the cross—now he did so humble himself under all that he was in confusion to appear before any. Notwithstanding, though he honoured all men, yet he found that they were not at all needful to him, as formerly they seemed to be, but that it was both better and easier for him to converse with God only.

10. 'Thenceforward he perceived that God had given him an internal light for the ordering both of himself and others under him, even in the smallest matters; and whereas solicitudes in government, &c., did formerly disquiet and oppress his spirit, now he found that businesses were far better discharged by casting his care on God, and putting them out of his thoughts till the time came that he was to execute his duty; so that in the midst of a throng of cares he lived without care. Now he was not, as formerly, troubled for that he had not time sufficient for prayer, because he found that God gives more in one hour to mortified resigned souls than to others in many days, and he found more profit to his spirit by a faithful discharge of employments imposed by God than in vacancy and reading spiritual books of his own election.

11. 'A sight of his defects now does him good, by humbling him and making him distrustful of himself and confident in God, knowing that no de-

fects not knowingly and deliberately persisted in do hinder God's counsels and designs for our perfection; and as for the defects of those under his government, he found it a great folly for him to disquiet himself about them, and that his former desire of making them sad and melancholy was an effect of his own impatience.

12. 'His prayer now was to place himself in God's presence, both inwardly and outwardly presented to him, and to rejoice with Him permanently and habitually. Now he understood the difference between imperfect and perfect souls on the point of enjoying the divine presence, expressed by St. Thomas (22 q. 24, a. 9 ad 3, et opusc. 63); and he perceived that those were blind that seek God with anxiety of mind, and call upon Him as if He were absent; whereas, being already His temples, in which His divine, majesty rests, they ought to enjoy Him actually and internally present in them. Sometimes in his prayer he pondered awhile on some text of Scripture, according to the inspirations and lights then given him; sometimes he remained in cessation and silence before God, which manner of prayer he accounted a great treasure; for then his heart, his desires, his secret intentions, his knowledge, and all his powers spake, and God understood their mute language, and with one aspect could expel his defects, kindle his desires, and give him wings to mount spiritually unto Him. Now he took comfort in nothing but in suffering contentedly the will of God to be performed in all things, which was as welcome to him in aridities as consolations, being unwilling to know more than God freely discovered unto him, or to make a more speedy progress, or by any other ways than such as God Himself prescribed unto him. If his heart, out of its natural infirmity, did at any time groan under his present burden, his answer thereto would be: "Is not that good which God wills to be, and will it not always incessantly remain so?" or, "Will God cease to perform His own will because thou dost not judge it to be for thy good?" In conclusion, his present established comfort was to see himself in God's presence to be a sufferer, and to be treated according to His divine pleasure.

13. 'If, sometimes leaving this quiet prayer to which God had brought him, he offered to apply himself to his former exercises of meditation, he found that God gave him an internal reprehension and restraint. For his greater assurance, therefore, he searched mystic authors, St. Dionysius Areopagita (de Myst. Theol. c. 1), St. Augustine (Epistol. 119), St. Gregory (Mor. lib. 30, 26, &c.), St. Bernard (in Cant. Serm. 55, &c.), out of which he satisfied himself, that as rest is the end of motion, and a quiet habitation the end of a laborious building, so this peaceful prayer and quiet enjoying of God in spirit was the end of the imperfect busy prayer of meditation, and therefore that all internal discoursing with the understanding was to cease whensoever God enabled souls to actuate purely by the will; and that to do otherwise would be as if one should be always preparing somewhat to eat, and yet af-

277

terwards refuse to taste that which is prepared. By this divine prayer of the will, the Holy Spirit of wisdom, with all the excellencies of it described in the Book of Wisdom (cap. viii.), is obtained, and with it perfect liberty.

14. 'In consequence hereto he proceeds by reasons to demonstrate the supereminent excellency of this reposeful prayer of the will, as: 1. That though in it there is no reasoning of the mind, yet the soul, silently presenting herself before God with a firm faith that her desires are manifest to Him, doth more than equivalently tell God her desires, and withal exercises all virtues, humbling herself before Him, loving Him only, and believing that leaving her own ways and constantly holding to God's, all good will proceed from thence to her; 2. that in this prayer a soul hath far more sublime and worthy notion of God; 3. that this still and quiet prayer may be far more prolixly and perseverantly practised than the tiring prayer of meditation, (yea, it may come to be continual and without interruption); 4. that all the good effects of meditation, as humility, obedience, &c., are far more efficaciously and perfectly produced by this prayer than by that which is joined with inward seasonings; 5. true indeed it is that the exercises instituted by St. Ignatius were more proper generally for souls than this, yet that this ought to be esteemed proper for those whom God had called and prepared to it, and that this was St. Ignatius's own practice, who, though in his less perfect state he purified the imperfect exercises instituted by him, yet afterwards he was exalted to this sublime prayer, by which he came to suffer divine things. That, therefore, as none ought to intrude into the exercise of this pure prayer till God has called and fitted them for it, so being called, none ought to be forbidden it (as Osanna in his alphabet teacheth); and that whosoever forbiddeth such shall give a strict account to God for so great a fault, insomuch, as a certain spiritual writer saith, that God will shorten the lives of those superiors who shall presume to discourage and affright any souls from these internal ways, except they desist from such an attempt.'

15. This is the sum of the account which the most venerable F. Baltazar Alvarez, after a retirement of fifteen days, with a most humble confession of his own defects and misery, and a magnifying of God's liberal goodness extended towards him, gave unto his General.

16. Now, besides this account, he wrote likewise a short discourse, in which he did more fully treat of the nature of this prayer of rest and silence, and gave a particular answer to several objections which certain of his brethren had made and dispersed against the said prayer. The sum of which objections, with his answers to them, I will here adjoin.

17. The first objection was, that one who exerciseth this prayer, which admitteth neither of discoursive meditation nor any such like use of

the understanding, seems to spend his time unprofitably in doing nothing, which might far better be bestowed in external exercises of virtues.

18. The answer hereto is, that though the understanding be in a sort suspended from exercising its activity, yet the soul is far from being idle; on the contrary, she performs that which St. Bernard calls the business of all businesses; for therein the stream of holy affections doth freely flow by loving, admiring, adoring, congratulating, resigning, and offering the soul to God contemplated with the eye of faith, &c., and all this sometimes in a few words, sometimes in silence. In a word, the soul behaves herself according to the variety of affections that the unction of the Holy Spirit, who is the principal master herein, doth teach and move her to, according to that of St. Dionysius Areopagita to Timotheus, *Converte te ad radium*, &c.,—'Turn thyself to the beam of divine light.' From hence that admirable union doth proceed which the same Saint calls 'The union of the unknown with the unknown,' which is the supreme height of mystical theology, and which, without experience of it, cannot be conceived by any.

19. The second objection is, that to leave meditation, out of an expectation of divine inspirations or revelations, seems to be a tempting of God and a favouring of the error of the heretics called Illuminates.

20. The answer is, that this prayer, exercised merely by holy affections without mental discoursings, cannot be practised but by such as have a long time been exercised in the inferior degree of discoursive prayer, except it be when God presents souls extraordinarily by a special invitation and enablement; and those, likewise, that from meditation do ascend to this quiet prayer, do it by the guidance of a supernatural light, and being in it, they exercise themselves therein not by desiring or expecting revelations, but by acknowledging the divine presence in the soul and producing the foresaid holy affections to Him. Neither is here any affinity with the doings of the Illuminates, who, without any call from God, without any preparation, did arrogantly presume to pray as they did, remaining in a distracted idleness and misspending the time in expectation of extraordinary visits, without any good effect at all toward the reformation of their inordinate affections; whereas, if an immortified soul should presume to betake herself to this prayer, she will be forced to quit it; for none can appear with a secure peacefulness before God's presence that doth deliberately resist His Spirit, which is the spirit of purity, sanctity, humiliation, and conformity to the Divine Will.

21. In the third place, it is objected that there is no way to discern when one undertakes this prayer by a divine inspiration, and when this is done out of presumption and a desire to enjoy spiritual gifts, which nourish self-love.

22. It is answered that this will evidently enough be known by the effects, as a tree by its fruits. Now the effects of this prayer, when it is practised upon a divine call, are a softness and flexibility of the heart to the Divine Will; a resigned acceptation of all things from His hand; a confidence of obtaining all good from Him upon whom the soul hath entirely bestowed herself; an imitation of the pattern of all perfection, our Lord Jesus; a renouncing of self-will, &c. Now surely that prayer which teaches these things is doubtless from God.

23. But, fourthly, it is replied that those which practise this kind of prayer are self-opinioned, adhering to their own ways, and, out of a presumptuous conceit of being spiritual, despise others, and refuse to submit themselves to the judgment of superiors.

24. The answer is, that such defects and miscarriages as these are not to be imputed to the prayer itself (which teaches quite the contrary), but to the imperfections and frailty of those that do not practise it as they ought; and therefore this is not a ground sufficient to condemn the prayer itself, no more than meditation ought to be condemned because the like or greater faults are committed by some that practise it, who are more obnoxious to a vain esteem of themselves upon occasion of some curious inventions found out by their internal reasonings therein. Yea, the sacraments we see are abused, but yet not, therefore, forbidden; as for superiors, none of them, except it be sometimes for a trial, ought to prohibit their subjects from praying according as God, by His inspiration, directs them; and if they shall absolutely prohibit this, they must expect that God will require an account of them; however, in such a case it would be a fault in subjects to disobey them, but yet, till such a prohibition do issue forth, the subjects surely may lawfully, yea ought to, follow the internal directions of God. Neither is it presumption in them, if by the advantage of experience they shall think themselves capable of judging of such matters better than those that have no experience at all in them; nor is it pride to acknowledge the gifts given us of God, as the apostle saith.

25. Fifthly, it is objected that some are so wholly given up to this fashion of prayer, that they are always in a kind of ecstasy, being so delighted with the gusts which they find in it, that they quite forget their obligations of charity, obedience, and exercise of virtues, from which they retire, to the end that they may immerse themselves in a prayer that affords them no truths which may profitably be communicated to their neighbours. Now all this is directly contrary to the institute of St. Ignatius; moreover, by this kind of prayer, many of the practisers of it become subject to divers corporal infirmities, which render them incapable to comply with the obligations of their state of life.

26. The answer is, that it is no wonder if some defects be found in these persons, since none are entirely free; but, however, the said defects are not to be imputed to the prayer, but to undue use of it; for contemplation itself doth even urge souls to the exercise of charity whensoever necessity and duty requires it (not otherwise). Hence is that saying of St. Augustine (lib. 19, *de Civit. D.* c. 19), *Otium sanctuna querit charitas veritatis,* &c.,—'Love of verity secketh a holy vacancy.' Necessity of charity undertaketh due employments, the which charge, if it be not imposed, one ought to remain in the fruition and contemplation of verity, and agreeable hereto is the doctrine of St. Gregory (in cap. vii. Job) and St. Bernard (Ser. 57 in Cant.). Moreover, a soul by meditation may perhaps find out finer conceits; but the will is more enriched with virtues by this prayer. Now it is virtue alone that renders a soul acceptable to God, and as for corporal infirmities, they proceed only from an indiscreet use of this prayer; for otherwise it being a prayer of stillness and repose, is far less dangerous to the head and health than the laborious imaginative exercise of meditation, and hence it is that those holy persons that practised it were enabled much longer to continue in it.

27. A sixth objection was that this manner of prayer doth draw souls so wholly to itself, that all devotion to Saints and all praying for common or particular necessities become too much neglected and forgotten.

28. It is answered that since such vocal prayers and voluntary exercises are only means to bring souls to perfect prayer of quietness, according to St. Thomas's doctrine (22 q. 83, a. 13) they ought to cease when the soul finds herself full of fervent affections; neither is this any proof of disesteem of such means, but a right understanding and use of them. It is said of St. Ignatius that by long practice of vocal prayer, &c., he was brought to such inward familiarity with God, that he could not proceed in the saying of his office by reason of the copious communication of ardent affections and graces that God bestowed on him, insomuch as his companions were forced to obtain for him a dispensation from that obligation, because the performance of his office took up almost the whole day, so abundant were the divine visitations in it towards him. Neither are we to think that a soul by following the divine conduct in pure prayer doth thereby omit due petitions for either common or particular necessities; on the contrary, since those necessities are known to God, who sees the hearts of His servants that ardently desire a supply to them, but yet do not busy themselves much in making express prayers for them, because they would rather employ their affections in such prayer as they know is more acceptable to God,—by such a not express asking, they do privily and most efficaciously ask and obtain the said petitions; and as for devotions to Saints, they account it to be their chiefest honour that God should be most honoured.

29. The seventh and last objection was the same that the author had before answered in his account to his General, viz. that this fashion of prayer calls souls from the spiritual exercises instituted by St. Ignatius, the answer to which need not be repeated. But whereas it was added that diversity of prayer might cause factions in the society, it was answered that the perfect may lawfully practise ways not common to the imperfect, without any fear of divisions or any intention of contradicting or despising of others.

30. This is the sum both of the account given by the V. R. Father Baltazar Alvarez to his General touching his prayer, as likewise of his answers to the objections made unto it, and the success of the tempest raised against him was, as to his own person, very prosperous and happy; for after a most strict examination his innocence and truth were asserted by his writings, and his most humble patience manifested in his whole behaviour. Moreover, the General conceived so great an esteem of him that he preferred him to two offices successively, of the greatest dignity and trust that the society then had in Spain. Notwithstanding, the same General (as the author of the Life, p. 493, saith), not approving that such a manner of prayer should so commonly be spread, did therefore restrain and moderate such a generality; and in his letters to the Provincial (p. 508) required superiors that they should direct and assist their religious so that they might highly esteem, and in their practice follow, the manner of prayer most conformable to their institute, prescribed in their exercises.

THE THIRD TREATISE
THE SECOND SECTION

OF THE FIRST DEGREE OF INTERNAL PRAYER, VIZ. MEDITATION.

Chapter I. The Degrees of Prayer

§§ 1, 2. 3. Several degrees and stations in an internal life; as the three ways, Purgative, Illuminative, and Unitive.

§§ 4, 5. They are best distinguished according to the three degrees of internal prayer.

§§ 6, 7, 8, 9, 10, 11, 12, 13, 14, 15. The grounds of the several degrees of prayer.

§§ 16, 17. How God is represented in the said degrees.

§§ 18, 19. How the operations of the soul grow more and more pure.

§§ 20, 21. The degrees of prayer are not so diverse but that sometimes they may be intermixed.

§§ 22, 23, 24. In what sense the exercises of an active life (to wit, meditation) are divided into three ways also, purgative, illuminative, unitive.

1. It is generally the custom of those that write treatises of spiritual doctrine to begin with a division of the several stations or ascents observed in the duties and exercises thereof, but such a division I have conceived most proper to be reserved to this place; and the reason is, because though in a spiritual progress there be an ascent in the practice of all duties universally of a spiritual life, as well of mortification as prayer, notwithstanding the true judgment of a progress is to be made with reference principally to prayer, according to the increase in the purity and spirituality whereof so is the per-

son to be esteemed to have made a proportionable progress in all other duties and virtues disposing to contemplation and perfection.

2. Now several mystic authors, according to the several notions that they had both of the end of a spiritual life and means conducing thereto, have by several terms made the division of its degrees. The most ancient division is into three states: 1. of beginners; 2. of proficients; 3. of such as are perfect. Yet withal they do not signify by what distinctive marks each of these states are separated from the others; but generally, in latter times, the whole course of a spiritual life is divided: 1. into the Purgative way, in which all sinful defects are purged out of the soul; 2. the Illuminative way, by which divine virtues and graces are introduced; 3. the Unitive way, by which a soul attains unto the end of all other exercises, to wit, an union with God in spirit by perfect charity.

3. Besides these many other divisions may be found, as of F. Benet Canfield, who, making the Divine Will (that is, God Himself) the sole object of all our exercises, doth by a division of the said Will into: 1. external; 2. internal; 3. essential or supereminent Will, virtually divide all spiritual exercises into such as are proper and conformable to these three notions of one and the same Will. Again, others divide all exercises into: 1. active; 2. contemplative, &c.; and it is of no importance which of these divisions is made use of so they be rightly understood.

4. But since, as hath been said, the degrees of perfection generally understood as relating to all the duties of an internal life are best conceived and measured by the degrees of internal prayer, which, indeed, are of a different nature one from the other, and therefore are not so properly called degrees, as several states of prayer (which is not so in mortification or the exercise of virtues, because the perfect do the same actions, though in a more perfect degree than the imperfect); hence it is that R. F. Constantine Barbanson, the most learned and experienced author of the book called *Secrets Sentiers de l'Amour Divin*, divides the whole progress of a spiritual contemplative life according to the progress of prayer, which (saith he) hath these degrees: 1. The exercises of the understanding in meditation. 2. The exercises of the will and affections without meditation (which at the first are very imperfect). 3. Afterward a soul comes to an experimental perception of the divine presence in her. 4 Then follows the great desolation. 5. This being past, there succeeds a sublime manifestation of God in the summity of the spirit. 6. From thence, after many interchangeable risings and fallings (which are found likewise in all the degrees), the soul enters into the divine yet most secret ways of perfection.

5. Now this order of his in gross (as being most natural and suitable both to reason and experience) my purpose is to follow, yet so as to collect

the four last degrees into one, so that I shall only distinguish three degrees of prayer, to wit: 1. Discursive prayer or meditation. 2. The prayer of forced immediate acts or affections of the will, without discourse preparatory thereto. 3. The prayer of pure active contemplation or aspirations, as it were naturally and without any force flowing from the soul, powerfully and immediately directed and moved by the Holy Spirit. Now this third degree, to which the prayer belonging is, indeed, truly the prayer of contemplation, beyond which there is no state of prayer, may very conveniently include all the four degrees mentioned by Barbanson, and so nicely distinguished by him; rather out of a particular experience of the effects passing in his own soul, which, perhaps, are not the same in all (for God works according to His own good pleasure in the souls of His perfect servants, and not according to any methods that man can conceive or express).

6. These, therefore, being the three degrees of internal prayer (which do most properly answer to the commonly assigned ways of spirituality, the purgative, illuminative, and unitive), of them the first is a prayer consisting much of discourse of the understanding; the other two are prayers of the will, but most principally and purely the last. Of these three I shall treat in order in the following discourse (to wit: 1. in pursuit of this second section of the most imperfect degree, to wit, meditation; 2. in the following section of the prayer of immediate acts of the will; 3. and in the last section of the prayer of aspirations or contemplation); but before I come to treat of each in particular, I conceive it requisite first to show the grounds upon which the propriety and reasonableness of this division of the succeeding degrees of prayer is built, and it may be evidently and convincingly demonstrated so far, that according to the dispensation of divine grace to souls that tend to perfection, it may be affirmed that they are conducted by these degrees in this order, and no other way; and this experience will make good even in souls that never heard of any degrees of prayer, but, without learning, reading, or instructions, are immediately guided by God's Holy Spirit in His internal ways. The reason hereof will appear by that which follows.

7. First, therefore, it is apparent and acknowledged that, generally speaking, a soul from a state of negligence and secularity first entering into a spiritual course, though she be supposed, by virtue of that grace by which she is moved to make so great and happy a change, to be really in the state of justification, yet there still remains in her a great measure of fear, conceived from the guilt of her former sins; and withal, strong inclinations to sin and vicious habits do yet abide, and will do so, till by long practice of virtue and piety they be abated and expelled. Moreover, a world of vain and sinful images do possess the soul, which distract her whensoever she sets her mind on God, calling on her to attend to her formerly pleasing objects, which took up all her affections, and which do still ofttimes insinuate themselves into her

memory with too much contentment to inferior nature, which contentment, though she, upon reflection, do resist and renounce with her superior soul, yet this resistance is ofttimes so feeble, that frequently she is really entangled and seduced, and more oft does find ground to doubt that she has given consent thereto.

8. Such being ordinarily the disordered condition of a soul at her first conversion, the remedy acknowledged to be proper and necessary for her is prayer, and the highest degree of prayer that for the present she is capable of is either a much distracted vocal prayer or discoursive meditation, in which the understanding and imagination are chiefly employed; and the reason is, because although God hath imprinted true charity in such a soul, yet seducing images so abounding, and vicious affections being as yet so predominant in sensitive nature, there is a necessity for the fortifying it to chase away the said images and subdue such affections, by storing the imagination with contrary good images, and setting on work affections contrary to these; and this is done by inventing arguments and motives (especially of fear). So that the exercises proper to a soul in this first imperfect state are those of sensible contrition and remorse for sin, &c., caused by the consideration of the foulness of it; of the misery that attends it; the certainty and uncertainty of death; the terrors of God's judgments; the horror of hell, &c., as likewise a consideration that no less a price would serve for the reparation of a soul from sin, than the bloody Passion of the Son of God, &c. Such matters as these are now the seasonable subjects of meditation; and the actions of mortification fit to attend such prayer are more sensible, gross, and exterior, proper to repress her grosser defects.

9. Now when by means of such exercises the soul is become well eased from remorse, and begins to be moved to the resistance and hatred of sin by the love of God rather than fear of His judgments, her discoursive prayer for all that does not cease, but there is a change made only in the objects of it, because, instead of the consideration of judgment, hell, &c., the soul finds herself more inclined to resist sin by the motives of love, or a consideration of the charity, patience, and sufferings of our Lord, as likewise out of a comfortable meditation of the future joys promised and prepared for her. Although charity be much increased, yet not yet to such a point but that she stands in need of motives and considerations to set it on work, as likewise of good, holy, and efficacious images of divine things to allure her to forget or neglect the vain images that yet do much distract her. The object of her thoughts now are the infinite joys of heaven, the sublime mysteries of faith, the blessed Humanity of our Lord, the glorious attributes of the Divinity, &c., and the mortifications answerable to the present state do grow more internal, being much exercised about inward defects, which by prayer are discovered to her and corrected. Now a soul whilst she continues in this sort

of prayer and mortification, standing in need of a much and frequent consideration of motives, is properly said to be in the purgative way, though toward the latter end there be a mixture of the illuminative.

10. In the second place, when a soul by perseverance in such discoursive prayer comes to find (as in time she will) that she stands in less need of inventing motives to induce her to exercise love to God, because good affections by exercise abounding and growing ripe do with facility move themselves, so that the mere presenting of a good object to the soul suffices to make her produce a good affection; thenceforward, by little and little, the soul in prayer quits discoursing, and the will immediately stirs itself towards God, and here (meditation ending) the second and more perfect degree or state of internal prayer begins, to wit, the prayer of immediate acts of the will.

11. Now a soul living a solitary or abstracted life, and being arrived to this prayer, if she should be obliged by others, or force herself to continue meditation, she would make no progress at all, yea, on the contrary, the extreme painfulness of inventing motives (now unnecessary) and tying herself to methods and prescribed forms would be to her so distractive, so void of all taste and comfort, and so insupportable, that not being suffered to follow God's invitation calling to an exercise of the will, she will be in danger to give quite over all internal prayer; whereas, by pursuing God's call, she will every day get light to discover more and more her secret inward defects, and grace to mortify and amend them; and such her mortification is exercised rather by transcending and forgetting the objects of her inordinate affections than a direct combating against them; and this state of prayer doth properly answer to that which is commonly called the illuminative way, because in it the soul with little reflection on herself or her own obscurity, by reason of sin, &c., tends directly and immediately to God, by whom she is enlightened and adorned with all virtues and graces.

12. In the third place, a soul after a long exercise in forced affections of the will to God, represented to the understanding by images far more subtle and spiritual than formerly, yea, endeavouring to contemplate Him in the darkness and obscurity of a blind and naked faith, void of all distinct and express images, will by little and little grow so well disposed to Him, that she will have less need of forcing herself to produce good affections to Him, or of prescribing to herself determinate forms of acts or affections; on the contrary, divine love will become so firmly established in the soul, so wholly and only filling and possessing it, that it will become, as it were, a new soul unto the soul, as constantly breathing forth fervorous acts of love, and as naturally almost as the lungs do send forth breath.

13. And here begins the state of pure contemplation (the end of all exercises of an internal life). In this blessed state the actuations and aspirations are so pure and spiritual, that the soul herself oftentimes is not able to give an account what she does; and no wonder, since they do not proceed from any forethought or election of her own, but are suggested to her by the Divine Spirit entirely possessing her; and although in these most sublime and blind elevations of the will, the imagination and understanding with their images are not absolutely excluded, yet so imperceptible are their operations, that it is no wonder if many mystical writers, speaking according to what they felt and experienced in themselves, have said that in pure contemplation the will without the understanding was only operative. As for the mortifications proper to this state, they are as inexpressible as the prayer; indeed, prayer and mortification seem to be now become the same thing, for the light in which the soul walks is so clear and wonderful, that the smallest imperfections are clearly discovered, and by prayer alone mortified. Prayer is the whole business of the life, interrupted by sleep only, and not always then neither; true it is that by other necessities of corporal nature, refections, study, conversation, or business, it may be depressed a little from the height in which it is when the soul sets itself to attend to God only; but still it continues with efficacy in the midst of all those avocations. And this is truly and properly that which mystics do style the unitive way, because herein the soul is in a continual union in spirit with God, having transcended all creatures and herself too, which are become as it were annihilated, and God is all in all.

14. There is no state of spirituality beyond this, but yet this state may infinitely increase in degrees of purity, the operations of the soul growing more and more spiritual in time, and divine without all limitation. In this state it is that the soul is prepared for divine inaction, passive unions and graces most admirable and most efficacious to purify her as perfectly as in the condition of this life she is capable. Now it is that God provides for souls dearly beloved by Him trials and desolations incomprehensible to the inexperienced, leading them from light to darkness, and from thence to light again; in all which changes the soul keeps herself in the same equality and tranquillity, as knowing that by them all she approaches nearer and nearer to God, plunging herself more and more profoundly in Him. A soul that is come to this state is above all instructors and instructions, a divine light being her guide in all manner of things; in a word, it is not she that now lives, but Christ and His Holy Spirit that lives, reigns, and operates in her.

15. These are the three states of a spiritual contemplative life, distinguished according to the three states or degrees of internal prayer. As for vocal prayer, it is not to be esteemed a peculiar degree of prayer; but it may and doth accompany all these states without any change in the substance of

the prayer, though with very great variety in the actuation of the soul during its exercise; for whilst the soul is in the imperfect degree of meditation, she performs her vocal prayer with the use of grosser images and much distractedness; but being arrived to the exercises of the will, she recites them with less multiplicity and some good measure of recollection, and being in the exercise of aspirations, her vocal prayers become likewise aspirative and unitive, not at all distracting her, but rather driving her more profoundly and intimately into God.

16. Now God being both the principle and object of all our internal exercises is, after several ways, represented to the mind in them; for, 1. In meditation the soul, as yet much immersed in sense, is forced to make use of a distinct grosser image by which to apprehend Him, as the Humanity of our Lord and the mysteries belonging thereto, and sometimes such attributes of the Divinity as are most obvious and easy to be conceived, and which do produce more sensible motions in our imperfect souls, as His justice, mercy, power, &c. 2. But in the practice of the acts of the will, the understanding endeavours to apprehend God in the obscure notion of faith; and when she is sometimes forced to make use of more particular sensible images, the mind, after a short reflection on them, gives place to the recollected actuations of the will alone. 3. But being arrived to aspirations (which is active contemplation) the soul makes use of no particular express images at all, but contents herself with the only general obscure notion of God which faith teaches her.

17. Now though it may seem that the most perfect have no great advantage in this regard over the more imperfect, since all that are imbued with ordinary knowledge do sufficiently believe and are assured that God, being infinite and incomprehensible, cannot be truly represented by any particular images and notions which are creatures of our own framing, notwithstanding we are to consider that there is a great difference between the acknowledging of this truth in the speculative judgment, and the operating according to such a truth by the will; for imperfect souls, notwithstanding the foresaid judgment, when they are to apply themselves to prayer, are forced in practice to contradict such their speculative judgment, and to represent God to their minds not only by particular and distinct, but even grosser sensible images, because they find that the said true and perfect notion of God by a general, negative, obscure conception of faith, will have little or no efficacy on their wills, the which will remain arid and void of all good affections, except they exchange the said notion for others more particular and express. Whereas, on the contrary, perfect souls having by long practice purified their internal operations, in time do come to such a state that they cannot, if they would, receive benefit, or warm their affections by sensible or particular images; except they do silence not only the imagination but understanding also, the will remains without motion or vigour; yea, in the particular case of the great

desolation, the elevations of the will also become so wonderfully pure, delicate, and even imperceptible, that the soul itself can scarce perceive or so much as believe that she operates towards God, insomuch as, on the contrary, she is oft perplexed with great fear and doubt that in truth she does not love God.

18. Now the foresaid division of the three states of prayer, together with the successive purification and spiritualizing of images, is so grounded on reason and even nature, that every one that experiences prayer will perceive it, and others cannot except against it. For as we see in all arts and sciences, as (for example) music or poetry, a person that sets himself to learn them is at the first obliged to make use of a world of gross distinct images, the which he applies particularly and leisurely to every string, every stop, and every finger moving the instrument, as likewise to every word and syllable in a verse; but by exercise having attained to a moderate skill, a far less number of images will serve to direct him; and the reason is because the images, by practice, becoming more pure and spiritual, are, by consequence, more universal, so that one will come to have the virtue of a great number which formerly were requisite; and at last the person becoming perfect in those arts will be able to make a verse exact, according to the rules of poetry, without any perceptible reflection upon any particular rules, and to play on an instrument not only in the dark, but even whilst he is conversing with another, by reason that the images are become so pure and universal, that the person using them perceives them not, neither knows by what he is directed.

19. Now if the operation of a soul in natural sensible things may come to be so pure and subtle, much more in spiritual and divine matters, in exercising about which her endeavours ought to be to exclude all manner both of sensible and intellectual images, or rather in exercising about which the will alone strives to be operative.

20. Notwithstanding what hath been said of the distinction of these three ways of a contemplative life, we are to observe that they are not so absolutely distinguished but that sometimes there may be a mixture of them; for it may happen that a soul, being as yet in the most imperfect purgative way, may in some fits be so abundantly supplied with grace, as that during the exercise of meditation she may oft be enabled to produce immediate acts of the will, yea, and perhaps aspirations too, so joining together exercises both purgative, illuminative, and unitive in one recollection; yea, it may be possible for such an imperfect beginner to spend the whole time of a recollection in those nobler exercises; but yet when such grace and devotion (which ordinarily lasts not long) does come to cease, she will be forced to return to her imperfect exercise of meditation; or, if out of an aversion from descending lower, she will needs stick to those higher exercises (which to her are but

temporary), she will, by means of aridity and indevotion, lose all the fruit of her recollections, which will indeed become insupportable to her.

21. So, on the other side, it may well happen that a soul that is ascended to the exercise of immediate acts, may sometimes for some short space find it necessary for her to help herself now and then, by using meditation and seeking motives in the understanding to move her affections. Therefore these three states are to be distinguished and separated with relation to the proper and constant exercises of souls.

22. Before we quit the present subject of the degrees of prayer and a spiritual life, it is, for the preventing of mistakes, to be observed that those writers likewise which teach and know no more sublime exercises than meditation do, notwithstanding, divide the whole course of their spirituality also into these three exercises of the purgative, illuminative, and unitive way, although the perfection both of their doctrine and practice reaches no further than the active life which they profess, as we may see in the books of De Ponte, Rodriguez, &c., to which we may add Louis of Granada also, &c.

23. But these three ways of active livers, though agreeing in name with the forementioned mystic exercises, yet are much different in their nature and qualities; for all the said three ways are exercised by the help and with the use of discourse, and do never arise to the exclusion of particular sensible images, so that the perfection of their exercise is to discourse with more subtlety, and from such discourse to derive and draw more fervent affections and good purposes of the will. Further than this active exercisers cannot go, because their life does not afford the leisure, freedom, and vacancy from external businesses which is necessary for enabling souls to contemplative exercises, which begin with those that I call proper aspirations, arising upon the expiration of imaginative exercises, as being the perfection of them.

24. And, indeed, if active livers should proceed further, they would then relinquish their institute, that refers all the doings of it to the exterior, which cannot be without the use and help of particular images, so that the forementioned general image of God, or rather non-image, is not at all proper for their course. They do not, therefore, ordain these their external imaginative exercises in order to contemplation, but only to enable them to perform their external deeds of charity with greater perfection and purity of intention. As therefore they do not themselves practise contemplation, so neither do they teach it to others, nor indeed can they, for want of experience.

Chapter II. Of Meditation

§§ 1, 2. Of Meditation: the first and lowest degree of internal prayer.

§§ 3, 4. Who are apt or unapt for Meditation.

§§ 5, 6. Generally most souls are to begin with it. And why?

§§ 7, 8, 9, 10. What those are to do that are unapt for Meditation.

§ 11. The misery of souls that are tied to a prayer improper for them.

1. The first and most imperfect degree of internal prayer is (as hath been said) Meditation, or discoursive prayer, of which we shall treat here—not with that exact niceness as may be found in many books current in all hands, yet sufficiently in order to our present design, which is to consider it only as a preparation to the perfect prayer of contemplation; and therefore the instructions concerning it shall be such as may be proper for those whom God hath called to that perfect state, and withal moved to comply with the said call. And to such many instructions will not be proper.

2. Meditation is such an internal prayer in which a devout soul doth, in the first place, take in hand the consideration of some particular mystery of faith, to the end that, by a serious and exact search into the several points and circumstances in it with the understanding or imagination, she may extract motives of good affections to God, and consequently produce suitable affections in virtue of the said motives as long as such virtue will last.

3. This is a prayer to the exercise whereof all sorts of persons are neither disposed nor enabled, neither is it a token either of excellency of wit and judgment or of true devotion to be apt for the practice of it; on the contrary, the more that a soul doth abound with devotion and good affections to God, the less is she enabled or disposed thereto, yea, incapable of continuing long in the exercise of it. And again, some superficial wits, full of fancy, but wanting solidity of judgment, and which are not naturally much disposed to devotion, yet if they be put to the exercise of this discoursive prayer they will perform it better and thrive more in it than others, though of sharp wits, solid judgments, and great abilities, both in learning and invention, and that withal have very good wills to seek our Lord.

4. Women are, generally speaking, less apt for meditation than men, and, by consequence, more fit for the more perfect exercises of the will, by reason that they are more disabled in judgment and invention, and more abounding in will and affections, so that in them the will draws the stream from the understanding; therefore great care is to be taken that they be not

compelled without necessity to tarry long in discoursive exercises, lest thereby they may be much prejudiced in the head and spirit, with little or no profit any way, but much harm in being detained from the more proper and beneficial exercise of the will in holy affections.

5. Now there being so great and inexpressible variety in the internal dispositions of persons, it is not possible to give certain and general rules to fit all, except this, that in the beginning of a spiritual contemplative course, all souls that are not naturally incapable of raising affections by internal discourse ought to apply themselves thereto, and to tarry therein till they find themselves ripe for a future exercise, to which they will attain sooner or later, either according to their diligence and constancy in practising meditation, or the measure and grace of devotion which God shall give them, or their natural aptness or inaptness for excrcises of the understanding.

6. This advice is of great concernment, and therefore souls are not easily and lightly to be permitted to apply themselves to exercises of the will till a convenient time spent in those of the understanding; for though, perhaps, whilst the *fervor novitius* lasts in the beginning of one's conversion, a soul, being then full of affection, may for a while have little need of motives to open the passage to the said affections, which of themselves will be apt enough to flow, yet that fervour ceasing, they will be at a miserable loss, full of nothing but aridities, obscurities, and desolations, having no refuge at all, except their understanding be stored with good motives of holy affections caused by former consideration and meditation.

7. Yet this is not so to be understood as if souls were to be obliged to those nice, distracting, painful methods of meditation which are described in many books, or to frame curious pageants and scenes of the mysteries to be meditated on, &c.; for though such an employment of the imagination in prayer may be proper and profitable for those that by their professions live active distracted lives, to the end by such workings of the fancy to wipe out, as it were, the vain images contracted abroad by superinducing or painting over them new and holy images, yet for those who are more solitary and abstracted such a way of meditating would be very painful, and the profit so little, as it would not countervail the pain. To such, therefore, it will suffice with moderate attention to think on the substance of the mystery proposed, or on such circumstances of it as either are expressed in the text or do even naturally attend it, and from thence to draw as strong, fervorous, and frequent affections as may be.

8. As for those that are naturally utterly disabled and incapable of meditating (as many women are), it is very requisite in the beginning that they should at least supply the benefit that comes from meditation by preparing themselves to their recollections with much serious and attentive reading

of some pious book, which may in some good proportion recompense meditation.

9. But in case a soul incapable of meditation and unable likewise to read shall undertake a spiritual contemplative course (as none are excluded), such an one must resolve to take a very great courage to pursue her exercises of the will and affections (which is but a dry exercise, and wanting sensible devotion is very ungrateful to the palate of the soul); she must be prepared not to be daunted with aridities and distractions, which distractions she has no other way to resist or expel, but only by pure obstinacy of the will not to attend to them or care for them; and, lastly, she must use more abstraction of life and solitude to prevent the multiplying of distracting images.

10. Those who, in the exercise of meditation, are more seriously affected to the discoursing part of it than to the good desires and purposes which should flow from such discourse, are in danger of many perils, as of pride, curiosity, extravagant opinions, yea, pernicious errors. The cause of which dangers is the predominancy that their imagination hath over their other faculties, which inclines them to please themselves with subtle, aerial, and curious discourses, and with framing of places and times, and other circumstances, in the consideration of a mystery, all which inconveniences are avoided in the exercises of the superior will, which being a blind faculty is best able to heave up herself unto God in darkness and vacancy of images, and being likewise a spiritual faculty is exempted from the devil's influences, who has great dominion over our corporeal powers to suggest representations, &c. For these reasons it is good to make the discoursing part of meditation as short as may be, so as that if the mere reflection on a mystery will suffice to produce a good affection, the person is to restrain the imagination.

11. To conclude, the great and inexplicable variety that is to be found in the dispositions of souls being considered, and likewise the great inconvenience that necessarily follows a misapplication of spirits to exercises improper for them, the sad condition of those good souls cannot sufficiently be bewailed who by their profession being, as it were, imprisoned in a solitary religious life, and being naturally inapt for discourse, are kept all their lives in meditation, repeating over and over again the same toilsome methods without any progress in spirit, to their great anguish and disquietness. And this misery is much greater in religious women, who, having no diversions of studies or employments, cannot possibly find exercise for their imagination; and therefore, seeing great defects and unsatisfactions in themselves, and not knowing the only cure of them (which is by ascending to the internal exercises of the will), their imperfections increase, and their anguishes proportionably, without any known means to amend them.

Chapter III. How Meditation is to be Exercised

§ 1. How a soul is to exercise Meditation.

§§ 2, 3, 4, 5, 6, 7, 8. What inconvenient practices and methods therein are to be avoided.

§§ 9, 10, 11, 12, 13, 14. What orders are positively to be observed.

§ 15. The grounds of these advices.

§§ 16, 17, 18, 19, 20, 21, 22. Further special instructions to the same purpose.

§ 23. A particular way of Meditation in Blosius.

1. Intending now to set down more particular instructions and advices how and in what manner a soul (by her choice or profession aspiring to contemplation) ought, in order thereto, to practise the lowest and most imperfect degree of internal prayer, which is Meditation, I will first show such a beginner what he is not to do—that is, what practices and orders he is to avoid; 2. and next, how he is to behave himself in the exercise thereof.

2. As to the former, therefore, I should be so far from commending, that I would scarce permit souls living a contemplative life (as all enclosed religious women do, &c.) to be strictly obliged to a prescribed method in meditation, or to those many and nice rules which are ordained by some modern authors, as: 1. that a soul should put herself in the divine presence; 2. that she should make acts of contrition; 3. that she should select points of meditation; 4. that she should consider them in such an order, with such framing of representations of the persons, times, places, postures, &c.; 5. that thence she should draw motives of good affections; 6. that thereupon she should draw petitions; 7. that afterwards she should make purposes; 8. that thereto she should adjoin thanksgiving; 9. moreover, that she should have a list of imperfections or faults committed the day, &c., before, and make expunctions of faults amended; 10. that, in conclusion, she should make an examination how her meditation hath been performed, to the end she may give an account thereof to her spiritual director, &c.

3. It is far from my intention to speak against the use of such methods and orders among those where they were first invented and are still practised, for they may well enough agree with their institute, which is far more active than contemplative. But among solitary contemplative spirits such orders are indeed a disorder, and a nice observance of such ceremonious methods would be more distractive and painful than the simple exercise it-

self; and particularly the expectation that an account is to be given of one's thoughts during meditation would afford more business to a soul than the mystery on which she meditates, so that she would be more solicitous to give satisfaction to her director than to perform her duty to God; and therefore St. Teresa with just reason complains against those directors which fetter and encumber their disciples' minds with orders and rules, which require more attention than the matter of the prayer itself.

4. How to meditate profitably (though not curiously) is quickly and without much difficulty learnt by such as are fit for it; but to observe all the said prescripts is both difficult, encumbering, and unprofitable, being, indeed, little better than a misspending of the time (I mean for souls tending to contemplation).

5. Moreover, in meditation I would not tie the will that it should not go beside or beyond the understanding; on the contrary, my advice and request is that the will, so it be carried towards God, should be suffered to go as far as it can, and that scope should be given to any good affection, not caring whether such affections be pertinent to the present subject to be considered on at that time, upon condition that the soul find that she bestows herself more efficaciously on God by such affections, than by those which would properly flow from the present motives considered.

6. Neither would I that when a soul has chosen one point or mystery to meditate on, she should strictly oblige herself to proceed on with it, but that if, without a voluntary roving and seeking, any other should offer itself to the mind more grateful and more gustful to the soul, she should entertain the latter, holding herself to it as long as the virtue of it well lasteth; and it ceasing, then let her return to the first proposed subject. And the like liberty I recommend in the following exercises of immediate acts, whensoever any act or good affection is suggested to the mind besides those which the soul finds in her paper proposed for the present recollection.

7. Notwithstanding, in case that the new matter (or affections) occurring be such as that it doth feed some over-abounding humour or passion in the soul, as fear (even of God Himself), tenderness, shedding of tears, scrupulosity, or dejectedness of spirit, &c., I would by no means permit a soul to entertain her mind with such matter, because she will thereby only plunge herself more deeply into nature and immortification, and not at all purify her inordinate affections. Such souls, even in the beginning, ought not to choose such matters for their prayers, and much less ought they to be permitted to quit other good matter for that. This advice extends likewise to the exercise of immediate acts of the will, forasmuch as concerns the matter of them.

8. Now such freedom of spirit and permission to change the present matter or affections is to be supposed to be allowed only when the said change proceeds not out of sloth, inconstancy, a vain pleasing of the fancy or affection, but out of a judicious election, or from an interior invitation, the which most probably is from the Spirit of God; hereto, therefore, may be applied that saying of St. Bernard, *Modus diligendi Deum, est diligere sine modo;* that is, the measure and manner of loving of God is to love Him immeasurably and freely without a prescribed manner.

9. In the next place, having showed what incumbrances a soul is to avoid in her exercise of meditation, I will proceed to declare positively and directly how I would advise her to behave herself therein.

10. Let a soul that begins mental prayer with the exercise of meditation make choice of some good books of that subject, as Fulvius Androtius, Granada, or the abridgment of De Ponte's Meditations (which I would especially recommend).

11. Let her begin with the matter of the purgative way, as concerning sin, death, the final judgment, hell, or the like, and let her abide in the exercises of that way till she finds in herself an aversion from sin, and that much of the fear and remorse that were formerly in her are deposed, so that she is come to have some good measure of confidence in God. When she finds these effects in her, let her (without regarding whether she has run over all the exercises and matters in her book belonging to the purgative way) pass to the exercises of meditation which respects the illuminative way (as they call it), that is to such whose matter or argument is some mystery of faith touching our Lord's Life, Passion, &c., and which are apt to beget and increase humility, patience, and other virtues in her.

12. Being entered into the illuminative way, let her in like manner abide in the exercises thereof till she find herself apt for resignation, love, and other affections of the unitive way, to the exercise of which let her thereupon apply herself.

13. It may happen that a soul that is duly and in right order come into the illuminative and unitive way (as those ways are distinguished by the masters of meditation), and after some time spent in the exercises proper to those ways may afterward find herself called back to the purgative, as after the committing of some fault extraordinary, or during some unusual temptation, in which cases she is to yield thereto and abide in those inferior exercises as long as she finds them proper and profitable for her (which is not like to be very long).

14. In like manner, whilst she is in the purgative way, if acts of resignation, love, &c., and much more if aspirations shall offer themselves to her (as sometimes they may), let her by all means correspond unto them as

long as they are relishing to her, neglecting and forbearing in the mean time to consider motives or to produce inferior acts of contrition, fear, &c., belonging to the purgative way.

15. The ground of the reasonableness and necessity of these advices is this: because the matter and manner of prayer are to be prescribed and ordered according to the temper and disposition of souls, and not the methods of books; and therefore souls are to be applied to such a manner of prayer as God calls them to, and is likely to subdue inordinate affections in them; therefore scrupulous and fearful souls, even in the beginning; are to be forbidden the exercises of terror, &c., which belong to the purgative way, and they are to be applied to such exercises as are apt to produce love, confidence in God, &c.

16. For some short space before a soul begins her exercise of meditation let her look upon the book, and therein peruse the points that she intends to meditate on; or rather, indeed, those points are to be thought upon and provided beforehand, that is, over-night for the morning meditation, and after dinner for the evening. So doing, she will be less to seek about them, and better employ the time appointed for her exercise.

17. Let her not trust her memory for the points that she is to meditate on, but have the book ready that she may look on it as she shall have need, and let her take one point after another as they lie in the book, or as she shall have determined before, when she prepared for the succeeding recollection.

18. In her meditating on each point let her behave herself after this manner: 1. With her memory and understanding let her think on the matter of that point; 2. out of which let her draw a reason or motive, by which the will may be inclined some way or other toward God; 3. and thereupon let her produce an act of the will (as of humiliation, adoration, resignation, contrition, &c.), abiding in such application of the soul to God as long as the will hath life and activity for it, or as long as she shall be able to do it; 4. the which failing and growing to be disgustful, let her proceed to the next point, therein behaving herself likewise after the same manner, so proceeding in order to the others following till she have spent a competent time in her recollection.

19. Now I conceive a competent time for one recollection spent in meditation to be an hour, or very little less. Whereas for the exercise of immediate acts of the will a lesser space will suffice; and the reason of the difference is: 1. because in this latter exercise more acts of the will (wherein all good doth consist) are produced than in meditation; 2. and, besides, the exercise of acts is more dry and wearisome (except in some few that abound in sensible affections) than is meditation to souls fit for it.

20. During meditation let the soul (neglecting the too common practice, in which meditation is made rather a study and speculation than an exercise of the spirit) spend no more time in inventing motives and in internal discoursings than shall be necessary to move the will to good affections; but as for such affections, let her abide in them as long as she can (for therein consists all the profit); and if upon one consideration or motive she can produce many acts of the will, let her not fail to do so, and to continue in each act as long as she finds that she is enabled. It is no matter though in the mean time the understanding should lie quiet, as it were asleep, and without exercise.

21. Indeed, in souls which have an effectual call to an internal life, their meditations will have little study or speculation in them; for after a short and quick reflection on the matter, mystery, or motive, they will forthwith produce acts of the will; and their consideration of the matter is not so much by way of reasoning or inferring, as a simple calling to mind or thinking on a subject, out of which the will may produce some act or other answerable to the point reflected on by the understanding. And this sort of meditating is proper for many ignorant persons, especially women, which have not the gift of internal discoursing.

22. A soul that practises meditation will find that at the first, she will, during one time of recollection, stand in need of many points to be thought upon, and of many motives to produce affections. But in continuance the will will become affected, as fewer points will suffice to employ it in producing good affections and purposes, which will take up almost the whole time appointed for the recollection; and a soul being come to this state, will be ready and ripe for a more sublime exercise of immediate acts of the will.

23. Another way of meditating like unto this, and proper for persons of good wills, is that which is recommended by Blosius, and seems to have been his own practice, which is, without much discoursing to represent to the mind any mystery to which the soul has an affection (as our Lord's agony, or *Ecce Homo,* or His dereliction on the Cross, &c.), and to regard Him in such a state with as much tenderness of affection as may be, exercising short acts of love, compassion, gratitude, &c. Moreover, he advises a person to endeavour (yet without much straining or force used) to preserve this object present to the mind all the day after, and to perform the daily employments as in our Lord's presence. By this means a soul will come well prepared with a tenderness of heart to her recollections, and so will have little need to spend time in employing the understanding.

Chapter IV. Of Set Retirements for Meditation

§ 1. Of the custom of set appointed Retreats for Meditation, &c.

§§ 2, 3. For what sorts of persons the said retirements are proper.

§ 4. They are improper for religious persons practising contemplation, especially women.

§§ 5, 6, 7. Except with certain conditions.

§§ 8, 9, 10. How seculars may and ought to make use of and benefit by the said Retreats.

1. Before I quit this subject of Meditation, or treat of the signs by which a soul, after a convenient time spent in the practice of it, may be able to judge of her ripeness for a higher exercise of prayer, it will not be amiss to consider what use or effect in souls by their profession or election aspiring to contemplation, and actually advanced in the same ways, the yearly, quarterly, or otherwise appointed Retreats for more serious meditation may have toward the same end, &c. Now just ground there is to take this into consideration, because experience shows that the said custom has of late been introduced into convents (even of women) professing the greatest solitude in order to contemplation.

2. The clearing of this doubt will depend upon a due consideration of what condition the persons are, and what are the proper ends and uses for which the said retreats and practices of recollection therein were (or ought to be) designed; which, in the first place, in regard to secular persons were: 1. To be an efficacious instrument for one in an imperfect extroverted course of life to be brought to discern the foulness of his soul, the peril of his state, &c., and from thence to procure remorse, contrition, and purposes of amendment. 2. Or for a secular person in a less perfect state of life to discern and know God's will concerning the undertaking of a more perfect state; for such recollections (proper for the imperfect condition of the said persons) being practised in solitude, do serve much to the illuminating of the understanding, purifying the intention, and fortifying the will in good purposes and designs. 3. By the same the said persons may be well instructed how to serve God better, remaining in the same less perfect state, on which ground they have been worthily recommended by the See Apostolic, and their practice promoted by the grant of indulgences.

3. Next in regard of religious persons, the said retirements: 1. Are very helpful in the beginning of such a spiritual state, by teaching with great exactness the rudiments of mental prayer, and for the same end they may likewise serve devout secular persons of active lives, that are desirous and have the courage, to undertake a more spiritual course. 2. In the progress of

an active religious life, religious persons, by their many distractive employments and studies, cannot but contract many stains and defects, the which are not easily perceived, and less are they perfectly corrected by the help of their daily usual meditations; and, therefore, such solemn and rigorous retirements were justly esteemed requisite to procure light and grace for the discovering and rectifying such defects and dissipations of the spirit.

4. These surely are the natural and proper ends of the said retirements, as they are usually practised at set times, respectively to each one's particular need. Now in none of these regards can they be proper for persons that in a life of religious solitude do actually practise contemplation, except only in the last point, viz. inasmuch as the said retreats are instituted to the end that religious persons may thereby take the benefit of a more strict solitude, and a freedom from distractive employments, there to enjoy a vacancy to attend to God alone in perfect liberty of spirit. For, indeed, in this regard religious persons of contemplative orders (especially such as are employed in offices, studies, &c.) may oft have need to recollect their dissipated and distracted spirits, as well as others, so that they may do very well monthly (or as occasion shall require) by such retirements to increase their light, and to lay up a treasure of good purposes and advices for the time following, by which practice an use and habitual state of recollectedness may be attained, and provision made that it be not extinguished by future employments.

5. But if the end of such retreats be only to oblige souls to a nice observance and practice of meditation, merely for the foresaid purposes, without any consideration of advancing them in affective prayer, it cannot be imagined what benefit contemplative souls can reap thereby, but rather a hindrance and distraction. For: 1. They are supposed not to stand in need now to learn how to pray mentally, to which kind of prayer the said exercises are but the first imperfect rudiments, 2. Much less do they stand in need of a total change of life, or of doing some extraordinary penitential satisfaction for former crimes, or to learn remorse for them. 3. By such exercises, as they are commonly taught and practised, such souls will not learn how well to practise their religious observances in solitude, or to use vocal prayer of obligation more perfectly. For all such exercises, unless they be practised in order to affective prayer, do end in themselves, not being intended to be means to lead souls to higher prayer, &c. 4. And in case the persons be naturally indisposed for internal discursive prayer, what is it that they can learn thereby (which is very ordinarily the case, especially of many religious women)?

6. All things therefore considered, nothing seems to me more improper than the said retreats for meditation for solitary contemplatives, to whom a due observance of the choir is both far more proper and efficacious

to all ends pretended to by such exercises than they are. Yea, moreover, great harm may come to souls professing contemplation by them; for so great attention, such an exact performance of nice observances, and such a captivity of spirit is required, that when all is passed, souls thereby ofttimes become disabled to continue the internal prayer proper for them, or to comply with many regular duties. To these we may add the great inconveniences which may come from strict examinations of conscience, repetitions of general confessions, &c., very prejudicial to tender souls.

7. Therefore, as touching contemplative persons, who (living, perhaps, under the conduct of those that are wholly devoted to the active way) shall be obliged to such retirements, and therein to exercises very unsuitable to their state, my advice to them is, that they should keep themselves in as much stillness of mind as may be, and having received instructions for their prayer, let them in practice give as much scope as they well can to their good affections, not much troubling themselves whether the said affections be proper to the matter proposed for meditation or no, nor distracting themselves with reflection upon their prayer, to the end to give an account of it to others. Let them likewise endeavour to preserve all due liberty in spirit in their examinations and confessions, therein proceeding no further than may consist with their spiritual profit, and by all means avoiding such particulars as are likely to nourish fear and scrupulosity, or to disturb the peace of their minds.

8. And as for secular livers, to whom, indeed, the said retreats (according to custom undertaken at set times) may prove of admirable profit and benefit, to the end the virtue of them may not quickly expire, they ought to be careful afterwards to make good use of the lights received in them, and to put in execution the good purposes made during such retirements; for they must not expect by a few days' solitude and prayer to get a habit of sanctity, but only a transient good passion and disposition thereto, which, without future care to cherish and increase it, will quickly vanish, and their fervour will be cooled.

9. Moreover, perceiving evidently by this experience the good effects of mental prayer, they ought to resolve the best they can to allow some reasonable time to the prosecution of it, when they return to their secular vocations, using likewise as much abstraction as their state of life will permit. Otherwise it is to be feared they will not only return to all their former defectuousness and sins, but will moreover thereto add the guilt of ingratitude to God, that so effectually called them from sin; and their following sins will be sins against clear light.

10. Certain it is that if souls shall so rely upon the repeating such retirements, and new taking of the same practices of meditation, &c., as by

them to make amends (*tones quoties*) for all faults past, they will be in great danger to find themselves deceived. For though in itself it be very good to seek all good means to procure remorse and contrition for past sins, yet if a soul, upon a consideration that she has such a special remedy in readiness, shall neglect the care and watchfulness over herself, it is to be feared, and not without just grounds, that that which she takes for contrition will prove to be no more than a natural remorse; for it is not likely that God will shower down His grace upon a soul so corrupted in her intention.

Chapter V. Signs when a Change of Prayer is Seasonable

§ 1. A change from meditation to prayer of the will is necessary in an internal life.

§ 2. It is otherwise in active livers.

§ 3. A soul of a contemplative profession, when to leave operating with the understanding.

§ 4. Exercises of the will more perfect than those of the understanding.

§ 5. Whether meditation on the Passion may be left.

§§ 6, 7, 8, 9, 10, 11. Reasons to prove the affirmative.

§§ 12, 13, 14, 15, 16, 17. Advices showing when a change of prayer is seasonable.

§§ 18, 19, 20, 21, 22, 23, 24, 25, 26. More particular signs showing the proper time of a change.

§ 27. The wonderful variety of changes in an internal life.

1. It is impossible for a soul that leads an abstracted life, and diligently pursues internal prayer, to fix continually in meditation, or to rest in any degree of affective prayer; because the nature of such intellectual and spiritual operations is to become more and more pure, abstracted, and universal, and to carry the will and affections of the soul still higher and further into God; the activity of the imagination and understanding continually abating, and the activity of the will continually increasing and getting ground upon the understanding, till at last all its operations become so quieted and silenced that they cease, or at least become imperceptible.

2. A soul, therefore, being thus invited and disposed to approach continually nearer and nearer unto God, if she be, either by her own or others' ignorance, so fettered with customs or rules that she is deprived of due liberty of spirit to correspond to such an invitation and to quit inferior exer-

cises, she will find no profit at all by her prayer, but, on the contrary, extreme pain, which will endanger to force her to relinquish her recollections.

3. It is otherwise with those whose profession is to live active distracted lives, though they do seriously aspire to the perfection answerable to that state. For such may continue all their lives in meditation, and follow the methods of it; because what they lose by their distractions they may recover by their following meditation, the good images used therein expelling the vain images contracted in their external employment. True it is that to such persons meditation will grow more and more pure, and more in spirit, yet never so as to exclude a direct use of the imagination.

4. When a contemplative soul, therefore, hath for some reasonable time practised meditation, and comes to perceive that a further exercise thereof is become dry and ungrateful to her spirit, causing great disgust and little or no profit, she ought then to forbear meditation, and to betake herself to the exercise of immediate acts, which she will then doubtless perform with great gust and facility, to her notable profit in spirit.

5. It is a great mistake in some writers who think the exercise of the will to be mean and base in comparison of inventive meditation and curious speculation of divine mysteries, inasmuch as none but elevated spirits can perform this, whereas the most ignorant and simple persons can exercise acts or affections of the will. On the contrary, it is most certain that no acts of the understanding (as speculation, consideration, deduction of conclusions, &c.), in matters pertaining to God, are of themselves of any virtue to give true perfection to a soul, further than as they do excite the will to love Him, and by love to be united to Him. And this union by exercise may be obtained in perfection by souls that are not at all capable of discourse, and that have no more knowledge of God than what is afforded from a belief of the fundamental verities of Christian faith; so that it is evident that the end of all meditation, &c., is the producing acts of the will. Therefore let no man neglect or scorn the exercise proper for him, out of a conceit that it is too mean; but let him first try the profit of it, and not till then make a judgment.

6. Others there are that do, indeed, persuade souls in due time to quit the exercises of the understanding for those of the will, but yet always with one exception and reservation, to wit, of the meditation on the Passion of our Lord; this, say they, is never to be set aside, but will be a subject fit for the contemplation of the most perfect. What an ingratitude it would be to God, say they, and what a neglect of our soul's good, purposely to forbear a frequent meditation of this mystery, the ground of all our happiness, the root of all merit, the supremest testimony of divine love towards us, the most inviting and winning object of love from us to God, the terror of all our spiritual

enemies, &c.! This is the position of many spiritual authors, and particularly of F. Benet Canfield.

7. Notwithstanding, I cannot join with these authors in this position, nor agree that a due liberty of spirit should be abridged for any pretext whatsoever. The ground of which liberty is this, that a soul is to make the experience and proof of her own spiritual profit to be the rule and measure of all her spiritual exercises, and upon no colours or conceits of perfection in any subject or exercise, to oblige herself thereto further than she finds it helpful and gustful to her spirit.

8. As for the mystery of the Passion, it does, doubtless, deserve all the titles given unto it; but yet souls are not to be discouraged if they find in themselves a disability to meditate on it, whether this disability proceed from some natural temper of the internal senses or from abundance of affections in the heart, that cannot expect, because they do not need curiously to search motives from the understanding and discourse; neither is it to be supposed that such persons, exercising immediate acts of the will toward God without discoursing on the Passion, are therefore bereaved of the true (yea, only true) exercise of our Lord's Passion. On the contrary, in such exercises of the will is contained the virtue of all precedent meditations. Neither are the persons driven to the pains and expense of time in finding out reasons and motives to raise their affections to our Lord, but immediately and without more ado suffer the affections to flow; and they do far more truly, efficaciously, and profitably exercise and, as it were, exemplify the Passion itself; and this in two manners, viz. 1. In their internal prayer, wherein they produce the same affections and acts of love, humility, and patience of which our Lord gave there a pattern in His Passion. 2. In their external doings, really on occasions practising the same virtues (which are proper to the Passion) with far more perfection in virtue of such prayer than they could by meditation, and so do show themselves to be more true disciples of His.

9. This divine object, therefore, is far from being lost or forgotten by such proceeding in prayer, yea, it is in a far more noble manner both commemorated and imitated; and surely to tie the soul generally in all recollections to a particular curious reflection on the circumstances belonging to our Lord's Passion, would be as if one would oblige a person that can read perfectly, and with one glance of his eye join a whole sentence together, to make an express and distinct reflection on each letter, syllable, and word. Such a framing and multiplying of images would only serve to obscure the mind and cool the affections. Well may such devout souls, out of time of prayer, in reading or discoursing, admit such images, and receive benefit by them in future recollections; but when they actually pray, then to be forced to stop and restrain the will from melting into divine love or from sacrificing

herself to God by perfect resignation, &c., till she have passed through her former imperfect method of imaginative meditation, is all one as to forbid souls to unite themselves in spirit to the Divinity.

10. Notwithstanding, when souls come to be perfect they will be in such a state as that the express consideration of this or any other good sensible object will be no impediment at all to their higher exercises, yea, it will very efficaciously advance the soul in them, and this is after that perfect contemplation is attained to; for then the imagination is so rectified and so perfectly subjected to the superior soul, that it will not only not obscure or distract, but, on the contrary, will with great readiness help to make contemplation more pure and clear. Then a view of the Humanity of our Lord will drive the soul more deeply into the Divinity, as we see that the glorified Saints, without the least distraction to their vision of God, yea, surely with an addition to the perfection of it, do in their thanksgiving reflect on the Humanity and Passion of our Saviour, saying, *Dignus est Agnus qui occisus est,* &c.

11. Till souls, therefore, do attain to such contemplation, let them (being in the exercise of immediate acts, &c.) content themselves to exercise the mystery of the Passion virtually, though not expressly, remembering the saying of a spiritual author, that in God nothing is neglected. All faith and all love is exercised in the contemplation and union of the spirit by love to the Divinity; all particular devotions are both sufficiently and perfectly performed when we perform our principal duty most perfectly. In doing this we do honour the Saints after a manner most acceptable to them; we do most perfectly discharge our vocal prayers (which are not of obligation), and we most efficaciously express our charity both to our friends, living and dead, so that there will be no need for such ends to interrupt or distract our recollections by obliging ourselves voluntarily to multiply the repeating of offices, &c.; and lastly, so far is this from being any disparagement to our gratitude unto our Lord for His sufferings, that we thereby acknowledge that all the good thoughts that we entertain, and all the good actions that we do, are produced in virtue of His Passion, adhered to by faith and love, although no express internal discourse on it be exercised.

12. Now what hath here been delivered, concerning the disobliging of souls that practise internal prayer from tying themselves to imaginative exercises about sensible objects, is not only suitable to reason, but is moreover confirmed by the authority of learned and experienced mystic writers, and particularly the devout reader may see what Barbanson in his *Secrets Sentiers* (Part I. cap. vi. Admonit. 2) hath written on this point.

13. Thus having shown the indispensable necessity for a soul aspiring to contemplation, with all due liberty of spirit to follow the divine

guidance from each inferior degree of prayer to another more sublime, then become more proper and profitable, I will now endeavour to give more particular advices concerning passing from the exercise of meditation to that of immediate acts of the will, and will show by what signs and marks a devout soul may reasonably judge and conclude that such a change and transition is proper for her. Yet so that my intention and desire is that souls should principally depend on their internal light, which God's Holy Spirit will afford them in and by prayer.

14. Let every devout soul diligently pursue her present exercise in prayer, advisedly undertaken or recommended to her by a prudent director, till there come a proper time for a change. Let her (saith the excellent author of *Scala Perfectionis*) content herself with this gift of God till He be pleased to bestow on her a better, which He will not fail to do when He shall see it to be for her good; and so doing she cannot but increase in charity, although she see no evident proof of her advancement in spiritual operations. Whensoever it shall be God's pleasure to make a change in her prayer, He will by degrees so press her thereto, that in the end she shall both clearly perceive and correspond to His invitation; and till that time come it is to no purpose for her to examine or frame any judgment of her progress. Her best is to do her duty, and leave the success to God.

15. A change, whensoever it is made as it ought to be, consists in this, that the activity of the fancy and discourse is abated, and the whole internal exercise of prayer by little is reduced to blind operations of the will, which operations (or affections) likewise grow by practice more and more natural, quiet, pure, silent, subtile, imperceptible, and profound, the Divine Spirit drawing the soul, in her exercises, ever more and more unto Itself.

16. Ordinarily, when a time of change from a more imperfect to a more sublime exercise of prayer cometh, it will not on the sudden or at once be perceived, or but very obscurely and doubtfully; only a soul will perceive a bettering in her exercises, her operations by little and little becoming more spiritual; and, indeed, in some persons there is almost daily a bettering and purifying of their prayer, which themselves do or may well enough observe, though, perhaps, they are not able to express the manner of it to another by reason of its subtilty.

17. Far less inconveniences would follow by detaining a soul somewhat too long in an humble inferior exercise (as of meditation) when she is fit and ripe for a more sublime one, than if (through inconsideration, levity, or an ambitious humour to imitate examples or instructions in books not pertinent to her) she should at the first, or before her time, be put into one above her present capacity; for in the former case an easy and present remedy may be found by exalting the soul afterward to a more perfect exercise suitable to

her present disposition, till which be done she will at least exercise her humility and submission of judgment, by which she will receive much profit. But it is very difficult to find a remedy in the other case; because, first the natural unwillingness and shame that is in souls to acknowledge their too hasty ambition and to descend lower will secretly hinder them; and, besides, they will be ready to justify themselves by misapplying certain documents in spiritual authors, which forbid souls to quit their present exercises for one inferior, through any discouragement from aridities or unsatisfaction found in them. Notwithstanding, except they will be content with the mortification of returning to meditation (in case they be not yet ripe for immediate acts of the will), they will be in danger of incurring an habitual dryness, melancholy, and stupidity; and, moreover, they will run into an endless labyrinth, perplexing and entangling themselves therein, to the great disquiet of their own minds and the troubling of others with questions and doubts.

18. Yet it cannot be denied but that God doth often invite souls to some change in prayer, according to that which before they had read in some books; and then they are to follow the instructions of such a book as a light sent them from God. In which case it is indeed the secret motion and invitation afforded them by God to apply such instructions that is their sure guide, without which they must apply nothing that they find in books.

19. More particularly by these following signs a devout soul may, for the most part, perceive and judge when it is fit for her to change her exercises of prayer (as, for example, to quit meditation, and to betake herself to a prayer of the will, &c.).

20. First, she will not find that pleasure, satisfaction, and profit in her present exercise which formerly she did, but, on the contrary, a sensible disgust and a kind of impotency to practise internal discourse any longer; or, if she will force herself to observe her method of meditating, it will produce no effect upon her affections, which, if they were left to themselves, would flow far more freely; and this disgust is not for once or twice, nor, as formerly, upon occasion of some corporal distemper, passion, aridity, or any unusual accident, but it is a lasting, disgust arising from a desire to please God and to grow in perfection, joined with an uncertainty or fear that the way wherein she now is is not proper to effect that desire.

21. Secondly, she will thereupon find in herself a certain motion or inward invitation to enter into some other new exercise, as yet not clearly known to her; or, if there be no new exercise proposed to her, there is, however, a motion to a cessation from the present exercise, at least forasmuch as concerns the manner of it; as it happens when, from aspirations, a soul is invited to a resting and repose in God, with a cessation of all active aspirations

or affections, which is an immediate disposition to a supernatural contemplation.

22. Thirdly, a devout soul, considering the benefit that she hath hitherto reaped by her present exercise and her accustomance to it (which is not easily left); considering, likewise, that for want of trial she doth not as yet know the worth and benefit of the new proposed exercise (which, at first appearing a little strange and uncouth to her, she will not easily see or believe that it will prove as profitable as her present exercise has already been); for these and the like reasons she will be apprehensive and unwilling to adventure upon the new one.

23. Fourthly, during these uncertainties and irresolutions, her distaste in her present exercise rather increasing than diminishing, and God still interiorly, though not grossly and sensibly, inclining her to the new proposed way, she at length, as it were forced thereto, adventures upon it, yet with some fear at the first whether this change will prove for her good or no.

24. Fifthly, as soon as she is well entered into this new exercise, presently she will find it gustful and delightful unto her, and withal much more profitable than was the other formerly practised; whereupon she will thenceforward with courage and joy persevere in it.

25. By such steps and degrees doth a soul that is purely under the guidance of God's Holy Spirit pass from one degree of prayer to another formerly unknown to her, till at last she come to contemplation; and she will clearly perceive that it was not herself but God only that did, as it were, lead her by the hand, and draw her forward into the new exercise, teaching her likewise how to behave herself in the beginning; whereas in the pursuance of it she afterwards proceeds, as it were, by her own habitual skill, though really God is in everything her secret Master and Helper. And He deals with an humble soul as a writing-master with his scholar, who at first moves and directs his hand to form and join letters, but afterwards directs him only with his eye and tongue; or as a father that carries his child over a ditch or stile, but lets him go alone in the even plain way.

26. And as for a soul that, by reading or teaching, is informed in the nature and degrees of internal prayer, her proceeding and transition is much after the same manner, excepting only that the next degree to which she is to ascend does not seem so strange to her; but the signs by which a necessity of change doth appear are, as formerly, a constant disgust in her present exercise (meditation, &c.), and a kind of disability to continue it with any profit to her spirit; by which means it comes to pass that in her recollections the meditating or discoursing part diminishes daily, and the affective part increases, the will by little and little getting ground of the understanding, till at last the prayer becomes entirely of the will; and thus she passes almost un-

awares into the next degree, her prayer becoming by little and little more and more purified. Into which degree, when she is in such a manner and order entered, then indeed she is not for any aridities or obscurities to quit it and to return to meditation, but to use a discreet violence upon the will to make it to produce good affections and acts, although nature take little comfort or satisfaction in the exercise; for by so doing she will much benefit herself, both by mortifying nature and fixing divine love more profoundly in the spiritual region of the soul.

27. To conclude this point: a spiritual life is subject to many and wonderful changes, interior as well as exterior, and all are according to the mere will and good pleasure of God, who is tied to no methods or rules; therefore, following Him in all simplicity and resignation, let us wonder at nothing; let us neither oblige ourselves too rigorously to any exercise, nor refuse any to which He shall invite us, seem it never so strange, or to natural reason even senseless. For in His guidance there can be no danger of error, but, on the contrary, there is all security; and this may and ought to be a great comfort and encouragement to a well-minded resolute soul.

THE THIRD TREATISE
THE THIRD SECTION

OF THE EXERCISES OF IMMEDIATE FORCED ACTS OF THE WILL, BEING THE SECOND DEGREE OF INTERNAL PRAYER.

Chapter I. Of Acts of the Will and Affections

§§ 1, 2, 3. Of exercises of the will: to wit, forced immediate acts, or affections and aspirations.

§§ 4, 5, 6, 7. Difference between acts of the will and affections.

§§ 8, 9. How the prayer of sensible affections is to be exercised.

§ 10. Of sublime pure affections of the spirit.

§§ 11, 12, 13, 14, 15, 16. Of the prayer of immediate acts of the will compared with meditation.

§§ 17, 18. Conditions of acts.

§ 19. Mere cessation of prayer to be avoided.

§ 20. An account not to be required touching the behaviour of souls in affective prayer.

§ 21. Acts proceeding from a good natural propension are most efficacious.

1. A soul that by a divine call, as being in a state of maturity for it, relinquisheth meditation to the end to betake herself to a more sublime exercise, which is that of immediate Acts or Affections of the will, then only begins to enter into the ways of contemplation; for the exercises of the will are the sublimest that any soul can practise, and all the difference that hereafter follows is only either in regard of the greater or lesser promptitude, or in regard of the degrees of purity wherewith a soul produces such acts.

2. So that the whole latitude of internal prayer of the will (which is contemplative prayer) may be comprehended under these two distinct exercises—to wit, 1. The exercise of forced acts or affections of the will,

produced either immediately according to the person's present disposition, without a distinct or express motive represented by the understanding, or else suitable to such a motive, yet without any formal discourse of the understanding: these are called forced acts, because after that a soul is become indisposed to prosecute the exercise of meditation, it will be long before that good affections do, as it were, naturally flow from her, so that she will need to use some force upon herself for the producing of the said acts of the will, which are imperfect contemplation. 2. The exercises of aspirations, which, though they be in substance little differing from the former, yet by reason of the facility wherewith they are produced without force, foresight, or election, purely flowing from an internal impulse of the Divine Spirit, we therefore give them another name, and call them not acts, but aspirations, the constant exercise of which is proper and perfect contemplation.

3. Of these two exercises I shall consequently treat, beginning with the more imperfect, which is that of forced immediate acts or affections of the will.

4. In this exercise I make some difference between acts and affections of the will, the former of which are made in and by the superior will only, without any concurrence of sensitive nature. Such are acts of humiliation, resignation, &c., the producing of which does not cause any gust in inferior nature; whereas affections of love, joy, hope, desire, &c. (being exercised by imperfect souls), are much immersed in sense; and they begin at the first almost wholly in inferior nature, but yet by practice they become more and more pure, being raised to the top of sensitive nature, where it is joined or combined with the superior spiritual will.

5. Now whether of these two, that is, acts or affections, are to be practised respectively by souls, that must depend upon the observation and experience that each soul has of her own natural disposition and inclination. Generally, souls are more disposed to the exercise of immediate acts, which, likewise, are both more profitable and more secure, and, therefore, in the following discourse I shall most insist upon them.

6. And as for the exercise of sensible affections, it belongs only to such souls as in their natural temper are more tender and affectionate; whose love expresses itself with great liquefaction in sensible nature, so that they are easily moved to tears, and do feel warmth and quick motions about the heart, &c. (which effects or symptoms do not argue love to be greater; for it may be as cordial and more firm, generous, and active in others who seldom or never feel such effects).

7. Such tender souls as these, having withal a natural good propension to seek God in their interior, can easily exercise their affections to God

in and by their corporal nature, without troubling themselves with seeking reasons and motives for it; yea, in a short time they come to have a kind of disgust in inventing or considering motives represented by the understanding.

8. As for the manner how such souls are to behave themselves in their recollections, the special instructions following concerning the exercising of immediate acts of the will will serve, so that there will be no need of repeating them twice.

9. The principal care that such souls ought to have is, to endeavour to raise this their love out of sensitive nature to the superior spiritual will, by whose operations alone the soul is truly perfected. Therefore, according to the advices formerly given touching sensible devotion, they are to mortify and restrain rather than to give scope to tears and other tendernesses of nature in prayer, &c.; and some other particulars which do concern affections, as distinct from acts of the will, shall hereafter be occasionally taken notice of.

10. Now besides these sensible acts of love there are others, which are purely in spirit, and which, among all the operations of the will, are the most sublime that can be exercised in this life; for they cannot be used by a soul (so as to be her constant usual exercise) till she be come to a perfect degree of mortification, which ordinarily is not before a passive union; after which they are exercised in a manner so spiritual and divine, that the unexperienced cannot conceive nor the experienced express. Those are certain painful yet delightful longings after God; certain languishing elevations of spirit towards an unknown, dark, Divine Object, the desire and absence of which causes a tedious disgust of all sensible contentments—yea, even in spiritual things also. But of such operations as these it will be seasonable to speak when we come to treat of perfect contemplation.

11. As touching the most profitable exercises of immediate acts of the will, the practice thereof in gross is after this manner. The soul's aim is to recollect herself by that general notion that faith gives her of God; but being not able to do this presently, she doth in her mind, and by the help of the imagination, represent unto herself some Divine Object, as some one or more perfections of God, or some mystery of faith, as the Incarnation, Transfiguration, Passion, Agony, or Dereliction of our Lord, &c.; and thereupon, without such discoursing as is used in meditation, she doth immediately, without more ado, produce acts or affections one after another towards God, or upon herself with reference to God, adoring, giving thanks, humbling herself in His presence, resigning herself to His will, &c.

12. This exercise is more easy to learn and comprehend than meditation, because so many rules are not necessary to it, neither is there in it such study or exercising the abilities of the understanding or imagination. It is, indeed, a very plain, downright, and simple exercise, consisting merely in the

efficacy of the will; but notwithstanding such plain simplicity, it is a far more noble exercise than that of meditation, as being the fruit and result of it; for whatsoever the understanding operates with reference to God can produce no good effect upon the soul further than it hath relation to and influence on the will, by disposing it to submit and resign itself to God, or to tend towards Him by acts of love, adoration, &c.

13. Now this exercise, although likewise it be not so busy and laborious as meditation, yet it may and will oftentimes seem to some souls, even after they have made a reasonable progress in it, to be more harsh and difficult; but the good-will and resolution of the soul persisting in it will, by God's grace, overcome all difficulties.

14. An advice, therefore, it is again and again to be repeated, and never to be forgotten—to wit, that the devout well-minded soul that shall be called by God to walk in these internal ways of prayer be courageous and diligent in the pursuance of them, after the best manner she can, amidst all desolations, obscurities, and distractions, practising these exercises as much as may be in the superior will, not caring whether sensitive nature concur therein or no.

15. In forced immediate acts of the will, especially at the beginning, there is some degree of meditation, which is the thinking on the object, and thereupon internally producing the act or affection itself, and quietly continuing and resting in it till all the virtue of it be spent. There is, likewise, always some use of images; and in the beginning these images are more gross, but afterwards, by practice, they grow more pure, and all manner of discourse ceaseth; yea, the soul will begin to reject all distinct images, and apprehend God without any particular representation, only by that obscure notion which faith informs us of His totality and incomprehensibility; and this only is truth, whereas all distinct images are but imperfect shadows of truth.

16. Now how great is the security of a soul thus operating purely by the will? How free is she from those errors and dangers into which she may be led by the curious searching subtilty of the understanding? Here God Himself is only her light, and not any imagination of her own; though images should intrude themselves perforce into the fancy, or be incited by the devil, yet the soul will not with the will apply herself to such images, but either diverts her mind from them or transcends and renounces them; and without images stirring up sensuality and the rational will, the devil cannot produce the least harm or danger to the soul, nor hinder her union with God.

17. The more plain and simple that acts of the will are (for the manner of expression), the more proper and efficacious are they to cause a good and profitable recollection; and therefore such elegant and sprightly expressions as are to be found in many places of St. Augustine's *Confessions,*

Soliloquies, &c., or in St. Bernard, St. Teresa's *Exclamations,* &c., though they be more full of life, and more apt to inflame affection, being read out of times of recollection, yet they are not so proper to be used in the recollection, because the pleasingness and exquisiteness of the expression gives too much exercise and contentment to the fancy, and by that means distracts and enfeebles the actuation of the will. This, I say, holds most generally true; yet if souls do find their profit more by the use of them, let them, in God's name, make choice of such.

18. The less impetuous that the operations of the will are in this exercise of *Immediate Acts,* and the more still, quiet, peaceable, and profound that they are (so there be no wilful negligence), the more effectual and profitable are they, and the more efficacious to still passions, as also to compose and settle the imagination.

19. There may come much harm to a soul by cessation from internal working, and from all tendence to God in her recollections, if so be the motive of such cessation be a desire and expectation to hear God speaking after any unusual manner within her, and telling her some new thing or other; for by giving way to such a foolish presumption she will deserve, and put herself in a disposition to receive, diabolical suggestions, or, at least, vainly to conceive and interpret her own imaginations to be internal speakings of God; and this may prove very perilous if a soul give credit to such fancies (as probably such souls will); but they ought to consider that if God's pleasure be such as to communicate His will internally after an extraordinary manner, He will speak and work whether the soul will or no, and whether she will or no she must hear and suffer. And, therefore, let her abstain from such indiscreet invitations or expecting such divine conversations; let her continue quietly her exercises, and not cease till God force her to cease them.

20. The custom practised by some spiritual directors of requiring from all their disciples an account of their internal prayer, formerly judged to be inconvenient, as causing distractions and too frequent reflections with solicitude upon their present actuations, to the end they may remember them, and so be able to relate them,—the said custom, I say, is moreover (besides this inconvenience and uselessness) of extreme difficulty in this exercise, which, being simple and plain, acted only or chiefly by the will, cannot well be explicated, inasmuch as the acts leave scarce any sensible impression in the memory; and lastly, they are exercised directly to God without any reflections. Now it is by the means of reflections that a soul takes notice of and remembers her actuations.

21. Where there is a good propension in the interior to introversion, an act produced by the will to God is not only much more prompt, facile, and profound, but also far more efficacious than any other without such a propen-

sion can be, though the party be never so learned, and employ never so much the faculty of reasoning. Yet do I not deny but that even souls of the greatest propensions may sometimes find themselves obliged to make use of some meditation. But (unless their director mislead and wrong them) they will not tarry long therein, but will presently break forth copiously into good affections.

Chapter II. Variety of Acts, how to be exercised

§§ 1, 2, 3, 4, 5, 6, 7, 8, 9, 10, 11, 12, 13, 14. Touching certain forms of immediate acts, &c., adjoined to the end of the book; and how they are to be used.

§§ 15, 16, 17, 18, 19, 20, 21, 22, 23. Great variety of acts there are—some directed to the pure Divinity, some to our Lord's Humanity, some to Saints, some to the soul herself, &c.—and what use is to be made of them.

§§ 24, 25, 26. To what souls one form of exercise without variety may be proper.

§ 27. Of exercising upon the Pater Noster. The excellency thereof.

§§ 28, 29. Souls are not to bind themselves to certain forms.

§§ 30, 31, 32. What use is to be made of the usual reading in preparation to recollection.

§§ 33, 34, 35, 36. How souls that cannot make use of images are to behave themselves.

§§ 37, 38, 39, 40. What order is to be observed in the change of acts.

§ 41. Souls must not bind themselves to these or any set form of exercises; but they must choose for themselves.

1. At the end of this book I have adjoined a collection of several patterns of exercises by acts of the will and holy affections, for the use and practice of those whom, either in the world or in religion, God shall call to an internal life of contemplation. I did not conceive any necessity to annex any exercises of meditation, partly because it was not my design to treat of that degree of prayer, but only passingly and in order to affective prayer, to which it is but a remote preparation; and, besides, there are patterns of such exercises, abundantly obvious to every one, which may suffice any internal liver, being practised according to the instructions here formerly given. And as for the supreme degree of affective contemplative prayer—to wit, perfect aspirations—I have contented myself with selecting a few, which are added in the conclusion, rather to show to imperfect souls the form and manner of them than for the use of perfect souls ripe for the exercise of them; for such are

conducted, immediately and entirely, by a divine light, and have no need of human prescriptions; neither, indeed, can they profitably make use of any other affections than only such as God's Holy Spirit shall suggest to them.

2. As touching, therefore, the foresaid exercises of forced immediate acts of the will and affections, I have compiled a sufficient variety of them proper for all states and dispositions of souls, as acts of remorse, fear, contrition, &c. (which belong to the purgative way), and likewise acts of adoration, glorification, humiliation, resignation, and love (which belong to the illuminative and unitive ways). I have, moreover, made some distinct exercises of affections, more proper for some souls than are those which I call acts of the will; besides, I have set down most copiously patterns of simple acts of resignation, as being generally the most useful and proper for most souls. And lastly, several exercises there are mixed and interlaced partly with acts and partly with affections, and those not of one, but several kinds, because many souls there are that cannot content themselves with being tied to any one kind of determinate exercise. And, therefore, my desire was to comply with all tempers, to the end that every one might find an exercise proper and profitable for him, or at least might be put in the way how to frame for himself such an one.

3. A soul that, after a sufficient time diligently spent in the practice of meditation, is maturely called and conducted by God to the exercise of immediate acts may, and indeed ought, at the first to take for the subject of her recollections those acts which belong to the unitive way—to wit, acts of divine love, resignation, &c.; but the case is otherwise with a soul that is found utterly unfit for meditation, and consequently must necessarily begin a spiritual course with the prayer of immediate acts; for, for such a soul (ordinarily speaking), it will be expedient that at the beginning she take for the matter of her acts such as are proper for the purgative way, as acts of contrition, fear of judgment, hell, &c.; and this advice is conformable to the directions of Blosius in the tenth and eleventh chapters of his Institutions.

4. Now for the use of the said exercises of immediate acts and affections, I would advise a soul that is well disposed and resolved to practise them that, at the first, she would rather use them mentally, because it is less distractive and more recollective, unless by experience she find that the using them vocally doth most relish with her spirit, and (as in some dispositions it may) cause a more intimate and perfect recollection.

5. Whereas every exercise consists of about ten clauses of acts or affections, let her not tie herself precisely to that number in any recollection; but if one exercise will not serve, let her borrow from the next following; and again, if one be too much for one time, let her use as many of those acts in

order as they lie as will suffice for the time, and no more, and in the next recollection let her begin where she last ended.

6. A devout soul will find that, by diligent practice, in progress of time the number of acts or affections to be exercised in each recollection will come to diminish, so that whereas at the beginning (perhaps) ten acts would scarce suffice for one recollection, afterwards five or three, yea, it may be, one will ofttimes be sufficient.

7. Let her generally observe the order and sequel of the said acts contained in the exercises proper for her, beginning and prosecuting them as they lie; for otherwise she will spend the precious time allotted for prayer in looking here and there for somewhat that may be pleasing to her fancy or humour, and yet in the end, perhaps, not content herself, or at the least the satisfaction that she may come to find will scarce countervail the distraction incurred and time lost. And again, it is an ill custom of some to take at random the acts or affections on which they would exercise themselves, opening the book and at adventure making use of what their eyes first light on.

8. Yet let her not tie herself so rigorously and superstitiously to any of the said acts, but that if without searching there should be offered to her any other kind of act or affection (be it resignation, love, or aspirations, &c.) which may be gustful to her, let her entertain it, and therein abide as long as the relish of it lasteth, and that ceasing let her return to prosecute the acts of the present exercise.

9. Yet one special case there is, in which a soul ought by no means to oblige herself to any order prescribed in the said exercises, and that is, when she finds that fear or scrupulosity do overmuch abound in her, causing unquietness, dejection, and want of confidence in God. In which case let her by all means omit such exercises or acts as are apt to raise or feed such passions in her, and instead of them let her apply herself to exercises of hope, love, and joy in God, which ought to be cherished in her.

10. Yea, souls that are of such a disposition ought, even in the beginning, after their first conversion, not to dwell long upon the exercises that concern remorse for sin or other matters of fear, as death, judgment, and hell, but rather to fix upon affections contrary to their present disposition; and in case of new faults committed, let their contrition or detestation of sin be rather exercised in a generality, or virtually in acts of conversion to God, than particularly, directly, and expressly; and let them not be scrupulous herein, out of an opinion that at such times God expects painful remorses from them, or earnest expressions of detestation of their sins; for such detestation is sufficiently involved in an act of direct love to God, which contains much

perfection besides. Such acts, therefore, being more beneficial to her, are consequently more acceptable to God.

11. A soul having pitched upon any act or affection contained in the said exercises, let her tarry as long upon each of them, without passing to another, as her gust unto such an affection lasteth, and as she finds profit to her spirit by it.

12. Whensoever in any clause there is contained matter of several desires or affections, let her in her mind and exercising separate them, and rest upon each of them severally, for by this means the said exercises will last longer and yield more profit.

13. After that all the exercises appointed for her have been passed over, let her repeat and pursue them again and again, unless she do find herself drawn by God to some other exercise more perfect, as is that of aspirations. And, indeed, whensoever in her exercise during her recollection she does find herself moved to perfect aspirations, elevations of the will, &c., or else to produce some other acts, as of resignation, &c., upon occasion of some present cross to be sustained, let her not fail to correspond to such an invitation.

14. Those that can find no profit or relish by any of these prescribed exercises, or the like, may conclude that they are not as yet ripe for them, and that, therefore, they are to continue in discoursive prayer till it loses its relish, and that they begin to find gust in affections.

15. The acts and affections in the following exercises are for the most part directed to God Himself, or the pure Divinity, as if they were internal conversations with God, which are perfect introversions, and of all active assumed exercises, are the most profitable.

16. But withal such actuations are ofttimes very painful, by reason that such introversions are exercised without the help of grosser images (which have some kind of recreating diversion in them), and when such images do offer themselves, the soul tending to the naked Divinity tarries not in them, but transcends or rejects them. And if her mind, finding no gust in an object so perfectly spiritual, becomes willing to ease itself by fastening upon some other good but inferior object, she is by some writers taught to withdraw her attention from anything but God; which violence and self-contradiction cannot be without much pain, insomuch that souls become thereby sometimes so tired with such introversions, and find so great difficulty in seeking the Divine presence so above the course of nature, that they lose all comfort and profit in their exercises, yea, and come to such a pass that they find an impossibility to introvert themselves, by reason that, to their seeming, they find not God so present as at other times.

17. Therefore in such cases it not only may be permitted, but ought to be enjoined, unto a soul to give ease unto herself, by quitting for a time such painful introversions and addresses to the pure Divinity, and, instead thereof, exercise herself in producing other acts less painful because less introverting, as acts or affections to the Humanity of our Lord, to Angels, Saints, &c.; yea, she may sometimes address her internal speech to her own soul, or to some person or creatures absent, yet all with reference to God, for otherwise it would not be an act of religion, nor profitable to the soul.

18. The truth is that, for the attaining to contemplation, it is not necessary (speaking of precise and absolute necessity) that the acts whereof the exercises consist, should immediately be directed to the pure Divinity (though it cannot be denied but that such are the most perfect and most efficacious, because the most introverting; and therefore a soul must give over all other addresses, either to the Humanity of our Lord, it to any Angel or Saint, &c., whensoever she is interiorly moved or enabled to actuate immediately towards God Himself, who is likewise the end and ultimate object of all other speakings and actuations).

19. To the end, therefore, to comply with the several dispositions of souls, I have in many places in the following exercises intermixed several other acts, for the most part addressed to our Lord's most sacred Humanity, likewise to our Blessed Lady, &c., and sometimes soliloquies to the soul herself.

20. And such acts and affections as these are frequent in the Psalms and other Scriptures; so David speaks to his own soul: *Nonne Deo subjecta eris, anima mea?*—'O my soul, wilt thou not be subject and resigned to God? And again: *Quare tristis es, anima mea,* &c.—'O my soul, why art thou sad, and why dost thou so disquiet thyself in me? Hope still in God, for,' &c. Again, sometimes he speaks to persons absent: *Venite et narrabo quanta fecit Deus animæ meæ,*—'Come hither, and I will tell you how great things God hath done for my soul.' Sometimes in Scripture the soul imagines that she hears God speaking to her, as, *Veni, electa mea, et ponam in te thronum meum,*—'O my chosen beloved soul, come, and I will place my throne in thee.' St. Augustine's *Soliloquies* and Thomas à Kempis are full of such kind of acts, and by any such change the soul will receive some refreshment, and be enabled to produce some good affections to God.

21. Now as I said that the form of the act is not of absolute necessity, so neither is the nature or matter of it, as whether it be of contrition, humiliation, adoration, resignation, &c., performed to God, or of congratulation to the Saints, veneration of them, or imploring their intercession, so that such acts be ultimately terminated in God; for it is perseverance in any exercises

of religious acts which is the principal, if not only, means to attain to contemplation.

22. The truth is, whatsoever kind of acts or devotions a soul useth, if they be constantly practised they will all end in God; so that even the most ignorant among those that God calls to contemplative prayer, though they know no other practice of devotion but the Rosary, and cannot begin their recollections any other way than by turning their thoughts towards the Blessed Virgin; whose protection and intercession they crave, yet being by that means become profoundly introverted they quickly leave all direct and express addresses to her, and are led, unawares, perhaps, to themselves, to the unknown obscure object of the Divinity, in which they plunge and lose themselves; for perfect introversion cannot consist with a continuation of direct and express internal acts made to any creature.

23. The general rule and advice, therefore, in this matter is, that accordingly as souls upon experience and observation do find themselves disposed to any kinds of acts or affections, whether of one kind only or several kinds mixed together, so they must order their exercises and recollections, preferring the savour and profit that their souls find in them, before any rules, methods, or authority of examples.

24. Some few souls there are to whom one only exercise, without any change or variety, may suffice for their whole life, till they arrive to perfect contemplation. So that their advancement will consist only in the degrees of purity and recollection with which they perform the said exercise. Now these are such souls as: 1. Are fitted naturally for acts of the will and not for meditation; because in discoursive prayer change of matter will be necessary, inasmuch as the same motive unvaried will not have the efficacy to produce sensible affections. And again, souls will be apt to be cloyed and to have an aversion from an affection or desire, after they have fed upon it for some reasonable time. 2. Such as withal have a very strong and urgent call from God to seek Him in His internal ways, joined with natural aptness to an internal life, which aptness consists in a stability of the imagination and a quietness of passions.

25. For such souls as these it will be best that they should be confined to one exercise, such an one as that is which Blosius in his Institutions hath framed, and professeth that by a diligent prosecution thereof (together with mortification) a soul may attain to perfection and mystic union. A pattern of such an exercise, conformable to the direction of Blosius (who seems to have practised it himself), I will set down among the following forms of exercises.

26. And, indeed, one singular benefit that such souls will reap by being constant to one exercise is this, that they will never have to seek for it nor

stand in need of books, because after a little practice they will have it in their hearts and memories; only good care must be had to fit the exercise to the soul, giving a scope and latitude sufficient to it, that it may comprehend in it acts suitable to several states of the soul; that is, both acts of contrition and likewise of the exercise of the principal virtues (among all which the most efficacious, profitable, and lasting are the acts of resignation). In the exercise of which it will be good for the soul to abide till she be fitted and called by God to pure aspirations, for then all manner of prescribed exercises must cease, because then a soul does not pray by her own election, but by an internal impulse of the Divine Spirit.

27. Some spiritual writers for this purpose recommend our Lord's Prayer for a constant exercise in daily recollections, advising such souls to exercise separately every petition as a several act, dwelling on each as long as they can find relish in it, and so doing they shall be sure not to omit anything that a soul can or ought to pray for; and this advice is suitable to the teaching of an ancient holy hermit, whose words, recorded by Cassian (9 Conf. c. 25), are these: *Hæc oratio licet omnem videatur perfectionis plenitudinem continere, utpote, &c.*; that is, 'This prayer of our Lord, although it may seem to contain in it the fulness of all perfection, as being either begun or established by our Lord's own authority, yet it doth promote those that are familiarly exercised in it to that far more sublime state which we mentioned before; conducting them to that inflamed prayer, that far more supereminent actuation of soul known or experienced by very few, yea (to speak more properly), altogether inexpressible, which, transcending all human sense or knowledge is not distinguished by any sound of speech or motion of the tongue, nor any pronunciation of words, but it is a degree of sublime prayer which the spirit, illustrated by an infusion of heavenly light, doth not design or express by human language; but having all the senses and faculties united and conglobated, it doth plentifully gush it forth out of the heart, as water out of a copious fountain, and ineffably poureth it out unto our Lord, in that one short moment of time sending forth so many and so great desires as the soul herself, making a reflection on her own operations, is not able to declare nor even to conceive.'

28. But it is not ordinary to find souls so composed in their imaginations and resolute in their wills as to content themselves with one only exercise; and for this reason I have made a collection of several kinds, with sufficient variety and mixture. These I have gathered out of several books, using mine own liberty and judgment in altering them so as to make them more proper for those that prosecute internal affective prayer, and for that purpose ofttimes leaving out many discourses and considerations intermingled with them in the books out of which they have been extracted.

29. Now I do not pretend nor desire that souls practising affective prayer should oblige themselves to these particular exercises, or to the order observed in them. They may, if they conceive it for their purpose, frame other exercises for their own use, either by selecting here and there out of these or out of any other books such acts or affections as they shall find agreeing to their spirit; but having framed such a collection, I would seriously advise them to practise according to the advices here set down, especially in this chapter.

30. The reading of some pious discourse before recollections, usually practised in communities, is a good and profitable practice, but especially proper for souls that are not advanced beyond meditation, who may do well to attend to the mystery read, that after they may make it the matter of their prayer; yet better it were they should have the matter of their meditation prepared beforehand, because it is to be feared that by once reading over the points of a mystery they will not be sufficiently imprinted in the memory so as to be made use of.

31. But as for souls that are in the practice of immediate acts of the will, I should not require of them the like attention, but rather that they would employ that time in chasing away distracting images, in placing themselves in the Divine presence, in begging God's assistance, and directing their following recollection to His glory; and if in their private recollections they shall premise some competent reading, I conceive that St. Augustine's *Confessions, Soliloquies,* the *Imitation of Christ,* and such other books affectuously written, will be most commodious for them; or, above all, certain passages of the holy Gospels containing some words spoken by our Lord Himself will likely be a most profitable and effectual preparation; but no certain rules can be prescribed for these things. Every one, therefore, is to choose that book and subject that he finds most proper for him.

32. When the preparation by reading is past, let the person applying himself to his recollection look upon the matter of the act or affection that he intends to employ his prayer upon; and after this, withdrawing his eyes from the book, let him think a while upon it, framing a suitable image or conception of it; and when that is done, let him forthwith produce an act or affection to God answerable to the matter, resting thereon as long as the virtue thereof lasteth, and so proceed to the following acts in like manner.

33. Some souls there are that, through a secret natural quality in their internal senses, cannot so work with the imagination as to produce an image that may become a matter of prayer to them; such persons, consequently, are not fit for the exercise of immediate acts of the will (and much less for meditation); they are, therefore, to apply themselves to the exercise of pious desires or amorous affections. But generally souls are so disposed as to be

rather enabled for acts of the will than affections, yet so that sometimes also they will find affections more flowing than acts, and, therefore, accordingly they are to give way to them.

34. It may happen sometimes to devout souls that they may find themselves disabled to either of them. In such case I would advise them to use a discreet violence on themselves to exercise some good acts most relishing to them (for where force is to be used, there acts to be exercised by the superior will are rather to be chosen than affections); but if after trial they find that they are not able to continue in so constrained an exercise, and so are at a stand, and likely to spend the time appointed in an unprofitable idleness, let them try if a more imperfect exercise will fit them, either speaking to God in the third person, as if He were absent or would not hear them, or addressing themselves to Angels, Saints, or to their own souls, &c.; and if they cannot perform even this mentally—that is, neither with attention nor gust—let them do it at least vocally, withal exercising as much patience, stillness, and quietness as may be; and doing thus, let them assure themselves that thereby they will afford unto their spirits a good, wholesome, and profitable, though tasteless, repast.

35. But if, after all this, it should happen (which would be very strange) that they should find all these ways insupportable to them, so that they can do nothing at all, both the understanding and will failing them, then, since no active working, external or internal, will help them, they may conceive it to be the case of an extraordinary desolation and desertion; so that their only recourse must be to pure suffering with patience and resignation, exercising these the best they can in such circumstances; which, if they will do, then will this afflicting desolation really prove more profitable than a state and prayer of light and comfort, which profit is scarce perceptible, because the Spirit of God works more intimately in the depth of the spirit, but, therefore, is more efficacious to the soul's advancement.

36. In this case I should scarce allow the suffering soul to divert and ease her mind by reading (and much less by any corporal exercise) during the time appointed for her recollection; or if so, as soon as ever she finds by a little glancing on a book an affection to be raised, let her pursue the said affection, and quit reading presently; for reading at such times, being allowed merely for necessity, ought to be used no further than necessity shall require.

37. No certain rules or determinations can be assigned for the time that souls are to be detained in the exercise of certain kinds of acts, as of contrition and others of the purgative way, before they pass into those of resignation or love (which are of the unitive way). Only in general it may be said, that the longer and deeper that souls have been plunged in vicious habits, the longer (probably) will it be before they be ripe for such a passage, yet

that time may be contracted by fervour in prayer and mortification. To some, a few months will suffice to remain in acts of contrition, &c.; to some, not many days; yea, some souls (as tender innocent virgins, &c.) are so well affected to God, and so unacquainted with vicious customs, that they may at the first be put into acts of resignation or love.

38. But herein every one is to regard the state of his soul and conscience, observing whether he find therein quietness and competent satisfaction, in which case he may reasonably judge that he may relinquish the acts of the purgative way.

39. But as for giving over the acts of resignation and love, &c., from thence to pass to the exercise of aspirations, God knows a much longer space of time is required, even in souls the most innocent. For this sublime exercise, arising out of a settled habitual charity fixed in the soul through long and constant practice of forced acts of the will (contrary to the teaching of Barbanson, who saith that souls may from meditation immediately pass to aspirations), it does not depend on man's choice when he will exercise aspirations, of which God alone is the mover and director; and whatsoever industry in prayer a soul shall use, it is very unusual that she should be enabled to arrive to this exercise in youth, before the boiling heat and activity of nature be well qualified.

40. Notwithstanding, in whatsoever exercise a soul shall be, if such aspirations do offer themselves she is to give way unto them; and as long as they continue she is to cease all other forced and elected acts.

41. To conclude these instructions, it is to be considered that the following patterns of exercises of acts, &c., are to be made use of only for a necessity, such as commonly beginners have, yea, and most souls even after they have for a good while pursued this internal prayer; but as for those whose interior, without seeking abroad, doth minister sufficient matter unto them of resignation, love, &c., either suggested by occasion of occurring difficulties, or coming of itself into their minds, such souls being enabled to pray without any forms prescribed, as long as they are so sufficiently furnished from within, are not to make use of exercises in books, and this may be the case even of some imperfect souls which may be prevented and much helped by God for the matter of their prayer; but, however, it is good that they should have a book in readiness to help them in case they come to stand in need, lest for want of matter so suggested they should be idle and at a stand. For such must not rely upon their first sensible fervour; but when that ceases (as they are to expect that it will) they must not scorn to descend, not only to make use of books, but also to apply themselves to inferior exercises and helps suitable to their imperfect state.

Chapter III. Of the Exercise of Acts of Resignation

§§ 1, 2. More special advices touching the exercise of affections of divine Love.

§§ 3, 4, 5, 6, 7, 8. Likewise touching acts of Resignation. The great profit and excellency of the said acts.

§ 9. Several objects of Resignation.

§§ 10, 11, 12, 13, 14, 15, 16, 17, 18, 19, 20, 21. Further instructions concerning the exercising of the said acts.

§ 22. All acts whatsoever must give way to aspirations.

1. Whereas all internal affective prayer consisteth either: 1. of such affections as are apt to cause suitable motions in corporal nature; 2. or of acts of the will, produced by and residing in the superior soul, as among holy affections the principal is Love, the source and mover of all the rest, so among all immediate acts of the will the most useful and considerable are those of Resignation or submission to the Divine will.

2. Now, having in the second treatise spoken sufficiently concerning the nature and qualities of Divine Love, I shall not need to give particular instructions how to employ that inward affection of charity immediately to God in the exercise of internal prayer, which is to be regulated according to the precepts formerly given; but as for the exercise of Resignation (which is, indeed, an exercise of love too, but so as that it regards external difficulties as the occasion or matter about which such love is expressed), it is an exercise that deserves to be more particularly treated of, and above all others most to be recommended, as being generally the most secure and profitable of all other exercises.

3. For though acts of pure melting love to God (in which all images of creatures, yea, all direct representations of God are excluded) be in themselves more perfect and unitive than are acts of Resignation, which involve in themselves images of external things (to wit, the special difficulties in which the soul intends to resign herself), notwithstanding, to recompense this disadvantage, there is in acts of Resignation far more security and less danger of propriety or self-interest than in acts of immediate love, which being apt to cause stirrings and pleasing motions in corporal nature, very few souls can practise them purely and without propriety, except they be exalted to a supreme degree of spiritual divine charity. Again, there is in Resignation exercised more directly true mortification and contradiction to self-love and interest than in any other kind of internal prayer, and consequently it is a prayer more purifying, and considering the daily and hourly use that we have

thereof in unavoidable occurring difficulties, it is of all other the most profitable; and though acts of Resignation (which are also the immediate fruits of divine love) do involve in themselves images of external things, yet this is only in the beginning of the act, so that the soul doth not tarry in such images, but presently passes from and out of them into God.

4. Good Lord, what millions of questions, debates, and perils doth total Resignation cut off! And this not only for *meum et tuum,* or worldly propriety in a secular state, for the regulating whereof there are such endless volumes of useless and perplexed cases dispersed everywhere, but also in external matters in a religious life, either with regard to superiors or among religious persons themselves, or towards externs, yea, and for matters of doubts merely internal, being such as are in question between God and fearful or scrupulous souls; all these, I say, are cut off by a total resignation, which doth tend to simplicity, peace, and the possession of that one thing which our Saviour saith is only to be counted necessary, to wit, the divine will (which is God Himself), and so doth reject all other things that may hinder or delay the soul from attaining to that one only necessary good.

5. Hence it follows that that soul which is resigned both for external and internal matters is not only freed from perils that may come from temptations or contradictions, but in a manner from all doubts, questions, and debates; whereas the unresigned soul is in a state wherein nothing can satisfy or secure her conscience.

6. A soul that is in the practice of the prayer of Resignation ought not to interrupt or omit the producing of acts conformable thereto, notwithstanding any failings or transgressings against good resolutions formerly made, if so be such failings proceed out of frailty or sudden passions (being then ofttimes more in sensuality than in the superior will, and so have less fault in them); for, notwithstanding such failings, resignations heartily made will not prove in vain, but in time will come to good issue.

7. In consideration of the eminent excellency of this duty of Resignation, I have adjoined several exercises of the acts of that virtue, exemplifying in all kinds of difficulties regarding either external or internal objects, touching outward goods, friends, &c., as likewise all accidents that may befall the body, as sickness, pains, want of conveniences or necessaries, &c.; and, lastly, touching the soul, as aridities, temptations, &c.; for the practising of which exercises, besides the advice given in the last chapter (which ought to be applied to this present purpose). I thought expedient to add certain more peculiar instructions here following.

8. When the exercise of Resignation in prayer comes to be the ordinary daily exercise of a soul, then she is established in the unitive way,

properly so called, and well-minded quiet souls will soon be ready and ripe for the practice, both external and internal, of this heavenly virtue.

9. Concerning the matter of objects of Resignation (which are generally matters of difficulty and contradiction to nature), either they are: 1. such difficulties as are sure to happen; 2. or only probably (of which probably there may be several degrees); 3. or very unlikely, but yet possible; 4. or, lastly, altogether impossible. Now in all these Resignation may be profitably exercised. But the better the more likely that the things are to happen; and the best and most necessary Resignation of all is in things sure to befall us, and which belong to our state especially such against which our nature finds the greatest difficulty.

10. Now since these last do most frequently occur to our minds in our recollections, therefore we must be the more industrious and courageous to overcome them by framing internal acts of our judgment and will to entertain the said difficulties, that so we may be prepared against the time that they do really befall us.

11. Now, having made efficacious and prevalent acts of internal Resignation, if, when the said difficulties do *de facto* happen, we do truly and really accept and embrace them with our superior will (whatsoever repugnance we find in our sensitive nature), this will much more advance the soul in Divine Love, and increase the good habit of Resignation, than many bare internal acts would do, by which the soul doth only represent a difficulty in the imagination, resolving with the will to accept it.

12. In performing these acts internally, a soul must be very careful to exercise them with most profound humility, and a distrust of her own ability to resist any temptation or contradiction, and with an entire trust and dependence on God's grace, with a firm faith in Him that He will assist her at all times whensoever He shall bring such trials upon her.

13. For this reason I have frequently expressed the acts of resignation either by way of oblation and delivery of the soul into God's hands, to be entirely disposed of by Him, or of petition, that in all such occurrences not our own will but God's will should be performed. As for the acts which are made by way of resolution or purpose, though they seem to argue some confidence in our own strength, yet the devout exerciser ought in his mind to exclude all such confidence.

14. The most perfect way of producing acts of Resignation (as likewise all other acts) is by intending purely the love of God and seeking His glory, renouncing all inferior unworthy interests of our own; and therefore Alphonsus, in his Method of Serving God, in his excellent chapter of Prayer, exhorts all devout souls, either expressly or virtually, to exercise prayer with this intention; but as for the exercise of Aspirations, an express and direct

intention of God's glory will scarce consist with it, because that sublime exercise will not admit any reflected act to be mixed, though implicitly and virtually they contain as much or more.

15. A soul needs not always to oblige herself in her recollections, in order to go through the following patterns and forms of Resignation according to all the examples given, as she was advised to do in other immediate acts; but she may alter, interrupt, omit, or add others as she shall see cause, or according to her present need, or as they shall be interiorly suggested to her by God or her own thoughts.

16. In the beginning of the exercising this degree of prayer, I conceive it will be the best course for a soul to single out and make choice of such acts of resignation as do regard such daily occurring difficulties, to which nature hath less aversion to resign herself, and from these to ascend afterwards by degrees to matters of more difficulty, till at last, by God's grace, she be enabled to accept even those things which nature doth most abhor; for if she should suddenly adventure upon acts above her present strength and forces of mind she will be in danger to be dejected, finding that she wants internal courage to undertake or submit to such difficulties represented to her mind.

17. And, indeed, according to this method, God Himself in His most wise and blessed providence deals with us, proportioning our trials and afflictions to our present strength, and to the measure of grace which He gives us, sending to imperfect souls only ordinary temptations (as St. Paul saith, 1 Cor. x. 13), and reserving the greater for such heroical spirits as are most advanced in the ways of perfection.

18. When special occasions of actual and real Resignation do not occur, a soul may make general and indefinite acts of Resignation, regarding in gross all occasions whatsoever without exception, either according to the form practised by St. Ignatius: *Deus meus et omnia, ecce me tibi penitus offero, et omnia mea tuæ subjicio voluntati.* Or saying, in our Lord's words, *Non mea voluntas fiat, sed tua, Domine, in terra sicut in cælo (Amen, Jesu);* or in any other form like to these. And this practice of universal Resignation may be begun very timely, and accordingly continued one's whole life; although, indeed, only perfect souls can purely, without reservation, exercise such acts. Yea, when a devout soul hath a particular occasion to resign herself in any special difficulty occurring, she may for that purpose make use of any such general form of Resignation, only reflecting internally upon the present occasion, and so applying the general form, without expressly naming the particular difficulty.

19. In exercising internally these acts, a soul is not to produce them overfast, and quick one upon another, to the hurt and oppression of the head

or spirit, but quietly and leisurely one after another, with reasonable pausings.

20. Though in the following examples of Resignation mention is only made of matters difficult and unpleasing to nature, yet may a soul with benefit exercise herself in the clean contrary; for example, as she may resign to sickness, pain, want, dishonour, &c., so she may also, for the glory of God, resign herself to health, pleasures, riches, honour, &c., intending, if God's will be such, to accept of these also, and to employ them only to His glory, and not to the satisfaction of corrupt nature, not diminishing but rather increasing humility and divine love by them. In which case, how pleasing soever to nature such things in themselves be, yet the Resignation is exercised with regard to that which is mortifying to nature, as he that for the glory and love of God submits himself to accept of an office imposed on him, and attended with dignity and power, intends thereby not the satisfying of his ambition, but rather frames a resolution to abate and mortify such a satisfaction, and to employ that office (not sought but obediently accepted by him) purely to the glory of God and the benefit of souls. Thus it is the nature of a spiritual life to make good use both of prosperity and adversity, in all things renouncing all self-seeking, and having an eye only to God; though, indeed, considering our frailty and inclination to be corrupted by prosperity, adversity is far more secure and profitable for us, and therefore such resignations are proper for few souls.

21. To conclude this matter, some souls there may be which will find it best for them to continue in acts of Resignation, yea, and perhaps even in the same acts, till they be thence brought to Aspirations; and others there will be whose exercises may consist of great variety both of acts and affections, and that confusedly both for matter and manner, and this either out of a book or from their own interior. And in the exercising of acts or affections, in some the said acts may be raised by a short reflection or by consideration of some motives, or even with a precedent light meditation. Lastly, some will find more relish in acts expressed in Latin, though they do but imperfectly understand the language, than in their own natural tongue (for whose sake I have in the following collection framed exercises in both languages); and all this manner of exercises are good, if the soul by experience and observation find profit by them, for by that alone must all our exercises be regulated.

22. But how perfect soever any acts or forced affections be, they must give way to aspirations whensoever a soul is invited or enabled to produce them; for as acts are the end of meditation, so are aspirations the proper end and fruit of acts, far more perfectly effecting and procuring that purity of soul and heavenly-mindedness to which we aspire by all our exercises.

Chapter IV. How Prayer is to be Exercised in Distractive Offices

§ 1. How internal exercises are to be practised in times improper and distractive.

§ 2. Particularly in a state of distractive offices and employments.

§ 3. Souls ought to prepare and furnish themselves beforehand for such times.

§§ 4, 5, 6, 7, 8. With what conditions and unwillingness offices ought to be undertaken.

§§ 9, 10, 11, 12, 13. How they are (being imposed) to be discharged.

§§ 14, 15, 16, 17, 18, 19, 20. No offices whatsoever ought to dispense with internal prayer.

§§ 21, 22. No distractions, aridities, &c., ought to hinder it.

§§ 23, 24. God will bless a soul that behaves herself well in distractive employments.

1. Before I quit this present argument of the prayer of forced immediate acts of the will, to treat of the supreme degree of prayer, to wit, Aspirations, I conceive it requisite to consider how a devout person is to behave himself, who, having undertaken a religious contemplative life in solitude, repose, and vacancy to attend to God and His holy inspirations, but afterwards coming to find some change in that life, either: 1. by being distracted with unavoidable external employments and offices imposed for the good of the community, &c., from which all cannot be exempted; 2. or else incumbered with the incommodities and solicitudes of sickness, to which all are obnoxious (which are generally two states that seem most disadvantageous for retired prayer); I say my intention is to give the best advices I can how souls are to behave themselves in these two states, as with regard to their prayer especially.

2. First, therefore, to the end that a well-meaning soul may with purity behave herself about external offices and employments, she is to consider: 1. That it is unlawful, contrary to humility, and a sign of a weariness of internal ways, and of a sensual desire to rule over others; yea, moreover, it is a wilful thrusting one's self into dangerous distractions and temptations for any one voluntarily to desire or seek such employments, dignities, or prelatures. 2. Yet because it is necessary that some should be employed in offices that regard the common good, spiritual or temporal, it is as unlawful utterly to refuse them, whensoever God shall by the command of superiors call a soul to the undertaking and discharge of such offices.

3. For this reason it will behove every religious devout soul, by assiduous prayer during the time of vacancy, to furnish herself with light and discretion, that she may proceed in this matter with the spirit of humility, prudence, and religious perfection.

4. In case, therefore, that superiors shall think good to impose an office upon a religious subject: 1. If the subject know of any real incapacity or disability in himself, or if he believe any other more sufficiently qualified, he ought, with all humility and simplicity, to rectify the superior's mistaken opinion concerning his sufficiency; yea, he may represent unto him his just grounds of fear lest such an employment should prove notably prejudicial to his soul, protesting likewise that he does not desire any kind of preëminence over others, &c. 2. Yet if the superior, notwithstanding such humble and sincere remonstrances of the subject, shall persist in a resolution to impose on him any such office (whatsoever the superior's motive be, whether necessity, reason, or even passion), the subject must submit himself, and accept of it willingly, whatsoever reluctance there be in the imagination or nature against it; but let him accept it with a pure intention for God in the spirit of obedience, especially if the office be grateful to nature, or to the sensual or ambitious desires of it. 3. Notwithstanding, considering his own frailty, and the temptations likely to accompany such an employment, he ought to undertake it with some fear and apprehension, lest without extraordinary watchfulness in prayer he may come to be corrupted or oppressed by it.

5. In this regard, therefore, the subject ought oftentimes to renew and rectify his intention about it, at least in his recollections twice a day. For, for want of care in this point, it oft falls out that the office which at first was undertaken out of obedience to God and superiors, comes afterward to be executed for self-will and sensual complacence, after that the spirit of devotion is abated or extinguished.

6. Indeed, so contrary and prejudicial to the spirit of contemplative prayer are the distractions and solicitudes which attend offices, that: 1. Religious subjects during the time of vacancy, when they are more illuminated, ought to forethink and imprint in their hearts good purposes never to offer themselves to such dangers; and when they shall befall them, to carry themselves in them vigilantly and prudently, according to their former light, lest, entering upon them unprovided, they should prove mischievous and destructive to all devotion. 2. And again, superiors, if they will consider that their principal care ought to be for the good of souls, will think it concerns them to be very nice in exposing to such perils their subjects before that the spirit of devotion and charity be firmly rooted in their hearts; for they also shall be accountable for the harm that their subjects' souls shall so incur.

7. Some superiors, either being of active spirits, and not knowing or not duly esteeming internal ways, or, perhaps, mistakingly believing their subjects to be more affected to external employments than interior, thereupon unwarily heap on them businesses to the hindrance of their recollections. In this case the subject ought to acquaint his superior with the inward disposition of his soul, how much good he finds by a constant exercise of prayer, and what damage the want of it causeth to his imperfect soul; but this being done, he must resolve to submit in case his superior still think fit to employ him.

8. In such circumstances, let not the subject be troubled if he finds it hard to abstain from showing some outward marks of unwillingness, however in his superior will he be resigned. For, indeed, to show cheerfulness argues in an imperfect soul rather a contentedness to be dispensed from prayer, not sufficiently esteemed by him, than a love to obedience; yea, such a seeming unwillingness will afford him a double mortification: 1. in that he contradicts sensuality in the discharge of obedience; 2. in that he incurs, in the opinion of others, an esteem of being immortified, the which will be a means to humble him.

9. When an internal liver is once actually and duly engaged in an office, in the first place he ought seriously to consider that, coming out of a state of abstraction and solitude, into business, he will thenceforward walk in less light than formerly; and yet will be exposed to far greater perils by reason of many unavoidable occasions of distraction, impatience, satisfaction of sensuality, &c., of which he had little experience in time past; therefore he must resolve to keep a more watchful guard over himself; lest business bring him to a forgetfulness of his soul and of all former instructions and good purposes.

10. Secondly, to the end to secure himself from such perils, he must in the actual execution of business be wary that he do not fix his mind more intently and affectionately on them than mere necessity shall require. Let him oft call to mind his former good resolutions, and review again and again these or the like instructions, for without such preventions it can scarce be avoided but that he will decay in spirit and grow negligently tepid in his spiritual exercises; since corrupt nature will be very forward to take any colourable pretences of quitting internal recollections (the only support of a spiritual life), which now will become more irksome by reason of greater dissipation of thoughts, and more frequent occasions of falling into immortifications; and therefore souls will be apt to think that the nature of their present employment is such as that it will not consist with the obligations of an internal life. Then they will catch hold of any advantage to dispense with

them, for that purpose making use of such popular sayings as this, that every good work is a prayer, &c.

11. Thirdly, more particularly in this state of active employments a soul must be careful, as far as the office will permit, not only to continue the practice of her former mortifications (and principally for the tongue and senses), but also to make good use of those many new mortifications which the discharge of her employment will afford her occasions to exercise; and, indeed, since probably she cannot enjoy that repose of spirit requisite to serious and perfect recollections, she ought the best she can to recompense that defect by increasing the practice of mortification and patience, by which means she will advance herself in spirit.

12 . Fourthly, she must remember that the doctrine of abstraction (most necessary in an internal life) has place also even in distractive offices, at least thus far, that the person is not to meddle in things that belong not to his present employment; and for such things as do belong thereto, he must be careful as to do them well and faithfully, so without bestowing on them more solicitude than shall necessarily be required, performing them seriously, but yet with composedness and tranquillity of mind, not suffering them to distract or encumber his memory before the time come for the executing of them, and then abstaining from passion and impetuousness, and from engaging his affections to them. A devout soul thus constantly discharging her office will come to that liberty, easiness, and settledness of spirit, that necessary employments will breed in her no harmful distractions (the cause of which is inordinate love to creatures).

13. But, fifthly and lastly, her principal care must be about her prayer. Although, by occasion of business, she cannot so habitually continue in a recollected state, yet at least she must resolve diligently and faithfully to pursue her daily appointed exercises, since prayer is the principal instrument by which divine light and grace against all temptation is administered to us; so that if prayer be duly performed, be it with distractions or without them, it will both urge a soul to use fitting mortifications out of prayer, and to make advantage (toward the perfecting and advancing of her spirit) even of the distractions and encumbrances of her office; whereas, if she be careless in prayer, she will become careless also in mortification, and by little and little will lose all that which with great pain and travail she had formerly gotten, yea, and be in very great peril never to find a way to return to her former state.

14. Certainly, if any distractions or employments can justify a soul for the neglect of this duty of internal prayer, those which attend the Popedom (the highest, weightiest, and most incessantly encumbering office that a soul is capable of) may do it. Yet St. Bernard, in those excellent books of

Consideration, written to Pope Eugenius III., seriously advises him not so wholly to plunge himself in business, but that every day he should borrow or steal from the affairs of the universal church some hours to employ in this holy exercise.

15. Hereupon Lewis of Granada will allow of no excuse, under pretence of business, to cease from pursuing daily recollections. For (saith he) no business can be so necessary and so continually urgent as to hinder our daily necessary refections. Now prayer, which is the food of the soul, is as necessary thereto, if not more so, than food to the body, and if it so fall out that businesses are to be despatched just at the hours appointed for daily spiritual refections, the person foreseeing that, ought to repair himself by taking some other vacant time for his prayer; and if that will not be allowed him, he may and ought, according to the judgment of Aquaviva, General of the Jesuits, to solicit his superior to give him some relaxation from such employments, which the superior is obliged to grant, otherwise God will require a severe account from him for the harm that must needs come to the subject's soul by the want of that which is only able to support the spirit, and to enable it with profit to discharge the most necessary duties of his calling.

16. If, either out of sloth, distractions, or remorse through some imperfections incurred, a soul find difficulty to apply herself any time to prayer, though she promise better for the future, yet, if upon any motives of sensual nature she omit it at any time, she will the day following have less mind to go to it, and so be in danger quite to abandon her recollections. If she have not the very same excuses and pretences that she had formerly, nature will be subtle enough to invent some other, for the longer she delays the more inapt will she be for it, according to that wise saying of the ancient Rabbins, *Qui protrudit horam, hora protrudet ipsum,* he that thrusts off the hour of doing any good duty till another time, that hour, when it comes, will thrust off and delay him; he will be less capable then of doing his duty than he was formerly, by means of some new impediment; whereas a soul, by using some violence upon herself to break through discouragements to prayer, will get such courage and grace from God that afterwards her employments will afford her less hindrance unto this holy duty.

. To this purpose, Johannes a Jesu Maria, General of the discalced Carmelites, relates concerning a devout gentleman, a penitent of his, who daily used at a certain time to recollect himself in prayer, how that treating with another upon some affairs of consequence, and the clock happening to strike the hour appointed for his prayer, he abruptly broke off the conversation, excusing himself that he had then an affair of such importance that it could not be delayed and must not be omitted; and so dismissing his friend, he retired to his recollection, wherein God was pleased, in reward for his diligence and fidelity to Him, to visit him after an extraordinary manner with some kind of supernatural contemplation, such as he had never had experience of before.

18. A well-minded soul, therefore, to the end she may be enabled to attend to this business of businesses (as St. Bernard calls it), ought to employ all her providence and subtlety so to order all her daily employments both for the time and manner as that they may be no hindrance thereto. Let her, if need be, make notes and remembrances of her several affairs each day (to the end her memory may not betray her), and beginning the morning with a serious recollection (which will sanctify all the following day's work), let her endeavour to despatch her task with such care and diligence, that towards evening she may be beforehand with her task of businesses, that solicitudes about them may not disquiet her mind, encumber her memory, nor distract her prayer.

19. It is morally impossible that in a religious state there should be any employment that should so wholly (and this constantly) take up one's thoughts as not to leave one hour each day to be given to God. Or if such an employment were, it would be absolutely unlawful, as being destructive to the obligation of a Christian, and much more that of a spiritual or religious person; no excuse, therefore, or pretence can justify a customary neglect of so essential a duty.

20. In case that sometimes by reason of some pressing affairs the devout soul cannot allow herself the whole time appointed for her recollections, let her at least take as much of it as possibly may be spared, or let her in exchange take some other hour of the day or night. However, let her preserve a thirsting desire and love to prayer, and by fervent interrupted actuations (as the present business will permit) and by some more than ordinary mortifications (especially of the tongue) repair the loss of a set recollection.

21. If a soul in employments cannot free her mind from distractions, aridities, and solicitudes in prayer, let her, however, be courageous to pursue it after the best manner she can, preserving as much resignation and tranquillity (at least in the superior soul) as may be, and let the sight of such imperfections humble but not disquiet her spirit. Let her consider and believe that God is not only as present to her in spirit during her greatest desolations as He was in her clearest recollections, but as loving also, and that this is the proper season for a soul to show her fidelity to God in adhering to Him in the top of her spirit, when not only the interior senses are diverted by images of businesses, but the affections also disordered by solicitudes.

22. To this purpose she may apply the point of election mentioned by Father Benet Canfield, who, to the great comfort of well-meaning souls, shows that in the midst of the greatest troubles, afflictions, passions, and dis-

336

tractions, a soul may as truly and efficaciously dispose of the operations of the superior spirit (which depends not upon our corporal organs) by fixing them upon God, making choice of Him for her final end, and submitting herself with resignation and love to Him even for sending her such trials, as she could in her greatest solitude and most quiet introversion; and this is best done without any violence or impetuosity, but with great tranquillity darting a spiritual regard to God, by means of which she may be as truly and effectually united to God (though not according to sense) in the midst of these troubles as in her greatest sensible unions.

23. A soul that will be thus vigilant and industrious may assure herself that God, who lays this office on her, doth it not for her harm, but for her greater good, and to give her occasion of exercising several virtues, which otherwise she would have wanted (at least the perfection of them), as likewise for the trial of her fidelity to Him amidst whatsoever incumbrances and temptations. Now by means of these virtues she will make great progress in the spiritual, at least forasmuch as concerns solid charity, if not for light of contemplation; and retaining a love to prayer, and practising it as well as she can, she will come to be in so good a disposition, that when she shall return to her former vacancy and solitude she will make a wonderful progress in the ways of contemplation. Thus she may see that as the office hath perils in it, so will God proportionably increase His grace and assistance.

24. For want of this care and vigilance over their interior, it is to be feared there be many in religious convents that fruitlessly spend their lives in employments in some sort beneficial to others, but of little profit, yea, perhaps, very prejudicial to themselves; as some that read lessons of philosophy or divinity, yea, even many that pass their whole time almost in spiritual employments, as preaching, hearing confessions, giving spiritual directions, &c.; for these works being performed not in virtue of spiritual prayer, and consequently not proceeding from the Divine Spirit, but the spirit of corrupt nature (which is the source of all actions performed in a state of distraction), God's Spirit seldom gives a blessing to them.

Chapter V. How Prayer is to be Practised in Sickness

§§ 1, 2. How internal livers ought to behave themselves in time of sickness. The benefits of sickness to such only.

§§ 3, 4, 5, 6, 7, 8. The great danger of souls unprovided for sickness, especially of tepid souls in a religious state.

§§ 9, 10, 11. How sickness is to be accepted.

1. The second state (before mentioned) that requires a more than ordinary care and provision (as seeming less proper for internal exercises) is the state of sickness; which, though it do exact a greater solicitude and vigilance, as being a disposition to a condition irreversible, yet in itself it is a more secure state than that of external employments, inasmuch as those are such as are apt to draw our affections from God to sensual objects; whereas in sickness all things do rather drive a soul to seek and adhere unto God, since all other comforts do fail her, and all pleasures become distasteful to her. Moreover, in sickness there are continual occasions of high resignations, and far less solicitudes about temporal matters; for the chief business of a sick person is forbearing and holding of patience; in a word, it is rather a not doing than doing.

2. Now, since it concerns a soul most deeply to be well-disposed in sickness, my purpose is to give some general advices to souls already practised in internal ways, and they shall be such as chiefly have a reference to prayer and mortification; the which advices, notwithstanding, our sick person ought only so far to make use of as he finds them proper for his spirit and case.

3. It was not without just reason that an ancient holy man said that a religious spiritual life is a continual meditation of death, because the principal end of all our exercises is to prepare ourselves against the day of our great account, to the end we may give it with joy and not with fear.

4. If, when sickness is come, a soul be to learn how she ought to behave herself, it will go hard with her, by reason that then such a soul will be in great blindness of understanding and deadness of will. All her thoughts and care will be employed in seeking to avoid pain, to pass away the tedious time, and to recover; and if any good thoughts come into her mind, it is fear that principally raises them; hence it is that serious conversion is seldom given in sickness, when passions do swell, and immortifications come thick upon one another; and a soul that in health hath neglected God and despised the means of conversion, cannot with any reason or confidence expect an extraordinary or miraculous grace to work a sudden cordial conversion. If that one's whole life spent in painful mortifications and serious recollections be but even little enough to conquer the perverseness of our wills and the glueyness of our affections adhering to sensual objects, what may be expected from a few interrupted inefficacious prayers or purposes in sickness, suggested merely by fear upon the approaches of death and judgment, whilst there still remains in the heart a secret love to those sinful delights that must now be forsaken? Upon which grounds St. Jerome hath a terrible saying, that among those that defer their conversion till their death, scarce one of a hundred thousand is saved.

5. And I believe the case of such a soul in religion is more perilous, because having enjoyed so great helps to a holy life, she has with so unpardonable an ingratitude neglected them; whereas a secular person, being touched in sickness, may resolve to seek those means of abstraction of life, a renouncing of the world, prayer, &c., the want of which was the principal cause (it may be) of his deordinations. Upon which grounds alone St. Bernard saith that he would give absolution presently to the greatest sinner (in sickness) if he would promise (upon supposition of recovery) to quit the world and embrace a penitential life in religion, because it is not possible to promise or perform a greater satisfaction. But I doubt whether he would be so indulgent to an unconverted religious person that can promise no higher state than he is in already, with so little good effect to his soul.

6. Yet God forbid that from hence any should advisedly give way to despair, or deliberately refuse to humble themselves, to mortify their inordinate affections, or to pray the best they can. Good purposes and actions performed merely out of fear will produce some good effect, and God's goodness (which is incomprehensible) may change fear into love, how imperfect soever.

7. Now though the case of tepid livers be not altogether so miserable, yet it is infinitely perilous, and the issue extremely to be suspected; for though they cannot be charged with many great sins of commission, yet their whole life has been a continual omission of duties to which their profession did in a special manner oblige them, and now what other new motive can they have to relinquish their negligence but only fear also? Or what prayers are they likely to make, when their necessity is so great and the helps to prayer so small?

8. The only secure way, therefore, to prevent the incurring this hazardous state in sickness is, during health to combat against tepidity, and by diligent prayer to provide one's self of internal strength and grace; for such souls by a prosecution of their accustomed duties of mortification and prayer make good use of their sickness and gain extremely by it; they are not forward to promise great matters (as tepid souls usually do, though they perform but little); they have forethought of sickness, and the temptations accompanying it, and now call to mind and execute former resolutions made to improve for their soul's advancement, all states and conditions; and by occasion of their present corporal infirmity or pains to fortify in their minds the virtue of patience, resignation, contempt of the world, and adhesion to God, this sickness proves to them a greater blessing than health; and if they do recover, they do yet more seriously and fervently perform their former exercises.

9. When sickness is actually come, a soul is to accept and embrace it as a special gift of God; yea, though such sickness happened through the person's own intemperance or other fault, as a malefactor is obliged with resignation to accept of death deserved for some crime. He ought, indeed, to be penitent and sorry for the faults which were the cause of such an harmful effect; but the effect itself he ought to consider as proceeding from the divine will and providence; yea, in such cases a soul may even rejoice that God is so merciful as to bring on her the smart and punishment of her sins in this world, giving her withal a profitable occasion to exercise her resignation, from whence she may infer a hope that He will therefore spare her after this life.

10. A soul must not forbear this willing acceptation of sickness, &c., because perhaps she finds great resistance thereto in sensuality; yea, she ought therefore the rather to accept it, as knowing that it is the superior will and not the will of sensuality that meriteth or demeriteth; and so doing, the repugnance of sensuality will, as well as the sickness, turn to the merit and advancement of the soul

11. Now a soul must not content herself for once or twice to accept sickness, but she must practise this almost continually, and especially when

any extraordinary pain or irksomeness does afflict her. And such acceptation must be not only for the present, but with a mind willingly to submit to the divine will, if His pleasure were that such pains should continue never so long.

12. She must particularly take heed of one notable temptation which often befalls good but imperfect souls, by means of which they yield too freely to impatience in sickness, which is this: nature being soon weary of suffering, will suggest unto the soul to justify impatience, among other incommodities of sickness this one, that thereby she is put in an incapacity to pray, or otherwise to serve God or her neighbour, upon which she will be apt to desire health with impatience, falsely justifying herself for such impatience, as if she did not so for the satisfaction of nature, but to the end she may perform spiritual duties more perfectly; but this is a mere delusion, for that is the true and perfect way of serving God which is suitable to the present condition wherein God hath placed a soul; and an imperfect interrupted prayer made with resignation in the midst of pains or troubles sent by God, is perhaps more efficacious to procure the good of the soul than the highest elevations exercised otherwise.

13. It is no great matter though the soul herself do not distinctly and clearly see how her present sufferings (external or internal) may be profitable to her; she is to refer all things to the infinite wisdom and goodness of God, who can bring light out of darkness; and therefore she must be contented (if such be His will) to be blindfolded, and humbly to remain in her simplicity, and in a reverential awe and admiration of the inscrutable ways of the divine providence.

14. A sick person is to account himself after an especial manner in God's hands as His prisoner, chained, as it were, by his own weakness, disabled from the ordinary solaces of conversation, walking, &c., debarred from eating what pleases the palate, become profitable to none, troublesome and chargeable to many, exposed ofttimes to bitter pains and sharper remedies of such pains, &c.; a grievous indeed, but yet a happy prison this is to a soul that will make a good use of it; for unless the internal taste of the soul also be depraved, she may by this occasion infinitely increase in spiritual liberty, health, and strength, by accepting with indifference these incommodities, and mortifying her natural exorbitant desire of remedies, not desiring to escape, but when and after what manner God shall ordain.

15. But to speak more particularly touching the duties of a soul during sickness, she is to assure herself of this one thing, whether she think that her sickness may justify her neglect of her spiritual exercises of mortification and prayer (the essential duties of an internal life); if these be not continued as well in sickness as health, the soul herself will become the more sick of

the two, and exposed to greater danger than the body; for most certainly, if sickness do not produce good effects of patience and resignation, &c., in the soul, it will produce the quite contrary, and such effects cannot be produced but only by the exercise of mortification and prayer.

16. First, therefore, for mortification, this is indeed the proper time wherein it is most seasonable and necessary. Store of matter for that virtue is almost incessantly afforded; pains, weakness, &c., in the body, and grief, fear, and other disquieting passions in the mind, which are oft more insupportable than outward torments; all these temptations the soul must be armed against.

17. Now among all internal temptations, the greatest and most painful is fear of death, and especially of the consequences of it—judgment and hell—without which, death to a faithful Christian could not rationally be object of fear, as he that knows it to be the universal inheritance of mankind, and to Christians the door of eternal happiness. In case, therefore, that such fear of death do remain in inferior nature, the superior reason ought to contradict it and use it as a subject of a very healthful mortification.

18. But as for the other far more considerable, more inward and painful subject of fear—which is the uncertainty of a future eternal condition after death, which doth usually much afflict and deject imperfect souls that are conscious of their manifold defects, small satisfaction paid for them, great weakness of divine love (a proof whereof is this very fear, which would be expelled if charity were perfect)—it is a hard matter to encourage such souls against it, or to persuade them to mortify it and resign themselves willingly to support it, it being indeed very profitable and healthful to the soul. On the contrary, they think resignation in this case to be scarce a fitting or lawful thing, though most certainly it is so.

19. I do not say that such souls ought to bring themselves to an indifference what way they shall be disposed of after death. But the point of resignation lies in this, that a soul ought to content herself not to know how and in what manner God will dispose of her after death. Her anchor is hope, which she ought to cherish and fortify all she can, and the best way for souls to fortify that is to make as few reflections on themselves as may be, and to employ all their thoughts and affections directly upon God. It is divine love alone that is at least the principal virtue that brings souls to beatitude, and therefore fearful souls, though they were in as dangerous a state as they suspect, must needs rationally argue thus: that the way to procure and strengthen love is by fixing their minds upon the mercies, goodness, and perfections of God, and to contradict or forget all arguments or motives of servile fear, the greatest enemy of love. What folly is it, because they are imperfect, therefore

wilfully to continue in their imperfections by nourishing fear! Surely, at the close of our lives we ought to practise after the best manner we can the best actions, and most acceptable to God, which is to relinquish ourselves, and to contemplate, trust, rely, and roll ourselves upon Him.

20. Let the afflicted soul, therefore, herein as in all other matters, not only with patience support such an ignorance, but with an amorous resignation congratulate with God His eternal most secret purposes and decrees concerning her, both for time and eternity, freely consenting and agreeing to the will of God that such secrets should be reserved to His own breast, hidden from our knowledge, therein acknowledging His divine wisdom and goodness, which moved Him (doubtless for our good) to conceal from us those things, the knowledge of which would have bred security, negligence, and perhaps pride, in our corrupt hearts. Let her desire be to know nothing, and to have nothing but what, when, and in what manner it, doth please Almighty God.

21. Such behaviour of hers towards her Creator and Redeemer (to whom she belongs both for her being and manner of it), as it is most just and reasonable, so it will make her most acceptable to God, and in conclusion, most assuredly bring her to happiness; whereas to be dejected and disquieted because God will not reveal His secret purposes to her is most unreasonable, and can proceed from no other ground but natural pride and self-love. And to give a deliberate scope to unquietness so grounded is both dishonourable to God and utterly useless to the soul herself; for assuredly God will not, to satisfy the inordinate desires of nature, alter the course of His divine providence.

22. It did not hinder or abate the tranquillity of Adam's state in innocence that he was uncertain of perseverance, yea, though he knew that one sin committed would exclude him utterly from his present happiness; whereas, in our present state, after thousands of sins, one act of true conversion to God and amorous resignation to His will is able to restore us.

23. Let the soul withal consider that He which hath denied unto her an assurance and forbidden her to presume, hath yet commanded her to hope, and to comfort herself in that hope. Let her therefore frequently and seriously exercise acts of hope (how little gust soever sensuality finds in them; for the greater repugnance there is in inferior nature, the more generous are such acts and more acceptable to God), which acts are to be grounded not upon any conceits of our own innocency or worth; for if the soul were never so perfect, yet a conceit of her own innocency would be but a rotten foundation of hope, which should regard only the free mercies of God, the merits of His Son, &c.

24. Moreover, let her exercise these acts, not as acts of her own will, but (far more perfectly and divinely) as acts of God's own will, who hath

commanded us thus to hope. She may withal, if need be, make use of considerations and motives in the understanding, by reading or hearing comfortable
promises in Scripture, &c., to incline the will to conform itself to the divine
will; to which conformity when a soul shall once perfectly be brought, there
remains to her no hell nor purgatory, no more than to God Himself; for where
there is no propriety of will there is nothing but the divine will, which is God
Himself, and according to the measure of this conformity such will be the
measure of our happiness.

25. As for other internal pains and anguishes arising from other
grounds, as scrupulosities about confessions, &c.: the instructions formerly
delivered in the second treatise are to be made use of, especially those of
submitting absolutely to the advice of a spiritual director, and of transcending
all imaginations and all risings in inferior nature; and surely now, above all
other times, the soul is to be careful not to yield to the suggestions of fear,
which is the only temptation left by which the devil can disquiet tender souls
(to whom now pleasures and ambition, &c., have lost all taste), and so draw
them from God and resignation to Him, from confidence in His mercies, &c.,
for which virtues this of all other is the most proper season.

26. And as concerning temptations to infidelity, despair, &c., besides
what has been already said, I will only add these two advices: 1 . that the soul
be sure to avoid all inventing of reasons or disputes to oppose the temptations; 2. to turn the mind neglectingly from the said temptations, and to fix it
with resignation and confidence on God. These, indeed, are the only proper
remedies for souls, especially those that walk in internal ways, for these require no study nor subtlety of wit to encounter the enemy, who is able to
entangle even the most learned that in confidence of their abilities dare contest with him; and yet these remedies are sufficient to quench even his most
fiery darts. And, moreover, this one expedient of turning the mind from all
objects but God, and adhering to Him, is an universal remedy, always ready
at hand, being the usual exercise of those souls for whom these instructions
were principally written.

27. To this purpose Cardinal Bellarmine (in his book *De Arte bene
Moriendi*) from Barocius, Bishop of Padua, relates a sad story of two doctors
in that university, famous for scholastic controversy, the one whereof, after
his death, did (according to a mutual agreement formerly made) appear to his
friend after a most affrightening manner, all burning in flames, giving this
account of the causes that brought him to that woful condition. 'A little before my expiring' (said he) 'the devil suggested to me doubts and arguments
against the Divinity of our Lord, the which I, out of confidence in my own
abilities, undertaking to resolve, found myself so pressed with new replies
that in the end, being quite overcome, I renounced the Catholic doctrine of

the Church, and assented to the Arian heresy, and in that state (a just judgment for my pride) I expired, so receiving this reward of heresy.' The living companion, astonished with this relation, revealed the case to some pious friends from whom he received advices directly conformable to these here before delivered; and thereupon spending the remainder of his time more in prayer and penance than study, and not long after approaching to his end, the same temptation assaulted him; for the devil requiring of him an account of his faith, could get no other answer of him but this: 'I believe what the Church teacheth;' and being thereupon asked what the Church taught, he answered, 'The Church teacheth that which I believe;' the which words he often repeated in the hearing of those that assisted him, by which means he eluded the subtlety of the enemy, and (as afterwards appearing to some of those his counsellors, in a glorious manner, he manifested) passed to heaven.

28. In the next place, as touching mortification to be practised about external things, it is a duty so necessary in all states, that it belongs as well to the infirmary as the refectory; for in all manner of things and occurrences in this life there lies a snare to be avoided, and an enemy to be combated; so that whosoever out of slothfulness shall forbear to continue the practice of mortification, will the next day be more averted from it, nature getting strength against the spirit.

29. Inasmuch, therefore, as sickness is a temptation and a snare, it is by consequence (well used) an occasion of victory against impatience and self-love, and of advancement in spiritual perfection.

30. More particularly the exercises of mortification proper in the time of sickness are: 1. not to be drawn by the pains and incommodities of it to impatience; 2. not to yield to an immoderate satisfaction of nature, when it suggests a desire either of seeking improper or unlawful remedies, or when pleasing nourishment, refreshment, &c., are offered to us; 3. to take heed of spiritual sloth, and neglect of our devotion to God (of which we will speak when we treat of the duty of prayer).

31. As concerning the mortification of impatience, by restraining the tongue from breaking out into complaints or murmurings, and the mind from yielding to melancholy and discontent, enough hath been said in the second treatise, which may easily be applied to the present subject of sickness. I will therefore only add these two advices: 1. That the infirm person would consider that impatience in sickness is not only harmful to the soul, but likewise to the body too; as, on the contrary, patience, peacefulness of mind, and a mortifying temperance, which are heavenly ornaments of the soul, are withal very efficacious means to restore health, inasmuch as thereby neither will the patient out of immortification refuse bitter things which are advantageous to health, nor greedily seek pleasing things which are harmful. 2. That patience

ought to be preserved at least in the superior soul, although violence of pain should force the patient to groan, or it may be to cry out (which, if they afford ease, are not wholly to be condemned).

32. Next, touching the mortification and moderation of the sensual appetite to be practised in sickness. In the first place, it cannot be denied that it is lawful and fitting for a sick person to desire and seek remedies proper in that case. Yet this is to be done without too much solicitude and disquietness of mind; and in case such remedies cannot be had, a contented submission of mind in the want or refusal of them is of admirable virtue to advance the soul; since necessity declares such a want to be the will of God, and this for the soul's greater good. A most perfect example hereof we have in our Lord, who, among the other insupportable torments of the cross, was most grievously afflicted with thirst, in which case He demanded refreshment, but all assuagement being denied Him, yea, gall being presented to Him to inflame His thirst, He complained not at all.

33. In the second place, it is to be considered that though the same manner of exercising temperance by repressing sensuality in the interior disposition of the soul be alike to be practised in health and sickness, yet there is a difference as in regard of the matters about which such temperance is to be exercised; for those meats and solaces which would misbecome a spiritual person in health may be very allowable and expedient in sickness; only care ought to be had that the yielding to some reasonable pleasure and recreation of the senses may be, by the direction of the spirit, according to spiritual discretion, for the good of the spirit, so as not to hinder internal exercises of the soul, and because such is God's will. And not that an undue liberty should be allowed upon the pretence of sickness to give the reins to sensual appetite, so as to make the state of sickness more easy and pleasurable, perhaps, than that of health. It is nothing considerable, as in itself, whether the body have ease or no; all the matter is how it fares with the spirit. If bodily ease may indeed be a help to the spirit, it is to be admitted for that purpose; for, as St. Bernardsays, as man was not made for the woman, but the woman for man, so spiritual exercises were not made for corporal, but corporal for spiritual.

34. Notwithstanding, there is beyond this a perfection to be recommended to the imitation of such internal livers whose grace and fervour have rendered them in a capacity of aspiring to it, the which the same St. Bernard hath both by his instructions and admirable example delivered. Hippocrates, saith he, doth teach to save lives in this world, but Christ and His apostles do teach to lose lives: he that will save his life shall lose it. Now which of these two masters do ye choose to follow? Truly that religious man plainly shows whom he chooses for his master, who saith, this meat is ill for the eyes, that for the head, the other for the stomach, &c. Now such niceness as this our

Holy Father so earnestly protests against, as almost to deny the use of physic to be lawful, the only proper medicinal remedy for religious persons being abstinence; yea, it is observed that he purposely made choice of unwholesome places to build his monasteries in, as being desirous that his religious should rather be infirm than robust.

35. However, in the choice and use of diet or physic every one must follow that divine light of discretion which God gives them, always avoiding superfluities, and sometimes contenting themselves with the want even of necessaries. They must account themselves obliged to continue the practice of the same internal duties, though after another manner, increasing the mortification of the will (which is a mortification far more pure and perfect), though they be forced to allow a little more to the body; their minds are to be set upon the benefits which sickness brings with it, and to use all endeavours to possess themselves of them; considering: 1. that they have a continual occasion of exercising patience and resignation (the greatest blessings that a soul is capable of); 2. that they have opportunity for more free, pure, and less distracted recollections, so that their prayer and mortifications do inseparably attend one another; 3. in a word, they are now in such a state by which the greatest saints have more surely and more speedily advanced themselves to perfection, than by many years' voluntary external and corporal labours and austerities.

36. Thaulerus hath a saying, that the condition of the dearest and most perfect servants of God is to have their souls full of the divine love and their bodies full of pains, and that when they feel no pain or other afflictions, they greatly apprehend lest God have forgotten them; but their comfort returns when God visits them with any corporal or worldly afflictions; then they even feel that it stands well with them, for then they are in a state that of all other doth best dispose for the divine union.

37. The sufferings of our Lord are never as perfectly understood by reading or meditation, as when devout souls themselves taste of the like; then they see and comfortably taste His love to them. If their pains be supportable, they do invite them to unite themselves to God by express acts of resignation; but if they be so excessive that they become incapable of making express formal prayers, then the very suffering of those pains with patience and peace of mind is a most sublime and efficacious prayer. Then is the proper season for those (*gemitus inenarrabiles*) those groans which cannot be uttered, which, as St. Paul saith, the Holy Spirit suggests to suffering, humble, and devout souls.

38. And here, by the way, I would recommend to those charitable persons that do attend on the sick, a care to behave themselves as becomes them in those mortifications that attend such an office; that they would bear

with the passionate humours of their patients, and not judge them for small excesses; that they would freely and charitably administer what shall be requisite to their present state, being assured that God will never be wanting to those that have left all for Him, and now depend only upon Him; He will rather enrich them more for their charity than suffer them to be endangered by it. It may be it is for the sick patient's sake that the healthful enjoy a comfortable subsistence. Let them herein imitate the tenderness of our Holy Father to the sick, and his care likewise, to admonish their attendants of their duty (as in the 36th chapter of his Rule).

39. But above all things a devout soul ought to judge that God hath sent her the most profitable trial of sickness, not to the end to discharge her of her daily recollections, but rather that she may pursue them after a more efficacious manner. Probably she will not be able to observe exactly her former appointed times of prayer, as also through disturbance of humours and spirits she will find great distractions; yet, if lifting up her spirit as well as she can, she offer both her pains and distractions to God, and withal, if in times out of prayer, she be watchful over herself not to give way either to the inordinate appetites or impatience of nature, but to be in a continual state of resignation, she will have little reason to complain of the imperfections of her prayer.

40. A soul can have no excuse for neglecting this most necessary duty of prayer, the times of which may more securely be observed in sickness than in health; for who would trouble or interrupt such an one against his will, or who would not permit him to be alone or to rest whensoever he has no mind to continue conversation? However, if the devout soul should stand in need, she may and ought to use all lawful foresight, industry, excuses, and sleights that may be, to prevent the being hindered or interrupted.

41. Now because physic, inwardly taken, does much encumber the stomach and indispose for prayer, therefore I would advise the sick person: 1. not to be forward to seek or accept of all receipts that friends and visitants are apt to prescribe; 2. when he is to take physic (whether in the morning or evening) so to order his times as not to take it till he have performed his recollection; 3. not to receive physic, no, nor repasts, often or more than shall be necessary; not too much neglecting the body, but yet being careful rather to attend to the necessities of the spirit. Let our patient therefore stoutly resist the invitations and tendernesses of friends that are apt to urge him to eat more or oftener than shall be needful. And whatsoever he shall receive, let him take it in the name of God and for His sake, neither with avidity, if it be pleasing to nature, nor with murmuring, if displeasing.

42. It will be exceeding difficult during pain or any great infirmity to use discoursive meditation; the exercise of acts of the will (and much more,

of aspirations) is a far more proper prayer in such a case. Therefore it is good even for those who are not yet so fully ripe for the exercise of acts as to make them their constant exercise, yet to use them sometimes in time of health, to the end that if they be overtaken with sickness, they may not be to seek for their exercise.

43. Among express voluntary acts the exercise of total resignation is the most perfect, and generally the most profitable; yet a soul in sickness, if she find herself indisposed for such acts, may content herself with acts of an inferior nature, yea, with devotions to any particular saints, to her angel guardian, and specially to our blessed Lady.

44. Those that are only infirm and languishing are (forasmuch as concerns the nature of their prayer) in a case little different from that they were in during health. Those whose sufferings are from outward pain merely, without sickness, may happen to have their prayer altered to the better by means of such pains, which themselves may prove a very profitable prayer, if the patient, with quietness and submission to the divine will, do offer such pains continually to God.

45. But as for sicknesses more inward, they do more indispose the patient to prayer, besides the great distractions that come from physic, blood-letting, diet, &c., so that none can prescribe any certain advices. The well-meaning soul therefore must, and with a moderate attention may, herself observe all circumstances, and, accordingly, for the manner practise both mortification and prayer. She will easily discern at what times, how long, and in what manner she ought to pray, as likewise wherein she is to mortify herself, and how far she may yield to the desires and necessities of nature. The truth is, the cases not only of several persons in several sicknesses, but even of the same person in the same sickness, are so wonderfully various, that it is impossible to fit advices for all; all that an instructor can say to the purpose is, that prayer and mortification are absolutely necessary to a soul as well in sickness as health; but for the special manner and matter, her own judgment and discretion, but especially the Spirit of God, must teach her, and doubtless will, if she attend to His holy inspirations.

46. I said before that the universal remedy against all inward temptations was actual prayer and conversion of the soul to God, which remedy is good for all souls in what state soever; but more proper for such as practise internal contemplative exercises (who are not now in a disposition to invent motives and arguments to contradict such temptations), but most necessary for the fearful and scrupulous. Notwithstanding, I would not oblige all imperfect souls, upon every thought of a temptation, to recur always to their prayer, but only when necessity and a just fear of being overcome shall require it. Otherwise, being in no such fear, they may content themselves with

some intermitted elevations of their minds to God, deferring their prayer till their next appointed recollection; for it would be too great a burden imposed on such souls as without some difficulty cannot enter into serious introversion, to bind them hereto upon every assault of an inward temptation, when a moderate care not to yield to the temptation will suffice.

47. God seldom sends great sicknesses to spiritual persons in the beginning of their course, before they have gotten a reasonable habitude of prayer to make good use thereof, lest thereby they should become disabled to pray; but after such an habitude gotten, if sickness come, it will advance their prayer; and as their bodily strength decays, their prayer proportionably will grow more easy, profound, and spiritual; but it is to be doubted that the prayer of meditation will be little bettered by sickness.

48. I will conclude this point of sickness with proposing one special consideration, which ought to induce souls to be careful that they do not deliberately turn sickness into a liberty of sense or spirit, by omitting or neglecting prayer and mortification; and it is this: In all sickness there is at least some degree of peril of being taken out of this life, which event, if it should happen to a soul whilst she continues in such a tepid, negligent state, God will assuredly judge her according to her present state in which depth finds her; yea, she will be in danger to lose the fruit that she might expect from all her former good purposes and resolutions, or at least to suspect that such purposes were not sincere and cordial, since now, the proper time of putting them in execution being come, they are ineffectual. (And above all other, the case of scrupulous souls would be miserable, if they should neglect to combat their scrupulosities by a simple obedience and transcending of their fears.) On the contrary, it is certain that a soul cannot possibly have a firmer ground of assurance of eternal happiness than a sanctified use of sickness.

Chapter VI. Of Spiritual Discretion

§ 1. Internal exercises weaken the body, yet oft prolong life.

§§ 2, 3, 4. The body ought to suffer for the good of the spirit, and not the spirit for the body.

§ 5. Yet with discretion, that the body be not unnecessarily prejudiced.

§§ 6, 7, 8, 9, 10, 11, 12. In the first place discretion is to be used about mortification, both by superiors and others.

§§ 13, 14, 15, 16. Secondly, discretion is to be used in sensible devotion.

§ 17. Thirdly, in meditation.

§§ 18, 19, 20. Fourthly, in the exercise of immediate acts.

§§ 21, 22. Fifthly, even in aspirations.

§ 23. Of languishing love mentioned by Harphius.

1. Internal prayer, seriously prosecuted (as it deserves to be), being contrary to our natural inclinations, cannot choose but cause some trouble and uneasiness to nature, and abate the vigorousness of the body, quenching those spirits and draining those humours which are superfluous and afford matter of temptations; yet, on the other side, it makes amends, even to nature itself, in contributing much to the prolonging of life by means of moderation of diet, a composedness of passions, and contentedness of mind, &c., which it causeth. Proofs whereof we have in the ancient holy fathers of the desert, and more lately in St. Romuald, who lived till he was a hundred and twenty years old, and St. David, of Wales, till a hundred and forty, &c.

2. However, if it were otherwise, the soul is not to serve the body, but the body the soul; so that if one of them must, for the benefit of the other, be a loser, it is most just that the loss should lie on the body's side. And, surely, since there is scarce any study or exercise of mind which does not abridge life or debilitate the functions of it, without making any amends to the soul for the future life—and yet for all that men are neither discouraged, nor do think it fit for such considerations to forbear such studies—much less certainly ought spiritual and divine exercises to be laid aside upon such pretences.

3. Notwithstanding, just it is that some due regard be had to the body, that it be not too much prejudiced by the exercises of the spirit, performed with overmuch violence and impetuosity, and this not so much for the body's sake as the spirit's, which, since in this life it cannot work without the body, by too violent workings it may so weaken the body as that it will not be enabled for continuance; and so those little short gains which are got by a few impetuous exercises will be dearly bought by an incapacity of continuing them, contracted in both soul and body. We must neither stretch our understandings to high seekings, lest we be plunged thereby in internal darkness, from which would proceed intolerable perplexities; neither must we force the affections even to good objects too much, nor suffer them to flow with too violent a stream; nor, lastly, must we exhaust bodily strength by unnecessary external austerities.

4. As for the painfulness, troubles, and uneasiness to nature, that without too much debility doth accompany spiritual exercises, those may well enough be digested, considering the unspeakable benefits and service that they produce unto the soul. And yet for our comfort this uneasiness will,

by custom and constancy, continually diminish; for, as Harphius observes, a soul after long practice of elevations of spirit will come to such a facility in them, that they will become as it were natural to her. And herein we may observe the wonderful wisdom and goodness of the Divine Providence over souls, how He tempers the exercises of the spirit to the exigence of the body; for while the body, being vigorous, is able to endure more, He gives her ruder and more laborious exercises; but when, by long-continued workings, it is become so feeble that any violent intention of the spirit or rude external mortifications (of which there is no need) would overwhelm it, then the exercises are most easy, peaceable, silent, and serene, yet infinitely more full of virtue than formerly.

5. Now the peculiar virtue by which all harmful inconveniences either to the body or spirit may be avoided, is that supernatural discretion by which a soul is enabled to hold a mean, and avoid the vicious extremes in the practising of all spiritual duties. It is justly called a supernatural virtue, because God only can bestow it (for all the wit and philosophy in the world are but mere folly and blindness in these matters); and this He does principally by the means of prayer, with the use of requisite abstraction and attandance to His divine inspirations, whereby we shall receive a celestial habitual light to direct us in all things suitably to our own particular dispositions and abilities, for no one man can in all matters be a rule unto another.

6. Now, as touching a particular application of this supernatural discretion to the exercises of an internal life, much hath already been set down dispersedly in these treatises. I will, therefore, only point at some few considerations which, in the practice of the several duties of a contemplative life, do regard this mistress of all virtues, discretion, which surely deserves above all other to be purposely and by itself treated of, inasmuch as without it all other virtues are imprudent, that is, not virtues at all.

7. First, therefore, in regard of the duty of mortification (I speak now only of necessary mortifications, of which kind all are to be esteemed that come from God, either immediately or by means of others, especially superiors). A soul is to esteem those mortifications which a superior, beyond the rule, shall voluntarily impose upon the subject, to be to the subject himself necessary, however voluntary to the superior.

8. Now superiors ought rarely to impose such kind of mortifications on their subjects, because so many circumstances are required to make them well imposed, that a great measure of illumination from God is requisite for those that practise the imposing of them. For, 1. The superior must evidently see that the subject in probability will make good use of them. 2. And that though they may do the subject good some one way, yet they will not harm

him more another. 3. He must take heed that others be not scandalised thereby.

9. The like circumstances are to be observed by a particular person that would voluntarily assume mortification, for want of which point of discretion Harphius saith: That such kind of strange, odd, and uncouth mortifications as are imposed and practised in some communities ought not to be voluntarily assumed, as if with a design therefore to be despised by another.

10. The author of the *Abridgment of Perfection* justly imputes indiscretion to those who will never give rest to nature, but will always have some cross or other (exterior or interior) by which to mortify nature; for (saith he) the highest perfection is not to desire to be always suffering, but to be content to suffer all that by God's providence shall befall us, which contentment is taken away by that continual anxiety which those most suffer that will needs be always upon the rack.

11. In like manner Harphius taxes those that think themselves ready for afflictions, and complain that they want occasions to exercise their resignation; for says he to such an one: Thou deceivest thyself by pride; God does see that as yet thou art not indeed ready and strong enough for extraordinary trials; for if He did, He would not fail to furnish thee with occasions. He will send an angel from heaven on purpose to exercise a soul, rather than she would want mortifications for her good. Therefore, let souls never be solicitous, nor set themselves to devise or procure mortifications, as if they thought God had forgotten them. Notable examples of this providence of God may be seen in the life of Thaulerus, where, likewise, we read how God reprehended the layman that converted Thaulerus, in his sleep, for certain assumed voluntary corporal austerities. To this purpose, there is a memorable passage in the life of Suso concerning a spiritual daughter of his, who of herself was disposed to have undertaken some great corporal mortifications, but was dissuaded by Suso, although himself, by a special call from God, did use very violent and sharp ones; in which discourse there are many excellent documents, very well deserving to be perused by the devout reader.

12. Let a soul, therefore, seriously practise that mortification of mortifications, which is pure internal prayer, and with it join a diligent good use of those mortifications attending her state of life, or sent her otherwise from God, not omitting those most efficacious internal mortifications by acts of humiliation and annihilation of herself; and so doing, she will have little reason to complain of want of exercise of this virtue. For corporal austerities do not by the excess of them, but by the fitness and proportion to the soul's present disposition, perfectionate an internal liver; so that some infirm but sincerely affected persons do advance themselves more by ordinary and tri-

fling mortifications than others that consume their strength and spirits with intolerable fastings, chains, disciplines, &c.; for, as Cassian says (in the preface to his *Institutions*), *Si rationabilis possibilium mensura servetur, eadem observantiæ perfectio est etiam in impari facultate;* that is, If a reasonable discreet measure of austerities, that ordinarily are not above our power, be observed; there will be the same perfection of observance where the external abilities are unequal.

13. In the next place, there is great use of discretion in sensible devotion, by which, saith Harphius, some souls are so far carried away, so besotted with self-love and self-will in the use of it, that no advice from the most experienced will avail to moderate them, till it be too late to amend, and till they find themselves unable to support any serious application to exercises of the spirit. Nevertheless, saith he, having thus by their indiscretion brought on themselves this inconvenience, they may for all that merit much, if with humility, patience, and resignation they will accept of such their infirmity.

14. We ought, therefore, much rather to mortify such sensible fervour than use force to increase it, applying hereto that saying of the wise man (Proverbs xxv. 16), '*Hast thou found honey, eat of it what may be sufficient for thee, lest thou be filled and vomit it up.*'

15. All the merit that is in sensible devotion consists in the concurrence of the superior will to those acts, without which it will not help to raise the soul out of her natural state. Yea, the more she is visited and even bathed in such sensible consolations (except she use mortification about them, and be wary not to rest in them, but turn them to the producing of more efficacious acts in the superior will), the more strong will she grow in self-love, and more defiled with a kind of spiritual lust. Unless souls, therefore, do grow more humble thereby, it is a sign of danger to be perverted by it, and quite to lose the end for which God gave it.

16. Yet souls during their imperfect state are not violently to strain themselves to work purely in spirit, but moderately to use sensible devotion when God sends it as a means to advance them in spirit. Neither ought they, on the other side, to be so carried away with a liking and gluttonous affection to it (which indeed affords delicacies more agreeable to nature than any sensible satisfactions) as for it to omit other duties belonging to their state, and which God would have them to do.

17. Thirdly, as touching the exercise of meditation, how far discretion is to be used in it hath been sufficiently declared when we treated of it. Indeed, souls during that exercise are to he directed rather by the discretion of others than their own, and this both in judging whether they be fit for it, how long they are to continue in it (the rule whereof must not be custom but

experience of profit), and what proportion of time they are to allow unto the understanding and will to operate in it; for that exercise doth not afford supernatural light enough to enable a soul to be her own guide.

18. Fourthly, forasmuch as concerns the exercise of immediate acts of the will, a soul that out of ripeness got by sufficient practice of meditation is arrived thereto, will have light and discretion sufficient to judge what acts are most proper for her, what time is to be spent in each recollection, when and what pauses shall be necessary, and when she is to change it for a higher.

19. A principal point of discretion in this exercise is not to be carried away with the examples of some saints in former times, who could remain almost continually in some mental actuation to God, without giving way to an extravagant thought, by which means they were almost continually in internal combatings. An indiscreet imitation of such examples, as likewise a too violent producing of acts upon one another, would so oppress ordinary spirits, that it would put them into an incapacity of ever being able to pray for the future.

20. They who do not use set recollections may and ought frequently to force themselves to interior acts towards God; yea, as oft as they please, not much regarding the season of the day, as whether it be after refection or before sleep. And when they have done all, their progress will be but small for want of more prolonged and continued exercises.

21. Lastly, discretion and mortification likewise are to be used also even in those exercises to which we are invited and enabled by God Himself; such are the exercises of aspirations and elevations of the spirit. The usual times, therefore, of set recollections are to be expected; for they do so weaken and consume corporal nature, that if souls should give way unto them as oft as they think themselves enabled (which is indeed almost continually, so perfectly are they disposed to God) they would utterly disable themselves to do any service to God for the future.

22. To this purpose Harphius relates an account that one brother Roger, a devout Franciscan, gave of himself, saying that a hundred times in a Matins he was in spirit drawn upward to a more high knowledge of divine secrets; all which tracts he forcibly resisted, being assured that if he had given his soul free scope to fix the eye of the understanding upon those objects so represented to him, he should have been so plunged in the abyss of the divine incomprehensibility, and so wholly driven out of himself, that he should never have been able to have retired himself alive from such a contemplation. But there is little peril of indiscretion in souls so highly elevated and so wholly in God's hands, who may do with souls and bodies what He pleaseth.

23. The same Harphius describes the state of some other souls (not so sublimely elevated) who yet are so languishing in their love to God, and in such an impatient ardour and thirst after Him, that it makes the body to faint and quite wither away, and therefore he calls them Martyrs of Love. Now, by this languishing love, I conceive, is understood a love much in sensuality (though the object thereof be God), and it is exercised about the heart much after the same manner that a violent but chaste love is oft exercised between absent persons of different sexes, so that I take it to be the highest degree of sensible devotion. Now, though Harphius says that such Martyrs of Love, dying corporally through the extremity of passion, do immediately pass into heaven, having been already purified in the purgatory and fire of love; notwithstanding, although no doubt such souls die in a most secure estate, yet it may be they will not escape some degree of purgatory for their indiscreet yielding to the impulses of nature in the exercising of this love, which, though truly divine, is yet far less perfect than that pure love which in perfect contemplation is exercised in the intellectual soul, without any sensible change or redundance of the body; for the tree of love is in no sort to be plucked up by the roots, as long as there is any hope that it may be in a disposition or capacity to bring forth more fruit.

Chapter VII. Of the Prayer of Interior Silence

[N.B. The instructions contained in this chapter are to be received with the utmost caution; and let the note which is inserted in § 2 be attended to.—J. N. S.]

§ 18. This prayer is far from the mere cessation or idleness of the illuminati.

*§§ 19, 20. A transition to the following discourse of contemplation, with a
serious exhortation of St. Teresa to aspire courageously thereto.*

1. Before we proceed to the supreme degree of prayer, which is pure
contemplation, it may be convenient, as it is also pertinent enough, to insert
here as an appendix to these instructions, concerning the prayer of forced acts
of the will, a certain exercise of internal prayer pertaining to this same degree, though in regard of the soul's behaviour much differing. It is a prayer
of internal silence, quietness, and repose, in which there is no meditation at
all, any acts of the will expressly and directly framed, being rather a kind of
virtual and habitual attention to God than a formal and direct tendence to
Him; yet is this a far inferior degree of prayer than is that prayer of quietness,
which St. Teresa speaks of and experienced; which was, indeed, supernatural
contemplation.

2. The first that published a treatise purposely of this kind of prayer
was Antonio de Rojas, a devout Spanish priest and doctor, in a book called
the *Life of the Spirit approved*, with large eulogies, by no less than nine eminent doctors, bishops, or inquisitors, so that there can be no reasonable
grounds to doubt of the lawfulness, convenience, and security of it; it hath,
moreover, been translated and published in French, and recommended by
several other doctors.

3. Now the order that the author advises a devout soul to observe in
the exercise of this prayer of internal silence, both in regard of preparation
thereto and actual exercise of it, is as followeth:

4. In the first place for preparation: 1. The soul is to examine and purify her conscience with a prudent, diligent search. 2. She is to endeavour
seriously and cordially to make an act of contrition for her sins, from a consideration of God's goodness, love, and mercy, &c. 3. She is to frame an act
of pure and entire resignation of herself into God's hands, with reference to
the present exercise of a silent recollection, determining to perform it purely
for God's glory, renouncing all inferior private interests and contentments,
&c. 4. She may (if need be) meditate a little upon one of the mysteries concerning the Incarnation and Passion, &c., of our Lord; also mixing certain
ejaculatory prayers. 5. She is to make a firm act of faith and acknowledgment
of God's presence in the centre of the soul before whom she intends to place
herself with most profound reverence, humility, and love.

5. In consequence to these preparations (in which she is to continue
till she find herself disposed to quit all such express and direct acts or affections, and having an implicit assurance by a bare and obscure faith that God,

who is incomprehensible universal goodness, is indeed present to and in her),
all that remains for her then to do is, with all humility and love, to continue
in His presence in the quality of a petitioner, but such an one as makes no
special direct requests, but contents herself to appear before Him with all her
wants and necessities, best, and indeed only, known to Him, who therefore
needs not her information; so that she with a silent attention regards God
only, rejecting all manner of images of all objects whatsoever, and with the
will she frames no particular request nor any express acts towards God, but
remains in an entire silence both of tongue and thoughts (the virtue of the
precedent direct acts remaining in her), with a sweet tacit consent of love in
the will permitting God to take an entire possession of the soul as of a temple
wholly belonging and consecrated to Him, in which He is already present.

6. In this state the soul behaves herself much after the manner of an
humble, faithful, and loving subject, that out of duty and with most entire
affection and respect approaches to the presence of his sovereign. At his first
access he uses such profound reverences and protestations of duty and fidelity as are befitting; but that being done, he remains silent and immovable in
his presence, yet with the same respect and reverence that he first entered;
and knowing that his prince only ought to dispose of his fortune and state,
and that he is both most wise to judge what favours may become the one to
give and the other to receive, and withal that he has a love and magnificence
to advance him beyond his deserts, he makes no particular requests at all.
Now the reverence that he shows him is not by making any express reflections, or inward saying, 'The king is here, to whom I owe all duty, love, and
obedience;' for, knowing him to be present, there is no need of renewing either speeches or thoughts that he is so; and really exhibiting all manner of
respect to him, it would be to no purpose to make either internal or external
professions of it. He is in readiness to hear and execute any commands; and
until he be informed by the king how he ought to perform his will and service, he is not forward to voluntary undertakings; so does the soul (according
to the instructions of Rojas) behave herself in God's presence, not renewing,
but only persevering in the virtue of those direct acts of faith, love, duty, &c.,
which she framed in the beginning. If, being in this vacancy and internal silence, God's Spirit shall suggest unto her any pure affections, she is attentive
and ready to entertain and quietly exercise them, and presently returns to her
silence.

7. If during this silence the soul find any aridity, obscurity, or insensibleness in inferior nature, &c., those things do not interrupt her persevering
in her silence and virtual exercise of faith, oblation, and resignation, joined
with a quiet attention to His will and inspirations; yet if, indeed, she should
forget herself, and that either wandering thoughts or sensual affections
should press upon her and divert her attention from God (which can scarce be

whilst she is vigilant to expel all images whatsoever that may cause her to break her internal silence), she can easily recover the said silent attention, by renewing (if need be) a short express act of faith of the divine presence, &c.

8. In this attention to God, she is far from expecting any extraordinary illuminations, favours, or visits, of which she accounts herself utterly unworthy.

9. Lastly, she has no suspicion or fear lest such a respectful silence should be mere idleness or cessation, for she knows it to be the effect of love and respect; and since an intellectual soul is all activity, so that it cannot continue a moment without some desires, the soul then rejecting all desires towards created objects, she cannot choose but tend inwardly in her affections to God, for which end only she put herself in such a posture of prayer; her tendence then being much like that of the mounting of an eagle after a precedent vigorous springing motion and extension of her wings, which ceasing, in virtue thereof the flight is continued for a good space with a great swiftness, but withal with great stillness, quietness, and ease, without any waving of the wings at all or the least force used in any member, being in as much ease and stillness as if she were reposing in her nest.

10. This seems to me to be in sum the fashion of that internal prayer of silence recommended by Rojas, which, without any variation, he would have exercised daily, morning and evening, allowing to each recollection about an hour.

11. Now the advantages that he (not without grounds of reason) attributes to it are: 1. That it causes far more profound recollections than any other kind of set internal prayer; because a soul having, either by a short discourse or exercise of faith, oblation, &c., found Him who is the centre of her repose, she then leaves all the rooms and apartments of sense (both external and internal) void and empty, and passes forward to those of the spirit, which are pure, clear, and secure. 2. It doth extremely abate the activity both of the imagination and passions, neither of which doth it suffer to stir at all. 3. God is most perfectly contemplated in it, being apprehended simply and truly by faith in the superior spirit. For as long as there are discourses in the understanding, images permitted to rest in the fancy, and sensible motions of tenderness in the heart, there God is not perfectly and entirely the object of such operations. *In spiritu, non in commotione Dominus,* saith the prophet Elias. God is not in the rushing wind (He is not in the stirrings of passions or of the imagination), but (*in sibilo auræ tenuis*) he is in the silent whisper of a soft air. And, saith David (*Factus est in pace locus ejus*), His place of abode is in the clear and peaceful regions of the spirit 4. Moreover, by this exercise we come to the most perfect operation of self-annihilation, by which both

ourselves and all creatures are so transcended and forgotten as if they were not at all, neither can the devil find where to fasten a temptation. We present to God the temple of our souls empty, to the end He alone may possess it, which He will not fail to do, and withal most richly adorn it, making it fit for such a guest.

12. To these benefits may be added this (which is a great one, and fruitful in many blessings), to wit, that in this exercise all divine virtues are in a very sublime manner exercised; viz. 1. Faith, by which the soul, quitting all discourse and doubting, believes and even perceives the divine presence, by which she conquers the world, exalting herself so much above all created things that they are out of her sight. 2. Hope, because the soul, placing herself before God in the posture of a beggar, confidently expects that He will impart to her both the knowledge of His will and ability to fulfil it. 3 Love, because the soul resolutely affects nothing but correspondence to the divine love. 4. Resignation, since the soul forgets all private interests, has nothing at all to ask, neither repose nor business, but only whatsoever God would have her to enjoy, do, or suffer. 5. Patience, because herein the soul must expect to suffer many aridities, desolations, obscurities, incumbrances of thoughts, temptations, and other internal afflictions; whence it is that Thaulerus gives unto an exercise, much resembling this, the name of the afflicting exercise. 6. Purity, for the soul is hereby separated from all adhesion to creatures, being united to God only. 7. Mortification, of which here is the very quintessence, for when the soul acts in spirit only, then the flesh becomes insipid and without taste, saith St. Gregory. The flesh with all its desires is here slain, as it were, and buried out of the way; the eyes see nothing pleasing to sense, the ears hear nothing, the tongue is silent, a curtain is drawn before all images and representations in the memory, the will is separated from all created things, neither willing nor nilling any of them, but permitting God to will for her. 8. Obedience, for the understanding contracts and abases the wings of all discourses and disputes against anything that God commands. 9. Humility, in the most perfect degree, because the soul therein and thereby is even reduced to nothing. 10. In a word, here is adoration, sacrifice, devotion, and all graces united together, where creatures are excluded, and God with all His perfections is alone exposed to all the faculties of the soul to be contemplated by the mind, embraced by the will, and to be the sole object of all her operations: here is abstraction in perfection, and (as Thaulerus saith) all virtues are learnt in learning abstraction.

13. This is an exercise fit for all sorts almost, and all dispositions of souls. Learning is but a small furtherance, neither need it be any hindrance to it; it excludes no other kind of prayer, exercise, or devotion, for any kind of prayer may be used as a preparation to find God in the spirit; and that being once done, the soul is to chase away all objects that are not God, that she

may be united to Him alone, knowing Him most perfectly by ignorance; approaching to Him by resting and forbearing all motion, and conversing with Him most comfortably and profitably by silence. By this holy idleness in pure recollective prayer the soul attains to a clear and most comfortable experience of that which is obscurely apprehended by faith, and cannot be known by discourse. This is that (*mors angelorum*) death of angels (that St. Bernard desired), by virtue of which they regard not, neither live in themselves (as the apostate angels did), but in God only, and God in them. There is no other act of the understanding exercised in this, but that only which is the most perfect, to wit, simple intelligence, which is incapable of error, and the will seeks nothing, desires nothing, but enjoys all.

14. Now as touching the forementioned preparations, souls ought not to think themselves obliged to make use always of these, but to use their own liberty. That was an excellent preparation which the good, simple, devout old woman is said to use, who, when she set herself to her devotions in the church, said only: 'O my God, let that come to Thee which I wish, and let that befall me which Thou desirest;' and having said this, presently, with a belief of God's presence, she abandoned herself into God's hands, remaining in this silent busy idleness and negative knowledge, more full of fervour and light than all the speculations of the schools or studious meditations of cloisters.

15. Now whereas the author commends this exercise, both the perfect and imperfect, confidently affirming that any one may securely begin with it, even at the first entrance into a spiritual course, as many have done with great and speedy profit, I conceive that in such a case there will be need of more than ordinary courage in beginners to prosecute it; for their understandings and inward senses not yet being stored with good images to chase away vain distractions, nor their wills sufficiently inflamed with holy desires, it is not possible but they must often be assaulted terribly with most tedious aridities, passions, &c. They will be oft suspicious that they spend most of their recollections in a mere fruitless idleness, and so will be apt to fall into doubts and to betake themselves to unquiet consultations with others. But if they can avoid this and resolutely go on, notwithstanding these discouragements, no doubt they will reap inestimable benefits by it. But considering these great temptations and dangers, I should judge that the most secure way is not to adventure upon this exercise at the beginning, till one be arrived to the practice of immediate acts; and also, in the prosecution of it, it will be necessary to use great abstraction of life, and to practise likewise out of time of prayer the same internal silence, calming both the busy working of the imagination and stilling the motions of (even) good desires, both in study, working, saying the Office, &c.

16. Though the exercise be the same in substance at all times, yet by long practice it grows more and more pure and abstracted, the silence and introversion grow more profound, and the operations more imperceptible, and it will in time securely bring a soul to that which St. Teresa calls the prayer of quietness, which is indeed perfect contemplation, to which this is but an imperfect degree, and of which this is but a slight imitation.

17. Some spiritual writers do express the state and behaviour of a soul in such a kind of prayer as this, by this phrase, that the soul is then *aux escouttes;* that is, she is watching and attending what God will speak to her or work in her. This phrase is to some very suspicious and offensive, as if it implied that the practisers of such prayer did pretend to extraordinary visitations and favours, from which notwithstanding they are wholly averse; and they mean no more by the phrase, but only to signify that the most perfect disposition that a soul can put herself in to receive divine lights, and to be enabled to tend purely and spiritually to God, is by silencing all noise of creatures and their images, by quieting all motions of passions, by admitting no other operation of the understanding but simple intelligence of objects apprehended by faith, and lastly, by a real embracing with the will no other object but God Himself, without reflecting or professing that the will adheres to Him. It is surely a far more perfect expression of resignation to the divine will in any difficulty and affliction really and quietly to embrace it with perfect silence than to busy one's self with profession that one does embrace it, as also actually and indeed to love, than to say one loves, &c.

18. Now though no distinct reflecting or otherwise express acts either of the understanding or will are admitted into this exercise, yet the soul is far from that mere cessation or nonactuation professed by the frantic illuminates; for here the soul is in a case like to a tender mother with unspeakable satisfaction regarding her most amiable child: she all the while says nothing, neither thinks any express distinct thought of which she can give any account, yet both her mind and will also are busy, yea, the mind in one simple regard has the virtue of many long discourses, and the will in one quiet continued application has the quintessence of a thousand distinct affections. In like manner, a soul does actually regard God, and being in His presence she does really with adoration, humility, resignation, and love behave herself towards Him; and what need is there that she should tell Him that she does acknowledge His presence, or that she does adore, love, and resign herself to Him? She rather chooses the Psalmist's way of praising and serving God, who (instead of the Latin interpretation, *Te decet hymnus Deus in Sion,* Psalm lxiv.), in the Hebrew expression followed by the Septuagint, saith, *Domine tibi silentium laus est,*—'Silence is praise to Thee, O Lord;' and, indeed, the most effectual becoming praise of all other it is, proceeding out of a deep sense of His incomprehensible perfections and majesty, whom the

Seraphim contemplate by covering their faces, and glorify most perfectly in that profound and awful half-hour's silence mentioned in the Apocalypse.

19. Thus we conclude our instructions concerning the two inferior degrees of internal affective prayer. The remainder of this book will be employed about the blessed fruit of all our labours, to wit, perfect contemplation, the advices about which are not meant for the informing of those that are arrived thereto (for they have a divine light shining brightly in their hearts, beyond all human instructions), but for the encouragement of those that tend towards so divine a state, that will abundantly recompense all the labours, pains, bitternesses, and contradictions that occur in the way. Yea, though the well-minded soul should never in this life attain thereto, yet faithfully tending toward it to her last hour, she will not want even here a sufficient recompense of divine light and graces with an inestimable comfort of mind at her death, and afterwards she will not fail of the peculiar crown due to those that here do aspire to contemplation.

20. Let no excuses, therefore, be admitted, no incumbrances hinder souls (those especially whose profession and state is contemplation) to pursue the ways of prayer proper thereto, with all courage and perseverance; for, as St. Teresa saith, it is of great importance to have a resolute determination and fixed purpose of mind never to desist from diligent endeavour, until at length we come to drink of this water of life, I mean supernatural prayer. Labour, therefore, for it, come what will come from your labour, succeed what may succeed, though it cost never so great a price and never so much travail; let who will murmur at it, whether we attain to it or die in the way, although the heart faint and break asunder with the excessive pains undergone for it; yea, though all the world be in an uproar against it, and would fright us with telling of the dangers that are in the way.

THE THIRD TREATISE
THE FOURTH SECTION

OF CONTEMPLATION

Chapter I. Of Contemplation in General

1. Hitherto the exercises of a devout soul have been exceedingly laborious, in which she hath been obliged to use force and constraint (more or less) upon herself to elevate the will above all created things, and to apply it unto God. She hath struggled through terrible oppositions of the devil and corrupt nature, the instability of the imagination, tumultuousness of passions, &c., all which would hinder her perseverance in her recollections; but notwithstanding all this, pursuing them still, sometimes in light and sometimes in darkness, sometimes allured by sweetness, and again sometimes afflicted (but not discouraged) with desolations, in the end God crowns her courage and patience by exalting her to a new, more perfect, and divine exercise of the prayer of union or Contemplation.

2. Contemplation (in the accepted general notion of the word) signifies a clear, ready, mental seeing and quiet regarding of an object, being the result and effect of a precedent diligent and laborious inquiry and search after the nature, qualities, dependencies, and other circumstantial conditions of it.

3. Now according to the nature of the object contemplated, and the disposition or end of the person contemplating, there are several sorts of contemplation (at least so called). For, in the first place, anciently there was a certain kind of false contemplation, which we may call philosophical, practised by some learned heathens of old, and imitated by some in these days, which hath for its last and best end only the perfection of knowledge, and a delightful complacency in it. Others there were (and it is to be feared are still) that contented themselves with an airy vain renown, which they hoped to gain by their knowledge; so that whatsoever was the object of their contemplation (whether things natural, moral, yea, or even divine, as far as by wit and subtilty or tradition they could be known), self-love and pride was the utmost end of all these contemplations. Yea, to this rank of philosophical contemplations may be referred those scholastic wits which spend much time in the study and subtle examination of the mysteries of faith, and have not for their end the increasing of divine love in their hearts; nay, these are indeed more imperfect and culpable (saith Albertus Magnus, *Lib. de Adhær. Deo*) inasmuch as they offend against a greater and supernatural light.

4. Yea, and those among them that do truly intend, as their last and principal end, the glory of God and seeking His divine love (which is the best sort of scholastic contemplatives), yet since their chief employment consists in much internal discourse and reasoning, which cannot be practised without various and distinct sensible images by which to represent God, &c., the knowledge which they attain to is not properly contemplative, and the highest degree of prayer that they arrive unto is only a perfect kind of meditation.

5. In the second place, there is a mystic contemplation which is, indeed, truly and properly such, by which a soul without discoursings and curious speculations, without any perceptible use of the internal senses or sensible images, by a pure, simple, and reposeful operation of the mind, in the obscurity of faith, simply regards God as infinite and incomprehensible verity, and with the whole bent of the will rests in Him as (her) infinite, universal, and incomprehensible good. This is true contemplation indeed, and as rest is the end of motion, so is this the end of all other both internal and external exercises; for therefore, by long discourse and much practise of affection, the soul inquires and tends to a worthy object that she may quietly contemplate it, and (if it deserve affection) repose with contentment in it.

6. So it is in prayer: the soul aspiring to a perfect union with God, as yet absent, begins with inquiry by meditation; for, as St. Augustine saith, *In-*

tellectus cogitabundus principium omnis boni; that is, All good proceeds from the understanding as its first principle. By meditation the soul labours to represent this divine object with all the sensible advantages and motives of admiration and love that it can invent, to the end the will by pure love may rest in Him; but this being done, the will being not yet at free liberty to dispose of itself, is forced with some violence to untwine and withdraw its adhesion from creatures, that it may elevate itself and be firmly fixed to this her only good, and at last, by long custom, the force by little and little diminishing, the object begins to appear in its own perfect light, and the affections flow freely, but yet with a wonderful stillness, to it; and then such souls are said to be arrived to perfect mystical union or contemplation.

7. This is properly the exercise of angels, for their knowledge is not by discourse; but by one simple intuition all objects are represented to their view at once, with all their natures, qualities, relations, dependencies, and effects; but man, that receives all his knowledge first from his senses, can only by effects and outward appearances with the labour of reasoning collect the nature of objects, and this but imperfectly; but his reasoning being ended, then he can at once contemplate all that is known unto him in the object.

8. Now in Holy Scripture our chiefest happiness and perfection are said to consist in this, that we shall be like unto angels both in our knowledge and love, for we shall (as they) have a perfect view and contemplation of God as He is, not by any created forms and representations; and so beatifical shall that contemplation be, that it will for ever ingulf all our affections. But in this life our perfection will consist in approaching as near as may be to such an angelical contemplation of God without sensible forms, and as He is indeed proposed by faith, that is, not properly represented, but obscure notions imprinted in our minds concerning Him, by which we do perceive that He is not anything that we can perceive or imagine, but an inexhaustible ocean of universal being and good, infinitely exceeding our comprehension; which being and good, whatsoever it is in itself, we love with the whole possible extension of our wills, embracing God beyond the proportion of our knowing Him; but yet even such a contemplation and love in this life, by reason of our bodily weakness and necessities, cannot be without many descents and interruptions.

9. This mystic contemplation or union is of two sorts: 1. Active and ordinary, being indeed an habitual state of perfect souls by which they are enabled, whensoever fit occasion shall be, to unite themselves actively and actually to God by efficacious, fervent, amorous, and constant, yet withal silent and quiet, elevations of the spirit. 2. Passive and extraordinary; the which is not a state but an actual grace and favour from God, by which He is pleased at certain times, according to His free good pleasure, to communicate

a glimpse of His majesty to the spirits of His servants, after a secret and wonderful manner. And it is called Passive, not but that therein the soul doth actively contemplate God, but she can neither, when she pleases, dispose herself thereto, nor yet refuse it when that God thinks good to operate after such a manner in the soul, and to represent himself unto her by a divine particular image, not at all framed by the soul, but supernaturally infused into her; which grace is seldom, if ever, afforded but to souls that have attained to the former state of perfect active union. Concerning this Passive Union and the several kinds of it, we shall speak more hereafter.

10. As for the former sort, which is active contemplation, of which we have already treated in gross in this chapter, we read in mystic authors, Thaulerus, Harphius, &c., that he that would become spiritual ought to practise the drawing of his external senses inwardly into his internal, there losing and, as it were, annihilating them. Having done this, he must then draw his internal senses into the superior powers of the soul, and there annihilate them likewise; and those powers of the intellectual soul he must draw into that which is called their unity, which is the principle and fountain from whence those powers do flow, and in which they are united. And lastly, that unity (which alone is capable of perfect union with God) must be applied and firmly fixed on God, and herein, say they, consist the perfect divine contemplation and union of an intellectual soul with God.

11. Now whether such expressions as these will abide the strict examination of philosophy or no, I will not take on me to determine; certain it is that by a frequent and constant exercise of internal prayer of the will, joined with mortification, the soul comes to operate more and more abstracted from sense, and more elevated above the corporal organs and faculties, so drawing nearer to the resemblance of the operations of an angel or separated spirit.

. Yet this abstraction and elevation (perhaps) are not to be understood as if the soul in these pure operations had no use at all of the internal senses or sensible images (for the schools resolve that cannot consist with the state of a soul joined to a mortal body); but surely her operations in this pure degree of prayer are so subtile and intime, and the images that she makes use of so exquisitely pure and immaterial, that she cannot perceive at all that she works by images, so that spiritual writers are not much to be condemned by persons utterly inexperienced in these mystic affairs, if delivering things as they perceived by their own experience they have expressed them otherwise than will be admitted in the schools.

13. Now to this kind of purely intellectual operations doth a soul begin to arrive after a sufficient exercise of immediate acts of the will, and

having attained thereto they do grow more and more spiritual and sublime by the exercise of aspirations and blind elevations without all limit.

14. I call them pure intellectual operations, in opposition to actuations imaginative, produced by mean of gross sensible images, and not as if the said operations were in the intellect or understanding; for, on the contrary, they are exercised in a manner wholly by the will, for in proper aspirations the soul hath no other use of the understanding but only antecedently to propose an object, which is no other but only a general obscure confused notion of God, as faith darkly teaches, and this rather virtually than directly and expressly, the main business being to elevate the will and unite it to God so presented.

15. In which union (above all particular images) there is neither time nor place, but all is vacuity and emptiness, as if nothing were existent but God and the soul; yea, so far is the soul from reflecting on her own existence, that it seems to her that God and she are not distinct, but one only thing; this is called by some mystic authors the state of nothingness, by others the state of totality; because therein God is all in all, the container of all things. And the prayer proper to this state is thus described by a holy hermit in Cassian (collat. x. c. ii.): *Ita ad illam orationis incorruptionem mens nostra perveniat,* &c.; that is, So will the mind ascend to that pure simplicity of prayer, the which is freed from all intuition of images, undistinguished with any prosecution of words or senses, but uttered internally by an inflamed intention of the mind, by an unutterable excess of affection, and inconceivable quickness and alacrity of spirit, which prayer, the spirit being abstracted from all senses and sensible objects, doth pour forth unto God by sighs and groans that cannot be expressed.

16. It is an error, therefore, of inexperienced persons, who think and say that all the exercises and thoughts of contemplatives are actually in heaven, in interior conversation with angels and saints, tasting of the joys of paradise, or wholly employed in sublime speculations about divine mysteries of the Trinity, Incarnation, &c.; true it is, that in a Passive Union, God may, after a clear and distinct but wonderful manner, represent any or all these things by a supernatural species imprinted in the soul. But as for the proper exercise of active contemplation, it consists not at all in speculation, but in blind elevations of the will, and ingulfing it more and more profoundly in God, with no other sight or knowledge of Him but of an obscure faith only.

17. This happy state of active contemplation is, for substance, the most perfect that the soul is capable of in this life, being almost an entire reparation and restitution of the soul to the state of primitive innocence for as long as it lasts; because then the soul is freed from all sinfully-distracting

images and affections that would separate her from God. Hereupon a holy hermit, in Cassian, says that, except in the very actual exercise of contemplation, a soul is not only in an imperfect state, but also in an immediate disposition to a sinful defect, by reason that where God doth not wholly possess the soul, the very images of creatures cannot but more or less defile her. How comfortable, therefore, and how only secure is a life of prayer!

18. Those that are inexperienced may, and often do, call this a state of idleness and unprofitable cessation, as Martha complained against her sister Mary; but those that have attained to a taste of it know it to be the *business of all businesses,* as St. Bernard calls it. True it is they do not, without a special and certain inspiration from God, interest themselves in external businesses, nor perhaps employ much of their time and devotions in express prayers for common necessities; yet those inexpressible devotions which they exercise, and in which they tacitly involve the needs of the whole Church, are far more prevalent with God than the busy endeavours and prayers of ten thousand others. A few such secrets and unknown servants of God are the chariots and horsemen, the strength and bulwarks of the kingdoms and churches where they live.

19. I know that some mystic authors do constitute several distinct states following active contemplation. As Barbanson makes mention of the state of the Divine Presence in the soul, and after that of the Manifestation of God to the spirit, &c., and in all these great variety of ascents and descents, &c.; likewise F. Ben. Canfield, in his last and most perfect state of the essential and supereminent will of God, makes mention of several distinct exercises, as denudation, an active and passive annihilation, &c. These authors, perhaps, spoke according to the experience of the divine operations in their own souls, and with regard to their particular manner of prayer. Therefore, I conceive that what they deliver needs not be esteemed a common measure for all; neither will I deny but that there may be distinct states (some of which I will mention), as the great desolation, &c.; but it will be to no purpose to search closely into then. Those happy souls whom God shall so highly favour as to bring them to the mount of vision and contemplation will have no need of light from any but God to conduct them in those hidden divine paths, and the inexperienced will reap but little profit from such curious inquiries.

20. I will therefore content myself with delivering in a general manner, 1. the nature of the prayer proper to the state of active contemplation; 2. and from thence I will proceed to treat modestly concerning Passive Union, and the several kinds of it; 3. to which I will add a brief discourse of that great desolation which usually follows the said union; 4. and then I will conclude the whole book with a very short description of the state of Perfection.

Chapter II. Of the Prayer of Aspirations

§§ 1, 2. Of the prayer proper to the state of contemplation: to wit, Aspira-
tions; and why they are so called.

§ 3. Examples of aspirations.

§§ 4, 5, 6, 7, 8, 9, 10. Agreement and difference between aspirations, and
other internal acts.

§§ 11, 12, 13, 14, 15. How a soul becomes ripe for aspirations, and passes to
them.

§§ 16, 17. Aspirations may be exercised in external business; and why?

§§ 18, 19, 20, 21, 22. Great variety of aspirations: to wit, with or without
words, &c.

§§ 23, 24, &c. The great benefit and fruits of aspirations.

1. Internal prayer proper to the state of active contemplation consists of certain most purely spiritual operations of the will, longing and thirsting after God, and an union with Him in the supreme point of the spirit, where His most proper dwelling is.

2. These perfect operations are by spiritual authors severally named, as elevations, inward stirrings of the spirit, Aspirations, &c.; we will in the following discourse make use, for the most part, of this last term of Aspirations, as most proper in a general notion to express the said operations. For, 1. By them the soul in a holy ambition doth aspire to raise and elevate herself out, of inferior nature, and to mount to the *apicem spiritus,* which is God's throne. 2. By them the soul being inflamed with divine love doth breathe forth her ardent affections to God, as the heart forces the lungs to send forth that air which they had formerly sucked in, that they may draw in fresher air to refrigerate it; so that in both there is a quick reciprocal motion of emptying and filling, of rising and falling; for after every aspiration there is a short descent, and then a mounting higher than before. 3. Because, as our outward breathing is an action, as it were, purely natural, performed without any labour at all, or so much as election, so a soul rooted in charity breathes forth these pure Aspirations without any force used upon herself, they flowing from her freely (both as to the matter and manner of them) and in a sort naturally. 4. Because, as the motions made in breathing do not hinder (but rather advance) all other motions and operations, so may Aspirations be exercised during other ordinary employments without any prejudice to either, or without any considerable distraction, except they be such businesses that do require a special fixed attention of the mind with serious study. Now in such employments, if they be imposed by necessity or obedience, the soul ought to

371

quit her Aspirations, and so doing she will gain as much by her obedience as she would by prayer.

3. Now these Aspirations are certain short and lively affections of the soul, by which she expresses a thirsty longing after God, such as these are: 'My God, when shall I love Thee alone? When shall I be united to Thee? Whom have I in heaven or earth but Thee alone? O that Thou wouldst live and reign alone in my soul! O my God, Thou alone sufficest me! Dost not Thou know, O my God, that I love Thee only? Let me be nothing, and be Thou all, O my God. O love! O love! O infinite, universal good! When shall I come and appear before the face of Thee, O my God? Let me love Thee only, and that is sufficient! When shall I die, that my God alone may live in me?' &c.

4. Now the same affections (such as these) that are used in the prayer of Aspirations, may also be used, forasmuch as concerns the expression and sense of them, in the exercise of immediate acts, and even in meditation itself; but yet the manner by which the soul produces the said affections are, in many respects, different in perfect and imperfect souls, and the said Aspirations are of a quite different nature from other forced immediate acts of the will.

5. For, first, such fervorous affections, tending directly and immediately to God, are the entire matter in the exercise of Aspirations; whereas in immediate acts they are only now and then interlaced; but the ordinary matter of such acts is the doing or forbearing anything for God, as in acts of resignation, &c.

6. Secondly, in those immediate acts and affections in which there are no images of creatures involved, but which respect God immediately, He is represented by some distinct image or express notion in the mind, as by some special attribute, perfection, name, similitude, &c. But a soul, after a long practice of internal abstraction and renouncing of all representations of God, contents herself with such a confused notion of Him as may be apprehended by an obscure general faith; that is to say, not simply and absolutely with no kind of image at all (for that is supposed inconsistent with the operations of the soul whilst it is in a mortal body), but not with a distinct, formal, chosen, particular image; for all such offering themselves are rejected by perfect souls; so that if they were to give an account of what they conceive in their minds when they intend to think of God, all that they could say would be, God is nothing of all that I can say or think, but a Being infinitely beyond it, and absolutely incomprehensible by a created understanding. He is what He is, and what Himself only perfectly knows, and so I believe Him to be, and as such I adore and love Him only; I renounce all pretending to a distinct knowing of Him, and content myself with such a blind believing. Now

though imperfect souls also (especially such as are learned) do acknowledge this negative apprehension of God to be only truly proper and perfect, yet, by reason that gross images are not yet chased out of their minds, they cannot in their internal operations proceed constantly according to such an acknowledgment. Such an obscure negative object will not ordinarily move their affections, whereas no other but such an object will move the affections of perfect souls.

7. Thirdly, proper Aspirations in perfect souls have no precedent discourse at all, as acts have, at least virtually; neither doth the will in Aspirations intend to employ or make use of the understanding, for they are sudden elevations of the will without any previous motive or consideration.

8. Fourthly, immediate acts are not only produced with deliberation and choice, but ordinarily with some degree of force used apon the will. But Aspirations proceed from an interior impulse, indeliberately, and as it were naturally flowing from the soul, and thereby they show that there is in the interior a secret, supernatural, directing principle, to wit, God's Holy Spirit alone, teaching and moving the soul to breathe forth these Aspirations, not only in set recollections, but almost continually. Now this doth not infer that the Holy Spirit is not also the principle of all other good acts and affections of the will (for none of them have any true good in them further than they proceed from this divine principle); but in them the will doth previously and forcibly raise up itself to the producing them, in which, likewise, much of nature is mixed; and so the Holy Spirit is not so completely and perfectly the fountain of them as He is of Aspirations.

9. Fifthly, in case that a soul, whose constant exercise as yet is but immediate acts or meditation, do sometimes merely by an internal impulse produce such indeliberate Aspirations, yet they are neither so pure and subtile, neither will they continue any considerable time; but the present invitation or fervour being passed, the soul must be content to return to her inferior exercises, or if she will needs force herself to continue them, her recollections will become dry, insipid, and without any profit at all.

10. Lastly, Aspirations (when they are a soul's usual exercise) do proceed from a more habitually perfect ground, and, therefore, are far more efficacious and noble than immediate acts; and, moreover, there being no violence at all used in them, they are much more frequently and continuedly produced, and, consequently, do procure more new graces and merits, and do far more increase the habit of charity.

11. No man can limit the time how long souls are to continue in inferior exercises before they will be enabled and made ripe for so sublime a prayer, and, therefore, there is no relying upon the instructions, practice, or examples of any; all depends 1. Upon the industry or diligence of souls in

prayer and mortification; 2. somewhat upon their special temper and disposition; 3. likewise upon the advantage that they may have from solitude and abstraction of life; 4. but principally upon the free grace and good pleasure of God, who may and does, by ordinary or extraordinary means, call and enable souls to Aspirations, some sooner and some later.

12. In passing from the exercise of acts to Aspirations there is, as to the manner of the cessation of forced acts, great variety in souls; for some will have their morning recollections to be suddenly and entirely changed from forced acts to Aspirations, and also the ability for a longer continuance increased; whereas, the evening recollections will be little altered. In other souls (and this is most ordinary), their exercising of acts will grow by degrees more and more aspirative, and this will happen sometimes in the beginning, sometimes in the middle, and sometimes in the conclusion of their recollections. And thus they in their recollections will get more and more ground upon acts, diminishing both the frequency and constraint or difficulty of them, and increasing Aspirations, till in progress they become wholly aspirative.

13. Some souls, whose exercise is acts mixed with Aspirations, at their first coming to their recollections, yea, and till they have for some reasonable space exercised themselves, may happen to find themselves in perfect distraction; in which case, if they be called away by occasion of businesses of no great solicitude, they may find much profit by such interruptions, and be disposed thereby to return with much eagerness to their recollections, and with an enablement to exercise Aspirations. Yea, sometimes they will find themselves enabled to exercise them during such employments, their spirits being refreshed by means of such pauses and distances caused by the said interruptions. And experience will teach them that it will be needful sometimes to break off the course of their present internal prayer for some little space, after which they will find themselves better disposed for more frequent and efficacious Aspirations.

14. But as for imperfect souls, this must be no rule for them, for they must not, by reason of distractions, interrupt their mental prayer (or, at least, very seldom), but must with discreet violence force themselves to begin with a serious recollection, by that means driving away, or, at least, abating their present distractions.

15. When the exercise is become wholly Aspirations, all the change that will happen afterward will not be in the substance of the exercise, but only in the degrees of purity, subtilty, and spiritualness of those Aspirations, for there is no active exercise more sublime.

16. A soul may come to that state that she may constantly breathe forth Aspirations, and yet, sufficiently to the discharge of her obligation, either work, read, hearken to a lesson recited, say or hear Mass, communicate, &c.; neither is there any negligence or irreverence committed by so doing; for by no operation so much as by Aspirations doth a soul enjoy a sublime and perfect union in spirit with God, which is the end of all exercises and duties. And this is the meaning of that saying of mystics, 'In God nothing is neglected;' yea, some of them do affirm that there may be souls so perfect, that even amidst the noises and disorders of a camp they may, without neglecting their present duty there, most efficaciously exercise themselves in Aspirations to God.

17. Now the reason why Aspirations are less hindered by external businesses than are meditation or immediate acts is, because in Aspirations the understanding is scarce at all employed, and, therefore, may well enough attend to other businesses; and, moreover, the will, abounding and even overflowing with divine love, will not find herself interested in affection, and, consequently, not distracted by such employments.

18. There is great variety in the manner of producing Aspirations; for, first, some are purely mental, being certain indeliberate quick elevations and springings up of the spirit to Godward, as sparkles of fire flying from a burning coal (which is the expression of the author of the *Cloud of Unknowing*) And of these some are more gross and imaginative, especially in beginners, and, therefore, not difficult to be expressed; others, in more perfect souls that are come to a higher degree of spiritual abstraction, grow more subtle and intellectual, insomuch as ofttimes the person himself cannot express what passed in his spirit, which was, indeed, nothing but a blind and almost imperceptible elevation of the will exercised in the summity of the spirit, as it happens ofttimes in the great desolation. Now this growth of immateriality in Aspirations is not easily perceptible, though it be real and certain, as we know that corn grows though we cannot perceive its growing, and, indeed, it is no great matter whether we observe such degrees or no; yea, the examination thereof were better neglected.

19. Again, other Aspirations are, moreover, externally expressed by the tongue, and in such expressions sometimes there is a proper sense and meaning, as *Deus meus et omnia* (which was St. Francis's aspiration), or, *Noverim Te et noverim me* (which was St. Augustine's); and in these sometimes a soul doth abide a good space, reiterating again and again the same aspiration; sometimes she doth vary, always proceeding according to her interior impulse from God's Holy Spirit: other aspirations have no sense at all, as were those practised by Br. Mussæus, a disciple of St. Francis, who, when, he was full of interior affection, could usually cry out nothing but *U. U. U.*

Such unusual aspirations as these do show a great excess of interior fervour, which, bursting out, forces the soul (not able to contain itself, nor yet to find out words by which to express its affection) to pour forth itself after such an insignificant manner.

20. Moreover, Aspirations and forcible elevations of the will there are which are signified, not by the tongue, but by some extraordinary action of the body, as clapping of hands, leaping, &c. To this purpose we have an example of another disciple of St. Francis, called Br. Bernard, who, out of an inward boiling fervour, was forced to run over mountains and rocky places, being agitated with a kind of holy frenzy. In such cases as these, tears are very rare, God's Holy Spirit not usually moving thereto, because they would then flow immeasurably, to the great prejudice of corporal health.

21. Now such actions and motions, though they may be yielded to sometimes when one is alone, yet in company they are to be suppressed. To which purpose Blosius gives this good instruction out of Thaulerus, that albeit these things be good, as flowing from a divine principle, yet they are not the things principally to be commended, for these unions of the spirit with God, to which corporal nature concurs, are not to be equalled to that most perfect union which some souls do experience in pure spirit; and, therefore, it is observable that such violent agitations do chiefly befall such souls as have had their exercise much in sensible devotion, as women and devout ignorant men; and on the same grounds such are more disposed to rapts, ecstasies, &c.

22. Lastly, to these several expressions of Aspirations may be added that of saying the Divine Office or other vocal prayers aspiratively, which is a far greater proof of sublime contemplation than any of those unusual motions, &c. This was the contemplation of many of the ancient hermits, and is, no doubt, of some in these days. As a certain spiritual writer says of himself, that being in the constant exercise of aspirations, using daily two recollections consisting of them, on a time he found himself invited to produce them vocally, and thereupon he took in hand the saying of our Lady's Office, choosing that because he could say it perfectly without book; he repeated it nine or ten times a day with a perfect attention of spirit, the which mental attention or operation was, in effect, but Aspirations (taking the word, as here we do, in a large sense); and so for a few days, as long as that invitation and enablement lasted, he used no other internal exercise, finding great benefit by this; but that invitation ceasing, he found himself again obliged to return to mere mental Aspirations.

23. I will conclude this point with setting down some of the great and inestimable benefits that accrue to souls by this sublime exercise; as, first, in regard of the interior senses and sensitive faculties: the dominion that the superior soul has over them is now become very great, for inasmuch as it is

God that helpeth, moveth, and directeth souls in their operations during this exercise of Aspirations, the heart also being estranged from the love of creatures and replenished with divine love, distractive thoughts and images of creatures either do not press into the mind, or if they do, yet they pass no further than into the imagination; or if the understanding do sometimes busy itself with them, yet they do scarce or not at all touch or affect the will, which is not by such extravagant thoughts interrupted or diverted in her pursuit of Aspirations and blind elevations; whereas, in immediate forced acts greater force is to be used against such distractions, which do not only busy the understanding, but likewise, more or less, withdraw the will from God.

24. Secondly, in regard of sensible devotion: though the devil may have great influence upon it in meditation, or even sometimes in immediate affections and acts, seeking thereby to seduce souls to extravagances and a spiritual gluttony, it is otherwise in the exercise of Aspirations, which are so much elevated above the imagination and sensitive nature, that here he has no advantage given him for such deceits; and if during that sensible devotion, which in some souls, during this exercise, flows from the spirit into inferior nature, he should endeavour to inject his baits, an humble and perfectly mortified soul will easily turn his malice to her own good and the enemy's confusion.

25. Thirdly, in regard of the understanding: whereas it was before all bepainted with images of creatures, yea, when it regarded God, it saw Him by an image of its own creating, now the soul loses all remembrance of itself and of all created things, and all that she retains of God is a remembrance that He cannot be seen nor comprehended. All creatures, therefore, being removed, and no particular distinct image of God admitted, there remains in the soul and mind, as it were, a nothing and mere emptiness, which nothing is more worth than all creatures, for it is all that we can know of God in this life; this nothing is the rich inheritance of perfect souls, who perceive clearly that God is nothing of all that may be comprehended by our senses or understanding. The state, therefore, of such souls, forasmuch as concerns knowledge, is worthily called the 'cloud of unknowing' and the 'cloud of forgetting' by the author of that sublime treatise so called; and this is the most perfect and most angelical knowing that a soul is capable of in this life. Now this perception of this nothing doth appear more clearly and comfortably the longer that a soul remains under this cloud and darkness, where God's dwelling is; for, as the Psalmist saith, this *darkness is* immediately *under his feet;* this knowledge of nothing is, by F. Benet Canfield, called an active annihilation.

26. Fourthly, in regard of the will: it is in this exercise so wholly possessed and inflamed with divine love, which doth so intimely penetrate

into the very centre of it, that it is become like fiery, burning steel, clean through shining with this fire. It is now a will deiform, and in a manner deified, for it is so closely united and hidden in the Divine Will, that God may be said to will and do all things in and by her.

27. Fifthly, in regard of the whole person: till a soul be arrived unto this exercise, she never attains to a perfect possession of all virtues universally; they are, indeed, all in an inferior degree and with much mixture of natural, sensual ends, produced by the former exercises; and if some special virtues seem to be in a high degree, it is either because nature disposes more to them, or because the practice of them may be more suitable to some designs of nature; but as soon as by the exercise of Aspirations divine love is far more perfectly exercised, the very root of all sin (self-love) is destroyed, and purity of intention is practised to God for Himself only, and only by His instruction and motion. The divine love that the soul exercised before was immediately upon herself with relation to God, and not directly and immediately to God Himself; or if so sometimes, yet it was with reflections upon herself; but in Aspirations she exercises love only to God Himself without reflections, which cannot be exercised but by souls perfectly mortified, being the highest mystic contemplation possible to be exercised in this life; for, as Alphonsus Madriliensis saith, a soul is never able to produce a proper act of love to God till she have first got a perfect hatred of herself, which is the supreme degree of mortification, which once attained, she is ripe for a passive union, and perhaps at the very door of it.

28. The author of the *Cloud,* and likewise Barbanson, do with great reason teach, that after a soul is mounted to this degree of exercising love constantly by Aspirations, she is not in any difficulty, aridity, &c., to descend to any inferior exercise; herein differing from F. Benet Canfield and some others, who require some exercise of the Passion in all estates.

Chapter III. Of Passive Unions

§§ 22, 23, 24, 25. How a soul is to behave herself with humility and disaffection in regard of these extraordinary favours.

§§ 26, 27, 28, 29, 30, 31, 32, 33, 34, 35. In what cases the judgment of a prudent director is necessary.

§§ 36, 37, 38. In what cases some souls may follow their own light.

§§ 39, 40. In what sense ecstasies are supernatural.

1. Hitherto, of the exercise of perfect Active Union or Contemplation: I call it perfect, because though in every degree of prayer there is a proportionable degree of union of the soul with God, yet perfect union is only in this of Aspirations, but so as that it may increase in degrees, and grow more and more immediate without all limits; but how much soever it increases, it will never exceed that obscure light which faith affords, which is the most perfect light that we can have in this life (for to see God as He is, is reserved for the future life). Now though even the most imperfect have this light of faith, yet in their inferior contemplations they do, for the most part, make use of and follow their natural light, regarding such images and representations of God as they frame in their imagination or by discourse; but in perfect contemplation this light of faith is the only light.

2. But besides these active unions, there are other unions and contemplations which are passive and extraordinary, by which God reveals Himself unto the soul by a supernatural species impressed in her, in which He is the only agent, and she the patient; not as if when a soul does contemplate God she were not in some sort active, but because by no dispositions or preparations that the soul can use can she assuredly procure them; but when God is pleased graciously to communicate them, the soul is taken out of her own disposal, and does and must see and think only what God will have her, and this no longer than His good pleasure is such.

3. Now such supernatural graces are either: 1. sensible; or, 2. purely intellectual. The former are the most imperfect and least efficacious to cause a gracious good disposition in the soul that receives them.

4. Of sensible unions, the most imperfect and least to be relied upon are: 1. Those which by God are communicated to the outward senses, as apparitions visible to the eyes; words framed in the air by the operation of Angels; alterations made in the other senses, as in the smell, by a grateful odour presented thereto; in the palate, by a pleasant taste caused therein, &c.; of which kind of favours, divers examples occur in spiritual authors, to which may be added the gift of tears, warmth about the heart, &c., and (which seems to be the highest kind of sensible favours) a splendour seen in the eyes and countenances of God's Saints, betokening an inward purity; likewise elevation of the body, ability to walk on the water, or to pass through doors

whilst they are shut, and other suchlike, resembling the qualities of glorified bodies. Now though the devil can counterfeit these, yet they are seldom given by God, but He withal gives an assurance that they are from Him.

5. A second sort of sensible graces, more sublime than the former, are such as are by God communicated to the internal senses, especially the imagination, infusing supernatural images into it, by which God sometimes makes known His will either immediately or by the disposition of Angels, so as the persons will perceive words imaginatively spoken, or think they see an Angel or Saint, as if such words had indeed been spoken, and those objects represented really to the outward senses; for such is the nature of the imagination that it can, after its manner, exercise all the functions of the outward senses.

6. Of such supernatural inactions of God upon the soul by means of the internal senses, the most notable effects are raptures or ecstasies, likewise internal visions and apparitions, which go together sometimes, and sometimes are separated.

7. Now a rapture or ecstasy is an elevation of the soul caused by God, by which the person is bereaved of the use of the outward senses, by reason that the soul in her internal operations cleaves wholly to supernatural things, and the imagination is environed with lights, visions, &c. And all this is done to the end that the person may internally know and see what is God's pleasure to reveal unto him, for the good either of himself or any other.

8. My purpose is not to treat nicely of these matters (for which the reader is referred to Joannes a Jesu-Maria, a discalced Carmelite, who treats of them with great exactness); I will content myself with insisting: 1. On the ways of discerning true visions, raptures, &c., from false; 2. and affording instructions how a soul ought to behave herself about them.

9. Now, for a preparation to the following rules of discerning, I will lay these grounds: 1. That the devil cannot immediately operate either on the understanding or will, but only by imprinting new, or disposing the images already in the fancy, or by moving the sensitive appetite. 2. By consequence, if the lights imprinted in the understanding by means of raptures, visions, &c., do direct to real good (as to the love of God, humility, &c.), and that the will entertains these good affections, a soul may prudently and rationally ascribe the cause to God.

10. The rules of discerning, delivered by both ancient and modern holy authors, are these which follow: the first, When the will is moved without the ordinary precedent action of the understanding or imagination, and also in the same instant a certain new light is communicated to the mind, a soul may be confident that it comes from the Divine Spirit.

11. The second rule: Good observation is to be made whether the persons be Christianly disposed, not much swayed by curiosity or pride, not addicted to melancholy, &c.; whether by such favours they be not invited to say or do something contrary to Catholic truth, peace, obedience, honesty, purity, humility, &c., and, accordingly, souls are to judge from what principles they flow.

12. The third rule: Divine spiritual unions, visions, &c., are ordinarily of short continuance.

13. The fourth rule: Apparitions of good spirits, although in the beginning they cause a trembling and amazement, yet in the end the soul receives courage and comfort, finds herself illuminated, inflamed with devotion, and in great peace; whereas, when the devil grows familiar with any, though he appear in never so fearful and horrible shapes, the persons are not affrighted, and he leaves them as he found them.

14. The fifth rule: It is ordinarily the mark of a good spirit: 1. When he effectually shows that his power accompanies his will, as when upon his saying, 'Fear not,' the person presently becomes quiet. 2. When his words are clear, intelligible, and so delightful, that the soul doth diligently observe and remember the pronunciation of every word and syllable. 3. When the person thinks himself obliged to attend to what is said. 4. When the soul conceives much more by those holy and divine words than in themselves they signify. 5. When there remains in the soul an assurance that what is said shall certainly be effected, &c. All these are signs of a good spirit, saith St. Teresa.

15. The sixth rule: The receiving of any extraordinary outward favours or gifts, as roses, rings, jewels, &c., is much to be suspected, unless such things happen to souls of a long-continued sanctity, and that they be rather miraculously revealed after their death than divulged during their life. The like judgment is to be made of outward characters imprinted on bodies, as the name of Jesus, marks of our Lord's wounds, &c.

16. The seventh rule: When souls, after the practice of long and severe austerities, come to enjoy much peace and contentment, both external and internal, especially if such favours be overmuch in sense, and not greatly relishing of the spirit, or if they be never so little indecent &c., it is much to be feared that the devil has a great influence upon such a change; and, therefore, such persons ought to persevere in fear and penance, not trusting upon their good works past, but humbly beseeching God to preserve them from the enemy's illusions.

17. The eighth rule: Ecstasies that do not produce considerable profit either to the persons themselves or others deserve to be suspected; and when any marks of their approaching are perceived, the persons ought to divert their minds some other way.

18. The ninth rule: The appearance of objects, how beautiful and celestial soever, ought not suddenly to be welcomed, nor affection to be placed upon them, for the devil hath been permitted to take on him the shape even of our Blessed Lord Himself; and if in such visitations the persons feel any impure motions, or fall into indecent postures, &c., whatsoever reluctance they make against them, they ought to judge that they proceed from an ill principle; yet if a soul, being surprised with any seemingly glorious false apparition, should either afford veneration or unfitting affection thereto, she ought not to be much dejected for what is past, since the error committed was only material.

19. The tenth rule: It is very suspicious to see a soul that is very young in a spiritual course, or that is not of extraordinary purity, to fall into raptures, &c.; for great mortification with prayer is requisite to make a soul ripe for the divine inaction.

20. The eleventh rule: It is no proof at all of the want of grace and charity in persons to be troubled with diabolical apparitions, &c., if thereby there be wrought in them no other ill effects besides molestations and affliction; yea, in that case it may reasonably be judged that they are strongly assisted with God's Holy Spirit, since they overcome so great temptations of the evil spirit.

21. The twelfth and last rule: It cannot proceed from a good spirit, when souls visited with revelations, &c., shall obstinately believe them to be of God, after they have been condemned by experienced superiors and directors, unless the persons be able to yield most convincing proofs thereof, and, moreover, shall seriously profess that God, together with the secrets revealed, hath imprinted in their souls this assurance and belief also. Certain it is that obedience is a most secure remedy against all possible inconveniences, and can do no harm in any cases. This is that that St. Teresa seriously enjoins, and most constantly practised herself; and this in very strange circumstances, when the confessarius condemning her was both unlearned and impertinent, &c. But withal, spiritual directors ought not to be rash in their proceedings, nor to judge till after a long experience and knowledge of the inward dispositions of the persons, and a due weighing of the nature of the revelations discovered to them. It is likewise requisite that those that take upon them to judge of these things be themselves devout, exercised in prayer, and in good state towards God, to the end that they may from Him receive light to direct others.

22. In the next place, as touching the manner how a soul, after receiving of such supernatural favours, is to behave herself. The principal care that she ought to have is, that she do not bear a deliberate and fixed love to such things (which is due to God only), and, consequently, that she do not,

either expressly or implicitly, pray to God to have such visions, revelations, &c.; or in case that God, without her prayers, hath sent them, that she do not usually, without necessity, talk of such matters, or love to hear others talk of them; for these are signs of an undue affection to them.

23. St. John of the Cross saith, that when God doth, after an extraordinary manner, make known unto humble souls His will that they should take in hand some great employment, by means whereof they may likely gain a great esteem of excellency, and, probably, will be in danger to conceive some extraordinary worth to be in themselves, for which they are so highly favoured by God (which conceit the devil will not fail to cherish and increase), He doth oftentimes rather increase than diminish the fear and repugnance that they had formerly to such things, causing in them a desire and readiness much rather to the undergoing of some vile or base offices. Thus He dealt with Moses, when He had sent him to Pharaoh, and thus with Jeremy, &c. But it happens quite contrary when the bidding is from the devil, counterfeiting privily a divine mission, for he, with his commissions, causeth a forwardness in souls to take upon them employments of excellency or otherwise grateful to nature, as also a great aversion from those that either suspect or would dissuade them from such undertakings.

24. A soul, therefore, is by serious consideration to raise and increase in herself an apprehension and aversion from such matters, saying with St. Peter, *Exi a me, &c.—Go from me, O Lord, for I am a sinful man;* and by exercising so profitable a mortification she will secure herself from all perils, and render herself very acceptable to God. Serious instructions to a disappropriation and mortifying our love to such things are to be found in *Scala Perfectionis, Angela. de Foligno;* and particularly in the book called *Interior Abnegation* there is this passage: 'To God it belongeth to give rare and excellent gifts, and to the soul it belongeth to refuse them. It is suitable to the divine goodness to approach unto a soul, and the soul's duty is, in humility, to draw back, as St. Peter did. It belongs to God to elevate the soul, and her duty is to humble and abase herself; for as our nature in everything and upon every occasion desireth a proper excellency and sublimity, yea, even in things holy and appertaining to God, so our spirit illuminated by Grace (which is superior to our nature) ought incessantly in all things and occasions to seek to be deprived of all excellency (except in essential virtues), and to embrace all poverty and lowness even in sacred things, that so she be not less careful and resolute to overcome herself than nature is to seek herself. Thus there must be a continual contestation between God and the humble soul, &c.; and especially those souls that are most inclined and forward to embrace these high and grateful things must necessarily make such resistance, not yielding till pure necessity forces them, and till God take from them all power to withdraw themselves, and to refuse the excellences of that grace,

whereunto He at the same time so continually and powerfully urgeth and draweth them.' Instructions to the same purpose we find in Avila's Epistles.

25. This was the practice of the holy Virgin St. Colette, who, when God offered to reveal unto her divers secrets, answered: 'Lord God, it sufficeth me only to know Thee, and the sins in which I have offended Thee, and to obtain Thy pardon for them.' But most notable in this regard is the example of Suso, when God commanded him to publish to all estates in the world (the Pope, bishops, abbots, &c.) their vices and enormities represented to him in the vision of the nine rocks; he, out of that habitual fear and humility that was in him, did so resist the executing such a charge, that till he was adjured and commanded in the name of the Holy Trinity, and so forced to it even against his will, he had never yielded; and then also he submitted himself with much bewailing his misery, expressing his fear of the danger of pride, and, therefore, humbly begging that his name might be concealed from the world; and, lastly, protesting his desire and love to be directed to nothing, but only to God Himself. His resistance, indeed, was so obstinate, that God told him that if He had not known that it proceeded from true (but indiscreet) humility, He would presently have cast him into hell for it.

26. Those, therefore, that are favoured with extraordinary graces, if they did duly consider their state and danger, would find little ground to exalt themselves, or to despise others that are in a more low, but withal far more secure way.

27. Now for the preventing and avoiding the great danger of ill-using such favours and divine graces, to the feeding of self-love and pride, spiritual authors do seriously enjoin such persons so visited by God not to trust their own judgments or to determine whether they come from God or not, and much less to put in practice anything of consequence upon such revelation, but to refer themselves to the judgment and advice of others.

28. And herein great care is to be had to choose pious and discreet directors, because too many there are that will too readily and suddenly resolve such matters to come from none but God, and will thereupon desire such persons to intercede for them, and to beg some particular favours of the like nature, &c. Now upon such indiscreet behaviour in those that should be directors, such persons will begin to think that God loves to treat with them, and will interpret the things declared unto them according to their own gust and humours; and if things shall fall out otherwise than they imagined, they will fall into melancholic suspicions, and great danger of the devil's snares.

29. The best course that a confessarius in this case can take is, if there be any rational grounds of probability that such visions, &c., do not come from God, to exhort and enjoin the persons to avoid and despise then; yea, and if after long and serious examination it should seem almost evident

to him that God is the Author of them, yet ought he so to behave himself both in words and actions, as to deter the soul from adhering to them with affection, rather inclining her to a suspicion and fear or, however, to an indifferency about then, with an aspect of love to God Himself only, who is above all His gifts, and ought to be the only object of our love; and thus, if the confessarius behave himself, he may be sure that he will prevent all harm to ensue, and he shall perform a service very acceptable to God.

30. Certainly the danger is far less to be too difficult in believing and esteeming such things than to be never so little too credulous and inclined to admire them, for it were better that good ones should be often suspected than that an ill one should be once believed. And, therefore, we do find that our Blessed Lord, appearing to St. Teresa, did neither take it ill from her nor from her director, when by his order she did spit at Him and defy Him so appearing to her; but He only informed her how she should give convincing proofs that it was no illusion.

31. St. John of the Cross gives very good advices touching this point, exhorting souls, as the surest way, that in case they cannot meet with a prudent and experienced confessarius, they should not speak one word concerning such graces, but to pass them over and to make no account of them; and, however, by no means of their own heads to proceed to the executing of anything signified after such an unusual manner.

32. And though it should happen that the soul, being so disposed as to make no great estimation of such things (which will be a great security from danger by them), shall therefore think it to no purpose to consult with a prudent director about such trifles; or if, on the other side, such revelations seem unto her so absolutely clear and unquestionable that there is no need at all to ask any one's judgment about them; yet, saith the same author, it will be necessary that she discover them to her spiritual master.

33. And the reasons are: 1. Because ordinarily such is God's order and disposition, to the end that by such an humble submission of herself a new light and grace may be communicated to her. 2. To the end that upon such an occasion she may be put in mind to restrain her affections from such things, and be established in true nakedness and poverty of spirit; for which end the confessarius ought not to insist upon the excellency of such favours, but (passing over them slightly) to encourage the soul rather to value, and tend to a perfect active union, by charity and pure prayer. 3. That by such an occasion offered, the soul may conquer that natural unwillingness which is in some to discover what things pass within them; and with such souls the confessarius is to deal mildly, not affrighting or scandalising them, nor disheartening them from dealing freely, that by this means such visions, ecstasies, &c., may produce in them that effect which probably God intended,

namely, by them to call souls to a nearer and more perfect active union by love; whereof one perfect act framed by the will is of more worth and more grateful to God, than all the visions and revelations of all things that pass in heaven and earth can be, and certain it is that many souls which are never visited with any such favours are yet far more advanced in spirit and more near to God than are some others who frequently enjoy such extraordinary favours.

34. Whatsoever it be that is suggested in such a revelation, whether it concern knowledge or practice, though in itself it be of never so small moment, yet without advice a soul ought neither to assent to it nor execute it; for whatsoever the thing itself be, yet considering the cause and means by which it comes (which is supposed to be supernatural), it becomes of great importance. Yea, the mere conversation and familiarity with an intellectual spirit is a matter of great consequence, and as being with a good spirit, it is likely to be occasion of much good; so being with a bad spirit (as it may well be supposed to be till the contrary be evident), it will probably cause very much harm.

35. A soul being to consult with others about such matters, ought to take heed that she fall not into impertinences, but, as Alvarez de Paz adviseth, let her humbly, briefly, and clearly manifest so much of these extraordinary matters to her director as may be sufficient to enable him to judge, and if he do not value them, let her simply hold on her course and securely proceed in her ordinary exercises of devotion.

36. If some eminently perfect souls have followed their own light in judging of these things and practising accordingly, with out consulting others, this ought not to prejudice the foregoing advises, which are, indeed, for souls less experienced and perfect, and such as, in St. Paul's phrase, have not their senses exercised in the discerning of good and evil (in matters of this nature).

37. In such cases, likewise, all souls are not so absolutely obliged to resign their judgments and wills to others, as utterly to neglect their own proper call received from God; for to a well-minded soul that walks and deals simply and plainly with God, and labours diligently to keep her affections free from all created things, aspiring to an indifference whether she have or wants them—yea, out of humility and a pious fear rather desires to want such extraordinary visitations—such a soul, doubtless, will be so guided and illuminated by God's Holy Spirit as she will perfectly know what to do and forbear, and whether, when, and of whom to ask counsel. Let, therefore, such a soul carefully observe her internal direction, and this is the advice of St. John of the Cross.

38. From these precedent advices it may appear how differently a soul ought to behave herself in this case of extraordinary calls or inspirations from that to which (as hath been said in the first treatise) we are obliged in those inspirations which, though indeed supernatural, yet are ordinary. For in ordinary ones we are not at all to trouble others with consultations, or to seek advice, but presently to put in execution what shall be inspired or internally suggested unto us, whereas in these extraordinary cases we must do the quite contrary.

39. Thus far concerning those Passive Unions and contemplations which God sometimes communicates to souls after a sensible manner, especially in ecstasies (and revelations), in which there is an alienation and suspension of the use of the outward senses, which I have styled supernatural graces of God; not as if the like might not be produced by a natural way, for history informs us of some that, by a wonderful intention of mind upon philosophical verities, have drawn the operations of the spirit so much inward that the exercise of the outward senses have been suspended, and an ecstasy ensued; and, therefore, no doubt the like may even naturally happen in the contemplating of divine verities; in which case, the imagination being full of divine and spiritual images only, no wonder if during such a suspension there be represented internal discoursings with God and angels, &c., which to the persons may seem to have been real. However, even in these circumstances, an ecstasy so following according to the exigence and disposition of natural causes may properly be termed supernatural, since the preceding contemplation, which caused it, did proceed from a more than ordinary supernatural grace, and the imaginations occurring during such an ecstasy are no doubt ordered by an especial and supernatural providence of God.

40. But, besides these, there are (no doubt) many ecstasies and revelations purely supernatural, in which God either immediately or by the disposition of angels doth communicate such divine lights, graces, &c., as could not possibly flow from any assemblance of natural causes. Such were many of those communicated to St. Teresa, St. John of the Cross, &c. Now which way soever of these two such graces do proceed, the foresaid advices ought to have place.

Chapter IV. Of a Passive Union Purely Intellectual

§§ 1, 2, 3, 4. Of the second and more perfect sort of passive unions, to wit, such as are purely intellectual.

§§ 5, 6, 7. How in these unions God is contemplated in caligine, &c.

§§ 8, 9, 10, 11, 12, 13. The excellency and wonderful benefits flowing from these intellectual unions (though very short). As first in regard of the understanding.

§ 14. Secondly in regard of the will.

§§ 15, 16. Thirdly in regard of the internal senses.

§ 17. Inexperienced persons cannot and ought not to be judges in these things.

1. The other before-mentioned Passive Union, which I called intellectual, is far more noble and sublime, in which God or some divine mystery is immediately presented or discovered to the understanding, without any representations, figures, or discoursings in the imagination. In the former sensible unions the contemplations pass from the outward senses to the inward, and thence to the understanding; but this begins in the understanding, and only by reflection returns to the imagination, there making use of some species for an apprehension (after a human manner) of the object intellectually discovered to the soul.

2. The former sensible unions, especially such as pass in the internal sense, with alienation from the exercise of the outward, do seldom befall very perfect souls, and less to men than to women; because such an alienation from sense proceeds partly from the infirmity of the soul and its incapacity to attend to divine inaction (perhaps not from a necessary exigence of the inaction itself), and partly from a customary exercise of prayer by strong and tender affections in sensitive nature, which do more push forward the soul to attend earnestly to divine objects, from whence is caused a suspension of the outward senses.

3. There are some degrees of this intellectual passive union to which a soul, by leading a pure spiritual life, may dispose herself, making herself worthy and capable of the said inactions, she behaving herself as an humble patient, and not an agent in the business.

4. By virtue of these inactions, many souls have received internal lights and resolutions to many difficulties concerning themselves or others; likewise many suggestions, strong and clear, concerning extraordinary matters to be said or done, and all this without any external or imaginative vision, by certain secret whispers of the Divine Spirit, silently but assuredly enlightening the mind concerning certain truths or purposes to be believed or performed; frequent examples whereof we have in the lives of B. Angela of Foligno, St. Teresa, &c.

5. Of these intellectual passive unions, the supreme and most noble that may be had in this life is, that whereby God is contemplated without any perceptible images, by a certain intellectual supernatural light darted into the

soul, in which regard it draws much towards an angelical contemplation; for herein though God be not seen as He is, yet He is clearly seen that He is, and that He is incomprehensible.

6. Mystic authors call this rather a divine passive union than contemplation; a union far more strait and immediate than any of the former; a union exercised more by the will than the understanding, although the effect thereof be to refund great light into the understanding, notwithstanding which light, yet the understanding's contemplation is said to be *in caligine,* in which darkness God is more perfectly seen, because there is nothing seen that is not God; yea, according to the doctrine of mystics, this union passes above both the understanding and will, namely, in that supreme portion of the spirit which is visible to God alone, and in which He alone can inhabit; a portion so pure, noble, and divine, that it neither hath nor can have any name proper to it, though mystics endeavour to express it by divers, calling it the summit of the mind, the fund and centre of the spirit, the essence of the soul, its virginal portion, &c.

7. Such passive unions are rather a reward and free grace bestowed by God on souls that have been extraordinarily faithful and diligent in mortification and internal exercises than an end to be intended by any; for even the most pure and perfect souls cannot, with all their industries, procure them at pleasure.

8. This most pure contemplation does so exceed all voluntary operations of the soul's faculties, that it usually causes an alienation and suspension of all the senses, as well external as internal; yet the continuance of it is but very short, as St. Bernard (who, no doubt, could speak from his own experience) observes, for it seldom lasteth above a quarter of an hour.

9. But the benefits, fruits, and graces which so short a visitation causeth in the soul are both wonderfully excellent and very lasting, and these both in regard: 1. of the understanding; 2. of the will; and 3. the sensitive faculties likewise.

10. First, in regard of the understanding, there is thereby a divine light communicated, not revealing or discovering any new verities, but affording a most firm clear assurance and experimental perception of those verities of Catholic religion which are the objects of our faith, which assurance the soul perceives to be divinely communicated to her.

11. O happy evidence of our Catholic belief! No thanks to them that believe after such sight, which is more evident than anything we see with our corporal eyes. Surely the first knowledge and assurance that the primitive Christians had of the mysteries of our religion came by such contemplations communicated to the Apostles, &c. (as St. Paul witnesses of himself for one),

who saw and even felt the truth of what they preached and delivered by tradition to others.

12. Such contemplations as this made St. Teresa so confident in the points of her belief, that it seemed to her that she was able to dispute with and confound all the heretics in the world; but yet therein she might perhaps be deceived, if that God did not further enable her than by such contemplations only; for though they served to establish most firmly her own belief, yet would they not suffice to enable her to dispute with and convince others, because neither could she intelligibly enough express what she had seen, and if she could, yet would not all believe her, nor were they rationally obliged to do so. And, therefore, doubtless she would never have undertaken, of her own accord, without a special motion and invitation from God, to have entered into any such disputes; indeed, if God had urged her thereto, then, doubtless, He would have given her an especial assistance and force.

13. A soul that is newly awakened, as it were, from such a contemplation or union, coming to read the Holy Scriptures or any spiritual book, will pierce far more deeply into the verities contained in them, and will see clearer lights and feel far more perfect tastes of the divine truths therein than ever before; so that all the knowledge that she formerly had will seem unto her mere darkness and a knowledge of the outward letter only, whereas now she penetrates into the internal spirit of the writings.

14. In the next place, the change that is made by this supernatural union with regard to the will and affections is equally admirable, insomuch as many years spent in mortification and other internal exercises will not so purify the soul as a few minutes passed in such a divine inaction. Here it is, indeed, that a soul perfectly feels her own nothing and God's totality, and thereby is strangely advanced in humility and the divine love; for being so immediately united to God, so illustrated with His heavenly light, and inflamed with His love, all creatures (and herself above all) are become as nothing, yea, perfectly odious to her. Besides, there are many secret defects in a soul, so subtle and intime, that they can neither be cured nor so much as discovered but by a passive union, insomuch as hereby the soul is advanced to perfection in a manner and degree not to be imagined, far more efficaciously than by all the former actions of herself put together, so that the following aspirations and elevations of the spirit become far more pure and efficacious than before. And, indeed, were it not for such good fruits and effects upon the will, such passive unions would be little profitable unto the soul; for our merit consists in our own free acts produced in virtue of divine grace assisting us, and not in the operations simply wherein God is only agent, and we patients.

15. In the third place, these supernatural unions are of that virtue that they do wholly subdue the imagination and other internal senses to the superior soul, so that they cannot, as they list, wander to and fro, but are reduced to such a happy servitude to the spirit, that without any stress or violence they are brought to attend it in all its employments and occasions; or, if the imagination do sometimes wander, yet it never fastens itself with delight on any external perishing objects, by reason that self-love is in a sort extinguished in the soul, so that it may easily be reduced; or, howsoever, by its wanderings it doth not hinder or interrupt the operations of the spirit.

16. Moreover, it is observed by mystics that souls which formerly during the precedent less perfect exercises were of quite different, even contrary dispositions and natural complexions, after such supernatural unions do come to a very near resemblance to one another (as we see that several ways or paths which from far distant places lead to a city, the nearer they approach to the city the nearer also do they come to one another, and at last fall into and make one common highway). And the reason hereof is, because nature and its particular affections and inclinations are now so worn and even burnt out by the fire of divine love and grace, that it is the Spirit of God that is the only principle of all their actions; which, therefore, must needs be uniform and like to one another.

17. It will be no wonder if these things here spoken of a supernatural passive union shall seem incredible, or, perhaps, to be but dreams of extravagant or melancholic spirits, not only to those that are strangers from the Catholic faith, but those Catholics also that are inexperienced in internal ways; yet if they would consider that all this hath been delivered by the testimony of most devout, humble, and spiritually prudent persons, some of them very learned also, who profess to write nothing but what themselves have had experience of, and this by an internal command of God's Spirit, and for the edification of others, they will perhaps judge more warily of these things. And withal, considering that out of the Catholic Church no such divine graces and communications were ever heard of, they will, however, reap this benefit by them, if not to dispose themselves the best they can for the enjoying them, at least they will abhor all novelties in doctrines, and continue unshaken and obedient children to the Church.

Chapter V. Of the Great Desolation

§§ 1, 2, 3. Of the great desolation usually following an intellectual passive union.

§§ 4, 5, 6, 7. A description of the nature and woful bitterness of this desolation.

§ 8. How a devout soul does, or ought to behave herself therein.

§ 9. The great benefits and fruits proceeding from this desertion well undergone.

1. A soul having once experienced such extraordinary divine favours will be apt to say with the Psalmist (*Non movebor in æternum*), 'I shall never be moved, Thou, Lord, of Thy goodness hast made my hill so strong.' But if she think so she will find herself strangely deceived; for as the whole course of a spiritual life consists of perpetual changes, of elevations and depressions, and an extraordinary consolation is usually attended by succeeding anguish and desertion, so above all other times this so supereminent and so comfortable a divine visitation is commonly followed by a most terrible unexpected desolation, a desolation so insupportable to souls unprovided or unaware of it, that many not enabled or not well instructed how to behave themselves in it have lost all heart to prosecute internal ways, and so bereaving themselves of the benefit of all their former exercises and, divine passive inactions, have returned to a common extroverted life.

2. This truly is a misery so great and so deplorable, that to prevent the like in others, I conceive requisite to give warning of it, and by a brief description of the nature and manner of such a desolation, together with the good ends for which God permits, yea, in a sort conducts souls into it, to encourage them to bear themselves in it with patience, resignation, and tranquillity of mind. I shall be brief in this point, remitting the readers for a farther explanation of it to Barbanson, as likewise to that excellent treatise called Interior Abnegation.

3. From the foresaid sublime familiarities, therefore, and communications between God and His chosen souls, He conducts them usually (especially after the first passive union) to another far different state of pure sufferance; but this is not a happy suffering (as formerly) from God, but a woful suffering from the soul herself; for God, for some time retiring Himself from her, permits her to feel her natural infirmity, and this He does by degrees, lest, if the extremity and bitterness of this state did at once seize upon her, she should be utterly oppressed by the temptation. Therefore, when by many inferior trials of her patience and resignation He sees her strong and courageously resolved to follow Him whithersoever He shall lead her, then He puts her to this last and of all other greatest trial.

4. For first He not only withdraws all comfortable observable infusions of light and grace, but also deprives her of a power to exercise any perceptible operations of her superior spirit and of all comfortable reflections upon His love, plunging her into the depth of her inferior powers. Here, con-

sequently, her former calmness of passions is quite lost, neither can she introvert her self; sinful motions and suggestions do violently assault her, and she finds as great difficulty (if not greater) to surmount them as at the beginning of a spiritual course. The feeling of all this is intolerable to her, and thereupon she begins to suspect that by some great unknown sin she has procured all this, or, however, that her resistance is now so feeble and inefficacious that she deserves that God should quite cast her off. She finds the corrupt inclinations of her nature so strong in her that she thinks she is nothing but nature: the rebelliousness whereof and its rage against God is inexpressible: she is now as full of images of vanities as ever she had been formerly, and it seems to her that she has far less power to expel them than when she lived in the world. If she would elevate her spirit she sees nothing but clouds and darkness; she seeks God and cannot find the least marks or footsteps of His presence; something there is that hinders her from executing the sinful suggestions within her, but what that is she knows not; for to her thinking she has no spirit at all, and, indeed, she is now in a region of all other most distant from spirit and spiritual operations—I mean such as are perceptible. Her prayers and recollections are most grievous unto her, because infinitely difficult, by reason that sense and nature (which most abhors them) is now almost only active and operative in her, and the recollections which she endeavours to make are not only insipid, but, as it seems to her, utterly inefficacious, so that she oft suspects that it were better, perhaps, if she were quite extroverted; yet for all that she dares not altogether quit her endeavours to practise recollections, but yet she knows not why.

5. Now if all these disorders continued only for some short time, she might without extreme difficulty practise patience as she did in her former aridities and desolations; but alas! this most afflicting martyrdom oftentimes continues many months, yea, in some persons several years (not always in extremity, but with some intercisions), so that the soul comes in a manner to lose all patience. She often complains in her prayers to God for deserting her that would fain not desert Him, yet when she makes such prayers, to her seeming her spirit will not join; if she had nothing to do but merely to suffer, it were not so much but she knows it is her duty to work and to raise herself up by prayer, and this she cannot do. She stands in need now of as gross operations to cause an introversion as ever, and yet those gross operations have not so good an effect as in her former imperfect state.

6. Moreover, the temptations which she now suffers are both so violent and her resistance so feeble, they are withal so unexpected, so secret, and subtle, that notwithstanding any information that she formerly had, by reading or other ways, touching such a condition of suffering to be expected, yet when it comes she will scarce be persuaded that this can be possibly a way to perfection or conducing to her good; all her former light and instructions will

scarce at all diminish her resentment of her deplorable condition; she loses nothing of her former light (for souls arrived to this state are not to seek or to learn how and in what manner they are to exercise themselves interiorly: they study no more for that than one would do how he may see with his eyes or hear with his ears, having the perfect use of his senses), but when she is to practise according to this light, she has no satisfaction at all. If she have any difficulties or obscurities, it is how she is to comport herself in external matters, and even this obscurity is but very small; but, however, she thinks that all the light she has serves to little purpose, finding that notwithstanding it she works as if she had no light at all. In a word, she now sees her own natural misery so perfectly (yea, and can see nothing but it) that she cannot see how God can comfort her if He would.

7. All this shows that notwithstanding all her precedent exercises, yea, that during the foregoing divine inactions, yet many dregs of corrupt nature did remain in her; they were only hid, but not extinguished. This, therefore, was the only forcible expedient left to destroy in a manner all the sinful inclinations of nature in her; indeed, to natural reason this seems a strange and most improper remedy—to destroy nature by suspending the influences and operations of grace, and by suffering nature to break forth violently without any control and restraint, all sensible light in the understanding and fervour in the will being in a manner extinguished; yet out of this darkness God produces light and strength from this infirmity.

8. For the truth is that in this case of desolation the soul doth by her free-will, or rather in the centre of the spirit beyond all her faculties, remain in a constant union and adhesion to God, although no such union do appear unto her; yea, though it seems to her that she is not only estranged but even averted from God, and by virtue of that most secret but firm adhesion she makes election of God as her only good, which may to any but herself sufficiently appear by her carriage during that state; for she breaks not out into any murmurings, she seeks not to comfort herself by admitting any inordinate external solaces, nor doth anything deliberately by which to rid herself from such an afflicting estate sooner or otherwise than God would have her to do. She practises tranquillity of mind in the midst of a tempest of passions in sensitive nature; she exercises resignation without the least contentment to herself therein; she learns patience in the midst of impatience, and resignation in the midst of irresignation; in a word, she yields herself as a prey unto Almighty God, to be cast into this most sharp purgatory of love, which is an immediate disposition to an established state of perfection.

9. More particularly the fruits and benefits flowing from this most sad estate (supported with patience and tranquillity of spirit) are wonderful. 1. For first, hereby the devout soul obtains a new light to penetrate into the

mystery of our Lord's desertion in the garden and on the cross, and from this light a most inflamed love to Him; now she ceases to wonder why He should deprecate a cup so mortally bitter as this, and that it should work such strange effects on Him, or that He should cry out, *Eli, Eli, lamma sabacthani,* and by this desertion of His (which lasted till the very last moment of His life) she hopes to have an end put to hers. 2. Now she learns by experience to make a division between the supreme portion of the spirit and inferior nature, yea, between the summity of the spirit and the faculties of the same; for that portion of her by which she cleaves to God seems to be another third person distinct from herself that suffers, complains, and desires, for she chooses God, and at the same time fears that her will chooses and consents to sin; she is mightily supported by God, and yet she thinks Him utterly estranged and separated from her. Thus at last she perceives that she can operate without any perceptible use of her faculties. 3. Hereby she learns a perfect disappropriation and transcendence even of the highest gifts and graces of God, and a contentation to be deprived of the greatest blessings that God has to bestow on her (except only Himself). 4. The sight of the inexpressible weakness and perverseness of nature, left to itself, without any sensible influences of grace upon the inferior faculties, produces in her a most profound humility and hatred of herself. 5. Lastly, by this most sharp purgatory of love she enters into a state of most perfect confidence in God, of tranquillity of mind, and security of God's unchangeable love to her, not to be disturbed by any possible future affliction. For what has a soul left to fear that can with a peaceable mind support, yea, and make her benefit of the absence of God Himself?

Chapter VI. Of the State of Perfection

§§ 1, 2, 3. Of the end of all the precedent exercises, and of all the changes in a spiritual life: to wit, a stable state of perfection and prayer.

§§ 4, 5. Wherein that state consists. The testimony of Suso.

§§ 6, 7. The wonderful purity and sublimity of the soul's operations in this state: out of Barbanson.

§§ 8, 9, 10. Of the union of nothing with nothing, &c.

§ 11. The sublimity of angelical love in perfect souls.

§ 12. A conclusion of the whole book.

1. It remains only for a conclusion of the whole book, that something be said of the end of all these exercises of Mortification and Prayer, in which there is so great variety of degrees and changes.

2. And surely that end must needs be supereminently excellent, for the attaining whereof such incredible labour (both interior and exterior) must be undertaken, and whereto such wonderful divine graces and visits are only instrumental dispositions. Suso, writing from his own experience concerning the foresaid passive union by which a soul hath a distinct view of God, her original, says: That though the said contemplation continued but as it were a moment, it so replenished his heart with joy, that he wondered it did not cleave asunder. On the other side, upon the subsequent most contrary visitation by a spiritual desertion, the heart becomes so replenished with bitterness and anguish, as if all Gilead had not balm enough to assuage it.

3. And for what end all this? Surely not that a man should rest finally in the joy conceived by such a fruition, nor merely to torture the soul by such a bitter desolation. Our supreme happiness is not receiving but loving; all these favours, therefore, and all these sufferings do end in this: namely, the accomplishment of this love in our souls, so that all our perfection consists in a state of love and an entire conformity with the divine will.

4. There are, therefore, in a spiritual life no strange novelties or wonders pretended to. Divine love is all; it begins with love and resignation, and there it ends likewise. All the difference is in the degrees and lustre of it; love, even in its most imperfect state, is most divinely beautiful, which beauty is wonderfully increased by exercise; but when by such fiery trials and purifications, as also by so near approaches as are made to the fountain of beauty and light in passive unions, this love is exalted to its perfection; how new, how admirable, and incomprehensible to us imperfect souls is the manner of the exercising of it! We must content ourselves to hear those speak of it that have had some experience in it, and if what they say be incomprehensible to us, we ought not to wonder at it.

5. That which the forementioned Suso (in his ninth Rock) writes of the nature of this love in gross is not so abstruse. O, how small (says he) is the number of those perfect souls! And yet as few as they are, God sets them as pillars to support His Church, so that if it were not for them, it would be in danger to be dissipated. The prayer of one such soul is of more efficacy than of all Christians besides; they approach very near to God, their original, and yet such is the vile esteem that they have of themselves, they themselves are not assured of this; yet by fits a certain clarity or glimpse of their prime principle is communicated to them, by which they easily infer that there is some other thing within them from whence those splendours do issue; but they are so purely, simply, and nakedly resigned to God in Catholic belief, that whensoever they receive any joyful consolation from Him, they are more apprehensive than when they find themselves deprived of it, for their only desire is simply to imitate the example of our Lord Jesus in simple faith.

They adhere so purely and simply to the Catholic faith, that they neither desire nor endeavour to know anything else; there is in them so profound a humility that they esteem themselves unworthy of any of those secret and comforting graces of God, and therefore dare not ask them; they desire no other thing but this, that God may be perfectly glorified. They are so absolutely resigned to the divine will, that whatsoever befalls them and all other creatures is most acceptable to them. Therefore, if God give them anything, they are contented with it; if he deprive them of it, they are as well pleased. Thus they challenge nothing, they appropriate nothing; yet if it were left to them, they would choose rather to avoid pleasing than bitter things, for the cross is their sovereign delight; they fear neither life nor death, purgatory nor hell, nor all the devils in it, for all servile fear is utterly extinguished in them, and the only fear remaining is this, that they do not as yet imitate the example of our Lord as they ought and desire. They are so humble that they despise themselves and all the works that ever they performed; yea, they abase themselves below all creatures, not daring to compare themselves with any; they love all men alike in God, and every one that loves God they love him likewise; they are totally dead to the world and it to them, and all the intellectual exercises and operations which formerly they pursued with propriety are altogether dead in them. They do neither by intention nor love seek themselves nor any proper honour nor profit in time or eternity; they have utterly lost themselves and all creatures both for time and eternity, and they live in a certain learned ignorance, not desiring to know anything; they resent no temptations nor afflictions; it is their joy to follow our Lord, bearing His cross; to the last gasp they desire to walk in no other way but this, and although they be unknown unto the world, yet the world is well known unto them; these are truly men, indeed, true adorers of God, that adore Him in spirit and truth; thus Suso.

6. But as for the internal actuations in the souls of the perfect, they are so inexplicably subtle and pure, that experience itself doth not sufficiently enable them to give an intelligible account of them. What soul can imagine how divinely spiritual and angelical must needs have been the internal exercises of divine love in St. Romualdus, after almost a hundred years spent in solitude, during all which time they continually grew more and more pure and divine?

7. In the active unions which souls, during a less perfect state have with God, God is in them as an object distinct from them, and so contemplated by them; but in the state of perfection He is not only the object and end, but the only perceivable principle also of all their operations; yea, saith Barbanson (cap. 12), He is the fund, the entire state, the stable foundation of the soul, by virtue of which the being, life, and respiration of the spirit is become as much exalted as the operations and contemplations thereof, for this

union is not now only a gift and operation of God, that is of a short continuance, nor only simple actual infusions, by which the soul may at some times be actually informed, and no more; but the very foundation, state, and disposition of the soul is changed, reversed, and reformed by divine grace, which being a participation of the Divine Being, and, consequently, making us partakers of the divine nature, confers on us a stable and permanent state in regard of our interior, to live according to the divine and supernatural life, conformable whereto are the consequents and effects of it, to wit, light, knowledge, experience, and inclination to divine things. Yea (saith the same author in another place), although the divine, actual, and special touches be not always really present, so as by means of their prevention to produce actual operations, the soul, notwithstanding, can maintain itself, yea, and perceive itself to persist in a state of life according to the Spirit of God, a life of peace, serenity, and repose, in which the spirit is continually attentive to what God will vouchsafe to speak in her.

8. By reason of this habitation and absolute dominion of the Holy Spirit in the souls of the perfect (who have wholly neglected, forgotten, and lost themselves, to the end that God alone may live in them, whom they contemplate in the absolute obscurity of faith), hence it is that some mystic writers do call this perfect union the UNION OF NOTHING WITH NOTHING, that is, the union of the soul, which is nowhere corporally, that hath no images nor affections to creatures in her; yea, that hath lost the free disposal of her own faculties, acting by a portion of the spirit above all the faculties, and according to the actual touches of the Divine Spirit, and apprehending God with an exclusion of all conceptions and apprehensions; thus it is that the soul, being nowhere corporally or sensibly, is everywhere spiritually and immediately united to God, this infinite nothing.

9. The soul now is so elevated in spirit that she seems to be all spirit, and, as it were, separated from the body. Here she comes to a feeling, indeed, of her not-being, and by consequence, of the not-being of creatures. This is, indeed, a real truth; not as if the soul or other creatures either did cease according to their natural being, or as if a natural being were, indeed, no real being (as Father Benet Canfield doth seem to determine), but because all sinful adhesion by affection to creatures being annihilated, then they remain (as to the soul) only in that true being which they have in God, by dependence on Him and relation to Him, so that He is all in all; whereas, whilst we sinfully adhere unto them by staying in them with love, we carry ourselves towards them as if we thought them to have a being or subsistence of and in themselves, and not of God only; and that they might be loved for themselves without reference to God, which is the fundamental error and root of all sin.

10. All sensible operations formerly exercised, yea, all express and deliberate intellectual operations bring the soul some-whither and to some determinate thing; but in this perfect state the soul's desire is to be nowhere, and she seeks nothing that either sense or understanding can fix upon. Such souls can taste and comprehend what St. Denis meant in his Instructions to Timothy (*Tu autem relinque sensus, &c.*): But thou, O Timothy, relinquish the senses and sensible exercises, yea, abandon all intellectual operations, and with a courageous force of mind repress all these things, and according to thy utmost possibility raise thyself in ignorance, and renouncing of all knowledge to an union with God above all substance (or being) and knowledge.

11. But these are secrets of divine love, which, except by experience they be tasted, can in no sort be comprehended. Blessed are those souls that thus lose themselves that they may find themselves! This loss is so infinitely gainful, that it is cheaply bought with all the anguishes of mortification, all the travails of meditation, and all the aridities, obscurities, and desolations attending the prayer of the will: this loss is the design of all these exercises and labours, this is the fruit of all divine inactions. We mortify our passions, to the end we may lose them; we exercise discursive prayer by sensible images, to the end we may lose all use of images and discourse; and we actuate immediately by operations of the will, to the end we may arrive to a state of stability in prayer above all direct exercises of any of the soul's faculties: a state wherein the soul, being oft brought to the utmost of her workings, is forced to cease all working, to the end that God may operate in her, so that till a soul be reduced to a perfect denudation of spirit and a deprivation of all things, God doth not enjoy a secure and perfect possession of it.

12. And thus by God's assistance we have passed through the several degrees of prayer, according to which, especially, the stations and degrees of an internal life are to be measured; we have endeavoured (it is to be hoped not altogether unprofitably) with all simplicity and perspicuity to declare the order and changes of them. If God, by the means of our prayers, give us the grace and courage to proceed *de virtute in virtutem,* according to these steps and these directions we shall, without doubt, sooner or later arrive unto the top of the mountain, where God is seen: a mountain, to us that stand below, environed with clouds and darkness, but to them who have their dwelling there, it is peace and serenity and light. It is an intellectual heaven, where there is no sun nor moon, but God and the Lamb are the light of it.

The blessed spirit of Prayer rest upon us all. Amen. Amen.

ACTS AND AFFECTIONS OF THE WILL

AN ADVERTISEMENT TO THE READER

Dear Christian Reader,

There was intended (and accordingly promises were made in two or three passages of the precedent Treatises) that hereto should be adjoined an Appendix consisting of a few chapters of several subjects; as: 1. A brief description of the nature, faculties, and operations of an intellectual soul (the knowledge of which may be conceived very expedient for the unlearned, to enable them the better to comprehend many passages in this book, both touching temptations and prayer, &c.). 2. A discourse to prove that it is no prejudice or disparagement to divine charity to love God for a reward, so that such a reward be the blessed enjoying of Himself, and not any inferior ends, pleasing to sense, &c. 3. A protestation (which in one word is here made) against the least intention of reflecting with censure or disparagement upon the ways or doings of others (whether directors or disciples) in the matter of Prayer, or any other good practices taught or used by them, as considered in themselves, and much more against all thought of decrying any ceremonious or solemn observances practised in or by any Communities, &c. The venerable Author of these instructions being of a spirit too full of charity and spiritual prudence, and too adverse from so mean an ambition, as to seek the procuring an esteem to himself or his own writings by the depressing of others. So that whensoever he gives any advices or cautions touching such matters, his intention only is, that the purifying of the soul and the exalting of Prayer should not be prejudiced by the foresaid practices: the which, whether indeed they be prejudicial hereto or no, only superiors are to be judges. 4. An answer to certain objections made by some, since the venerable Author's death, against the publishing of these instructions, especially touching Divine Inspirations.

401

These are the principal points that the author of this Abridgment purposed to annex here at the end of the Third Treatise. But certain pressing occasions obliging us to hasten the publishing of this present work, and likewise an unwillingness that it should at first swell to too great a proportion and bulk, for these reasons it was judged expedient to omit the said discourses, which to a charitable reader will not be necessary; or, however, to remit them to another impression, if we shall be encouraged thereto. Only notice may be taken, that for as much as concerns the last of these particular points, viz. the answer to such objections as have been made against the exposing indifferently to the world instructions intended only for a few solitary devout religious souls, and especially those that concern the duty of attending to and executing Divine Inspirations and calls, it was judged very expedient and almost necessary that it should not be omitted, but rather premised (as it is) in the beginning of the book.

I will detain thee no longer (devout Reader) but only to tell thee, that if by God's Grace these instructions prove instrumental to the teaching or promoting thee in pure Prayer, my hope is thou wilt not in thy prayers be unmindful of the poor unworthy author of this Abridgment.

A POSTSCRIPT TO THE READER

Beloved Charitable Reader,

To recompense with some advantage the want of a promised Appendix, which was to have contained certain discourses framed by the unworthy author of this methodical Abridgment, for a clearer (though not necessary) explication of a few passages in the foregoing Treatises, I here present unto thee the Testimonies and Approbations of the doctrine here delivered, given by two of the most learned and pious fathers of our Congregation, famous through all Christendom for the more than ordinary eminency of their endowments, to wit, the Very Rev. F. Leander à Sancto Martino, and the Very Rev. F. Rudesind Barlow, both Doctors in Divinity, and who had several times been Presidents-General of our holy Congregation, &c. The which Approbations they gave first voluntarily, upon the request of the Venerable Author, and submission of his writings to their judgment; and a second time by the commission and order of the General Chapter assembled at Douay, A.D. 1633, in which an attempt had been made by a certain Religious Father to cast some aspersions on the said doctrine (specially concerning Divine Inspirations and calls), as if the lawful authority of superiors did receive prejudice thereby. But when the said Reverend Father had in a short writing delivered the grounds of his suspicions and allegations, and that in consequence thereto the late Venerable Author had as briefly, with great sincerity and clearness, presented his sense in that matter, the VV. RR. Fathers in Chapter did presently absolve the V. Author, causing withal his opponent to subscribe to a writing conceived in a manner *verbatim* out of the account given by the Author. But on that occasion they imposed on the two aforesaid VV. RR. Approvers, once more diligently to peruse the several Treatises composed by the V. Author, who most freely and humbly submitted them to their censure; so that on that occasion they renewed their former testimonies and approbations.

From hence, beloved Reader, thou wilt perceive and canst not but give thy testimony and approbation also to the prudent care expressed by our holy Congregation, not to permit any books of this nature even to the private reading and use of their religious subjects, till all possible circumspection and diligence had first been used, that nothing therein should be contained that might produce the least danger, prejudice, or inconvenience. And after all this, way was not given to a publishing the said books, till twenty years were passed, when in a General Chapter assembled in A.D. 1653, at Paris, the VV. RR. Fathers, perceiving the many blessed fruits proceeding from the said writings, to the advancement of all regular duties of solitude, humility, obedience, and devotion, especially in the Convent of our RR. Dames of Cambray and elsewhere; and, moreover, finding that many among the Secular Clergy in England, yea, that several devout persons of the laity, both men and women, did, to the wonderful profit of their souls, make use of some of the said Treatises, and not any one appearing that did make any opposition at all to any part of the doctrine;—on these and the like grounds by unanimous agreement (*nemine contradicente*) it was ordered, 'that a Methodical Abridgment of the spiritual instructions dispersed throughout the numerous Treatises of the late Venerable F. Augustine Baker should, for the good and benefit of souls, be exposed to the public.'

To the said Approbations I will adjoin a short discourse written for the satisfaction and encouragement of the Religious Dames of Cambray, by the foresaid most R. Father Leander a S. Martino, and by him called 'A Memorial,' in which he briefly explains the principal advices delivered by our Venerable Author: as likewise a scheme of the doctrine of Divine calls and Inspirations, at one glance representing to the Reader the sum of the said doctrine, acknowledged by our Author to be perfectly conformable to his sense of it.

The Approbations Follow.

The first books written by our Venerable Author were certain collections out of several spiritual writers, which he entitled with the letters A, B, C. After which he composed himself several Treatises, the which he entitled with the following letters, D, F, G, H, &c.

Now the first of these, viz. D, consisting of about 300 Aphorisms, in which is contained the sum of spiritual doctrine, or Directions for Contemplation, has these Approbations:

Legi et approbavi hunc Libellum pro usu Monialium nostrarum.

Ego Fr. LEANDER, S. Theol. Doctor et Prior Sancti Gregorii, hujus Monasterii B. Mariæ de Consolatione Ordinarius indignus. Augusti 17, 9.

Again in the Reëxamination.

Allowed.

Br. Leander. Br. Rosendo.

Again. Lectus est hic libellus, et admissus et approbatus a me Fr. Leandro de S. Martino, pro usu Monialium nostrarum.

F. Leander de S. Martino, Ordinarius.

To the book F, (being the second part of Directions for Contemplation and) treating of certain erroneous opinions frequent in these days; also of matters of Confession in a Spiritual Life: together with a Catalogue of choice spiritual books, &c.

The Approbations.

This second part of Directions for Contemplation is not only lawful to be read, but necessary to be known of such as be not instructed in a Spiritual Life, to the end they may learn something here, and know where to learn more, and to perform their obligations without trouble of mind and loss of time to themselves and others.

F. Leander de S. Martino, Prior S. Gregorii, ejusdem Ordinis et Congr.

Ordinarius Monialium.

B. Rosendo Barlow, President of the English Congregation of the Order of St

Bennet.

To the book G (the third part), of varieties of Contemplations, &c.

The Approbations.

I have read over diligently this book, and find it in all points worthy of allowance, full of very wholesome doctrine, and fit for our spirit and calling. And therefore I do allow of it for the use of our Nuns, and commend much unto then the practice thereof, according to the rules herein contained. 27 Aug. 9.

F. Leander de S. Martino, Prior of S. Gregories, and Ordinary of the
Monastery of our Ladies of Comfort in Cambray.

This book, called Directions for Contemplation, the third part, is a brief sum of what is largely handled by the best mystic authors that write of this subject, and therefore worthy to be read, and read again.

B. Rosendo Barlow, President of the English Congregation of the Holy Order

of St. Bennet.

To the book H, treating of Purity of Intention, Custodia Cordis, and of Meditation on the Passion.

The Approbations.

This fourth part of Directions for Contemplation is replenished with passing good documents, and very fine explications of the nature and effects of Prayer, and therefore most serviceable to such as seriously seek a perfect course of life. Doway, 24 Dec. 9.

F. Leander de S. Martino, Prior of St. Gregories, ejusd. Ord. et Congr.

B. Rosendo Barlow, President of the English Congr. of the Order of St.

Bennet.

To the first part of Doubts and Calls are

These Approbations.

I have carefully read over these three Books of Doubts and Calls, and find them to contain nothing against Faith or good order: but rather very many necessary and secure Instructions and rules for the Direction of internal Prayer; all conformable to the teaching of the best Masters of Spirit that have written of these matters. May 12, 1630.

F. Leander de S. Martino, Prior of the English Benedictines of S. Gregories

in Doway.

Again,

Item probatus a me F. Leandro, Præside Congregationis, 1634, Aprilis 4.

To the second part of Doubts and Calls are

These Approbations.

This book, called The second part of Doubts and Calls, may lawfully be read: It containeth nothing but that which is true and profitable to the Reader. 4 Jan. 1630.

B. Rosendo Barlow, President of the English Congregation of the Order of

S. Bennet.

Seen and allowed, as containing very profitable and necessary Doctrine, according to the Spirit and vocation of our Rule. 7 Sept. 9.

F. Leander de S. Martino, Prior of S. Gregories, and Ordinary of the

Monastery of Our Ladies of Comfort in Cambray.

Again,

Item approbavi. F. LEANDER de S. Martino, Præses Cong., 1634. Apr. 4.

To the third part of Doubts and Calls are

These Approbations.

Seen and allowed as containing very profitable and wholesome Doctrine, fit and agreeable to the vocation of our Rule. 7 Sept. 9.

F. Leander de S. Martino, Prior of S. Gregories, and Ordinary of the Monastery of Our Ladies of Comfort in Cambray.

Again,

This Treatise of Doubts and Calls is a very good one. 1630.

B. Rosendo Barlow, President of the English Congregation of the Order of

S. Ben.

To the Book of Confession (the Original whereof is lost, but a Perfect transcript remaining) is

This Approbation.

I have read this Book, and have found nothing in it against Faith or Good manners. For although the Author dispute much against the urging of Confession of Venial sins, as unnecessary to Spiritual profit: yet he doth not in any sort condemn the discreet use of frequent Confession of Venial sins but only the needless renumeration of them and of daily defects, which cannot be used without great loss of time and anxiety of mind. In testimony of this I subscribe my Name at Cambray. 17 Sept. 9.

B. Rudisind Barlow, President of the English Congregation of the Order of

S. Bennet.

Besides these many more Approbations might be added annexed by the same VV. RR. FF. to other Books: as to that of Discretion; of Sickness; Directions for the Idiot's Devotions (contained in 16 several Books), Remedies; The Stay of the Soul in Temptations, in two volumes; A Book called The Five Treatises; The Alphabet and Abstract, etc.

But I made choice only of the fore-mentioned, because they treated of subjects more likely to meet with contradiction. Supposing, therefore that these will suffice, which are taken from the originals extant at Cambray, in the Approvers' own handwriting, I will here adjoin the fore-mentioned Memorial, containing both an Approbation and explication of the general doctrine of our V. Venerable Author.

A MEMORIAL

Written by the late V. R. F. Leander À S. Martino, and placed in the Book of Collections

I have read over carefully the book A, B, C, and the *Alphabet and Abstract,* as also the three parts of *Doubts and Calls,* besides divers other Treatises of the same Author, in all which are to be seen my Approbation and allowance in the beginning of them. They do all contain very sound and wholesome doctrine for the direction of devout souls, and fit and agreeable to our calling and Rule, and especially for the use of our Dames; the spirit of our Holy Rule consisting principally in a spiritual union of our soul with God in affective Prayer, and exercise of the will immediately upon God, rather than intellectual and discursive Prayer, busying the understanding, as appeareth plainly by our Rule, and the daily use of our Choir Office, which for the most part consisteth of Aspirations and Affections, and hath very few discourses.

Yet because the Author referreth the Dames his scholars to his larger explication by word of mouth in many places, and to his practice in which he settled them, both which cannot be known but by those who knew the Author; and this mystic way, though most plain, most secure, and most compendious to perfection, containeth many hard and delicate points, which will seem most strange to such as have been only accustomed to intellectual Meditation, and little to affective Prayer, by reason of the great abstraction which it requires from all things that are not God; lest the ensuing confessors and directors should mistake the meaning of the Author, and thereupon alter the course of prayer begun and settled in the house (as we hope, to the glory of God and spiritual profit of souls in perfection proper to our calling), I have thought it convenient to note these few points following.

First of all, that the reader of these books and collections have always before his eyes, that they are written precisely and only for such souls as by God's holy Grace do effectually and constantly dedicate themselves to as pure an abstraction from creatures as may with discretion be practised in the Community; and consequently for such as abstain from all manner of levity, loss of time, notable and known defects, vain talk, needless familiarity, and in a word do take as much care as they can to avoid all venial sins and occasions of them, and all things which they shall perceive, or be warned of, to be impediments to the divine union of their souls with God.

Secondly, let him consider that it is supposed as a ground in all those collections and observations, that the Office of Choir, and actions of obedience, and conventual acts, and all other things prescribed by Rule and statute, are most exactly to be kept and observed: yea, preferred before all other private exercises whatever. So that all these instructions are to be understood always with reservation of the conventual discipline and public observance prescribed by obedience.

Particularly let the reader observe a note which is given in one of these books, and found but in few spiritual writers, yet necessary for those religious that are addicted to the Choir, viz. that although the Author commendeth so highly mental Prayer, yet that Prayer which is perfectly *mental and vocal too is* far more excellent than that which is mental only; as will be the exercise of the Saints in heaven after the Day of Judgment, when in body and soul they shall praise and contemplate Almighty God. Whereupon it followeth, that although in this life our frail and weak body hindereth our soul, so that our Prayer cannot be so perfectly mental and vocal as it shall be in heaven, yet must our mental Prayer be so practised, that by the Grace of God and loyal perseverance in union with Him, our vocal Prayer in Choir may be converted into mental, that is, that our vocal saying and singing may be so lively animated, as it were, and informed with affect of the soul, as if it were altogether spiritual Prayer. And so shall we fulfil the words of our Rule: *Nihil præponatur operi Dei,*—Let nothing be preferred before the Office of the Choir. Whereas in divers places the Author saith that all bodily exercises, even frequenting the Sacraments, without mental Prayer and abstraction and mortification, do not advance the soul one jot in spirit, although it be plain enough to them that know these three instruments of spiritual perfection, yet lest any should mistake his meaning, as if these former exercises did not profit a soul at all, without these instruments practised by few, out of the former advices the reader must understand that by 'Advancement in spirit' is meant here, not the bare avoiding of grosser sins and some perfection too in active life, which is gotten by these bodily exercises, but a clear and experimental knowledge of the will of God, and a spiritualising of the soul by adhering to God, and transcending all creatures whatsoever; for this do the mystic doctors call 'Advancement in spirit'; and this cannot be attained unto but by the above three named instruments continually practised and employed by God's Grace. Which notwithstanding, the Author denieth not, but that a soul without the foresaid exercises may so profit in spirit (as active souls do that live in worldly manner), that they carefully avoid sin and keep God's commandments, and be truly united to God in following His will, by the use of bodily exercises and frequency of Sacraments, although they use not much mental Prayer, abstraction, and mortification. For if they use none at all (as no good Christian but useth them in some degree), undoubtedly they will not profit at all in spirit, neither actively nor contemplatively, nor avoid sin, nor be in any sort united to God.

About the doctrine of Confession: whereas the Author disputeth much against the using of Confession of venial sins, as necessary to spiritual profit, it is to be understood that he doth not in any wise condemn the discreet use of frequent Confession, but only the needless enumeration of venial sins and daily defects which some souls do make in their confessions with great anxiety of mind, and which some confessors do oblige their penitents unto, with great prejudice of that cheerful liberty of spirit which a soul should have to converse with God in Prayer, and is commonly a cause of scruples, one of the greatest banes of spiritual perfection. So that for souls that are by nature prone to fear and scrupulosity, the director must of necessity moderate them both in the frequency of Confession, and the matter to be confessed. Yea, he may advise them to confess fewer times than other freer souls do. Otherwise for souls that are cheerful and valiant and courageous in the way of the Spirit, the Author obligeth them in his practice to keep the ordinary time of Confession; much more those that are not so careful in avoiding occasions of ordinary defects; I say, he obligeth them in such sort as the Constitutions oblige, which is not under any sin, as if they should sin as often as they omit the ordinary time of Confession; but as a laudable counsel and profitable observance, which under a penalty and regular correction is to be kept, and not omitted but by advice from the spiritual father, or leave of the Superior.

Note also that he doth worthily advertise a defect of many who come to Confession, making the principal intention of it only the absolution from sin. I say this is a defect, because the principal part of the intention must be the increase of Grace and love of God, by which, formally infused or poured into ourselves, God Almighty doth blot out sins and wipe them away. Now although absolution from sin is never given without infusion of Grace, yet ought the intention of the penitent to be principally the obtaining of Grace; for if he principally intend the absolution from sin, it is a reflection of the soul upon its own profit by self-love, desiring to avoid the wrath of God and punishment due to sin, and to be freed from the deformity of guiltiness; which, though it be a good desire, yet is but a property of beginners in love, and nothing comparable to the intention of Grace, which is the perfect love of God, and is an elevation of the soul to transcend itself and all creatures, to live only in God.

About the doctrine of set Examinations of Conscience, the Author doth not condemn it, especially for souls who are not greatly advanced in perfection; but for souls which daily profit and grow in Grace he prefers the exercise of Love; and not without cause; for his meaning is, that in our recollection it is an easier and speedier way to amend ourselves by wrapping all our defects in a generality, and so endeavour to consume them, as it were casting them into the fire of love, than by particularising them and discussing them in singular; because in so doing they distract the mind, that may be better employed. Yet this doctrine hinders not, but if any notable defect have been committed, it should be by a particular reflection amended; yet rather by an amorous conversion of the soul to God by Humility, than by turning itself to look upon the defect in particular. And doubtless a soul that, according to the Author's doctrine, doth so carefully avoid all defects that it presently, upon sight of any default, exacteth an amendment of itself, such a soul needeth no set examen, but supplieth the use thereof by a more noble exercise, which is, as I termed it, an humble consuming of all her defects in one bundle in the heavenly fire of charity or love of God.

Nevertheless a set examen is profitable for such as are not yet come to such a height of unitive love, and is counselled by our Father Blosius in divers places, and by St. Bernard in his book to the Carthusians in these words: *Nemo te plus diligit, nemo te fidelius judicabit,* &c.—that is, 'None loves thee more, none will judge thee more faithfully, than thine own self.' In the morning, then, exact an account of the night past, and appoint thyself a caution for the day ensuing. At evening take account of the day past, and order the course of the night following. Thus strictly examining thyself, thou wilt find no leisure to play wanton. And long before St. Bernard, the holy Abbot St. Dorotheus commends the same exercise (Serm xi.) as usual amongst all monks: *Quo pacto per singulos dies nosipsos purgare,* &c.—that each night every one ought to inquire diligently with himself how he has spent the day, and each morning how he spent the night, and let him do penance and renew himself before God, if, as is possible, he may have sinned. And long before him St. Ephrem, who lived only years after Christ our Lord's Passion, hath the commendation of a set examination, exhorting that

410

each day, morning and evening, we should diligently examine whether we have earned our wages.

Neither doth our Author discommend this set examen, but the defective use of it, which is: first, to make it in order to Confession, which doubtless in a soul well advanced breedeth needless images, since such a soul will call to mind what sufficeth for her ordinary confession without this examen. Second, too much particularising of our defects: which is likewise distractive, it being sufficient to examine the performance of our duty and obligatory actions, or if any notable defect have carelessly crept upon us; all other defects being more profitably wrapt up in a generality, and so cast into our Saviour's Passion, than particularly stirred up, which would but in a manner raise up a new dust in the soul. Third, the anxious looking upon the defects in themselves and in their peculiar matter or object; whereas it is better and safer to turn the eye of our soul from the matter in particular unto God Almighty, humbling ourselves before Him, and with loving reverence craving pardon of Him. A fourth defect is to imagine that it is a sin in careful souls to omit this examen, whereas indeed it is none at all; though in souls that are careless of their actions, it is ordinarily a defective negligence worthy to be reprehended. In a word, a set examen may be used profitably by all souls with those cautions above mentioned, and is to be counselled to all beginners in the way of Perfection, and to all that be not so wary in their actions. But if the director perceive a soul to be so wary, that she is perpetually careful of progress in spirit, and never deferreth correction and amendment of her defects, but out of hand redresseth what she discovereth to be amiss, to such a soul may the director permit, instead of a set examen, to use her ordinary elevation of heart to God, and by virtual contrition or actual (as God moveth her) included in the exercise of love, deface all the defects of her life.

Let none likewise be scandalised at that which is said, that there be higher exercises than Meditation on the Passion; and that it is not always the profitablest way to busy our soul in that object. For since our Religious hear ordinarily two Masses, or at least one daily, in that they do actually celebrate the memory of our Saviour's Passion; and at divers other times they have leisure to think lovingly thereupon, that they need not in all their recollections take that only object; especially since their manner of Prayer is more by act of will, than by consideration of the understanding; and (as is very well declared in one place) all their recollections and actions that have any other special object are virtually intended in honour of our Saviour's Passion.

What is said about passive Contemplation, that it is rather received into the soul than produced or wrought by our own action or endeavour, is most true; supposing always that this reception of it in our soul is a vital op-

411

eration (which, whether it be called an action of the soul or a mere passion, is a school question and nothing to our purpose). Certain it is that by all our own power we could not produce it, and therefore it is called the *Inaction of God* in our soul by many mystics, to which we only concur by vitally receiving it, and by a willing consent to let God work His Will in us.

What is said about the immediate operation of God in the very essence and substance of our soul, and not in the powers thereof, nor by meditation of the powers, although it be against the general doctrine of the Philosophers and Schoolmen, yet it is a probable opinion, and grounded upon experience of devout men, that were also great scholars, and therefore may securely be followed. As also that which is there said, that God can move the will to love without the operation of the understanding, though many deny it, yet it is most probable and befitting the almighty power of God, and is held by Gerson and St. Bonaventure, who were no small School Divines.

Lastly, the vehement urging that great heed be taken in the choice of a confessor and director in these mystic ways of God is necessary, and not intended to the dispraise of any, nor to the disabling of such as perhaps have not all the qualities required. But it seems especially for two ends: the one for an advertisement to the directors and confessors that they presume not to judge or proceed rashly in the directing of our Religious, but according to these cautions and instructions; especially if they themselves have not been accustomed to this affective Prayer of the will. And we do conjure them in behalf of our Saviour Christ to cherish this way, and to set it forward as the peculiar exercise belonging to our spirit and calling; yet so as intellectual prayer be not altogether neglected in the occasions which in these books are sufficiently assigned. The other end is to cut off a dangerous curiosity which women used to have of desiring to confer upon their interior with every learned or devout man they hear of; which is a very great defect, and by those vehement persuasions of our Author very deservedly and warily prevented. And although St. Teresa did give way to this universal communication of interior to divers learned men, and commended it to her daughters, yet we are credibly informed that in her latter days with tears she hath said, that by it occasion was given to discontented minds to vent forth their disgusts, with harm to themselves and the Community. Therefore, out of this point let the Religious resolve to communicate their interior to their lawful superiors, and to directors by them appointed, who will have care that the spirit of Prayer be not extinguished or hindered in them by any unskilful or heedless guides. Thus much we thought convenient to note under our hands in commendation of these holy instructions, and for a caution and warning to future confessors and spiritual directors.

ACTS AND AFFECTIONS OF THE WILL

F. Leander de S. Martino, Prior of St. Gregory in Douay, and Ordinary of the Cloister of the Dames of our Lady of Comfort in Cambray, of the Holy Order of St. Benedict.

In the last place I will adjoin a scheme clearly and at once representing the sum of the Ven. Author's Doctrine, of Divine Calls, composed by the same V. R. F. Leander de S. Martino.

Whatsoever action or omission occurs unto us in all our life, what occasion soever of doing, forbearing, suffering, or receiving from God or any creature, is of such condition, that either

1. It hath some exterior rule commanding it, or forbidding it, which is to be esteemed undoubtedly as the Call of God; and in all such occurrences

1. The exterior rule is to be faithfully kept and practised, in the performing or omitting the action occurring.

2. The interior Call is likewise as carefully to be kept and practised, in the manner of omitting or performing; that it may be done or omitted, with the true spirit and life of Grace, by the exercise of the will.

Or 2. It hath no exterior rule allotted to the occurrence at that time, and is otherwise against no exterior rule of lawful authority: as certainly an infinity of such things happen and occur in time of silence and rest, in our cells; being alone in our labour, recreation, refection, c&c.: and in such cases

1. If it be *extraordinary* in *matter,* as long fasting, much watching, &c.; or in *manner,* as if it be ecstatical or in some strange manner of illumination or inspiration unaccustomed or unwonted to the soul, it is not to be practised till it be examined and allowed by the ordinary exterior rule; yet in no sort to be neglected, but remembered and noted for use and direction, when occasion occurreth in ourselves or others.

2. If it be *ordinary* in *matter* and *manner,* neither implying any inconvenience nor notable singularity, then is the inward Call in a spiritual and true-minded soul a sufficient and secure guide, and ought to be carefully observed and obeyed, lest otherwise the soul ungratefully take God's graces in vain, and so be worthily deprived of them.

F. Leander de S. Martino, President.

18 March 1634.

After the above written paper there follows this, in Father Baker's own hand

The doctrine of Divine Calls here above expressed by our Reverend Father, Father Leander de S. Martino, being at the present our worthy President, I do profess to be the self-same in substance (and by my intention) which more largely, but less sufficiently, I have expressed and delivered in divers books and treatises that are of my penning concerning that subject.

B. Augustine Baker, the 20th of March 1634, Stilo Romano

CERTAIN PATTERNS
OF
DEVOUT EXERCISES
OF
IMMEDIATE ACTS AND AFFECTIONS
OF
THE WILL

TO THE DEVOUT READER

Devout Reader,

According to promises made in several passages of the foregoing Instructions (especially in the second and third chapters of the third section of
the Third Treatise), I here have provided for thee a sufficient number of exercises of holy Affections and Acts of the Will, &c.; in the first place
beginning with devout exercises upon the Life and Sufferings, &c., of our
Saviour, consisting of almost all sorts of Acts and Affections, to wit, of Contrition, Humiliation, Resignation, Love, &c.

2. Now though the said exercises be more sublime and perfect than
some others that follow, to wit, those of Fear, Hatred of Sin, Remorse, Reflections upon the *Quatuor Novissima,* &c., yet have I placed them first,
because they are a kind of exercise of Meditation (the lowest degree of internal Prayer), and may be proper enough for such well-disposed souls as by
means of some unknown natural indisposition are incapable of practising
Meditation, according to the common laborious method and rules. They may
likewise be useful and proper for souls also that are advanced to the second
degree of internal Prayer, viz. that of immediate Acts of the Will.

3. It was not needful to divide these into several distinct exercises, as
those that follow. Therefore the devout soul that shall practise them may in
each recollection make use of as many good affections or acts in them as will
suffice; and in the following recollection begin where she last ended (observ-

415

ing the directions prescribed in the precedent instructions touching internal Prayer of immediate Acts of the Will).

4. Now it is not to be supposed that, in annexing these exercises, we have any intention to confine the readers and practisers of these directions unto them; for in practice each one is to make use of such acts as are most relishing to his spirit, whether composed by the exerciser himself, or found in this or any other book. And particularly the books most proper to be made use of for the Prayer of immediate Acts or Affections of the Will are, St. Augustine's *Confessions, Soliloquies,* &c.; the *Imitation of Christ* (especially the third book); the *Divine Exercises* of Eschius, in Latin, and likewise long since translated into English and enlarged by Doctor Peryn; the *Actus Virtutum* of Blasius Palma; *Paradisus Animæ;* the *Igniarium Divini Amoris* of Blosius, &c.

HAIL, JESUS
OR ACTS UPON THE LIFE AND PASSION OF OUR SAVIOUR JESUS CHRIST:

Which contain in them Acts of almost all Kinds of Prayer, as Contrition, Resignation., Love, &c.

1. Hail, Sweet Jesus; praise, honour, and glory be to Thee, O Christ, who for my sake hast vouchsafed to come down from Thy royal seat, and from the mellifluous bosom of Thy Divine Father, into this valley of misery, and to be incarnate and made man by the Holy Ghost in the most chaste womb of the most sacred Virgin Mary;

2. Choose, I beseech Thee, my heart for Thy dwelling-place; adorn it, replenish it with spiritual gifts, and wholly possess it.

3. O that I were able, by profound humility, to unite Thee to it, and with an ardent affection to receive Thee; and after having received Thee, to retain Thee with me!

4. O that I were so fastened unto Thee, that I might never depart or turn away my mind from Thee.

5. Hail, sweet Jesus; praise, honour, and glory be to Thee, O Christ, who hast vouchsafed to be born of Thy Virgin Mother, poor and passible, without any pain or detriment to her virginity, in a poor stable;

6. Whom, being born, she humbly adored.

7. O that it were Thy will to be continually born in me by a new fervour of spirit,

8. And that I may be wholly burnt with the fire of Thy love!

9. O that Thou wert the only comfort, desire, and solace of my heart!

10. O that I sought after Thee alone, thought on Thee alone, and loved Thee alone!

11. Hail, sweet Jesus; praise, honour, and glory be to Thee, O Christ, who, being born in the depth of winter, didst not refuse to be swaddled in poor clothes, and weeping to be laid in a manger, and as a little infant to be nourished at Thy Mother's breast;

12. I adore Thee, most dear Redeemer, King of angels.

13. Hail, Prince of Peace, Light of the Gentiles, and most desired Saviour;

14. Grant, O Lord, that I may always stand in Thy sight, truly humble and truly poor in spirit;

15. Grant that for Thy holy name's sake I may willingly endure all kinds of mortification, and may love nothing in the world besides Thee, nor wish to possess anything but Thee.

16. Hail, sweet Jesus; whom the celestial legions of angels did honour, newly born, with joyful praises; and the shepherds, devoutly seeking and finding, adored with admiration;

17. Grant that I may joyfully, without tediousness, persevere in Thy service and praises.

18. Hail, sweet Jesus, who wouldst upon the eighth day, like other children, be circumcised, and, being yet an infant, shed Thy Precious Blood;

19. And for our singular comfort wouldst be called Jesus, which signifieth a Saviour:

20. O that it would please Thee to admit me, circumcised from all bad thoughts, words, and works, into the number of Thy children!

21. Thou, O Lord, art called Jesus, that is to say, a Saviour: be Thou therefore my Saviour, and save me.

22. Hail, sweet Jesus, whom the sages, with a devout seeking, found by the direction of a star, and having found, most humbly adored,

23. Offering unto Thee gifts of gold, frankincense, and myrrh;

24. Grant, O Lord, that with these blessed men I may always seek and adore Thee in spirit and truth;

25. Grant that I may offer daily unto Thee the gold of bright shining charity, the frankincense of sweet-smelling devotion, and the myrrh of perfect mortification.

26. Hail, sweet Jesus, who for our sake wouldst be subject to the law, and, to give us an example of humility, wouldst be carried to the temple by Thy

Blessed Mother, and be redeemed with an offering ordained for such as were poor;

27. Where just Simeon and Anna the Prophetess, rejoicing greatly at Thy presence, gave very glorious testimony of Thy dignity:

28. O that all pride were utterly thrown down in me!

29. O that all desire of human favour and itch of self-love were cooled and cured in me!

30. Hail, sweet Jesus; praise, honour, and glory be to Thee, O Christ, who, staying in the temple, wert for the space of three days with great grief sought by Thy devout Mother, and at length with great joy found by her sitting in the midst of the doctors, hearing them and proposing questions to them:

31. Would to God Thou wouldst give and communicate Thyself in such sort unto me, that I might never be separated from Thee, nor ever be deprived of Thy comfort!

32. Hail, sweet Jesus, who, for the space of thirty years remaining unknown, hast vouchsafed to be reputed the son of Joseph the carpenter and of his wife the Blessed Virgin Mary;

33. Let Thy grace, I beseech Thee, pluck up and utterly root out of the fund of my soul all pride and ambition:

34. O that I may delight to be unknown, and to be esteemed vile and base!

35. Hail, sweet Jesus, who hast not disdained to come to the river Jordan, and entering into it to be baptised by Thy servant John the Baptist;

36. I would, through Thy merits, I might become most clean and pure, even in this life.

37. Hail, sweet Jesus, who, for our sakes abiding amongst wild beasts in the desert, and fasting forty days and forty nights, and persevering in prayer, hast permitted Thyself to be tempted by Satan;

38. And overcoming him, hast been honoured with the ministry and service of angels;

39. Give me grace that I may chastise and subdue my flesh, with all the vicious affections thereof;

40. Give me grace that I may constantly persevere in prayer and other spiritual exercises;

41. Let no temptation, I beseech Thee, defile me, but rather let temptations purge me and unite me unto Thee.

42. Hail, sweet Jesus, who, to the end Thou mightest gather together the dispersed children of God, hast vouchsafed to preach penance, to call disciples, and out of them to choose twelve Apostles to be eminent preachers of Thy faith;

43. Draw me after Thee, and powerfully stir up my heart to love Thee;

44. Grant that I may adhere to Thee alone. Amen.

45. Hail, sweet Jesus; praise, honour, and glory be to Thee, O Christ, who for me hast suffered many afflictions, heat, cold, hunger, thirst, labours, and miseries;

46. Grant that I may receive from Thy hand cheerfully all kinds of adversity.

47. Hail, sweet Jesus, who, thirsting for the conversion of souls, hast passed whole nights in prayer,

48. Hast been wearied with travelling, hast passed from country to country, from city to city, from town to town, from village to village;

49. Let Thy love make me quick and ready to all good things, that I be never slothful in Thy service;

50. Grant that everywhere I may have a zeal for Thy honour, and employ myself wholly in Thy service.

51. Hail, sweet Jesus; praise, honour, and glory be to Thee, O Christ, who, conversing with men, hast vouchsafed most willingly to comfort them, and by many miracles most mercifully to cure their maladies and diseases;

52. Give me a devout heart full of affection and compassion, whereby I may pity other men's afflictions, and may have as great feeling of their miseries as if they were my own;

53. Whereby also I may bear patiently with all men's imperfections, and to the best of my ability succour them in their necessities.

54. Hail, sweet Jesus; praise, honour, and glory be to Thee, O Christ, who hast not shunned the company of publicans and sinners, but hast afforded them Thy most loving familiarity and ready pardon of sins, to Matthew, Zacheus, Mary Magdalen, and to the woman taken in adultery, and to the rest that were repentant;

55. Grant that I may embrace all men with cheerful love and charity;

56. May readily forgive those who offend me;

57. May perfectly love those who hate me.

58. Hail, sweet Jesus, who for my soul's sake hast suffered many injuries, many blasphemies, many reproaches, and infinite abuses from those on whom Thou hadst bestowed many benefits;

59. Give me a heart truly innocent and simple, that I may sincerely love my enemies and unfeignedly pity them;

60. And rendering good for evil may, through perfect charity and meek patience, perfectly please Thee. Amen.

61. Hail, sweet Jesus; praise, honour, and glory be to Thee, O Christ, who, coming to Jerusalem in a meek and gentle manner, didst ride upon an ass, and amidst the praises which were sung by the people who came to meet Thee didst pour forth tears, bewailing the ruin of the city and destruction of those ungrateful souls:

62. O that I might never be delighted with the praises and favours of men;

63. But always be profitably employed in internal tears of compunction and devotion!

64. Hail, sweet Jesus, whom Judas, the treacherous disciple, sold for a little money to the Jews who persecuted Thee and conspired Thy death;

65. Root out of my heart all evil desires of transitory things;

66. Grant that I may never prefer anything before Thee.

67. Hail, sweet Jesus; praise, honour, and glory be to Thee, O Christ, who in Jerusalem, according to the law, didst eat the Paschal lamb with Thy disciples, and giving them an example of humility and holy charity, kneeling upon the ground, didst wash their feet, and having washed them didst wipe them with a towel:

68. Would to God this example might pierce my heart, and utterly throw down in me all pride and loftiness!

69. Give me, O Lord, a most profound humility, by which I may without difficulty cast myself at all men's feet.

70. Hail, sweet Jesus, who with an unspeakable charity hast instituted the Sacrament of the Eucharist, and with a wonderful liberality hast in it given Thyself to us;

71. Stir up in me a desire and enkindle in the interior of my soul a vehement thirst of this most venerable Sacrament;

72. Grant that when I come to this table of life I may with a chaste affection, singular humility, and perfect purity of heart receive Thee.

73. Hail, sweet Jesus, who immediately before Thy Passion didst begin to fear, to grieve, and be sad, taking upon Thyself our weakness,

74. That by this Thy infirmity thou mayest comfort and strengthen those that tremble at the expectation of death;

75. Preserve me, I beseech Thee, as well from vicious sadness as from foolish joy;

76. Grant that all the grief I have hitherto sustained may redound to Thy glory and the remission of my sins.

77. Hail, sweet Jesus, who, falling upon the ground, prayedst unto Thy Father, and humbly offeredst up Thyself wholly unto Him, saying, 'Father, Thy will be done;'

78. Grant that in all necessities and tribulations I may have recourse unto Thee by prayer;

79. That I may give and resign myself wholly to Thy will;

80. That I may with a quiet mind receive all things as from Thy hands.

81. Hail, sweet Jesus; praise, honour, and glory be to Thee, O Christ, who, being in an agony, didst pray very long;

82. And being Creator of heaven and earth, the King of kings and Lord of angels, didst not disdain to be comforted by an angel;

83. Grant that in all adversity and desolation, in all tribulation and affliction, I may seek comfort from Thee only,

84. And that I may find help and assistance at Thy hands.

85. O that I could in all events wholly rely on Thee,

86. And leave myself wholly to Thy Fatherly care!

87. Hail, sweet Jesus, who, by reason of the greatness and vehemency of Thy grief, hadst Thy Body moistened all over with a bloody sweat:

88. O that all the parts of my interior man would sweat out holy tears of contrition!

89. Hail, sweet Jesus, who of Thine own accord offeredst Thyself to be taken by Judas the traitor, and Thine other enemies thirsting after Thy blood, and desiring Thy death;

90. Grant, for the honour of Thy name, I may not fly adversities,

91. But may cheerfully go to meet them,

92. And joyfully receive them, as precious tokens sent from Thee;

93. And humbly and constantly endure them as long as it shall please Thee.

94. Hail, sweet Jesus, who didst lovingly kiss the traitor Judas coming deceitfully to Thee;

95. Showing, by the calmness of Thy countenance and sweetness of Thy words, that Thou didst love him;

96. Grant that I may show myself loving and mild to all my enemies;

97. That I may pardon them from my heart, howsoever they shall offend me;

98. And tolerate and love them as the ministers of Thy will and promoters of my salvation.

99. Hail, sweet Jesus, who didst permit Thine enemies most furiously to lay their sacrilegious hands upon Thee;

100. And, being cruelly bound by them, didst not revenge but mildly endure the reproaches, blasphemies, and injuries wherewith they did most wickedly affront Thee:

101. O that, being freed from the bonds of vice, I may be fast tied to Thee with the sweet chains of love!

102. O that Thou wouldst bestow upon me the grace of true patience! Amen.

103. Hail, sweet Jesus; praise, honour, and glory be to Thee, O Christ, who didst restore and heal the ear of Malchus, one of Thy furious persecutors, cut off by Peter, Thy chief disciple;

104. That so, rendering good for evil, the riches of Thy mercy and mildness might shine forth to us;

105. Grant, I beseech Thee, that the desire of revenge may never have place in my heart;

106. Grant that I may bear intimate compassion and affection towards all such as offend me;

107. Strengthen my too great weakness, and make steadfast my too great inconstancy, with the most strong support of Thy grace.

108. Hail, sweet Jesus, who sufferedst Thyself to be led, bound as a malefactor and thief, by a troop of soldiers unto Annas, and to be presented before him:

109. O unspeakable mildness of my Redeemer!

110. Behold, whilst Thou art taken, whilst Thou art drawn, whilst Thou art haled, Thou dost not complain, Thou dost not murmur, Thou makest no resistance;

111. Grant, O Lord, that these examples of Thy virtues may shine in me to my good and everlasting glory.

112. Hail, sweet Jesus, King of heaven and earth, who, standing, humble, like a base and abject person, before the proud High-priest, didst with great modesty receive a cruel blow given Thee upon the Face by one of his servants;

113. Suppress, I beseech Thee, in me all motions of anger and wrath; dull all the stings of indignation, and extinguish all desire of revenge;

114. That, even provoked with injuries. I may not be troubled;

115. That I may not strive or make any tumult;

116. But, suffering all things with a meek and patient mind, I may render good for evil, and ever be ready to favour those who most cross and molest me.

117. Hail, sweet Jesus; praise, honour, and glory be to Thee, O Christ, who didst suffer Thyself to be shamefully led bound to Caiphas, that Thou mightest restore us to true liberty, freeing us from the bonds of everlasting death;

118. Grant that in the very midst of derisions and contumelies I may give Thee thanks with all my heart,

119. And that by them I may be advanced in Thy love.

120. Hail, sweet Jesus, whom Peter the chief of the Apostles thrice denied; and yet Thou most mercifully lookedst upon him, and provokedst him to repentance and holy tears for his offence:

121. O that it might please Thee in like manner to look upon me with that lovely eye of Thy mercy!

122. That, with due tears of repentance, I may bewail my past sins;

123. And having bewailed them, may not hereafter any more return to them again.

124. Hail, sweet Jesus, who with a pleasing countenance and modest look, standing before the priests and the elders of the people of the Jews, didst not disdain to be falsely accused and suffer many injuries;

125. Grant that I may never utter any falsity or calumniate any man;

126. But may suffer such calumnies as are laid against me with great tranquillity of heart;

127. And, referring all difficulties to Thee, with silence I may expect Thy grace and comfort.

128. Hail, sweet Jesus, who, whilst Thou didst make profession of the truth, affirming Thyself to be Son of God, yet didst Thou not disdain to be esteemed a blasphemer;

129. Grant that in all places and before all men I may stand to the truth, and in awe of the presence of Thy Divinity and Majesty I may not fear the censures and judgments of men.

130. Hail, sweet Jesus, who by the wicked Jews wast proclaimed guilty of death, and without cause condemned;

131. That by Thy unjust condemnation Thou mightest deliver us from the guilt of our sins wherewith we were justly attainted;

132. Grant that I may reject all sinister and rash suspicions;

133. That I may suffer, without any bitterness of heart, all such wrongful detractions and wicked judgments as others shall devise against me;

134. And that on all occasions I may retain, by the help of Thy grace, a quiet and untroubled mind.

135. Hail, sweet Jesus; praise, honour, and glory be to Thee, O Christ, who for my sake wast made the disgrace and scorn of men, and the outcast of the people;

136. And didst not turn away Thy sacred Face, which the angels desire to behold, from the filthy spittle of Thy adversaries;

137. Grant that I may imitate Thy meekness and patience.

138. Hail, sweet Jesus, who didst vouchsafe to be most cruelly beaten and buffeted, and most unworthily reproached and reviled for my sake;

139. Grant, I beseech Thee, that I may never refuse to be despised and to be reputed base and vile,

140. And that, according to Thy permission, I may be contented to be exercised with all kinds of injuries;

141. That I may receive them, not as from men, but from Thee, and of Thy Fatherly mercy.

142. Hail, sweet Jesus, who didst permit Thyself to be mocked and scoffed, and Thy lovely Face (which to behold is the chiefest happiness), for Thy greater derision, to be blindfolded;

143. Grant that, the veil of ignorance being taken away, I may be endued with the knowledge of Thy will;

144. Imprint in my heart a continual remembrance of Thee;

145. Thou knowest, O Lord, how hard a thing it is for me to suffer, though never so small a matter;

146. Out of Thy mercy, therefore, assist my frailty, that I may not cowardly fall or faint at the coming of any adversity.

147. Hail, sweet Jesus, who didst permit Thyself (being mocked and bound) to be led to the profane tribunal of Pilate the judge, and in a disdainful manner to be presented before him, Thou Thyself being the Judge of the living and the dead;

148. Grant that I may be truly subject to my superiors and all powers over me ordained by Thee;

149. That I may obey my equals, and love and honour all men;

150. Grant that I may not fear other men's judgments of me, but may receive them with a ready and meek mind. Amen.

151. Hail, sweet, Jesus, who, standing before Pilate, didst Humbly hold Thy peace, whilst the Jews did wrongfully accuse and calumniate Thee:

152. Grant, O Lord, that I may never be troubled at other men's slandering me,

153. But that I may with silence overcome all injuries;

154. Give me the perfect grace of humility, by which I may neither desire to be praised nor refuse to be contemned;

155. Grant that I may imitate Thy innocency and patience;

156. That I may both live well, and, living well, be contented to be ill spoken of and despised.

157. Hail, sweet Jesus, who, with great exclamations and much noise of people, like a most heinous malefactor wast drawn from tribunal to tribunal, from Pilate to Herod, through the midst of the city;

158. Grant that I may not be dejected with any injuries of my enemies,

159. And that I be not much ashamed of contempt,

160. To the end that, by Thy gracious assistance, I may possess my soul in patience.

161. Hail, sweet Jesus; praise, honour, and glory be to Thee, O Christ, who, by Thy silence condemning Herod's vain desire, wouldst not, without good cause and for a good end, delight his curious eyes by working a miracle; and didst thereby give us a lesson to avoid ostentation in the presence of great men;

162. Pour into my soul Thy spirit of profound humility;

163. Mortify and extinguish in me all tickling of vain glory:

164. Grant that I may not seek to gain the praises of men, but do all and purely for Thy honour and glory.

165. Hail, sweet Jesus, who didst not disdain to be scoffed at by Herod and his whole army, and to be clothed in a white garment, like a fool or a madman;

166. Grant that I may rather choose to be reputed base and abject with Thee than glorious with the world;

167. That I may esteem it better and more worthy to suffer disgrace for Thy love, than to shine in the vain honour of the world;

168. Grant that, knowing thoroughly my own unworthiness, I may grow base in my own conceit, and despise, reprehend, and bewail myself.

169. Hail, sweet Jesus, who, being compared with the notorious thief Barabbas, wast judged more wicked and more worthy of death than he:

170. The murderer is set at liberty, and the impious Jews demand Thy death, who art the Author of life;

171. Thou art indeed that Living Stone rejected by man but chosen by God:

172. O that I may prefer nothing before Thee, nor change Thee for anything!

173. O that I could esteem all things as dung and filth, to the end I might gain Thee!

174. Grant, O Lord, that the blot of envy may never stain my soul.

175. Hail, sweet Jesus, who, being stripped naked in the palace and bound to a pillar, didst suffer Thy naked and most immaculate Flesh to be rent with most cruel scourges, that with Thy sores Thou mightest heal our wounds:

176. O amiable Jesus, I make choice of Thee, covered with stripes, for the spouse of my soul,

177. Desiring to be inflamed and burned with the fire of Thy most sweet love;

178. Strip my heart naked, I beseech Thee, from all indecent cogitations;

179. Grant that I may now patiently suffer the scourges of Thy Fatherly correction. Amen.

180. Hail, sweet Jesus; praise, honour, and glory be to Thee, O Christ, upon whom are discharged unspeakable injuries and contumelies;

181. For they clothed Thee, the King of Glory, with a purple garment for Thy greater affront;

182. They fastened upon Thy divine head a crown of thorns;

183. They put into Thy hands a sceptre of a reed, and, kneeling down in a scornful manner, saluted Thee, saying, 'Hail, King of the Jews!'

184. Plant, I beseech Thee, in my heart the memory of Thy Passion;

185. Let scorn for Thy sake be my glory, and injuries and affronts my crown.

186. Hail, sweet Jesus, who didst not refuse for my sake to be beaten with a reed, to be buffeted, to be spit upon, and to be the object of all kinds of derision;

187. I beseech Thee, by Thy wounds, by Thy Blood, by Thy disgrace, and by all the grief and sorrow Thou sufferedst for me, to endow my soul with all Thy patience and graces;

188. That Thou wouldst convert me and all I have to Thy everlasting praise and glory.

189. Hail, sweet Jesus, who, being defiled with spittle, rent and disfigured with stripes, bound and wholly miserable, wast brought forth as a spectacle to the enraged people, wearing a crown of thorns and a robe of purple;

190. Grant that with my heart I may utterly tread under foot, and have in detestation, all ambition, ostentation, worldly pomp and vanity, and all earthly dignity;

191. That, by profound humility and true contempt of myself, I may incessantly run towards the glory of Thy heavenly felicity.

192. Hail, sweet Jesus, who, being declared innocent by Pilate the judge, didst not refuse to hear the furious outcries of the Jews, by which they demanded that Thou shouldst be crucified;

193. Grant that I may live innocently, and not be troubled by reason of other men's evil will towards me;

194. Give me this grace, that I may neither backbite other men, nor willingly give ear to those that do it;

195. But that still I may have a good opinion of others, and bear other men's imperfections with a true compassion;

196. And love all men for God and in God with a pure, sincere, and cordial affection.

197. Hail, sweet Jesus; praise, honour, and glory be to Thee, O Christ, who didst permit Thyself in the presence of Thy people to be unjustly condemned to the most ignominious death of the cross,

198. That Thou mightest free us from the sentence of eternal death;

199. Grant that I may seek Thy honour, and rather choose to be exercised with Thee in adversity, than by forsaking Thee to enjoy the commodities of life.

200. Hail, sweet Jesus, who, with many disgraces and injuries offered Thee, didst carry Thy cross with great pain upon Thy sacred and torn shoulders,

201. And, being weary and breathless, didst languish under the burden;

202. Grant that, with fervent devotion, I may embrace the cross of my own abnegation,

203. And with an ardent charity imitate the example of Thy virtues,

204. And may humbly follow Thee unto death.

205. Hail, sweet Jesus, who, in that lamentable journey in which Thou wentest to Thy death, didst meekly admonish the women, that they should bewail themselves and their children;

206. Give me acceptable tears of compunction, with which I may truly bewail my sins and my own ingratitude;

207. Give me tears of devout compunction and of holy love, which may melt my hard heart, and make it grateful unto Thee,

208. That I may love Thee alone, and rest in Thee only.

209. Hail, sweet Jesus; praise, honour, and glory be to Thee, O Christ, who, having Thy shoulders bruised with the weight of the cross, didst at length arrive weary at the place of execution,

210. Where wine, mingled with gall, was offered Thee to refresh Thy languishing strength:

211. O that Thou wouldst extinguish in me the allurements of gluttony and the concupiscence of the flesh,

212. And cause in me an aversion and horror of all impure and unlawful delights;

213. And that I may eat and drink soberly to the glory of Thy name,

214. That I may hunger and thirst after Thee alone,

215. And in Thee place my delight and joy!

216. Hail, sweet Jesus, who didst not disdain to be stripped naked upon Mount Calvary in the sight of the people,

217. And to suffer a most bitter pain by Thy sores, renewed with the pulling off Thy clothes;

218. Grant that I may love poverty of spirit, and not be troubled with any worldly want;

219. Grant that by Thy example I may endure and suffer any corporal necessities or calamities whatsoever.

220. Hail, sweet Jesus, who, being naked, didst not refuse to be rudely stretched out upon the wood of the cross, and cruelly fastened with nails unto the same;

221. In this manner Thou didst suffer Thy innocent hands and delicate feet to be most grievously wounded, and all Thy sacred joints to crack and be put out of joint;

. Grant me, O Lord, that with a faithful and grateful mind I may consider this Thy unspeakable charity, with which of Thy own accord Thou didst stretch forth Thy arms, and willingly offer Thy hands and feet to be pierced;

223. Vouchsafe, O Lord, to enlarge and extend my heart with the perfect love of Thee;

224. Pierce it, and fasten it unto Thyself with the most sweet nail of charity;

225. And all my senses, cogitations, and affections enclose only on Thee.

226. Hail, sweet Jesus; praise, honour, and glory be to Thee, O Christ, who didst hang (Thy hands and feet being pierced) three hours upon the shameful wood of the cross, and, shedding in great abundance Thy Precious Blood, didst of Thy own accord endure unspeakable torments throughout Thy whole Body;

227. Lift up, I pray Thee, upon the wood of Thy cross, my miserable soul grovelling on the ground:

228. O healthful Blood, O reviving Blood!

229. O that Thou wouldst purge and thoroughly heal me, being washed with this Thy Precious Blood!

230. O that Thou wouldst offer this Thy Blood to Thy Father for a perfect satisfaction of all my iniquities!

231. Grant, I beseech Thee, that mine inward man may, with ardent affection, mentally receive the lively drops of Thy Precious Blood, and may truly 'taste how sweet Thy Spirit is.'

232. Hail, sweet Jesus, who wast so good even to those that were so wicked, that for the very same persons who did crucify Thee Thou didst pray unto Thy Father, saying, 'Father, forgive them, for they know not what they do;'

233. Give me, I beseech Thee, the grace of true meeknes and patience, by which I may, according to Thy commandment and example, love my enemies,

234. And do good to those that hate me;

235. I heartily pray unto Thee for those that hurt and persecute me.

236. Hail, sweet Jesus, who wouldst that the title written in Hebrew, Greek, and Latin (as it were the trophy of Thy victory) should be fastened to the cross, that we beholding it might courageously fight against our invisible enemies;

237. Protect me, under this title, against the wiles and deceits of the devil:

238. Teach me, under this title, to overcome all temptations, and to subdue all vices;

239 That, having by grace conquered them, I may freely praise and glorify Thy holy name. Amen.

240. Hail, sweet Jesus; praise, honour, and glory be to Thee, O Christ, whose garments the soldiers divided amongst themselves, but did leave Thy coat, which was without seam (and signifieth the unity of the Church), undivided;

241. Pour down into my heart, I beseech Thee, the spirit of peace and union,

242. That I may never, through my fault, divide or trouble the concord and union of my brethren;

243. But that I may always endeavour to repair divisions and pacify troubles.

244. Hail, sweet Jesus, who, suffering upon the altar of the cross incomprehensible torments and ineffable anguishes, wert shamefully reproached and scorned by the Jews, who vomited out of their wicked mouths sundry blasphemies against Thee;

245. Grant, O Lord, that, being mindful of Thy humility, patience, and mildness, I may quietly and cheerfully suffer pain, disgrace, persecution, infamy, &c.,

246. And may remain with Thee nailed to the cross even to the end;

247. Let no violence of temptation, no storm of adversity, no tempest of contumely, hinder me from effecting my good purposes;

248. Let not death, nor life, nor things present nor to come, nor any creature separate me from Thy love.

249. Hail, sweet Jesus, who didst tolerate one of the thieves to upbraid Thee, and didst most mercifully and bountifully promise the glory of Paradise to the other, who humbly acknowledged his own injustice, and with a devout faith confessed Thee to be his King and God;

250. Behold me, I beseech Thee, with those eyes of mercy which Thou didst cast upon the thief repentant for his sins:

251. O that, by Thy holy help and grace, I may lead a life so innocent, that I may faithfully serve Thee and purely love Thee!

252. That at the end of my life I may deserve to hear, most merciful Redeemer, that most desired voice, 'This day thou shalt be with Me in Paradise.'

253. Hail, sweet Jesus, who, from the cross beholding Thy most sweet Mother full of grief and tears, with inward compassion didst commend her to Thy disciple John, and again John to her, and us all in John unto Thy said Mother;

254. Grant that I may love and honour her with a most chaste and ardent affection;

255. That, having her for my Mother, I may deserve also to be acknowledged by her for her son;

256. Grant that in all necessities, and especially at the hour of my death, I may find her present assistance.

257. Hail, sweet Jesus; praise, honour, and glory be to Thee, O Christ, who in a most pitiful manner, hanging upon the cross with wide gaping wounds, didst profess Thyself to be destitute of all comfort;

258. Grant that with a firm confidence I may always have recourse to Thee, my most merciful Saviour, in all adversities, temptations, and desolations,

259. And wholly distrusting myself, I may trust in Thee alone,

260. And commit and resign myself entirely to Thee;

261. Wound the intime of my soul with the remembrance of Thy wounds;

262. Imprint them in my heart, and make my spirit even drunk with Thy Sacred Blood;

263. That I may attend to Thee, and Thee only seek, find, hold, and possess.

264. Hail, sweet Jesus, who, panting upon the cross, Thy Body being drawn dry for want of Blood, becamest very thirsty, and didst burn with an unspeakable desire of our salvation;

265. Grant that I may ardently thirst after Thy honour and the salvation of souls,

266. And may with courage employ myself in this affair;

267. Grant that I may not be hindered nor entangled by any transitory thing.

268. Hail, sweet Jesus, who wouldst that a sponge dipped in vinegar and gall should be offered Thee to drink, being then thirsty even to death, that by taking thereof Thou mightest satisfy for our gluttony and leave us an example of poverty;

269. Give me grace to despise unlawful pleasures and avoid all excess in meat and drink;

270. Also to use those things moderately which Thou givest for the sustentation of the body;

271. Pacify the inordinateness of my desires, that whatsoever doth please Thee may please me, and whatsoever displeaseth Thee may be displeasing also to me.

272. Hail, sweet Jesus, most enamoured of mankind, who, duly performing the work of our redemption, didst offer up Thyself upon the altar of the cross a holy sacrifice for the expiation of the sins of all men,

273. Be Thou, I beseech Thee, the scope of all my thoughts, words, and works,

274. That in all things I may with a right and simple intention seek Thy honour;

275. Grant that I may never grow cold nor faint in Thy service;

276. But that fervour of spirit may be renewed in me, and that I may daily more and more be inflamed to praise and love Thee. Amen.

277. Hail, sweet Jesus; praise, honour, and glory be to Thee, O Christ, who of Thy own accord didst embrace death, and recommending Thyself to Thy Heavenly Father, bowing down Thy venerable head, yieldedst up Thy Spirit;

278. Truly thus giving up Thy life for Thy sheep, Thou hast shown Thyself to be a good Shepherd;

279. Thou didst die, O Only-begotten Son of God; Thou diedst, O my beloved Saviour, that I might live for ever:

280. O how great hope, how great confidence have I reposed in Thy Death and Thy Blood!

281. I glorify and praise Thy holy name, acknowledging my infinite obligations to Thee;

282. O good Jesus, by Thy bitter Death and Passion, give me grace and pardon;

283. Give unto the faithful departed rest and life everlasting.

284. Hail, sweet Jesus, at whose death the sun withdrew his light, the veil of the Temple was rent asunder, and the monuments opened;

285. O Sun of Justice, permit not, I beseech Thee, that the beams of Thy grace at any time forsake me;

286. But let them continually enlighten the inmost parts of my soul;

287. Withdraw wholly from me the veil of hypocrisy;

288. Shake the earth of my soul with wholesome repentance;

289. Rend my stony heart,

290. That, being wholly renewed, I may contemn all transitory things, and love only that which is eternal.

291. Hail, sweet Jesus, who wouldst that Thy side should be opened with a soldier's lance,

292. And out of it pour blood and water to revive and wash our souls;

293. Thou wouldst, O my best Beloved, that Thy mellifluous Heart should be wounded for me;

294. O that it might please Thee to make a most deep wound in my heart with the lance of Thy love,

295. And unite it to Thy most Sacred Heart,

296. In such manner that I may have no power to will anything but that which Thou wilt!

297. Bring in, O my Lord, bring in my soul, through the wound of Thy side, into the bosom of Thy charity and the treasure-house of Thy Divinity,

298. That I may joyfully glorify Thee, my God, crucified and dead for me. Amen.

299. Hail, sweet Jesus; praise, honour, and glory be to Thee, O Christ, who sufferedst all that the malice of men or devils could devise;

300. Behold, with as much devotion as possibly I can, I salute the five principal Wounds of Thy blessed Body.

301. Hail, ruddy, glorious, and mellifluous Wounds of my Redeemer and my King!

302. Hail, glorious seals of my reconciliation and salvation!

303. I humbly desire to abide and be hidden in you, and be by that means secure from all evil.

304. Hail, sweet Jesus, who, being with great lamentations of Thy friends taken down from the cross, wouldst be anointed with precious ointments, wrapped in a winding-sheet, and buried where no man was buried before;

305. Bury, I beseech Thee, all my senses, all my forces, and all my affections in Thee,

306. That, being joined to Thee by efficacious love, I may become insensible in respect of all other things.

307. Hail, sweet Jesus, who hast vanquished the power of the devil, and, powerfully and lovingly in soul descending into hell, didst make joyful with Thy presence the Fathers there detained,

308. And didst translate them thence at Thy glorious Ascension to the delightful garden of the celestial Paradise and to the clear vision of God;

309. Let the virtue of Thy Passion and Thy Blood descend now, I beseech Thee, into Purgatory, upon the souls of my parents, kinsfolks, friends, benefactors, and all the faithful departed,

310. That, being delivered from pains, they may be received into the bosom of eternal rest.

311. Hail, sweet Jesus, who like a conqueror with glorious triumph didst arise out of Thy closed sepulchre,

312. And, revested with Thy lovely countenance, didst replenish Thy friends with new joy and gladness;

313. Grant, O Lord, that, leaving the old paths of my wicked conversation, I may walk in the newness of life,

314. And seek and savour those things which are above in heaven, and not those things which are here upon earth,

315. To the end that when Thou my life shalt appear at the last day, I may appear with Thee in glory.

316. Hail, sweet Jesus; praise, honour, and glory be to Thee, O Christ, who, forty days after Thy Resurrection, didst gloriously ascend into heaven in the sight of Thy disciples, where Thou sittest on the right hand of Thy Father, blessed for evermore:

317. O that my soul might always languish on earth, and ascend and aspire towards heaven!

318. May it hunger and thirst always after Thee!

319. Hail, sweet Jesus, who didst give Thy Holy Ghost to the elect disciples persevering together with one mind in prayer,

320. And didst send them to teach all nations throughout the whole world;

321. Cleanse, I beseech Thee, the interior of my heart;

322. Give me true purity and constancy of mind, that the Holy Ghost may find a grateful habitation in my soul,

323. And may replenish me with the special gifts of His grace;

324. May comfort, strengthen, fill, govern, and possess me.

325. Hail, sweet Jesus, who, coming as a Judge at the last day, wilt render unto every one according to his works, either punishment or reward;

326. O my most merciful Lord God, grant that according to Thy will I may so innocently pass the course of this miserable life,

327. That, my soul departing out of the prison of my body, I may be vested with Thy merits and virtues,

328. And be received into Thy everlasting joy,

329. And with all the Saints I may bless and praise Thee for ever.

330. Hail, sweet Jesus, whom I have most grievously offended all the days of my life;

331. Alas, I have never ceased to be ungrateful to Thee, resisting Thy grace in divers manners, and always adding new faults unto my former;

332. Behold, O my sweet Refuge; behold me, the outcast of all creatures, bringing with me nothing but bundles of sins;

333. I prostrate myself at the feet of Thy mercy, and humbly implore pardon and remission;

334. Pardon, I beseech Thee, and save me, for Thy name's sake;

335. For I believe and am assured that no sins are so grievous and heinous but, by the merits of Thy most Sacred Passion, may be forgiven and, washed away. Amen.

PSALMUS DE PASSIONE D. N. JESU CHRISTI.

1. Memor ero ab initio mirabilium tuorum Domine: et misericordias Tuas in æternum cantabo.

2. Tu splendor Paternæ gloriæ, et figura substantiæ Ejus, Teipsum exinanisti, formam servi accipiens.

3. Parvulus natus es nobis, et Filius datus es nobis: quia Tu es qui mittendus eras, Tu es expectatio Gentium.

4. Pauper factus es, et in laboribus a juventute Tua: expandisti manus Tuas tota die ad populum incredulum.

5. Omnes nos quasi oves erravimus: et posuit Dominus in Te iniquitatem omnium nostrum.

6. Tacebas consternatus super faciem Tuam: et vultus Tuus hærebat terræ.

7. Non remansit in To fortitudo: sed et species Tua immutata est in Te.

8. Rubrum factum est vestimentum Tuum: quia torcular calcasti solus.

9. Vere languores nostros Ipse tulisti: et dolores nostros Ipse portasti.

10. Circumdederunt Te canes multi: concilium malignantium obsedit Te.

11. Homo pacis Tuæ, qui edebat panes Tuos, magnificavit super Te supplantationem.

12. Amici Tui et proximi Tui a longe steterunt: et vim faciebant qui quærebant animam Tuam.

13. Tu spiritus oris nostri, Christe Domine: captus es in peccatis nostris.

14. Data sunt super To vincula et ligabant Te in eis: et noti Tui quasi alieni, recesserunt a Te.

15. Dedisti percutienti Te maxillam: saturatus es opprobriis.

16. Suscitatur falsiloquus adversus faciem Tuam: Tu redemisti eos, et ipsi locuti sunt contra Te mendacia.

17. Hostis Tuus terribilibus oculis intuitus est Te: et quasi Agnus coram tendente oo obmutuisti

18. Aperuerunt super Te ora sua: et exprobrantes percusserunt maxillam Tuam.

19. Corpus Tuum dedisti percutientibus: et gonas Tuas vellentibus.

20. Faciem Tuam velarunt: quia portentum dedit Te Dominus domui Israel.

21. Abominati sunt Te: et faciem Tuam conspuere non verebantur.

22. Inquilini domus Tuæ, sicut alienum habuerunt Te: et quem maxime diligebas adversatus es Te.

23. Contumelia et tormento interrogaverunt Te: morte turpissima condemnaverunt Te.

24. Astiterunt reges terræ, et principes convenerunt in unum, adversus Christum Domini.

25. Quæ ignorabas interrogabant Te: Tu vero tacuisti, semper siluisti, patiens fuisti.

26. Dorsum Tuum fabricaverunt peccatores, prolongaverunt iniquitatem suam.

27. Sicut ovis ad occisionem ductus es: factus est principatus super humerum Tuum.

28. Egredimini filiæ Sion: videte Regem Salomonem in diademate quo coronavit illum Mater sua.

29. Cui comparabo te Virgo filia Jerusalem: magna est enim velut mare contritio tua: quis medebitur tui?

30. Recordare Domine, paupertatis et nuditatis: absinthii et fellis.

31. Federunt manus Tuas et pedes Tuos: dinumeraverunt omnia ossa Tua.

32. Abjectionem Te posuit Dominus in medio populi Tui, et cum sceleratis deputatus es.

33. Ipsi consideraverunt et inspexerunt Te: Diviserunt sibi vestimenta Tua, et super vestem Tuam miserunt sortem.

34. Dederunt in escam Tuam fel: et in siti Tua potaverunt Te aceto.

35. Plauserunt super Te manibus omnes transeuntes per viam: sibilaverunt inimici Tui, et moverunt caput suum.

36, Dixerunt, Devorabimus: en ista est dies quam expectabamus; invenimus, vidimus.

37. Omnia luminaria coeli moerere fecisti: et dedisti tenebras super terram.

38. Occidit sol in meridie; et tenebrescere fecisti terram in die luminis.

39. Tradidisti in mortem animam Tuam; abscissus es de terra viventium: propter scelus populi Tui percussus es.

40. Circumdederunt To lanceis suis: consciderunt To vulnere super vulnus.

41. Lapsa est in lacum vita Tua: et posuerunt lapidem super Te.

42. Requiescens accubuisti ut leo: et quasi leæna; quis suscitabit Te?

43. Tu quoque in sanguine testamenti Tui emisisti vinctos Tuos de lacu, in quo non est aqua.

44. Quantas ostendit tibi Pater tribulationes, multas et malas? et conversus vivificavit Te, et de abyssis terræ iterum reduxit Te.

45. Ascendisti in altum, cepisti captivitatem, dedisti dona in hominibus: etenim non credentes inhabitare Dominum Deum.

46. Ecce quomodo dilexisti me: facta es at mors dilectio Tua.

47. Te laudent coelum et terra: quia To decet laus, O expectatio Israel, Salvator ejus in die malorum.

48. Memor esto verbi Tui servo Tuo: in quo mihi spem dedisti.

49. Dixisti enim: Ego si exaltatus fuero, omnia traham ad Meipsum.

50. Ecce exaltaris super coelos Deus: trahe nos ad Te: curremus in odorem unguenturum Tuorum. Amen.

HOLY EXERCISES OF CONTRITION.
AN ADVICE TO THE READER.

These following Exercises of Contrition are useful and proper first, for such devout souls as, being naturally indisposed for discursive prayer, are consequently obliged to begin an internal course of prayer with such immediate acts or affections. Such, therefore, at the beginning, may do well to make these Exercises of the purgative way the entire subject of their recollections, until they find that, remorse ceasing, they are enabled for the following Exercises of Love, &c.

Secondly, these Exercises may be useful also for souls that have made a greater progress in the prayer of immediate acts; but this is when, by occasion of some sin committed, they judge it fit to raise contrition in their hearts for it. In which case it will not be necessary that their whole recollection should be spent in these acts; but it will suffice to exercise one or two of them at first, and to employ the remainder of the time in their usual former matter of prayer.

The First Exercise.

1. Who will give to mine eyes a fountain of tears, that I may bewail both day and night my sins and ingratitude towards God my Creator?

2. Consider (O my soul) the multitude of the benefits that God hath bestowed upon thee, and be thou confounded and ashamed of thy wickedness and ingratitude.

3. Consider who thy Creator is, and who thou art; how He hath behaved Himself towards thee, and how thou towards Him.

4. Thou hast made me, O Lord, when I was not; and that according to Thine own image.

5. Thou from the very first instant of my being hast been

My God,

My Father,

My Deliverer,

All my Good.

6. Thou, with the benefits of Thy providence, hast preserved my life even till this present. O, let it be spent in Thy service!

7. But because these things, O gracious Lord, cost Thee nothing, to bind me more fast to Thee, Thou wouldst need give me a present bought by Thee most dearly.

8. Thou hast come down from heaven, to seek me in all those ways in which I had lost myself. O, draw up my soul unto Thee!

9. Thou hast exalted and made noble my nature by uniting it in One Person with Thy Divinity.

10. By Thy captivity Thou hast loosed my bonds, and by delivering Thyself into the hands of sinners Thou hast delivered me from the power of the devil; and by taking upon Thee the form of a sinner Thou hast destroyed my sins.

The Second Exercise.

1. These things Thou didst to allure and bind me unto Thee, and to strengthen my hope.

2. To make me detest sin, by beholding what Thou hast done and suffered to overthrow the kingdom of sin.

3. And also that, being overcome and overwhelmed with the multitude of Thy benefits, I should love Him who did so much for me, and loved me so dearly.

4. Behold, O God, Thou hast redeemed me; but what had this availed me if I had not been baptised? Among so many infidels as are in the world Thou hast brought me to Thy Faith and Baptism.

5. There that covenant was made that Thou shouldst be mine, and I Thine; Thou my Lord, and I Thy servant; Thou my Father, and I Thy child; that Thou shouldst behave Thyself as a Father towards me, and I as a child towards Thee.

6. What shall I say of the other Sacraments which Thou hast instituted for remedies of my evils, making a plaster for my sins of Thine own most Precious Blood!

7. Having these helps, yet have I not remained in goodness; but my wickedness hath been so great, that I have lost my first innocency.

8. And Thy mercy on the other side is so great, that Thou hast patiently hitherto expected me.

9. O my hope and Saviour, how can I without tears call to my remembrance how oftentimes Thou mightest justly have bereaved me of my life?

10. To Thee, therefore, be given the glory which is due; and to me shame and confusion of face, as it is this day.

The Third Exercise.

1. How many thousand souls now peradventure burn in hell, who have less sinned than I, and yet I burn not there!

2. What had become of me, if Thou hadst taken me away when Thou tookest them?

3. Who then, O Lord, bound the hands of Thy justice? who held the rod of Thy judgments when I by sinning provoked Thee?

4. What pleased Thee in me that Thou didst deal more mercifully with me than with others?

5. My sins cried unto Thee, and Thou stoppedst Thine ears. My malice every day increased against Thee, and Thy goodness every day increased towards me.

6. I was wearied in sinning, and Thou wast not wearied in expecting.

7. In the midst of my sins I received from Thee divers good inspirations, which I neglected.

8. What shall I now render, O Lord, unto Thee, for all these benefits which I have received of Thee I because Thou hast given me Thyself, what shall I render to Thee?

9. If all the lives of angels and men were mine, and that I should offer them all unto Thee as a sacrifice, what were this oblation if compared with one drop of Thy Blood, which Thou hast shed for me so abundantly?

10. Who, therefore, will give tears to mine eyes, that I may bewail my ingratitude and wicked retribution or requital of these Thy so many benefits? Help me, O Lord, and give me grace, that I may worthily bewail mine iniquities.

The Fourth Exercise.

1. My God, I am Thy creature, made according to Thy image; take away from me that which I have made, and acknowledge that which Thou hast made.

2. I have bent all my forces to do Thee injury, and have offended Thee by the works of my hands.

3. The things which Thou hast given and created for me, to be employed and used for Thy service and honour, I have wrongfully and most unthankfully converted and employed the same to Thy offence and dishonour.

4. My feet have been swift to evil, and my eyes have been dissolute to vanity, and mine ears have been always open to trifles and toys.

5. My understanding, which should have contemplated Thy beauty and have meditated both day and night on Thy commandments, hath considered transitory toys and meditated day and night how to transgress Thy said commandments.

6. My will was by Thee invited to the love of celestial delights and delicacies; but I preferred the earth before heaven.

7. Alas, what can I, a wretch, answer, if Thou enterest with me into judgment, and wilt say: I have planted thee a chosen vineyard, all true seed; how then, O strange vineyard, art thou turned in My sight into that which is depraved?

8. I have not only been ungrateful for Thy benefits, but used Thy benefits also themselves as weapons against Thee.

9. Thou hast made all creatures for my use, to allure me to love Thee; I have abused them, and of them have divers times taken occasion of sin. I have made choice rather of the gift than the Giver.

10. What shall I say? Wherefore have not all the calamities and miseries which I have known to have fallen upon other men, and touched not me, been a sufficient argument to me that my delivery from every one of them was a peculiar benefit from Thee?

The Fifth Exercise.

1. But if a most strict account shall be demanded for these things which cost Thee so little, what account wilt Thou ask of those which Thou hast bought Thyself with Thy most Precious Blood?

2. My God, how have I perverted all Thy counsels for my salvation!

3. How have I violated the mystery of Thine Incarnation!

4. Thou wert made man to make me partaker of the Divine Nature. I have made myself a beast and the slave of the devil.

5. Thou hast come down to the earth to bring me to heaven; and I have not hearkened to or acknowledged this high vocation, but have persevered in wickedness and in the mire of my baseness.

6. Thou hast made me one body with Thee; and I have joined myself again with the devil.

7. Thou hast humbled Thyself even to the dust of the earth; I puff myself up with pride.

8. Thou wouldst die to kill my sins; and I, presuming in Thy said mercy, goodness, and love, have not feared to sin against Thee. What greater impiety can be imagined?

9. I have taken occasion of Thy goodness to work malice; and by that means which Thou hast used to kill sin, I have taken occasion to raise again sin in myself.

10. Because Thou wert so good, I thought I might without prejudice be evil. Woe to mine ingratitude! And because Thy benefits were so many, I thought I might without punishment render unto Thee as many injuries.

The Sixth Exercise.

1. Thus have I made Thy medicines occasions of sin, and I have turned that sword, which I received of Thee to defend myself from mine enemies, against my own bowels, and with the same murdered mine own soul.

2. Thou diedst, that they that now live may not live to themselves, but unto Thee.

3. O most patient Lord, who for sinners hast suffered buffets, but far more patient in suffering sinners, will this Thy patience endure for ever towards me? What shall I do, my Lord I what shall I do? I confess I am not worthy to appear in Thy sight nor to behold Thee. Whither shall I fly from Thy face?

4. Art not Thou my Father, and in very truth a Father of mercies which have no end or measure?

5. What, then, shall I do, but cast myself down at Thy feet, and humbly crave mercy? Art not Thou
My Creator?
My Preserver?My Redeemer?
My Deliverer?
My King?
My Pastor?
My Priest? and
My Sacrifice?

6. If Thou repellest me, who will receive me? If Thou rejectest me, of whom shall I seek succour?

7. Behold, I come full of wounds; Thou canst heal me: I come all blind; Thou canst give me sight: I come all dead; Thou canst raise me: I come all full of leprosy; Thou canst make me clean.

8. Thou shalt sprinkle me, O Lord, with hyssop (with Thy Precious Blood shed for me), and I shall be made clean.

9. Thou, O God, who art able to do all things, convert me unto Thee; renew my spirit, enlighten my understanding, sanctify my will, increase my strength of body and soul, that I may depend only on Thee, fear and love Thee above all things, and serve Thee fervently; and that in all my affections hereafter I may conform myself to Thy blessed will and pleasure.

10. I beseech Thee, finally, to impart unto me Thine abundant effectual grace, by which I may be able to begin to lead a perfect and holy life, and to serve Thee perfectly and thoroughly even to the end. For therefore Thou, O my God, gavest me a being, that I may employ it in Thy service.

The Seventh Exercise.

1. Take pity, O Lord, take pity, O merciful Saviour, of me, most miserable sinner, doing things of blame, and worthily suffering for the same.

2. If I ponder the evil which I daily commit, that which I endure is nothing in comparison of it.

3. Thou, O Lord our God, art just and full of goodness, neither is there in Thee any wickedness.

4. Because when we offend, Thou dost not unjustly and cruelly afflict us; who when we were not, hast powerfully made us; and when for our sins we were guilty of damnation, Thou hast by Thy wonderful mercy and goodness set us in the state of salvation.

5. I know, O Lord God, and am assured that our life is not governed by uncertain chances, but wholly disposed and ordered by Thy awful power and providence.

6. Wherefore I humbly beseech Thee, that Thou wilt not deal with me according to my iniquities, by which I have deserved Thine anger, but according to Thy manifold mercies which surmount the sins of the whole world.

7. Take pity on me, Thy son, whom Thou hast begotten in the great grief of Thy Passion; and do not so attend to my wickedness that Thou forget Thy goodness.

8. Is it possible for a woman to forget the child of her own womb? And though she should forget, O most loving Father, Thou hast promised not to be unmindful.

9. Truly it is better for me not to be at all, than to be without Thee, sweet Jesus.

10. It is better not to live, than to live without Thee, the only true life.

The Eighth Exercise.

1. Woe to me at the Day of Judgment, when the books of our consciences shall be opened (wherein our actions are registered), when of me it shall be openly proclaimed, See here a man and his works!

2. Alas, what shall I say? I will call and cry unto Thee, O Lord my God; why am I consumed being silent?

3. Weep, O my soul, and make lamentation, as a young married woman for the death of her husband.

4. O anger of the Almighty, rush not upon me, for I cannot subsist against Thee.

5. Take pity on me, lest I despair of Thy mercy; that by despairing of myself, I may find comfort in confiding in Thee.

6. And albeit I have done that for which Thou must justly condemn me, yet Thou hast not lost Thy accustomed property of showing mercy and pity.

7. Thou, O Lord, dost not desire the death of sinners, neither dost Thou take pleasure in the perdition of those that die.

8. Nay, rather that those who were dead might live, Thou Thyself hast died; and Thy death hath been the death that was due to sinners; and they by Thy death are come to life.

9. Grant me, I beseech Thee, O Lord, that Thou living I may not die; since that Thy death hath given life, much more let Thy life give life.

10. Let Thy heavenly hand help me, and deliver me from the hands of those that hate me, lest they insult and rejoice over me, saying, We have devoured him.

The Ninth Exercise.

1. How is it possible, O good Jesus, that ever any one can despair of Thy mercy? who, when we were Thine enemies, hast redeemed us with Thy Precious Blood, and hast reconciled us to God.

2. Behold, O Lord, protected by Thy mercy, I run, craving pardon, to the throne of Thy glory, calling and knocking until Thou take pity on me.

3. For if Thou hast called us to pardon, even when we did not seek it, how much more shall we obtain pardon if we ask it!

4. Forget my pride provoking Thee to displeasure, and weigh my wretchedness imploring Thy favour.

5. O Saviour Jesus, be Thou my succour and protection, and say unto my soul, I am thy Salvation.

6. I do presume very much on Thy bounty, because Thou Thyself dost teach us to ask, seek, and knock at the door of Thy mercy.

7. Thou therefore, O Lord, who willest me to ask, grant that I may receive. Thou dost counsel me to seek; grant me likewise to find. Thou dost teach me to knock; open unto me, knocking at the door of Thy mercy.

8. Behold, besides my heart I have nothing else to give Thee; neither can I give Thee this without Thee. Take me, therefore, and draw me unto Thee, that so I may be Thine by imitation and affection, like as I am by condition and creation, who livest and reignest world without end.

9. O Lord God Almighty, who art Trinity in Unity, who art always in all things, and wert before all things, and wilt be in all things everlastingly, one blessed God for all eternity;

10. To Thee, this and all the days of my life, I commend my soul, my body, my seeing, my hearing, taste, smell, and touching; all my cogitations, affections, words, and actions; all things that I have without and within me; my sense and understanding; my memory, faith, and belief; and my constancy in well-doing; all these I commend into the hands of Thy powerful protection, to the end that all the nights and days, hours and moments of my life, Thou mayest preserve and direct me.

The Tenth Exercise.

1. If Thou, O Lord, examine my righteousness, I shall be found as a dead man, stinking through rottenness.

2. But if Thou behold me with the eye of Thy mercy, Thou wilt thereby raise me (being through sin but a carcase) from the sepulchre of mine iniquity.

3. Whatsoever Thou hatest in me, O Lord, expel and root out of me.

4. Bestow on me, O Lord, Thy fear, compunction of heart, humility, and a conscience free from all sin.

5. Grant me grace, O Lord, that I may be always able to live in charity with my brethren; not forgetting my own sins, or prying into the sins or doings of other men.

6. Visit me weakened;
Cure me diseased;
Refresh me wearied;
Raise me dead.

7. Grant me, O Lord, a heart that may fear Thee, a mind that may love Thee, a sense that may conceive Thee, eyes that may see Thee.

8. Give me, O Lord, discretion to be able to discern betwixt good and evil, and endue me with an understanding ever watchful.

9. O Mary, Mother of God, Mother of Jesus Christ our Lord, thou sacred and unspotted Virgin, vouchsafe to make intercession for me unto Him who made thee a worthy temple for Himself to dwell in.

10. Be pleased to pray for me, a poor sinner, unto our God; that I may be delivered from the furious jaws of the infernal fiend, and from that death which never shall have end.

The Eleventh Exercise.

1. O most mild and merciful Lord and Saviour, Son of the living God, the world's Redeemer, amongst all men and in all things I confess myself to be a miserable sinner.

2. Nevertheless I beseech Thee, most sweet and sovereign Father, that as an abject I may not be cast out of Thy favour.

3. Yea, rather, O Lord, Thou who art King of kings, and hast determined and decreed the length of each man's life, grant me a devout desire to amend mine.

4. Stir up my sluggish soul, to the end that at all times and in all things it may seek, desire, love, and fear Thee, and may put in practice that which is pleasing to Thee.

5. I most humbly and heartily beseech Thee (who art Alpha and Omega, the beginning and ending), that when the time is come I must die, Thou wilt be a mild and merciful Judge, and a perpetual protector to me against the accusations and snares of the devil, mine old adversary.

6. Admit me for ever into the society of the holy Angels and of all Thy Saints in Thy heavenly city, where Thou art blessed and praised for all eternity.

7. O hope of my heart, O strength of my soul, may it please Thy omnipotent goodness to accomplish what my wonderful great weakness doth attempt to perform, seeing Thou art my life and the scope of my intention!

8. And albeit hitherto I have not deserved to love Thee so much as I ought, yet such is my desire that I would most gladly do it.

9. Grant me to accomplish and perform Thy holy inspirations.

10. Transform, most sweet Saviour, my tepidity into a most fervent love of Thee. For the only thing I desire to attain unto by this my prayer is, that I may be able to love Thee with a most ardent affection.

ACTUS CONTRITIONIS, &c.
ET DE IV. NOVISSIMIS.
1. Exercitium Contritionis.

1. Infelix ego homo, quis me liberabit de corpore mortis hujus?

2. Heu quam multa habeo quæ defleam! cum nihil sit unde merito gaudeam.

3. Ah Domine Deus meus, quid unquam fiet de me cum deficiam quotidie, et non desinam offendere Te!

4. Quando resurgam? putasne mortuus homo rursum vivet?

5. Domino ante Te omne desiderium meum, et gemitus meus a Te non est absconditus.

6. Cur non tollis peccatum meum? Nam sicut onus grave gravatæ sunt super me iniquitates meæ; et non potero ut viderem.

7. Si Tu præterieris, Domine, quis miserebitur mei: aut quis alligabit vulnera mea?

8. Numquid voluntatis Tuæ est mors impii? Nonne miserationes Tuæ super omnia opera Tua.

9. Quid dicam Tibi, O immensa bonitas? Peccavi, sed parce mihi: et noli me damnare, qui pro me condemnari voluisti.

10. Volo ego quidem servire Tibi: sed sine Te non valeo: Tu ergo qui dedisti velle, da perficere.

2. Exercitium de Morte.

1. O anima mea, quid fiet de nobis si nos ultima hora tot et tantis peccatis onustos occupet?

2. O mors, finis temporis O, initium æternitatis! Quam terribilis es iis quibus peccatum est jucundum!

3. Doimine per omnes miserationes Tuas da mihi ut ultimum hoc momentum non sit mihi infaustum: sit mihi potius tota mea vita doloribus et afflictionibus plena.

4. Heu Deus meus et omne bonum meum: esto Tu solus liberator meus et amicum refugium meum in die illa terribili.

5. Da mihi ut ab hoc momento non cessem providere quæ ad pacem mihi erunt in illa periculosa tempestate.

6. Recogitabo Tibi Domine, omnes annos meos in amaritudine animæ meæ.

7. O mortis stimule peccatum, ab hac hora blanditiis tuis mortiferis renuncio.

8. Dicam Deo susceptor meus es Tu: illumina oculos meos, ne unquam obdormiam in morte.

9. Hie ure, hic seca Domine: modo in æternum parcas.

10. Recordare, Jesu pie, quod sum causa Tum viæ, ne me perdas illa die!

3. Exercitium de Judicio.

1. O peccatum! O æternitas!

2. Væ mihi, cum aperientur libri, et dicitur, Ecce homo et opera ejus. Heu mihi Domine in illa die si inventus fuero minus habens.

3. Per omnes miserationes Tuas Domine, da mihi ut meipsum hic judicando, terribile illud judicium Tuum præveniam.

4. Nunc scio et video, quia malum et amarum est dereliquisse Te Deum meum.

5. O anima stulta et insipiens! times offendere homines qui tecum judicandi sunt, et non times Supremum Judicem offendere?

6. O quam bonus es Domine, qui mihi spatium et opportunitatem dedisti providendi contra istius diei terrorem.

7. Ecce offero Tibi cor meum: purifica illud ab omni labe quæ Tibi displicere poterit.

8. Recte vereor omnia opera mea: nam delicta quis intelligit? ab occultis meis munda me Domine.

9. Super custodiam meam stabo: sed frustra vigilo nisi Tu custodias.

10. Confige timore Tuo carnes meas: a judiciis enim Tuis timui.

4. Exercitium de Inferno.

1. Domine, quis novit potestatem viæ Tuæ: aut præ timore viam Tuam dinumerare?

2. O anima mea, nunquid poteris habitare cum igne devorante? nunquid habitabis cum ardoribus sempiternis?

3. Abominor, O Inferne, blasphemias et maledictiones tuas stridores dentium et ululatus: et horum omnium infelicissimam æternitatem.

4. Recordare Domine Jesu, quia Tuum non est perdere ex eo quod Pater Tuus dedit Tibi.

5. Quod enim debuimus Tu solvisti: quod peccavimus Tu luisti: quod negleximus Tu supplesti.

6. Conserva me opus Tuæ pietatis: ne incassum circa ipsum laboraveris, et ne infructuosa sit in me immaculati Cruoris Tui effusio.

7. Non est auxilium mihi in me: libera me, Domine, et pone me juxta Te et cujusvis manus pugnet contra me.

8. Mirifica misericordias tuas, qui salvos facis sperantes in Te.

9. Qui certamen forte dedisti nobis: da ut vincamus.

10. Ut confiteamur Tibi dicentes: Benedictus Deus qui non dedit nos in captionem dentibus inimicorum nostrorum: anima nostra sicut passer erepta est de laqueo venantium: laqueus contritus est et nos liberati sumus.

5. Exercitium de Paradiso.

1. Gloriosa dicta sunt de te, civitas Dei: sicut lætantium omnium habitatio est in te: fundaris enim exaltatione universæ terræ.

2. Unam petii a Domino, hanc requiram: ut inhabitem in domo Domini omnibus diebus vitæ meæ: et in lumine ejus videam lumen.

3. Domine, modo ut videam decorem tuum in regno Tuo: duc me per lucem aut tenebras; per vitam aut mortem.

4. Libenter moriar mihi ipsi et omnibus creaturis: ut Tibi soli et Tecum in æternam vivam.

5. O anima mea, festinemus ad patriam nostram: ubi nulli sunt laquei: ubi nunquam Deum tuum offendes.

6. Heu mihi quia incolatus meus prolongatus est: habitavi cum habitantibus Cedar: multum incola fuit anima mea.

7. Mihi adhearere Deo bonum est: quid enim mihi est in coelo et a Te quid volui super terram? Deus cordis mei, et pars mea Deus in æternum.

8. O Deus charitas! ad quid me creasti? nonne ut amem Te et ut amando in æternum fruar Te?

9. Da mihi, Domine aut amare aut mori: imo da mihi mori, ut digne amem Te.

10. Ecce cor meum quod offero Tibi: et quid volo nisi ut sit holocaustum charitatis ad æternam gloriam Tuam. Amen.

HOLY EXERCISES OF PURE LOVE TO GOD.

The First Exercise.

1. I do rejoice in all the perfections that are in Thee, O my God, as in Thy wisdom, goodness, power, and all other Thy divine prerogatives and perfections.

2. Let it please and suffice me that Thou art infinitely happy and rich (my most benign and loving Father).

3. I do rejoice at the presence of Thee, my God, in heaven (where Thou reignest as in Thy kingdom), and that Thou art there worshipped, adored, and loved by all Thy Angels and Saints.

4. So that if it were in my power, I would love and honour Thee with all that love and worship wherewith all the Angels and Saints do there love Thee.

5. I do rejoice in all the loves and services that the just men in the Church (especially the perfect) in all former ages, in the present or in the future ages have and do, or shall bear and perform towards Thee.

6. And I desire to love Thee with the love of them, and would for Thy love do and perform, if it lay in my power, all their works, as well internal as external, and would undergo all their labours, and endure all their afflictions.

7. I do heartily rejoice in all the good things that are in the elect servants of God, but especially for the wonderful gifts of the perfect, and that they are by Thee, O my God, illuminated, inflamed, and sanctified.

8. My love and desire towards Thee, O my God, is such, and so great, that if it were possible to me, and acceptable to Thee, I would of each soul (especially my own) make a kingdom of heaven, that Thou mightest be beloved and praised in so many heavens by the dwellers in them.

9. Which, if it lay in my power, should be more in number than the grass piles on the earth, the sands in the sea, or drops of water therein.

10. I do here in Thy presence, O my God, hold and repute myself as nothing; and whatsoever I have above nothing, natural or supernatural, I acknowledge it to be Thine only.

11. And because of myself I am nothing, and that my God is all good, and that all good things come only from Him, I do greatly rejoice, and with all my heart confess that I am nothing, can do nothing, and have nothing; for both my being and ability to do, and all I have, is Thine and from Thee.

The Second Exercise.

1. I do here, in the presence of God, repute and judge myself the most vile of all creatures; and because I cannot feel or perceive this in myself, but rather the contrary (having a good and great opinion of myself), I do acknowledge, therefore, that I am the most proud and ungrateful of all others; and I do bewail myself as such an one.

2. O my God, I love and desire to love Thee, with a love pure and free from all respect of proper commodity and self-interest.

3. I love Thee, my Lord, with a perseverant love, purposing by the help of Thy holy grace and assistance never to be separated from Thee by sin.

4. And if I were to live for millions of years, yet would I ever remain Thy faithful servant and lover.

5. I wish all creatures would adore and serve Thee, and that infidels may be converted to Thy faith, and all sinners to a good life; and all this only for Thy supreme honour and glory.

6. I wish that neither myself nor any other had ever offended Thee, my God; and that in particular I myself had ever served Thee faithfully from the instant of my nativity.

7. I wish and desire that both I myself and all others may Hereafter serve and love Thee most faithfully, and this for the love and good-will I bear Thee.

8. I rejoice and congratulate that Thou, my Lord God, art so rich and happy, that all creatures can add no more to Thy happiness than already Thou hast;

449

9. Nevertheless, because Thou mayest have external honour and worship from Thy creatures, I do wish sincerely that all of them may accordingly perform their service and the worship due unto Thee the best they can.

10. I am sorry for all the sins and indignities that are, have, or shall be done unto Thee, by myself or any others.

11. And this principally and only I am sorry for, because these sins are injuries done to Thy Divine Majesty, who only art worthy to be honoured and served by all Thy creatures.

12. I do joyfully accept and am glad of all that is pleasing to God, be it prosperity or adversity, sweet or bitter, and this merely for the love I bear Him.

13. I am sorry for all that doth displease God, or is contrary to His divine will or commandments, and all this only for the love of Him and His glory.

The Third Exercise.

1. I congratulate with Thee, O my God, for the blessedness and all the perfections that are in Thee, and which for all eternity Thou hast ever had; as Thy omnipotence, wisdom, goodness, &c.

2. I congratulate with Thee also, and am glad that Thou hast need of no extrinsical thing, but art in Thyself most rich and fully sufficient both for Thyself and all creatures.

3. I likewise with Thee, O my Lord, rejoice in the sweet ordinance and disposition of heaven and earth, and for all the things which are in the marvellous creation of this world, and for all the works which Thou hast made, or shalt yet make unto the end of the world.

4. I congratulate, approve, and rejoice in all the judgments of my Lord God, as well manifest as secret: concerning the devils, the souls of the damned, the unbaptised children in Limbo, the souls that are in Purgatory, and the wicked men that live in this world.

5. I congratulate and rejoice with Thee, O my God, in all the lauds and praises which the Angels and Saints in heaven and Thy servants on earth do give Thee, and for all the worship they yield unto Thee.

6. Because I find myself altogether insufficient to praise my God, I do for my help and assistance therein invite and call upon the holy angels and all creatures;

7. And with them I join my own soul, with all the powers of it, that all of them together may glorify my God for His infinite excellency.

8. I am sorry I am not perfect, and wish that (so far as it may please my God to grant) I may be perfect the more worthily to praise Thee;

9. And not out of any commodity by it to myself, but purely for the love I bear Thy Divine Majesty, who art infinitely worthy of more love and honour than all creatures that are or can be, are able to perform towards Thee.

10. Exult and rejoice and be thou delighted, O my soul, for all the excellency and good things that are in thy God.

11. I rejoice in the dignity that our Saviour Christ now hath in heaven, and congratulate Him in it.

The Fourth Exercise.

1. Blessed be Thy Eternal Father, O Heavenly Lord Jesus, who so abundantly bestowed these felicities on Thee; do Thou blessedly and gloriously enjoy them for all eternity.

2. I congratulate the most Blessed Virgin Mary and all the Angels and Saints in heaven for the glory and happiness which they now enjoy;

3. And I praise and exalt my God for His great goodness and liberality therein showed towards those His most faithful and elect friends.

4. I do exceedingly rejoice that since all creatures together are in no sort able to praise, Thee, my God, according to the very least worth that is in Thee, yet Thou Thyself, and Thou only, art able sufficiently and perfectly to praise and glorify Thyself,

5. I do rejoice indeed at this, and do heartily desire Thee to do it evermore.

6. Yea, I do heartily crave of Thee that Thou mayest incessantly and most intensively praise Thyself, since Thou only art able to do it, and deservest to have it done.

7. I do congratulate and rejoice with Thee, O my Lord God, in all the works which Thou hast done; and this only because they are the works of Thy hands.

8. As for the creation of the world, Thy providence about it, Thy redemption of it; wonderfully esteeming all these works, because they are Thine.

9. And I rejoice as well in that Thou hast made a hell for the punishment of the wicked, as a heaven for the reward of the good.

10. I wish and desire, out of my love to God, that He may be praised and known of all men; and I do invite all creatures to do the same with myself.

11. I offer myself, for the love of my God, to bear and suffer all things which may be to His honour and glory; though no manner of commodity accrue to me thereby, but purely I do it out of the free love I bear, and desire to bear, towards my God.

12. Lastly, I profess that if I could desire anything wherein I might show or exercise my love towards my God, I hope (with the help of His grace) I should and would do it most cheerfully and readily out of the pure and sincere love that I bear and wish to bear towards my God, without respect of any commodity by it to myself: which God grant me to do for His glory and my happiness. Amen.

CERTAIN AMOROUS DESIRES, &c.

TO BE USED ACCORDING TO THE DISPOSITION OF THE SOUL

1. O Domine da quod jubes et jube quod vis.
Grant me to do what Thou commandest, O my Lord, and command what Thou wilt.

2. O vita animæ meæ!
O life of my soul!

3. In manus Tuas Domine commendo spiritum meum.
Into Thy hands, O Lord, I do commend my spirit.

4. Paratum cor meum Deus, paratum cor meum.
My heart is ready, O my God, my Heart is ready.

5. Ecce ego; mitte me.
Lo, here I am; send me.

6. Domine quid mihi est in coelo et a Te quid volui super terram?
O Lord, what is there in heaven, or what upon earth, that I would have besides Thee?

7. Domine quid me vis facere?
Lord, what wilt Thou have me to do?

8. Heu mihi quia incolatus meus prolongatus est!
O woe is to me, that my sojourning is prolonged!

9. Domine Tu scis quia amo Te, et animam meam ponam pro Te.
Thou knowest, O Lord, that I love Thee, and will bestow my life for Thee.

10. Quemadmodum desiderat cervus ad fontes aquarum, ita desiderat anima me ad Te Deus.
Even as the hart doth thirst after the fountain of waters, so doth my soul thirst after Thee, O God.

11. Cupio dissolvi et esse cum Christo.
I desire to be dissolved and to be with Christ.

12. Quando veniam et apparebo ante faciem Domini?
When shall I come and appear before the face of our Lord?

13. Precor cœlestem Regem, ut me dolentem nimium faciat eum cernere.
I beseech the Heavenly King to cause me (who am very much grieved for want of it) to come to the sight of Him whom I so much love.

14. Domine si inveni gratiam in oculis Tuis, ostende faciem Tuam
Lord, if I have found favour in Thy sight, show unto me Thy face.

15. Benedic anima mea Domino, et omnia quæ intra me sunt nomini sancto Ejus.
O my soul, and all that is within me, bless ye our Lord, and praise His holy name.

16. Benedicam Dominum in omni tempore, semper laus Ejus in ore meo.
I will bless our Lord at all times, His praise shall ever be in my mouth.

17. Sanctus, Sanctus, Sanctus, Dominus Deus Sabaoth; pleni sunt cœli et terra majestatis gloriæ Tuæ.
Holy, Holy, Holy, Lord God of Sabaoth; heaven and earth are full of the majesty of Thy glory.

18. Deus, Deus, meus respice in me; quare me dereliquisti?
O my God, my God, look upon me; why hast Thou forsaken me?

19. Deus meus, adjutor meus, sperabo in Te.
O my God, my Helper, I will hope in Thee.

20. Domine in cœlo misericordia Tua, et veritas Tua usque ad nubes.
O Lord, Thy mercy is in heaven, and Thy truth reacheth to the clouds.

21. Ad Te levavi oculos meos qui habitas in cœlis.
To Thee have I lifted up mine eyes, who dwellest in heaven.

22. Dilectus meus mihi et ego Illi.
My Beloved is mine, and I am His.

23. Regnum Tuum regnum omnium sæculorum, et dominatio Tua in omni generatione et generatione.
Thy kingdom is a kingdom for ever, and Thy reign is for all generations and generations.

24. Vulnerasti cor meum Sponse mi, vulnerasti cor meum.
Thou hast wounded my heart, my Spouse, Thou hast wounded my heart.

25. Adjuro vas filiæ Jerusalem, si inveneritis dilectum meum, ut nuntietis Ei quia amore langueo.
I adjure you, O daughters of Jerusalem, if you shall find my Beloved, tell Him that I languish with love.

26. Veni dilecte mi, veni.
Come, Thou my Beloved, come.

27. Quo abiit dilectus tuus? quo declinavit dilectus tuus? et quæremus eum tecum.
Whither is thy Beloved gone? whither is thy Beloved turned aside? and we will seek Him with thee.

28. Quis mihi det ut inveniam Te et deosculer Te?
Who shall procure unto me, that I may find Thee and kiss Thee?

29. Trahe me post Te, curremus in odorem unguentorum Tuorum.
Draw me after Thee, we shall run in the odour of Thine ointments.

30. Indica mihi quem diligit anima mea, ubi pascas, ubi cubes.
Thou whom my soul loveth, show unto me where Thou dost eat, where Thou dost lodge.

31. Ostende mihi faciem Tuam; sonet vox Tua in auribus meis.
Show me Thy face; let Thy voice sound in mine ears.

32. Quæsivi quem diligit anima mea, quæsivi Illum et non inveni.
I have sought for Him whom my soul loveth; I have sought for Him, and have not found Him.

33. Paululum cum transissem, inveni quem diligit anim mea.
When I had gone a little farther, I found Him whom my soul loveth.

34. Anima mea liquefacta est, ut locutus est mihi.
My soul melted as He spoke to me.

35. Diligam te Domine fortitudo mea, firmamentum meum, et refugium et liberator meus.
I will love Thee, O Lord, my strength, my firm foundation, my refuge, and my deliverer.

36. Illumina oculos meos ne unquam obdormiam in morte: ne quando dicat inimicus meus, prævalui adversus eum.
Enlighten mine eyes, that I may never sleep in death; lest mine enemy may come at length to say, I have prevailed against him.

37. Dignus es Tu Domine Deus accipere gloriam et honorem et virtutem et benedictionem.
Thou art worthy, O Lord God, to have glory and honour and power and praise.

38. Confiteantur Tibi Domine omnia opera Tua, et sancti Tui benedicant Tibi.
Let Thy works, O Lord, confess unto Thee, and let Thy Saints praise Thee.

39. Si oportuerit me mori non te negabo.
Though I were to die for it, yet I would not deny Thee.

40. Jesu, Jesu, Jesu, &c. Non dimittam Te nisi benediceris mihi.
I will not let Thee go till Thou hast blessed me.

41. Miserere mei Deus, miserere mei, quoniam in Te confidit anima mea.
Have mercy on me, O Lord, have mercy on me, because my soul doth confide in Thee.

42. Beati qui habitant in domo tua Domine, in sæcula sæculorum laudabunt Te.
Blessed are they who dwell in Thy house, O Lord; they praise Thee for ever and ever.

43. O all my hope!

44. O all my glory!

45. O all my refuge, and all my joy!

46. O life of my soul, and the pleasant repose of my spirit!

47. Mortify in me whatsoever displeaseth Thy sight, and make me according to Thy Heart.

48. Wound me, O Lord, wound the most inward part of my soul with the darts of Thy love,

49. And make me drunk with the wine of Thy perfect charity.

50. When shall all die in me which is contrary to Thee?

51. When shall I live to be no more mine own?

52. When shall nothing else live in me, but Thou, O Jesus?

53. When shall the flames of Thy love wholly consume me?

54. When shall I be utterly melted and pierced through with the wonderful efficacy of Thy sweetness?

55. When wilt Thou free me from all these impediments and distractions, and make me one spirit with Thee, that I may not any more depart from Thee?

56. O dearly beloved! O dearly beloved of my soul!

57. O sweetness of my heart!

58. O God of my soul, why guidest not Thou Thyself to Thy poor creature?

59. Thou fillest heaven and earth, and wilt Thou leave my heart empty?

60. Too late have I known Thee, O infinite goodness!

61. Too late have I loved Thee, O beauty so ancient and so new!

62. Woe to me, I have loved Thee not!

63. Blind I was that I saw Thee not.

64. Thou wert within me, and I went, seeking Thee abroad;

65. But now that I have found Thee, though late, suffer not, good Lord, that I ever leave Thee. Amen. Amen. Amen.

CERTAIN AMOROUS SPEECHES OF THE SOUL TO HERSELF IN PRAYER:

THE WHICH ARE A GOOD FORM OR MATTER OF PRAYER TO BE NOW AND THEN MADE USE OF, WHEN THE SOUL IS NOT ABLE OR APT TO CONTINUE SPEAKING IMMEDIATELY TO GOD.

The like is to be said of the following Devotions to our Blessed Lady, &c.

1. O my soul, when wilt thou be ready to follow the humility of thy Lord Jesus Christ?

2. When shall the example of His patience shine in thee?

3. When wilt thou be wholly free from passions and vicious affections?

4. When wilt thou peaceably and gently endure all tribulation and temptation?

5. When wilt thou perfectly love thy God?

6. When wilt thou be pure, simple, and resigned before Him?

7. How long will it be ere thou be hindered no more from His most chaste embraces?

8. O that thou didst fervently love God!

9. O that thou didst inseparably cleave unto thy chiefest good!

10. O my soul, where is thy love? where is thy treasure? where is thy desire? where is all thy good? where is thy God? when shalt thou be with Him? when shalt thou most happily enjoy Him?

11. If thou hast sinned and art wounded, behold thy God, behold thy Physician is ready to cure thee.

12. Peradventure thou art afraid, because He is thy judge; but take heart, for He who is thy judge is also thy advocate.

13. His mercy is infinitely greater than is or can be thy iniquity.

14. Thy God is most gentle, most sweet; He is wholly amiable, wholly desirable, and loveth all things which He has created.

15. Let not thine imperfections discourage thee too much, for thy God doth not despise thee, because thou art frail and infirm; but loveth thee exceedingly, because thou desirest and labourest to be more perfect.

16. Arise, my soul; arise out of the dust, thou captive daughter of Sion.

17. Arise, forsake the puddle of thy negligent life.

18. How long must thou take pleasure in perils? how long wilt thou esteem anxiety and torments to be rest? how long wilt thou securely sleep in destruction?

19. Return unto our Lord thy God, for He expecteth thee.

20. Make haste, be not slack, for He is ready to receive thee.

21. Join thyself to Jesus, He will illuminate thee.

22. Alas, my soul, how ungrateful hast thou been to thy God!

23. He hath promised those things unto thee, which neither eye hath seen, nor ear hath heard, nor can the heart of man comprehend.

24. O my soul, if it were necessary daily to suffer torments, yea, to endure hell itself for a long time together, that we might see Christ in His glory and be joined in fellowship of the Saints in His heavenly city, were it not meet, thinkest thou, to sustain all manner of misery that we may be made partakers of so great a good and so great a felicity?

25. Love Him, then, love Him of whom thou art beloved; attend to Him that attendeth to thee, and seek Him that seeketh thee.

26. Love this Lover, of whom thou art beloved, with whose love thou art prevented, and who is the fountain from whence thy love floweth.

27. O my soul, sigh vehemently and aspire fervently to that glorious city so highly spoken of!

28. Heaven and earth and all therein contained do continually exhort thee to love thy Lord God.

29. Why art thou sad, O my soul? and why art thou troubled? Hope in our Lord, for He will be thy comfort and solace.

30. Sweet and amiable Jesus is present with thee; thou must with reverence and love attend unto Him.

AN EXAMPLE OF ACTS WHICH A SOUL MAY EXERCISE TOWARDS GOD AS ABSENT FROM HER.

1. I will bless our Lord at all times, His praises shall ever be in my mouth.

2. Our Lord have mercy on us, enlighten His countenance upon us and take pity on us.

3. It is good for me to seek after our Lord and get near unto Him, for He is our hope and our all.

(*The Psalms of David are full of these acts.*)

AN EXAMPLE OF SPEAKING SUPPOSED TO BE MADE BY GOD TO THE SOUL.

1. Son, it behoveth thee to give all for all, and reserve nothing to thyself.

2. Son, where is true peace to be found? is it not in Me?

3. Son, thou canst not attain to perfect liberty if thou dost not wholly forsake thyself.

4. Son, abide constant, and hope in Me: this is all in all.

AN EXERCISE OF DEVOTION TO OUR BLESSED LADY MOTHER OF GOD.

1. Hail, sweet Mary; hail, most sacred Virgin, whom God before all ages did choose for His most sacred Mother;

2. Thou art betwixt God and man, that blessed mediatrix by whom the highest things are joined to the lowest;

3. Thou art the beginning of life, the gate or entry of grace, the safe haven of the world suffering shipwreck;

4. Obtain for me, I beseech thee, perfect pardon of my sins and the perfect grace of the Holy Ghost;

5. That I may diligently worship, chastely and fervently love thy Son my Saviour, and thee the Mother of mercy.

6. Hail, sweet Mary, whom, foreshadowed in sundry figurative speeches, and promised in divers oracles of the Prophets, the ancient fathers did covet most earnestly;

7. O my Lady, receive me for thy poor servant; adopt me, O Mother, for thy son;

8. Grant that I may be numbered among them whom thou dost love (whose names are written in thy virginal breast), and whom thou dost teach, direct, help, cherish, and protect.

9. Hail, sweet Mary, whom God by a most Honourable privilege did preserve from sin,

10. And adorned with most singular graces and most excellent gifts;

11. O glorious Virgin, O gracious Virgin, O most pure Virgin, O most pure Virgin chosen amongst thousands;

12. Do not repel me, wicked sinner; do not despise and reject me, defiled with the filth of sin;

13. But hear me, a miserable wretch, crying unto thee; comfort me, desiring thee; and help me, trusting in thee. Amen.

AN EXERCISE TO THE HOLY ANGELS, AND ESPECIALLY THE ANGEL GUARDIAN.

1. I salute you, O holy spirits, and with all my heart congratulate your happiness, who continually contemplate the Divine Face and all-satiating Goodness:

2. You, O Seraphim, Cherubim, and Thrones, who are of the higher hierarchy; you, O Dominations, Virtues, and Powers, of the middle; you, O Princes, Archangels, and Angels, of the lowest, who continually sing, Holy, Holy, Holy, Lord God of Sabaoth.

3. Thou, O my Lord, hast made these holy spirits angels for my benefit, and hast commanded them to keep me in all Thy ways.

4. They do therefore assist us with great care, and with watchful endeavour at all times and in all places succouring us.

5. They present our sighs and sobs to Thee, O Lord; they inflame our wills, illuminate our understandings, and replenish our minds with holy thoughts.

6. They walk with us in all our ways, rejoicing at our virtues and contristated at our vices.

7. Their love is great and excessive towards us.

8. They help such as are taking pains; they protect such as are at rest; they encourage such as fight; they crown the conquerors; they rejoice with such as joy (I mean such as joy in Thee); and they suffer with such as suffer (I mean such as are in sufferance for Thee).

9. Great and very great is the honour done to man to have angels to wait on and assist him.

10. O my dear Angel Guardian, govern, protect, and defend me; illuminate, comfort, and direct me, now and evermore.

11. O blessed angels, be you ever blessed and praised for all and every favour and benefit you have most lovingly and powerfully bestowed on me and vouchsafed me.

12. Grant, O Father of heaven and earth, that they may ever rejoice concerning us (that is, by our practice of virtue), and that Thou mayest ever be praised by them and us; and that both they and we may be brought into one sheepfold, that together we may confess to Thy holy name, O Thou Creator of men and angels. Amen

AN EXERCISE OF DEVOTION TOWARDS OUR HOLY FATHER AND RELIGIOUS FOUNDER, ST. BENEDICT.

1. Hail, most blessed and glorious Father; I congratulate with all my heart thy glory and grace with God.

2. I praise likewise and thank the Divine Goodness that made thee worthy and brought thee to thy fame,

3. Bestowing on thee in this life very great natural and supernatural gifts and graces, by means whereof thou hast obtained thy present most glorious and happy condition.

4. In particular I praise and magnify the same Divine Goodness for that it gave thee the grace in the very flower or prime of thy youth, with a thirsty mind to seek after the sole felicity of the future life.

5. And for that end to forsake all the vain pleasures of this life; the solaces of thy parents, kindred, and country; the desire of human sciences and learning; and (generally) all things that might not be needful for thee towards attaining the foresaid felicity.

6. And I praise and magnify the same Divine Goodness that, by such calling and taking of thee so timely out of the world and the snares of it, He freed and secured thee from worse habits and multitudes of sins which the world (if thou hadst remained longer in it) had been apt to breed and cause in thee.

7. I praise and magnify the same Divine Goodness for leading thee to a place of solitude, and there providing for thee all corporal necessaries towards His holy service and thine own soul's good;

8. And especially for that the same Divine Goodness itself vouchsafed to become thy immediate Master and Director, inspiring thee and teaching thee what to do continually;

9. And gave thee grace and strength to perform and accomplish the things necessary and expedient to the end He called thee to;

10. And, namely, to live in mortification of body and will, and, as it were, in continual prayer and high contemplation.

11. I praise and glorify the same Divine Goodness for bestowing on thee the most necessary gift of perseverance, by which thou didst remain constant in such perfect divine service from thy first call to the very period of thy life;

12. That, coming to die, even ripe for most holy death, thou didst, as it were, pass from life to life, as one who feels not what corporal death means;

13. So that thy expiration was aspiration, according to what St. Gregory said of thee: 'Ultimum spiritum inter verba orationis efflavit;' to wit, His last breath was prayer: passing forth of the faithful contemplation of this life to the real and beatifical contemplation of the other.

14. I now cordially congratulate the perfect felicity thou enjoyest.

15. And since I am called by the divine grace (as I truly hope) to live according to thy holy rite for my salvation and perfection, vouchsafe thy holy intercession for that end, that I may, through God's grace, live accordingly and die consummated and perfect therein and thereby, for without His grace I can do nothing;

16. And, as the said St. Gregory saith, thou framest thy rule according to thy holy life. Sweet Jesus, give me grace interiorly and exteriorly to be a faithful imitator thereof;

17. That I may be led by the same guide, the Holy Ghost,

18. And exercise true spiritual prayer, the only means to all virtues;

19. That I may in all things abandon myself with all purity of intention,

20. And do all good and abstain from all evil which interiorly and exteriorly may concern me,

21. Especially in all things occurring, patiently to suffer all injuries and crosses

22. And that all may be accomplished, God grant me, as He did to thee, the gift of perseverance;

23. That I expiring may be admitted into the happy society of thee and thy faithful followers, Which God grant, Father, Son, and Holy Ghost. Amen.

(This exercise to St. Benedict was the devotion of the Venerable Father Baker, to give God thanks for the happiness of his religious vocation.)

HOLY EXERCISES
OF ACTS OF THE WILL.
The First Exercise.

1. My God, Thou art of a most simple being, therefore infinite in all perfections;

2. I do adore Thee with my whole heart, with most profound humility and reverence;

3. And because Thou only art most worthy of all love, I do and for ever will (through Thy grace) love Thee with a most entire and sincere love.

4. Thy being, O my God, is incomprehensibly immense, filling and penetrating all things;

5. O, teach me, therefore, so to live as being always in Thy presence;

6. Possess my heart as Thy temple, and reign in it as Thy throne.

7. I offer unto Thee, my life and all my faculties and strength, to be employed only in Thy service.

8. Thou, O my God, art alone from everlasting to everlasting; eternally and unchangeably perfect and happy.

9. O my soul, never cease to bless our infinitely great and bountiful Lord, all whose perfections and happiness shall eternally be contemplated and enjoyed by thee.

10. O, bless our Lord, all the works of our Lord; praise Him and exalt Him for ever.

The Second Exercise.

1. Great art Thou, O Lord, and great is Thy power; yea, and Thy wisdom is infinite.

2. Send, O God, out of Thy inexhaustible fountain of light, one beam into my soul, that I may perfectly see, admire, and adore all Thy most wise and secret judgments.

3. O my soul, how filthy and odious is sin, when thou lookest upon it by a divine light!

4. O, how ungrateful have I been to my most merciful God, whose infinite power and wisdom have been continually watchful over me!

5. Whom need I to fear, having a Saviour infinite both in power, wisdom, and goodness?

6. Thou, my God, art good, not with this or that kind of goodness, or after such or such a manner; but simple good, without all limitation or measure.

7. O my soul, if a small shadow and appearance of good here on earth doth, with such violence, draw our affections, how ought we to love Him by whom all good is communicated to creatures!

8. My God, if I had in my heart all the capacity of loving that is in all men and angels, it were all due to Thee alone. How much more, then, ought I to employ all that little power that is in me!

9. My God, give me this proof of sincere love to Thee, to make me as well love Thee commanding as promising; as well chastising as comforting.

10. How happy were we, O my soul, if we had no other will but the will of Jesus!

The Third Exercise.

1. My God, Thou art the author, end, and measure of all purity and holiness; before whom folly is found even in the angels.

2. How infinite is Thy goodness, then, since Thou desirest that my heart may become a temple for Thy holiness to dwell in!

3. O that Thy presence would purify it from all strange and unworthy affections to creatures!

4. O that there I might have my only conversation with Thee in a holy silence and solitude!

5. O my soul, conceive if thou canst how ugly and abominable sin (which is impurity itself) is in the eyes of our God, who is purity itself.

6. Thy divine providence, O my God, stretcheth to all creatures whatsoever; by its law all things arise, fall, move, and rest: even the very hairs of our heads are numbered by Thee.

7. O ungrateful and foolish wretch that I am, how oft have I desired and even endeavoured to withdraw myself from this all-comprehending providence, having a will to live according to mine own most imprudent judgment! My God, I repent me of this from the bottom of my heart, and most humbly beg pardon of Thee.

8. From this hour my purpose, through Thy grace, is to accept and welcome all occurrences, whether pleasing or distasteful to sense, as coming from Thy heavenly providence: this shall be my comfort and stay in all my afflictions; in dangers, security; and perfect rest of mind in expectation of future events.

9. Do Thou alone, O my God, provide, determine, will, and choose for me.

10. Hast not Thou, O my God, provided for me Thine own kingdom? What, then, can make me dejected?

The Fourth Exercise.

1. Who can declare the mercies of my God towards my soul? Of nothing He raised me to the dignity of an intellectual, immortal nature; from the low state of nature He exalted me to the divine state of grace; from thence He will raise me to a participation of His glory and happiness.

2. Bless thou our Lord, O my soul; and all that is in me, praise His holy name.

3. And with me let all His holy Angels and Saints sing forth the praises of my God, my most merciful and liberal Benefactor.

4. Let it suffice, O my soul, that hitherto we have been so unpardonably ungrateful.

5. My God, through Thy grace I will consecrate the remainder of my life to the glorifying of Thy holy name, directing all the powers of my body and soul to the accomplishing of Thy will and increasing of Thy glory and praise.

6. Thy right hand, O my God, is full of righteousness: Thou art a most just Judge, and with Thee is no acceptation of persons; but Thou renderest to every one according to his works.

7. This Thy justice is as truly acceptable to me as Thy goodness.

8. Be Thou therefore exalted in the punishing of all obstinate impenitent sinners; for just and reasonable it is that Thou shouldst be feared.

9. But Thy will it is, O my God, that I should appeal from Thy tribunal of justice to that of mercy, being desirous to amend and correct all my past sins and provocations of Thee.

10. However, O my God, if Thou wilt exercise Thy justice on me, let it be in this world, that Thou mayest spare me in the next.

The Fifth Exercise.

1. My God, as Thou art the Author of the being of all things, so art Thou the End also; for Thy glory all things were and are created.

2. And a great proof hereof Thou hast given to all the sons of Adam, for we see that our hearts find no rest at all whilst we adhere by affection to creatures.

3. Therefore, my God, I do here offer myself as a holocaust, to be even consumed to Thy glory.

4. I offer unto Thee my understanding, firmly to adhere to all divine verities revealed by Thee to Thy Church, renouncing all doubt or questioning of any of them; and herein my purpose irrevocable is, through Thy grace, to live and die.

5. O that it would please Thee that all mankind might know Thee, and with a firm faith confess Thee!

6. My God, I do willingly offer unto Thee my blood to seal this my faith, whensoever by Thy providence an occasion shall be presented, hoping that then Thou wilt be my strength and my salvation; and being assured that, whilst I hope in Thee, I shall not be weakened.

7. O my God, that Thou wouldst wholly possess my mind, which is Thine, and which I here offer to Thee! Fill it with good thoughts of Thee only; expel out of my memory all vain seducing objects of vanity.

8. I offer unto Thee, O my God, all my will and affections; to will, love, and desire only that which Thou willest and lovest.

9. If Thou wilt have me to be in light, be Thou ever praised; and if Thou wilt have me to be in darkness, be Thou likewise praised.

10. I renounce all propriety in myself, for I am wholly Thine, both for life and death, for time and eternity.

The Sixth Exercise.

1. My God, in union with that most perfect and acceptable oblation of Thy Son my Saviour Jesus Christ, I offer unto Thee my whole self entirely, and all things that belong unto me, to be employed only in Thy service and worship.

2. Let His worthiness recompense for my unworthiness, that I may obtain that for His merits which I cannot for my own.

3. I offer unto Thee my watching and my sleeps, in union with His waking from the sleep of death.

4. I offer unto Thee all my thoughts, speeches, and actions, to be sanctified and purified to Thy glory by all His most holy thoughts, words, and actions.

5. I offer unto Thee my refections, in union of that Blessed Refection in which He gave His most Precious Body and Blood to nourish the souls of His disciples.

6. I offer unto Thee all the prayers and other exercises of piety which, through Thy grace, I have or shall perform, beseeching Thee to accept them in union with those most perfect merits and heavenly prayers which Thy Son offered to Thee on Mount Olivet or elsewhere.

7. My God, I offer unto Thee all the afflictions, pains, desertions, and tribulations which I either have or ever shall suffer in union with the most bitter Passion of Thy only-begotten Son, my only Saviour.

8. O most sweet and merciful Jesus, as Thou in infinite goodness didst offer Thyself unto Thy Father for the expiation of my sins, and to purchase for me an inheritance of glory, behold I here offer my whole self entirely to Thee, to be employed purely to Thy glory.

9. Do Thou likewise offer me with Thyself, Thy merits and sufferings, to Thy Heavenly Father, that my poverty may be enriched with Thy abundance, and my sins cancelled by Thy merits.

10. O Holy Spirit, the greatest gift that our Heavenly Father had to bestow upon the sons of men, without whose inspiration we cannot so much as think a good thought, behold I offer my heart and my whole self unto Thee, beseeching Thee so to purify my soul with Thy sevenfold graces that I may serve Thee with a chaste body, and please Thee with a pure heart. Amen.

The Seventh Exercise.

1. My God and all my good, I am nothing, I have nothing, I can do nothing that is good as of myself; Thou art all, and all our sufficiency is from Thee only.

2. I do here humbly prostrate my soul before Thee, plunging myself in the abyss of mine own nothing.

3. How infinitely good art Thou, O my God, that vouchsafest to behold and take care of so vile, so unclean a creature as I am!

4. I beseech Thee that even for this most undeserved goodness of Thine I may yet more humble myself before Thee and all others.

5. I am content that my inexpressible vileness were known unto all, to the end that all may treat me according to my demerits, out of a just zeal to Thy glory.

6. O my God, the God of love, I would to God that as I live only in Thee and by Thee, so likewise my living may be for Thy honour and service.

7. My God, even because I am indeed nothing, and Thou alone art all, therefore will I utterly distrust and abandon myself, and securely trust in Thee only, who alone art able to supply my infinite wants and cure my defects.

8. To Thee, O Lord Jesus, is this poor and wretched soul of mine left, to Thy guard is it committed by Thy Heavenly Father; behold I cast all my care and solicitude upon Thee, both for this life and that which is to come.

9. My God, Thou alone art my love, and Thou only shalt be my fear.

10. My God, Thou hast made me unto Thee, and my heart is unquiet (and so let it be more and more) till it rest in Thee; let me find bitterness in all undue love to creatures.

HOLY EXERCISES OF RESIGNATION
TO THE DEVOUT READER

Devout Reader,

Above all other acts of the will, our venerable author doth most recommend to practise those of Resignation. For thy use, therefore, I have selected certain forms which thou mayest either exercise as they be, or according to them frame exercises for thyself. Now here thou wilt find both examples of general illimited resignations (most proper for the more perfect, which yet may be used indifferently by any), and likewise of resignations in all particular difficulties and afflictions, either actually pressing or only in imagination and supposition. Now for the use and application of all these I refer thee to the foregoing instructions in Treat. iii. sect. iii. chap. iii. The particular resignations are taken from four heads, in which any person may receive damage, and consequently may have occasion to resign himself, viz.: 1. Goods of fortune, as riches, houses, clothes, &c.; 2. Goods of fame, honour, authority, office, &c.; 3. Goods of the body, as health, strength, beauty, agility, &c.; 4. Goods of the soul, as endowments, natural or supernatural, learning, &c.

Now in regard of these, there first follow short patterns of resignation, according to this order, one after another. If thou desirest acts of this nature and order more largely expressed, I refer thee to the book called the *Idiot's Devotions.* After these I have several other more extended exercises of particular resignations, consisting of acts relating to the foresaid heads, without any order, one mixed with another. And those which I judged most necessary, and the occasions of them most frequently occurring, I have oft repeated.

ACTS OF GENERAL RESIGNATION

1. My God, whatsoever I have, whatsoever I can do, all this Thou hast freely bestowed on me. Behold I offer myself and all that belongs to me to Thy heavenly will. Receive, O Lord, my entire will and liberty; possess my understanding, memory, and all my affections; only vouchsafe to bestow upon me Thy love, and I shall be rich enough; nothing more do I desire; Thou alone, O my God, sufficest me.

2. O my God and all my good, I have and do consecrate to Thy love and honour both my body and soul. Conserve them as it shall please Thee, and employ them according to Thine own will in Thy service.

3. My Lord, I here prostrate myself before Thee, to do Thee homage for what I am and may be by Thy grace.

4. My God, I beseech Thee to glorify Thyself by me, according to whatsoever manner Thou shalt please.

5. My God, hereafter I will never search any object of my affections out of Thee, since I see that all good is to be found in Thee.

6. Ecce Domine, ecce cor meum quod offero Tibi, et quid volo nisi ut sit holocaustum charitatis ad æternam gloriam Tuam?

7. O most desirable goodness of my God, let it be to me even as Thou wilt, O eternal, most holy, and well-pleasing will of my Saviour; do Thou reign in and over all my wills and desires from this moment for ever.

8. My God and all my good, for that infinite love of Thine own self, grant that as I live in and by Thee, so may I live only to and for Thee.

9. Deus meus et omne bonum meum, in voluntate Tua vita est; in meâ mors: non meâ voluntas fiat, sed Tua Domine in terra sicut in cœlo. Amen. Jesus.

10. O my soul, let us live to Him, and for Him only, that died for us; let us disengage ourselves from this base world; let us pass from sense to reason, and from reason to grace; let us enter into commerce with the angels, that our conversation may be with Jesus, that so by all manner of ways we may be His, both in life and death, in time and eternity.

11. O my soul, let us freely submit ourselves to our Lord's judgments, renouncing our own judgment; let us adore them, though we be ignorant of them. Let us most assuredly believe that He doth nothing but for our greater good. Whatsoever befalls us, let us take it willingly and thankfully from His hands, which are always full of blessings for us.

12. Let Jesus only live and reign in my heart, and let the world and all its vain desires perish.

FORMS OF PARTICULAR ACTS OF RESIGNATION.

1. About External Goods.

For the love of God, and in conformity to His will, I resign myself: 1. To be deprived of any of the clothes that I have, or may have, though never so necessary; 2. or of books; 3. or of convenient lodgings; 4. and to have those things bestowed on me from which my nature is most averted. 5. To be driven to wear clothes that seem base, unfit, or inconvenient for the season. 6. To be ill accommodated in lodging, bedding, &c. 7. To want even necessary clothes. 8. To be forced to wear such clothes as will make me appear ridiculous. 9. To want meat or drink; 10. or to have only such as is ungrateful to nature. 11. To endure crosses that in any sort, spiritually or corporally, may fall on my friends or kindred, as loss of state, infirmity, death, &c.; 12. and, on the other side, to restrain all inordinate complacency in their prosperity. 13. To endure that my friends should neglect, forget, yea, hate and persecute me. 14. To be abandoned of all creatures, so that I may have no man or thing to cleave unto, save only Thee my God, who wilt abundantly suffice me. 15. To be indifferent in what place, company, &c., I shall live; 16. yea, to live with those from whom my nature is most averted. 17. To live in all sorts of afflictions, as long as shall please Thee my God; 18. and not to yield to the motion of nature, which perhaps out of wearisomeness would fain have life at an end. But wholly to conform my will to Thy good will and pleasure; 19. yea, to take pleasure that Thy will may be fulfilled in me any way.

2. Acts of Resignation about our Good Name.

For the love of Thee my God, and in conformity to Thy will, I resign myself: 1. To suffer all manner of disgraces, contempts, affronts, infamies, slanders, &c., be they done to my face or behind my back; 2. though I have given no cause or provocations; 3. yea, after I have done the greatest kindnesses to my defamers; 4. if I have deserved them by my fault I am sorry for it and beg pardon, but am glad of this good effect of it, that it is an occasion of procuring this mortification and humiliation. 5. To suffer injuries either from superiors, equals, or inferiors. 6. To be in life or manner of my death shameful and odious to others; 7. and after death to be evil thought and evil spoken of by others; 8. yea, not to have any that will vouchsafe to pray for me; 9. yea, to be esteemed to have died in the state of eternal damnation; 10. yea, moreover, to have it expressed so to the world in a chronicle, to the shame of all that have relation to me; 11. in this life to be held for the scum of mankind, forsaken by all both in their doings and affections. 12. To be mortally persecuted by professed enemies (though I will account none such); 13. yea, by such as have had great proofs of my charity to them; 14. in sickness and other necessities to be driven to be chargeable and troublesome to others; 15. whereas I in the mean time am profitable to none at all; 16. so that all men do grow weary of me, and long to be rid of me; 17. and in this case to remain several years, yea, all my life long; 18. dying a natural death (so it be in Thy grace), to be esteemed by others to have destroyed myself; 19. and thereupon to have my body ignominiously used, buried in the highway or under the gallows, to the eternal loss of my fame and unspeakable confusion of my kindred, friends, &c.

3. Acts of Resignation about the Body.

For the love of Thee, O my God, and in conformity to Thy will, I resign myself: 1. to suffer weaknesses, sickness; 2. pains; 3. deformity; 4. horror in the sight of others, as was the case of Job and Lazarus. 5. To suffer extremity of heat or cold; 6. want of necessary sleep, and hunger or thirst; 7. indigestion; 8. torments and defects about my five senses. 9. To be affrighted with horrible and hideous sights of devils, &c. 10. To be afflicted with fearful noises. 11. To suffer scourgings, beatings, &c. 12. To be spit upon, as Thou my Saviour wast. 13. To suffer incisions, torments, &c., external and internal. 14. To suffer loss of eyes, hearing, &c.; to be overtoiled with all sorts of labours; 15. and this being in feebleness of body. 16. To lose all pleasure and gust in meats and drinks. 17. To suffer any disfiguring in my face, or distortions in other parts of my body. 18. To suffer the loss of any of my members. 19. To receive harm in my imagination, and thereby to lose my perfect judgment, so as to become a fool or mad. 20. That my body should by little and little putrefy and rot away. 21. To die suddenly, or after long sickness and tokens of death. 22. To die without senses or memory, and distracted or mad. 23. To endure the agony of death, and the long torments that do accompany it, 24. To suffer the unwillingness and terror that nature feels in the separation of the soul from the body. 25. To die a natural death, or else a violent and painful one, procured by others. 26. To die at what time, in what place and manner it shall please Thee my God. 27. To die without the help of any of the Sacraments, being not able to come by them. 28. In the agony of death to endure such terror, afflictions, and temptations as the devil doth then usually procure. 29. Being dead, to want not only all decent or honourable, but even Christian burial, so as that my body may be made a prey to beasts and fowls.

4. Particular Acts of Resignation about the Soul.

For the love of God, and in conformity to His will, I do resign myself: 1. To undergo all sorts of temptations that shall please Thee my God to lay on me or permit to befall me; 2. and to suffer them to the end of my life, ever adhering to Thee. 3. To endure all manner of desolations, aridities, and indevotions. 4. To suffer all obscurity and darkness in my understanding; all coldness and dulness of affection in my will to Thee, so far as I am not able to help it; 5. in all which I renounce the seeking any solace in creatures. 6. To want all manner of gifts and graces not necessary to my salvation; 7. nor to desire inordinately nor rest with affection in supernatural contemplations, sweetnesses, or other extraordinary visits or favours. 8. To resign myself to all things, be they never so contrary to sensuality. 9. To bear with the repugnance that I find in sensuality, till with Thy grace (sooner, or later, or never) it may be brought to perfect subjection to my spirit; in the mean time suffering patiently the difficulty that is in fighting against it, or resisting the desires of it. 10. To endure all the difficulties, tediousnesses, and expectations that are in a spiritual life; also such various changes, chances, and perplexities as are in it; notwithstanding all which my purpose is (through Thy grace) to persevere and go through them all. 11. To bear with my own defectuousness, frailty, and proneness to sin; yet using my best industry, and bearing with what I cannot amend. 12. To die before I can reach to perfection. 13. To live and die in that degree of a spiritual life as shall seem good to Thee, and not according to my own will; 14. yet ever desiring and endeavouring that I may not be wanting in coöperating with Thy calls and graces. 15. To be contented to serve Thee according to that manner Thou hast provided and appointed; that is, with regard to my natural talents, complexion, &c., as likewise such supernatural helps and graces as Thou shalt afford me, and not according to the talents and gifts bestowed on others. 16. To be contented that Thou hast bestowed greater gifts on other men than on me. 17. To understand and know no more nor no otherwise than Thy will is, and to remain ignorant in what Thou wilt have me to be ignorant of. 18. To give up and offer to Thee my God whatsoever honour and contentment may come by such knowledge; for all is Thine. 19. To want all knowledges but such as are necessary to my salvation. 20. To follow Thee by all the ways whatsoever that Thou shalt call me, externally or internally, though I cannot understand how they can lead to a good issue; so walking, as it were, blindfold. 21. To be contented that others excel me in virtues, and that they be better esteemed; yet ever desiring that I may not be wanting in my industries. 22. To be content not to know in what case I am as to my soul; nor in what degree of perfection, nor whether I go backward or forward; 23. nor to know whether I be in the state of grace; only beseeching Thee that I be industrious to please Thee. 24. To be content that another should receive the fruit of all my endeavours and actions, though never so perfect, so purely do I desire to serve Thee. 25. To endure with patience all manner of injuries; 26. and yet to be esteemed by others that I endure them against my will, without humility, with murmuring, revengefulness, and pride, and that the fear of danger or discredit only hinders me from executing such revenge. 27. To serve Thee purely for Thine own sake, so as that I would serve Thee though there had been no reward or punishment. 28. To suffer the pains of Purgatory, though never so bitter, that Thou shalt ordain; 29. and this for as long a time as Thou shalt please. 30. To do and suffer in this life both in soul and body what, and in what manner, and for how long as it shall please Thee my God. 31. To be content to enjoy the lowest place in heaven; 32. and this, although Thou shouldst enable me to merit as much as any or all Thy Saints in heaven have done.

OTHER MIXED RESIGNATIONS.

§ 1. O, how good art Thou, O my God, to those that trust in Thee, to the soul that truly seeks Thee! What art Thou, then, to those that find Thee!

1. Whatsoever I shall suffer, O my God, by Thy ordinance, either in body or soul, and how long soever I shall suffer, I renounce all consolation but what comes from Thee.

2. My God, though Thou shouldst always hide Thy face from me, and never afford me any consolation, yet will I never cease to love, praise, and pray unto Thee.

3. For Thy sake I renounce all pleasure in eating and drinking, being resolved to make use of Thy creatures only in obedience to Thy will, and to the end thereby to be enabled to serve Thee.

4. I resign myself to abide all my lifetime among strangers; yea, or among such as have an aversion towards me, and which will never cease to molest me.

5. My God, casting myself wholly on Thy Fatherly providence, I renounce all care and solicitude for to-morrow concerning anything belonging to this life.

6. I offer unto Thee, O my God, this desire and resolution of my heart, that notwithstanding my continual indevotion, my infinite distractions and defects, &c., I will never give over the exercises of an internal life.

7. My desire is always to be in the lowest place, beneath all creatures, according to my demerit.

8. For Thy love, O my God, I renounce all inordinate affections to my particular friends or kindred.

9. I resign myself to suffer any lameness or distortedness in any of my members.

10. I resign myself to abide all my life among those that are enemies to Thy Catholic Church, and there to be in continual fears, dangers, and persecutions.

§ 2. Draw me, O God, we will run after Thee, because of the odour of Thy precious ointments.

1. For Thy love, O my God, I resign myself to want necessary clothing, or to be deprived of those which I have.

2. I resign myself patiently to bear with the repugnance I find in my corrupt nature, and the difficulty in resisting the unruly passions of it. Yes, through Thy grace, my purpose is to use my best industry and vigilance against it.

3. For Thy love I renounce the seeking after all curious and impertinent knowledge.

4. I renounce all sensual contentment in sleep or other corporal refreshments, being desirous to admit no more of them than shall be necessary, and in obedience to Thy will.

5. My God, through Thy grace, neither hard usage from others, nor any mere outward corporal extremity or want, shall force me to seek a change of my present condition.

6. My God, I do consecrate myself to Thee alone, for the whole remnant of my life to pursue the exercises of an internal life, leaving the fruit and success of my endeavours to Thy holy will.

7. For Thy love, and in conformity to Thy blessed will, I resign myself to be abandoned of all creatures, so as to have none to have recourse unto but Thee only.

8. I offer myself unto Thee, with patience to suffer whatsoever Thou shalt inflict on me, and never to yield to the inclination and feebleness of nature, which perhaps out of wearisomeness would have life at an en

9. When obedience or charity shall require it, I resign myself to go and abide in a place haunted with evil spirits, being assured that as long as I adhere to Thee they cannot hurt my soul.

10. I renounce rashness, readiness, and forwardness to judge the actions of others, employing all my severity in censuring against myself only.

§ 3. My God and all my good, in Thy heavenly will is life; but death is mine. Not my will, therefore, but Thine be done in earth as it is in heaven.

1. For Thy love, O my God, I do resign myself to be deprived of all the gifts and privileges which in my nature I do most affect, and to see them conferred on the person for whom I have the greatest aversion.

2. I resign myself not only to want the esteem or favour of my superiors, but also to be despised, and hardly, yea, injuriously treated by them.

3. When through my own demerit I do deserve such ill usage from them, I will be sorry and humbled for my fault, and bless Thee for punishing it so easily in this life.

4. O tepidity, I do detest thee.

5. I do resign myself, and am even desirous to find such usage in this world, that I may know and feel it to be only a place of exile.

6. My God, whatsoever affliction or desertion Thou shalt suffer to befall me, through Thy grace I will neither omit, neglect, nor shorten my daily appointed recollections.

7. I offer myself to Thee, O my God, entirely to be disposed of by Thee, both for life and death. Only let me love Thee, and that is sufficient for me.

8. Whatsoever natural or other defectuousness shall be in me, either for mind or body, by which I may incur disesteem from others, I do willingly embrace such occasions of humiliation.

9. I renounce all forwardness to give counsel to others, being much rather desirous to receive it from any other.

10. I do utterly renounce all familiarity and all unnecessary conversation or correspondence with persons of a different sex.

§ 4. *My Lord Jesus, Thou who art Truth hast said, My yoke is easy and My burden light.*

1. I have received from Thy hands a cross of religious penitential discipline; through Thy grace I will continue to bear it till my death, never forsaking any ways to ease it by external employments, or to escape from it, and shake it off by missions, &c.

2. For Thy love, O my God, and in conformity to Thy will, I resign myself to die when, where, and in what manner Thou shalt ordain.

3. I am content to see others make a great progress in spirit, and to do more good in Thy Church than myself.

4. I renounce all that satisfaction and false peace which is got by yielding to my inordinate passions, and not by resisting and mortifying them.

5. My God, till Thou hast humbled that great pride which is in me, do not spare to send me daily yet more and greater humiliations and mortifications.

6. I offer myself unto Thee, to suffer with patience and quietness whatsoever desolations, obscurity of mind, or deadness of affections that shall befall in a spiritual course; notwithstanding all which, through Thy grace, I will never neglect a serious tendency to Thee.

7. I am content to serve Thee with those mean talents that Thou hast given me.

8. I yield myself to endure all manner of injuries and contempts, and yet to be esteemed by others to be impatient and revengeful.

9. I do renounce all solicitude to please others, or to gain the affections of any one to myself.

10. I do resign myself to such painful and withal base offices as my proud and slothful nature doth abhor, whensoever obedience, charity, or Thy will shall impose them on me.

§ 5. My God, Thou art faithful, and wilt not suffer us to be tempted above that we are able; but wilt with the temptation give an issue that we may be able to bear it.

1. My God, my desire is to serve Thee gratis, like a son, and not as a mercenary.

2. I came into religion to suffer and to serve; I renounce, therefore, all desires of procuring ease, plenty, or superiority.

3. In love to Thee, O my God, I resign myself to follow Thee, by whatsoever ways, external or internal, that Thou shalt conduct me, although I be not able to understand them, nor can see how there can be any good issues of them.

4. I am content to see all become weary and desirous to be rid of me.

5. I am resigned to want whatsoever gift and graces are not necessary to my salvation.

6. In love to Thee, O my God, and in submission to Thy will, I do renounce all inordinate love and correspondence with the world, that so I may attend to Thee only.

7. I resign myself to become a spectacle horrible and loathsome to men's eyes, as was Job or Lazarus.

8. I do adore and most humbly submit myself to Thy most wise and secret judgments concerning my death or future state.

9. I resign myself to suffer those most bitter pains of the stone, gout, colic, &c., if Thou shalt ordain them to fall on me.

10. I renounce all obstinacy in defending mine own opinions, and all desire of victory in discourse.

§ 6. My God, who is like unto Thee, who hast Thy dwelling most high, yet humblest Thyself to regard the things which are (done) in heaven and earth!

1. I resign myself to abide in this place and in this present state of life wherein Thou hast put me; neither will I seek or ever procure a change for any outward sufferings till Thou shalt appoint.

2. Let all creatures scorn, abandon, and persecute me, so that Thou, O my God, wilt accompany and assist me; Thou alone sufficest me.

3. Through Thy grace I will never cease to approach nearer and nearer to Thee by prayer and abstraction from creatures.

4. I do resign myself, whensoever necessity, obedience, or charity shall require it, to visit and assist any one lying sick, though of the plague, or any other infectious or horrible disease.

5. I am contented that those who are nearest to me in blood or friendship should be so averted from me as to abhor my name.

6. I resign myself to die a natural or violent death, and as soon as it shall please Thee.

7. I offer unto Thee this desire and purpose of my heart, that I will esteem no employment to be necessary but the aspiring to a perfect union with Thee, and that I will not undertake any other business but in order to this.

8. I do heartily renounce all affection to all, even venial imperfections and the occasions of them.

9. I renounce all propriety in any dignity or office that I have or may have hereafter.

10. I desire to have no more to do with the world than if I were already dead and buried.

§ 7. My God, it is my only good to adhere unto Thee, who art the God of my heart and my portion for ever.

1. I offer myself unto Thee to be afflicted with whatsoever temptation, external or internal, Thou shalt permit to befall me; and though I should fall never so oft, yet will I not yield to dejection of mind or despair, but will rise up as soon as by Thy grace I shall be enabled.

2. I resign myself to follow Thee, O my Lord Jesus, in the same poverty of which Thou hast given me an example, renouncing all propriety in anything, and being contented and pleased to enjoy only what shall be necessary in all kinds.

3. I resign myself not only to be disfavoured by my superiors, but also to see those most favoured that are most averted from me.

4. My God, although Thou shouldst kill me, yet will I never cease to hope and trust in Thee.

5. I am content not to learn or know any more than Thou wouldst have me to know.

6. I do offer myself to all manner of contradictions and injuries to be sustained from my superiors or brethren, in patience, silence, and without complaining.

7. I renounce all impatience and unquietness for my many defects and hourly imperfections.

8. I do offer unto Thee my desire and resolution never to relinquish an internal spiritual course, notwithstanding any difficulties whatsoever that shall occur in it.

9. My God, I do not desire a removal of all temptations, which show me: 1. How impossible it is to enjoy a perfect peace in this life; and, 2. how necessary unto me Thy grace and assistance is. I embrace the pain of them. Only let me not offend Thee by yielding to them.

10. For Thy love I resign myself to be deprived of all proper and certain habitation.

§ 8. Holy, Holy, Holy, Lord God of Sabaoth! All the earth is full of Thy glory. Glory be to Thee most High.

1. For Thy love, O my God, and in conformity to Thy holy will, I resign myself unto Thee, with all that I am, have, can do, or suffer, in soul, body, goods, fame, friends, &c., both for time and eternity.

2. For Thy love I do renounce all desire of authority, especially all charge over the souls of others.

3. I am content not to learn or know more than Thou wouldst have me to know.

4. I resign myself, whensoever Thou shalt call me to it, to sacrifice my life, in what manner soever Thou shalt ordain, for the defence of Thy Catholic truth, trusting in Thy merciful promise that Thou wilt assist me in such trials.

5. My God, I am content to be blotted out of the memory of all (except those that would afflict me).

6. My God, let me be the universal object of the contempt and hatred of all creatures, so that I may love Thee and enjoy Thy presence and grace.

7. Jesus, who art the Prince of peace, and whose habitation is in peace, I offer my heart unto Thee, that Thou mayest establish a firm peace in it, calming the tempestuous passions that so oft rage in it.

8. I renounce all affection to speaking.

9. I resign myself in sickness to be burdensome and chargeable to others, so as that all should become weary and desirous to be rid of me.

10. I renounce all facility in hearkening to or believing any ill that is reported concerning others, and much more to be a disperser of such report.

§ 9. I adore Thee, O my God, the blessed and only Potentate, King of kings and Lord of Lords, who dwellest in unapproachable light: to Thee be glory and eternal dominions. Amen.

1. I resign and offer myself unto Thee, to follow the conduct of Thy Holy Spirit in an internal life, through bitter and sweet, light and darkness, in life and death.

2. I do renounce all solicitous designs to gain the affections of superiors or of any others; with any intention thereby to procure ease or contentment to nature.

3. I do renounce all propriety in any endowments that Thou hast or shalt give me.

4. I am contented with whatsover Thou shalt provide for my sustenance, how mean, how little, and how disgustful soever it be.

5. I resign myself in the agony of death to endure whatsoever pains, frights, or temptations Thou shalt permit to befall me, only let my spirit always adhere to Thee.

6. My God, I do here again renew and ratify my vows of religious profession, consecrating myself and all that I have or can do to Thy glory and service only.

7. I resolve, through Thy grace, that my great and daily defects shall not destroy my peace of mind nor confidence in Thy goodness.

8. I resign myself, for the humiliation and good of my soul, to be deprived of any endowments and gifts that may any way make me be esteemed by others.

9. I resign myself in sickness to want the assistance and comfort of friends, yea, even the use of Sacraments.

10. I resign myself (yea, would be glad) to lose all sensual pleasure in meats and drinks, if such were Thy will.

§ 10. *Blessed is the man whose hope is only in the name of Thee my God, and that regardeth not vanities and deceitful frenzies.*

1. Though Thou shouldst always hide Thy face from me, yea, my God, although Thou shouldst kill me, yet will I never cease to approach to Thee, and to put my whole trust in Thee only.

2. I consecrate my whole life to Thee, to be spent in a continual tendency in soul to Thee; not presuming to expect any elevated contemplations or extraordinary graces, but referring to Thy holy pleasure whether I shall ever be raised above my present mean exercises.

3. I resign myself to be esteemed fit and capable only of the basest and most toilsome offices; the which if they shall be imposed upon me, I will not avoid them.

4. I resign myself to be guided only by Thee and Thy holy inspirations.

5. I resign myself to be continually tormented, and to have my sleeps broken with any kind of troublesome noises or frights, &c.

6. My God, I resign myself to Thee alone, to live and die in that state and degree of a spiritual life to which it shall seem good to Thee to bring me; only I beseech Thee, that I may not be negligent in coöperating with Thy grace and holy inspirations.

7. I resign myself to suffer the straits and tediousness of a prison, and there to be deprived of books, or any thing that may divert my mind.

8. I resign myself to suffer the extremity of heat and cold, and to want the comfort of all refreshments against heat, and of necessary clothes against cold.

9. I resign myself to be obliged to take meats and drinks loathsome to my nature.

10. I resign myself to see others, my inferiors, provided of all things, and myself only neglected.

§ *11. Our Lord is my light and salvation: whom, then, should I fear?*

1. There is not any spiritual exercise so displeasing or painful to my nature which I would not embrace, if I knew or did believe Thy will to be such.

2. My God, so I may die in Thy grace and holy love, I resign myself to the infamy of being reputed to have procured my own death; and that therefore my body should be ignominiously cast out, and none to have the charity to pray for my soul.

3. I resign myself to be affrighted with horrible noises, hideous apparitions, &c.

4. Through Thy grace, my God, I will not rest with affection in any of Thy gifts how sublime soever; but will only make use of them to pass by their means in to Thee, who art my only increated, universal, and infinite good.

5. I esteem this life to be a mere prison or place of exile.

6. My God, I offer my soul unto Thee, that Thou mayest establish a firm peace in it, not to be interrupted as now it is by every contradiction and cross.

7. I resign myself to have my superiors, and all others whom my nature would wish to be most friendly, to be in all things a continual contradiction and cross to me.

8. For Thy love I would be content rather to have no use of my tongue at all, than thus continually to offend Thee with it.

9. Let all creatures be silent before Thee, and do Thou, O my God, alone speak unto me; in Thee alone is all that I desire to know or love.

10. My God, I know that to fly Thy cross is to fly Thee that diedst on it; welcome, therefore, be (these) Thy crosses and trials.

§ 12. My God, with Thee is the fountain of life, and in Thy light we shall see light.

1. My God, to Thee only do I consecrate the remainder of my life, purposing to account no business to be necessary, but only tendency to Thee by prayer and abnegation.

2. I resign myself, if such be Thy pleasure, even to be deprived of all use of these eyes, that are still so much delighted with vanity, curiosity, and all distracting objects.

3. O that I were nothing, that so Thou, my God, mayest be all in all!

4. I resign myself to be deprived of all certain habitation, and to live a vagabond in the world, so that none should take care of me or own me.

5. My God, my desire is to serve Thee in a state wherein I may be deprived of all propriety and election in all things, as well internal as external: do Thou, my Lord, choose for me.

6. In conformity to Thy heavenly will, O my God, I do accept the pain and trouble that I feel from my continual indevotion, my unruly passions, and (almost) unremediable imperfections; and I will with patience expect Thy good time, when I shall be enabled with Thy grace to rectify them.

7. For Thy love I renounce all conversations and correspondences, which I do find to be occasions to me of falling into defects, by nourishing inordinate affection or unquietness.

8. I renounce the folly of being disquieted with seeing that others are not such as I would have them to be, since I cannot make myself such an one as I fain would.

9. I offer myself to become a fool unto all for Thee, my God.

10. So that thereby my pride may be humbled, I even beg of Thee, my God, that Thou wouldst not spare to send me crosses and contradictions.

§ 13. I know, my God, that Thou art the God that triest hearts and lovest simplicity, therefore in the simplicity of my heart I offer myself unto Thee.

1. O my God, when will the time come that Thou wilt lead my soul into Thy solitude?

2. For Thy love I renounce all complacency in any kind of endowment or skill in any arts (as far as any of these are in me), consecrating all that by Thy free gift is in me to Thy glory and service only.

3. I do utterly renounce all familiarity and unnecessary conversations or correspondences with persons of a different sex.

4. My God, it is Thou that hast placed me in this my present condition; and Thou only shalt displace me.

5. O tepidity, I abhor thee. My God, teach me an effectual cure and remedy against it; let not my latter end be worse than my beginning.

6. My God, I offer unto Thee my heart, that whatsoever yet unknown inordinate desires are in it, Thou mayest teach me to mortify them by any ways Thou shalt please.

7. I resign myself, in case that obedience shall unavoidably oblige me thereto, to undertake that most fearful employment of the charge of souls (in the mission, &c.).

8. For Thy love and for the mortification of sensuality, I could content to be freed from all necessity of eating and drinking, if such were Thy pleasure.

9. I offer unto Thee, my God, this desire of my heart, that at last, this day, I may begin perfectly to serve Thee, having spent so much time unprofitably.

10. Feed me, O Lord, with the bread of tears, and give me drink in tears, according to the measure that Thou shalt think fit.

§ 14. My Lord and my God, from Thee are all things, by Thee are all things, to Thee are all things: to Thee only be glory, love, and obedience for ever.

1. My God, if Thou wilt that I be in light, be Thou blessed for it, and if Thou wilt that I be in darkness, still be Thou blessed for it. Let both light and darkness, life and death, praise Thee.

2. Blessed be Thy holy name that my heart doth not (and never may it) find rest or peace in anything that I seek or love inordinately, whilst I do not love it in Thee and for Thee only.

3. I offer unto Thee this resolution of mine, that by all lawful and fitting ways I will endeavour to avoid any office of authority.

4. I resign myself to live and abide in any state or place where I shall daily have my health or life endangered.

5. I resign myself to suffer in Purgatory whatsoever pains, and as for as long a time, as shall seem good to Thee.

6. Through Thy grace and assistance, O my God, no hard usage from others, nor any desire of finding any ease or contentment to my nature, shall force me to change my present condition.

7. My God, if Thou shalt so ordain or permit, I resign my body to be possessed or tormented by evil spirits, so that my spirit may always adhere by love to Thee.

8. I resign myself to take part in any calamity, disgrace, &c., that Thy Divine Providence shall permit to befall the country or community in which I live.

9. I renounce all resting affection to sensible gusts in my recollections, resolving to adhere firmly to Thee, as well in aridities as consolations.

10. My God, I am nothing, I have nothing, I desire nothing, but Jesus, and to see Him in peace in Jerusalem.

§ 15. *Blessed art Thou, O my God, in all Thy gifts, and holy in all Thy ways.*

1. I offer unto Thee the desire and resolution of my heart, that no employment which cannot without sin be avoided, nor much less any complacency in conversation with others, nor any unwillingness to break off conversation through impertinent civility, shall cause me to omit or shorten my daily appointed recollections.

2. Far be it from me that my peace should depend on the favour or affection of any creature, and not in subjection to Thy will only.

3. I renounce all knowledge that may hinder or distract me from the knowledge of my own defects and nothingness.

4. My God, I have neither devotion nor attention, and indeed do not deserve either; only I beseech Thee that Thou wilt accept of my sufferings.

5. My God, so that I may die in Thy holy fear and love, I resign myself to want all comforts and assistance from others, both in my death and after it, if such be Thy will.

6. My God, through Thy grace I will never voluntarily undertake any employment or study, but such as shall serve to advance my principal and most necessary business of seeking Thee by prayer, to which all other designs shall give way.

7. My God, I beseech Thee not only to forgive, but to crown with some special blessing all those that despise, depress, or persecute me, as being good instruments of Thy grace to abate pride and self-love in me.

8. Whatsoever dignity or privilege I enjoy, I am content to relinquish it whensoever it shall be Thy will; and if I were wrongfully deprived of it, I will not for the recovering endanger the loss of mine own peace or that of others.

9. I resign myself not only to suffer for mine own faults, but also the faults of my brethren.

10. My God, my desire is to live to Thee only. Place me, therefore, where Thou wilt; give me or take from me what Thou wilt. Only let me live to Thee and with Thee; that suffices me.

N.B. The reader may take notice that before every one of these fifteen exercises of particular resignations there is premised a proper passage of Holy Scripture, which may be conceived as the ground of the following acts, and will moreover be a fit subject to exercise some good affection or act of the will upon.

A DAILY CONSTANT EXERCISE.
TAKEN OUT OF BLOSIUS.

TO THE READER.

According to our promise (Treatise iii. section iii. chap. iii. § 25) we here present thee a peculiar exercise, consisting of all variety of affections and acts of the will, &c. Thou wilt there find for what dispositions it will be proper, and how by it a soul, without any other variety, may attain to a perfect active contemplation, according to the testimony of Lud. Blosius in *Instit. Spirit.* chap. xi., from whence the exercise itself is taken.

I have, moreover, added another like exercise in Latin, which perhaps may be agreeable to some. It also consists of several divisions and sorts of prayer, as contrition, reflections on the Passion, resignation, amorous desires, &c.; and each division, moreover, contains subdivided parts, to the end that if the whole exercise prove too large for one recollection, the exerciser in each division may content himself with one only of the parts. And, indeed, the devout soul is to be advised that she ought not to make any resolution to go through the whole exercise each recollection; but wheresoever she finds any act or prayer relishing to her, let her insist and dwell upon it with her mind as long as the gust thereof shall last; so that if only three or four, yea, if but one of the acts will suffice her, let her seek no further.

A DAILY CONSTANT EXERCISE
1. Of Contrition.

My Lord and my God, what shall I, sinful wretch, say unto Thee?

I bow the knees of my heart, acknowledging in Thy sight my manifold and grievous sins.

I have sinned, O God, I have sinned and done evil before Thee.

I have sinned against Thee, my most omnipotent Creator.

I have sinned against Thee, my most merciful Redeemer.

I have sinned against Thee, my most liberal Benefactor.

Woe unto me, I have continually been most ungrateful to Thee.

I am a most vile creature, dust and ashes.

Be merciful, O Lord; be merciful, be merciful unto me.

Behold my sorrow and contrition for my sins.

O, would to God I had never offended Thee!

Would to God I had never resisted and hindered the operation of Thy grace in my heart!

Would to God I had always pleased Thee, and observed Thy holy will and inspirations!

My purpose and firm resolution, through Thy grace, is to avoid henceforward whatsoever may offend Thee, and rather to die than willingly to provoke Thy wrath and hatred against me. Therefore, O merciful Jesus, by Thy most bitter Passion and all the merits of Thy most Sacred Humanity, I beseech Thee to pardon and blot out all my sins.

Wash me with Thy Precious Blood; heal, purge, and sanctify me.

2. Reflections on the Merits and Passion of our Saviour Jesus Christ.

I do adore, glorify, and bless Thee, O my only Saviour Jesus Christ, for all Thy unspeakable mercies and benefits.

O Son of the living God, I do most humbly give thanks to Thee for that for me Thou hast vouchsafed in Thine infinite love:

1. To become man.

2. To be born in a poor stable and laid in a manger.

3. To suffer poverty with Thy poor Virgin Mother.

4. For more than thirty years to be wearied with continual labours and travails for our good.

5. Out of inexpressible anguish to sweat drops of Blood.

6. To be ignominiously apprehended by sinners, unworthily bound and arraigned before Thine enemies.

7. To be shamefully defiled with spittings, cruelly beaten, and dishonourably clothed with a white and purple garment, like a fool and a mock king.

8. To be unjustly condemned to death.

9. To be cruelly torn with whips and crowned with thorns.

10. To be most tormentingly fastened with nails to the cross.

11. To be most inhumanely presented with gall and vinegar to drink in Thy extreme thirst.

12. For me to hang naked, wounded, and condemned in inconceivable torments many hours on the cross;

13. There to shed Thy most Precious Blood, and to offer Thy life a propitiation for my sins.

14. To be sealed up in the grave, from whence, notwithstanding, Thou didst raise Thyself, conquering death for me.

O blessed Jesus, my only Hope and Salvation, grant that I may love Thee with a most fervent and constant love.

O rosy wounds of my Lord, inflicted for me, I salute you. With what love were you suffered by Him! And what love do you deserve from me!

3. Acts of Humiliation, &c.

Behold, O most merciful Saviour, I, a most abominable sinner, in imitation of Thy most glorious humility, do submit myself to all creatures, acknowledging myself unworthy to live on earth; and, after the example of Thy most admirable charity, I do with sincere love, according to my utmost ability, embrace all those that do afflict or persecute me.

For Thy love I do renounce all iniquity and vanity, all inordinate delectations, all self-will and immortification.

I do relinquish and reject all things below Thee; and above all I do make election of Thee, as my only good.

I do commit and resign myself entirely to Thee.

I do desire and beseech Thee that Thy most perfect and well-pleasing will may be accomplished in me and concerning me, in time and eternity.

For Thy love and glory I am ready to want any consolation, and to suffer any injury, contempt, or tribulation. If such be Thy pleasure, my Heavenly Lord, let me live in the same poverty and afflictions that Thou didst suffer all Thy life long.

4. Address to the Blessed Virgin, &c.

O Mary, the most sweet Virgin Mother of our Lord, the most glorious Queen of Heaven, intercede for me to thy Son.

O merciful protectress of the oppressed,

Support of the weak and infirm,

Refuge of afflicted sinners, look with thine eyes of pity on me.

By thine intercession let my heart be inflamed with a most ardent love unto our Lord Jesus Christ.

O all you glorious Angels and blessed Saints, intercede for me.

O thou blessed angel appointed by God to be my sure guardian and most comfortable companion in this valley of tears, pray for me.

O thou my most special patron S. Benedict, intercede in my behalf unto our Lord, that, living according to thy perfect rule and example, I may with thee contemplate His beautifying face.

5. Petitions to our Lord for Grace, &c.

My Lord and my God, with the company and assistance of these Thy beloved Saints, I take the boldness to make known unto Thee my miseries and defects, beseeching Thee to cure them all.

Mortify in me whatsoever is displeasing to Thee.

Adorn me with merits and graces acceptable in Thy sight.

Give me true humility, obedience, meekness, patience, and charity.

Grant me a perfect restraint and dominion over my tongue and all my senses and members.

Give me true internal purity, nakedness, liberty, and most profound introversion.

Illuminate my soul with Thy most pure divine light.

I acknowledge that Thou art most immediately and intimely present to me, and in the very centre of my spirit.

Vouchsafe, I beseech Thee, to see with my eyes, to hear with my ears, and to operate with my external members.

Possess my memory and understanding, and inflame my will and affections with Thy love.

Lead me into the naked fund of my spirit, and translate me into Thee, my God and original; that I may clearly know Thee, ardently love Thee, be immediately united to Thee, and, by a quiet fruition, rest in Thee, to the glory of Thy name. Amen.

6. Supplication in Behalf of the Church, &c.

O my God, be graciously merciful to all those whom Thou hast redeemed with Thy most Precious Blood.

Convert all miserable sinners to Thee.

Restore all heretics and schismatics unto the bosom of Thy Church; illuminate all infidels that are ignorant of Thee.

Be present to all that are in any tribulation or necessity.

Bless all my parents, kindred, acquaintance, and benefactors.

Give unto the living pardon and grace; and to all the faithful departed light and rest everlasting.

7. Adoration, of the Most Blessed Trinity

O most Holy, Glorious, and Ever-blessed Trinity, Father, Son, and Holy Ghost; One omnipotent, most wise, most holy, and most merciful God;

I do in the profound abyss of mine own nothing adore Thee, my most gracious God.

Vouchsafe to teach and assist me, whose hope is only in Thee.

O Heavenly Father, by Thine infinite power establish my memory in Thee, fill it with holy and divine thoughts; O eternal Son of Thy coeternal Father, by Thine infinite wisdom illuminate mine understanding, and adorn it with the knowledge of Thy supreme excellency and mine own incomprehensible vileness.

O Holy Spirit, the most pure love of the Father and Son, by Thine infinite goodness inflame my soul with an inextinguishable ardour of divine love.

O my God and all my good, O that I could love and praise Thee as perfectly and incessantly as all Thy Angels and Saints do!

According to the utmost extent and capacity that Thou hast given me, I do glorify, adore, love, and magnify Thee. But because I cannot worthily praise Thee, do Thou vouchsafe to praise and glorify Thyself in and by me.

If I had the love of all creatures, I would most willingly expend and employ it on Thee only.

8. Amorous Aspirations, &c.

My Lord and my God.

O Being infinitely peaceable and infinitely amiable;

O infinite abyss of goodness, infinitely delicious and desirable;

O torrent of inestimable delectations and joys;

O my all-sufficient reward;

Thou art my only immutable good.

What do I desire but Thee!

O, draw me after Thee;

Inflame me with the fire of Thy most fervent love.

O my God, my God and All,

Plunge me in the abyss of Thy Divinity, swallow me entirely, and make me one spirit with Thee, that Thou mayest take Thy delights in me.

Nothing but Jesus, nothing but Jesus.

O Jesus, do Thou alone live and reign in my soul.

My God, let me only love Thee, and that suffices me.

N.B. If this or the following exercise seem to any too long, it may be divided into several hours for recollection; or it may be comprehended briefly in a few words, or even without words. So saith Blosius.

EXERCITIUM QUOTIDIANUM

1. Confessionis et Doloris de Peccatis

Ecce ego, Domine, quia vocasti me.

Ecce venio ad Te, et in conspectu Tuo vias meas arguam.

Væ mihi Domine, quia peccavi Tibi.

Aversus sum a Te, O pulchritudo æterna!

O immensa Bonitas, Te offendi.

O amabilitas infinita, Te dereliqui.

O peccatum! O æternitas!

Væ mihi, cum aperientur libri, et dicetur, ecce homo et opera ejus.

Heu, heu mihi, Domine, in illa die si inventus fuero minus habens.

Nunc scio et video, quia malum et amarum mihi est dereliquisse Te Deum meum, universum bonum meum.

Tribularer utique si nescirem misericordias Tuas, Domine.

O Jesu! O nomen sub quo nemini desperandum est.

Etiamsi occideris me, sperabo in Te: et Ipse eris Salvator meus.

O Pater misericordiarum, respice in faciem Christi Tui, quia copiosa apud Eum redemptio est.

Non ponar amplius contrarius Tibi: non committam illud amplius in æternum.

2. Hymnus Passionis

Et nunc quæ est expectatio mea? nonne Tu Domine Jesu Deus meus, misericordia mea.

Memor ero ab initio mirabilium Tuorum: et misericordias Tuas, Domine, in æternum cantabo.

HOLY WISDOM

Omnes nos quasi oves erravimus et posuit Dominus in Te iniquitatem omnium nostrum?

* * * * * * * * *

Jacebas consternatus super faciem Tuam: et vultus Tuus hærebat terræ.

Non remansit in To fortitudo: sed et species Tua immutata est in Te.

Rubrum factum est vestimentum Tuum: quia calcasti torcular solus.

* * * * * * * * *

Circumdederunt Te canes multi: concilium malignantium obsedit Te.

Amici Tui et proximi Tui a longe steterunt: et vim faciebant qui quærebant animam Tuam.

Tu Spiritus oris nostri, Christe Domine, captus es in peccatis nostris.

* * * * * * * * *

Dedisti percutienti Te maxillam: saturatus es opprobriis.

Suscitatur falsiloquus adversus faciem Tuam: hostis Tuus terribilibus oculis intuitus est Te.

Contumelia et tormento interrogaverunt Te: morte turpissima condemnaverunt Te.

Dorsum Tuum fabricaverunt peccatores: prolongaverunt iniquitatem suam.

* * * * * * * * *

Sicut ovis ad occisionem ductus es: et quasi agnus coram tondente se, obmutuisti.

Apernerunt super Te ora sua: et exprobantes percusserunt maxillam Tuam.

Recordare paupertatis et nuditatis Tuæ: absinthii et fellis.

* * * * * * * * *

Foderunt manus Tuas et pedes Tuos: dinumeraverunt omnia ossa Tua.

Ipsi vero consideraverunt et inspexerunt Te: diviserunt sibi vestimenta Tua et super vestem Tuam miserunt sortem.

Plauserunt super Te manibus omnes transeuntes per viam sibilaverunt inimici Tui et frenduerunt dentibus suis.

Dixerunt devorabimus eum: en ista est dies quain expee tabamus; invenimus, vidimus.

* * * * * * * * *

Facies Tua intumuit a fletu; et palpebræ Tuæ caligaverunt.

Conclusit Te Deus apud iniquos: et posuit Te sibi quasi in signum.

Hæc passus es absque iniquitate manus Tuæ: cum haberes mundas ad Deum preces.

* * * * * * * * *

Ecce quomodo dilexisti me! facta est ut mors dilectio Tua.

Salvete, salvete, salvete, salutiferæ plagæ Domini amatoris mei; in quibus descripsit me.

Te laudent coelum et terra: quia Te decet laus.

O expectatio Israel, salvator ejus in die malorum.

3. Oblationis et Resignationis, &c.

Quid retribuam Tibi, Domine Jesu, pro omnibus quæ retribuisti mihi?

Tu Teipsum totum pro me obtulisti: factus es pro me maledictum.

Ecce, Domine, totum me offero Tibi: et omnia mea Tuæ subjicio voluntati.

Suscepi de manu Tua crucem: portabo eam usque ad mortem, sicut imposuisti mihi.

Omnes homines et maxime eos qui me persequuntur, sincera charitate, sicut possum, complector.

* * * * * * * * *

Omnia quæ infra Te sunt, Domine, relinquo et respuo: Teque prea omnibus eligo.

Desidero Tibi soli vivere: pone me ubi vis: des et auferas mihi quiquid vim tantummodo vivam Tibi et Tecum, nam hoc sufficit mihi.

In infimum locum infra omnem creaturam me recipio: et pro Tuo honore omnium servum me constituo.

Pro tuo amore, Tua gratia adspirante, omnem futuram vitam meam consecro Tibi in quotidianis internæ conversationis exercitiis transigendam

Quidquid ex Tua ordinatione perpetiar, et quamdiucunque perpetiar, omni consolationi renuntio, quæ a Te non procedit.

* * * * * * * * *

Deus, meus, nihil sum, et nihil possum: nihil habeo et nihil desidero, nisi solum Jesum, ut videam Eum in pace in Jerusalem.

Domine Deus meus, adoro et cum profundissima humilitate submitte me Tuis secretissimis et sapientissimis decretis de morte et futuro statu meo.

Omnes creaturæ me rejiciant, contemnant, et persequantur: tantummodo Tu, Domine, mihi protector adstes: Tu solus mihi sufficis.

Abrenuncio (falsæ illi) paci quæ completionem carnalium meorum desideriorum sequitur; et non eorumdem mortificationem.

Non recuso vivere, si its volueris, in eadem paupertate et derelictione, in qua Tu, Domino Jesu, vixisti.

* * * * * * * * *

Domine quæcumque mihi ex Tua permissione contigerit afflictio, desertio vel ariditas, Tua mihi adsistente gratia, nec omittam, nec ex negligentia contraham quotidiana mea internæ vitæ exercitia.

Deus meus, ex toto corde oro Te, ut glorifices Teipsum in me, et de me, quocumque demum modo Tibi placuerit.

Domino, pro Tuo amore renuntio omni desiderio auctoritatis aut prælationis.

Utinam tandem, Domine, meipsum a meipso abstraheres et a pereuntibus omnibus et perdentibus desideriis.

Ecce meipsum Tibi resigno, Domino, non solum ut superiorum meorum favore priver, sed ut ab ipsis contemnar, et quovis modo affligar.

* * * * * * * * *

Domine, corpus et animam meam dicavi Tibi: conserva hæc sicut placet; et impende ea sicut placet Tibi: in obsequium et gloriam Tuam.

Deus meus, donec perfecte humiliaveris superbum cor meum, ne parcas immittere vel multiplicare quascumque volueris cruces aut contradictiones.

Offero meipsum Tibi, ad perferendas quascumquedesolationes et obscuritates, quæ contingere solent in internæ vitæ exercitiis: quibus nihil obstantibus, propositum cordis mei perficias de non interrupta in eis perseverentia. Domine, pone me juxta te et cujusvis manus pugnet contra me.

* * * * * * * * *

Domino, quamvis faciem Tuam semper a me averteres, et nunquam mihi aliquam consolationem indulgeres: tamen auxilio gratiæ Tuæ nunquam cessabo Te diligere, adorare et quærere.

O tepiditas, quantum abominor te! Deus meus, non sint novissima mea pejora prioribus.

Domine, ex amore Tuc resigno me Divinæ voluntati Tuæ, ad moriendum, quando, ubi et quomodo ordinaveris.

Deus meus, Tu me hic collocasti: et Tu solus me alio transferes.

Domine, nihil a me necessarium æstimabitur nisi ut attendam ad Te per orationem et mei abnegationem.

* * * * * * * * *

Domine, Jesu, novi quia qui fugit crucem, fugit Crucifixum gratissima ergo erit mihi crux, quam imponere dignaberis.

Domine, si vis me esse in luce, sis benedictus: et si vis me esse in tenebris, sis benedictus. Lux et tenebræ benedicite Dominum.

Deus meus et omne bonum meum! quando duces animam meam in solitudinem Tuam?

Nihil sum Domine, et nihil sim, ut Tu solus sis omnia.

Non solum ignoscas, Domine Deus, tribulantibus me: sed et peculiarem aliquam gratiam eis conferas, utpote salutis meæ efficacissimis instrumentis.

4. Precatio ad B. Virginem et Sanctos.

O beatissima Virgo Mater Dei, respice in me et intercede pro me!

Regina coeli:

Refugium peccatorum;

Consolatrix afflictorum;

Salus infirmorum; me in tuam benedictam fidem, ac singularem custodiam, et in sinum misericordiæ tuæ hodie et quotidie et in hora exitus mei commendo.

O Sancti beatorum spirituum ordines;

Omnes Sancti et Sanctæ Dei; adjuvate me precibus, vestris ut ad societatem vestram pervenire merear.

5. Intercessio pro Ecclesia, &c.

Benigne fac Domine, in bona voluntate Tua Ecclesiæ Tuæ, pro qua Sacrosanctum Sanguinem Tuum fudisti.

Convertere miseros, peccatores.
Revoca hæreticos atque schismaticos.

Illumina infideles.

Juxta sis, Domine iis, qui tribulato sunt corde.

Adesto propinquis et benefactoribus meis, omnibusque qui precibus meis commendati esse cupiunt.

Benefac iis qui mihi inimico sunt animo.

Da vivis veniam et gratiam: da fidelibus defunctis requiem lucemque sempiternam.

6. Adspirationes ad SS. Trinitatem, &c.

O adoranda Trinitas, Pater et Filius et Spiritus Sanctus. Tibi gloria et benedictio in sæcula sæculorum.

Sanctus, Sanctus, Sanctus, Dominus Deus Sabaoth.

Ecce Domine, sicut possum magnifico sapientem et benignam Omnipotentiam Tuam.

Benedico Omnipotenti et benignæ sapientiæ Tuæ.

Glorifico Omnipotentem et Sapientem benignitatem Tuam.

O essentia summe simplex, summe tranquilla et summe amabilis.

O utinam a meipso totus deficerem.

O summa sufficientia mea! Quid volo præter Te?

O serena lux intimorum meorum! Tu in fundo animæ meæ habitas.

O jucunda requies spiritus mei! usquequo non me liberas ab omni proprietate?

O incircumscripta plenitudo omnis boni! Quicquid Tu non es, relinquo.

O ardens incendium! O dulce refrigerium! Amare Dei Filium.

Deus meus, non videbit Te homo et vivet: eia Domine moriar, ut videam: videam ut moriar.

Domine, quando dabis mihi immolari?

O quando duces animam meam in solitudinem Tuam?

O charitas! O charitas! O charitas!

Diligam totum Te ex toto me.

Aut amare, aut mori Domine.

Visibilia omnia mihi invisibilia sint; et invisibilia sola, visibilia.

Nihil sum; et nihil sim, ut Tu solus sis omnia.

Deus meus, merces mea magna nimis.

Væ, væ, væ! Amor non amatur.

Ecce cor meum Domine, quod offero Tibi et quid volo nisi ut sit holocaustum charitatis ad æternam gloriam Tuam.

Deus meus, omne bonum meum: Tibi silentium laus est.

Quem Tuus amor ebriat.

Novit quid Jesus sapiat:

Quam felix est, quem satiat.

Jesu, spes poenitentibus,

Quam pius es quærentibus!

Sed quid invenientibus!

THE END OF THE EXERCISES.

TO THE DEVOUT READER

Devout Reader,

There was a promise made of an Exercise of Aspirations at the end here of the rest; but it will not be needful to repeat them again, having not only in the two precedent exercises, but also in that of amorous desires, given thee sufficient patterns of them. Farewell, and pray for me.

Soli Deo Gloria.

FINIS.

Also from Benediction Books ...

Wandering Between Two Worlds: Essays on Faith and Art

Anita Mathias

Benediction Books, 2007

152 pages

ISBN: 0955373700

Available from

www.amazon.com, www.amazon.co.uk

www.wanderingbetweentwoworlds.com

In these wide-ranging lyrical essays, Anita Mathias writes, in lush, lovely prose, of her naughty Catholic childhood in Jamshedpur, India; her large, eccentric family in Mangalore, a sea-coast town converted by the Portuguese in the sixteenth century; her rebellion and atheism as a teenager in her Himalayan boarding school, run by German missionary nuns, St. Mary's Convent, Nainital; and her abrupt religious conversion after which she entered Mother Teresa's convent in Calcutta as a novice. Later rich, elegant essays explore the dualities of her life as a writer, mother, and Christian in the United States-- Domesticity and Art, Writing and Prayer, and the experience of being "an alien and stranger" as an immigrant in America, sensing the need for roots.

About the Author

Anita Mathias was born in India, has a B.A. and M.A. in English from Somerville College, Oxford University and an M.A. in Creative Writing from the Ohio State University. Her essays have been published in The Washington Post, The London Magazine, The Virginia Quarterly Review, Commonweal, Notre Dame Magazine, America, The Christian Century, Religion Online, The Southwest Review, Contemporary Literary Criticism, New Letters, The Journal, and two of HarperSanFrancisco's The Best Spiritual Writing anthologies. Her non-fiction has won fellowships from The National Endowment for the Arts; The Minnesota State Arts Board; The Jerome Foundation, The Vermont Studio Center; The Virginia Centre for the Creative Arts, and the First Prize for the Best General Interest Article from the Catholic Press Association of the United States and Canada. Anita has taught Creative Writing at the College of William and Mary and at regional writers' conferences in the United States. She now lives and writes in Oxford, England.

"Yesterday's Treasures for Today's Readers"

Titles by Benediction Classics available from Amazon.co.uk

Religio Medici, Hydriotaphia, Letter to a Friend, Thomas Browne

Pseudodoxia Epidemica: Or, Enquiries into Commonly Presumed Truths, Thomas Browne

Urne Buriall and The Garden of Cyrus, Thomas Browne

The Maid's Tragedy, Beaumont and Fletcher

The Custom of the Country, Beaumont and Fletcher

Philaster Or Love Lies a Bleeding, Beaumont and Fletcher

A Treatise of Fishing with an Angle, Dame Juliana Berners.

Pamphilia to Amphilanthus, Lady Mary Wroth

The Compleat Angler, Izaak Walton

The Magnetic Lady, Ben Jonson

Every Man Out of His Humour, Ben Jonson

The Masque of Blacknesse. The Masque of Beauty,. Ben Jonson

The Life of St. Thomas More, William Roper

Pendennis, William Makepeace Thackeray

Salmacis and Hermaphroditus attributed to Francis Beaumont

Friar Bacon and Friar Bungay Robert Greene

Holy Wisdom, Augustine Baker

The Jew of Malta and the Massacre at Paris, Christopher Marlowe

Tamburlaine the Great, Parts 1 & 2 AND Massacre at Paris, Christopher Marlowe

All Ovids Elegies, Lucans First Booke, Dido Queene of Carthage, Hero and Leander, Christopher Marlowe

The Titan, Theodore Dreiser

Scapegoats of the Empire: The true story of the Bushveldt Carbineers, George Witton

All Hallows' Eve, Charles Williams

The Place of The Lion, Charles Williams

The Greater Trumps, Charles Williams

My Apprenticeship: Volumes I and II, Beatrice Webb

Last and First Men / Star Maker, Olaf Stapledon

Last and First Men, Olaf Stapledon

Darkness and the Light, Olaf Stapledon

The Worst Journey in the World, Apsley Cherry-Garrard

The Schoole of Abuse, Containing a Pleasaunt Invective Against Poets, Pipers, Plaiers, Iesters and Such Like Catepillers of the Commonwelth, Stephen Gosson

Russia in the Shadows, H. G. Wells

Wild Swans at Coole, W. B. Yeats

A hundreth good pointes of husbandrie, Thomas Tusser

The Collected Works of Nathanael West: "The Day of the Locust", "The Dream Life of Balso Snell", "Miss Lonelyhearts", "A Cool Million", Nathanael West

Miss Lonelyhearts & The Day of the Locust, Nathaniel West

The Worst Journey in the World, Apsley Cherry-Garrard

Scott's Last Expedition, V1, R. F. Scott

The Dream of Gerontius, John Henry Newman

The Brother of Daphne, Dornford Yates

The Poetry of Architecture: Or the Architecture of the Nations of Europe Considered in Its Association with Natural Scenery and National Character, John Ruskin

The Downfall of Robert Earl of Huntington, Anthony Munday

Clayhanger, Arnold Bennett

The Regent, A Five Towns Story Of Adventure In London , Arnold Bennett

The Card, A Story Of Adventure In The Five Towns , Arnold Bennett

South: The Story of Shackleton's Last Expedition 1914-1917, Sir Ernest Shackketon

Greene's Groatsworth of Wit: Bought With a Million of Repentance, Robert Greene

Beau Sabreur, Percival Christopher Wren

The Hekatompathia, or Passionate Centurie of Love, Thomas Watson

The Art of Rhetoric, Thomas Wilson

Stepping Heavenward, Elizabeth Prentiss

Barker's Delight, or The Art of Angling, Thomas Barker
The Napoleon of Notting Hill, G.K. Chesterton

The Douay-Rheims Bible (The Challoner Revision)

Endimion - The Man in the Moone, John Lyly

Gallathea and Midas, John Lyly,

Mother Bombie, John Lyly

Manners, Custom and Dress During the Middle Ages and During the Renaissance Period, Paul Lacroix

Obedience of a Christian Man, William Tyndale

St. Patrick for Ireland, James Shirley

The Wrongs of Woman; Or Maria/Memoirs of the Author of a Vindication of the Rights of Woman, Mary Wollstonecraft and William Godwin

De Adhaerendo Deo. Of Cleaving to God, Albertus Magnus

Obedience of a Christian Man, William Tyndale

A Trick to Catch the Old One, Thomas Middleton

The Phoenix, Thomas Middleton

A Yorkshire Tragedy, Thomas Middleton (attrib.)

The Princely Pleasures at Kenelworth Castle, George Gascoigne

The Fair Maid of the West. Part I and Part II. Thomas Heywood

Proserpina, Volume I and Volume II. Studies of Wayside Flowers, John Ruskin

The Endeavour Journal of Sir Joseph Banks. Sir Joseph Banks

Christ Legends: And Other Stories, Selma Lagerlof; (trans. Velma Swanston Howard)

Chamber Music, James Joyce

Blurt, Master Constable, Thomas Middleton, Thomas Dekker

Since Yesterday, Frederick Lewis Allen

The Scholemaster: Or, Plaine and Perfite Way of Teachyng Children the Latin Tong , Roger Ascham

The Wonderful Year, 1603, Thomas Dekker

Waverley, Sir Walter Scott

Guy Mannering, Sir Walter Scott

Old Mortality, Sir Walter Scott

The Knight of Malta, John Fletcher

The Double Marriage, John Fletcher and Philip Massinger

Space Prison, Tom Godwin

The Home of the Blizzard Being the Story of the Australasian Antarctic Expedition, 1911-1914, Douglas Mawson

Wild-goose Chase , John Fletcher

If You Know Not Me, You Know Nobody. Part I and Part II, Thomas Heywood

The Ragged Trousered Philanthropists, Robert Tressell

The Island of Sheep, John Buchan

Eyes of the Woods, Joseph Altsheler

The Club of Queer Trades, G. K. Chesterton

The Financier, Theodore Dreiser

Something of Myself, Rudyard Kipling

Law of Freedom in a Platform, or True Magistracy Restored, Gerrard Winstanley

Damon and Pithias, Richard Edwards

Dido Queen of Carthage: And, The Massacre at Paris, Christopher Marlowe

Cocoa and Chocolate: Their History from Plantation to Consumer, Arthur Knapp

Lady of Pleasure, James Shirley

The South Pole: An account of the Norwegian Antarctic expedition in the "Fram," 1910-12. Volume 1 and Volume 2, Roald Amundsen

A Yorkshire Tragedy, Thomas Middleton (attrib.)

The Tragedy of Soliman and Perseda, Thomas Kyd

The Rape of Lucrece. Thomas Heywood

Myths and Legends of Ancient Greece and Rome, E. M. Berens

In the Forbidden Land, Henry Savage Arnold Landor

Illustrated History of Furniture: From the Earliest to the Present Time, Frederick Litchfield

A Narrative of Some of the Lord's Dealings with George Müller Written by Himself (Parts I-IV, 1805-1856), George Müller

The Towneley Cycle Of The Mystery Plays (Or The Wakefield Cycle): Thirty-Two Pageants, Anonymous

The Insatiate Countesse, John Marston.

Spontaneous Activity in Education, Maria Montessori.

On the Art of Writing, Sir Arthur Quillaer-Couch

The Well of the Saints, J. M. Synge

The Little World of Don Camillo, Giovanni Guareschi

and many others…

Tell us what you would love to see in print again, at affordable prices!
Email: **benedictionbooks@btinternet.com**